Optical Signal Processing, Computing, and Neural Networks

Optical Signal Processing, Computing, and Neural Networks

FRANCIS T.S. YU
Department of Electrical and Computer Engineering
The Pennsylvania State University

SUGANDA JUTAMULIA
Kowa Company, Ltd.
Silicon Valley Office

KRIEGER PUBLISHING COMPANY
MALABAR, FLORIDA
2000

Original Edition 1992
Reprint Edition 2000 w/corrections

Printed and Published by
**KRIEGER PUBLISHING COMPANY
KRIEGER DRIVE
MALABAR, FLORIDA 32950**

Copyright ©1992 by John Wiley & Sons, Inc.
Transferred to Authors 2000
Reprinted by Arrangement

All rights reserved. No part of this book may be reproduced in any form or by any means, electronic or mechanical, including information storage and retrieval systems without permission in writing from the publisher.
No liability is assumed with respect to the use of the information contained herein.
Printed in the United States of America.

> **FROM A DECLARATION OF PRINCIPLES JOINTLY ADOPTED BY A COMMITTEE OF THE AMERICAN BAR ASSOCIATION AND A COMMITTEE OF PUBLISHERS:**
> This publication is designed to provide accurate and authoritative information in regard to the subject matter covered. It is sold with the understanding that the publisher is not engaged in rendering legal, accounting, or other professional service. If legal advice or other expert assistance is required, the services of a competent professional person should be sought.

Library of Congress Cataloging-in-Publication Data

Yu, Francis T.S., 1932-
  Optical signal processing, computing, and neural networks / Francis T.S. Yu, Suganda Jutamulia.
    p. cm.
  Reprint. Originally published: New York : Wiley, 1992.
  Includes bibliographical references and index.
    ISBN 1-57524-157-9 (alk. paper) — ISBN 1-57524-158-7 (pbk. : alk. paper)
    1. Optical data processing. 2. Signal processing. 3. Neural networks (Computer science) 4. Computers, Optical. I. Jutamulia, Suganda. II. Title.

TA1632 .Y78 2000
621.36'7—dc21   00-042027

10   9   8   7   6   5   4   3   2

*To the creator of light,
who made the objects observable
to the eye*

Contents

PREFACE   xi

1 Partial Coherence and Optical Transform   1

    1.1 Aspects of Partial Coherence   1
    1.2 Spatial and Temporal Coherence   6
    1.3 System Transform   10
    1.4 Phase Transform by Thin Lenses   13
    1.5 Fresnel–Kirchhoff Theory   17
    1.6 Fourier Transformation by Lenses   20
    References   23
    Problems   23

2 Optical Signal Processing   34

    2.1 Coherent and Incoherent Processors   34
    2.2 Fourier Transform Processor   38
    2.3 Complex Spatial Filter Synthesis   39
    2.4 Joint Transform Processor   42
    2.5 Optical Signal Processing with Area Modulation   45
    2.6 Optimum Spatial Filtering   47
    2.7 Nonconventional Joint Transform Correlator   50
    References   57
    Problems   57

3 Applications of Optical Signal Processing   69

    3.1 Synthetic-Aperture Radar   69
    3.2 Inverse Synthetic-Aperture Radar   75
    3.3 Restoring Blurred Images   79
    3.4 Image Subtraction   83
    3.5 Wide-Band Signal Processing   85

	3.6	Homomorphic Filtering	91
	3.7	Mellin-Transform Processing	95
	3.8	Circular Harmonic Expansion Processing	97
	3.9	Hough Transform	100
		References	104
		Problems	105
4	**Partially Coherent Processing**	**117**
	4.1	Optical Processing under a Partially Coherent Regime	117
	4.2	Complex Amplitude Processing Using Incoherent Light	120
	4.3	White-Light Optical Processing	123
	4.4	Source Encoding and Image Sampling	124
	4.5	Noise Performance	127
	4.6	Applications	135
		References	149
		Problems	150
5	**Spatial Light Modulators and Detectors**	**160**
	5.1	Acoustooptic Modulator	160
	5.2	Magnetooptic Modulator	162
	5.3	Pockel's Readout Optical Modulator	164
	5.4	Microchannel Plate Modulator	167
	5.5	Liquid Crystal Light Valve	169
	5.6	Liquid Crystal Television	171
	5.7	Deformable Mirror Device	174
	5.8	Optical Disk	174
	5.9	Photoplastic Device	177
	5.10	Photographic Film	178
	5.11	Electron-Trapping Materials	185
	5.12	Photorefractive Materials	187
	5.13	Charge-Coupled Devices	189
	5.14	Quantum Well Modulators	190
		References	192
		Problems	194
6	**Hybrid-Optical Signal Processing**	**203**
	6.1	Microcomputer-Based Optical Processors	203
	6.2	Programmable Joint Transform Correlator	205
	6.3	High Efficiency Joint Transform Correlator	209
	6.4	Autonomous Target Tracking	213
	6.5	Data Association Multitarget Tracking	219
	6.6	Acoustooptic Space Integrator	226
	6.7	Multiple-Frequency-Shift Keying Signal Detection	232

6.8	Optical-Disk-Based Correlator	237
	References	240
	Problems	241

7 Photorefractive Crystal Signal Processing 249

7.1	Phase Conjugation Optical Correlator	249
7.2	Reconfigurable Interconnections	254
7.3	Multiplexed Photorefractive Matched Filters	269
7.4	Optical Novelty Filter	276
7.5	Compact Joint Transform Correlator Using a Thick Crystal	280
	References	283
	Problems	285

8 Digital–Optical Computing 287

8.1	Shadow-Casting Logic	288
8.2	Polarization Logic	293
8.3	Electron Trapping Logic	297
8.4	Symbolic Substitution Logic	301
8.5	Holographic Logic	304
8.6	Logic Based on Optical Bistability	305
8.7	Optical Interconnect and Perfect Shuffle	308
8.8	Matrix–Vector Multiplier and Crossbar Switch	311
8.9	Systolic Processor and Digital Transform	313
8.10	Matrix–Matrix Multiplier	316
8.11	Expert System and Artificial Intelligence	319
	References	326
	Problems	329

9 Optical Neural Networks 339

9.1	Aspects of Neural Networks	339
9.2	Optical Associative Memory	342
9.3	Hopfield Model	348
9.4	Back-Propagation Model	350
9.5	An Adaptive Optical Neural Network	353
9.6	Orthogonal Projection Algorithm	357
9.7	Multilevel Recognition Algorithm	358
9.8	Interpattern Association Model	361
9.9	Heteroassociation Model	366
9.10	Space–Time-Sharing Algorithm	370
9.11	The Compact Optical Neural Network	376
9.12	Information Storage Capacity	378
9.13	Moment-Invariant Neurocomputing	382

9.14 Self-Organizing Neural Network 386
9.15 Optical Implementation of the Hamming Net 396
References 403
Problems 405

Index **415**

Preface

An optical processor can perform a myriad of complicated computing operations; its success must be due to the profound diffraction phenomena of light. The essential merit of an optical processor is its capability to process a signal in complex amplitude, parallelism, large capacity, high speed, and massive interconnection. Several processing operations have proved to be more efficient with optical techniques, such as Fourier transforms, convolutions, correlations, and space interconnections. The major advantages of electronic computers are, however, that they are flexible, programmable, accessible. The question is, "Can we exploit the efficient operation of optics and the flexibility of electronics to come up with a realistic hybrid architecture that meets our computational needs?" The answer to this question is "yes."

The profound relationship between optical processing and computing has stimulated vigorous interest among electrical engineers in recent years. This trend has continued, not only because optical systems are capable of performing certain complex operations but also because the underlying optical theory is analogous to system theory. Because of the vast demand for engineering applications, about a decade ago we produced a book entitled *Optical Information Processing*. It was based mostly on lecture notes that we used in our classes. Because of the rapid advances in this area, the book quickly fell behind the current trend of research. In order to close this gap, we have now updated the text.

The first chapter of this text contains the basic coherence theory and the phenomenon of optical transformation, as a general background. The second chapter introduces the fundamental concept of optical signal processing and architectures. The third chapter presents selected applications in coherent optics, and the fourth chapter discusses white-light processing and its applications. These four chapters provide the background of basic optical signal processing. We begin our discussion of the advances of spatial-light modulators and detectors in Chapter 5, which covers the key devices that make the real-time processing and computing with optics possible. Several hybrid-optical architectures using some of these devices are given in Chapter 6, and applications of photorefractive crystal to optical signal processing are given in Chapter 7. In Chapter 8, digital–optical computing is discussed. Finally, optical neural networks, architectures, designs, and models are provided in Chapter 9.

It is our aim to provide the students with a comprehensive background in modern optical signal processing and computing, and to make available an up-to-date book for interested technical staffs. The material in this book has been used in a series of two-semester courses in the Electrical and Computer Engineering Department at The Pennsylvania State University, as well as at a few additional seminars. The students were mostly senior and first-year graduate students. We have found that it is possible to teach the whole book without any significant omissions in a two-semester period. It should be emphasized that the book is not intended to cover the vast domain of optical computing and processing, but rather a few restricted areas of considerable importance.

In view of the great number of contributors in this area, we have not been able to cite all of them in this book.

Finally, we would like to express our appreciation to our students for their constant interest, enthusiasm, and motivation. Without their support, this book could not have been brought to completion. We are indebted to Mrs. Debby Pruger for her typing of parts of the manuscript, and last but not least, we are grateful to our spouses for their encouragement, patience, and support in the course of writing this book.

FRANCIS T. S. YU
SUGANDA JUTAMULIA

University Park, Pennsylvania
San Jose, California
October, 1992

CHAPTER ONE

Partial Coherence and Optical Transform

The coherent optical signal processor can perform a myriad of complicated processing operations. Its success is due primarily to the coherence properties of light, so we begin our discussion with the basic aspects of the partial coherence of light. Optical signal processors are capable of performing any linear operation as a function of one or two variables. Its essential merit is its capability of performing complex optical transformations, for which the linear system theory applies. We also discuss the basic optical transform in this chapter. In fact, most optical signal processors can be represented by analog linear systems.

1.1 ASPECTS OF PARTIAL COHERENCE

When radiation from two sources maintain a fixed phase relation between them, they are said to be *mutually coherent*. Therefore an extended source is coherent if all points of the source have fixed phase differences between them. We begin our discussion with the aspects of partial coherence.

In the classic theory of electromagnetic radiation, as in the development of Maxwell's equations, it is usually assumed that the electric and magnetic fields are always measurable at any position. Thus, in these situations no account of partial coherence theory is needed. There are situations, however, for which this assumption of known fields cannot be made and for which it is often helpful to apply partial coherence theory. For example, if we want to determine the diffraction pattern caused by the radiation from several sources, we cannot obtain an exact result unless the degree of coherence from the separate sources is taken into account. In such a situation, however, it is desirable to obtain an overall average to represent the *statistically* most likely result from any such combination of sources. It may thus be more useful to provide a statistical description than to follow the dynamical behavior of a wave field in detail.

Our treatment of partial coherence uses such ensemble averages. Let us assume an electromagnetic wave field propagating in space, as depicted in Figure 1.1, where $u_1(t)$ and $u_2(t)$ denote the instantaneous wave disturbances at positions 1 and 2, respectively. We choose the second-order moment as the quantity to be averaged, which is why it is called the *mutual coherence function*. This function is defined in the following equation:

$$\Gamma_{12}(\tau) \triangleq \langle u_1(t + \tau) u_2^*(t) \rangle, \tag{1.1}$$

where the asterisk denotes the complex conjugate, and $\Gamma_{12}(\tau)$ is the mutual coherence function between these points for a time delay τ. The angle brackets $\langle \rangle$ denote a time average, which can be written as

$$\Gamma_{12}(\tau) = \lim_{T \to \infty} \frac{1}{T} \int_0^T u_1(t + \tau) u_2^*(t)\, dt. \tag{1.2}$$

It is apparent that the mutual coherence function defined by Eq. 1.2 is essentially the temporal *cross-correlation function* between the complex disturbances of $u_1(t)$ and $u_2(t)$.

The *normalized mutual coherence function* can therefore be defined as

$$\gamma_{12}(\tau) \triangleq \frac{\Gamma_{12}(\tau)}{[\Gamma_{11}(0)\Gamma_{22}(0)]^{1/2}}, \tag{1.3}$$

where $\Gamma_{11}(\tau)$ and $\Gamma_{22}(\tau)$ are the *self-coherence functions* of $u_1(t)$ and $u_2(t)$, respectively. The function $\gamma_{12}(\tau)$ may also be called the *complex degree of coherence* or the degree of correlation.

We now demonstrate that the normalized mutual coherence function $\gamma_{12}(\tau)$ can be measured by applying Young's experiment on interference. In Figure 1.2, Σ represents an extended source of light, which is assumed to be inco-

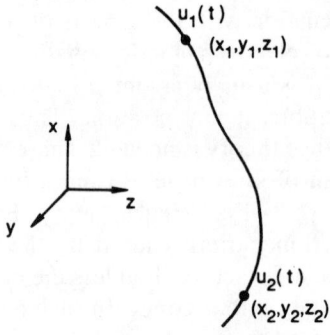

FIGURE 1.1 A wavefront propagation in space.

ASPECTS OF PARTIAL COHERENCE 3

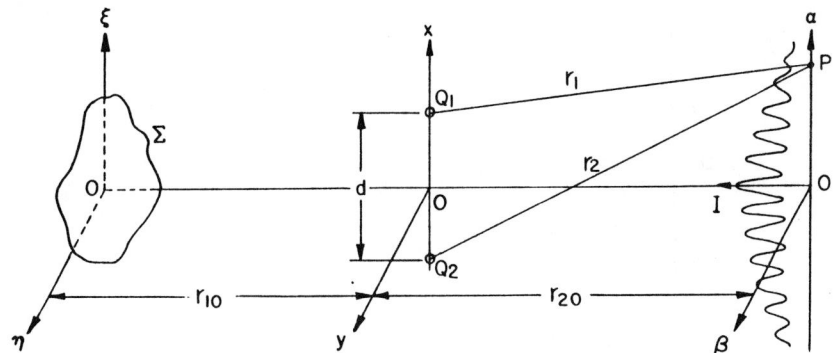

FIGURE 1.2 Young's experiment.

herent but nearly monochromatic; that is, its spectrum is of finite width. The light from this source falls upon a screen at a distance r_{10} from the source, and upon two small apertures (pinholes) in this screen, Q_1 and Q_2, separated by a distance d. On an observing screen located r_{20} away from the diffracting screen, an interference pattern is formed by the light passing through Q_1 and Q_2. Now let us suppose that the changing characteristics of the interference fringes are observed as the parameters of Figure 1.2 are changed. As a measurable quantity, let us adopt *Michelson's visibility* of the fringes, which is defined as

$$v \triangleq \frac{I_{max} - I_{min}}{I_{max} + I_{min}}, \qquad (1.4)$$

where I_{max} and I_{min} are the maximum and minimum intensities of the fringes.

For the visibility to be measurable, the conditions of the experiment, such as the narrowness of the spectrum and the closeness of the optical path lengths, must be such that they permit I_{max} and I_{min} to be clearly defined. Let us assume that these ideal conditions exist.

As we begin, our parameters change. First, we find that the average visibility of the fringes increases as the size of the source Σ is made smaller. Next, as the distance between pinholes Q_1 and Q_2 is increased, while Σ is held constant (and circular in form), the visibility shifts in the manner shown in Figure 1.3. When Q_1 and Q_2 are very close together, the intensity between the fringes falls to zero, and the visibility becomes unity. As d is increased, the visibility falls rapidly and reaches zero as I_{max} and I_{min} become equal. An additional increase in d causes the fringes to reappear, although they are shifted on the screen by half a fringe; that is, the areas that were previously light are now dark, and vice versa. As the distance d between pinholes is made even greater, the fluctuations in visibility shown in the figure are repeated. A curve similar to that in Figure 1.3 is obtained when the pinhole spacing is kept constant while the size of Σ is changed. These effects can be predicted from the *Van Cittert–Zernike theorem* (see Section 1.2). The visi-

4 PARTIAL COHERENCE AND OPTICAL TRANSFORM

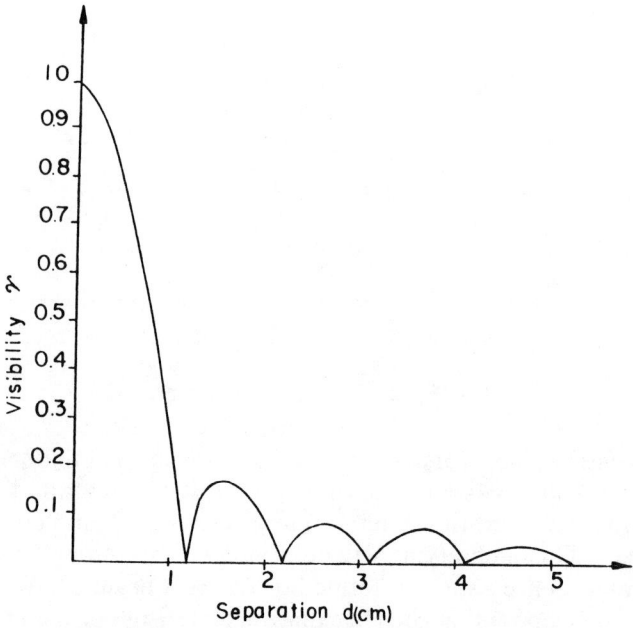

FIGURE 1.3 Visibility as a function of separation.

bility versus pinhole separation curve is sometimes used as a measure of *spatial coherence*, as discussed in Section 1.2. Screen separations r_{10} and r_{20} are both assumed to be large compared with the aperture spacing d and with the dimensions of the source. Beyond this limitation, changes in r_{10} nd r_{20} shift the scale of effects, as shown in Figure 1.3, but without altering their general character.

When the point of observation P is moved away from the center of the observing screen, visibility decreases as the path difference $\Delta r = r_2 - r_1$ increases, until it eventually becomes zero. The effect also depends on how nearly monochromatic the source is. The visibility of the fringe has been found to be appreciable only for a path difference of

$$\Delta r \simeq \frac{2\pi c}{\Delta \omega}, \qquad (1.5)$$

where c is the velocity of light and $\Delta\omega$ is the spectral width of the source. Equation 1.5 is often used to define the *coherence length* of the source, which is the distance at which the light beam is longitudinally coherent.

The preceding discussion has indicated that it is not necessary to have completely coherent light to produce an interference pattern, but that under the right conditions such a pattern may be obtained from an incoherent source. This effect is called *partial coherence*.

It will be helpful to develop the preceding equations further. Thus $u_1(t)$

and $u_2(t)$, the complex wave fields at points Q_1 and Q_2, are subject to the scalar wave equation in free space,

$$\nabla^2 u = \frac{\partial^2 u}{c^2 \partial t^2}, \tag{1.6}$$

where c is the velocity of light. This is a linear equation, and the wave field at point P on the observing screen is the sum of the fields from Q_1 and Q_2,

$$u_p(t) = c_1 u_1\left(t - \frac{r_1}{c}\right) + c_2 u_2\left(t - \frac{r_2}{c}\right), \tag{1.7}$$

where c_1 and c_2 are the appropriate complex constants. The corresponding irradiance at P may be written as

$$I_p = \langle u_p(t) u_p^*(t) \rangle = I_1 + I_2 + 2\,\mathrm{Re}\left\langle c_1 u_1\left(t - \frac{r_1}{c}\right) c_2^* u_2^*\left(t - \frac{r_2}{c}\right)\right\rangle, \tag{1.8}$$

where I_1 and I_2 are proportional to the squares of the magnitudes of $u_1(t)$ and $u_2(t)$. We now define the variables

$$t_1 = \frac{r_1}{c} \quad \text{and} \quad t_2 = \frac{r_2}{c}. \tag{1.9}$$

Then Eq. 1.8 can be written as

$$I_p = I_1 + I_2 + 2 c_1 c_2^* \mathrm{Re}\langle u_1(t - t_1) u_2^*(t - t_2)\rangle. \tag{1.10}$$

Thus, we see that the averaged quantity in Eq. 1.10 is the cross-correlation of the two complex wave fields.

If we make $t_2 - t_1 = \tau$, Eq. 1.10 can be written as

$$I_p = I_1 + I_2 + 2 c_1 c_2^* \mathrm{Re}\langle u_1(t + \tau) u_2^*(t)\rangle,$$

and combining this with Eq. 1.1, we obtain

$$I_p = I_1 + I_2 + 2 c_1 c_2^* \mathrm{Re}[\Gamma_{12}(\tau)]. \tag{1.11}$$

The *self-coherence functions* (i.e., the autocorrelations) of the radiations from the two pinholes can therefore be defined as

$$\Gamma_{11}(0) = \langle u_1(t) u_1^*(t) \rangle \quad \text{and} \quad \Gamma_{22}(0) = \langle u_2(t) u_2^*(t) \rangle. \tag{1.12}$$

6   PARTIAL COHERENCE AND OPTICAL TRANSFORM

If we let the following relations hold,

$$|c_1|^2 \Gamma_{11}(0) = I_1 \quad \text{and} \quad |c_2|^2 \Gamma_{22}(0) = I_2,$$

the intensity at P can then be written in terms of the degree of complex coherence, as given in Eq. 1.3

$$I_p = I_1 + I_2 + 2(I_1 I_2)^{1/2} \text{Re}[\gamma_{12}(\tau)]. \tag{1.13}$$

Let us write $\gamma_{12}(\tau)$ in the form

$$\gamma_{12}(\tau) = |\gamma_{12}(\tau)| \exp[i\phi_{12}(\tau)] \tag{1.14}$$

and assume that $I_1 = I_2 = I$, which can be called the *best condition*. Then Eq. 1.13 becomes

$$I_p = 2I[1 + |\gamma_{12}(\tau)| \cos \phi_{12}(\tau)]. \tag{1.15}$$

Thus we see that the maximum value of I_p is $2I[1 + |\gamma_{12}(\tau)|]$, and the minimum value is $2I[1 - |\gamma_{12}(\tau)|]$. By substituting these values into the visibility equation of Eq. 1.4, we have

$$v = |\gamma_{12}(\tau)|. \tag{1.16}$$

That is, under the best condition, the visibility of the fringes is a measure of the degree of coherence.

1.2   SPATIAL AND TEMPORAL COHERENCE

The term *spatial coherence* is applied to the effects of the size—in space—of the source of radiation. For example, if we consider a point source, and look at two points that are at equal light path distances from the source, the radiations reaching these points will be exactly the same. This mutual coherence will be equal to the self-coherence at either point. That is, if the points are Q_1 and Q_2, then

$$\Gamma_{12}(Q_1, Q_2, \tau) = \langle u(Q_1, t + \tau) u^*(Q_2, t) \rangle = \Gamma_{11}(\tau). \tag{1.17}$$

As the source is made larger, we can no longer claim an equality of mutual coherence and self-coherence. This lack of complete coherence is a *spatial* effect. *Temporal coherence* is an effect that is due to the finite spectral width of the source. The coherence is complete for strictly monochromatic radiation, but becomes only partial as other wavelengths are added, giving a finite spectral width to the source. It is never possible to separate completely the

1.2.1 Spatial Coherence

We utilize Young's experiment to determine the angular size of a spatially incoherent source (e.g., an extended source) as it relates to spatial coherence. Thus, we see that spatial coherence depends on the size of a light source. Let us now consider the paths of two light rays from a point on a linearly extended source ΔS, as they pass through the two narrow slits Q_1 and Q_2 depicted in Figure 1.4. If we let $r_{10} \gg d$, the intensity distribution at observation screen P_3 can, as a consequence of Eq. 1.13, be written as

$$I_p(\alpha) = I_1 + I_2 + 2\sqrt{I_1 I_2} \cos\left[k\left(\frac{d}{r_{10}}\xi + \frac{d}{r_{20}}\alpha\right)\right]. \tag{1.18}$$

Here I_1 and I_2 are the corresponding intensity distributions that are produced by the light rays passing through Q_1 and Q_2, respectively, and $k = 2\pi/\lambda$ is the wave number.

Equation 1.18 describes a set of parallel fringes along the α axis that comes from a single radiation point on the extended source, ΔS. Thus, we see that the other points on the extended source cause the superimposition of the fringes on the observation screen P_3. For a uniformly one-dimensional extended source of size ΔS, the resulting fringe pattern can be written as

$$\begin{aligned} I'_p(\alpha) &= I_1 \Delta S + I_2 \Delta S + 2\sqrt{I_1 I_2} \int_{-\Delta S/2}^{\Delta S/2} \cos\left[k\left(\frac{d}{r_{10}}\xi + \frac{d}{r_{20}}\alpha\right)\right] d\xi \\ &= \Delta S \left\{ I_1 + I_2 + 2\sqrt{I_1 I_2} \operatorname{sinc}\left[\left(\frac{\pi d}{\lambda r_{10}}\right)\Delta S\right] \cos\left(k\frac{d}{r_{20}}\alpha\right) \right\}, \end{aligned} \tag{1.19}$$

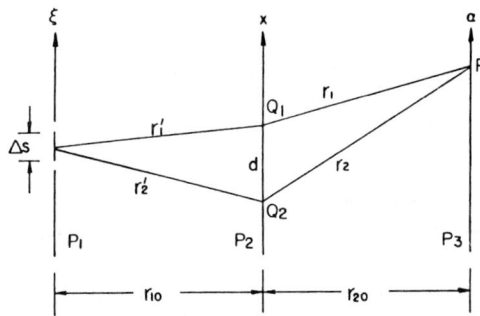

FIGURE 1.4 Measurement of spatial coherence.

PARTIAL COHERENCE AND OPTICAL TRANSFORM

where

$$\text{sinc } \pi\chi \triangleq \frac{\sin \pi\chi}{\pi\chi}.$$

The sinc factor of Eq. 1.19 indicates that the fringes vanish at

$$d = \frac{\lambda r_{10}}{\Delta S}. \tag{1.20}$$

Similarly, we can write Eq. 1.20 in terms of the angular size of the source θ_s,

$$d = \frac{\lambda}{\theta_s}, \tag{1.21}$$

where $\theta_s \triangleq \Delta S/r_{10}$. We note that the sinc factor of Eq. 1.19 is primarily due to the incoherent addition of the point radiators over the extended source ΔS. Equation 1.19 presents a useful example for the discussion of coherent and incoherent illumination. For completely coherent illumination there are interference fringes, while for completely incoherent illumination the interference fringes vanish. Moreover, Eq. 1.19 shows that the interference pattern (i.e., the cosine factor) is weighted by a broad sinc factor, whereby the interference fringes go to zero and reappear as a function of d, ΔS, or $1/r_{10}$. If the extended source had been circular in shape, the sinc factor of Eq. 1.19 would have been

$$2\frac{J_1(\pi \Delta S d/\lambda r_{10})}{\pi \Delta S d/\lambda r_{10}}, \tag{1.22}$$

where J_1 is the first-order *Bessel function*. The pinhole separation at which the fringes vanish would then be

$$d = 1.22 \frac{\lambda}{\theta_s}, \tag{1.23}$$

where $\theta_s \triangleq \Delta S/r_{10}$ is the angular size of the circular source.

Since the region of spatial coherence is determined by the visibility of the interference fringes, the coherence region increases as the size of the source decreases or as the distance of the source increases. In other words, the degree of spatial coherence increases as the distance of the propagated wave increases.

In addition, there is a relation between the intensity distribution of the source and the degree of spatial coherence. This relation is described in the *Van Cittert–Zernike theorem*. The theorem essentially states that the normalized complex degree of coherence $\gamma_{12}(0)$ between two points on a plane, which comes from an extended incoherent source at another plane, is proportional to the normalized inverse Fourier transform of the intensity distribution of the source:

$$\gamma_{12}(0) = \frac{\int_{\Delta S} I(\xi)\exp\left[i\frac{k}{r_{10}}(x_1 - x_2)\xi\right]d\xi}{\int_{\Delta S} I(\xi)\,d\xi}. \qquad (1.24)$$

Here subscripts 1 and 2 denote the two points on the diffraction screen P_2; x_1 and x_2 are the corresponding position vectors; ξ is the position vector at the source plane, $k = 2\pi/\lambda$; $I(\xi)$ is the intensity distribution of the source; and the integration is over the source size. Thus, it is apparent that if the intensity distribution of the source is uniform over a circular disk, the mutual coherence function is described by a rotational symmetric Bessel function J_1. On the other hand, if the source intensity is uniform over a rectangular slit, the mutual coherence function is described by a two-dimensional sinc factor.

1.2.2 Temporal Coherence

It is possible for us to split a light wave into two paths, to delay one of them, and then to recombine them to form an interference fringe pattern. In this way, we can measure the temporal coherence of the light wave. The degree of temporal coherence is the measure of the cross-correlation of a wave field at one time with respect to another wave field at a later time. Thus, the definition of temporal coherence can also refer to *longitudinal coherence* as opposed to transverse (i.e., spatial) coherence. The maximum difference in the optical path lengths of two waves derived from a source is known as the *coherent length* of that source. Since spatial coherence is determined by the wave field in the transverse direction, and temporal coherence is measured along the longitudinal direction, spatial and temporal coherences together describe the degree of coherence of a wave field within a volume of space.

The *Michelson interferometer* is one of the instruments most commonly used to measure the temporal coherence of a light source (see Figure 1.5). Looking at this figure, we can see that the beam splitter (BS) divides the light beam into two paths, one of which goes to mirror M_1 and the other to mirror M_2. By varying the path length (i.e., τ) to one of the mirrors, we can observe the variation in the interference fringes at observation screen P. Thus, the measurement of the visibility of the interference fringes corresponds to the measurement of the degree of temporal coherence $\gamma_{11}(\tau)$ at a time delay τ, where subscript 11 signifies the interference derived from the same point in space. Therefore, when the difference in path lengths is zero, the measurement of visibility corresponds to $\gamma_{11}(0)$.

Since the nature of the source affects coherence, the spectral width of the source affects the temporal coherence of the source. The time interval Δt,

10 PARTIAL COHERENCE AND OPTICAL TRANSFORM

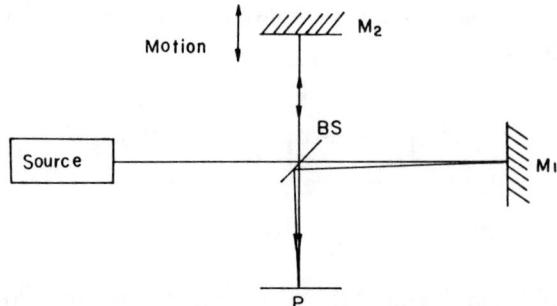

FIGURE 1.5 The Michelson interferometer. Note: BS, beam splitter; M, mirrors; P, observation screen.

during which the wave is coherent, can be approximated by

$$\Delta t \simeq \frac{2\pi}{\Delta\omega}, \qquad (1.25)$$

where $\Delta\omega$ is the spectral bandwidth of the source. Thus, the coherence length of the light source can be defined as

$$\Delta r = \Delta t c \simeq \frac{2\pi c}{\Delta\omega}, \qquad (1.26)$$

where $c = 3 \times 10^8$ m/sec is the velocity of light.

By substituting the relations

$$c = \frac{\omega\lambda}{2\pi} \quad \text{and} \quad \frac{\omega}{\Delta\omega} = \frac{\lambda}{\Delta\lambda},$$

we can also write

$$\Delta r \simeq \frac{\lambda^2}{\Delta\lambda}, \qquad (1.27)$$

where λ is the center wavelength, and $\Delta\lambda$ is the spectral width of the light source.

1.3 SYSTEM TRANSFORM

Generally speaking, an optical system can be represented by an input–output block diagram. In most instances the concept of the system theory can be easily applied to optical imaging and processing systems. Except for a few special cases, however, there are no general techniques for solving nonlinear optical systems. Nonlinear problems are usually solved by means of graphical and approximation procedures. Although no optical system is strictly linear, a large number of optical systems can be treated as linear, and these can be approached by linear system analysis. The analysis of optical systems usually involves linear spatially invariant concepts. It is the aim of this section to introduce some of the fundamentals.

It is well known that the behavior of a physical system can be described by the relationship of the output response to the input excitation, as shown in Figure 1.6. We assume that the output response and the input excitation are measurable quantities. Let us say that the output response $g_1(x, y)$ is caused by an input excitation $f_1(x, y)$, and a second response $g_2(x, y)$ is produced by $f_2(x, y)$. The input–output relationships are written in the following forms:

$$f_1(x, y) \to g_1(x, y) \tag{1.28}$$

and

$$f_2(x, y) \to g_2(x, y), \tag{1.29}$$

where (x, y) represents a two-dimensional spatial coordinate system.

If the sum of these two input excitations is applied to the input of the physical system, the corresponding output response would be a linear combination of $g_1(x, y)$ and $g_2(x, y)$, that is,

$$f_1(x, y) + f_2(x, y) \to g_1(x, y) + g_2(x, y). \tag{1.30}$$

Equation 1.30 in conjunction with Eqs. 1.28 and 1.29 represents the well-known *additivity* property of a linear system, which is also known as the *superposition* property. In other words, a necessary condition for a physical system to be linear is that the *principle of superposition* be included. The principle of superposition implies that the presence of one excitation in the system does not affect the response caused by other excitations.

If we multiply the input excitation by an arbitrary constant K, that is, $Kf_1(x, y)$, and the output response is equal to $Kg_1(x, y)$,

$$Kf_1(x, y) \to Kg_1(x, y), \tag{1.31}$$

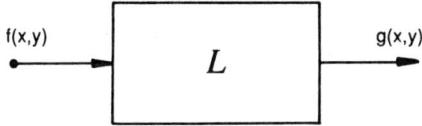

FIGURE 1.6 Block diagram of a physical system.

then the system is said to possess the *homeogeneity property*. In other words, a linear system is capable of preserving the scale factor of an input excitation. Thus, if a physical system is to be a linear system, the system must include the additivity and homeogeneity properties given in Eqs. 1.30 and 1.31.

There is, however, another important physical aspect that characterizes a linear system with constant parameters. This physical property is *spatial invariance*, which is analogous to the *time invariance* of an electrical network. If the output response of a physical system remains unaltered (except with appropriate translation) with respect to the input excitation, the physical system is said to possess the spatially invariant property. The qualification of a spatially invariant system is that if

$$f(x, y) \rightarrow g(x, y),$$

then

$$f(x - x_0, y - y_0) \rightarrow g(x - x_0, y - y_0), \quad (1.32)$$

where $f(x, y)$ and $g(x, y)$ are the corresponding input excitation and output response, respectively, and x_0 and y_0 are some arbitrary constants.

Thus, if a linear system possesses the spatially invariant property of Eq. 1.32, the system is known as a *linear spatially invariant system*.

We note that the concept of linear spatial invariance is rather important in the analysis of the electrooptic systems, because it simplifies otherwise quite complicated formulations.

One of the apparent distinctions of a linear spatially invariant system is that the system's *transfer function* can be uniquely described by the *spatial impulse response*. In contrast with the temporal (i.e., time) impulse response $h(t)$, the spatial impulse response $h(x, y)$ describes a function of two spatial variables x and y. In other words, if we assume that an impulse excitation $\delta(x, y)$ is applied to a linear spatially invariant system, as shown in Figure 1.7 then the output response must be the spatial impulse response of the system. The important aspect of a spatial impulse response of a linear spatially invariant system is that the system response can be uniquely described by an impulse response. The Fourier transform of a spatial impulse response describes the *system transfer function* $H(p, q)$,

$$H(p, q) = \iint_{-\infty}^{\infty} h(x, y)\exp[-i(px + qy)] \, dx \, dy, \quad (1.33)$$

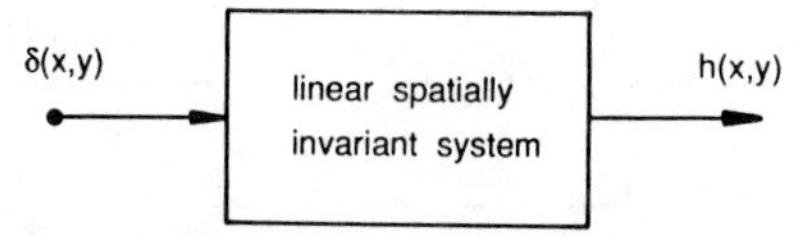

FIGURE 1.7 Description of a spatial impulse response.

where p and q are the angular spatial-frequency variables, in radians per unit distance, as opposed to the temporal frequency ω, in radians per unit time.

Consequently, if a system is linear spatially invariant, then the output response can be shown by the following convolution integral, that is

$$g(x, y) = \int\!\!\int_{-\infty}^{\infty} f(x', y')h(x - x', y - y')\, dx'dy', \qquad (1.34)$$

for which the Fourier space representation is shown in Figure 1.8, that is,

$$G(p, q) = F(p, q)H(p, q), \qquad (1.35)$$

where $G(p, q) = \mathcal{F}[g(x, y)]$, $F(p, q) = \mathcal{F}[f(x, y)]$, and $\mathcal{F}$ denotes the Fourier transformation.

1.4 PHASE TRANSFORM BY THIN LENSES

An important property of thin lenses is *phase transform* or *delay*. As we know that, light rays that propagate in a dielectric medium can be described by *wave theory*. Thus, a wavefront that propagates through a transparent dielectric medium (e.g., a lens) exhibits severe wavefront deformation.

Let us consider a light ray entering at a point on one side of a thin lens and emerging from the same point on the other side of the lens. Since the lens is assumed to be thin, the transversal displacement of the light ray inside the lens is negligible. Therefore, only the phase is retarded when a wavefront passes through a thin lens. We stress that the amount of phase transform is proportional to the thickness of the lens.

In order to calculate the phase transform of a lens, let us first consider the variation in thickness of a convergent (i.e., positive) lens, as shown in Figure 1.9. The phase transform $\phi(x, y)$ on the wavefront as it passes through (i.e.,

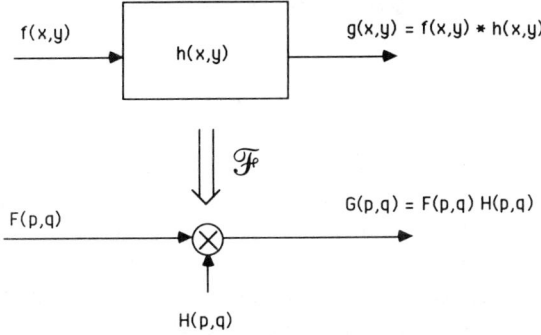

FIGURE 1.8 Analog system representations.

14 PARTIAL COHERENCE AND OPTICAL TRANSFORM

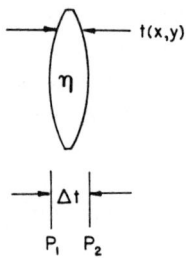

FIGURE 1.9 Thickness variation of a positive lens.

is refracted by) the lens can be written as

$$\phi(x, y) = k[\Delta t + (\eta - 1)t(x, y)]. \tag{1.36}$$

where $t(x, y)$ is the variation in thickness of the lens, Δt is its maximum thickness, η is its refractive index, $k = 2\pi/\lambda$ is the wave number, λ is the wavelength, and x and y are the spatial coordinates of the lens. We note that the quantity

$$\phi_1(x, y) = k\eta t(x, y)$$

represents the phase retardation caused by the lens alone, and

$$k[\Delta t - t(x, y)]$$

represents the phase retardation caused by free space (or air) alone. Notice that the *phase transform* function of the lens can be represented by the following:

$$T(x, y) = \exp[i\phi(x, y)] = \exp\{ik[\Delta t + (\eta - 1)t(x, y)]\}. \tag{1.37}$$

If the thin lens is illuminated by a monochromatic wavefront $u_i(x, y)$ at plane P_1 (see Figure 1.9), the wavefront that emerges through the lens can be expressed as

$$u_g(x, y) = u_i(x, y)T(x, y), \tag{1.38}$$

where $T(x, y)$ is the phase transform of the thin lens. Thus, we see that the output wavefront is the product of the input wavefront multiplied by the phase transform function of the lens. For convenience, an analog system representation of Figure 1.9 is given in Figure 1.10.

To derive the phase transform of a lens, we first consider the variation in thickness of a positive lens. If we divide the lens into left and right halves, as shown in Figure 1.11, the variation in thickness of the left half can be written as

PHASE TRANSFORM BY THIN LENSES   15

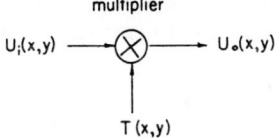

FIGURE 1.10 Analog system representation of a lens transform.

$$t_1(x, y) = \Delta t_1 - [R_1 - (R_1^2 - \rho^2)^{1/2}]$$
$$= \Delta t_1 - R_1\left\{1 - \left[1 - \left(\frac{\rho}{R_1}\right)^2\right]^{1/2}\right\}, \quad (1.39)$$

where Δt_1 is the maximum thickness variation of the left half of the lens. R_1 is the radius of curvature, and

$$\rho^2 = x^2 + y^2.$$

Similarly, the variation in thickness in the right half is

$$t_2(x, y) = \Delta t_2 - [R_2 - (R_2^2 - \rho^2)^{1/2}]$$
$$= \Delta t_2 - R_2\left\{1 - \left[1 - \left(\frac{\rho}{R_2}\right)^2\right]^{1/2}\right\}. \quad (1.40)$$

Thus, the overall thickness variation of the lens is

$$t(x, y) = t_1(x, y) + t_2(x, y)$$
$$= \Delta t - R_1\left\{1 - \left[1 - \left(\frac{\rho}{R_1}\right)^2\right]^{1/2}\right\} \quad (1.41)$$
$$- R_2\left\{1 - \left[1 - \left(\frac{\rho}{R_2}\right)^2\right]^{1/2}\right\},$$

where $\Delta t = \Delta t_1 + \Delta t_2$.

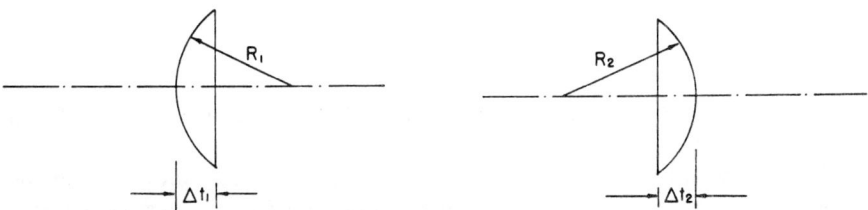

FIGURE 1.11 Left and right halves of a positive lens.

To simplify Eq. 1.41, we consider only the relatively small region of the lens that lies near the optical axis. In this case, we have

$$R_1 \gg \rho, \qquad R_2 \gg \rho.$$

Using the binomial series expansion, we can make the following approximations:

$$\left[1 - \left(\frac{\rho}{R_1}\right)^2\right]^{1/2} \simeq 1 - \frac{1}{2}\left(\frac{\rho}{R_1}\right)^2 \tag{1.42}$$

and

$$\left[1 - \left(\frac{\rho}{R_2}\right)^2\right]^{1/2} \simeq 1 - \frac{1}{2}\left(\frac{\rho}{R_2}\right)^2, \tag{1.43}$$

which are known as *paraxial approximations*. Thus, the overall thickness of the positive lens can be approximated as

$$t(x, y) \simeq \Delta t - \frac{\rho^2}{2}\left(\frac{1}{R_1} + \frac{1}{R_2}\right). \tag{1.44}$$

It should also be noted that the paraxial approximations of Eqs. 1.42 and 1.43 provide the same result by replacing the spherical surfaces of the lens with *parabolic* surfaces.

Thus, the phase transform function of a positive lens can be written as

$$T(x, y) = e^{ik\eta\Delta t} \exp\left[-ik(\eta - 1)\frac{\rho^2}{2}\left(\frac{1}{R_1} + \frac{1}{R_2}\right)\right]. \tag{1.45}$$

and its focal length can be identified as

$$f = \frac{R_1 R_2}{(\eta - 1)(R_1 + R_2)}. \tag{1.46}$$

By substituting Eq. 1.46 into Eq. 1.45, we have

$$T(x, y) = C_1 \exp\left(-i\frac{k}{2f}\rho^2\right), \tag{1.47}$$

where $C_1 = e^{ik\eta\Delta t}$ is a complex constant, f is the focal length of the lens, and $\rho = \sqrt{x^2 + y^2}$.

We stress that Eq. 1.47 is very useful in the processing of optical signals. The negative exponent expresses the convergent effect of a wavefront after it is refracted by the lens. In other words, if parallel light rays (in the form of a plane wavefront) are normally incident on the lens, the wavefront emerges as a spherical wavefront after being refracted by the lens, as illustrated in Figure 1.12.

Furthermore, the phase transform function of a divergent (or negative) lens can also be derived by the same approximation. Thus, we obtain

$$T(x, y) = C_2 \exp\left(i\frac{k}{2f}\rho^2\right), \quad (1.48)$$

where C_2 is a complex constant. Notice that Eq. 1.48 is essentially identical to Eq. 1.47, except that it contains a *positive* quadratic phase factor rather than a negative one. Thus, a plane wavefront will emerge as a divergent wavefront after passing through a negative lens, as shown in Figure 1.13.

1.5 THE FRESNEL–KIRCHHOFF THEORY

The Fresnel–Kirchhoff theory can generally be derived from the *scalar wave theory* by the application of Green's theorem. However, this approach is rather tedious and mathematically involved. So in this section we shall approach the Fresnel–Kirchhoff integral by simple *linear system theory*.

According to Huygens' principle, the complex amplitude observed from a point p' in the coordinate system $\sigma(\alpha, \beta, \gamma)$, caused by a monochromatic light source located in another coordinate system $\rho(x, y, z)$, as shown in Figure 1.14, may be calculated by assuming that each point of the light source is an infinitesimal spherical radiator. Thus, the complex light amplitude $h_l(\alpha - x, \beta - y, \gamma - z)$ in coordinate σ contributed by a point p in the ρ coordinate system must come from an unpolarized monochromatic point source, for which

$$h_1(\alpha - x, \beta - y, \gamma - z) = -\frac{i}{\lambda r}\exp[i(kr - \omega t)], \quad (1.49)$$

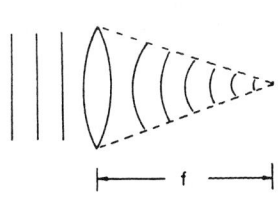

FIGURE 1.12 Convergent effect of a positive lens.

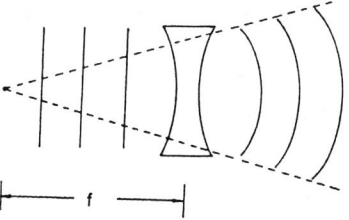

FIGURE 1.13 Divergent effect of a negative lens.

18 PARTIAL COHERENCE AND OPTICAL TRANSFORM

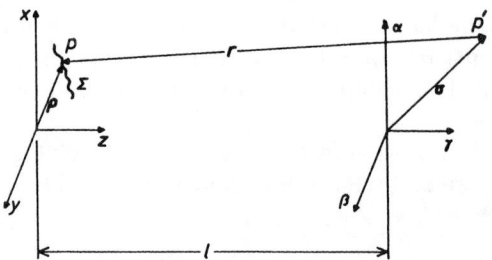

FIGURE 1.14 The Fresnel–Kirchhoff theory.

where λ is the wavelength, $k = 2\pi/\lambda$ is the wave number, and ω is the angular time frequency of the point source p, respectively, and r is the distance between the point source p and the point of observation p', which can be written as

$$r = [(l + \gamma - z)^2 + (\alpha - x)^2 + (\beta - y)^2]^{1/2}. \qquad (1.50)$$

If the separation l of the two coordinate systems is assumed to be large compared with the regions of interest in the ρ and σ coordinate systems, then the r in the denominator of Eq. 1.49 can be approximated by l, and that in the exponent is replaced by

$$r \approx (l + \gamma - z) + \frac{(\alpha - x)^2}{2l} + \frac{(\beta - y)^2}{2l}. \qquad (1.51)$$

Therefore, Eq. 1.49 can be written as

$$h_l(\alpha - x, \beta - y, \gamma - z) \qquad (1.52)$$
$$\approx -\frac{i}{\lambda l} \exp\left\{ik\left[l + \gamma - z + \frac{(\alpha - x)^2}{2l} + \frac{(\beta - y)^2}{2l}\right]\right\}.$$

where the time-dependent part of the exponent, ωt, has been dropped for convenience. Since Eq. 1.52 represents the free-space radiation from a monochromatic point source, it is known as the free-space or *spatial impulse response*. In other words, the complex amplitude produced at the σ coordinate system by a monochromatic radiating surface located in the ρ coordinate system can be written in the following abbreviated form:

$$g(\sigma) = \iint_\Sigma f(\rho) h_l(\sigma - \rho; k) \, d\Sigma, \qquad (1.53)$$

which is essentially a two-dimensional convolution integral, where $f(\rho)$ is the complex light field of the monochromatic radiating surface, Σ denotes the surface integral, and $d\Sigma$ is the incremental surface element. We note that the convolution integral of Eq. 1.53 is called the *Fresnel–Kirchhoff integral*.

For simplicity, we assume that a complex monochromatic radiating field $f(x, y)$ is distributed over the x, y plane. The complex light disturbances at the α, β coordinate plane can be obtained by the following convolution integral:

$$g(\alpha, \beta) = \iint_{-\infty}^{\infty} f(x, y) h_l(\alpha - x, \beta - y) \, dx \, dy, \qquad (1.54)$$

where

$$h_l(x, y) = C \exp\left[i \frac{k}{2l} (x^2 + y^2)\right] \qquad (1.55)$$

is the spatial impulse response between the spatial coordinate systems (x, y) and (α, β), and

$$C = -\frac{i}{\lambda l} e^{ikl}$$

is a complex constant. Equation 1.54 can be represented by the block diagram shown in Figure 1.15.

In addition, if the complex light disturbance at (α, β) is known, the monochromatic radiating field of $f(x, y)$ can be determined in a similar manner,

$$f(x, y) = \iint_{-\infty}^{\infty} g(\alpha, \beta) h_l^*(x - \alpha, y - \beta) \, d\alpha \, d\beta, \qquad (1.56)$$

where the superscript asterisk denotes the complex conjugate,

$$h_l^*(\alpha, \beta) = C^* \exp\left[-i \frac{k}{2l} (\alpha^2 + \beta^2)\right], \qquad (1.57)$$

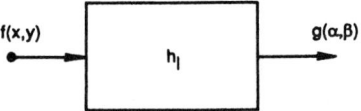

FIGURE 1.15 A system representation of forward diffraction.

and

$$C^* = \frac{i}{\lambda l} e^{-ikl}.$$

Notice that Eq. 1.57 represents a convergent spherical wavefront instead of a divergent wavefront. A block diagram representing the *backward diffraction* of Eq. 1.56 is shown in Figure 1.16.

1.6 FOURIER TRANSFORMATION BY LENSES

We now demonstrate the Fourier transform property of a lens. With reference to the optical system of Figure 1.17, we assume that a monochromatic complex wave field at P_1 is $f(\xi, \eta)$. Then by applying the Fresnel–Kirchhoff theory of Eq. 1.54, the complex light distribution at P_2 can be written as

$$g(\alpha, \beta) = C\{[f(\xi, \eta) * h_l(\xi, \eta)]T(x, y) * h_f(x, y)\}, \qquad (1.58)$$

where C is a proportionality constant, $*$ denotes the convolution operation, $h_l(\xi, \eta)$ and $h_f(x, y)$ are the corresponding spatial impulse responses, and $T(x, y)$ is the phase transform of the lens, as given in Eq. 1.47.

A linear system representation of Eq. 1.58 is shown in Figure 1.18. Equation 1.58 can be written in integral form, such as,

$$g(\alpha, \beta) = C \iint_{S_1} \left[\iint_{S_2} \exp\left(i\frac{k}{2}\Delta\right) dx\, dy \right] f(\xi, \eta)\, d\xi\, d\eta, \qquad (1.59)$$

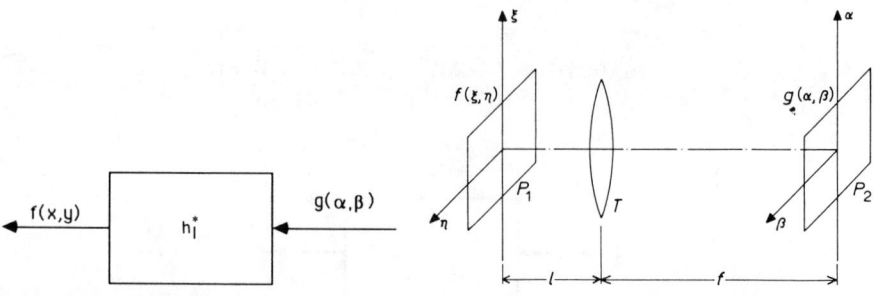

FIGURE 1.16 A system representation of backward diffraction.

FIGURE 1.17 Fourier transform property of a lens.

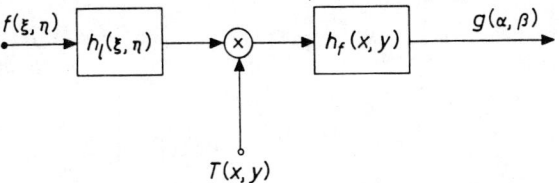

FIGURE 1.18 An analog system representation of Figure 1.17.

where

$$\Delta \triangleq \left\{ \frac{1}{l}[(x-\xi)^2 + (y-\eta)^2] \right. \\ \left. + \frac{1}{f}[(\alpha-x)^2 + (\beta-y)^2 - (x^2+y^2)] \right\}, \quad (1.60)$$

and S_1 and S_2 denote the surface integration over P_1 and the lens T, respectively. Since the lens is assumed paraxially large compared to the spatial regions of interest at P_1 and P_2, the surface integral of the lens can be assumed to be of infinite extent.

Equation 1.60 can be written in the following form:

$$\Delta = \frac{1}{f}[v\xi^2 + vx^2 + \alpha^2 - 2v\xi x - 2x\alpha \\ + v\eta^2 + vy^2 + \beta^2 - 2v\eta y - 2y\beta], \quad (1.61)$$

where $v = f/l$.

By completing the square Eq. 1.61, it can be shown by

$$\Delta = \frac{1}{f}\left[(v^{1/2}x - v^{1/2}\xi - v^{-1/2}\alpha)^2 - \alpha^2\left(\frac{1-v}{v}\right) - 2\xi\alpha \\ + (v^{1/2}y - v^{1/2}\eta - v^{-1/2}\beta)^2 - \beta^2\left(\frac{1-v}{v}\right) - 2\eta\beta \right]. \quad (1.62)$$

By substituting Eq. 1.62 into Eq. 1.59, we have

$$g(\alpha, \beta) = C \exp\left[-i\frac{k}{2f}\left(\frac{1-v}{v}\right)(\alpha^2 + \beta^2)\right] \\ \cdot \iint_{S_1} f(\xi, \eta) \exp\left[-i\frac{k}{f}(\alpha\xi + \beta\eta)\right] d\xi\, d\eta$$

22   PARTIAL COHERENCE AND OPTICAL TRANSFORM

$$\cdot \iint_{S_2} \exp\left[i\frac{k}{2f}(v^{1/2}x - v^{1/2}\xi - v^{-1/2}\alpha)^2\right.$$

$$\left. + (v^{1/2}y - v^{1/2}v - v^{-1/2}\beta)^2\right] dx\, dy, \quad (1.63)$$

for which we see that the integral over S_2 is a Fresnel integral. Since S_2 is assumed to be infinitely extended, the Fresnel integral will converge to a complex constant, which can be incorporated with C. Thus, Eq. 1.63 reduces to the following form:

$$g(\alpha, \beta) = C_1 \exp\left[-i\frac{k}{2f}\left(\frac{1-v}{v}\right)(\alpha^2 + \beta^2)\right]$$

$$\cdot \iint_{S_1} f(\xi, \eta) \exp\left[-i\frac{k}{f}(\alpha\xi + \beta\eta)\right] d\xi\, d\eta, \quad (1.64)$$

which is essentially the Fourier transform of $f(\xi, \eta)$, except with a quadratic phase factor. Notice that the quadratic phase factor vanishes if $l = f$. In other words, if the signal plane P_1 is placed at the front focal plane of the lens, it leaves an exact Fourier transformation, such as

$$G(p, q) = C_1 \iint_{S_1} f(\xi, \eta) \exp[-i(p\xi + q\eta)]\, d\xi\, d\eta,$$

$$= C_1 F(p, q), \quad \text{for } v = 1, \quad (1.65)$$

where $p = k\alpha/f$ and $q = k\beta/f$ are the angular spatial frequency coordinates. A block diagram representing Eq. 1.65 is shown in Figure 1.19.

In conventional Fourier transform theory, the transformation from the spatial domain to the spatial frequency domain requires a negative transform kernel, that is, $\exp[-i(px + qy)]$, and the transformation from the spatial frequency domain to the spatial domain requires a positive transform kernel, that is, $\exp[i(px + qy)]$. Since a positive lens always introduces a negative kernel, an optical system would take only successive Fourier transformations, rather than a transform followed by its inverse, as shown in Figure 1.20. Therefore, to achieve the respective inverse Fourier transformation, the co-

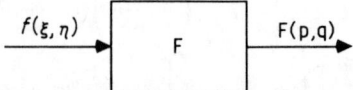

FIGURE 1.19   A block diagram representing the Fourier transformation of Eq. 1.65.

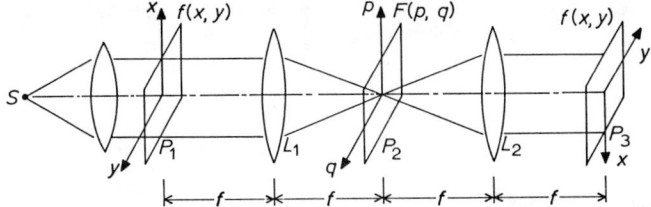

FIGURE 1.20 Successive Fourier transformations by lenses.

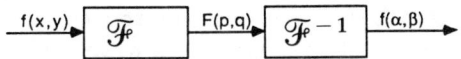

FIGURE 1.21 Block diagram presentation of Figure 1.20.

ordinate system of P_3 is rotated 180°, as shown in the figure. A block diagram representing the successive direct and inverse Fourier transformations is shown in Figure 1.21.

REFERENCES

1.1 M. Born and E. Wolf, *Principles of Optics*, 6th rev. ed., Pergammon, New York, 1980.
1.2 F. T. S. Yu, *Optical Information Processing*, Wiley–Interscience, New York, 1983.
1.3 F. T. S. Yu and I. C. Khoo, *Principles of Optical Engineering*, Wiley, New York, 1990.
1.4 G. O. Reynolds, J. B. DeVelis, G. G. Perent, Jr., and B. J. Thompson, *Physical Optics Notebook: Tutorials in Fourier Optics*, SPIE Optical Engineering Press, Bellingham, Wash., 1989.
1.5 B. E. A. Saleh and M. C. Teich, *Fundamentals of Photonics*, Wiley–Intescience, New York, 1991.

PROBLEMS

1.1 Two beams of strictly coherent light illuminate a diffraction screen. Determine the condition by which maximum visibility occurs at the diffraction screen.

1.2 Let us consider the Young's interference experiment as shown in Figure 1.22 where $d \ll l_1, l_2$. Show that the degree of coherence $|\gamma_{12}| = 1$ when the source converges to a point source, and that $|\gamma_{12}| = 0$ as the surface of the monochromatic source Σ becomes infinitely large.

24 PARTIAL COHERENCE AND OPTICAL TRANSFORM

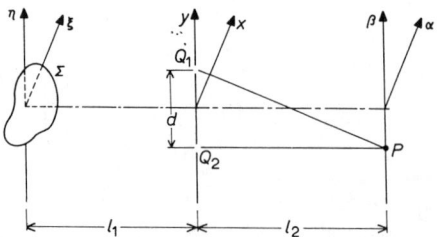

FIGURE 1.22

1.3 Instead of using an extended monochromatic light source as in Figure 1.22, assume that the light source is a narrow-slit monochromatic source perpendicular to the η axis. Given the wavelength of the light source 5000 Å, the separation between the source plane and the diffraction screen is $l_1 = 1$ meter, the separation between Q_1 and Q_2 is $d = 2.5$ mm, and the minimum-to-maximum irradiance ratio at the observation plane (α, β) is $I_{min}/I_{max} = 0.22$. Calculate the slit width of the light source.

1.4 With reference to Young's experiment in Problem 1.2, which contains a circular light source of radius ρ. Show that the visibility at the observation plane is dependent upon the product of radius ρ and the separation d between Q_1 and Q_2, for a fixed value of l_1.

1.5 We consider the illumination of two monochromatic plane waves on an observation plate in which the plate produces an interference fringe pattern as given by,

$$I(x, y) = K_1 + K_2\cos(p_0 x),$$

for all y, where K_1 and K_2 are arbitrary positive constraints, p_0 is the spatial frequency in radians per millimeter, and (x, y) is the coordinate system of the observation plate. Calculate the degrees of coherence between these two light waves.

1.6 Consider two sources both emitting two discrete frequencies, ω_1 and ω_2. One source emits the radiation as given by,

$$u_1 = a_{11}\exp[-i(\omega_1 t + \phi_{11})] + a_{12}\exp[-i(\omega_2 t + \phi_{12})]$$

and the other is

$$u_2 = a_{21}\exp[-i(\omega_1 t + \phi_{21})] + a_{22}\exp[-i(\omega_2 t + \phi_{22})].$$

(a) Determine the degree of coherence $|\gamma_{12}(\tau)|$.
(b) From the result obtained in part (a), show that $|\gamma_{12}(\tau)| \leq 1$ for all τ. If $\omega_1 = \omega_2$, so that we may set a_{12} and a_{22} equal to zero, show that the degree of coherence is unity.

PROBLEMS 25

1.7 Let us consider the infinitely large plane source of Figure 1.22, which is overlaid by a sinusoidal grating of spatial frequency p_0 rad/mm, that is, $T(\xi, \eta) = \frac{1}{2}[1 + \cos(p_0\eta)]$. Find the relationship between this spatial frequency p_0 and the separation d, at which high visibility fringe patterns can be observed.

1.8 Given an experiment setup like that in Figure 1.23, the (quasi-monochromatic) light source is assumed to be a uniform circular source of radius ρ. If the two pinholes Q_1 and Q_2 have the same radius r, where $r \ll d$, and $\rho < d$, then evaluate the corresponding irradiance at the observation plane P.

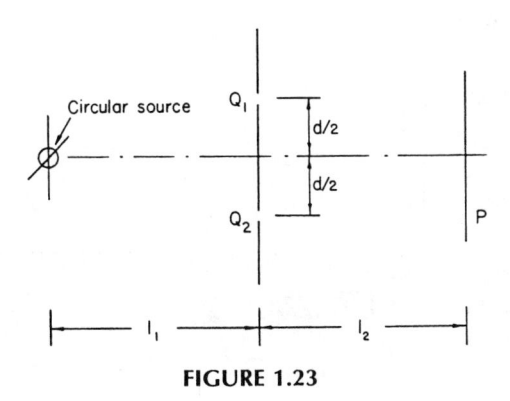

FIGURE 1.23

1.9 In order to maintain a high spatial coherence between Q_1 and Q_2 for a fixed separation d, it is desirable to sample the extended monochromatic source with narrow slits of Figure 1.22.
  (a) Calculate the locations of these narrow slits to fulfill this requirement.
  (b) Evaluate the corresponding spatial coherence function.
  (c) Show that the mutual coherence function is invariant for any two vertical points with separation d over the diffraction screen.

1.10 Refer to Young's experiment, shown in Figure 1.22. We assume that the source is a monochromatic slit source 0.1 mm wide, that the distance between this source and the narrow slits is 1 meter, that the separation between the slits is 3 mm, and that $\lambda = 600$ nm.
  (a) Determine the complex degree of coherence between the slits.
  (b) Calculate the visibility of the fringe pattern.

1.11 Let us consider two monochromatic point radiators separated by a distance of $\Delta\eta$. With reference to Young's experiment of Figure 1.22:
  (a) Calculate the mutual coherence Γ_{12} for the case where the radiators are derived from a common monochromatic source.

(b) Repeat part (a), assuming these point radiators are derived from two independent monochromatic sources.

1.12 Assume that two monochromatic plane waves of equal intensity are falling obliquely over an observation plane, as shown in Figure 1.24a. The fringe intensity distribution is as plotted in Figure 1.24b.
- **(a)** Calculate the degree of coherence between these two beams of light.
- **(b)** Determine the spatial frequency of the fringe pattern and the oblique angle of the plane waves. The wavelength of illumination is assumed to be $\lambda = 0.633$ μm.
- **(c)** If the intensity ratio is equal to 2 (i.e., $I_A/I_B = 2$), calculate the visibility of the interference fringes.

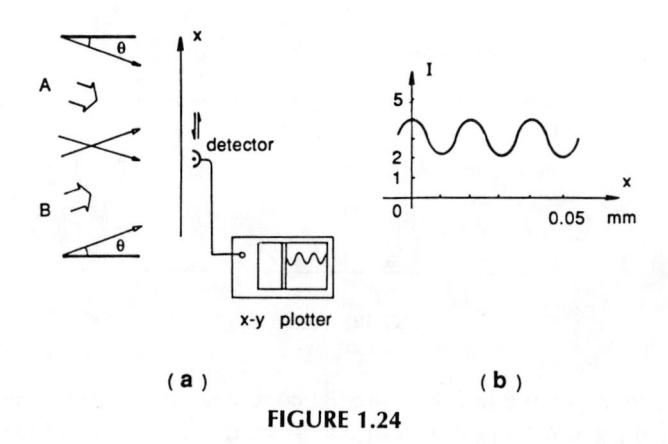

FIGURE 1.24

1.13 Referring to the depiction of Young's experiment in Figure 1.22, we assume that $d = 1$ mm, $\lambda = 600$ nm, and $l_1 = 1.2$ m. If Σ is replaced by two point sources with a separation, b, calculate the degree of coherence for $b = 0.5$ mm and 0.1 mm, respectively.

1.14 The time interval Δt during which the wave is coherent can be approximated by

$$\Delta t \simeq \frac{1}{\Delta \nu},$$

where $\Delta \nu$ is the spectral bandwidth of the light source.
- **(a)** Evaluate the coherent length of the light in terms of the center wavelength λ and $\Delta\lambda$ spectral width of the light source.
- **(b)** If the spectral width of the laser is $\Delta\lambda = 0.03$ Å and the center wavelength is $\lambda = 4880$ Å, compute the coherent length of the laser.

1.15 The intensity distribution of a one-dimensional monochromatic source is given by

$$I(\xi) = \begin{cases} 1, & |\xi| \leq W/2, \\ 0, & \text{otherwise}. \end{cases}$$

If the light source illuminates a diffraction screen (as shown in Figure 1.25):

(a) Calculate the complex degree of coherence (i.e., the normalized spatial coherence) at the screen.
(b) Sketch the two-dimensional complex degree of coherence at the diffraction screen.
(c) Determine the coherent distance along the x and the y directions of the diffraction screen.

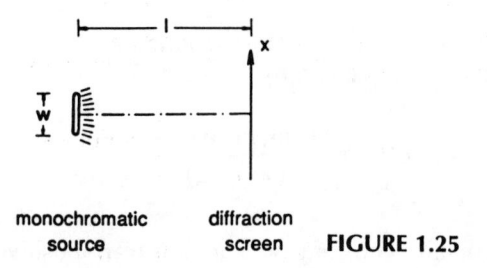

FIGURE 1.25

1.16 Refer to the depiction of Young's experiment in Figure 1.26, where Δs is a linear extended monochromatic source, $d = 1$ mm, $\lambda = 6330$ Å, and $L = 1$ m. Using these parameters, calculate the degrees of coherence between Q_1 and Q_2 for $\Delta s = 0.1$ mm and 0.5 mm, respectively.

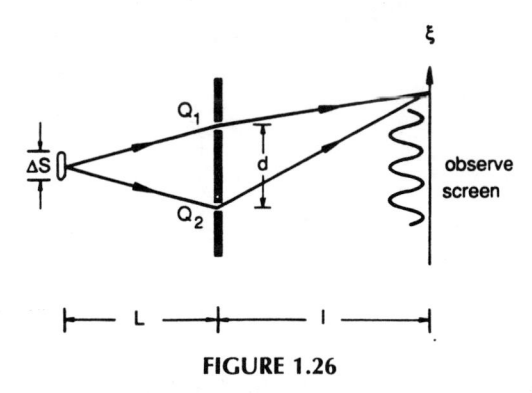

FIGURE 1.26

1.17 Two partially coherent monochromatic plane waves of equal amplitude are obliquely incident on an observation screen, as shown in the Figure 1.27.

28   PARTIAL COHERENCE AND OPTICAL TRANSFORM

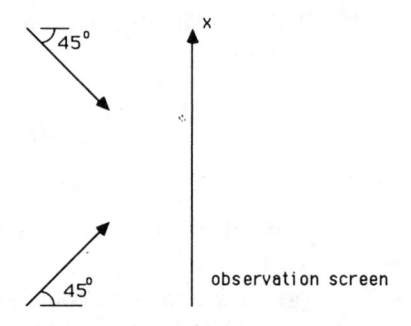

FIGURE 1.27

(a) If we assume that the wavelength of these monochromatic sources is $\lambda = 450$ nm, calculate the spatial frequency of the fringes.
(b) If the visibility of the fringes is equal to 50 percent, what is the degree of coherence between these two beams of light.
(c) Evaluate the I_{max} and I_{min} of the fringes.

1.18 The complex light distribution of a coherent illumination at a diffraction screen, shown in Figure 1.28, is given by

$$g(\alpha) = Ce^{i(\pi/\lambda l)\alpha^2}\left[\frac{\sin(\pi w\alpha/\lambda l)}{(\pi w\alpha/\lambda l)}\right],$$

where C is a proportionality constant, w is an arbitrary positive constant, and λ is the wavelength.

(a) Draw an analog system diagram for the calculation of the complex light field at P_1.
(b) Calculate the complex light distribution at P_1.

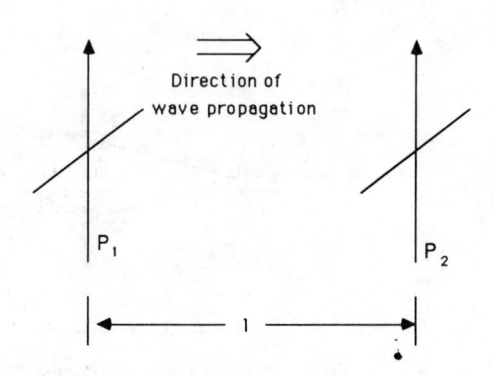

FIGURE 1.28

1.19 Assume that a coherent wave field at the (α, β) spatial coordinate system is shown in Figure 1.29. It is our responsibility to evaluate the complex wave field at the (x, y) plane.
(a) Draw an analog system diagram to represent this problem.

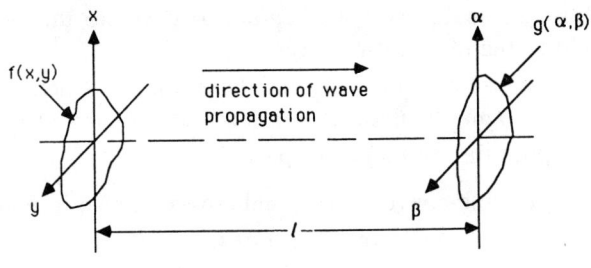

FIGURE 1.29

(b) If $g(\alpha, \beta)$ is given by

$$g(\alpha, \beta) = \exp\left[i\frac{\pi}{\lambda l}(\alpha^2 + \beta^2)\right],$$

evaluate $f(x, y)$.

1.20 Repeat Problem 1.19, assuming that a transparency $T(x, y)$ has been inserted in the (x, y) plane.
  (a) Draw an analog system diagram to determine the monochromatic wave field that is impinging the transparency
  (b) If we assume that $g(\alpha, \beta)$ and $T(x, y)$ are given by

$$g(\alpha, \beta) = \exp\left[i\frac{\pi}{\lambda l}(\alpha^2 + \beta^2)\right]$$

and

$$T(x, y) = \exp\left[-i\frac{2\pi}{\lambda l}(x^2 + y^2)\right],$$

then calculate the complex wave field impinging $T(x, y)$.

1.21 A diffraction screen is normally illuminated by a monochromatic plane wave of $\lambda = 500$ nm. It is observed at a distance of 30 cm from the diffraction screen as shown in Figure 1.30.

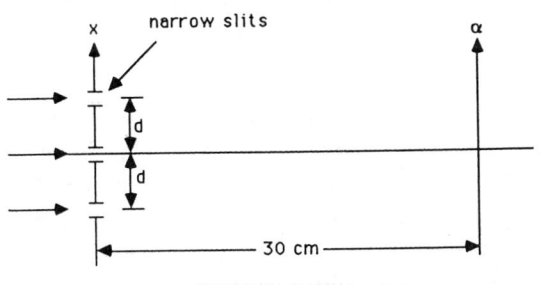

FIGURE 1.30

30 PARTIAL COHERENCE AND OPTICAL TRANSFORM

   (a) Draw an analog system diagram to evaluate the complex light field at the observation screen.
   (b) Calculate separations between these slits, by which the irradiance at the origin of the observation screen would be the minimum.
   (c) Compute the irradiance of part (b).

1.22 Consider a double-convex cylindrical lens as shown in Figure 1.31.
   (a) Evaluate the phase transform of the lens.
   (b) If the radii of the first and the second surfaces of the lens are $R_1 = 10$ cm and $R_2 = 15$ cm, respectively, and the refractive index of the lens is assumed to be $\eta = 1.5$, calculate the focal length of the lens.
   (c) If the lens is submerged in a tank of fresh water, in which the refractive index of the water $\eta = 1.33$, determine the focal length of the lens in the water.

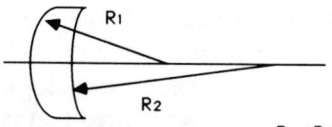

FIGURE 1.31 $R_1 < R_2$

1.23 The compound lens, as shown in Figure 1.32, consists of a thin positive lens of focal length 30 cm, separated by a distance of 10 cm from a thin negative lens of focal length 30 cm.
   (a) Find the focal length of the compound lens.
   (b) Draw an analogous system diagram to represent the optical system.
   (c) Calculate the location of the focal point from the negative lens.

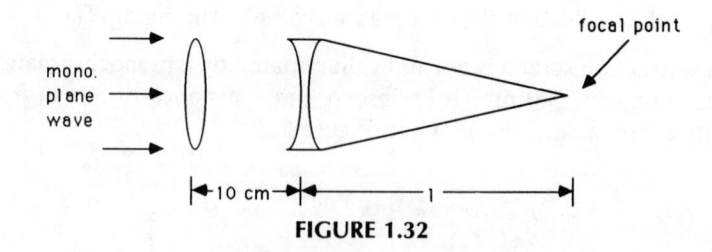

FIGURE 1.32

1.24 Assume that an optical processor is illuminated by a monochromatic plane wave, as shown in Figure 1.33, where the amplitude transmittance of the transparency is denoted by $f(\xi, \eta)$, and $l < f$.
   (a) Calculate the output complex light field at the back focal length of the transform lens.
   (b) Determine the output irradiance.

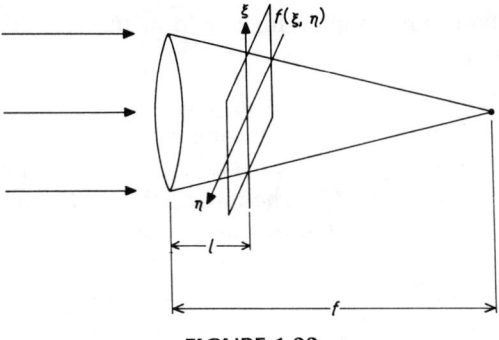

FIGURE 1.33

(c) What is the *effective* focal length of this Fourier transform system?

(d) Show that the scale of the Fourier spectrum is proportional to the effective focal length.

1.25 Consider a lens cut from a thin section of a cone, as shown in Figure 1.34. By means of the paraxial approximation, determine the corresponding phase transformation. Explain and sketch the effect of the lens upon a normally incident monochromatic plane wave.

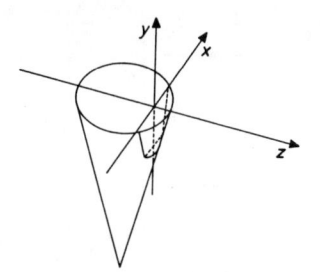

FIGURE 1.34

1.26 The amplitude transparency of a one-dimensional Fresnel zone-lens is given by

$$T(x, y) = \frac{1}{2}(1 + \cos ax^2), \quad \text{for all } y,$$

where a is an arbitrary constant.

(a) Show that this transparency is composed by three lenses, the flat, the concave, and the convex cylindrical lenses.

(b) Determine the corresponding focal lengths of this transparency.

(c) If this transparency is illuminated by a normally incident monochromatic plane wave, draw an analog system diagram to evaluate the complex light field behind the zone-lens.

(d) Calculate the complex light field at the rear focal plane of the zone-lens.

1.27 A spatial filter with time-varying characteristics can be realized by means of the Fabry–Perot interferometric technique. The filter consists of thin transparent glass plates that are used to support a highly reflective substance spread on the inner surfaces (Figure 1.35). A monochromatic plane wave is normally incident upon the surface of one of the glass plates. If r and t denote, respectively, the reflection and transmission coefficients of the reflective substance, and the effect of the glass plates is neglected, show that the complex wave field transmitted through the filter is

$$E(\omega) = K \frac{t^2 \exp(-i\omega d/c)}{1 - r^2 \exp(-i2\omega d/c)},$$

where ω is the angular frequency of the incident plane wave, c is the velocity of the wave propagation, d is the separation of the glass plates, and K is an arbitrary constant.

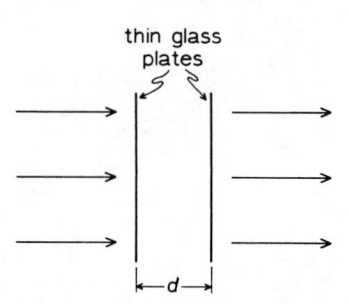

FIGURE 1.35

1.28 Given two positive, thin lenses of focal lengths f_1 and f_2:
  (a) Calculate the resultant focal length of these two lenses when they are touching.
  (b) If these two lenses are separated by a distance d, where $d < f_1$ and $d < f_2$, evaluate the distance of the focal point behind the second lens.

1.29 (a) Calculate the temporal mutual coherence function of a light source whose spectrum is approximated by rect $[|\lambda - \lambda_0|/\Delta\lambda]$, where the center wavelength $\lambda_0 = 6000$ Å and spectral width $\Delta\lambda = 2$ Å.
  (b) How many fringes can be formed in a Michelson interferometer before the visibility drops to 50 percent?

1.30 A monochromatic source consists of two parallel slit sources, one with a finite width, and the other that is assumed infinitely small. These two sources may be described as $I_s(x) + a_0\delta(x - x_0)$, where a_0 is a positive constant.

(a) Sketch a Young's experiment to show that the degree of mutual coherence λ_{12} can be measured.

(b) Determine the portion of $I_s(x)$ that can be completely derived from $|\gamma_{12}|^2$.

1.31 Given the coherent optical processor shown in Figure 1.36, denote the input transparency by $f(x, y)$ and the output complex light field by $F(p, q)$ [the Fourier transform of $f(x, y)$].

(a) Draw a block diagram showing Fourier transform representation of the optical system.

(b) Assuming that the output irradiance is recorded on a linear photographic plate, if this recorded transparency is inserted in the input plane in place of the original transparency, show that the output light distribution is proportional to the autocorrelation function of $f(x, y)$.

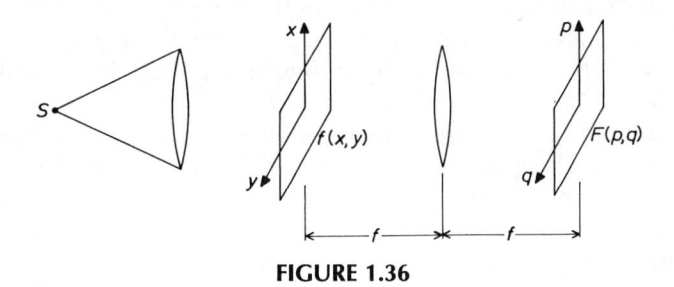

FIGURE 1.36

1.32 A monochromatic plane wave is normally incident on an aberration-free objective lens. Due to some alignment error, the irradiance observed on a plane is displaced slightly from the focal plane of the lens. Determine the largest error in distance at which the irradiance is still sufficiently accurate to represent the Fraunhofer diffraction pattern.

CHAPTER TWO

Optical Signal Processing

Advances in quantum electronics have brought the infrared and the visible range of electromagnetic waves into use. The invention of intensive coherent light sources has permitted us to build more efficient optical systems for communication and signal processing. Most of the optical processing architectures to date have been confined to cases of either complete coherence or complete incoherence. However, a continuous transition between these two extremes is possible.

The recent advances of real-time spatial light modulators and electrooptic devices have brought optical signal processing to a new height. Much attention has been focused on high-speed and high-data-rate optical signal processing and computing. In this chapter we discuss the basic principles of optical signal processing, most of it within the coherent regime.

2.1 COHERENT AND INCOHERENT PROCESSORS

Consider the hypothetical optical system as depicted in Figure 2.1, in which the light emitted by the source Σ is assumed monochromatic and the complex light distribution at the input plane comes from the incremental light source $d\Sigma$. To determine the light field at the output plane, we let the complex light distribution at the input plane be $u(x, y)$. If the complex amplitude transmittance of the input plane is $f(x, y)$, the complex light field immediately behind the signal plane would be $u(x, y)f(x, y)$.

We assume that the optical system under consideration is a linear and spatially invariant system with a spatial impulse response of $h(x, y)$. The complex light field at the output plane of the system, which comes from $d\Sigma$, can then be determined by the following convolution equation:

$$g(\alpha, \beta) = [u(x, y)f(x, y)] * h(x, y), \qquad (2.1)$$

where the asterisk denotes the convolution operation.

COHERENT AND INCOHERENT PROCESSORS

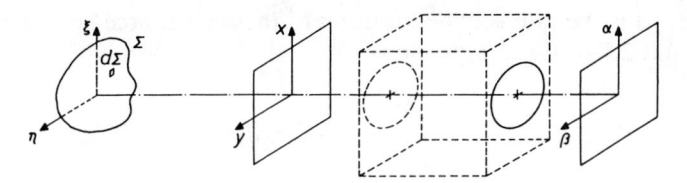

FIGURE 2.1 A hypothetical optical signal-processing system.

The corresponding intensity distribution at the output plane, which is due to $d\Sigma$, is

$$dI(\alpha, \beta) = g(\alpha, \beta)g^*(\alpha, \beta) d\Sigma, \qquad (2.2)$$

where the asterisk represents the complex conjugate. Thus, the overall intensity distribution at the output plane is

$$I(\alpha, \beta) = \iint |g(\alpha, \beta)|^2 d\Sigma, \qquad (2.3)$$

which can be written in the following convolution form,

$$I(\alpha, \beta) = \iiiint_{-\infty}^{\infty} \Gamma(x, y; x', y') h(\alpha - x, \beta - y) h^*(\alpha - x', \beta - y')$$
$$\cdot f(x, y) f^*(x', y') \, dx \, dy \, dx' \, dy', \qquad (2.4)$$

where

$$\Gamma(x, y; x', y') = \iint_{\Sigma} u(x, y) u^*(x', y') \, d\Sigma \qquad (2.5)$$

is the *spatial coherence function*, which is also known as the *mutual intensity function*.

Let us now choose two arbitrary points Q_1 and Q_2 at the input plane. If r_1 and r_2 are the respective distances from Q_1 and Q_2 to $d\Sigma$, the complex light disturbances at Q_1 and Q_2 that come from $d\Sigma$ can be written as

$$u_1(x, y) = \frac{[I(\xi, \eta)]^{1/2}}{r_1} e^{ikr_1} \qquad (2.6)$$

and

$$u_2(x', y') = \frac{[I(\xi, \eta)]^{1/2}}{r_2} e^{ikr_2}, \qquad (2.7)$$

where $I(\xi, \eta)$ is the intensity distribution of the light source. By substituting Eqs. 2.6 and 2.7 in Eq. 2.5, we have

$$\Gamma(x, y; x', y') = \iint_\Sigma \frac{I(\xi, \eta)}{r_1 r_2} \exp[ik(r_1 - r_2)] d\Sigma. \tag{2.8}$$

When the light rays are paraxial, $r_1 - r_2$ can be approximated by

$$r_1 - r_2 \simeq \frac{1}{r}[\xi(x - x') + \eta(y - y')], \tag{2.9}$$

where r is the distance between the source plane and the signal plane. Then Eq. 2.8 can be written as

$$\Gamma(x, y; x', y')$$
$$= \frac{1}{r^2} \iint I(\xi, \eta) \exp\left\{i\frac{k}{r}[\xi(x - x') + \eta(y - y')]\right\} d\xi\, d\eta, \tag{2.10}$$

which represents the inverse Fourier transform for intensity distribution at the source plane. Equation 2.10 is also known as the *Van Cittert–Zernike theorem*. The normalized form of this theorem is given in Eq. 1.24.

Now let us consider two extreme situations. In one we let the light source become infinitely large, and we assume that it is uniform, that is, $I(\xi, \eta) \simeq K$. Thus, Eq. 2.10 becomes

$$\Gamma(x, y; x', y') = K_1 \delta(x - x', y - y'), \tag{2.11}$$

where K_1 is a proportionality constant. This equation describes a completely *incoherent* optical system.

On the other hand, if we let the light source be vanishingly small, then $I(\xi, \eta) \simeq K\delta(\xi, \eta)$, and Eq. 2.10 becomes

$$\Gamma(x, y; x', y') = K_2, \tag{2.12}$$

where K_2 is an arbitrary constant. This equation describes a completely *coherent* optical system. In other words, a monochromatic point source describes a strictly coherent regime, whereas an extended source describes a strictly incoherent system. Furthermore, an extended monochromatic source is also known as a *spatially incoherent* source.

For the completely incoherent optical system described in Eq. 2.11, $[\Gamma(x, y; x', y') = K_1\delta(x - x', y - y')]$, the intensity distribution at the output plane, given in Eq. 2.4, becomes

$$I(\alpha, \beta) = \iiiint_{-\infty}^{\infty} \delta(x' - x, y' - y) h(\alpha - x, \beta - y)$$
$$\cdot h^*(\alpha - x', \beta - h') f(x, y) f^*(x', y') \, dx \, dy \, dx' \, dy', \quad (2.13)$$

which can be reduced to

$$I(\alpha, \beta) = \iint_{-\infty}^{\infty} |h(\alpha - x, \beta - y)|^2 |f(x, y)|^2 \, dx \, dy. \quad (2.14)$$

It is therefore apparent that for incoherent illumination, the intensity distribution at the output plane is the convolution of the input signal's intensity in relation to the intensity of the spatial impulse response. In other words, an incoherent optical system is linear in *intensity* or

$$I(\alpha, \beta) = |h(x, y)|^2 * |f(x, y)|^2, \quad (2.15)$$

where the asterisk denotes the convolution operation. An analog system diagram of an incoherent system is shown in Figure 2.2. The output intensity response can be determined by

$$I_0(\alpha, \beta) = \iint_{-\infty}^{\infty} I_i(x, y) h_i(\alpha - x, y - \beta) \, dx \, dy, \quad (2.16)$$

where $I_i(x, y)$ is the input intensity excitation and $h_i(x, y) = |h(x, y)|^2$ is the intensity of the spatial impulse response.

However, for the strictly coherent illumination described in Eq. 2.12 [$\Gamma(x, y; x', y') = K_2$], Eq. 2.4 becomes

$$I(\alpha, \beta) = g(\alpha, \beta) g^*(\alpha, \beta) = \iint_{-\infty}^{\infty} h(\alpha - x, \beta - y) f(x, y) \, dx \, dy$$
$$\times \iint_{-\infty}^{\infty} h^*(\alpha - x', \beta - y') f^*(x', y') \, dx' \, dy'. \quad (2.17)$$

It is therefore apparent that the coherent optical system is linear in *complex amplitude*, or

$$g(\alpha, \beta) = \iint_{-\infty}^{\infty} h(\alpha - x, \beta - y) f(x, y) \, dx \, dy, \quad (2.18)$$

An analog system diagram of Eq. 2.18 is given in Figure 2.3.

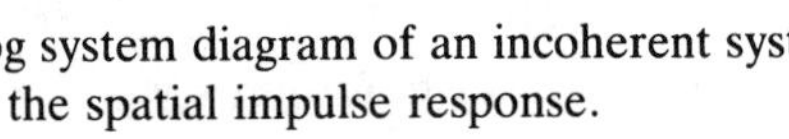

$I_i(x,y) \longrightarrow \boxed{h_i(x,y)} \longrightarrow I_0(\alpha,\beta)$

FIGURE 2.2 An analog system diagram of an incoherent system. *Note:* $h_i(x, y)$ represents the intensity of the spatial impulse response.

38   OPTICAL SIGNAL PROCESSING

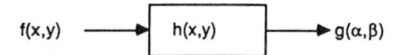

f(x,y) → h(x,y) → g(α,β)

FIGURE 2.3 An analog system diagram of a coherent system; $h(x, y)$ represents the spatial impulse response.

2.2 FOURIER TRANSFORM PROCESSOR

As we have shown in Section 1.6, successive Fourier transformations can be performed by lenses. Thus, a *Fourier transform processor*, which is commonly known as a coherent optical processor, can be constructed, as shown in Figure 2.4, where P_1, P_2, and P_3 represent the input, the Fourier, and the output planes, respectively, and a monochromatic point source S is located at the front focal length of a collimating lens. If an object transparency of amplitude transmittance $f(x, y)$ is inserted at the input plane P_1, the complex light field distributed at P_2 would be the Fourier transform of $f(x, y)$, or

$$F(p, q) = \mathcal{F}[f(x, y)], \tag{2.19}$$

where $p = (2\pi/f\lambda)x$ and $q = (2\pi/f\lambda)y$ are the angular spatial-frequency coordinates.

Let us now assume that a spatial filter of complex amplitude transmittance $H(p, q)$ is inserted in the Fourier plane P_2. The complex light field P_2 immediately behind the spatial filter is then

$$E(p, q) = KF(p, q)H(p, q), \tag{2.20}$$

where K is a proportionality constant.

Since the second lens L_2 performs an inverse Fourier transformation, the complex-amplitude light distribution at P_3 can be shown by

$$g(\alpha, \beta) = K \iint_S F(p, q)H(p, q)\exp[i(p\alpha + q\beta)] \, dp \, dq, \tag{2.21}$$

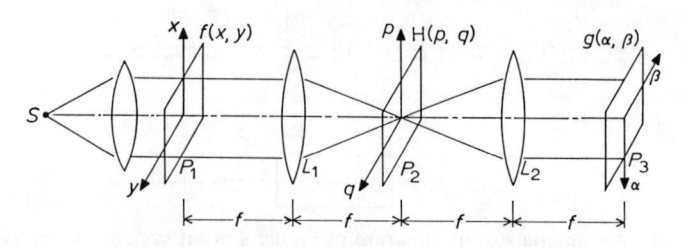

FIGURE 2.4 Fourier transform signal processor.

which can be written as

$$g(\alpha, \beta) = K \iint_S f(x, y)h(\alpha - x, \beta - y)\, dx\, dy$$

$$= Kf(x, y) * h(x, y), \quad (2.22)$$

where the integral is taken at the input spatial plane, and $h(x, y)$ is the spatial impulse response of the filter:

$$h(x, y) = \mathscr{F}^{-1}[H(p, q)]. \quad (2.23)$$

An analog system diagram of the optical signal processor is shown in Figure 2.5, and the Fourier transform processor can be represented by a linear system as shown in Figure 2.6.

It is important to stress that the spatial filter $H(p, q)$ can consist of apertures or slits of any shape. Depending on the arrangement of the apertures, it can act as a low-pass, high-pass, or band-pass spatial filter. Clearly any opaque portion of the filter represents a rejection of the spatial-frequency band, but note that the inclusion of a phase plate would produce a phase delay. Since we are able to construct amplitude filters and phase filters separately, in principle we can also construct any complex spatial filter as we wish.

2.3 COMPLEX SPATIAL FILTER SYNTHESIS

A complex spatial filter can be described by a complex amplitude transmittance function as given by

$$H(p, q) = |H(p, q)|e^{i\phi(p, q)}. \quad (2.24)$$

In practice, optical spatial filters are generally of the *passive* type. The physically realizable conditions of optical spatial filters are

$$|H(p, q)| \leq 1 \quad (2.25)$$

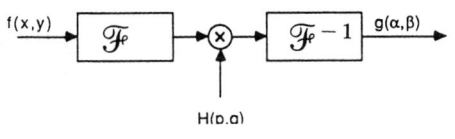

FIGURE 2.5 An analog system diagram of the signal processor in Figure 2.4.

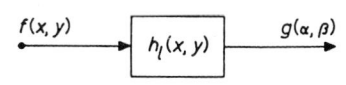

FIGURE 2.6 A linear system representation of Figure 2.4 or 2.5.

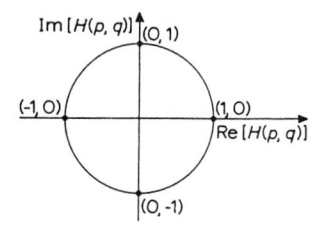

FIGURE 2.7 A complex amplitude transmittance.

and

$$0 \le \phi(p, q) < 2\pi. \tag{2.26}$$

We note that such a transmittance function can be represented by a set of points within or on a unit circle in the complex plane, as shown in Figure 2.7. The amplitude transmission of the filter changes with the optical density, and the phase delay varies with the thickness. Thus, a complex spatial filter can be constructed by combining an amplitude filter and a phase-delay filter.

Let us now discuss the technique developed by Vander Lugt for constructing a complex spatial filter using the interferometric method, as shown in Figure 2.8. The complex light field over the spatial-frequency plane is

$$E(p, q) = F(p, q) + e^{-ip\alpha_0} \tag{2.27}$$

where $\alpha_0 = f \sin \theta$, f is the focal length of the transform lens, and $F(p, q) = |F(p, q)|e^{i\phi(p,q)}$.

The corresponding intensity distribution over the recording medium is

$$I(p, q) = 1 + |F(p, q)|^2 + 2|F(p, q)|\cos[\alpha_0 p + \phi(p, q)]. \tag{2.28}$$

We assume that if the amplitude transmittance of the recording is linear, the corresponding amplitude transmittance function of the spatial filter is

$$H(p, q) = K\{1 + |F(p, q)|^2 + 2|F(p, q)|\cos[\alpha_0 p + \phi(p, q)]\}, \tag{2.29}$$

which is, in fact, a *real positive function*.

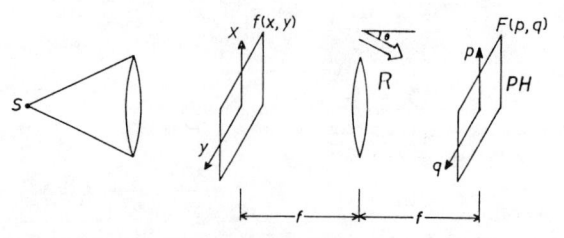

FIGURE 2.8 Construction of a complex spatial filter. *Note*: $f(x, y)$, input object transparency; R, reference plane wave; PH, photographic recording medium.

COMPLEX SPATIAL FILTER SYNTHESIS

If this complex spatial filter is inserted in the Fourier plane of a coherent optical signal processor, as shown in Figure 2.4, the complex light immediately behind the spatial filter would be

$$\begin{aligned} E(p, q) &= F(p, q)H(p, q) \\ &= K[F(p, q) + F(p, q)|F(p, q)|^2 + F(p, q)F(p, q)e^{ip\alpha_0} \\ &\quad + F(p, q)F^*(p, q)e^{-ip\alpha_0}], \end{aligned} \quad (2.30)$$

where the asterisk denotes the complex conjugate. The complex light field at the output plane can be determined by

$$\begin{aligned} g(\alpha, \beta) &= \iint E(p, q)\exp[\ i(\alpha p + \beta q)]\ dp\ dq \\ &= K[f(x, y) + f(x, y) * f(x, y) * f^*(-x, -y) \\ &\quad + f(x, y) * f(x + \alpha_0, y) + f(x, y) * f^*(-x + \alpha_0, -y)], \quad (2.31) \end{aligned}$$

where the first and second terms represent the zero-order diffraction, which appears at the origin of the output plane, and the third and fourth terms are the convolution and cross-correlation terms, which are diffracted in the neighborhood of $\alpha = -\alpha_0$ and $\alpha = \alpha_0$, respectively, as sketched in Figure 2.9.

It is interesting to see that if the input object function is translated to a new location, that is $f(x - x_0, y - y_0)$, then the correlation term of Eq. 2.31 can be shown that,

$$\iint f(x - x_0, y - y_0)f^*(x - \alpha + \alpha_0, y - \beta)\ dx\ dy$$

$$= R_{11}(\alpha - \alpha_0 - x_0, \beta - y_0),$$

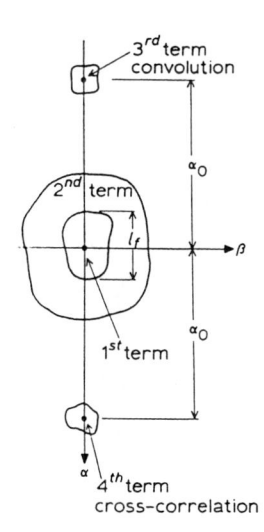

FIGURE 2.9 Sketch of output diffraction.

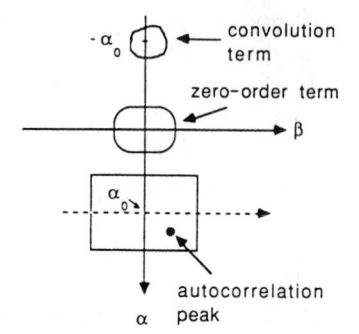

FIGURE 2.10 The autocorrelation peak shows the location of the input object.

where R_{11} represents the autocorrelation function. Thus we see that the correlation peak translates to the same amount as does the object function. A sketch of the output correlation spot with reference to the input coordinate plane is shown in Figure 2.10.

2.4 JOINT TRANSFORM PROCESSOR

In a conventional coherent optical processor, the processing operation is usually carried out at the Fourier plane with a complex spatial filter. This type of coherent optical processor can perform many complicated processing operations. In this section, we show that complex signal processing can also be performed by a joint transform processor.

Let us now consider a joint Fourier transform optical signal processor, as depicted in Figure 2.11. We assume that both an object function $f(x, y)$ and an inverted spatial impulse response $h(x, y)$ are inserted in the input plane P_1 at $(\alpha_0, 0)$ and $(-\alpha_0, 0)$, respectively. By coherent illumination, the complex light distribution at the Fourier plane P_2 is given by

$$U(p, q) = F(p, q)e^{-i\alpha_0 p} + H^*(p, q)e^{i\alpha_0 p}, \qquad (2.32)$$

where (p, q) represents the angular spatial frequency coordinate system and

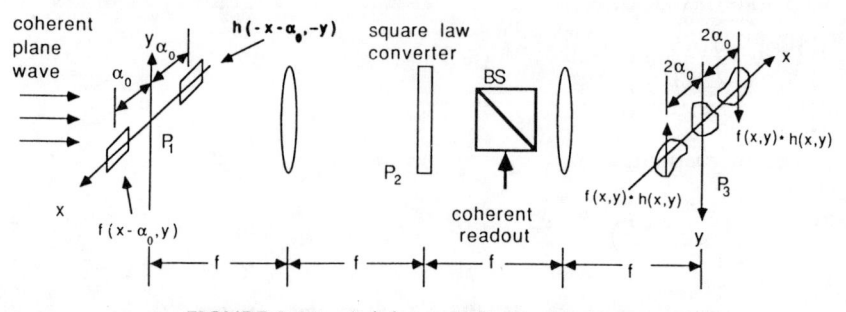

FIGURE 2.11 A joint transform processor.

the asterisk represents the complex conjugate, $F(p, q) = \mathcal{F}[f(x, y)]$, and $H(p, q) = \mathcal{F}[h(x, y)]$.

The output intensity distribution from the square-law detector can be written as

$$I(p, q) = |U(p, q)|^2$$
$$= |F(p, q)|^2 + |H(p, q)|^2 + F(p, q)H(p, q)e^{-i2\alpha_0 p}$$
$$+ F^*(p, q)H^*(p, q)e^{i2\alpha_0 p} \qquad (2.33)$$

By coherent readout, the complex light distribution at the output plane P_3 is given by

$$g(x, y) = f(x, y) \circledast f(x, y) + h(-x, -y) \circledast h(-x, -y)$$
$$+ f(x, y) * h(x - 2\alpha_0, y) + f(-x, -y) * h(-x - 2\alpha_0, -y), \qquad (2.34)$$

where $\circledast$ and $*$ denote the correlation and convolution operations, respectively. We see that the object function $f(x, y)$ convolved with the spatial impulse response $h(x, y)$ would be diffracted around $(-2\alpha_0, 0)$ and $(2\alpha_0, 0)$, respectively. It is therefore apparent that the joint transform processor can, in principle, perform all the processing that a conventional coherent optical processor can offer.

The inherent advantages of using joint transform processor are (1) the avoidance of complex spatial filter synthesis, (2) a higher input space–bandwidth product, (3) a lower spatial carrier frequency requirement, and (4) a generally higher output diffraction efficiency.

Matched filtering can be easily performed with a joint transform correlator, as opposed to the Vander Lugt correlator described in previous sections. We assume that the two identical object functions $f(x - \alpha_0, y)$ and $f(x + \alpha_0, y)$ are inserted in the input plane. Then the complex light distribution arriving at the square-law detector in Fourier plane P_2 will be

$$E(p, q) = F(p, q)e^{-i\alpha_0 p} + F(p, q)e^{i\alpha_0 p}, \qquad (2.35)$$

where $F_1(p, q)$ is the Fourier spectrum of the input object. The corresponding irradiance at the input end of the square-law detector is

$$I(p, q) = 2|F(p, q)|^2[1 + \cos 2\alpha_0 p].$$

By coherent readout, the complex light distribution at the output plane P_3 will be

$$g(\alpha, \beta) = 2f(x, y) \circledast f^*(x, y) + f(x, y) \circledast f^*(x - 2\alpha_0, y)$$
$$+ f^*(x, y) \circledast f(x + 2\alpha_0, y), \qquad (2.36)$$

44 OPTICAL SIGNAL PROCESSING

where ⊛ denotes the correlation operation; the first term represents the auto correlation function of $f(x, y)$, which is diffracted at the origin of the output plane; and the last two terms are the two autocorrelation terms, which are diffracted around $\alpha = 2\alpha_0$ and $\alpha = -2\alpha_0$, respectively. Notice that a square-law converter, such as a photographic plate, a liquid crystal light valve, or a charge-coupled-device camera, can be used.

To illustrate the space invariant property of the joint transform correlator, we assume a target "B" is located at (α_0, y_0) and a reference image is located at $(-\alpha_0, 0)$, as shown in Figure 2.12a, for which the set of input functions can be written as $f(x - \alpha_0, y - y_0)$ and $f(x + \alpha_0, y)$, respectively. Thus the complex light distribution at the input end of the square-law detector is

$$E(p, q) = F[\exp[-i(\alpha_0 p + y_0 q)] + e^{i(\alpha_0 p)}], \qquad (2.37)$$

and the corresponding power spectral distribution can be written as

$$I(p, q) = 2|F|^2[1 + \cos(2\alpha_0 p + y_0 q)].$$

By taking the inverse Fourier transform of $I(p, q)$, we have the following complex light distribution at the output plane:

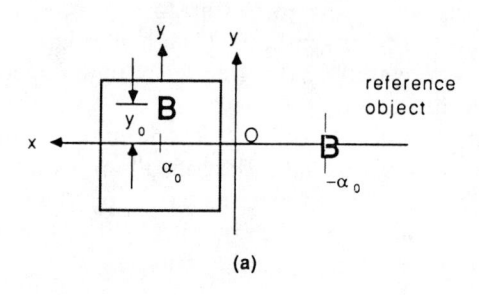

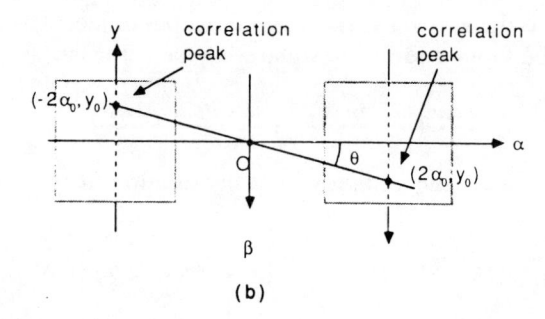

FIGURE 2.12 Space invariant property of a joint transform correlator.

$$g(\alpha, \beta) = 2f(x, y) \circledast f^*(x, y) + f(x, y) \circledast f^*(x - 2\alpha_0, y - y_0)$$
$$+ f^*(x, y) \circledast f(x + 2\alpha_0, y + y_0),$$

which is sketched in Figure 2.12b. Thus, we see that the joint transform correlator has the space invariant property.

2.5 OPTICAL SIGNAL PROCESSING WITH AREA MODULATION

Area modulation has been used for sound track recording in motion pictures for some time. We now demonstrate the use of area modulation for coherent optical spectrum analysis.

Area modulation is a simple operation that produces a binary transmittance of two discrete tones. The basic forms of area modulation, *unilateral* and *bilateral*, are described in Figure 2.13. We chose these two forms in our present application because of their simplicity, but be aware that other forms of area modulation may also be used. Since an area-modulated signal is in binary form (i.e., transparent and opaque), the problem of the nonlinearity of the recording material or electrooptic device can be avoided. As a matter of fact, high-contrast films that are highly nonlinear are preferable to assure a good tonal separation. Besides allowing less stringent control of the input object, the area-modulation technique makes it possible to use a much larger class of recording materials or electrooptic devices. However, these devices may be unacceptable for the density-modulation technique because of their nonlinear transmittance characteristics.

A two-dimensional amplitude transmittance function for a bilateral area-modulated signal can be described by

$$T_1(x, y) = \text{rect}\left(\frac{x}{L}\right) \text{rect}\left\{\frac{y}{2[B + f(x)]}\right\}, \quad (2.39)$$

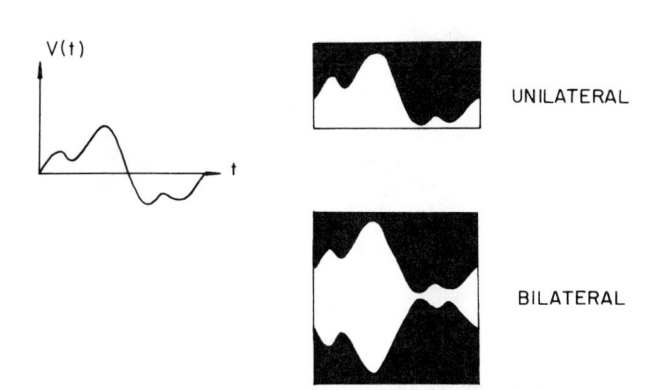

FIGURE 2.13 Unilateral and bilateral area-modulation formats.

46 OPTICAL SIGNAL PROCESSING

while for a *unilateral* area-modulated signal it is given by

$$T_2(x, y) = \text{rect}\left(\frac{x}{L}\right) \text{rect}\left\{\frac{y - [f(x) + B]/2}{B + f(x)}\right\}, \quad (2.40)$$

where (x, y) is the spatial coordinate system, L is length of the input transparency in the x direction, B is the bias level, $f(x)$ is the input signal function,

$$\text{rect}\left(\frac{x}{L}\right) \triangleq \begin{cases} 1, & |x| \leq L/2, \\ 0, & \text{otherwise}, \end{cases}$$

and the bias level is chosen such that $B \geq f(x)$, for all x.

If the area-modulated transparency of Eqs. (2.39) or (2.40) is inserted into the input plane of the coherent optical processor shown in Figure 2.14, the output complex light distribution would be

$$G(p, q) = C \iint T(x, y) \exp[-i(px + qy)] \, dx \, dy, \quad (2.41)$$

where (p, q) is the spatial frequency coordinate system, C is a complex constant, and $T(x, y)$ is the input transparency. Since the evaluation of Eq. (2.41) is forbidden, we restrict the evaluation over the p axis. For the case of a *bilateral* area-modulated signal we have

$$G_1(p, 0) = 2C \int \text{rect}\left(\frac{x}{L}\right)[B + f(x)] \exp(-ipx) \, dx$$

$$= 2C \left[\int_{-L/2}^{L/2} B \exp(-ipx) \, dx + \int_{-L/2}^{L/2} f(x) \exp(-ipx) \, dx\right], \quad (2.42)$$

which represents a one-dimensional Fourier transformation of a constant B and $f(x)$.

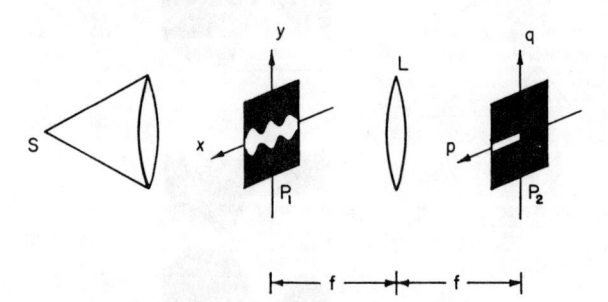

FIGURE 2.14 Spectrum analysis with area modulation. *Note*: S, monochromatic point source.

For the case of a *unilateral* area-modulated signal, the complex amplitude distribution along the p axis would be

$$G_2(p, 0) = C\left[\int_{-L/2}^{L/2} B \exp(-ipx)\,dx + \int_{-L/2}^{L/2} f(x)\exp(-ipx)\,dx\right]$$
$$= \frac{1}{2} G_1(p, 0), \qquad (2.43)$$

which is identical with the result obtained for the bilateral case, except that the irradiance is reduced by a factor of 4.

Let us consider a bilateral sinusoidal area-modulated signal as given by,

$$f(x) = A \sin(p_0 x + \theta), \qquad (2.44)$$

where p_0 is some arbitrary angular spatial frequency, and θ is a constant phase factor. Substituting into Eq. 2.42, we show that

$$G_1(p, 0) = K_1 \delta(p) + K_2 \delta(p - p_0) + K_3 \delta(p + p_0), \qquad (2.45)$$

where K is a proportional constant. From the preceding result, except the zero-order diffraction, two spectra points are located at $p = p_0$ and $p = -p_0$, respectively. Thus we see that the coherent optical processor can indeed perform spectrum analysis with an area-modulated signal. The basic advantage of the area-modulation technique is that, since the recording is not restricted to the linear region of the devices, a larger class of recording material or spatial light modulator can be used.

2.6 OPTIMUM SPATIAL FILTERING

In Section 2.3, we saw that a matched spatial filter is indeed a Fourier transform hologram. Since the input signal can be considered as the summation of a large number of resolvable object points, the Fourier transform of the signal can be treated as the superposition of a large number of coherent wavefronts. Thus, it can be shown that an optimum spatial filter can be synthesized with a one-to-one (unity) signal–reference-beam ratio.

We show that optimum signal detection can be achieved with an optimum nonlinear spatial filter. In Section 2.3, the intensity distribution of a complex matched filter construction is given by

$$I(p, q) = S^2(p, q) + R^2 + 2RS(p, q)\cos[x_0 p + \phi(p, q)], \qquad (2.46)$$

where $S(p, q) = |S(p, q)|\exp[i\phi(p, q)]$ is the signal spectrum, R is the reference beam, and (p, q) is the angular spatial frequency coordinate system.

From this equation we see that the signal spectrum is spatially modulated by a spatial carrier frequency x_0. In order to ensure separation from the zero-order diffraction, the carrier frequency must satisfy the following inequality:

$$x_0 > l_f + \frac{3}{2}l_s. \qquad (2.47)$$

where l_f and l_s are the spatial lengths in the x direction of the input object $f(x, y)$ and the signal $s(x, y)$, respectively. Moreover, it is evident that the nonlinear distortion caused by the transfer characteristic of the device can occur only through amplitude modulation, and not phase modulation. Therefore, the nonlinear spatial filter can be approximated by the Fourier decomposition, as given by

$$H(p, q) \simeq H_0(p, q) + \sum_{n=1}^{\infty} H_n(p, q), \qquad (2.48)$$

where $H_0(p, q) = \frac{1}{2}B_0(p, q)$ and $H_n(p, q) = B_n(p, q)\cos\{n[x_0 p + \phi(p, q)]\}$. Notice that the Fourier components $B_n(p, q)$ can be found by finite-point analysis, on a cycle-by-cycle basis with respect to the spatial carrier frequency x_0.

Although $B_1(p, q)$ is not identical to $S(p, q)$, there is a great similarity between them, particularly between their inverse Fourier transforms:

$$\mathcal{F}^{-1}\{B_1(p, q)\exp[i\phi(p, q)]\} \sim Ks(x, y), \qquad (2.49)$$

where $\mathcal{F}^{-1}$ represents the inverse Fourier transform, $\sim$ means the similarity, and K is an arbitrary constant.

If the complex nonlinear filter is located in the frequency plane of the coherent processor of Figure 2.4, the output signal is given by

$$g(\alpha, \beta) \simeq \sum_{n=0}^{\infty} \iint_{-\alpha}^{\alpha} B_n(p, q)F(p, q)\cos[x_0 p + \phi(p, q)]$$

$$\times \exp[-i(p\alpha + q\beta)]\, dp\, dq, \qquad (2.50)$$

which can be written as

$$g(\alpha, \beta) \simeq f(x, y) * b_0(x, y) + \sum_{n=1}^{\alpha} f(x, y) * b_n(x + nx_0, y)$$

$$+ \sum_{n=1}^{\alpha} f(x, y) * b_n(-x - nx_0, -y), \qquad (2.51)$$

where the $b_n(x, y)$ are the corresponding inverse Fourier transforms of $\frac{1}{2}B_n$

$(p, q)\exp[i\phi(p, q)]$. It can be seen that the first summation covers the convolution operations, while the second summation represents the cross-correlation operations.

If the input signal is assumed to be

$$f(x, y) = s(x, y) + n(x, y), \qquad (2.52)$$

where $s(x, y)$ is the signal and $n(x, y)$ is an additive white Gaussian noise, then the cross-correlation terms would be

$$R_{12}(\alpha, \beta) = \sum_{n=1}^{\alpha} [s(x, y) + n(x, y)] * b_n(-x - nx_0, y). \qquad (2.53)$$

Notice that the cross-correlations between $n(x, y)$ and $b_n(x, y)$ are approximately zero, and that $b_1(x, y)$ is similar to $s(x, y)$, that is,

$$b_1(x, y) \sim Ks(x, y), \qquad (2.54)$$

where K is an arbitrary constant. Equation 2.53 can therefore be reduced to

$$\begin{aligned} R_{12}(\alpha, \beta) &\simeq s(x, y) * b_1(-x - x_0, -y) \\ &\simeq s(x, y) * Ks(-x - x_0, -y), \end{aligned} \qquad (2.55)$$

which is the autocorrelation of $s(x, y)$. We stress that optimum detection requires an optimum value of $b_1(x, y)$, which may be obtained by the linear optimization technique as proposed in the following: The transfer characteristic of an electrooptic device is, in general, nonlinear, for which the amplitude transmittance can be expanded by a finite power series, as given by

$$T(E) = \sum_{n=0}^{N} a_n E^n, \qquad \text{for } E \geq 0, \qquad (2.56)$$

where T is the amplitude transmittance, E is the exposure, and the a_n are the real coefficients. Let us now replace Eq. 2.56 with a linear approximated transmittance

$$T^+(E) = \lambda_0 + \lambda_1 E, \qquad (2.57)$$

where λ_0 and λ_1 are the chosen parameters for which $T^+(E)$ is the best fitted linear approximation of $T(E)$. To determine the optimum value of λ_1, we look for the *minimum mean-square error* of $(T - T^+)$, such as

$$\frac{\partial}{\partial \lambda_n} \iint_s (T - T^+)^2 \, dx \, dy = 0, \qquad n = 0, 1. \qquad (2.58)$$

The solution to Eq. 2.58 is given by

$$\lambda_1 = \frac{\sum_{n=0}^{N} a_n(\langle E^{n+1}\rangle - \langle E^n\rangle\langle E\rangle)}{\langle E^2\rangle - \langle E\rangle^2}, \tag{2.59}$$

where

$$\langle E^n\rangle \triangleq \iint_s E^n(x, y)\,dx\,dy, \qquad n = 1, 2, 3, \ldots, N. \tag{2.60}$$

Referring to the matched filter of Eq. 2.46, the ensemble average of E^n can be written as

$$\langle E^n\rangle = \langle I^n\rangle t^n = t^n \sum_{2r=0}^{n} \frac{n!}{(n-2r)!(r!)^2}(S^2 + R^2)^{n-2r}(SR)^{2r}. \tag{2.61}$$

The optimum value of λ_1, with respect to the signal-to-reference beam ratio, can be determined by

$$\frac{\partial \lambda_1}{\partial R} = 0, \tag{2.62}$$

and the solution is

$$R = |S(p, q)|_{\max}. \tag{2.63}$$

Thus, an optimum matched filter can be achieved with a unity signal-to-reference-beam ratio. Since we have ignored the amplitude spectral variation, the optimum filter is essentially a *phase-preserving filter*. We stress that it is basically the *phase-only filter* that has gained widespread attention in recent years.

2.7 NONCONVENTIONAL JOINT TRANSFORM CORRELATOR

A conventional joint transform correlator (JTC) has the advantages of avoidance filter synthesis, a higher space–bandwidth product, a lower carrier frequency, a higher degree of modulation, and suitability for real-time implementation. However, the conventional JTC also has several major drawbacks, for example, its inefficient use of illuminating light, it requires a large transform lens and stringent spatial coherence, and the overall small size of the joint transform spectrum. We now describe an alternative approach that alleviates some of these limitations.

NONCONVENTIONAL JOINT TRANSFORM CORRELATOR

FIGURE 2.15 The quasi-Fourier transformation, P'_2, is the image of P_2.

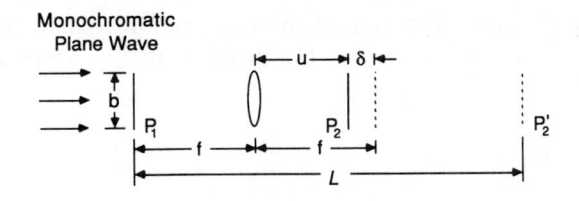

P'_2 = virtual image of P_2

The quasi-Fourier transform of an optical system as defined here is shown in Figure 2.15. We assume that the detection plane P_2 is located at a small distance δ from the back focal plane of the transform lens. Using the usual Gaussian lens equation, the image of P_2 can be shown to be located at a distance

$$L = \frac{f^2}{\delta} \tag{2.64}$$

from input plane P_1. We now refer to the far-field (i.e., Fraunhofer) diffraction arrangement of Figure 2.16. To achieve a Fourier diffraction pattern at plane P'_2, $\Delta L'$ must be sufficiently small compared with the illuminating wavelength λ, that is,

$$\Delta L' \leq \frac{\lambda}{4}. \tag{2.65}$$

In view of similar right triangles, L' can be approximated by

$$L' \simeq \frac{(b/2)^2}{2\Delta L'}, \tag{2.66}$$

where b is the size of the input object.

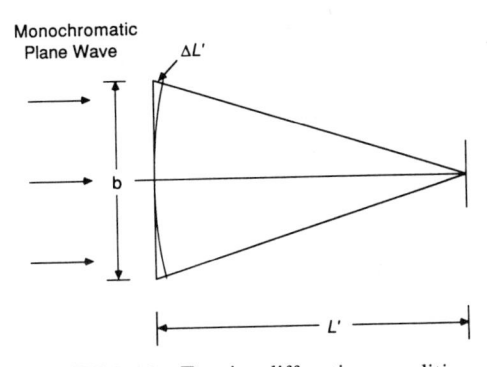

FIGURE 2.16 Fourier diffraction condition.

To obtain a Fourier diffraction at the observation screen, the inequality of relation (2.65) must hold. Thus the distance to the observation screen should be

$$L' \geq \frac{b^2}{2\lambda}. \tag{2.67}$$

It is apparent that to achieve a quasi-Fourier transformation at P_2, one should have

$$L \geq L'. \tag{2.68}$$

The allowable deviation from the focal length should be

$$\delta \leq 2\lambda \left(\frac{f}{b}\right)^2 \tag{2.69}$$

Note that this result is known as the *focal tolerance* or *focal depth* of the optical system.

One of the most important aspects of an optical correlator is the shift-invariant property of the Fourier transformation, from which the position of the object can be determined.

We now investigate the constraints in object translation under the quasi-Fourier-transform regime. Consider the quasi-joint-Fourier-transform configuration of Figure 2.17, where the displacement of the object spectrum at the quasi-Fourier domain P_2 is anticipated. Thus, referring to the triangular configuration in Figure 2.17, the amount of displacement along the vertical direction is

$$\alpha = \frac{\delta}{f} d, \tag{2.70}$$

where d is the translation of the object.

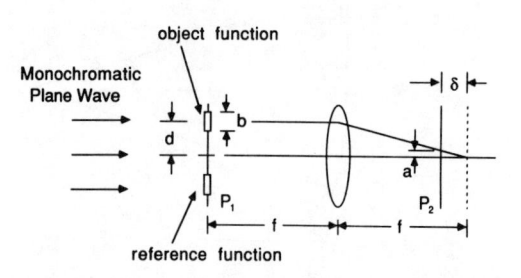

FIGURE 2.17 Quasi-joint-Fourier transformation.

To ensure good overlapping object and reference spectra at the quasi-Fourier domain P_2, the amount of displacement should be small compared with the size of the main lobe of the object spectrum, that is,

$$\alpha \leq \frac{\lambda f}{2b}. \qquad (2.71)$$

If we simply substitute Eq. 2.70 into relation 2.71, the amount of allowable object displacement is

$$d \leq \frac{f^2 \lambda}{2b\delta}. \qquad (2.72)$$

To recapitulate, the separation between the object and the reference functions should be within the constraint of relation 2.72. Thus, due to this condition, the object and reference spectra will be mostly overlapped, producing interferometric fringes (i.e., carrier frequency) such that the shift-invariant property can be preserved.

We now describe the nonconventional joint transform technique, as illustrated in Figure 2.18. Let us assume that $2\alpha_m$ is the size of the object spectrum, with α_m written as

$$\alpha_m = f\lambda f_{max} = \frac{f\lambda W}{b}, \qquad (2.73)$$

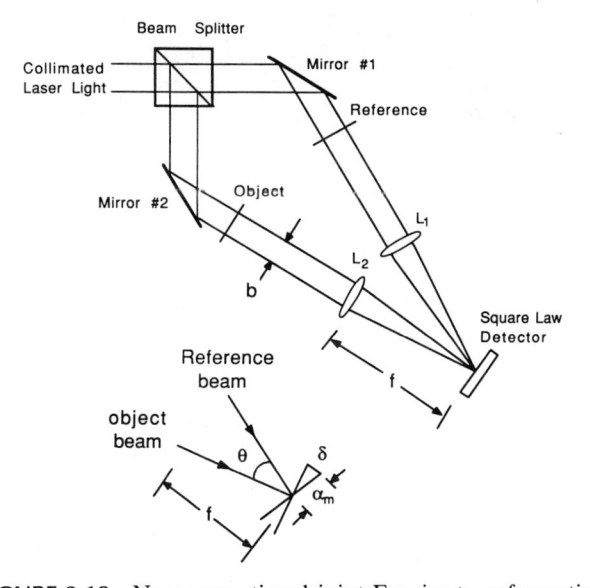

FIGURE 2.18 Nonconventional joint-Fourier transformation.

where f_{max} is the upper spatial frequency content of the object and $W = bf_{max}$ is the space–bandwidth product of the object. Note that the incident angle at the square-law detector, formed by the object and the reference beams, can be written as

$$\theta \simeq \arctan \frac{\delta}{\alpha_m}, \qquad (2.74)$$

where δ is the maximum focal depth of relation 2.69. By substituting relation 2.69 and Eq. 2.73 into relation 2.74, the constraint of the incident angle is

$$\theta \leq \arctan \frac{2f}{bW}. \qquad (2.75)$$

As an example, we let $f = 500$ mm, $b = 10$ mm, and $W = 200$, and the incident angle is $\theta \leq 27°$.

We also note that the proposed nonconventional joint-Fourier transformation may be achieved with a different arrangement, as shown in Figure 2.19, in which we assume that the constraints of the focal depth of relation 2.66 and the allowable incident angle of relation 2.75 hold. These optical setups have the advantage that they produce a larger joint transform spectrum, for which a higher readout correlation peak can be obtained. Furthermore, if the object displacement is within the shift-invariant constraint of relation 2.72, the nonconventional JTC (NJTC) can extract the spatial location of the object.

To illustrate the shift-invariant property of the NJTC, we used an input transparency with four English characters and a reference letter (Figure 2.20). The NJTC structure used in the experiment is shown in Figure 2.18. The joint transform power spectrum was recorded by a photographic transparency, which is called a *joint transform hologram* (JTH). By simply illuminating the

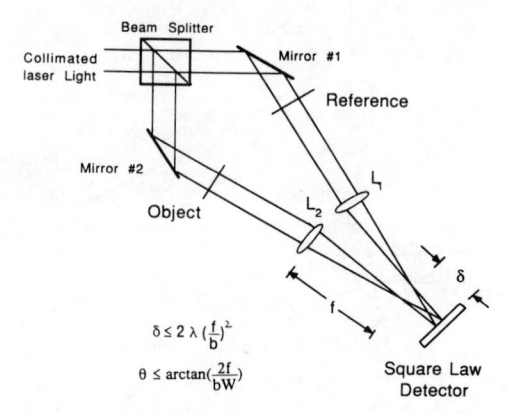

FIGURE 2.19 Nonconventional quasi-joint-Fourier transformation.

NONCONVENTIONAL JOINT TRANSFORM CORRELATOR   55

G A
B G   G

Input Object   Reference

(a)

(b)

FIGURE 2.20 (*a*) Input object and reference function. (*b*) Output correlation spots.

recorded JTH with coherent light, cross-correlations of input characters with the reference letter can be viewed at the output plane shown in Figure 2.20*b*. Two autocorrelation peaks, representing the locations of the input character G, can be observed. Thus we see that the shift-invariant property of the NJTC is preserved. The incident angle for this experiment was set at $\sim 10°$.

To illustrate the results obtained by using the quasi-Fourier-transformation arrangement of Figure 2.19, the input object and reference function of Figure 2.21 were used. In this experiment three JTHs—for $\delta = 0$, $\delta = f/10 = 50$

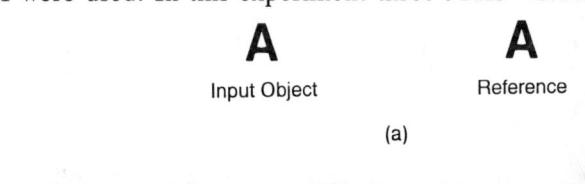

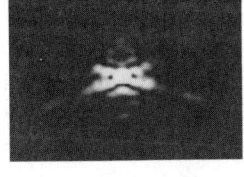

A   A
Input Object   Reference

(a)

$\delta = 0$ $\delta = f/10 = 50$ mm $\delta = f/5 = 100$ mm

(b)

FIGURE 2.21 (*a*) Input and reference objects. (*b*) Joint transform holograms.

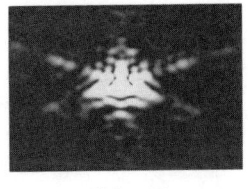

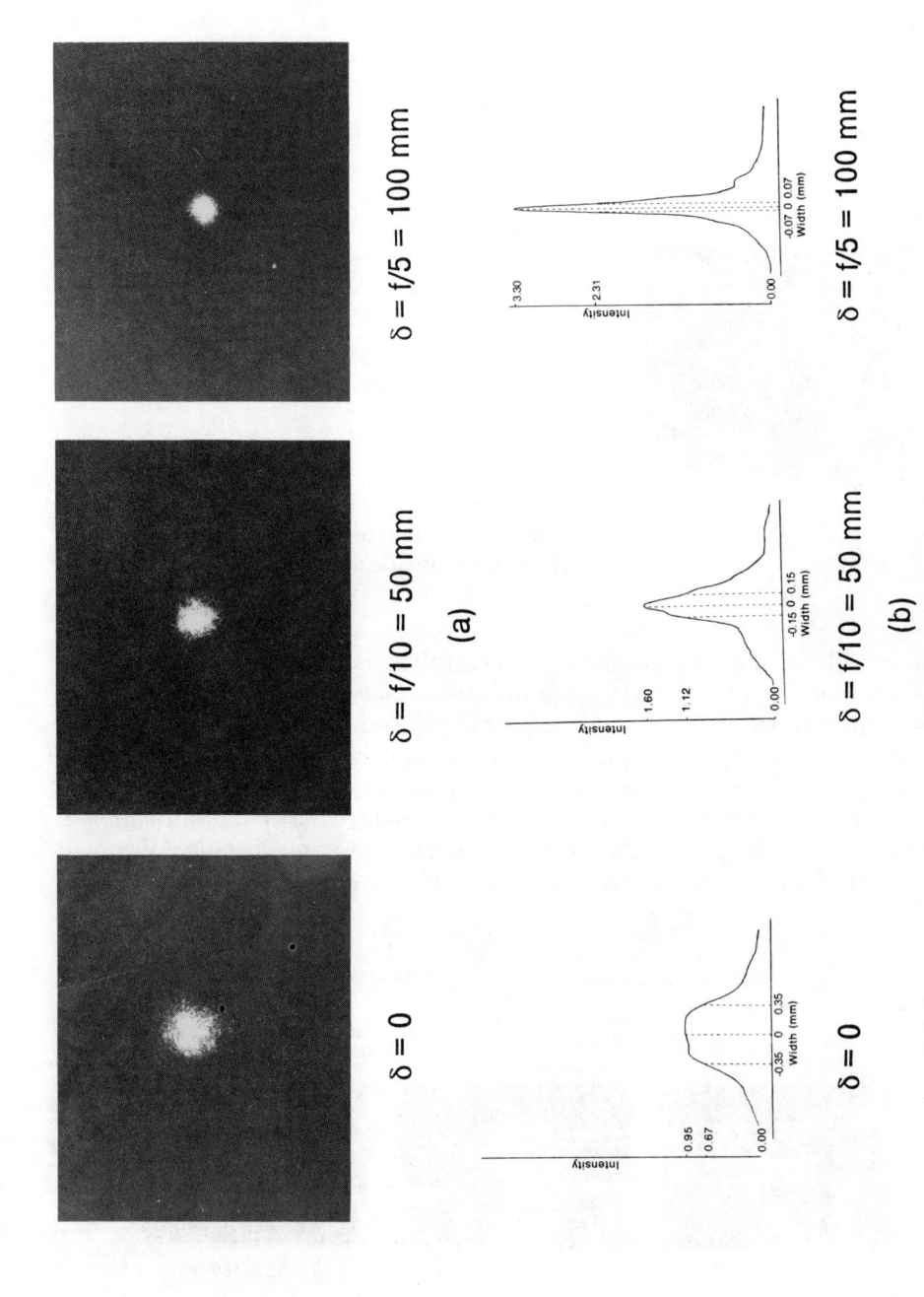

FIGURE 2.22 (*a*) Output correlation spots. (*b*) Photometer traces of the output correlation peaks.

mm, and $\delta = f/5 = 100$ mm—were recorded (Figure 2.21b). Throughout the making of the set of holograms, the incident angle was maintained at $\theta \simeq 10°$. Note that the scale of the joint power spectrum expands as δ increases. Again, the output correlation peaks of the JTHs were obtained by simple coherent illumination (Figure 2.22). Photometer traces of the corresponding correlation peaks are shown in Figure 2.22b. From these results we see that the peak intensity increases as δ increases, while the size of the correlation spot decreases as δ increases. These phenomena are primarily due to the size of the joint transform spectrum. Thus the proposed NJTC has the ability to improve the output signal-to-noise ratio and the accuracy of the signal detection.

Since the processor can, in principle, process all the information that a conventional coherent optical processor can, we believe that the NJTC possesses many capabilities beyond those discussed here.

REFERENCES

2.1 F. T. S. Yu, *Optical Information Processing*, Wiley–Interscience, New York, 1983.
2.2 J. W. Goodman, *Introduction to Fourier Optics*, McGraw-Hill, New York, 1968.
2.3 G. O. Reynolds, J. B. DeVelis, G. B. Parent, Jr., and B. J. Thompson, *Physical Optics Notebook: Tutorial in Fourier Optics*, SPIE Optical Engineering Press, Bellingham, Wash., 1989.
2.4 F. T. S. Yu and I. C. Khoo, *Principles of Optical Engineering*, Wiley, New York, 1990.
2.5 F. T. S. Yu, C. Zhang, Y. Jin, and D. A. Gregory, "Nonconventional Joint-Transform Correlator," *Opt. Lett.* 14 (1989): 922.
2.6 B. E. A. Saleh and M. C. Teich, *Fundamentals of Photonics*, Wiley–Interscience, New York, 1991.

PROBLEMS

2.1 Consider the spatial impulse response of an input–output optical system that is given by

$$h(x, y) = \text{rect}\left(\frac{x}{\Delta x}\right) - \text{rect}\left(\frac{x - \Delta x}{\Delta x}\right).$$

(a) If the optical system is illuminated by a spatially limited incoherent wavefront such as

$$f(x, y) = \text{rect}\left(\frac{x}{\Delta x}\right),$$

calculate the corresponding irradiance at the output plane.

(b) If the spatially limited illumination of the optical system is a coherent wavefront, compute the corresponding complex light field at the output plane.

(c) Sketch the irradiances of parts (a) and (b), respectively, and comment on the major differences.

2.2 The transfer function of the optical system shown in Figure 2.1 is given by

$$H(p, q) = K_1 \exp[i(\alpha_0 p + \beta_0 q)],$$

where K_1, α_0, and β_0 are arbitrary positive constants. We assume that the complex amplitude transmittance at the input plane is

$$f(x, y) = K_2 e^{i\phi(x,y)},$$

where K_2 is an arbitrary positive constant. Calculate the output responses under incoherent and coherent illuminations, respectively.

2.3 Given an input–output linear and spatially invariant optical system under strictly incoherent illumination:

(a) Derive the incoherent transfer function in terms of the spatial impulse response of the system.

(b) State some basic properties of the incoherent transfer function.

(c) What are the cutoff frequencies of the system under coherent and incoherent illuminations?

2.4 Consider an optical imaging system that is capable of combining two Fraunhofer diffractions resulting from input objects $f_1(x, y)$ and $f_2(x, y)$, as shown in Figure 2.23. Compute the irradiance at the output plane under coherent and incoherent illuminations, and comment on these results.

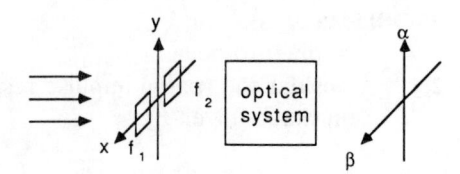

FIGURE 2.23

2.5 Given the spatial impulse response of an optical system, as given by

$$h(x, y) = \cos(px),$$

(a) We assume the input amplitude distribution of a coherent object is

$$f(x, y) = \cos(px).$$

Calculate the output irradiance.

(b) If the input object is translated, as given by

$$f(x, y) = \cos(px + \vartheta),$$

calculate the output irradiance.

(c) Sketch the output irradiance of (a) and (b), respectively. What is the major difference between these sketches?

2.6 Assume an *all-pass* optical system in which the spatial impulse response can be represented by a delta function,

$$h(x, y) = \delta(x, y).$$

If the binary-phase grating of Figure 2.24 is inserted at the input plane of the optical system, compute the image irradiance at the output plane under coherent and incoherent illuminations. Cite a conclusive distinction between the observed images.

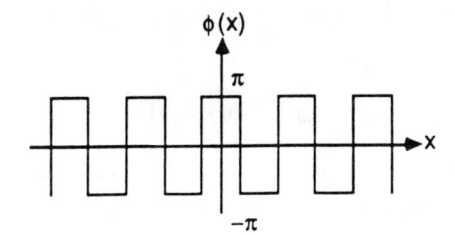

FIGURE 2.24

2.7 Assume that the amplitude transmittance of an object function is given by

$$f(x, y)[1 + \cos(p_0 x)],$$

where p_0 is an arbitrary angular carrier spatial frequency, and $f(x, y)$ is assumed to be spatial-frequency limited. If this object transparency is inserted at the input plane of the coherent optical signal processor in Figure 2.4, then:

(a) Determine the corresponding spectral distribution at the Fourier plane P_2.

(b) Design a stop-band filter for which the light distribution at the output plane P_3 will be $f(x, y)$.

2.8 Consider the coherent optical signal processor shown in Figure 2.25. The spatial filter is a one-dimensional sinusoidal grating,

$$H(p) = \frac{1}{2}[1 + \sin(\alpha_0 p)],$$

FIGURE 2.25

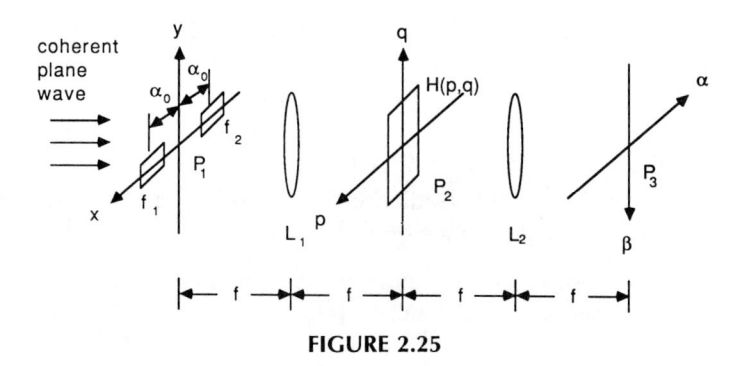

where α_0 is an arbitrary constant that is equal to the separation of the input object functions $f_1(x, y)$ and $f_2(x, y)$. Compute the complex light field at the output plane P_3.

2.9 Assume that a noisy object transparency, such as $f(x, y) + n(x, y)$, is inserted in the input plane of the coherent optical signal processor of Figure 2.4. If a matched spatial filter $H(p, q)$ is inserted in the Fourier plane of the optical processor,

$$H(p, q) = K_1 + 2K_2|F(p, q)|\cos[\alpha_0 p + \phi(p, q)],$$

where the K's are proportionality constant and $F(p, q) = \mathcal{F}[f(x, y)]$:
(a) Calculate the complex light distribution at the output plane.
(b) If the input object is translated to $f(x - x_0, y - y_0)$, calculate the location of the output correlation peak. Sketch the output orders of diffraction.

2.10 Referring to the coherent optical processor of Figure 2.4, design an appropriate spatial filter such that the output signal is the spatial derivative of the input transparency.

2.11 Let the input signal transparency of a coherent signal processor shown in Figure 2.4 be given by

$$f(x, y) = \exp[-(x^2 + y^2)]\exp[i\beta(x^2 + y^2)^{1/2}],$$

where β is a positive real constant, and the additive spatial noise is assumed to be white Gaussian.
(a) Synthesize a matched filter such that the signal-to-noise ratio at the output plane will be optimum.
(b) Determine the corresponding light amplitude distribution on the output plane of the processor.

2.12 Certain relationships between the real and imaginary parts of an analytic function are expressed by means of Hilbert-transform pairs,

$$f_r(x) = -\frac{1}{\pi} \int_{-\infty}^{\infty} \frac{f_i(\alpha)}{x - \alpha} d\alpha$$

and

$$f_i(x) = \frac{1}{\pi} \int_{-\infty}^{\infty} \frac{f_r(\alpha)}{x - \alpha} d\alpha,$$

where $f(x) = f_r(x) + if_i(x)$, with $f_r(x)$ and $f_i(x)$ the respective real and imaginary parts. Design a coherent optical system that is able to perform the respective Hilbert transformations.

2.13 The optical processing technique of Problem 2.12 can be extended to a two-dimensional Hilbert-transform pair,

$$f_r(x, y) = \frac{1}{\pi^2} \int_{-\infty}^{\infty} \int_{-\infty}^{\infty} \frac{f_i(\alpha, \beta)}{(x - \alpha)(y - \beta)} d\alpha \, d\beta$$

and

$$f_i(x, y) = \frac{1}{\pi^2} \int_{-\infty}^{\infty} \int_{-\infty}^{\infty} \frac{f_r(\alpha, \beta)}{(x - \alpha)(y - \beta)} d\alpha \, d\beta,$$

where $f(x, y) = f_r(x, y) + if_i(x, y)$. Design an optical system that can perform these transformations.

2.14 A method for synthesizing a complex spatial filter is shown in Figure 2.26a. If a signal transparency $s(x, y)$ is inserted at a distance d behind

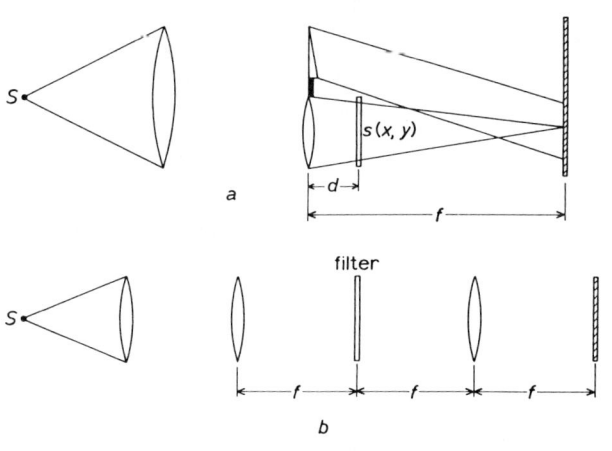

FIGURE 2.26

the transform lens, and the amplitude transmittance of the recorded spatial filter is linearly proportional to the signal transparency:
(a) What is the spatial carrier frequency of the spatial filter.
(b) If the spatial filter is used for signal detection, determine the appropriate location of the input plane of the system shown in Figure 2.26b.

2.15 The complex spatial filter of the previous problem is inserted in the input plane of the optical processor shown in Figure 2.27. What is the complex light distribution at the output plane?

2.16 A spatial filter, $H(p, q) = i(p + q)$, is inserted at the Fourier plane of the coherent optical signal processor in Figure 2.4.
(a) Calculate the complex light distribution at the output plane.
(b) If the input object is an open rectangular aperture, what would the image irradiance at the output plane be?

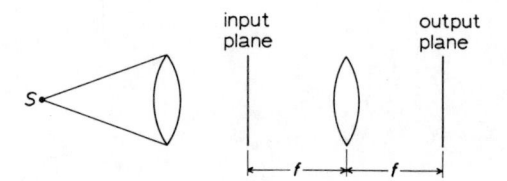

FIGURE 2.27

2.17 Suppose that the input object function of the coherent optical signal processor in Figure 2.4 is a rectangular grating of spatial frequency p_0, as shown in Figure 2.28.
(a) Evaluate and sketch the spectral content of the object at the Fourier plane.
(b) If we insert a π-phase filter,

$$H(r) = \begin{cases} e^{i\pi}, & r \leq r_0, \\ 0, & \text{otherwise}, \end{cases}$$

at the origin of the spatial-frequency plane, sketch the light distribution at the output plane and state your conclusion.

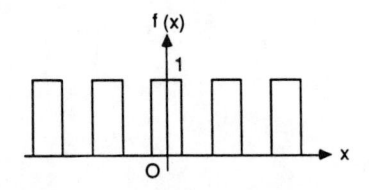

FIGURE 2.28

2.18 Consider the polychromatic coherent optical processor shown in Figure 2.29, in which the point source emits λ_1 and λ_2 (e.g., red and green) wavelengths. If the input object transparency $f(x, y)$ is superimposed with a phase grating,

$$T(x) = e^{i\alpha_0 x},$$

where α_0 is an arbitrary constant:
(a) Calculate the output complex light distribution.
(b) Assuming that $f(x, y)$ is spatial-frequency limited, design an optical system by which complex spatial filters for λ_1 and λ_2 can be synthesized.
(c) Calculate the amplitude transmittance of the polychromatic spatial filter.

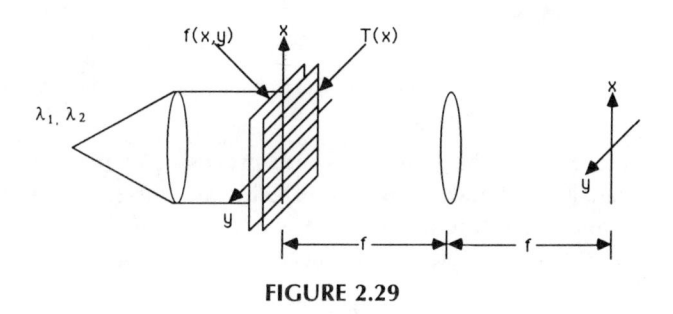

FIGURE 2.29

2.19 If the polychromatic spatial filter of part (c) in Problem 2.18 is inserted in the filter plane of Figure 2.30:
(a) Calculate the output complex light field.
(b) Sketch the output intensity distribution and show that the detected signal is, in fact, polychromatic.

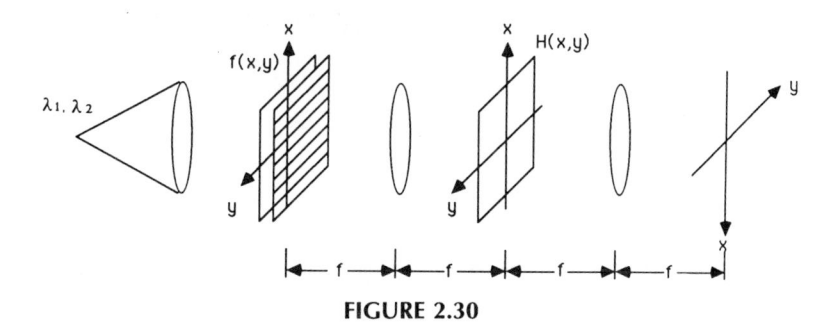

FIGURE 2.30

2.20 The transaxial location of an input transparency introduces a quadratic phase factor in a spatial filter synthesis:

64   OPTICAL SIGNAL PROCESSING

(a) Show that the quadratic phase factors produced in the optical setup of Figure 2.31 would be mutually compensated.

(b) If the recorded $H(p, q)$ (joint transform filter) is inserted back at the input plane of Figure 2.31, calculate the output complex light field.

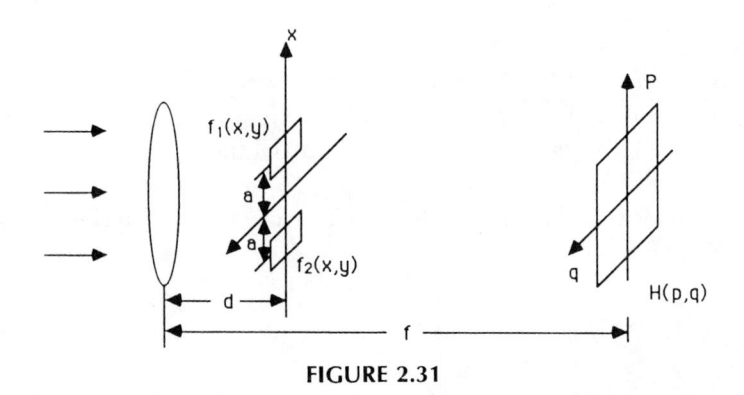

FIGURE 2.31

2.21 With reference to the joint transform processor of Figure 2.11, if the input signal is imbedded with white Gaussian noise, that is, $f(x, y) + n(x, y)$, and the reference function is $h(x, y) = f(x, y)$, show that the joint transform correlator is, in fact, an optimum correlator.

2.22 In the synthesis of a joint transform filter:

(a) Show that the filter is signal dependent, in contrast to the matched filter.

(b) Calculate the output correlation-peak intensities for input signal-to-noise ratio, $S/N = 10$ dB, 7 dB, and 5 dB, respectively.

(c) Sketch the output S/N as a function of input S/N. Comment on these results.

2.23 Consider the input plane of the joint transform correlator depicted in Figure 2.32:

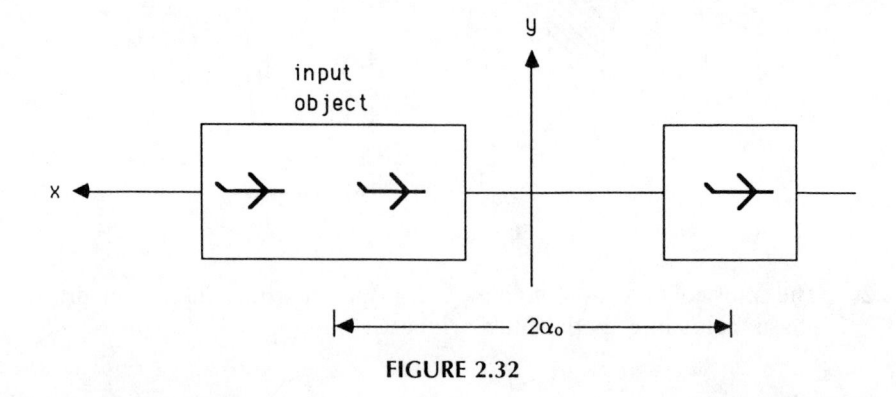

FIGURE 2.32

(a) Show that if the joint transform filter (i.e., JT power spectrum) were binary, a false alarm would be introduced.
(b) Sketch the output light distribution.

2.24 We assume that the joint transform spectrum is recorded by a photographic plate.
(a) Show that the modulation index of the joint transform filter decreases as the number of input objects increases.
(b) Sketch the correlation diffraction efficiency as a function of the number of input objects.

2.25 (a) What are the major differences between the Vander Lugt and joint transform filter syntheses?
(b) State the advantages and disadvantages of these two correlators.

2.26 Consider a spatial-multiplex transparency, which is the sequential record of two images $A_1(x, y)$ and $A_2(x, y)$ made through a sinusoidal grating on contact with the film. The corresponding transmittance may be written as

$$T(x, y) = K + A_1(x, y)\cos p_0 x + A_2(x, y)\cos q_0 y,$$

where K is an arbitrary constant, and p_0 and q_0 are the respective carrier frequencies in the (p, q) spatial-frequency coordinates. The images $A_1(x, y)$ and $A_2(x, y)$ are assumed to be spatially band limited within a circular region of radius $r = r_0$, where $r_0 < \frac{1}{2}p_0$, and $r_0 < \frac{1}{2}q_0$. This transparency is placed at the input plane P_1 of the optical processor in Figure 2.4.
(a) Determine the complex light distribution on the spatial-frequency plane P_2.
(b) Design a spatial filter so that the output light field will reimage $A_1(x, y)$ and $A_2(x, y)$, one at a time.

2.27 Let $f(x)$ represent a sinusoidal signal recorded on a bilateral area-modulation sound track. The amplitude transmittance function can be described by Eq. 2.39. If this transparency is inserted in the input plane of a coherent optical processor, then:
(a) Calculate the complex light distribution at the back focal plane of the transform lens.
(b) If the signal spectrum of part (a) is filtered by a narrow-slit filter, as shown in Figure 2.14, evaluate the corresponding inverse Fourier transform.

2.28 Assume a cathode-ray scanner with a spatial resolution of about 0.5 line/mm. The scanner is used to generate a bilateral area-modulated speech signal, from 25 and 4000 Hz. Determine the minimum modulating frequency and the velocity of the scanning electron beam.

66 OPTICAL SIGNAL PROCESSING

2.29 Consider the bilateral area modulation for coherent optical processing. If the focal length of the Fourier-transform lens is about 300 mm, determine the size of the input optical window by which the speech spectrographic generation at the output plane would be equivalent to a bandwidth of 300-Hz analysis, assuming the wavelength of the coherent source is $\lambda = 600$ nm.

2.30 Given the T–E transfer characteristic of a certain recording material shown in Figure 2.33:
(a) By a trial-and-error curve-fitting process, approximate a third-order polynomial to the corresponding T–E curve.
(b) With the polynomial obtained in part (a), compute the optimum exposures of the matched filter synthesis for signal–reference-beam ratios S/R = 1, S/R = 1/2, S/R = 1/10, and S/R = 1/30, respectively.
(c) Determine the corresponding optimum first-order linear transmittance for the S/R beam ratios specified in part (b).

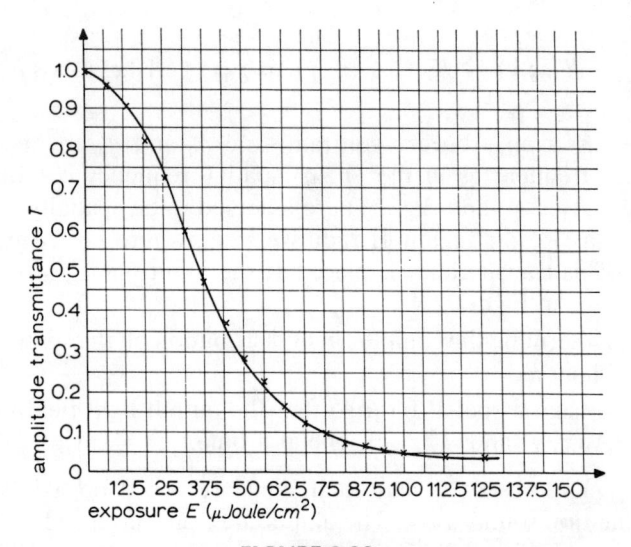

FIGURE 2.33

2.31 Given the same T–E transfer characteristic as described in Problem 2.30, consider the following problems:
(a) By means of a five-point analysis, make a rough plot of the first-order diffraction efficiency as a function of exposure, for the object–reference-beam ratios S/R = 1, S/R = 1/2, S/R = 1/10, and S/R = 1/30.
(b) From the plotted curves of part (a), determine the corresponding optimum exposures. Compare these results with the calculated values obtained in Problem 2.30.

(c) Comment on the linear optimization of a matched filter synthesis that is, in fact, a *phase-only* preserving filter.

2.32 Let us assume that the transmittance of a certain recording medium can be approximated by the nonlinear equation

$$T(E) = 1 + a_1 E + a_3 E^3, \quad \text{for } E \geq 0,$$

where E is the exposure. If the input exposure is a sinusoidal grating,

$$E(x, y) = E_0 + E_1 \cos px, \quad \text{for every } y,$$

where E_0 and E_1 are arbitrary constants and p is the spatial frequency, determine the first-order and the higher order transmittances.

2.33 Repeat Problem 2.32, but assume that the input exposure represents a spatial random noise that follows the one-sided Gaussian probability distribution

$$p(E) = \frac{2}{\sqrt{2\pi}\,\sigma} \exp\left(-\frac{E^2}{2\sigma^2}\right), \quad \text{for } E \geq 0 \text{ and every } (x, y),$$

where σ^2 is the variance of the Gaussian statistics. By means of the mean-square error criterion of Eq. 2.58, determine the optimum linear transmittance.

2.34 We see that, with the optical arrangement shown in Figure 2.34, the light distribution at the focal plane would not correspond to the exact Fourier transform of the input signal $s(x)$. Find the focal length of a lens that we can insert behind the lens L such that we would have the exact Fourier transform of the input at the focal plane.

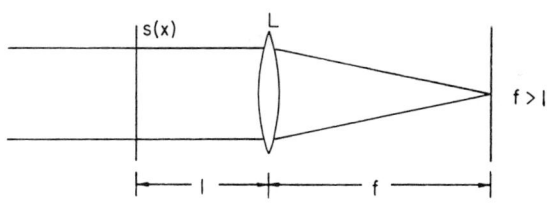

FIGURE 2.34

2.35 Referring to the nonconventional joint transform correlator, in which the focal depth is given by Eq. 2.69:
   (a) Plot the allowable deviation δ as a function of the focal length f of the transform lens.
   (b) Plot δ as a function of object separation b.

68 OPTICAL SIGNAL PROCESSING

- (c) In view of parts (a) and (b), comment on the focal tolerances (i.e., focal depth) of the joint transform correlator.

2.36 To ensure adequate overlapping between the input and reference spectra at the quasi-Fourier domain, the allowable object displacement is given by Eq. 2.72.
- (a) Plot the allowable signal displacement d as a function of focal length f.
- (b) Assuming that $\delta = 50$ mm, $\lambda = 600$ nm, and $b = 40$ mm, calculate the allowable signal displacement for $f = 100$ mm, $f = 500$ mm, and $f = 1$ m, respectively.

2.37 By referring to the nonconventional JTC of Figure 2.18 and assuming that $f = 400$ mm and $\lambda = 550$ nm:
- (a) Calculate the size of the signal spectrum for object spatial frequency limit of $f_m = 5$, 10, and 30 lines/mm, respectively.
- (b) Assuming $f_m = 10$ lines/mm, calculate the incident angle of the square-law detector for $\delta = 10$ mm, 40 mm, and 80 mm, respectively.

2.38 Referring to the preceding problem:
- (a) Calculate the size of the joint transform Fourier spectra.
- (b) We assume that the signal spectrum is given by

$$F(p, q) = \text{cir}\left[\frac{\rho}{2\pi f_m}\right],$$

where $\rho = \sqrt{p^2 + q^2}$, by which the recorded joint transform power spectra are inversely transformed by a monochromatic plane wave of $\lambda = 500$ nm. Calculate the autocorrelation peak intensities for $\delta = 0$, 10, 40, and 80 mm, respectively.
- (c) Sketch the output correlation functions of part (b), and calculate the widths of the distributions.
- (d) Determine the relative diffraction efficiencies of the joint transform filters.

CHAPTER THREE

Applications of Optical Signal Processing

Signal theory was originated by a group of electrical engineers who were mainly interested in electrical communication. However, from the very beginning interest in the optical aspect has never been totally absent. The recent advances in various electrooptic devices have made the relationship between optics and signal processing more profound than ever.

During the past two and a half decades, optical signal processing has received increased attention from a growing number of engineers and physicists. This interest originated in part from the discovery of lasers and in part from the realization that optical systems can be used to perform a variety of signal processing applications. In this chapter, we devote our efforts to discussing the applications of optical signal processing. Because there is such a large number of applications, we confine our discussion to a few cases that are of general interest.

3.1 SYNTHETIC-APERTURE RADAR

One of the more interesting applications of optical signal processing is the processing of synthetic-aperture antenna data. Let us assume that an aircraft, flying level, is carrying the radar system shown in Figure 3.1. Suppose that a sequence of pulsed radar signals is directed onto the earth from the radar system, that the return signals are received back on board, with an azimuth resolution of the order of $\lambda r_1/L$, where λ is the wavelength of the radar signals, r_1 is the slant range, and L is the along-track dimension of the antenna aperture. Since the radar wavelength is on the order of tenth centimeters, a very long antenna aperture is required to have an angular resolution comparable to a photoreconnaissance system. The antenna would have to be hundreds, or even thousands of feet, which is obviously impractical for any aircraft.

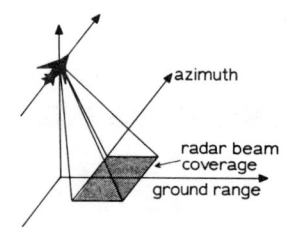

FIGURE 3.1 Side-looking radar.

This difficulty can be resolved, however, by means of the synthetic-aperture technique. Let us assume that the aircraft carries a small side-looking antenna, such that the broad-beam radar signal scans the terrain to the side of the flight path. The radar pulses are emitted at a series of positions along the flight path; these positions can be treated as if they were the positions bombarded by a linear array of antennas. The return radar signal from each of the positions is then recorded "coherently" as a function of time. It is assumed that the radar receiver has a reference signal, against which the amplitude and the phase information of the return signal can be recorded. By properly combining these recorded complex waveforms along the flight path, a synthetic aperture, equivalent to a very long antenna, can be achieved.

To examine this synthetic-aperture technique we first consider a target point like the one located at x_1 in Figure 3.2. The radar pulses are modulated by a sinusoidal carrier signal of radian frequency ω. This periodic pulsing provides range information and fine azimuth resolution, provided that the distance traveled by the aircraft between sample pulses is smaller than $\pi/\Delta p$, where Δp is the spatial bandwidth of the ground reflections. The return radar signals to the aircraft from the target point can be written as

$$S_1(t) = A_1 \exp\left[i\omega\left(\frac{2r}{c} - t\right)\right], \tag{3.1}$$

where A_1 is an appropriate complex constant. The complex quantity A_1 contains factors such as transmitted power, target reflectivity, phase shift, and the inverse fourth-power propagation law.

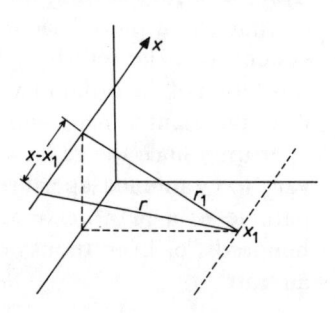

FIGURE 3.2 Flight-path geometry.

Since r can be approximated by

$$r \simeq r_1 + \frac{(x - x_1)^2}{2r_1}, \tag{3.2}$$

Eq. 3.1 can be written as,

$$S_1(t) = A_1(x_1, r_1)\exp\left\{i\left[\omega t - 2kr_1 - \frac{k}{r_1}(x - x_1)^2\right]\right\}, \tag{3.3}$$

which is a function of time t and space x. Thus, the aircraft motion links the space variation to the time variable by

$$x = vt, \tag{3.4}$$

where v is the velocity of the aircraft and $k = 2\pi/\lambda$.

It is apparent that if the terrain at range r_1 consists of N target points, the complete returned radar signal can be written as

$$\begin{aligned} S(t) &= \sum_{n=1}^{N} S_n(t) \\ &= \sum_{n=1}^{N} A_n(x_n, r_1)\exp\left\{i\left[\omega t - 2kr_1 - \frac{k}{r_1}(vt - x_n)^2\right]\right\}. \end{aligned} \tag{3.5}$$

By synchronously demodulating the returned signal, Eq. 3.5 can be written as

$$S(t) = \sum_{n=1}^{N} |A_n(x_n, r_1)|\cos\left[\omega_c t - 2kr_1 - \frac{k}{r_1}(vt - x_n)^2 + \phi_n\right], \tag{3.6}$$

where ω_c is the carrier frequency and ϕ_n is the arbitrary phase angle. This demodulated signal, used to modulate the intensity of the electron beam, sweeps vertically across the cathode-ray tube (CRT) in synchronization with the return radar pulses, as shown in Figure 3.3. By imaging this modulated cathode-ray display onto a strip of photographic film, which is pulled at a constant horizontal speed, the successive range traces will be recorded side-by-side, producing a two-dimensional format, as illustrated in Figure 3.4. The vertical lines represent the successive range sweeps and the horizontal dimension represents the azimuthal position, which is the sample version of $S(t)$. This sampling is carried out in such a way that, by the time the samples have been recorded on the film, the sampled version is essentially indistinguishable from the unsampled version. In this recording it is clear that the time variable is converted to a space variable defined in terms of the distance

72   APPLICATIONS OF OPTICAL SIGNAL PROCESSING

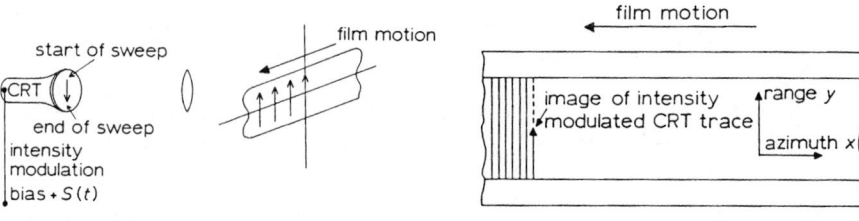

FIGURE 3.3 Return-signal recording.

FIGURE 3.4 Recording format.

along the recorded film. With proper reading exposure, the transparency of the recorded film represents the azimuthal history of the returned radar signal. By considering the recorded data along the line $y = y_1$, the amplitude transmittance can be written as

$$T(x, y_1) = K_1 + K_2 \sum_{n=1}^{N} |A_n(x_n, r_1)| \cos\left[\omega_x x - 2kr_1 - \frac{k}{r_1}\left(\frac{v}{v_f}\right)^2 (x - x_n)^2 + \phi_n\right], \quad (3.7)$$

where K_1 and K_2 are bias and proportionality constants, $x = v_f t$ is the film coordinate, v_f is the velocity of the film motion, and $\omega_x = \omega_c/v_f$.

Since the cosine can be written into the sum of two exponential conjugate forms, the summation of Eq. 3.7 can be written as the sum of two terms T_1 and T_2, respectively, as given by

$$T_1(x, y_1) = \frac{K_2}{2} \sum_{n=1}^{N} |A_n(x_n, r_1)| \exp\left\{i\left[\omega_x x - 2kr_1 - \frac{k}{r_1}\left(\frac{v}{v_f}\right)^2 \left(x - \frac{v_f}{v} x_n\right)^2 + \phi_n\right]\right\}. \quad (3.8)$$

and

$$T_2(x, y_1) = \frac{K_2}{2} \sum_{n=1}^{N} |A_n(x_n, r_1)| \exp\left\{-i\left[\omega_x x - 2kr_1 - \frac{k}{r_1}\left(\frac{v}{v_f}\right)^2 \left(x - \frac{v_f}{v} x_n\right)^2 + \phi_n\right]\right\}. \quad (3.9)$$

For simplicity, we restrict ourselves to a single target point as given by

$$T_1(x, y_1) = C \exp(i\omega_x x) \exp\left[-i\frac{k}{r_1}\left(\frac{v}{v_f}\right)^2 \left(x - \frac{v_f}{v} x_n\right)^2\right], \quad (3.10)$$

where C is an appropriate complex constant. The first exponent introduces a linear phase factor, that is, a simple tilt of the transmitted wavefront, in which the angle of obliquity is given by

$$\sin \theta = \frac{\omega_x}{k_1}, \qquad (3.11)$$

where $k_1 = 2\pi/\lambda_1$, with λ_1 the wavelength of the illumination. From the second exponent of Eq. 3.10, it can be seen that a positive cylindrical lens is centered at

$$x = \frac{v_f}{v} x_n, \qquad (3.12)$$

with a focal length of

$$f = \frac{1}{2} \frac{\lambda}{\lambda_1} \left(\frac{v_f}{v}\right)^2 r_1. \qquad (3.13)$$

Therefore it can be seen that, except for a linear phase function, Eq. 3.8 is a superposition of N positive cylindrical lenses, centered at locations

$$x = \frac{v_f}{v} x_n, \qquad n = 1, 2, \ldots, N. \qquad (3.14)$$

Similarly, Eq. 3.9 contains a linear phase factor $-\theta$, and represents a superposition of N negative cylindrical lenses, with centers given by Eq. 3.14 and focal lengths given by Eq. 3.13.

In order to reconstruct the image, the transparency that yields Eq. 3.7 is illuminated by a monochromatic plane wave, as shown in Figure 3.5. Then by the Fresnel–Kirchhoff theory, we show that the real images produced by $T_1(x, y_1)$ and the virtual images produced by $T_2(x, y_1)$ will be reconstructed

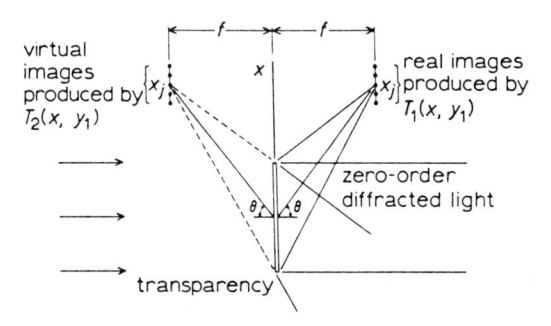

FIGURE 3.5 Image reconstruction from a radar signal format for $y = y_1$.

74 APPLICATIONS OF OPTICAL SIGNAL PROCESSING

at the front and back focal planes, respectively, of the film. The relative positions of the target point images are located along the line foci, since the centers of the lenslike structure are determined by the positions of the point scatterers. However, the reconstructed image will be spread in the y direction, because the recorded format exerts no focal power in that direction.

Our aim is to reconstruct an image not only in the azimuthal direction but also in the range direction. It is therefore necessary to image the y coordinate directly onto the focal plane of the azimuthal image. Since the focal length of the azimuthal image distribution is linearly proportional to the range r_1, as shown in Eq. 3.13, the focal distance is linearly related to the y direction. Thus, to construct the terrain map we must image the y coordinate of the transmitted signal onto a tilted plane that is determined by the focal distances of the azimuthal direction. This imaging procedure can be carried out by inserting a positive conical lens immediately behind the recorded format, as shown in Figure 3.6. The transmittance of the conical lens is

$$T_1(x, y_1) = \exp\left(-i \frac{k_1}{2f} x^2\right), \qquad (3.15)$$

where f is a linear function of r_1, as shown in Eq. 3.13. It is then possible to remove all the virtual diffractions from the entire tilted plane to the points at infinity, while leaving the transmittance in the y direction unchanged. Thus, if the cylindrical lens is placed at the focal distance from the recorded format, it will create a virtual image of the y direction at infinity. Now the azimuthal and the range images (i.e., the x and y directions) coincide at the points of infinity, which can be brought back to a finite distance by a spherical lens. In this final operation, a real image of the azimuthal and range coordinates of the terrain is mapped in focus at the output plane of the system. In practice, however, the desired image may be recorded through a slit in the output plane.

Figure 3.7 is an example of the images obtainable by optical processing of

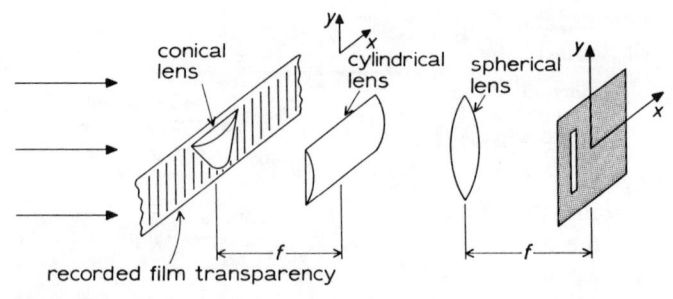

FIGURE 3.6 Optical processing for imaging synthetic-aperture radar.

INVERSE SYNTHETIC-APERTURE RADAR 75

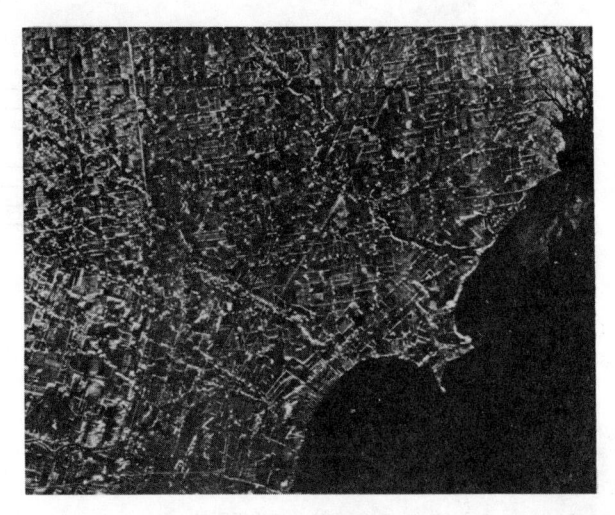

FIGURE 3.7 Synthetic-aperture radar image of the Monroe, Michigan, area. (By permission of L. J. Cutrona)

synthetic-aperture radar data. The radar image was obtained in the Monroe, Michigan, area, located south of Detroit. The photograph shows a variety of scatterers, including city streets, wooded areas, and farmland. Lake Erie, with some broken ice floes, can be seen on the right.

3.2 INVERSE SYNTHETIC-APERTURE RADAR

We have seen that synthetic-aperture radar (SAR) can produce high-resolution ground maps. In general, this is accompanied by using the motion of the aircraft to synthetically produce a large effective antenna aperture cross-range by coherently integrating the returned signal. A variation of this radar is called the inverse synthetic-aperture radar (ISAR) [3.3]. This variation can be used to produce the image of a moving target from either a stationary or moving platform. The ISAR technique requires target motion, while target motion will degrade the SAR image. The discussion in this section for the most part follows that of Brown and Fredricks [3.4].

Consider a rigid rotating body, as depicted in Figure 3.8. Let the body rotates with the axis of rotation normal to the paper at the origin. If the illuminating radar is far from the rotating body, then the lines of constant range are parallel to the x axis. Let $f(x, y)$ be the reflectivity of the object as a function of the coordinates fixed on the body. At $\theta = 0$, the center of our processing interval, x and y are also the range and cross-range coordinates of the body relative to the radar; however, when the body is rotated by an angle θ, the range and cross-range radar coordinates on the body are (u, v),

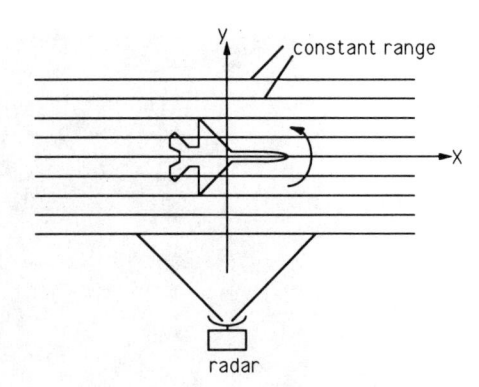

FIGURE 3.8 Geometry of inverse synthetic-aperture radar.

where

$$u = x \cos \theta - y \sin \theta$$
$$v = x \sin \theta + y \cos \theta, \qquad (3.16)$$

and

$$x = v \sin \theta + u \cos \theta$$
$$y = v \cos \theta - u \sin \theta, \qquad (3.17)$$

as depicted in Figure 3.9.

Let $f_0(u, v)$ be $f(x, y)$ with x and y transformed into u, v, as indicated by Eq. 3.17. For a particular pulse, the returned signal is responsive to the cross section as a function of range, that is, to

$$g(v) = \int f_0(u, v) \, du. \qquad (3.18)$$

Let $\hat{w}$ be the complex modulation on each transmitted pulse so that $\hat{w}(t - 2v/c)$ is the return from a unit point target at range v. For convenience, we

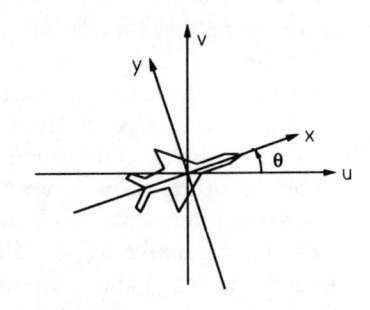

FIGURE 3.9 Target rotates through an angle θ.

measure time relative to when the pulse is centered on the body. If $w(r) = \hat{w}(2r/c)$, then the modulation of the return from a particular pulse is

$$g(r) = \int w(r, v) g(v) \exp(i4\pi v/\lambda) \, dv. \qquad (3.19)$$

That is, $\hat{g}(ct/2)$ are the data, or range sweep, received in response to a pulse transmitted when the body is at a particular disposition θ. It is assumed that the body does not move during a time equal to the duration of a single pulse; on the other hand, body motion over a sequence of pulses is the primary concern. In more detail, the observable data are

$$g(\theta, r) = \iint w(r - v) f_0(u, v) \exp(i4\pi v/\lambda) \, du \, dv. \qquad (3.20)$$

If the variables of integration are changed as in Eq. 3.16, we have

$$g(\theta, r) = \iint w[r - (x \sin \theta + y \cos \theta)] f(x, y) \exp[ik(x \sin \theta + y \cos \theta)] \, dx \, dy, \qquad (3.21)$$

where $k = 4\pi/\lambda$ [see Problem 3.12].

The fundamental observation to be made by this technique is that if we take the Fourier transform of $g(\theta, r)$ over r, the processing required to extract the image $f(x, y)$ of a rotating object becomes quite reasonable. Let $g(\theta, r)$ of Eq. 3.21 be transformed over r:

$$\begin{aligned}
G_0(\theta, \omega) &= \int g(\theta, r) \exp(-i\omega r) \, dr \\
&= \iiint w[r - (x \sin \theta + y \cos \theta)] \exp\{-i\omega \\
&\quad \cdot [r - (x \sin \theta + y \cos \theta)]\} \, dr \\
&\quad \cdot f(x, y) \exp \\
&\quad \cdot [ik(x \sin \theta + y \cos \theta)] \exp[-i\omega(x \sin \theta + y \cos \theta)] \, dx \, dy.
\end{aligned} \qquad (3.22)$$

By changing variables, Eq. 3.22 can be expressed as

$$G(\alpha, \beta) = Y(\omega) \iint f(x, y) \exp[i(\alpha x + \beta y)] \, dx \, dy, \qquad (3.23)$$

where

$$Y(\omega) = \int w(r) \exp(-i\omega r) \, dr, \qquad (3.24)$$

and

$$\alpha = (k - \omega)\sin\theta$$
$$\beta = (k - \omega)\cos\theta. \tag{3.25}$$

The optical processing system for the reconstruction of an ISAR image is depicted in Figure 3.10. As in SAR processing, the returned radar signal can be properly recorded on a two-dimensional photographic film. The recorded two-dimensional data $g(\theta, r)$ are placed in the input plane. A combination of a spherical and a cylindrical lens is required to form a lens that Fourier transforms $g(\theta, r)$ in the r direction while it images $g(\theta, r)$ in the θ direction to generate $G_0(\theta, \omega)$ [see Problem 3.11]. We then multiply $G_0(\theta, \omega)$ by $1/Y(\omega)$ in the (θ, ω) plane, where $Y(\omega)$ is the transform of the known transmitted pulse as shown in Eq. 3.24. The filtered output is coordinate-transformed from the (θ, ω) plane to the (α, β) plane by a specially fabricated holographic lens. Optical coordinate transforms have been reported by Bryngdahl [3.5]; the interested reader should refer to his article. Finally, a spherical lens performs a two-dimensional Fourier transform to yield the object image $f(x, y)$.

A difficulty in ISAR imaging is that variables θ and r must be determined in order to format the returned signal in a two-dimensional (θ, r) plane. Variable r can be determined from the relation $r = ct/2$, where t is the signal traveling time, and c is the signal propagation speed. However, θ is provided by the motion of the target, which is usually uncontrollable by the radar. Under such circumstances, the radar has to estimate the target rotation with respect to the radar to obtain the information necessary for the image scaling. Failure to do the proper scaling results in skewed images because of the disparity between the range and the cross-range resolutions. Prickett and Chen [3.3] report various methods used in digital processing to estimate the cross-range scale in the ISAR image:

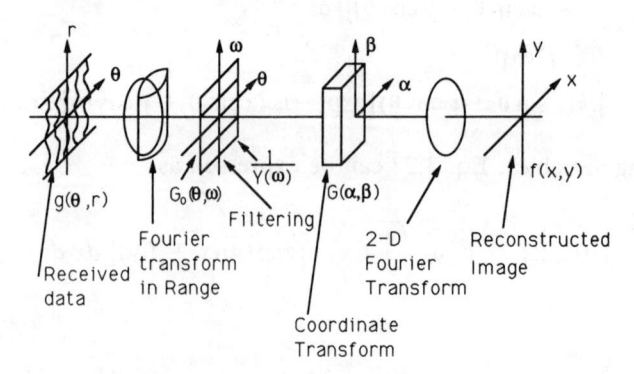

FIGURE 3.10 Schematic diagram of an optical processor for inverse synthetic-aperture radar.

1. Derive the target aspect from its range and azimuth history as seen by the radar.
2. Use the apriori information about the target shape, size, length–width ratio, or other characteristics to scale the images.
3. Determine the scale factor from the relationships among the positions of various target scatterers in a sequence of images.

Although this technique was proposed over twenty years ago, apparently no optical implementation has been realized yet. On the other hand, digital processing based on this principle has been used successfully in taking ISAR images of targets with yaw, pitch, and roll [3.3].

3.3 RESTORING BLURRED IMAGES

Another interesting application of optical signal processing is the restoration of blurred photographic images. The Fourier transform of a linearly blurred image can be expressed by

$$G(p) = S(p)D(p), \tag{3.22}$$

where $G(p)$, $S(p)$, and $D(p)$ are the blurred image, the unblurred image, and the distorting function, respectively, and p is the spatial frequency. The inverse filter function is

$$H(p) = \frac{1}{D(p)}. \tag{3.23}$$

We note that the inverse filter is generally not physically realizable, particularly for blurred images that were caused by linear motion or defocusing. Let the transmission function of a linear smeared-point image be

$$f(\xi) = \begin{cases} 1, & -1/2\Delta\xi \leq \xi \leq 1/2\Delta\xi, \\ 0, & \text{otherwise}, \end{cases} \tag{3.24}$$

where $\Delta\xi$ is the smear length. If a transparency satisfying Eq. 3.24 is inserted in the input plane P_1 of a coherent optical data processor, as shown in Figure 3.11, the resulting complex light field on the spatial frequency plane is

$$F(p) = \Delta\xi \frac{\sin(p\Delta\xi/2)}{p\Delta\xi/2}, \tag{3.25}$$

which is essentially the Fourier transform of the smeared-point image. The plot of the Fourier spectrum given by Eq. 3.25 is shown in Figure 3.12.

80 APPLICATIONS OF OPTICAL SIGNAL PROCESSING

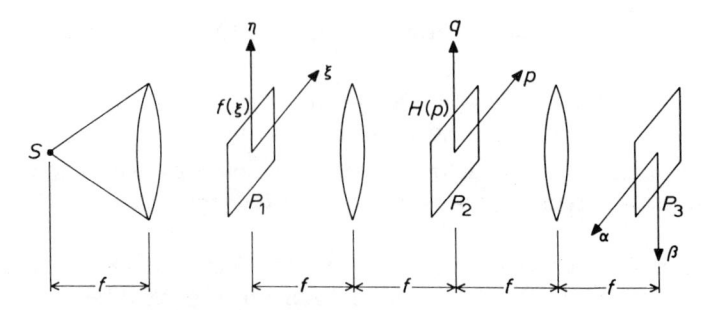

FIGURE 3.11 A coherent processing system.

In principle, the smeared image can be corrected by means of inverse filtering, as shown by

$$H(p) = \frac{p\Delta\xi/2}{\sin(p\Delta\xi/2)}. \tag{3.26}$$

This inverse filter is a bipolar function with an infinite number of poles, and it is not physically realizable. However, if one would sacrifice some degree of restoration, an approximate filter function can be realized. To do so, we combine the amplitude filter with a phase filter as shown in Figures 3.13 and 3.14, respectively. The transfer function of this combination is

$$H(p) = A(p)e^{i\phi(p)}. \tag{3.27}$$

If the inverse filter is inserted in the spatial-frequency plane of the data processor of Figure 3.11, the restored Fourier transfer function would be

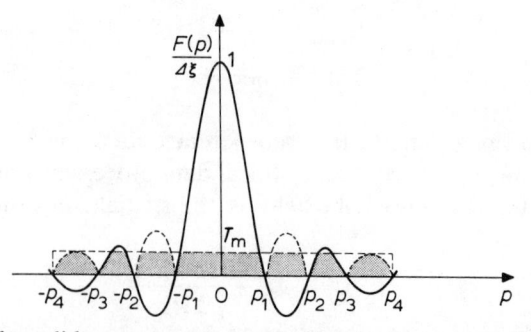

$$F_1(p) = F(p)H(p). \tag{3.28}$$

FIGURE 3.12 The solid curve represents the Fourier spectrum of a linear smeared point image. The shaded area represents the corresponding restored Fourier spectrum of a point image. The zeros are given by $p_n = 2n\pi/\Delta\xi$, $n = 1, 2, 3, \ldots$.

RESTORING BLURRED IMAGES   81

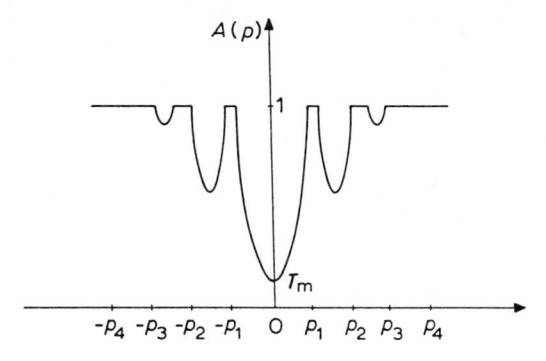

FIGURE 3.13 Amplitude filter.

If T_m is the minimum transmittance of the amplitude filter, then the restored Fourier spectrum of the point image is the shaded spectrum shown in Figure 3.12. Let us define the relative degree of image restoration as, for example,

$$\mathcal{D}(T_m)(\text{percent}) = \frac{1}{T_m \Delta p} \int_{\Delta p} \frac{F(p)H(p)}{\Delta \xi} \, dp \times 100, \quad (3.29)$$

where Δp is the spatial bandwidth of interest. In Figure 3.12, for example, $\Delta p = 2p_4$. Using Eq. 3.29, the degree of image restoration as a function of T_m is plotted in Figure 3.15. Although perfect restoration may be achievable as T_m approaches zero, the amplitude of the restored Fourier spectrum would be zero, leaving no light to be diffracted. Thus, perfect restoration cannot be achieved in practice. These considerations aside, it seems that noise (film granularity and speckling) is the major limiting factor in image restoration.

Notice that a phase filter can be synthesized by a holographic technique, perhaps by a computer-generated hologram. Let us assume that the transmittance of a phase filter is

$$T(p) = \frac{1}{2} \{1 + \cos[\phi(p) + \alpha_0 p]\}, \quad (3.30)$$

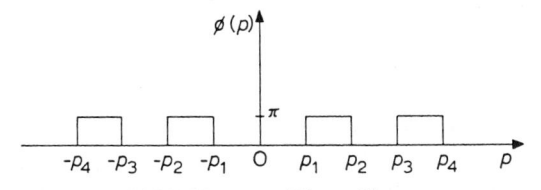

FIGURE 3.14 Phase filter.

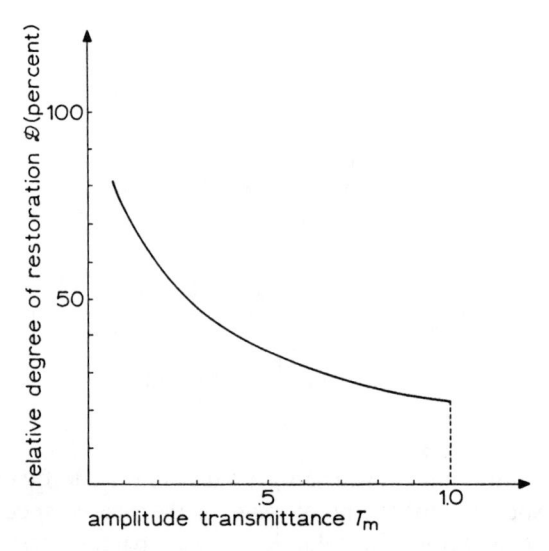

FIGURE 3.15 Relative degree of restoration as a function of T_m.

where α_0 is an arbitrarily chosen constant, and

$$\phi(p) = \begin{cases} \pi, & p_n \leq p \leq p_{n+1}, \quad n = \pm 1, \pm 3, \pm 5, \ldots, \\ 0, & \text{otherwise.} \end{cases} \quad (3.31)$$

If we add the amplitude filter, the complex filter function can be written as

$$H_1(p) = A(p)T(p) = \frac{1}{2}A(p) + \frac{1}{4}[H(p)e^{i\alpha_0 p} + H^*(p)e^{-i\alpha_0 p}]. \quad (3.32)$$

Notice that $H(p) = H^*(p)$ is the approximate inverse filter of Eq. 3.27. If $H_1(p)$ is inserted in the spatial frequency plane of Figure 3.11, the emerging light field is

$$F_2(p) = \frac{1}{2}F(p)A(p) + \frac{1}{4}[F(p)H(p)e^{ip\alpha_0} + F(p)H^*(p)e^{-ip\alpha_0}], \quad (3.33)$$

The first term is the restored Fourier spectrum, caused by the amplitude filter. This term will be diffracted on the optical axis at the output plane. The second and third terms are the restored Fourier spectra of the smeared image, and will be diffracted away from the optical axis and centered at $\alpha = \alpha_0$ and $\alpha = -\alpha_0$, respectively. Figure 3.16 shows the calculated irradiances of a restored object point blurred by linear motion. An experimental demonstration using such an inverse filter is shown in Figure 3.17. It is worth pointing

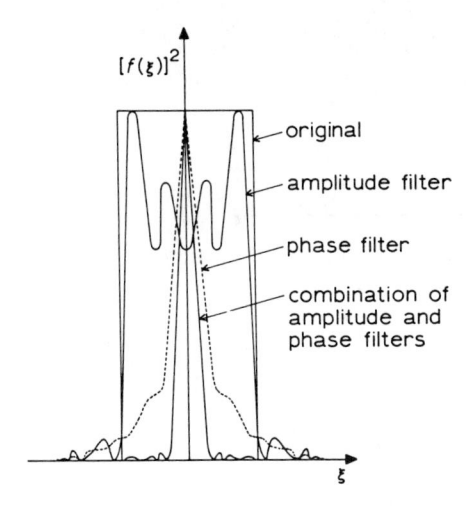

FIGURE 3.16 Calculated restorations of an object point blurred by linear motion.

out that the restoration of unfocused images can be accomplished by a similar procedure such that the spatial filter must be rotational symmetry.

3.4 IMAGE SUBTRACTION

Another interesting application of optical signal processing is image subtraction. Image subtraction may be of value in many applications, such as urban development, highway planning, earth resources studies, remote sensing, meteorology, automatic surveillance, and inspection. Optical image subtraction can also apply to communications as a means of bandwidth compression; for example, when it is necessary to transmit only the differences between images in successive cycles, rather than the entire image in each cycle.

Let us insert two image transparencies in the coherent optical processor shown in Figure 3.18. At the spatial frequency plane P_2, the complex light distribution is given by

$$F(p, q) = F_1(p, q)e^{-iap} + F_2(p, q)e^{iap}, \qquad (3.34)$$

where $F_1(p, q)$ and $F_2(p, q)$ are the Fourier spectra of $f_1(x, y)$ and $f_2(x, y)$, respectively. In image subtraction we would use a sinusoidal grating in the spatial frequency plane, for which we assume that

(a)   (b)

FIGURE 3.17 Smeared image restoration (a) Smeared image. (b) Restored image.

84 APPLICATIONS OF OPTICAL SIGNAL PROCESSING

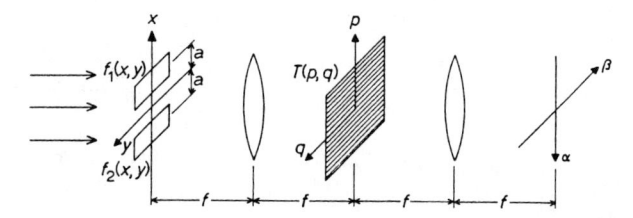

FIGURE 3.18 A coherent processor for image subtraction.

$$T(p) = \frac{1}{2}(1 + \sin ap). \tag{3.35}$$

Then the complex light distribution behind $T(p)$ is given by

$$E(p, q) = F(p, q)T(p)$$

$$= \frac{1}{2}[F_1(p, q)e^{-iap} + F_2(p, q)e^{iap}]$$

$$+ \frac{1}{4i}[F_1(p\,q) - F_1(p, q)e^{iap} - F_2(p, q) + F_2(p, q)e^{-i2ap}]. \tag{3.36}$$

The output complex light field can be shown to be

$$g(\alpha, \beta) = \frac{1}{2}[f_1(\alpha - a, \beta) + f_2(\alpha + a, \beta)]$$

$$+ \frac{1}{4i}[f_1(\alpha, \beta) - f_2(\alpha, \beta)]$$

$$- \frac{1}{4i}[f_1(\alpha - 2a, \beta) + f_2(\alpha + 2a, \beta)], \tag{3.37}$$

for which a subtracted image $[f_1(\alpha, \beta) - f_2(\alpha, \beta)]$ is diffracted around the optical axis at the output plane. For experimental demonstration, we provide the result shown in Figure 3.19.

3.5 WIDE-BAND SIGNAL PROCESSING

An important application of coherent optical systems is in spectrum analysis of broad-band signals. To begin, let us consider an optical processor that is capable of handling broad-band signals. By using the two-dimensional Fourier-transform property of lenses, a large space–bandwidth signal can be processed by means of a slightly different technique. The broad-band signal can

FIGURE 3.19 Image subtraction. (a) Input object transparencies. (b) Subtracted image.

be recorded with a cathode-ray tube raster pattern without interleaving, as shown in Figure 3.20. The time signal modulates the intensity of the electron beam, thus adjusting the scan rate so that the maximum frequency content of the signal is properly recorded. The required scan velocity of the electron beam is given by

$$v \geq \frac{f_m}{R}, \qquad (3.38)$$

where v is the scan velocity, f_m is the maximum frequency content of the time

86 APPLICATIONS OF OPTICAL SIGNAL PROCESSING

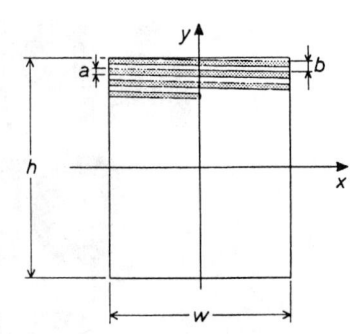

FIGURE 3.20 Raster scan signal transparency.

signal, and R is the resolution limit of the optical system. We assume that the return sweep of the electron beam is much faster than $1/f_m$, so that the transmittance of the recorded format can be represented by

$$f(x, y) = \sum_{n=1}^{N} f(x)f(y), \qquad (3.39)$$

where $N = h/b$,

$$f(x) = \begin{cases} f\left[x + (2n-1)\dfrac{w}{2}\right], & -\dfrac{w}{2} \leq x \leq \dfrac{w}{2}, \\ 0, & \text{otherwise} \end{cases} \qquad (3.40)$$

and

$$f(y) = \operatorname{rect}\left[\dfrac{y - nb}{a}\right], \qquad (3.41)$$

If this format is inserted in the input plane of the analyzer, then the complex light field at the spatial frequency domain is given by

$$F(p, q) = C \sum_{n=1}^{N} \int f(x)e^{-ixp}\,dx \int f(y)e^{-iyq}\,dy, \qquad (3.42)$$

where C is a complex constant. By substituting Eqs 3.40 and 3.41 in Eq. 3.42, we obtain

$$F(p, q) = C_1 \sum_{n=1}^{N} \operatorname{sinc}\left(\dfrac{qa}{2}\right)\left\{\operatorname{sinc}\left(\dfrac{pw}{2}\right) * F(p)\exp\left[i\dfrac{pw}{2}(2n-1)\right]\right\}$$

$$\times \exp\left\{-i\dfrac{q}{2}[h - 2(n-1)b - a]\right\}, \qquad (3.43)$$

where C_1 is a complex constant, and

$$F(p) = \int f(x')e^{-ipx'}\,dx',$$

$$x' = x + (2n-1)\frac{w}{2} \quad \text{and} \quad \text{sinc}\,X \triangleq \frac{\sin X}{X}.$$

For simplicity, we assume a simple sinusoid signal [i.e., $f(x') = \sin p_0 x$], $w \simeq h$, and $b \simeq a$, by which Eq. 3.43 can be written as

$$F(p, q) = C_1 \text{sinc}\left(\frac{qa}{2}\right) \sum_{n=1}^{N} \left\{ \text{sinc}\left(\frac{pw}{2}\right) * \frac{1}{2}[\delta(p-p_0) + \delta(p+p_0)]\right.$$
$$\left. \times \exp\left[i\frac{wp_0}{2}(2n-1)\right]\right\} \exp\left\{-i\frac{q}{2}[w - (2n-1)b]\right\}. \quad (3.44)$$

To simplify the analysis, we only consider the $\delta(p - p_0)$ component, for which we have

$$F_1(p, q) = C_1 \text{sinc}\left[\frac{w}{2}(p - p_0)\right] \text{sinc}\left(\frac{qa}{2}\right) \exp\left(-i\frac{qw}{2}\right)$$
$$\times \sum_{n=1}^{N} \exp\left[i\frac{1}{2}(2n-1)(wp_0 + bq)\right]. \quad (3.45)$$

The corresponding irradiance is given by

$$I_1(p, q) = |F_1(p, q)|^2 = C_1^2 \text{sinc}^2\left[\frac{w}{2}(p - p_0)\right] \text{sinc}^2\left(\frac{qa}{2}\right)$$
$$\times \sum_{n=1}^{N} e^{i2n\theta} \sum_{n=1}^{N} e^{-i2n\theta}, \quad (3.46)$$

where

$$\theta = \frac{1}{2}(wp_0 + bq). \quad (3.47)$$

Since

$$\sum_{n=1}^{N} e^{i2n\theta} \sum_{n=1}^{N} e^{-i2n\theta} = \left(\frac{\sin N\theta}{\sin \theta}\right)^2,$$

$I_1(p, q)$ can be written as

$$I_1(p, q) = C_1^2 \text{sinc}^2\left[\frac{w}{2}(p - p_0)\right] \text{sinc}^2\left(\frac{qa}{2}\right)\left(\frac{\sin N\theta}{\sin \theta}\right)^2. \qquad (3.48)$$

The first sinc factor represents a relatively narrow spectral line in the p direction, located at $p = p_0$, which is derived from the Fourier transform of a pure sinusoid truncated with the width w of the input transparency. The second line sinc factor represents a relatively broad spectral band in the q direction, which is derived from the Fourier transform of a rectangular pulse of width a (i.e., the channel width). This last factor deserves special mention, because for large values of N, it approaches a sequence of narrow pulses. The locations of the pulses (i.e., the peaks) can be obtained by letting $\theta = n\pi$, which gives

$$q = \frac{1}{b}(2\pi n - wp_0), \qquad n = 1, 2, \ldots \qquad (3.49)$$

Notice that this factor yields a fine spectral resolution in the q direction.

From Eq. 3.48, we see that irradiance in the p direction is confined within a relatively narrow region that essentially depends on w. The half-width of the spectral spread (i.e., from the center to the first zero) is

$$\Delta p = \frac{2\pi}{w}, \qquad (3.50)$$

which is the resolution limit of an ideal transform lens. In the q direction, the irradiance is first confined within a relatively broad spectral band (which primarily depends on the channel width a) centered at $q = 0$, and then modulated by a sequence of narrow periodic pulses. The half-width of the broad spectral band is

$$\Delta q = \frac{2\pi}{a}. \qquad (3.51)$$

The separation of the narrow pulses is obtained from a similar equation, that is,

$$\Delta q_1 = \frac{2\pi}{b}. \qquad (3.52)$$

It may be seen from Eqs. 3.51 and 3.52 that there are only a few pulses located within the spread of the broad spectral band for each p_0, as shown in Figure 3.21.

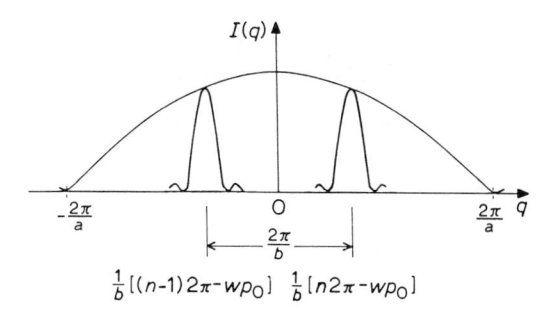

FIGURE 3.21 A broad spectral band modulated by a sequence of narrow pulses.

The actual location of any of the pulses is determined by the signal frequency. Thus if the frequency changes, the position of the pulses also changes, in accordance with

$$dq = \frac{w}{b} dp_0. \tag{3.53}$$

The displacement in the q direction is proportional to the displacement in the p direction. Since the pulse width decreases as the number of the scan lines N increase, the output spectrum yields a frequency separation equivalent to that obtained with a one-dimensional processor for a continuous signal that is NW long.

In order to avoid the ambiguity in reading the output plane, all but one of the periodic pulses should be ignored. This may be accomplished by masking out all the output plane except the region

$$-\frac{\pi}{b} \leq q \leq \frac{\pi}{b}, \qquad 0 \leq p \leq \infty, \tag{3.54}$$

as shown in Figure 3.22. Because the periodic pulses are $2\pi/b$ apart, as the input signal frequency advances, one pulse leaves the open region defined by Eq. 3.54 at $q = -\pi b$, while another pulse enters the region at $q = \pi b$. As a result, a single bright spot would be scanned out diagonally at the output plane. In other words, the frequency locus of the input signal can be traced out and appear as a bright spot. To remove the nonuniform characteristic of the second sinc factor of Eq. 3.48, a graded transparency can be placed at the output plane.

So far the analysis has been carried out on a one-frame basis. However, the operation could also be performed on a continuously running basis, making it possible to synthesize a wide-band real-time spectrum analyzer.

A convenient mode of real-time operation would be the use of a programmable spatial light modulator for which the scanned format can be vertically adjusted as the input signal advances.

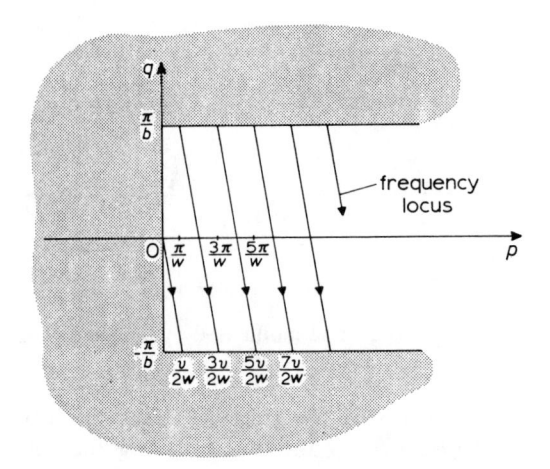

FIGURE 3.22 Output frequency locus.

The wide-band optical spectrum analyzer offers considerable flexibility in data handling. To name just one application, the output time-varying spectrum can be directly connected to an appropriate analog–digital converter and then to a digital computer for signal processing. This application may be important to the future of automatic recognition. A near-real-time continuous optical spectrum analyzer with a space–bandwidth product capability greater than 10^7 is within the current state of the art.

3.6 HOMOMORPHIC FILTERING

In preceding sections we have discussed techniques that relied on linear spatial invariant operations. There are, however, techniques available for nonlinear processing operations. One such approach is a homomorphic processing system, shown in Figure 3.23, which has been successfully applied with the digital processing technique. In this section we demonstrate a technique that makes use of the inherent nonlinearity of the photographic film (or devices) to perform the logarithmic transformation. The advantage of using photographic film is that several hundred lines per millimeter can be resolved. This capability of transforming images with very high spatial resolution remains the basic advantage of the optical method over the digital techniques.

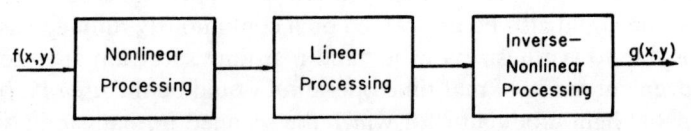

FIGURE 3.23 A homomophic processing system.

To produce a nonlinear transform, a two-step contact-printing process can be used. First, a negative transparency is produced. The intensity transmittance of the negative transparency as a function of the input exposure can be described as $K_1 E^{-\gamma}$, where K_1 is the proportionality constant, E is the exposure, and γ is the gamma of the film used. Using this transparency in contact printing, the relative exposure for the final positive transparency would be equal to the intensity transmittance of the negative transparency. We wish to find the amplitude transmittance characteristics required for the second exposure so that the amplitude transmittance of the final transparency would be proportional to the logarithm of the original exposure, that is

$$T_A = K_2 \log E. \tag{3.55}$$

Since the amplitude transmittance is dependent on both the gamma of the first film and the proportionality constant K_2 (i.e., exposure range), we examine the amplitude transmittance required in the second exposure for different ranges with a given gamma for the first exposure. Figure 3.24 shows

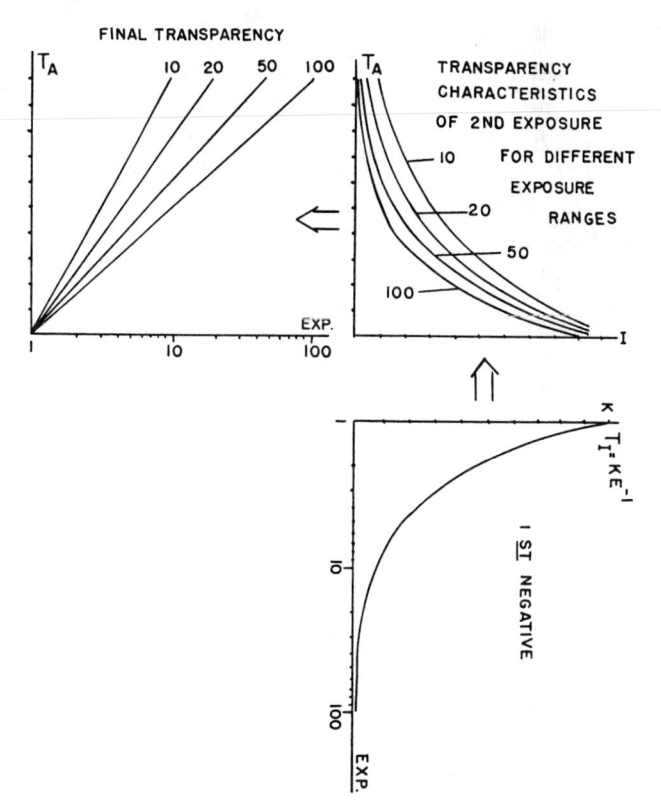

FIGURE 3.24 Logarithmic transformation using two-step contact-printing process.

92 APPLICATIONS OF OPTICAL SIGNAL PROCESSING

the different characteristics required to produce logarithmic transformation for exposure ranges of 10, 20, 50, and 100, with the gamma of the film used in the first exposure equal to 1. However, to produce a logarithmic transformation of different exposure ranges, it is not necessary to find different films for the second exposure, because any one of these characteristics can be used with any gamma value in the first exposure to obtain a logarithmic transformation, as illustrated in Figure 3.25.

Similarly, the inverse transformation (i.e., exponential transformation) can be obtained by a two-step contact-printing process, for which the intensity transmittance of the first exposure is given by

$$T_{f1} = C_1 \exp(K_3 T_A)$$
$$= C_1 \exp[K_3 K_2 \log E], \qquad (3.56)$$

where C_1 and K_3 are arbitrary constants. By contact printing onto another film having a gamma γ, the intensity transmittance of the final film can be shown as

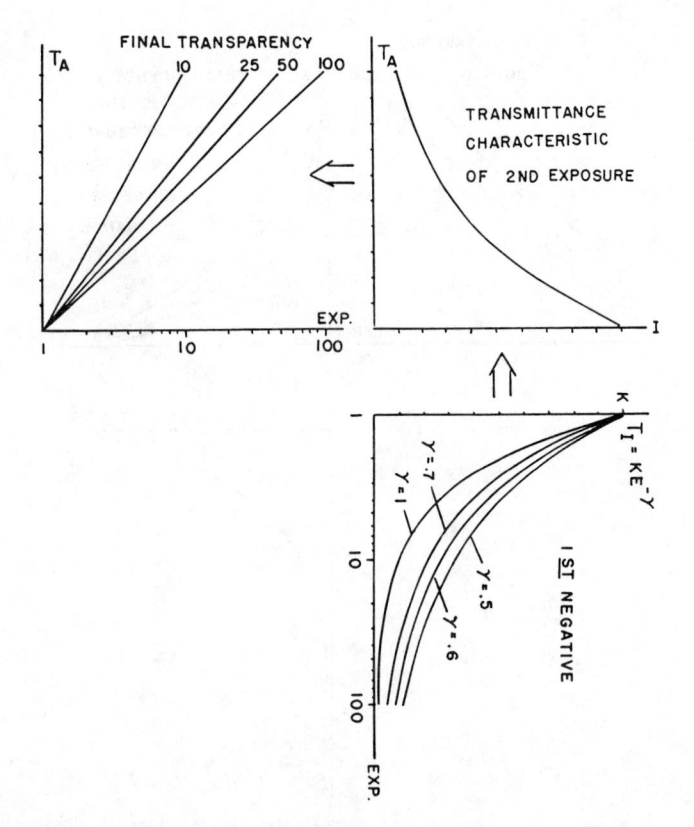

FIGURE 3.25 Logarithmic transformation using various film gammas.

$$T_{f2} = C_2 \exp(\gamma K_3 K_2 \log E). \tag{3.57}$$

It is therefore apparent that if $\gamma = 1/(K_2 K_3)$, the final intensity transmittance would be

$$T_{f2} = C_2 E, \tag{3.58}$$

which is proportional to E.

Figure 3.26 shows the characteristics required to produce the exponential transformation with the final intensity transmittance proportional to the original exposure. The input to the exponential transformation is the positive transparency resulting from the square root transformation.

As an experimental demonstrations, we have shown the results of filtering out multiplicative noise from a continuous-tone signal using a logarithmic and a linear transformation, as shown in Figure 3.27. The input consisted of the

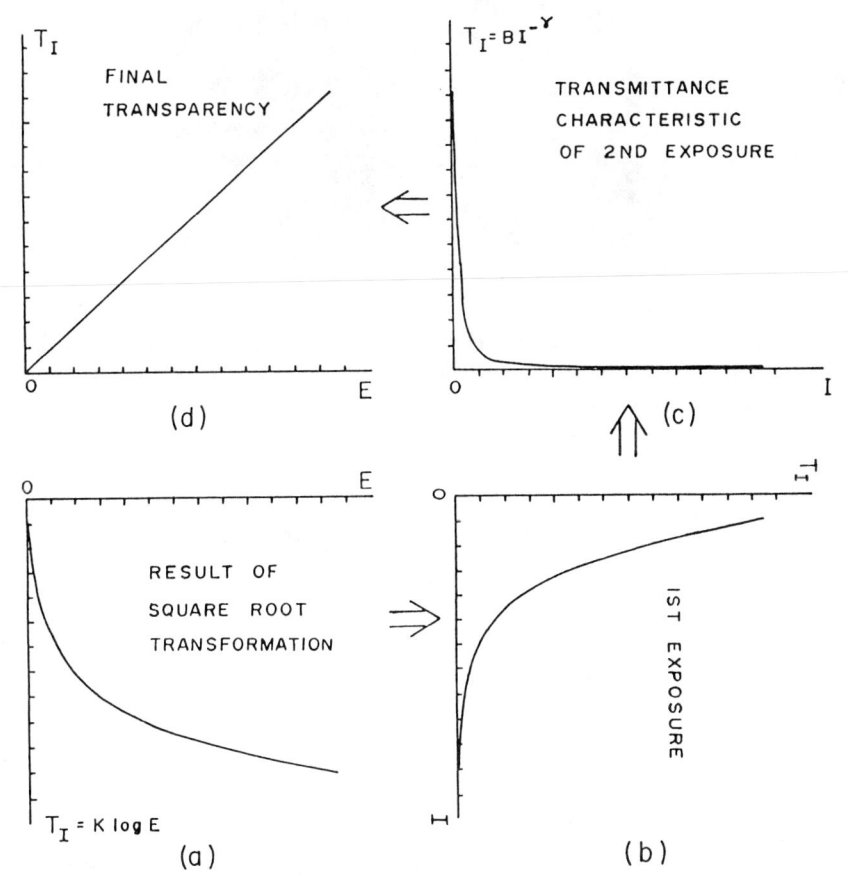

FIGURE 3.26 Exponential transform using two-step contact-printing process.

94 APPLICATIONS OF OPTICAL SIGNAL PROCESSING

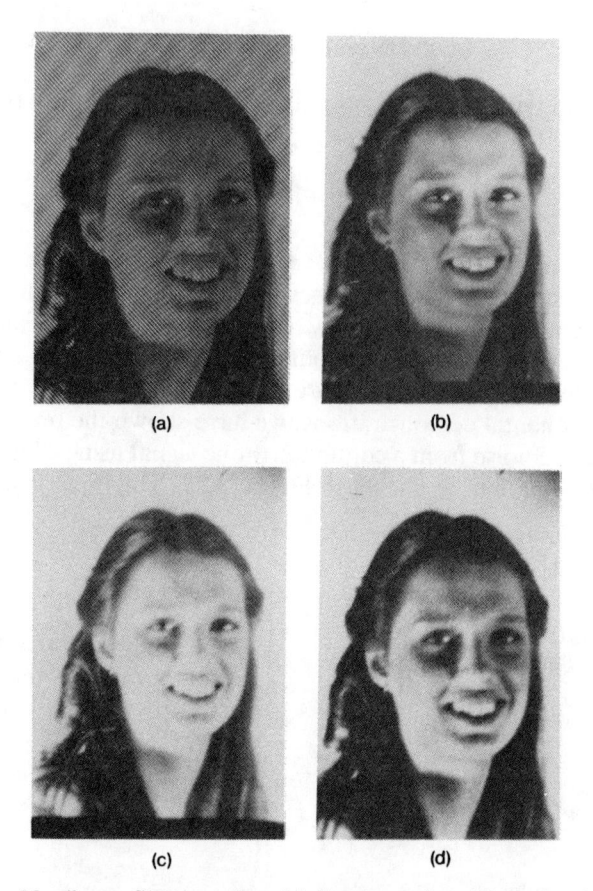

FIGURE 3.27 Nonlinear filtering of multiplicative noise. (*a*) Input object. (*b*) Spatially filtered linearly transformed signal. (*c*) Spatially filtered logarithmically transformed signal. (*d*) Inverse transformation of (*c*).

product of a continuous-tone picture and a Ronchi-type grating. The transparencies resulting from the linear and logarithmic transformations were illuminated by a collimated white light. The results of placing a simple absorptive filter in the spatial frequency plane at the location of the spectral harmonics for both the linear and logarithmic transformations are shown in Figure 3.27*b* and *c*, respectively. Using the same filter in both cases, the logarithmic filtering process is shown to be more successful than linear filtering in removing the multiplicative noise. The exponential transformation of the logarithmically filtered image is shown in Figure 3.27*d*. The image is changed to render a gray-scale distribution that more closely matches the original input image. For this case, the intensity transmittance of the final transparency was made proportional to the original exposure. The tonal differences between the high-intensity areas, decreased by the logarithmic transformation, are increased by the exponential transformation.

3.7 MELLIN-TRANSFORM PROCESSING

We note that correlation detection by complex spatial filterings is sensitive to any orientation and scale changes of the input target. The scale of the input from which the complex spatial filter is formed must be precisely matched, otherwise a large decrease of correlation peak will result. Although methods have been proposed to overcome this misscaling problem, most of them fall short of solving it. In this section we demonstrate a technique by which the misscaling problem can be alleviated by using the Mellin-transform technique.

The Mellin transformation has been successfully applied in time-varying circuits and in space-variant image restoration. The two-dimensional Mellin transform along the imaginary axis is given by

$$M(ip, iq) = \int\int_0^\infty f(\xi, \eta)\xi^{-(ip+1)}\eta^{-(iq+1)} \, d\xi \, d\eta, \tag{3.59}$$

where (p, q) is the transform-plane coordinate system.

The main reason to use the Mellin transform for optical correlation detection is the synthesis of the transformation. Since the information-processing operation relies on the Fourier-transformation properties of lenses, the synthesis must involve the same transformation operation. It can be shown that if we replace the variables $\xi = e^x$ and $\eta = e^y$, then the Fourier transform of $f(e^x, e^y)$ yields the Mellin transform of $f(\xi, \eta)$:

$$M(p, q) = \int\int_{-\infty}^{\infty} f(e^x, e^y)\exp[-i(px + qy)] \, dx \, dy, \tag{3.60}$$

where we let $M(ip, iq) = M(p, q)$ to simplify the notation, and (p, q) is the spatial frequency coordinate system. An inverse Mellin transform can also be written as

$$M^{-1}[M(p, q)] = f(\xi, \eta) = \frac{1}{2\pi}\int\int_{-\infty}^{\infty} M(p, q)\xi^{ip}\eta^{iq} \, dp \, dq, \tag{3.61}$$

where M^{-1} denotes the inverse Mellin transformation. It can be shown that the preceding equation is equivalent to the inverse Fourier transform by replacing the variables $\xi = \exp(x)$ and $\eta = \exp(y)$.

The basic advantage of applying the Mellin transform to optical processing is its scale-invariant property. In other words, the Mellin transforms of two different-scale, but otherwise identical, spatial functions are *scale invariant*, that is,

96 APPLICATIONS OF OPTICAL SIGNAL PROCESSING

$$M_2(p, q) = a^{i(p+q)} M_1(p, q), \qquad (3.62)$$

where a is an arbitrary factor, $M_1(p, q)$ and $M_2(p, q)$ are the Mellin transforms of $f_1(x, y)$ and $f_2(x, y)$, respectively, and $f_1(x, y)$ and $f_2(x, y)$ are the identical but different-scale functions. From the preceding equation we see that the magnitudes of the Mellin transforms are

$$|M_2(p, q)| = |M_1(p, q)|, \qquad (3.63)$$

which are of the same scaling. Thus we see that the Mellin transform of an object function is *scale invariant*, that is,

$$|M[f(\xi, \eta)]| = |M[f(a\xi, a\eta)]|. \qquad (3.64)$$

However, unlike the Fourier transform, the magnitude of the Mellin transforms is not *shift invariant*, that is,

$$|M[f(x, y)]| \neq |M[f(x - x_0, y - y_0)]|. \qquad (3.65)$$

In optical correlation detection, we assume that a complex spatial filter of $M[f(x, y)] = M(p, q)$ has been constructed, as given by

$$H(p, q) = K_1 + K_2 |M(p, q)|^2$$
$$+ 2K_1 K_2 |M(p, q)| \cos[\alpha_0 p - \phi(p, q)], \qquad (3.66)$$

where $M(p, q) = |M(p, q)| \exp[i\phi(p, q)]$. If the spatial filter is inserted in the spatial frequency plane of the coherent optical processor shown in Figure 3.28, the output light distribution can be shown to be

$$g(\alpha, \beta) = K_1 f(e^x, e^y) + K_2 f(e^x, e^y) * f(e^x, e^y) * f^*(e^{-x}, e^{-y})$$
$$+ K_1 K_2 f(e^x, e^y) * f(e^{x-\alpha_0}, e^y)$$
$$+ K_1 K_2 f(e^x, e^y) * f^*(e^{-x-\alpha_0}, e^{-y}), \qquad (3.67)$$

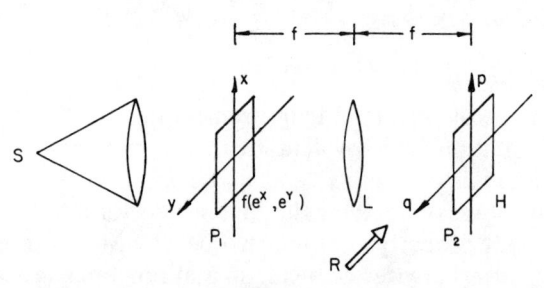

FIGURE 3.28 Optical generation of a Mellin-transform matched filter. *Note*: S is the monochromatic point source; R is the reference beam; H is the photographic plate.

where * denotes the convolution operation and the superscript * denotes the complex conjugate. The first and second terms represent the zero-order diffractions, which appear at the origin of the output plane; the third and fourth terms are the convolution and correlation terms, which appear in the neighborhood of $\alpha = \alpha_0$ and $\alpha = -\alpha_0$, respectively. Thus it is possible to use the Mellin-transform technique to optically correlate two object functions of different size. The importance of the Mellin transform as used in correlation detection might lie in its role in the implementation of a coherent optical pattern-recognition system. Methods for implementing Mellin transforms in real-time mode with an electronically addressed device have been reported by Casasent and Psaltis [3.10].

3.8 CIRCULAR HARMONIC EXPANSION PROCESSING

One of the most common problems in pattern recognition is identifying objects of different sizes, angular orientations, and perspectives. In this section, we use circular harmonic expansion to alleviate the object rotation problem in a matched filtering system.

If a function $f(r, \theta)$ is continuous and integrable over the region $(0, 2\pi)$, it can be expanded into a Fourier series as

$$f(r, \theta) = \sum_{m=-\infty}^{+\infty} F_m(r) e^{im\theta}, \tag{3.68}$$

where

$$F_m(r) = \frac{1}{2\pi} \int_0^{2\pi} f(r, \theta) e^{-im\theta} \, d\theta. \tag{3.69}$$

$F_m(r, \theta) = F_m(r) e^{im\theta}$ is called the mth-order *circular harmonic*.

If the object is rotated by an angle α, Eq. 3.68 can be written as

$$f(r, \theta + \alpha) = \sum_{m=-\infty}^{\infty} F_m(r) e^{im\alpha} e^{im\theta}. \tag{3.70}$$

Let us denote $f(x, y)$ and $f_\alpha(x, y)$ as object functions of $f(r, \theta)$ and $f(r, \theta + \alpha)$, respectively. By referring to the classic theory of matched filtering, when a rotated object $f_\alpha(r, \theta + \alpha)$ is applied to the input end of an optical correlator, the output light field is given by

$$g_\alpha(x, y) = \int_{-\infty}^{+\infty} \int_{-\infty}^{+\infty} f_\alpha(\xi, \eta) f^*(\xi - x, \eta - y) \, d\xi \, d\eta. \tag{3.71}$$

It is apparent that if $\alpha = 0$, the autocorrelation peak appears at $x = y = 0$.

98 APPLICATIONS OF OPTICAL SIGNAL PROCESSING

However, for an arbitrary value of α, g_α may not attain peak correlation at $x = y = 0$. By transforming the convolution integral in terms of polar coordinates, the center of correlation $C(\alpha)$ is defined as

$$C(\alpha) = \int_0^\infty r\, dr \int_0^{2\pi} f(r, \theta + \alpha) f^*(r, \theta)\, d\theta. \tag{3.72}$$

By substituting Eqs. 3.68 and 3.70 into Eq. 3.72, we have

$$C(\alpha) = \sum_{m=-\infty}^{+\infty} A_m e^{im\alpha}, \tag{3.73}$$

where

$$A_m = 2\pi \int_0^\infty |F_m(r)|^2 r\, dr. \tag{3.74}$$

Since, in orienting an object, the circular harmonic function is determined by different angles $m\alpha$ and not by a simple α, it is evident that object rotation poses severe problems for conventional matched filtering. Nevertheless, by using one of the circular harmonic functions as the reference function, such as,

$$f_{\text{ref}}(r, \theta) = F_m(r) e^{im\theta}, \tag{3.75}$$

the central correlation value between the target $f(r, \theta + \alpha)$ and the reference $f(r, \theta)$ can be expressed by

$$C(\alpha) = A_m e^{im\alpha}. \tag{3.76}$$

And the output center of irradiance is

$$|C(\alpha)|^2 = A_m^2, \tag{3.77}$$

which is independent of the object orientation.

We stress that the technique of circular harmonic expansion is based upon the use of one of the circular harmonic components of the object, for which the output correlation is invariant. We now show that the circular harmonic component can be easily implemented in a joint transform correlator.

We further note that, in practice, $f(r, \theta)$ is represented by a real quantity, for which Eq. 3.68 can be written as

$$f(r, \theta) = F_0(r) + 2 \sum_{m=1}^{+\infty} R_e[F_m(r) e^{im\theta}]$$

$$= F_0(r) + 2 \sum_{m=1}^{+\infty} |F_m(r)| \cos(m\theta + \phi_m), \tag{3.78}$$

where $F_m(r) = |F_m(r)|e^{i\phi_m}$. For real value implementation, we define two reference functions as follows:

$$R_{k1}(r, \theta) = 2|F_k(r)|\cos(k\theta + \phi_k), \quad (3.79)$$

$$R_{k2}(r, \theta) = 2|F_k(r)|\sin(k\theta + \phi_k). \quad (3.80)$$

These functions are the real and imaginary parts of the circular harmonic $F_k(r, \theta)$. Using R_{k1} as the reference function and $f(r, \theta + \alpha)$ as the input object function, the central value of the cross-correlation becomes

$$C_{k1} = \int_0^{2\pi} \int_0^\infty f(r, \theta + \alpha) R_{k1} r \, dr \, d\theta. \quad (3.81)$$

By substituting Eqs. 3.78 and 3.79 into Eq. 3.81, we have

$$C_{k1} = \int_0^{2\pi} \int_0^\infty \left\{ F_0(r) + 2 \sum_{m=1}^\infty |F_m(r)| \times \cos[m(\theta + \alpha) + \phi_m] \right\}$$
$$\times \{2|F_k(r)|\cos(k\theta + \phi_k)\} r \, dr \, d\theta. \quad (3.82)$$

Since all terms vanish except $m = k$, the equation is reduced to

$$C_{k1}(\alpha) = 4\pi \cos(k\alpha) \int_0^\infty r|F_k(r)|^2 \, dr$$
$$= 2C_k(0)\cos(k\alpha), \quad (3.83)$$

and its intensity is

$$I_{k1}(\alpha) = 4C_k^2(0)\cos^2(k\alpha), \quad (3.84)$$

which varies with cosine square with respect to the object orientations. Likewise, if $R_{k2}(r, \theta)$ is used as the reference function, the intensity of the correlation center is

$$I_{k2}(\alpha) = 4C_k^2(0)\sin^2(k\alpha). \quad (3.85)$$

Thus, by adding the correlation intensities given in Eqs. 3.84 and 3.85, we have

$$I_k = I_{k1}(\alpha) + I_{k2}(\alpha) = 4C_k^2(0), \quad (3.86)$$

100 APPLICATIONS OF OPTICAL SIGNAL PROCESSING

which is independent of the angular orientation. Thus, the rotation invariant is preserved. Equations 3.84 and 3.85 can be used to determine the value of α:

$$\alpha = \frac{1}{k} \tan^{-1} \sqrt{\frac{I_{k2}}{I_{k1}}}. \tag{3.87}$$

Since I_{k1} and I_{k2} are positive definite, the value of α is confined to region $[0, \pi/(2k)]$. Thus for each computed α, there are $4k$ possible orientations of the object. Notice that, to ensure a nonnegative value, bias terms can be added to R_{k1} and R_{k2}.

As an experimental demonstration, we give object function "5" in the lower half of Figure 3.29, and the real and the imaginary parts of the second-order circular harmonic expansion in the upper half. If the input transparency of Figure 3.29 is inserted at the input plane of a joint transform correlator, two sets of correlation peaks of the real and imaginary parts of the circular harmonic expansion are as shown in Figure 3.30. A plot of calculated angle of rotation α versus the input object orientation is shown in Figure 3.31, in which we see that accuracy is within $\pm 5°$. Thus, the peak intensity is independent of the object rotation.

3.9 HOUGH TRANSFORM

A technique for recognizing a pattern using a line-to-point transformation was first given by Hough [3.13], and was originally used for the interpretation of particle-track events taken from a bubble chamber [3.14]. The Hough

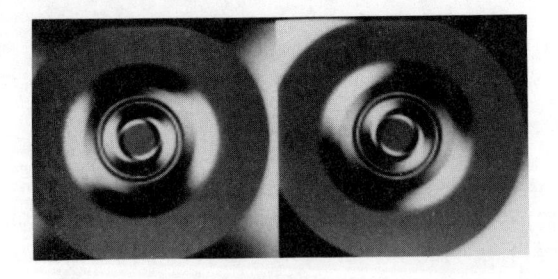

FIGURE 3.29 Real and imaginary circular harmonic functions are shown in the upper half of the figure, and the input object is shown in the lower half.

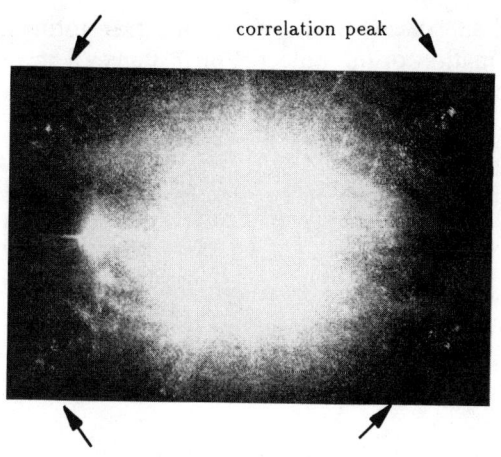

FIGURE 3.30 Output correlation peaks obtained from a joint transform correlator.

transformation can also be used in a variety of other applications, such as detection of curves from a photographic image, tracking moving targets, and optical pattern recognition. In fact, the Hough transform is a special case of the Radon transform, which has been used in digital signal processing for a number of years. Although the definition of the Hough transform can be derived from the Radon transform, the basic distinction between them is that the Radon transform deals with the projection of an object into various

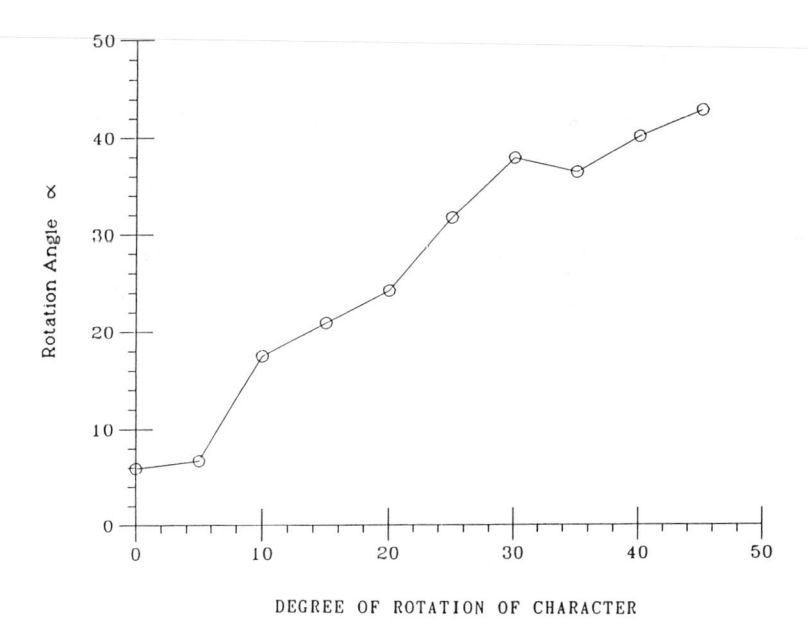

FIGURE 3.31 Plot of the calculated rotation angle versus input object orientation.

102 APPLICATIONS OF OPTICAL SIGNAL PROCESSING

multidimensional subspaces, while the Hough transform deals with the coordinate transformation of the object. For instance, a straight-line equation in a Cartesian coordinate system can be Hough transformed as given by

$$H(\vartheta, r) = \int\int_{-\infty}^{\infty} f(x, y)\delta(r - x\cos\vartheta - y\sin\vartheta)\,dx\,dy$$

$$= \begin{cases} 1, & \text{for } (\vartheta_1, r_1) \\ 0, & \text{otherwise,} \end{cases} \qquad (3.88)$$

where

$$f(x, y) = \begin{cases} 1, & (x, y) \in r_1 = x\cos\vartheta_1 + y\sin\vartheta_1, \\ 0, & \text{otherwise,} \end{cases}$$

as shown in Figure 3.32. Thus we see that a straight line has been transformed into a point (ϑ_1, r_1) in the parameter space (ϑ, r). On the other hand, an arbitrary point $\delta(x - x_0, y - y_1)$ in the (x, y) coordinate space can be Hough transformed as given by

$$H(\vartheta, r) = \int\int_{-\infty}^{\infty} \delta(x - x_0, y - y_0)\delta(r - x\cos\vartheta - y\sin\vartheta)\,dx\,dy$$

$$= \delta(r - x_0\cos\vartheta - y_0\sin\vartheta), \qquad (3.89)$$

which describes a pseudosinusoidal function in the (ϑ, r) plane, as shown in Figure 3.33. Since a point in the (x, y) plane can be represented by the intersection of many straight lines, it can be mapped into a pseudosinusoidal curve in the (ϑ, r) coordinate plane.

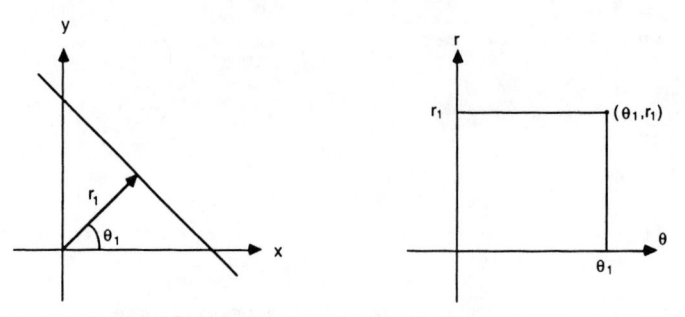

FIGURE 3.32 A straight line in the (x, y) plane is Hough transformed into a point in the (ϑ, r) parameter plane.

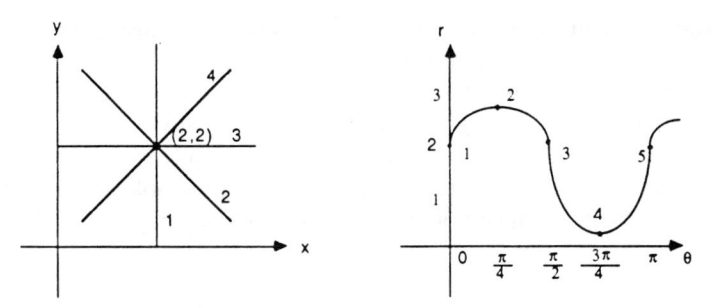

FIGURE 3.33 A point in the (x, y) plane is Hough transformed into a pseudo-sinusoidal curve in the (ϑ, r) plane.

In view of Eq. 3.88, we note that the kernel does not represent the convolution operation, for which the Hough transform is space variant. In order to obtain a convolution-type kernel, we must rotate the coordinate system. Thus to perform the Hough transformation in a coherent optical processor, the input object must be rotated. Therefore, by filtering one angular frequency using a narrow-slit bandpass filter in the Fourier plane, the output irradiance can be picked up by a translating photodetector through a narrow vertical slit. In this manner, the angular dimension can be mapped onto one of the dimensional coordinates. However, performing a two-dimensional integration requires two-dimensional scanning, which can be overcome by using a Dove prism, as suggested by Gindi and Gmitro [3.15], and as shown in Figure 3.34. The optical system images an input object and performs a one-dimensional Fourier transform in the vertical and the horizontal directions, respectively. Thus, by picking up the zero-order Fourier spectrum with a linear (horizontal) charge-coupled device (CCD), a line of Hough transform can be obtained for a given value of ϑ. It is apparent that by rotating the Dove prism, ϑ can be scanned angularly, so that the Hough transformation can be picked up by the linear CCD at the scanning rate.

Although optical implementation for straight-line mappings with Hough transforms works well to some extent, the space variant of the Hough transform may create serious problems for generalized transformation. Moreover,

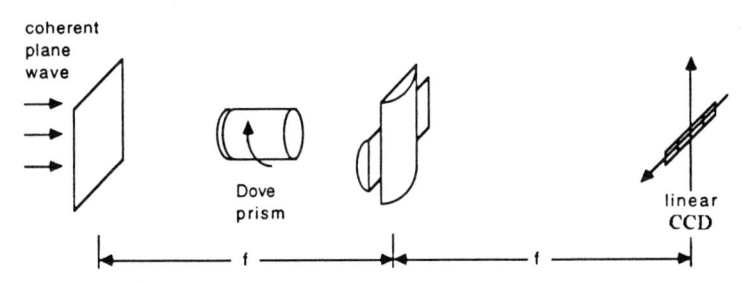

FIGURE 3.34 A coherent optical processor to perform Hough transformation.

the usefulness of the Hough transform depends on the accuracy of mapping the input object into the parameter space, and the performance of the optical system depends on the input signal-to-noise ratio, the clutter, and the multiobject problems. Most Hough transforms have been done in the digital image processing sector, where such applications are generally concentrated on line detection. Nevertheless, with the progress of real-time holographic elements, the Hough transform may find some practical applications in the area of optical signal processing.

REFERENCES

3.1 F. T. S. Yu, *Optical Information Processing*, Wiley-Interscience, New York, 1983.
3.2 L. J. Cutrona, E. N. Leith, L. J. Porcello, and W. E. Vivian, "On the Application of Coherent Optical Processing Techniques to Synthetic-Aperture Radar," *Proc. IEEE* 54 (1966): 1026.
3.3 M. J. Prickett and C. C. Chen, "Principles of Inverse Synthetic Aperture Radar (ISAR) Imaging," in *EASCON '80 Record* (IEEE Electronics and Aerospace Systems Conventions, Sept. 29, 30 and Oct. 1, 1980), IEEE Publication 80CH 1578-4, pp. 340-345.
3.4 W. W. Brown and R. J. Fedricks, "Range-Doppler Imaging with Motion Through Resolution Cells," *IEEE Trans. Aerosp. Electron. Syst.* AES-5 (1969): 98.
3.5 O. Bryngdahl, "Geometrical Transformation in Optics," *J. Opt. Soc. Am.* 64 (1974): 1092.
3.6 S. H. Lee, S. K. Yao, and A. G. Miles, "Optical Image Synthesis (Complex Amplitude Addition and Subtraction) in Real Time by Diffraction-Grating Interferometric Method," *J. Opt. Soc. Am.* 60 (1970): 1037.
3.7 C. E. Thomas, "Optical Spectrum Analysis of Large Space-Bandwidth Signal," *Appl. Opt.* 5 (1966): 1782.
3.8 A. Tai, T. Cheng, and F. T. S. Yu, "Optical Logarithmic Filtering Using Inherent Film Nonlinearity," *Appl. Opt.* 16 (1977): 2559.
3.9 M. S. Dymek, A. Tai, T. H. Chao, and F. T. S. Yu, "Exponential Transformation Using Film Nonlinearity for Optical Homomophic Filtering," *Appl. Opt.* 19 (1980): 829.
3.10 D. Casasent and D. Psaltis, "Scale Invariant Optical Transform," *Opt. Eng.* 15 (1976): 258.
3.11 Y.-N. Hsu and H. H. Arsenault, "Optical Pattern Recognition Using Circular Harmonic Expansion," *Appl. Opt.* 21 (1982): 4016.
3.12 F. T. S. Yu, X. Li, E. Tam, S. Jutamulia, and D. A. Gregory, "Rotation Invariant Pattern Recognition with a Programmable Joint Transform Correlator," *Appl. Opt.* 28 (1989): 4725.
3.13 P. V. C. Hough, "Methods and Means for Recognizing Complex Patterns," U.S. Patent 3 069 654, 1962.
3.14 T. Szoplik, "Line Detection and Directional Analysis of Images," in *Optical*

Processing and Computing, H. H. Arsenault, T. Szoplik, and B. Macukow, Eds., Academic Press, New York, 1989.
3.15 G. R. Gindi and A. F. Gmitro, "Optical Feature Extraction via the Radon Transform," *Opt. Eng.* 23 (1984): 499.

PROBLEMS

3.1 Referring to the synthetic-aperture radar systems of Section 3.1:
  (a) Derive expressions for the cross-track (ground-range) and azimuthal (along-track) resolutions.
  (b) Compare part (a) with the conventional radar system.

3.2 Assuming that the slant range $r_1 = 30{,}000$ m, the radar wavelength $\lambda = 2$ cm, the size of the along-track antenna $D = 2$ m, and the pulse width $\tau = 10^4$ ns:
  (a) Calculate the cross-track and the azimuthal resolutions of the synthetic-aperture radar system.
  (b) Sketch the cross-track resolution as a function of slant range. We assume that the aircraft maintains a constant altitude of 25,000 m.

3.3 Consider a range-Doppler radar system, which is not a synthetic-aperture radar, that radiates a single pulse of duration, $\tau = 10^{-7}$ sec., that permits a radial-velocity resolution Δv of up to 0.1 m/sec.
  (a) Use the ambiguity concept to design a wavelength of the pulse to achieve this resolution.
  (b) What is the range resolution of such a pulse?

3.4 Consider the synthetic-aperture radar system of Section 3.1. If the aircraft collects data from a point object over a travel distance L, then:
  (a) Determine the azimuthal angular resolution.
  (b) If all the available data are used, show that the along-track resolution in a synthetic-aperture radar system is equal to half the length of the actual antenna carried by the aircraft. (*Note*: an antenna of size l has a radiated beamwidth $\theta = \lambda/l$).

3.5 Referring to the preceding problem, if a radar pulse function is

$$s(t) = \text{rect}\left(\frac{t}{T}\right) e^{i\omega t},$$

where ω is in radians per second:
  (a) Calculate the corresponding ambiguity function.
  (b) Sketch the result of part (a).

106 APPLICATIONS OF OPTICAL SIGNAL PROCESSING

3.6 If we consider the side-looking radar system of Figure 3.2, the slant range is about 30,000 m from a point target on the ground terrain. Assuming that the wavelength of the radar is 3 cm, the wavelength of the illumination light source is 600 nm, and velocity of the aircraft to the film velocity ratio is 10^9:
   (a) Determine the focal length of the recorded Fresnel zone lens.
   (b) If the f-number of the signal impinging on the aircraft flight path is r_1/A, where A is the beam width at range r_1, what is the f-number of the zone lens that results from recording this signal?

3.7 Consider that a synthetic-aperture radar system, as depicted in Figure 3.2, is looking at a moving vehicle. We assume that the vehicle is traveling in the same direction as the aircraft, but with a velocity of v'. If the wavelength of the radar is λ:
   (a) Derive an expression for the recorded signal on the film.
   (b) What is the focal length of the recorded format?

3.8 Referring to the preceding problem, we assume that the wavelength of the radar is 3 cm, the velocity of the vehicle is 100 km/hr, the velocity of the aircraft is 500 km/hr, the velocity of the film transport is 0.15 mm/sec, and the slant range is about 20,000 m. Calculate:
   (a) The antenna beam width requirement.
   (b) The resolution requirement of the CRT scanner.
   (c) The focal length of the recorded format.
   (d) If we assume that the aircraft travels a distance of 2 km, what would be the azimuthal angular resolution with respect to the vehicle?
   (e) Calculate the f-number of the recorded Fresnel zone lens with respect to the moving vehicle.

3.9 Repeat Problem 3.7, assuming that the vehicle is traveling in the opposite direction with respect to the aircraft.

3.10 In formatting the returned-order signal in the (θ, r) plane for the ISAR imaging, we mistakenly estimate that the angular speed r is $2r_0$, where r_0 is the actual angular speed of the target. Assuming that r is small and that t is also small, we make the approximations $\sin \theta \approx \theta$ and $\cos \theta \approx 1$. How does the reconstructed image change its size in the x and y directions as compared with the correct image?

3.11 In the optical processing system for the reconstruction of the ISAR image in Figure 3.10, a spherical lens together with a cylindrical lens are required to form an assemblage that Fourier transforms $g(\theta, r)$ in the r direction while it images $g(\theta, r)$ in the θ direction to generate $G_0(\theta, \omega)$. Show how to form this assemblage.

3.12 An assumption saying $du\, dv = dx\, dy$ is made to derive Eq. 3.21 from

Eq. 3.20. Prove that the assumption is correct. (*Hint*: Use the Jacobian definition as follows:

$$x = g_1(u, v)$$

$$y = g_2(u, v)$$

$$J = \frac{\partial(x, y)}{\partial(u, v)} = \begin{vmatrix} \dfrac{\partial x}{\partial u} & \dfrac{\partial x}{\partial v} \\ \dfrac{\partial y}{\partial u} & \dfrac{\partial v}{\partial v} \end{vmatrix};$$

$$dx\, dy = J\, du\, dv.$$

3.13 The image of stationary irradiance from a distant object is projected on the recording medium of a camera. The object moves at a variable speed during the time that the shutter is open, such that the image is severely smeared. If the amplitude transmittance of the recorded film is given by

$$T(x, y) = A(x, y) * \left[e^{-x^2/2} \mathrm{rect}\left(\frac{x}{4}\right) \right],$$

where $A(x, y)$ is the unsmeared image of the object, design a coherent optical processor and an appropriate inverse spatial filter to sharpen the image.

3.14 If the object of Problem 3.13 is moving at a constant acceleration, the transmission function of the recorded film may be written

$$T(x, y) = A(x, y) * \left[\left(-\frac{x}{2a}\right) \mathrm{rect}\left(\frac{x - a/2}{a}\right) \right],$$

where a is an arbitrary constant. Synthesize a complex inverse filter to sharpen this image.

3.15 Consider the transmission function of a linear smeared image as given by

$$T(x, y) = A(x, y) * \mathrm{rect}\left(\frac{x}{\Delta x}\right),$$

where $A(x, y)$ is the smeared image, and Δx is the corresponding smear distance. For some reason, the minimum transmittance T_m of the filter is not allowed to go below 25 percent.

108 APPLICATIONS OF OPTICAL SIGNAL PROCESSING

- (a) Design an optimum complex spatial filter.
- (b) Compute the relative degree of image restoration.

3.16 In image sharpening, we want to synthesize an inverse filter with the combination of an amplitude and holographic filters.
- (a) Sketch an optical arrangement wherein the holographic and the amplitude filters are separately synthesized.
- (b) By controlling the film gamma, show that the amplitude filter can be obtained.
- (c) By combining the amplitude and the holographic filters, show that such an inverted filter can be synthesized.
- (d) If the reversed filter of part (c) is inserted in the spatial-frequency domain of the coherent optical processor, compute the output deblurred image irradiance.

3.17 Refer to the joint transform processor of Section 2.4. If the amplitude transmittance of a smeared transparency is given by

$$T(x, y) = A(x, y) * e^{-x^2/2}:$$

- (a) Design an impulse response of the deblurring filter.
- (b) Computer the corresponding output light field of the sharpened image.

3.18 Using the joint transform architecture in Section 2.4:
- (a) Design a phase-reversal function to sharpen a linear smeared image.
- (b) Calculate the output complex light distribution.
- (c) Show that a reasonable degree of restoration may be achieved using the phase-reversal technique.

3.19 Consider the complex image subtraction of Figure 3.18. If we let one of the input transparencies be an open aperture, say $f_2(x, y) = 1$, determine the output irradiance distribution around the optical axis.

3.20 Referring to the preceding problem, if $f_1(x, y) = \exp[i\phi(x, y)]$ is a pure phase object, show that the phase variation of $f_1(x, y)$ can be observed at the output plane of the optical processor.

3.21 Consider a multisource coherent optical processor for image subtraction, as shown in Figure 3.35. We assume that the two input object transparencies are separated by a distance of $2h_0$.
- (a) Determine the grating spatial frequency and the spacing of these coherent point sources.
- (b) Evaluate the intensity distribution of the subtracted image at the output plane.

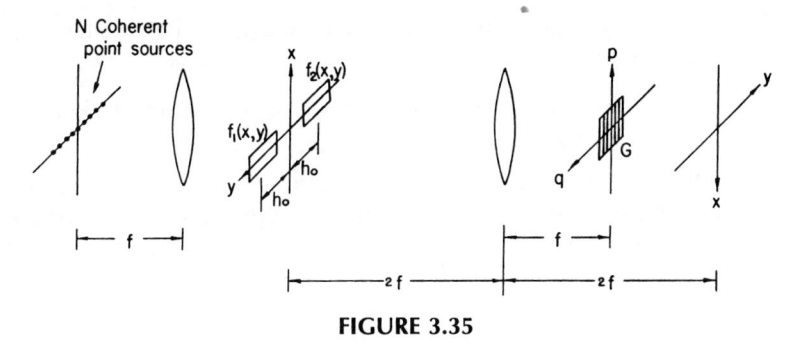

FIGURE 3.35

3.22 Referring to the optical architecture of Figure 3.18:
  (a) Show that the image subtraction is a one-dimensional processing operation, in which cylindrical transform lenses can be employed.
  (b) Draw a one-dimensional optical image subtractor.
  (c) What is the source size requirement?

3.23 Consider the one-dimensional coherent image processor shown in Figure 3.36.
  (a) Calculate the complex light field at the back focal length of the first transform length.
  (b) Design a grating filter in the Fourier domain by which image subtraction can be performed at the output plane.
  (c) Calculate the output light distribution and show that subtraction can be observed around the optical axis.
  (d) What happens to the quadratic phases introduced by the optical system?
  (e) Since image subtraction requires a point-pair coherence relationship between the input images, design a linear array of mono-

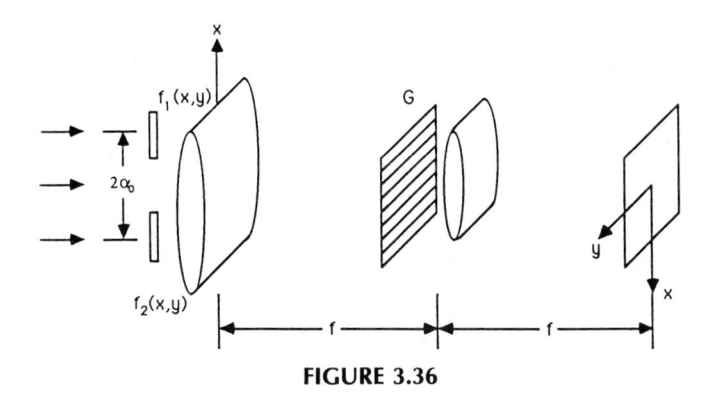

FIGURE 3.36

chromatic line sources to achieve the point-pair coherence requirement.

3.24 Refer to the one-dimensional joint transform processor of Figure 3.37.
  (a) Evaluate the irradiance at the Fourier plane.
  (b) We assume that the joint transform power spectrum is recorded on a photographic transparency H. If the recorded transparency is inserted back at the input plane of the joint transform processor, compute the output light distribution.

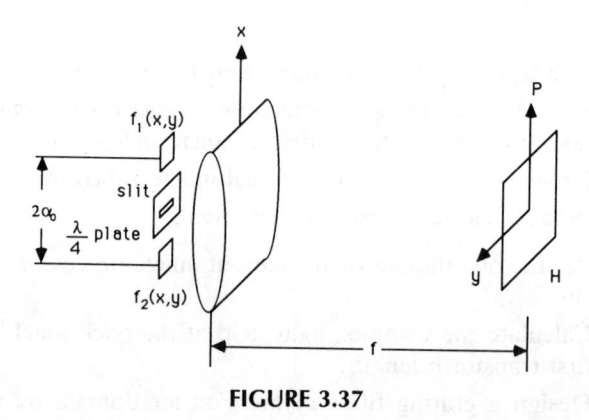

FIGURE 3.37

3.25 Referring to the wide-band optical spectrum analyzer described in Section 3.5.
  (a) Determine the frequency resolution of the analyzer.
  (b) For a large number of scan lines, compute the number of resolution elements at the output plane.
  (c) Compute the space–bandwidth product of the optical system.
  (d) Compare part (c) with respect to the wide-band analyzer of Section 3.5.

3.26 The spatial resolution of a CRT scanner is 2 lines/mm and the scanner area is 10×13 cm. If the CRT is used for wide-band intensity modulation:
  (a) Compute the space–bandwidth product of the CRT.
  (b) If the time duration of the processing signal is 2 sec and we assume that the separation between the scanned lines is equal to the resolution of the CRT, determine the highest temporal frequency limit of the CRT.

3.27 It is known that wide-band signal processing can be obtained by using bilateral area-modulation scanning. We assume that the two-dimensional recorded format is given by

$$f(x, y) = \sum_{n=1}^{N} \text{rect}\left(\frac{x}{L}\right) \text{rect} \frac{y - nD}{2[B + f_n(x)]},$$

where $N = H/D$ is the number of scan lines, $f_n(x) = f[x + (nL/2)]$ is the nth line transmittance function, B is the bias level, D is the separation between the scan lines, H and L are the dimensions of the input format shown in Figure 3.38. Evaluate the output frequency locus within the region $(P \geq 0, -(\pi/D) \leq q \leq \pi/D)$.

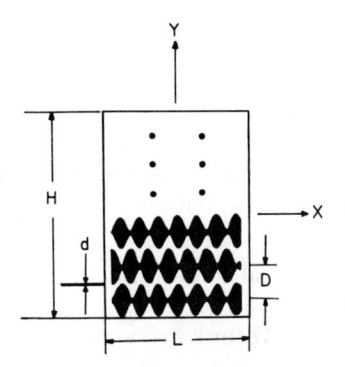

FIGURE 3.38

3.28 Repeat the preceding problem for unilateral area modulation.

3.29 Consider a wide-band unilateral area-modulation spectrum analyzer, in which the separation between the modulated channel is equal to the resolution (i.e., spot size) of the CRT scanner.
  (a) Evaluate the space–bandwidth product of the optical processing system.
  (b) Compare the result obtained from part (a) with the wide-band density modulation case.

3.30 Repeat the preceding problem for bilateral area modulation.

3.31 Refer to the wide-band spectrum analysis and area modulation of Problem 3.27. Assume that the input is a periodic triangular signal as shown in Figure 3.39.
  (a) Determine the minimum bias level required for the wide-band area modulation.
  (b) Sketch the corresponding wide-band area-modulated format.
  (c) If the recorded format of part (b) is inserted in a coherent spectrum analyzer, evaluate the spectral distribution within a narrow slit along the q axis of the spatial-frequency plane, that is,

$$H(p, q) = \begin{cases} 1, & -\dfrac{\pi}{D} \leq q \leq \dfrac{\pi}{D}, \\ 0, & \text{otherwise,} \end{cases}$$

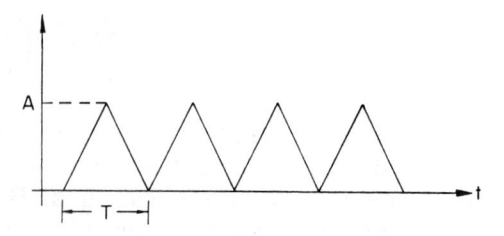

FIGURE 3.39

where D is the separation between the channels, as shown in Figure 3.38.

(d) Compare part (c) with the direct Fourier transformation of the triangle signal of Figure 3.39.

3.32 Assume an intensity-modulated optical spectrum analyzer, as shown in Figure 3.40. The input signal represents a continuous density-modulated speech signal, from 25 to 4000 Hz.

(a) Determine the width Δx of the optical window required for narrow- and wide-band spectrum analysis. (*Note*: A 300-Hz bandwidth is used for wide-band and 25 Hz for narrow-band analysis.)

(b) Show that the time and frequency resolutions cannot be resolved simultaneously.

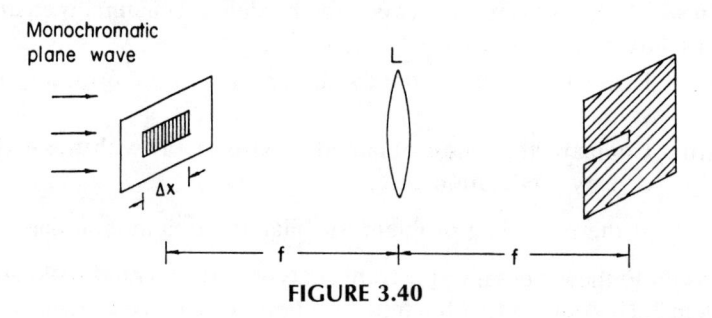

FIGURE 3.40

3.33 Figure 3.41 shows the intensity transmittance distribution of a halftone screen. The screen is used for contact printing on a high-contrast film with a collimated white light. We assume that the film's thresholding exposure is set at $T_{in} = 0.6$.

(a) Determine the transmittance distribution of the recorded film.

(b) If the recorded transparency is inserted at the input plane of the coherent optical processor, evaluate the irradiance distribution at the spatial-frequency plane.

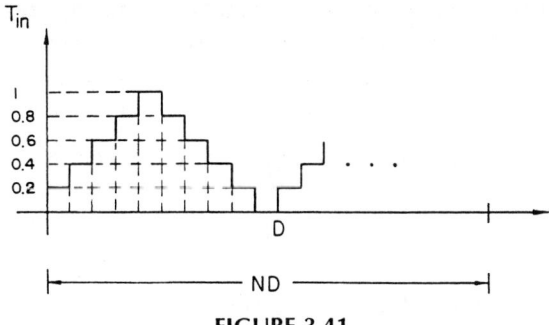

FIGURE 3.41

3.34 (a) Describe a method of applying a halftone screen processing technique to achieve a logarithmic transformation.

(b) Is it possible to utilize a halftone screen processing technique to obtain an exponential transformation? State the major difficulties.

3.35 With reference to the nonlinear processing system of Figure 3.23, show that a higher correlation peak may be obtained through the homomorphic filtering system.

3.36 When compared to the halftone processing technique, what are the major advantages and disadvantages of obtaining a logarithmic transformation utilizing the film nonlinearity?

3.37 The intensity transmittance of a photographic process is given by

$$T_{in} = KE^{-\gamma_n},$$

where E is the exposure and γ_n is the gamma of the photographic film. In contact printing, the intensity transmittance of the second film is

$$T_{ip} = K_1 E^{\gamma_{n1}\gamma_{n2}},$$

where K's are the proportionality constants, and γ_{n1} and γ_{n2} are the gammas of the first and second films. Let us assume that the amplitude transmittance of a noisy target is given by $n(x, y)f(x, y)$.

(a) In a block diagram, show a homomorphic matched filtering system for multiplicative noisy target detection.

(b) By using the contact-printing process, show that it is possible to transform the multiplicative noisy image into the additive type.

(c) Evaluate the matched filter synthesis for part (b).

3.38 (a) Identify the Fourier and Mellin transformations, which are either shift or scale invariant?

114 APPLICATIONS OF OPTICAL SIGNAL PROCESSING

    (b) Illustrate an optical arrangement so that the resultant Fourier transformation is both shift and scale invariant.

    (c) Evaluate the optical setup of part (b), and show that the resultant Fourier spectrum is indeed scale and shift invariant.

3.39 Consider a rectangular impulse function as given by

$$f(x) = \text{rect}\left(\frac{x}{a}\right).$$

    (a) Evaluate the Mellin transform of $f(x)$.
    (b) Sketch the result of part (a).
    (c) Show that the Mellin transform of $f(x)$ is scale invariant.

3.40 Consider a two-dimensional rectangular impulse function as given by

$$f(x, y) = \text{rect}\left(\frac{x}{a}\right)\text{rect}\left(\frac{x}{b}\right).$$

    (a) Evaluate the Mellin transform of $f(x, y)$.
    (b) Sketch the result of part (a).
    (c) Prove that the Mellin transform is indeed scale invariant.
    (d) By preprocessing $f(x, y)$, draw a coherent optical system that is capable of performing the Mellin transform.

3.41 Given a circular impulse function as given by

$$f(r) = \text{cir}\left(\frac{r}{a}\right),$$

show that the Mellin transform of $f(r)$ is scale invariant.

3.42 Given a circularly symmetric function such as

$$f(r) = \begin{cases} 1, & r \leq R_0 \\ 0, & \text{otherwise,} \end{cases}$$

where $r = \sqrt{x^2 + y^2}$:

    (a) Perform the circular harmonic expansion at the origin of the (x, y) coordinate system.
    (b) Assuming that the center of the circular disk of part (a) is located at $x = 0$, $y = R_0$, perform the circular harmonic expansion of this disk at $x = 0$, $y = 0$.

3.43 Perform the circular harmonic expansion of a circular sector around the vertex as shown in Figure 3.42.

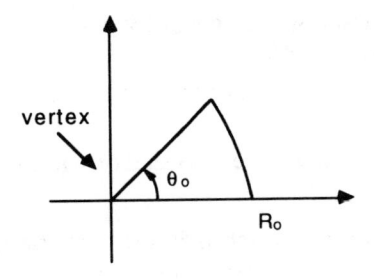

FIGURE 3.42

3.44 Given the spoke-like function shown in Figure 3.43, that is

$$f(r, \vartheta) = \text{rect}\left[\frac{\vartheta}{\vartheta_0} + \frac{1}{2}\right] * \sum_{n=1}^{N} \delta(\vartheta - n\vartheta_s),$$

where $\vartheta_0 \leq \vartheta_s$ and $\vartheta_s = 2\pi/N$, evaluate the circular harmonic expansion of $f(r, \vartheta)$ around the origin. *Hint:* Assume that $\vartheta_0 \simeq \vartheta_s$ and ϑ_0 and ϑ_s are very small, so that N can be assumed to approach infinity.

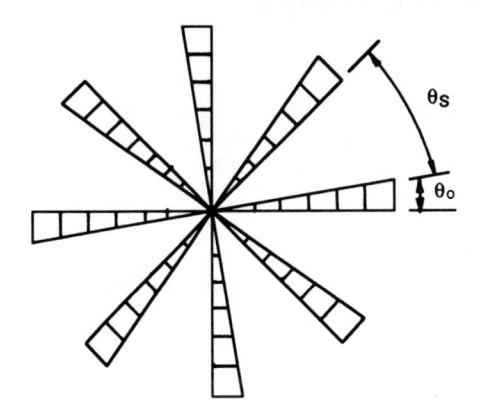

FIGURE 3.43

3.45 (a) Discuss the synthesis of an optical circular harmonic filter (CHF).
(b) Illustrate the optical implementation in a joint transform correlator and in a Vander–Lugt correlator, respectively.

3.46 The transform from a two-dimensional function to its projections (the Radon transform), usually defined as

$$R(\vartheta, r) = \int_{-\infty}^{\infty} f(\hat{p})\delta(r - \hat{p} \cdot \hat{n})\,d\hat{p}$$

where $\hat{p} = x\hat{i} + y\hat{j}$ and $\hat{n} = \cos\vartheta\hat{i} + \sin\vartheta\hat{j}$, shows that the Hough transform is, in fact, a special case of the Radon transform.

116 APPLICATIONS OF OPTICAL SIGNAL PROCESSING

3.47 An input object contains two narrow slits as given by $y = m_1 x + b_1$ and $y = m_2 x + b_2$, $m_1 \neq m_2$ and $b_1 \neq b_2$.
   (a) Design a conventional coherent optical processor to perform the Hough transform.
   (b) Derive the output irradiance that is to be recorded on a translating photographic film.

3.48 Given a binary object function $f(x, y)$, which is inserted at the input plane of Figure 3.34, show that the Hough transform of $f(x, y)$ can be registered on a linear CCD. If the object is a gray-level function instead of the binary type, show that the proposed optical system is not capable of performing the Hough transformation.

3.49 We assume that an input object represents a family of concentric circles, as given by

$$C(x_0, y_0; p_i) = \begin{cases} 1, & (x, y) \in (x - x_0)^2 + (y - y_0)^2 = r_i^2, \\ 0, & \text{otherwise}, \end{cases}$$

Derive the corresponding Hough transform.

CHAPTER FOUR

Partially Coherent Processing

Although coherent optical processors can perform a myriad of complicated signal processing functions, coherent processing systems are usually plagued by coherent artifact noise. This difficulty has prompted us to look at optical processing from a new standpoint: to consider whether it is necessary for all optical processing operations to be carried out by pure coherent sources. We have found that much optical processing can be carried out by partially coherent light or white-light light. The basic advantages of partially coherent processing are: (1) the suppression of coherent artifact noise; (2) that the partially coherent sources are usually inexpensive; (3) that the constraints on the processing environment are generally very relaxed; (4) that the partially coherent system is relatively easy and economical to operate; and (5) that the partially coherent processor is particularly suitable for color image processing.

4.1 OPTICAL PROCESSING UNDER A PARTIALLY COHERENT REGIME

Optical systems under the partially coherent regime have been studied since 1967. These studies have shown that there are difficulties in applying the linear system concept to the evaluation of the performance at high spatial frequencies. These difficulties are primarily due to the inapplicability of the linear system theory under a partial coherence regime. However, under the strictly coherent regime (i.e., spatially and temporally coherent), the optical system operates in a complex wave field. The output complex light field can be described by a complex amplitude convolution integral, like

$$g(\alpha, \beta) = \iint_{-\infty}^{\infty} f(x, y) h(\alpha - x, \beta - y) \, dx \, dy, \qquad (4.1)$$

which yields a spatially invariant property of the complex amplitude transformation, where $f(x, y)$ is a coherent complex wave field that impinges at the input end of an optical system, and $h(x, y)$ describes the spatial impulse response of the optical system. Equation 4.1 can be written in the following Fourier-transform form:

$$G(p, q) = F(p, q)H(p, q), \qquad (4.2)$$

where $G(p, q)$, $H(p, q)$, and $F(p, q)$ are the Fourier transforms of $g(x, y)$, $h(x, y)$, and $f(x, y)$, respectively. Thus Eq. 4.2 describes the optical system operation in the spatial frequency domain, where $H(p, q)$ can be referred to as the *coherent* or *complex amplitude transfer function* of the optical system.

On the other hand, if the optical system is under a strictly incoherent regime, the system processes intensity signals, such that the output irradiance is described by the following intensity convolution integral

$$I(\alpha, \beta) = \iint_{-\infty}^{\infty} f_i(x, y) h_i(\alpha - x, \beta - y) \, dx \, dy, \qquad (4.3)$$

which yields a spatially invariant form of the intensity operation, where $f_i(x, y) = |f(x, y)|^2$ is the input irradiance and $h_i(x, y) = |h(x, y)|^2$ is the intensity spatial impulse response of the optical system. Similarly, Eq. 4.3 can be written in Fourier-transform form, that is,

$$I(p, q) = F_i(p, q) H_i(p, q), \qquad (4.4)$$

where $I(p, q)$, $F_i(p, q)$, and $H_i(p, q)$ are the Fourier transforms of $I(x, y)$, $f_i(x, y)$, and $h_i(x, y)$, respectively, and $H_i(p, q)$ is the *incoherent* or *intensity transfer function* of the optical system.

We now define the following normalized quantities:

$$\hat{I}_i(p, q) = \frac{\iint_{-\infty}^{\infty} I(\alpha, \beta) \exp[-i(p\alpha + q\beta)] \, d\alpha \, d\beta}{\iint_{-\infty}^{\infty} I(\alpha, \beta) \, d\alpha \, d\beta}, \qquad (4.5)$$

$$\hat{F}_i(p, q) = \frac{\iint_{-\infty}^{\infty} f_i(x, y) \exp[-i(px + qy)] \, dx \, dy}{\iint_{-\infty}^{\infty} f_i(x, y) \, dx \, dy}, \qquad (4.6)$$

and

$$\hat{H}_i(p, q) = \frac{\iint_{-\infty}^{\infty} h_i(x, y) \exp[-i(px + qy)] \, dx \, dy}{\iint_{-\infty}^{\infty} h_i(x, y) \, dx \, dy}. \qquad (4.7)$$

These normalized quantities would give a set of convenient mathematical forms and also provide a concept of image contrast interpretation. Since the quality of a visual image depends to a large extent on the contrast (or the relative irradiance) of the image, a normalized intensity function would certainly enhance its information-bearing capacity. With the application of the Fourier convolution theorem to Eq. 4.3, the following relationship can be written:

$$\hat{I}_i(p, q) = \hat{F}_i(p, q)\hat{H}_i(p, q), \tag{4.8}$$

where $H_i(p, q)$ is commonly referred to as the *optical transfer function* (OTF) of the optical system, and the modulus of $|\hat{H}_i(p, q)|$ is known as the *modulation transfer function* (MTF) of the optical system.

We further note that Eq. 4.7 can also be written as

$$\hat{H}_i(p, q) = \frac{\iint_{-\infty}^{\infty} H(p', q')H^*(p' - p, q' - q)\, dp'\, dq'}{\iint_{-\infty}^{\infty} |H(p', q')|^2\, dp'\, dq'}. \tag{4.9}$$

By changing the variables $p'' = p' - (p/2)$, $q'' = q' - (q/2)$, Eq. 4.9 results in the following symmetrical form:

$$\hat{H}_i(p, q)$$
$$= \frac{\iint_{-\infty}^{\infty} H[p'' + (p/2), q'' + (q/2)]H^*[p'' - (p/2), q'' - (q/2)]\, dp''\, dq''}{\iint_{-\infty}^{\infty} |H(p'', q'')|^2\, dp''\, dq''}.$$
$$\tag{4.10}$$

We note that the definition of OTF is valid for any linearly spatial invariant optical system regardless of whether the system is with or without aberrations. Furthermore, Eq. 4.10 serves as the primary link between the strictly coherent and strictly incoherent systems. There are, however, threefold limitations associated with the strictly coherent processing. First, coherent processing requires the dynamic range of a spatial light modulator to be about 100,000:1 for the input wave intensity, or a photographic density range of 4.0. Such a dynamic range is often quite difficult to achieve in practice. Second, coherent processing systems are susceptible to coherent artifact noise, which frequently degrades the image quality. Third, in coherent processing, the signal being processed is carried out by a complex wave field. However, what is actually measured at the output plane of the optical processor is the output wave intensity. The loss of the output phase distribution may seriously limit the applicability of the optical system in some applications.

The drawbacks of coherent processing can be overcome by reducing either the temporal coherence or the spatial coherence, and there are several techniques available that use those approaches. In the following sections we briefly describe four frequently used concepts. The first method is based on a spatially partially coherent source, and the other three methods utilize a broad spectral band light source (e.g., a white-light source) to perform complex wave field operations.

4.2 COMPLEX AMPLITUDE PROCESSING USING INCOHERENT LIGHT

4.2.1 Spatially Partially Coherent Processing

Techniques of using spatially partially coherent light to perform complex data processing have been proposed. These techniques share a basic concept: The optical system is characterized by the use of a point spread function (PSF), which is not constrained to the class of nonnegative real functions used in conventional incoherent processing. The output intensity distribution can be adjusted by changing the PSF, that is,

$$I(x', y') = \iint O(x, y)h(x', y'; x, y) \, dx \, dy, \qquad (4.11)$$

where $h(x, y; x', y')$ is the PSF, and $I(x', y')$ and $O(x, y)$ are the image and object intensity distributions, respectively. If the pupil function of an optical system is $P(\alpha, \beta)$, the PSF is equal to the square of the Fourier spectrum of the pupil function. Therefore, the output intensity distribution can be adjusted by selecting an adequate pupil function. A typical processing system, as proposed by Rhodes, is shown in Figure 4.1. This optical processing system, which is characterized by an extended pupil region, has two input pupil functions, $P_1(\alpha, \beta)$ and $P_2(\alpha, \beta)$. With the optical path lengths of the two arms of the system being equal, the overall system pupil function is given by the sum of $P_1(\alpha, \beta)$ and $P_2(\alpha, \beta)$. If the path length in one arm is changed slightly, however, for example, by moving mirror M_2 a small distance, a phase factor

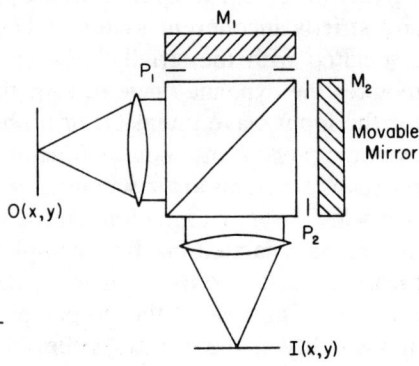

FIGURE 4.1 A two-pupil incoherent processing system.

COMPLEX AMPLITUDE PROCESSING USING INCOHERENT LIGHT   121

is introduced in one of the component pupil functions, with the result,

$$P(\alpha, \beta) = P_1(\alpha, \beta) + P_2(\alpha, \beta)\exp[i\phi(\alpha, \beta)]. \qquad (4.12)$$

It is evident that if the pupil transparencies $P_1(\alpha, \beta)$ and $P_2(\alpha, \beta)$ are recorded holographically, arbitrary PSFs can then be synthesized using the 0°–180° phase switching operation. Thus we see that this optical system is capable of performing complex data processing with spatially partially coherent light.

4.2.2 Achromatic Optical Processing

An achromatic optical signal processing technique with a broad-band source (e.g., white light) is shown as Figure 4.2. Lens L_0 colimates the white-light point source S, illuminating hologram R. The diffraction wavefront is spatially filtered by the aperture A, which removes the zero-order term and the lower sideband. The upper sideband is imaged onto the signal plane P; lens L_3 Fourier transforms the resulting wavefront; and observation in the transform plane is confined to the optical axis by a slit in the output plane O. The convolution of the demodulated input signal with the desired reference function is recorded by synchronously translating the signal and output films. Such a system, termed *an achromatic system*, thus has the flexibility of a coherent optical signal processor along with the potential for the noise immunity of an incoherent system.

4.2.3 Band-Limited Partially Coherent Processing

A matched-filter technique for operation with band-limited illumination is shown in Figure 4.3. The matched filter consists of a frequency-plane holographic filter, an achromatic-fringe interferometer, a color-compensating grating, and an achromatic doublet. The matched filter, a Fourier hologram, is made by recording the object spectrum and a collimated reference beam with an exposure wavelength λ_0. The reference-beam angle is at θ_0 with respect to the object beam axis. In the correlation operation the object is illuminated by using a broad spectral source. The various spectral components have dispersed angles due to the grating-like structure of the matched filter. A laterally dispersed correlation signal is generated in plane c, which is the conventional

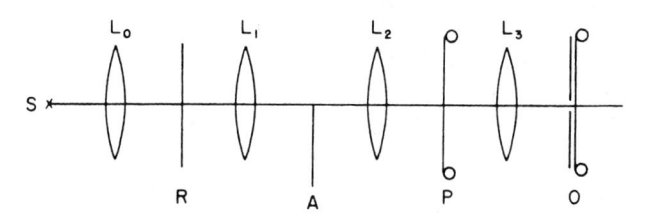

FIGURE 4.2 An achromatic optical processing system.

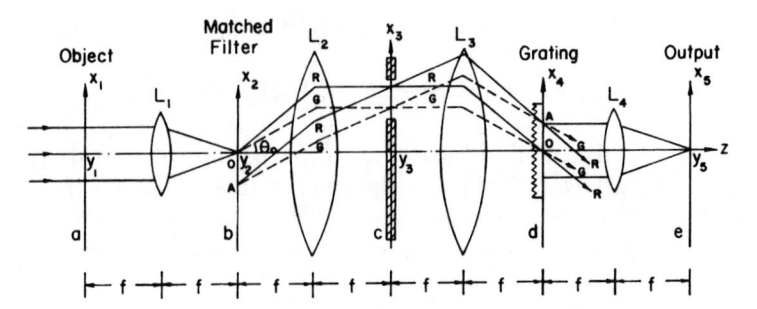

FIGURE 4.3 Band-limited partially coherent processing system.

correlation plane. These spectral components are recombined by imaging the matched filter into plane d, where a compensation grating produces a color dispersion that is equal but opposite to that introduced at plane b. The color-corrected correlation signal is observed in the output plane. However, the compensated signal is still wavelength-dependent, since the illumination wavelength changes the scale of the object spectrum at plane b. Insertion of a slit in plane c provides a convenient way to bandlimit the correlation signal to $\Delta\lambda$. Bandlimiting improves the signal-to-noise ratio (SNR) of the compensated correlation output. Broad-band illumination can be used for automatic scale search and object-size determination. Since spatially incoherent light, as well as coherent light, can be used to perform matched filtering, an extended white-light source is used together with a slit at plane c to provide a band-limited partially coherent processing.

4.2.4 Achromatic Partially Coherent Processing

An achromatic partially coherent optical processing technique with a white-light source was introduced by Yu in 1978. Figure 4.4 illustrates the processing system, where all the transform lenses are assumed achromatic. A high-diffraction-efficiency phase grating with an angular spatial frequency P_0 is used at the input plane P_1 to disperse the input object spectrum into rainbow-color spectra in the Fourier plane P_2. Thus the complex spatial filter creates

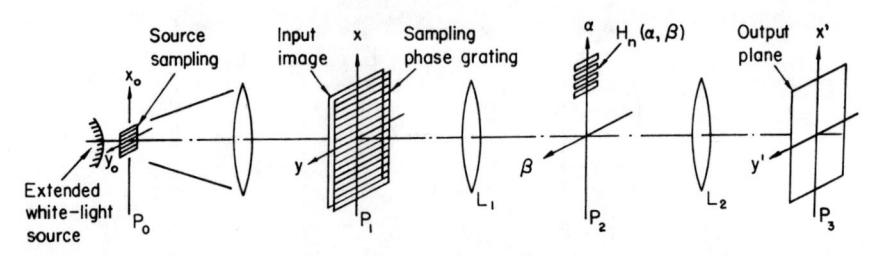

FIGURE 4.4 An achromatic partially coherent optical processing system.

a strip design for each narrow spectral band in the Fourier plane. The achromatic output image irradiance can therefore be observed at the output plane P_3. The advantage of this technique is that each channel (e.g., each spectral band filter) behaves as a partially coherent channel, while the overall output noise performance is primarily due to the incoherent addition of each channel, which behaves as if under incoherent illumination. Thus this partially coherent system is capable of coherent noise suppression.

4.3 WHITE-LIGHT OPTICAL PROCESSING

We now describe a partially coherent processor that uses a white-light source, as shown in Figure 4.4. The partially coherent processing system is similar to a coherent processing system, except that it uses an extended white-light source, a source encoding mask, a signal sampling grating, multispectral band filters, and achromatic transform lenses. For example, if we place an input object transparency $s(x, y)$ in contact with the sampling phase grating, the complex wave field at the Fourier plane P_2 would be (assuming a white-light point source), for every wavelength λ

$$E(p, q; \lambda) = \iint s(x, y)\exp(ip_0 x)\exp[-i(px + qy)]\, dx\, dy = S(p - p_0, q), \tag{4.13}$$

where the integral is over the spatial domain of the input plane P_1, (p, q) denotes the angular spatial frequency coordinate system, p_0 is the angular spatial frequency of the sampling phase grating, and $S(p, q)$ is the Fourier spectrum of $s(x, y)$. If we write Eq. 4.13 in the form of a spatial coordinate system (α, β), we have

$$E(\alpha, \beta; \lambda) = S\left(\alpha - \frac{\lambda f}{2\pi} p_0, \beta\right), \tag{4.14}$$

where $p = (2\pi/\lambda f)\alpha$, $q = (2\pi/\lambda f)\beta$, and f is the focal length of the achromatic transform lens. Thus we see that the Fourier spectra is dispersed into rainbow colors along the α axis, and each Fourier spectrum for a given wavelength λ is centered at $\alpha = (\lambda f/2\pi)p_0$.

In complex spatial filtering, we assume that a set of narrow spectral band complex spatial filters is available. In practice, all the input objects are spatial frequency limited. The spatial bandwidth of each spectral band filter $H(p_n, q_n)$ is therefore

$$H(p_n, q_n) = \begin{cases} H(p_n, q_n), & \alpha_1 < \alpha < \alpha_2, \\ 0, & \text{otherwise,} \end{cases} \tag{4.15}$$

124 PARTIALLY COHERENT PROCESSING

where $p_n = (2\pi/\lambda_n f)\alpha$, $q_n = (2\pi/\lambda_n f)\beta$, λ_n is the main wavelength of the filter, $\alpha_1 = (\lambda_n f/2\pi)(p_0 + \Delta p)$ and $\alpha_2 = (\lambda_n f/2\pi)(p_0 - \Delta p)$ are the upper and lower spatial limits of $H(p_n, q_n)$, and Δp is the spatial bandwidth of the input image $s(x, y)$.

Since the limiting wavelengths of each $H(p_n, q_n)$ are

$$\lambda' = \lambda_n \frac{p_0 + \Delta p}{p_0 - \Delta p} \quad \text{and} \quad \lambda'' = \lambda_n \frac{p_0 - \Delta p}{p_0 + \Delta p}, \tag{4.16}$$

its spectral bandwidth can be approximated by

$$\Delta\lambda_n = \lambda_n \frac{4p_0 \Delta p}{p^2 - (\Delta p)^2} \approx \frac{4\Delta p}{p_0} \lambda_n. \tag{4.17}$$

If we place this set of spectral band filters side by side and position them properly over the smeared Fourier spectra, the intensity distribution of the output light field can be shown as

$$I(x, y) \simeq \sum_{n=1}^{N} \Delta\lambda_n |s(x, y; \lambda_n) * h(x, y; \lambda_n)|^2, \tag{4.18}$$

where $h(x, y; \lambda_n)$ is the spatial impulse response of $H(p_n, q_n)$ and $*$ denotes the convolution operation. Thus the proposed partially coherent processor is capable of processing the signal in the complex wave field. Since the output intensity is the sum of the mutually incoherent narrow-band spectral irradiances, the annoying coherent artifact noise can be suppressed.

4.4 SOURCE ENCODING AND IMAGE SAMPLING

We now discuss a linear transform relationship between the spatial coherence (i.e., mutual intensity function) and the source encoding. Since the spatial coherence depends on the image-processing operation, a more relaxed coherence requirement may be used for specific image-processing operations. The object of source encoding is to alleviate the stringent coherence requirement so that an extended source can be used. In other words, source encoding is capable of generating an appropriate spatial coherence for specific optical signal processing, such that the available light power from the source can be efficiently utilized.

4.4.1 Source Encoding

We begin our discussion with Young's experiment with an extended source illumination, as shown in Figure 4.5. First, we assume that a narrow slit is

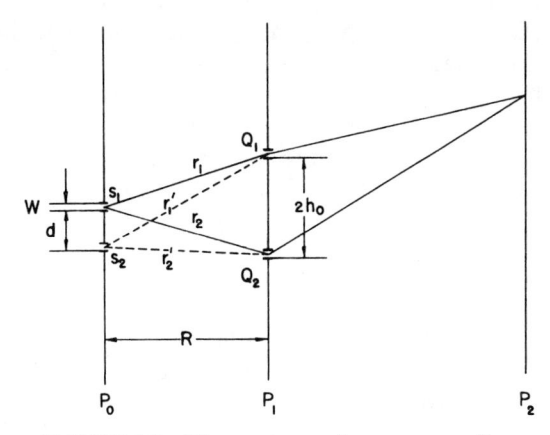

FIGURE 4.5 The concept of source encoding.

placed in the source plane P_0 behind an extended monochromatic source. To maintain a high degree of coherence between the slits Q_1 and Q_2 at plane P_2, the source size should be very narrow. If the separation between Q_1 and Q_2 is large, then a narrower slit size S_1 is required. Thus the slit width should be

$$w \leq \frac{\lambda R}{2h_0}, \tag{4.19}$$

where R is the distance between planes P_0 and P_1, and $2h_0$ is the separation between Q_1 and Q_2. Let us now consider the two narrow slits S_1 and S_2 located in source plane P_0. We assume that the separation between S_1 and S_2 satisfies the following path length relation:

$$r_1' - r_2' = (r_1 - r_2) + m\lambda, \tag{4.20}$$

where the r's are the respective distances from S_1 and S_2 to Q_1 and Q_2, m is an arbitrary integer, and λ is the wavelength of the extended source. Then the interference fringes due to each of the two source slits S_1 and S_2 should be in phase and a brighter fringe pattern can be seen at plane P_2. To further increase the intensity of the fringes, one would simply increase the number of slits in appropriate locations in plane P_0 such that the separation between slits satisfies the fringe condition of Eq. 4.20. If separation R is large, that is, if $R \gg d$ and $R \gg 2h_0$, then the spacing d becomes

$$d = m \frac{\lambda R}{2h_0}. \tag{4.21}$$

Thus by properly encoding an extended source, it is possible to maintain a high degree of coherence between Q_1 and Q_2, and at the same time to increase the intensity of the fringes.

To encode an extended source, we would first search for a coherence function for a specific image-processing operation. With reference to the partially coherent processor of Figure 4.4, the mutual intensity function at input plane P_1 can be written as

$$\Gamma(\mathbf{x}_1, \mathbf{x}_1') = \iint \gamma(\mathbf{x}_0) K(\mathbf{x}_0, \mathbf{x}_1) K^*(\mathbf{x}_1, \mathbf{x}_1') \, d\mathbf{x}_0, \qquad (4.22)$$

where the integration is over the source plane P_0, superscript * denotes the complex conjugation, $\gamma(\mathbf{x}_0)$ is the intensity distribution of the encoding mask, and $K(\mathbf{x}_0, \mathbf{x}_1)$ is the transmittance function between the source plane P_0 and the input plane P_1, which can be written

$$K(\mathbf{x}_0, \mathbf{x}_1) \approx \exp\left(i2\pi \frac{\mathbf{x}_0 \mathbf{x}_1}{\lambda f}\right). \qquad (4.23)$$

By substituting $K(\mathbf{x}_0, \mathbf{x}_1)$ into Eq. 4.22, we have

$$\Gamma(\mathbf{x}_1 - \mathbf{x}_1') = \iint \gamma(\mathbf{x}_0) \exp\left[i2\pi \frac{\mathbf{x}_0}{\lambda f}(\mathbf{x}_1 - \mathbf{x}_1')\right] d\mathbf{x}_0. \qquad (4.24)$$

From the preceding equation we see that the spatial coherence and source encoding intensity form a Fourier-transform pair, that is,

$$\gamma(\mathbf{x}_0) = \mathcal{F}[\Gamma(\mathbf{x}_1 - \mathbf{x}_1')], \qquad (4.25)$$

and

$$\Gamma(\mathbf{x}_1 - \mathbf{x}_1') = \mathcal{F}^{-1}[\gamma(\mathbf{x}_0)], \qquad (4.26)$$

where $\mathcal{F}$ denotes the Fourier-transformation operation. It is evident that the relationship between Eqs. 4.25 and 4.26 is the well-known *Van Cittert–Zernike theorem*. In other words, if a required spatial coherence is given, then a source encoding transmittance can be obtained through Fourier transformation. In practice, however, the source encoding transmittance should be a positive real quantity that satisfies the physically realizable condition:

$$0 \leq \gamma(\mathbf{x}_0) \leq 1. \qquad (4.27)$$

4.4.2 Image Sampling

There is, however, a temporal coherence requirement for partially coherent processing. If we use wavelength spread to restrict the Fourier spectra to within a small fraction of the fringe spacing d of a narrow spectral band filter $H_n(\alpha, \beta)$, then we have

$$\frac{P_m f \Delta \lambda_n}{2\pi} \ll d, \tag{4.28}$$

where $1/d$ is the highest spatial frequency of the filter, P_m is the angular spatial frequency limit of the input image transparency, f is the focal length of the achromatic transform lens, and $\Delta\lambda_n$ is the spectral bandwidth of $H_n(\alpha, \beta)$. The temporal coherence requirement of the spatial filter is therefore

$$\frac{\Delta\lambda_n}{\lambda_n} \ll \frac{\pi}{h_0 P_m}, \tag{4.29}$$

where λ_n is the central wavelength of the nth narrow spectral band filter, and $2h_0 = \lambda_n f/d$ is the size of the input object transparency.

4.5 NOISE PERFORMANCE

Partially coherent processors are known to perform better under noisy conditions than their coherent counterparts. We now show some effects of the noise performance under white-light illumination.

An experimental setup for the study of the noise performance of a partially coherent processor is shown in Figure 4.6. First, we investigate the noise performance under the spatially coherent illumination, that is, the effects of source size ΔS. For convenience, we assume that the source irradiance is uniform over a square aperture at source plane P_0, which can be written as,

$$\gamma(x_0, y_0) = \text{rect}\left(\frac{x_0}{a}\right)\text{rect}\left(\frac{y_0}{a}\right), \tag{4.30}$$

where

$$\text{rect}\left(\frac{x_0}{a}\right) \triangleq \begin{cases} 1, & |x_0| \leq \frac{a}{2}, \\ 0, & |x_0| > \frac{a}{2}. \end{cases}$$

For simplicity, we assume that the input signal is a one-dimensional object independent of the y axis. The Fourier spectrum is also one-dimensional in the β direction, but smeared into rainbow colors along the α direction. Let the width of the nth narrow spectral band filter be $\Delta\alpha_n$. If the filter is placed in the smeared Fourier spectra, the spectral bandwidth of the filter can be

128 PARTIALLY COHERENT PROCESSING

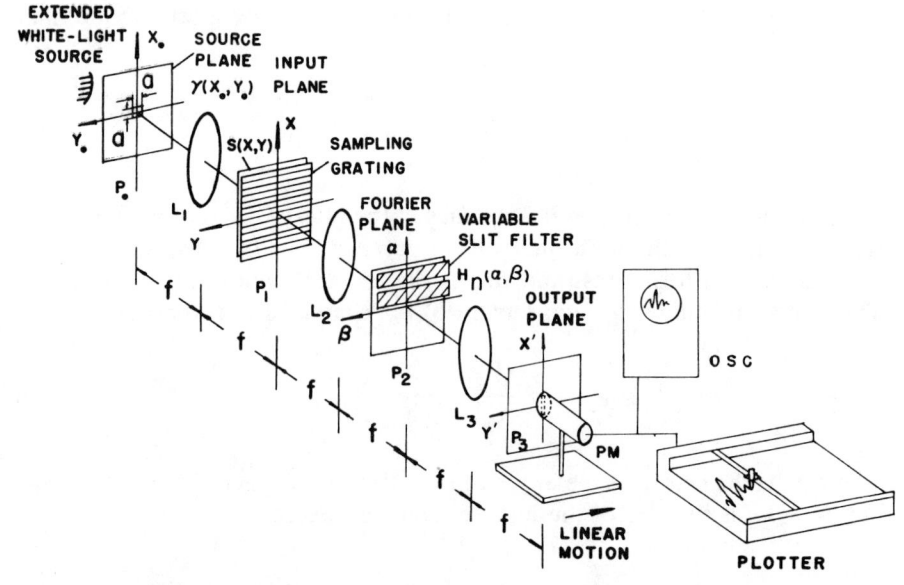

FIGURE 4.6 Noise measurement of a partially coherent processor. *Note:* $\gamma(x_0, y_0)$ is the source intensity distribution; P_0 is the source plane; P_1, P_2, and P_3 are input planes; $s(x, y)$ is the object transparency; $H_n(\alpha, \beta)$ denote the slit filters; PM is the photometer; and OSC is the oscilloscope.

written as

$$\Delta\lambda_n = \frac{\Delta\alpha_n}{\nu_0 f}. \tag{4.31}$$

The total number of filter channels can therefore be determined as

$$N \triangleq \frac{\Delta\lambda}{\Delta\lambda_n} \approx \frac{\Delta\lambda \nu_0 f}{\Delta\alpha_n}, \tag{4.32}$$

where $\Delta\lambda$ is the spectral bandwidth of the white-light source. Thus, we see that the degree of temporal coherence at the Fourier plane increases as the spatial frequency of the sampling grating ν_0 increases.

For the noise performance under the temporally coherent regime, we use a variable slit representing a broad spectral filter in the Fourier plane. The output noise fluctuation can be traced out with a linearly scanned photometer, as illustrated in Figure 4.6. It is apparent that the output noise fluctuation due to the spectral bandwidth of the slit filter and to the source size can then be determined separately. We use the following definition of an output signal-to-noise ratio (SNR) to evaluate the noise performance of the partially coherent processor:

$$\text{SNR}_n(y') \equiv E[I_n(y')]/\sigma_n(y'), \tag{4.33}$$

where $I_n(y')$ is the output irradiance of the nth channel, $E[\ ]$ denotes the ensemble average, and $\sigma_n^2(y')$ is the variance of the output noise fluctuation, that is,

$$\sigma_n^2(y') \equiv E[I_n^2(y')] - \{E[I_n(y')]\}^2. \tag{4.34}$$

Evidently, the output intensity fluctation $I_n(y')$ can be traced out by a linearly scanned photometer. The dc component of the output traces is obviously the output signal irradiance (i.e., $E[I_n]$), and the mean square fluctuation of the traces is the variance of the output noise (i.e., σ_n^2). Thus we see that the effect of the output SNR due to spectral bandwidth (i.e., temporal coherence) and source size (i.e., spatial coherence) can be readily obtained.

First, we demonstrate the noise performance due to perturbation at the input plane. For amplitude noise at the input plane, the experiments have shown that there is no apparent improvement in noise performance under partially coherent illumination. However, for phase noise at the input plane, the noise performance of the system is greatly improved by partially coherent illumination. We first utilize a weak phase model as an input noise. We consider the situation of an input object transparency superimposed with a thin phase noise at the input plane. The effect of the noise performance of the optical system can then be obtained by varying the source size and the spectral bandwidth of the slit filter. Figure 4.7 shows a set of output images

FIGURE 4.7 Effect on an output image (with a section of photometer traces) due to phase noise at the input plane for different spectral bandwidths. (*a*) For $\lambda_n = 1500$ Å. (*b*) For $\lambda_n = 1000$ Å. (*c*) For $\lambda_n = 500$ Å.

130 PARTIALLY COHERENT PROCESSING

with photometer traces illustrating the output noise due to the spectral bandwidth of the slit filter. From these pictures, we see that the SNR improves as the spectral bandwidth of the slit filter increases.

A quantitative measurement of the noise performance due to phase noise at the input plane is plotted in Figures 4.8 and 4.9. From these figures, we see that the output SNR increases monotonically as the spectral bandwidth $\Delta\lambda_n$ of slit filter increases, and increases linearly as the source size enlarges. Thus, the noise performance for a partially coherent processor improves as the degree of coherence (i.e., temporal and spatial coherence) relaxes. In other words, to improve the output SNR of the partially coherent processor, one can relax either the spatial coherence, the temporal coherence, or both.

Let us now demonstrate the effect of the noise performance due to strong phase noise. Conventional shower glass was used as an input phase noise. Figure 4.10 shows a set of results obtained under various spectral bandwidth illuminations. Figure 4.10a shows the output result obtained entirely with broad-band white-light illumination. Although this image is somewhat aberrated by the thick phase perturbation, the image is relatively free of random noise fluctuation. Comparing the results shown in Fig. 4.10a to those in b to c, we see that the output SNR decreases rapidly as the spectral bandwidth of the slit filter decreases. Figure 4.10d shows the result obtained with a HeNe laser. Besides the poor noise performance, we see that the output image is severely corrupted by coherent artifact noise.

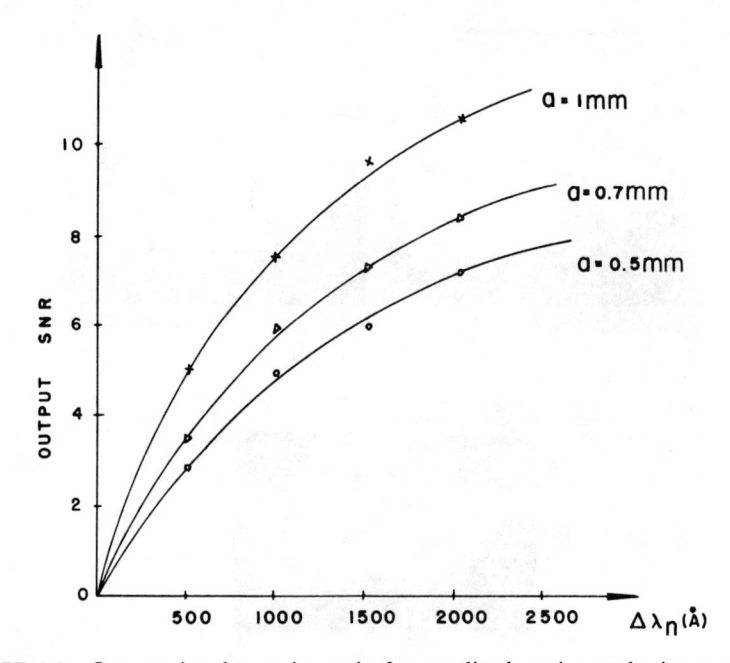

FIGURE 4.8 Output signal-to-noise ratio for amplitude noise at the input plane for various score signs.

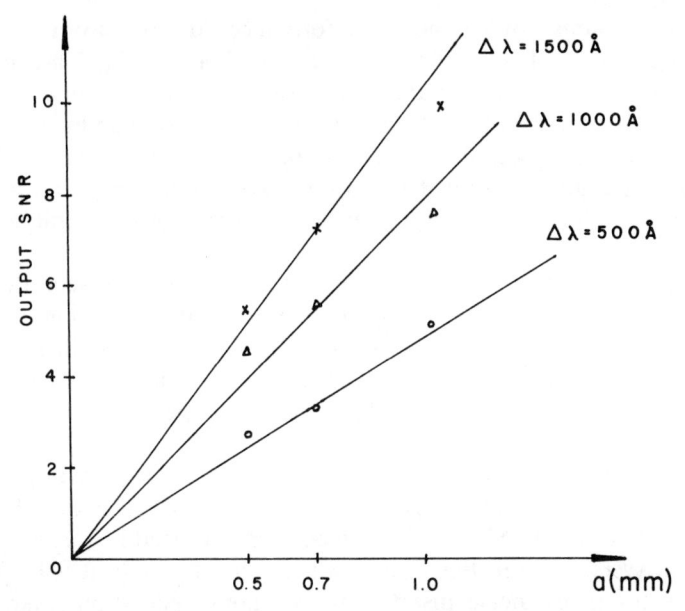

FIGURE 4.9 Output signal-to-noise ratio for phase noise at the input plane for various spectral bandwidths.

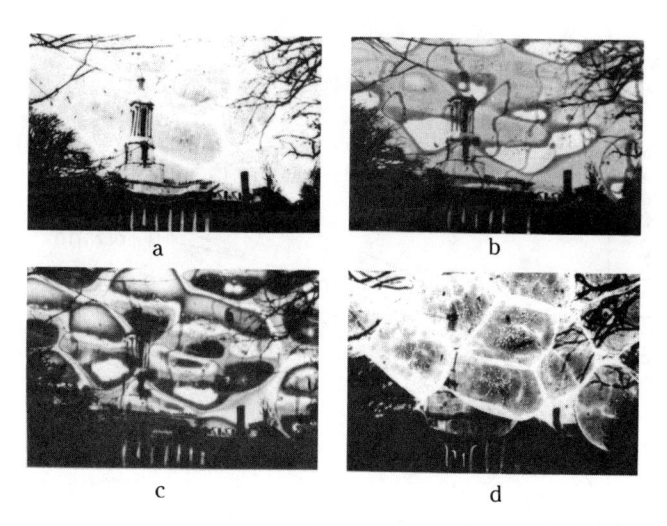

FIGURE 4.10 Effect on output image due to strong phase perturbation at the input plane. (*a*) For $\Delta\lambda_n = 3000$ Å. (*b*) For $\Delta\lambda_n = 1500$ Å. (*c*) For $\Delta\lambda_n = 500$ Å. (*d*) Obtained with an HeNe laser.

132 PARTIALLY COHERENT PROCESSING

We now demonstrate the noise performance due to noise at the Fourier plane. The effects of amplitude noise at the Fourier plane are plotted in Figure 4.11. In contrast to the amplitude noise at the input plane, we see that the output SNR increases monotonically as the spectral bandwidth of the slit filter increases. The output SNR also improves as the source size enlarges. Thus, for amplitude noise at the Fourier plane, the noise performance of a partially coherent processor improves as the degree of temporal and spatial coherence decreases.

Figure 4.12 shows the noise performance due to phase noise at the Fourier plane. From this figure, we again see that the output SNR is a monotonically increasing function of spectral bandwidth $\Delta\lambda_n$. The SNR also increases as the source size increases. However, as compared with the case of phase noise at the input plane of Figure 4.9, improvement in noise performance is somewhat less.

We now provide the result of noise performance due to thin phase noise along the optical axis (i.e., Z axis) of the optical system. Figure 4.13 shows the variation of output SNR due to phase noise inserted in various planes of the optical system. From this figure, we see that the output SNR improves drastically for phase noise inserted at the input and output planes under temporally and spatially partially coherent illumination. The noise performance is somewhat less effective for the phase noise at the Fourier plane, even though under partially coherent illumination. Nonetheless, the phase noise at the Fourier plane can, in principle, be totally eliminated under very broadband illumination if each of the noise channels is uncorrelated. We have also

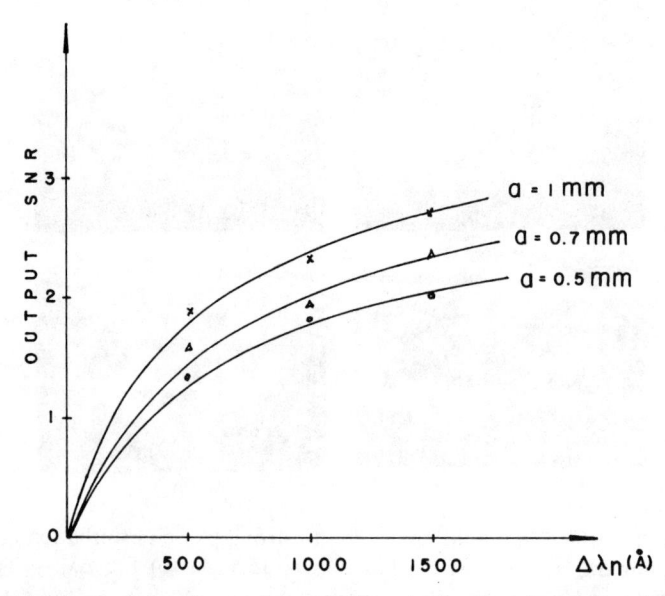

FIGURE 4.11 Output signal-to-noise ratio for amplitude noise at Fourier plane for various source sizes.

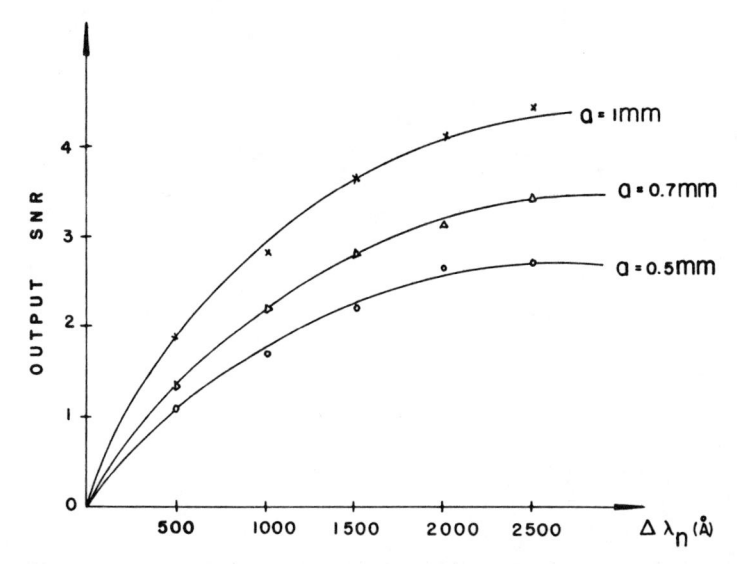

FIGURE 4.12 Output signal-to-noise ratio for phase noise at Fourier plane for various source sizes.

noted that the output SNR is somewhat lower for higher spatial coherent illumination. In other words, the output SNR can also be improved with extended source illumination.

The noise performance due to amplitude noise along the Z axis is plotted in Figure 4.14. From this figure, we see that the output SNR improves as the

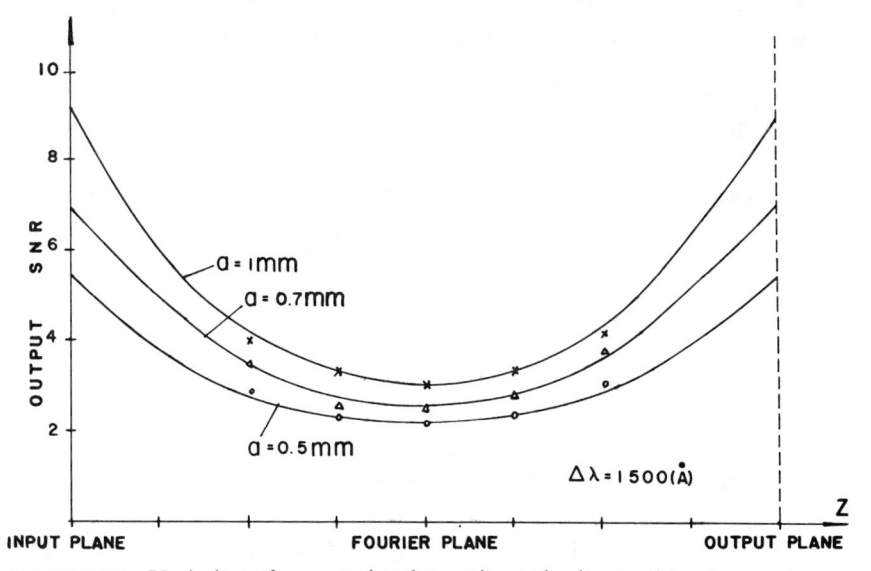

FIGURE 4.13 Variation of output signal-to-noise ratio due to thin phase noise as a function of the Z direction for various source sizes.

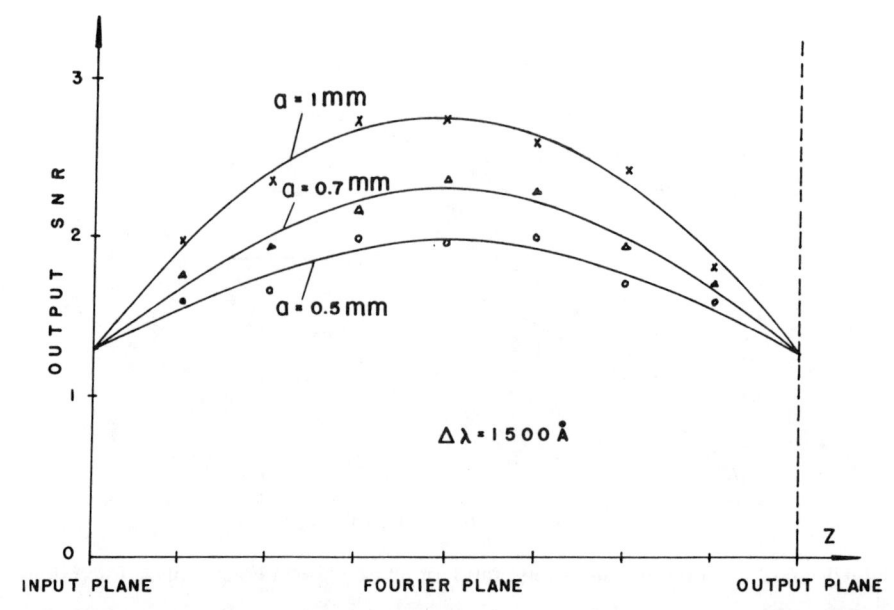

FIGURE 4.14 Variation of output signal-to-noise ratio due to thin amplitude noise as a function of the Z direction for various source sizes.

noise perturbation is moved away from the input and the output planes, and that the optimum SNR occurs at the Fourier plane. Again, we see that the output SNR is somewhat higher for larger source size (i.e., lower degree of spatial coherence). It is apparent that if the amplitude noise is placed either at the input or at the output plane, the noise performance cannot be improved by either partially coherent or incoherent illumination.

4.6 APPLICATIONS

It would take many pages to describe all the applications of partially coherent processing, so in this section, we restrict ourselves to those few applications that are of greatest interest to our readers. Because, as we noted earlier, the partially coherent processor is very suitable for color image processing, we confine ourselves to that process.

4.6.1 Restoration of Blurred Images

One of the interesting applications of partially coherent processing is the restoration of blurred color photographic images. Since linear smeared image is a one-dimensional restoration problem and the deblurring operation is a point-by-point filtering process, we use a *fan-shape*-type deblurring filter to compensate for the scale variation of the smeared Fourier spectra due to wavelength.

APPLICATIONS   135

We now describe a color image deblurring technique that uses a fan-shape-type deblurring filter. We assume the blurred image is due to the linear motion described by

$$\hat{s}(x, y) = s(x, y) * \text{rect}\left(\frac{y}{W}\right), \quad (4.35)$$

where $\hat{s}(x, y)$ and $s(x, y)$ denote the blurred and unblurred images, respectively, and

$$\text{rect}\left(\frac{y}{W}\right) = \begin{cases} 1, & |y| \le \frac{W}{2}, \\ 0, & \text{otherwise}, \end{cases}$$

and W is the smeared length.

If we insert this blurred image transparency into the input plane, P_1, of the partially coherent processor of Figure 4.4, the complex light distribution for every wavelength, λ, at the back focal length of the achromatic transform lens, L_2, would be

$$E(\alpha, \beta; \lambda) = S\left[\alpha - \left(\frac{\lambda f}{2\pi}\right)p_0, \beta\right]\text{sinc}\left(\frac{\pi W}{\lambda f}\beta\right), \quad (4.36)$$

where p_0 is the angular spatial frequency of the phase grating, and $S[\cdot]$ represents the smeared Fourier spectrum of $s(x, y)$. Equation 4.36 shows that the image spectrum is smeared into a rainbow-color spectrum.

We use a fan-shaped deblurring filter as described in the following equation:

$$H(\alpha, \beta; \lambda) = \delta\left(\alpha - \frac{\lambda f}{2\pi}p_0, \beta\right)\left\{\int\left[\text{rect}\left(\frac{y}{W}\right)\right.\right.$$
$$\left.\left.\exp\left(-i\frac{2\pi}{\lambda f}\beta y\right)\right]dy\right\}^{-1},$$
$$= \delta\left(\alpha - \frac{\lambda f}{2\pi}p_0, \beta\right)\left[\text{sinc}\left(\frac{\pi W}{\lambda f}\beta\right)\right]^{-1}. \quad (4.37)$$

If this deblurring filter is inserted in the spatial frequency plane, the complex light distribution, for every λ, at the output image plane would be

$$g(x, y; \lambda) = \mathcal{F}^{-1}\left[S\left(\alpha - \frac{\lambda f}{2\pi}p_0, \beta\right)H(\alpha, \beta; \lambda)\right]$$
$$= s(x, y)\exp(ip_0 x), \quad (4.38)$$

where $\mathcal{F}^{-1}$ denotes the inverse Fourier transform. The resultant output image intensity is therefore

$$I(x, y) = \int_{\Delta\lambda} |g(x, y; \lambda)|^2 \, d\lambda \approx \Delta\lambda |s(x, y)|^2, \qquad (4.39)$$

which is proportional to the spectral bandwidth $\Delta\lambda$ of the white-light source. Thus, we see that the partially coherent processor is capable of deblurring color images.

Figure 4.15a shows a black-and-white version of a color picture that was blurred by linear motion, and Figure 4.15b is the deblurred image obtained by white-light processing. Compared with the blurred photo, the letters USAF on the wing and YF-16 on the tail can be more clearly seen. The overall shape of the entire airplane is more distinctive than in the blurred picture. Also, the color reproduction of the deblurred image is rather faithful and the coherent artifact noise is virtually nonexistent.

4.6.2 Image Subtraction

Another interesting application of white-light optical processing is color image subtraction. Two color image transparencies are inserted in the input plane of the white-light optical processor of Figure 4.4. At the spatial frequency plane, the complex light distribution for each wavelength λ of the light source can be described as

$$\begin{aligned} E(\alpha, \beta; \lambda) = & S_1\left(\alpha - \frac{\lambda f}{2\pi} p_0, \beta\right) \exp\left(-i \frac{2\pi}{\lambda f} h_0 \beta\right) \\ & + S_2\left(\alpha - \frac{\lambda f}{2\pi} p_0, \beta\right) \exp\left(i \frac{2\pi}{\lambda f} h_0 \beta\right), \end{aligned} \qquad (4.40)$$

where $S_1(\alpha, \beta)$ and $S_2(\alpha, \beta)$ are the Fourier spectra of the input color images $s_1(x, y)$ and $s_2(x, y)$, $2h_0$ is the main separation of the two color images s_1

FIGURE 4.15 Restoration of blurred images. (a) A black-and-white blurred color picture due to linear motion. (b) A black-and-white deblurred color picture.

and s_2, and p_0 is the angular spatial frequency of the sampling phase grating. Again we see that the two input image spectra disperse into rainbow colors along the α axis of the spatial frequency plane.

For image subtraction, we insert a sinusoidal grating in the spatial frequency plane. Since the scale of the Fourier spectra varies with respect to the wavelength of the light source, we must use a fan-shaped grating to compensate for the scale variation. Let us assume that the transmittance of the fan-shaped grating is

$$H(\alpha, \beta; \lambda) = \left[1 + \sin\left(\frac{2\pi}{\lambda f} h_0 \beta\right)\right], \quad \text{for all } \alpha. \quad (4.41)$$

Then the output image irradiance is

$$I(x, y) \approx \Delta\lambda \left[|s_1(x, y - h_0)|^2 + |s_2(x, y + h_0)|^2 \right.$$
$$+ \frac{1}{2}|s_1(x, y) - s_2(x, y)|^2 + |s_1(x, y - 2h_0)|^2$$
$$\left. + |s_2(x, y + 2h_0)|^2 \right], \quad (4.42)$$

where $\Delta\lambda$ is the spectral bandwidth of the white-light source. Thus, the subtracted color image can be seen at the optical axis of the output plane. In practice, it is difficult to obtain a true white-light point source, but this difficulty can be overcome with the source encoding technique described in Section 4.4.

To ensure a physically realizable source encoding function, we let a spatial coherence function with an appropriate point-pair coherence requirement be

$$\Gamma(|y - y'|) = \frac{\sin\left(\frac{N\pi}{h_0}|y - y'|\right)}{N \sin\left(\frac{\pi}{h_0}|y - y'|\right)} \operatorname{sinc}\left(\frac{\pi w}{h_0 d}|y - y'|\right), \quad (4.43)$$

where N is a positive integer $\gg 1$, and $w \ll d$. Equation 4.43 represents a sequence of narrow pulses that occur at every $|y - y'| = nh_0$, where n is a positive integer, and their peak values are weighted by a broader sinc factor. Thus, a high degree of spatial coherence can be achieved at every point-pair between the two input color image transparencies. By applying the Van Cittert–Zernike theorem of Eq. 4.25, the corresponding source encoding function is obtained:

138 PARTIALLY COHERENT PROCESSING

$$\gamma(|y|) = \sum_{n=1} \text{rect} \frac{|y - nd|}{w}, \quad (4.44)$$

where w is the slit width, $d = (\lambda f/h_0)$ is the separation between the slits, f is the focal length of the achromatic collimated lens, and N is the total number of the slits. Alternatively, Eq. 4.44 can be written in the following form:

$$\gamma(|y|) = \sum_{n=1}^{N} \text{rect} \frac{|y - n\lambda f/h_0|}{W}, \quad (4.45)$$

for which we see that the source encoding mask is essentially a fan-shape-type grating. To obtain lines of rainbow-color spectral light sources for the subtraction operation, we would use a linear extended white-light source with a dispersive phase grating, as illustrated in Figure 4.16. For broad-spectral-band image subtraction operation, a fan-shaped sinusoidal grating is utilized in the Fourier plane, such as

$$G = \frac{1}{2}[1 + \sin(2\pi\alpha h_0/\lambda f)]. \quad (4.46)$$

The output image irradiance around the optical axis can be shown as

$$I(x, y) = K|s_1(x, y) - s_2(x, y)|^2. \quad (4.47)$$

Thus we assert that a color subtracted image can readily be obtained.

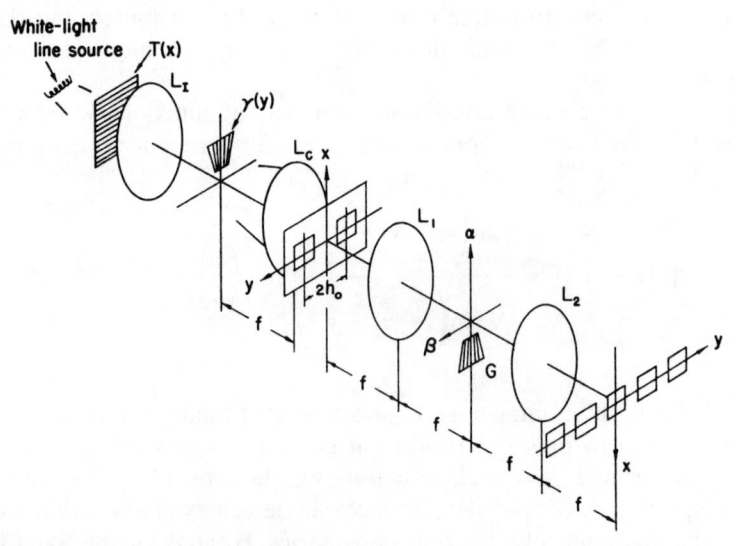

FIGURE 4.16 A white-light image subtraction system. *Note*: $T(x)$ is the phase grating; L_1 is the imaging lens; L_c is the collimated lens; L_1 and L_2 are achromatic transform lenses; $\gamma(y)$ is the fan-shaped source encoding mask; G is the fan-shaped diffraction grating.

APPLICATIONS 139

Figures 4.17a and b show a set of black-and-white pictures of input color transparencies. The first picture shows an F-16 fighter plane taking off over a mountainous coastline area, and the second picture shows the same scenic view but without the fighter plane. Figure 4.17c shows the corresponding subtracted image at the output plane. From this figure, we see that the shape of the F-16 fighter plane can be recognized. Although the resolution of the

(a)

(b)

(c)

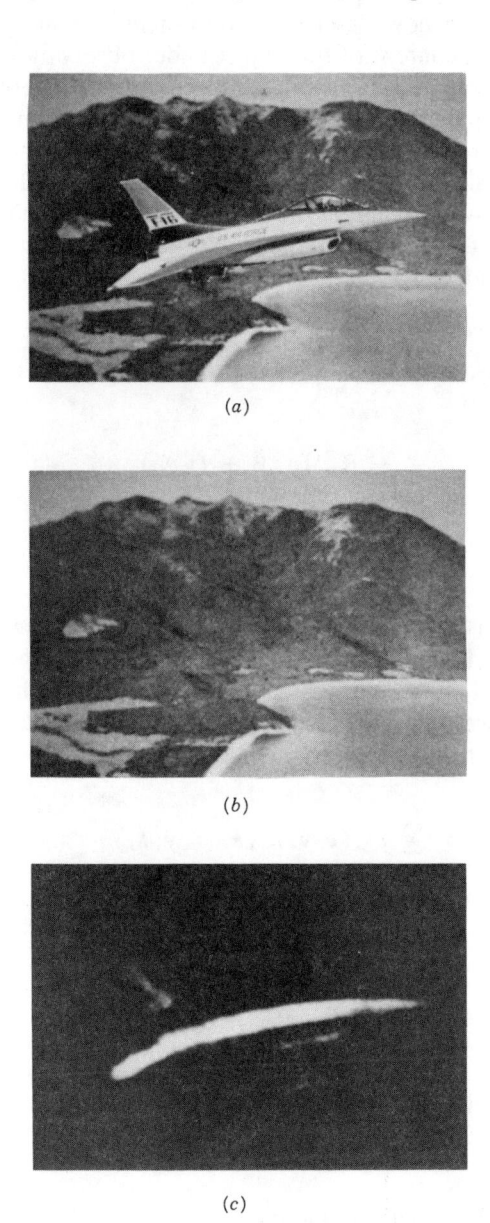

FIGURE 4.17 Image subtraction. (a) and (b) Black-and-white pictures of input color objects. (c) A black-and-white picture of the output subtracted color image.

140 PARTIALLY COHERENT PROCESSING

result is still below the generally acceptable standard, this drawback may be overcome by utilizing higher quality optics.

4.6.3 Complex Signal Detection

One of the most important applications of optical signal processing is complex signal detection. We now describe a white-light optical correlator that can exploit the spectral content of the object under observation. In other words, the correlator is capable of recognizing multiple-color objects of different shapes. There is much need for color-pattern recognition, and it has many applications. There are, for instance, two large categories where color is extremely important: natural color variations, and objects deliberately colored for identification—for example, in robotic vision applications.

We assume that a broad-band matched filter, as described in the following equation, is provided:

$$H(\alpha, \beta) \simeq \sum_{\substack{n=-N \\ n \neq 0}}^{N} \left\{ K_1 |S(\alpha, \beta + f v_0 \lambda_n)|^2 \right.$$

$$+ K_2 |S(\alpha, \beta + f v_0 \lambda_n)|$$

$$\left. \times \cos\left[\frac{2\pi h}{\lambda_n f} \alpha + \phi(\alpha, \beta + f v_0 \lambda_n)\right] \right\}, \quad (4.48)$$

where $S(\alpha, \beta; \lambda)$ is the input object spectrum; v_0 is the sampling grating frequency; K_s, C_s, and h are arbitrary constants; and λ_n is the main wavelength of the nth spectral band filter. If this filter is inserted in the Fourier plane of a white-light processor, as depicted in Figure 4.4, the output complex light filter can be shown to be

$$g(x, y; \lambda) = \sum_{n=1}^{N} C_1 s(x, y; \lambda_n) * s(x, y; \lambda_n) * s^*(-x, -y; \lambda_n)$$

$$+ \sum_{n=1}^{N} C_2 s(x, y; \lambda_n) * [s(x + h, y; \lambda_n)$$

$$+ s^*(-x + h, -y; \lambda_n)], \quad (4.49)$$

where $s(x, y; \lambda_n)$ is the color input object, * denotes the convolution operation, and the superscript * represents the complex conjugation. The corresponding output irradiance is

$$I(x, y) = \int_{\Delta \lambda_n} |g(x, y; \lambda)|^2 \, d\lambda$$

$$\approx \sum_{n=1}^{N} \Delta\lambda_n \{K_1 |s(x, y; \lambda_n) * s(x, y; \lambda_n) \circledast s^*(x, y; \lambda_n)|^2$$
$$+ K_2 |s(x, y; \lambda_n) * s(x + h, y; \lambda_n) \quad (4.50)$$
$$+ s(x, y; \lambda_n) \circledast s^*(x - h, y; \lambda_n)|^2 \},$$

where ⊛ denotes the correlation operation, and K_s are the proportionality constants. Thus, we see that an autocorrelation of the input image is diffracted at $x = h$ at the output plane. Since we utilized a broad-spectral-band white-light source, the spectral content of the image can be exploited.

Figure 4.18a is a black-and-white copy of a color aerial photograph of a (red) guided missile in flight. Figure 4.18b shows a visible (red) correlation spot obtained at the output plane of the correlator. Thus the white-light correlator can, uniquely, recognize color-patterns based on both the spectral content and the shape of an input object.

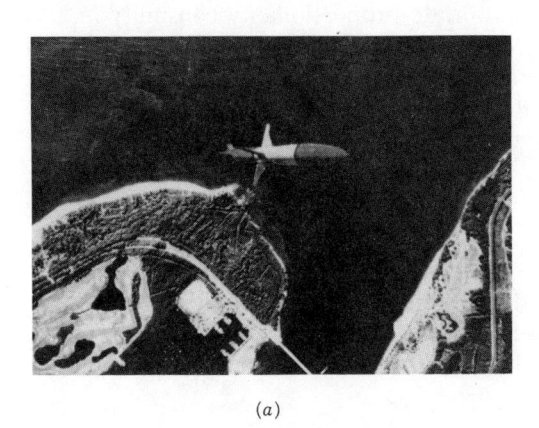

(a)

(b)

FIGURE 4.18 Complex signal detection. (a) A black-and-white picture of an input color object. (b) A black-and-white picture of the output correlation spot.

4.6.4 Color Image Retrieval

We now describe a spatial encoding technique for color image retrieval. A color transparency is used as the object to be encoded by sequentially exposing the primary colors of light onto a black-and-white film. The encoding takes place by spatially sampling the primary color images of the color transparency with a specific sampling frequency and a predescribed direction onto a monochrome film. In order to avoid the moire fringe pattern, the primary color images are sampled in orthogonal directions. Thus the intensity transmittance of the encoded film can be shown as

$$T(x, y) = K\{T_r(x, y)[1 + \text{sgn}(\cos \omega_r y)]$$
$$+ T_b(x, y)[1 + \text{sgn}(\cos \omega_b x)]$$
$$+ T_g(x, y)[1 + \text{sgn}(\cos \omega_g x)]\}^{-\gamma}, \tag{4.51}$$

where K is an appropriate proportionality constant; T_r, T_b, and T_g are the red, blue, and green color image exposures; ω_r, ω_b, and ω_g are the respective carrier spatial frequencies, (x, y) is the spatial coordinate system of the encoded film, γ is the film gamma, and

$$\text{sgn}(\cos x) \triangleq \begin{cases} 1, & \cos x > 0, \\ 0, & \cos x = 0, \\ -1, & \cos x < 0. \end{cases}$$

To improve the diffraction efficiency of the encoded film, it is advisable to bleach it to convert it into a phase-type transparency. The amplitude transmittance of the bleached transparency can be written as

$$t(x, y) = \exp[i\phi(x, y)],$$

where

$$\phi(x, y) = M\{T_r(x, y)[1 + \text{sgn}(\cos \omega_r y)]$$
$$+ T_b(x, y)[1 + \text{sgn}(\cos \omega_b x)]$$
$$+ T_g(x, y)[1 + \text{sgn}(\cos \omega_g x)]\}, \tag{4.52}$$

and M is an appropriate proportionality constant.

If we place this bleached encoded film in the input plane of the white-light optical processor of Figure 4.19, the first-order complex light distribution for every λ at the spatial frequency plane P_2 can be shown as

$$S(\alpha, \beta; \lambda) \approx \hat{T}_r\left(\alpha, \beta \pm \frac{\lambda f}{2\pi}\omega_r\right) + \hat{T}_b\left(\alpha \pm \frac{\lambda f}{2\pi}\omega_b, \beta\right)$$

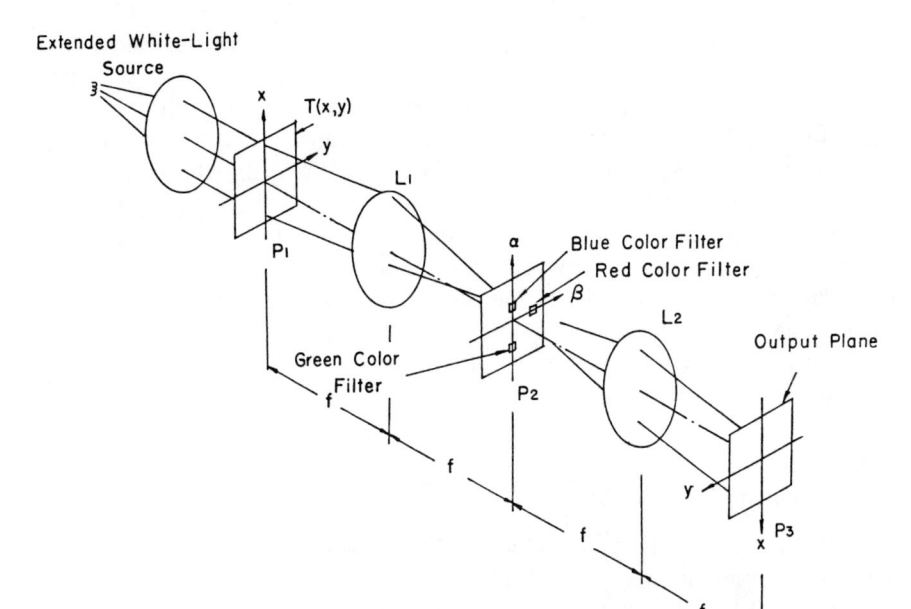

FIGURE 4.19　A white-light processor for color image retrieval.

$$+ \hat{T}_g\left(\alpha \pm \frac{\lambda f}{2\pi}\omega_g, \beta\right)$$

$$+ \hat{T}_r\left(\alpha, \beta \pm \frac{\lambda f}{2\pi}\omega_r\right) * \hat{T}_b\left(\alpha \pm \frac{\lambda f}{2\pi}\omega_b, \beta\right)$$

$$+ \hat{T}_r\left(\alpha, \beta \pm \frac{\lambda f}{2\pi}\omega_r\right) * \hat{T}_g\left(\alpha \pm \frac{\lambda f}{2\pi}\omega_g, \beta\right) \quad (4.53)$$

$$+ \hat{T}_b\left(\alpha \pm \frac{\lambda f}{2\pi}\omega_b, \beta\right) * \hat{T}_g\left(\alpha \pm \frac{\lambda f}{2\pi}\omega_g, \beta\right),$$

where $\hat{T}_r$, $\hat{T}_b$, and $\hat{T}_g$ are the Fourier transforms of T_r, T_b, and T_g respectively, * denotes the convolution operation, and the proportionality constants have been neglected for simplicity. We note that the last cross-product term would introduce a moire fringe pattern, which can be easily masked out at the Fourier plane. It is apparent that by proper color filtering of the smeared Fourier spectra, a true color image can be retrieved at the output image plane. Thus, the output image irradiance would be

$$I(x, y) = T_r^2(x, y) + T_b^2(x, y) + T_g^2(x, y), \quad (4.54)$$

which is a superposition of three primary encoded color images.

144 PARTIALLY COHERENT PROCESSING

We now provide the retrieved color image obtained with this technique, as shown in Figure 4.20. As compared with the original color transparency, we can see that the retrieved color image is spectacularly faithful and has virtually no color cross talk. The resolution and contrast are still below those necessary for widespread applications; however, these drawbacks might be overcome by utilizing a more suitable film.

The following technique for using computer-generated tricolor grating for color image retrieval [4.10] is worth mentioning. A tricolor grating is mounted on a camera where it is close to the film. Thus, by taking pictures of a color subject, an encoded transparency can be made (Figure 4.21). A retrieval color image using this technique is shown in Fig. 4.22. Again we see that the color reproduction is very faithful and has no moire fringe pattern.

4.6.5 Density Pseudocolor Encoding

Most of the optical images obtained in various scientific applications are gray-level density images—for example, the scanning electron micrographs, multispectral-band aerial photographic images, x-ray transparencies, and infrared scanning images. However, humans can perceive details in color better

FIGURE 4.20 A retrieved color image.

APPLICATIONS 145

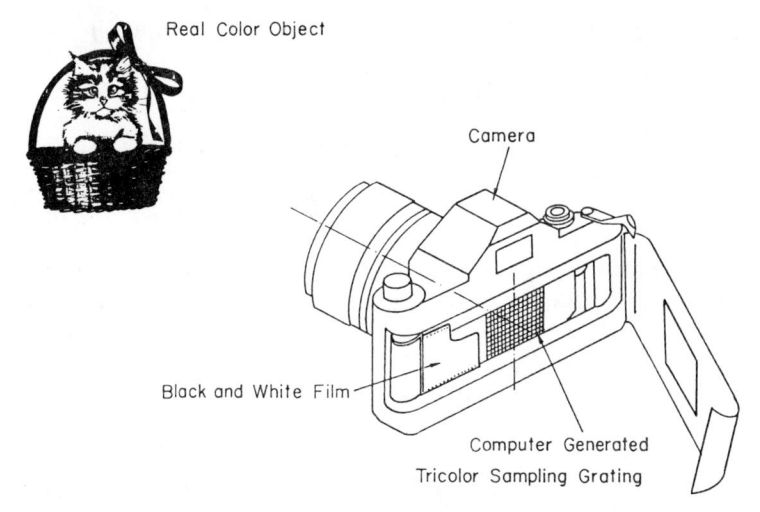

FIGURE 4.21 Color image encoding on black-and-white film using a tricolor grating.

FIGURE 4.22 The black-and-white color picture retrieved from the camera-encoded transparency.

than in gray levels. In other words, a color-coded image can provide better visual discrimination.

We now describe a density pseudocolor encoding technique for monochrome images. We start by assuming that a gray-level transparency (called T_1) is available for pseudocoloring. Using the contact printing process, a negative and a product (called T_2 and T_3, respectively) image transparency can be made. It is now clear that spatial encoding onto monochrome film can be accomplished by the procedure described for color image retrieval. The intensity transmittance of the encoded film can be written as

$$T(x, y) = K\{T_1(x, y)[1 + \text{sgn}(\cos \omega_1 y)] \\ + T_2(x, y)[1 + \text{sgn}(\cos \omega_2 x)] \\ + T_3(x, y)[1 + \text{sgn}(\cos \omega_3 x)]\}^{-r}, \quad (4.55)$$

where K is an appropriate proportionality constant. To improve the diffraction efficiency of the encoded film, we again use the bleaching process, so the phase-encoded transparency becomes,

$$t(x, y) = \exp[i\phi(x, y)],$$

where

$$\phi(x, y) = M\{T_1(x, y)[1 + \text{sgn}(\cos \omega_1 y)] \\ + T_2(x, y)[1 + \text{sgn}(\cos \omega_2 x)] \\ + T_3(x, y)[1 + \text{sgn}(\cos \omega_3 x)]\}, \quad (4.56)$$

where M is an appropriate proportionality constant. If we insert this encoded phase transparency at the input plane of the white-light processor of Figure 4.19, the complex light distribution due to $t(x, y)$ for every λ at the spatial frequency plane is

$$S(\alpha, \beta, \lambda) \approx \hat{T}_1\left(\alpha, \beta \pm \frac{\lambda f}{2\pi}\omega_1\right) + \hat{T}_2\left(\alpha \pm \frac{\lambda f}{2\pi}\omega_2, \beta\right) \\ + \hat{T}_3\left(\alpha \pm \frac{\lambda f}{2\pi}\omega_3, \beta\right) \\ + \hat{T}_1\left(\alpha, \beta \pm \frac{\lambda f}{2\pi}\omega_1\right) * \hat{T}_2\left(\alpha \pm \frac{\lambda f}{2\pi}\omega_2, \beta\right) \\ + \hat{T}_1\left(\alpha, \beta \pm \frac{\lambda f}{2\pi}\omega_1\right) * \hat{T}_3\left(\alpha \pm \frac{\lambda f}{2\pi}\omega_3, \beta\right) \quad (4.57) \\ + \hat{T}_2\left(\alpha \pm \frac{\lambda f}{2\pi}\omega_2, \beta\right) * \hat{T}_3\left(\alpha \pm \frac{\lambda f}{2\pi}\omega_3, \beta\right),$$

where $\hat{T}_1$, $\hat{T}_2$, and $\hat{T}_3$ are the smeared Fourier spectra of the positive, negative, and product images, respectively; * denotes the convolution operation; and the proportional constants have been neglected for simplicity. Again, we see that the last cross product (i.e., the moire fringe pattern) can be avoided by spatial filtering. Needless to say, by proper color filtering of the first-order smeared Fourier spectra, a moire-free pseudocolor encoded image can be obtained at the output plane. The corresponding pseudocolor image irradiance is therefore,

$$I(x, y) = T_{1r}^2(x, y) + T_{2b}^2(x, y) + T_{3g}^2(x, y), \qquad (4.58)$$

where T_{1r}^2, T_{2b}^2, and T_{3g}^2 are the red, blue, and green intensity distributions of the three spatially encoded images.

Figures 4.23a and b show a set of black-and-white pictures of color-coded images of a woman's pelvis. The x-ray was taken following a surgical procedure, in which a section of the bone between the sacroiliac joint and spinal column was removed. In Figure 4.23a, the positive image is encoded in red, the negative image is encoded in blue, and the product image is encoded in green. When we compare this image with the original x-ray picture, it appears that the soft tissue is better differentiated in the color image, as demonstrated by the fact that the image contrast in the region of the gastrointestinal tract is evidently superior in the color-coded image. It is worth noting that reversal of the color coding can be easily implemented, as shown in Figure 4.23b, where the positive and negative images are encoded in blue and red while the product image remains in green. This possibility of switching colors could be beneficial because an image in a different color combination may reveal subtle features that were otherwise undetected. For instance, the air pockets in the colon on the patient can be identified more easily in Figure 4.23b than in Figure 2.23a. Moreover, a wide variety of other pseudocolor encoded images can also be obtained by simply alternating the color filters in the Fourier plane of the white-light processor.

4.6.6 Generation of Speech Spectrograms

We now describe a technique for generating a multicolor speech spectrogram with a white-light optical signal processor. This technique utilizes a cathode-

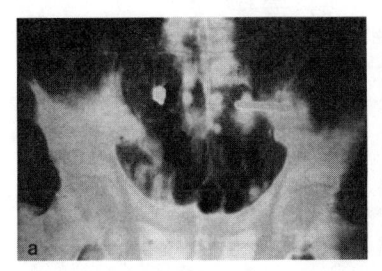

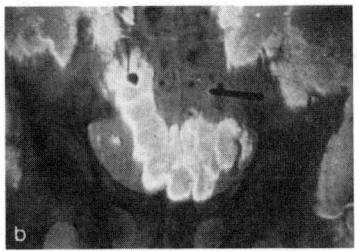

FIGURE 4.23 Black-and-white pictures of density pseudocolor images. (*a*) The positive image is coded in red, the negative image is coded in blue, and the product image is coded in green. (*b*) The positive image is coded in blue, the negative image is coded in red, and the product image is again coded in green.

ray-tube (CRT) scanner to convert a temporal signal to a spatial signal onto a photographic film. If this encoded film is moved across the input optical window of a white-light spectrum analyzer as shown in Figure 4.24, a speech spectrogram can be generated at the output plane.

We stress that for time to spatial signal conversion, the velocity of the film needs to satisfy the following inequality

$$v \geq \nu/R, \quad (4.59)$$

where R is the spatial resolution of the film and ν is the highest frequency content of the time signal.

When the encoded signal format moves across the input plane of the white-light processor of Figure 4.24, a slanted set of nonoverlapping smeared color spectra in the spatial-frequency plane can be observed. It is now clear that if a slanted narrow slit is utilized at the Fourier plane, a frequency color-coded spectrogram can be recorded at the output plane. We also note that by simply varying the width w of the input optical window, one obtains the so-called *wide-band* and *narrow-band* spectrograms. In other words, if a broader optical window is used, a narrow-band speech spectrogram, with correspondingly higher spectral resolution, can be obtained. On the other hand, if the optical window is narrower, then a wide-band spectrogram will be obtained. The loss of the spectral resolution due to the narrower optical window would, however, improve the time resolution of the spectrogram. This time–bandwidth relationship is, in fact, a consequence of the well-known Heisenberg uncertainty relation in quantum mechanics.

Figure 4.25 shows a black-and-white picture of a frequency color-coded speech spectrogram obtained by the proposed white-light technique. The frequency content is encoded with red for high frequency, green for inter-

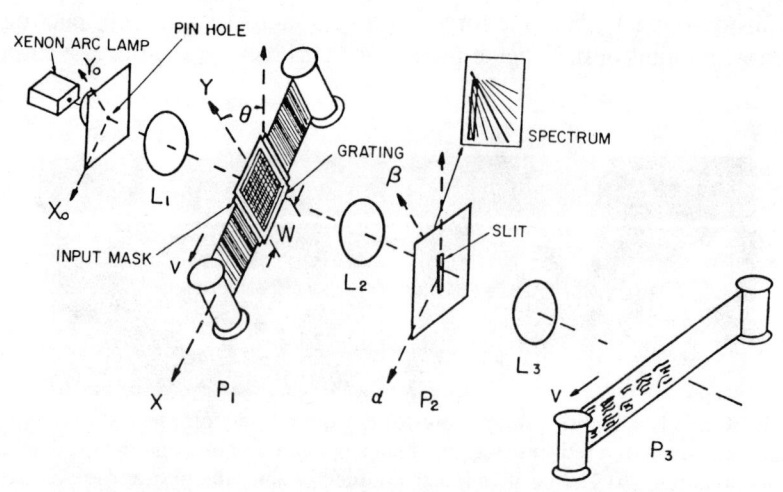

FIGURE 4.24 A white-light optical sound spectrograph.

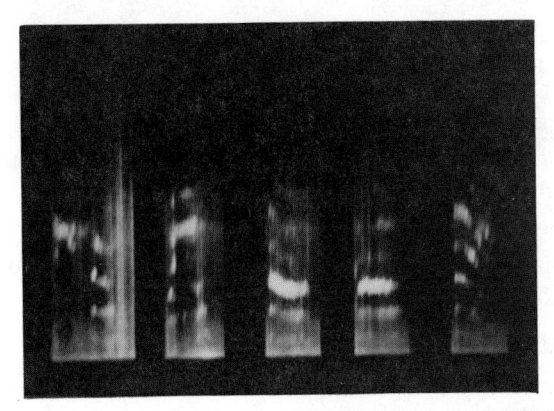

FIGURE 4.25 A black-and-white picture of a frequency color-coded speech spectrogram.

mediate frequency, and blue for low frequency. This speech spectrogram depicts a sequence of English words spoken by a male voice. The words are "testing, one, two, three, four." The format variation can readily be identified from this speech spectrogram. As compred with its electronic and digital counterparts, the optical technique simplifies the processing procedure. The system is also rather easy to operate.

REFERENCES

4.1   F. T. S. Yu, *White Light Optical Signal Processing*, Wiley–Interscience, New York, 1985.
4.2   E. Leith and J. Roth, "White-Light Optical Processing and Holography," *Appl. Opt.* 16 (1977): 2565.
4.3   G. M. Morris and N. George, "Matched Filtering Using Band-Limited Illumination," *Opt. Lett.* 5 (1980): 202.
4.4   A. W. Lohmann, "Incoherent Optical Processing of Complex Data," *Appl. Opt.* 16 (1977): 261.
4.5   W. T. Rhodes, "Bipolar Pointspread Function by Phase Switching," *Appl. Opt.* 16 (1977): 265.
4.6   W. Stoner, "Incoherent Optical Processing via Spatially Offset Pupil Masks," *Appl. Opt.* 17 (1978): 2454.
4.7   F. T. S. Yu, "A New Technique of Incoherent Complex Signal Detection," *Opt. Commun.* 27 (1978): 27.
4.8   P. Chavel and S. Lowenthal, "Noise and Coherence in Optical Image Processing II Noise Fluctuations," *J. Opt. Soc. Am.* 68 (1978): 721.
4.9   P. F. Mueller, "Color Image Retrieval From Monochrome Transparencies," *Appl. Opt.* 8 (1969): 2051.
4.10 F. T. S. Yu, X. X. Chen, and K. E. McClure, "Computer Generated Linear Sampling Pattern and its Application," *J. Opt.* 17 (1986): 270.

PROBLEMS

4.1 An input–output optical processing system is assumed under strictly incoherent illumination.
  (a) Derive the incoherent transfer function of the optical system, in terms of the spatial impulse response of the system.
  (b) Derive a set of basic properties of part (a).
  (c) What are the major differences between the coherent and the incoherent optical processing systems?

4.2 Given an optical processing system:
  (a) Derive the cutoff frequencies for coherent and incoherent illuminations.
  (b) What are the resolution limits for the same optical imaging system under the strictly coherent and the strictly incoherent illumination?

4.3 Draw an analog system diagram of the processing operation carried out by the partially coherent optical signal processor of Figure 4.4. Assume a white-light point source, and that the object transparency inserted at the input plane is illuminated by a spatially coherent white-light plane wave. The complex wave field immediately behind the object transparency is

$$\sum_n s(x, y; \lambda_n).$$

4.4 The amplitude transmittance of a one-dimensional Fresnel zone lens is given by

$$T(x) = \frac{1}{2}\left[1 + \cos\left(\frac{\pi}{\lambda_0 R} x^2\right)\right],$$

where $\lambda_0 = 600$ nm and $R = 20$ cm. If the zone lens is normally illuminated by a white-light plane wave, whose spectral bandwidth is uniformly distributed from 700 nm to 350 nm, then:
  (a) Show that the focal length of the zone lens depends on the wavelength of the illuminating light.
  (b) Calculate the smeared length of the focal point under white-light illumination.

4.5 An input transparency with an object size of 5 mm is to be processed by the white-light processor of Figure 4.4. Assume that the focal length of the transform lenses is $f = 500$ mm.
  (a) Calculate the size of the source required.
  (b) If the spatial frequency of the input object is assumed to be ten

lines per millimeter, estimate the required size of the spatial filter H_n and the required spatial frequency of the phase grating.

4.6 We assume that the light source of Figure 4.4 is a point source. If we ignore the input signal transparency:
  (a) Determine the smeared length of the Fourier spectra as a function of the focal length f of the achromatic transform lens and the spatial frequency p_0 of the sinusoidal phase grating $T(x)$.
  (b) If the spatial frequency of the diffraction grating is $p_0 = 80\pi$ rad/mm and $f = 30$ cm, compute the smeared length of the rainbow color.

4.7 Referring to Problem 4.6, if the white-light source is a uniformly circular extended source of diameter D, then:
  (a) Determine the size of the smeared Fourier spectra as a function of f and p_0.
  (b) If $D = 2$ mm, $p_0 = 80\pi$ rad/mm, and $f = 30$ cm, determine the precise size of the smeared Fourier spectra.

4.8 Consider the effect of the input signal transparency of Problem 4.6. If the spatial bandwidth of the input object transparency is p_1, which is smaller in comparison with the spatial frequency of the diffraction grating (i.e., $p_1 \ll 2p_0$), then:
  (a) What is the smearing length of the Fourier spectra, if the white-light is a point source?
  (b) If the white-light source is a uniformly circular extended source of diameter D, what is the size of the smeared Fourier spectra?
  (c) If the spatial bandwidth of the input object is $p_1 = 20\pi$ rad/mm, the spatial frequency of the phase grating is $p_0 = 80\pi$ rad/mm, and the focal length of the achromatic transform lens is $f = 30$ cm, what is the size of the smeared Fourier spectra?

4.9 For a coherent processing operation, the spatial filter function is a binary wedge-shaped filter, as shown in Figure 4.26. Show that the

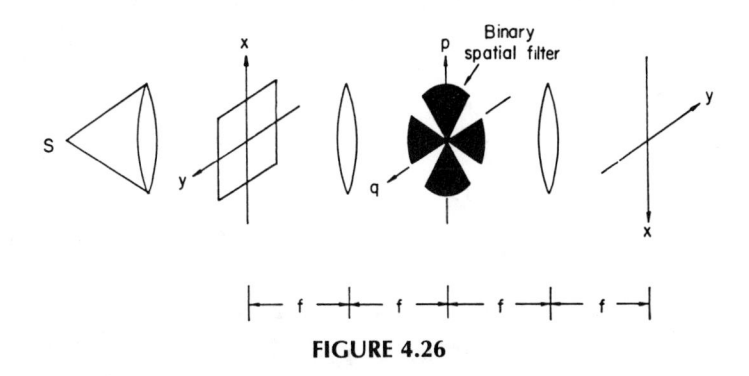

FIGURE 4.26

optical processing operation can be used with a white-light source instead of a coherent source.

4.10 Consider a white-light processing system as given in Figure 4.27. We assume a uniform circular source size of $\Delta s = 2$ mm in diameter. The spectral distribution is uniformly flat from 700 nm to 350 nm, and the maximum spatial frequency content of the object $f(x, y)$ is about 20 lines/mm. Calculate the minimum sampling frequency of the grating such that the first-order smeared Fourier spectrum can be made entirely separate from the zero-order spectrum.

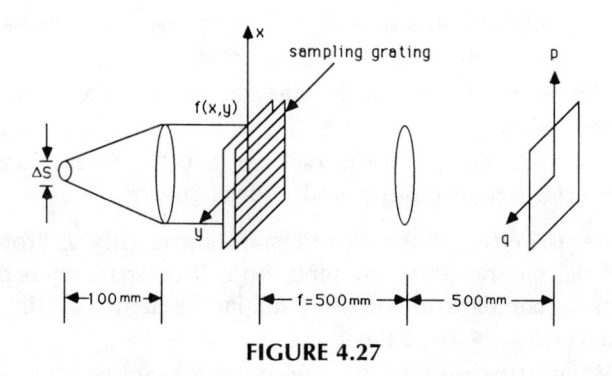

FIGURE 4.27

4.11 Given a temporal coherent image subtractor as shown in Figure 4.28:
  (a) Determine the spatial-frequency requirement of the filter grating G at the Fourier plane.
  (b) Evaluate the output complex light distribution.
  (c) Calculate the source size requirement for this subtractor.
  (d) Assuming that the separation of input objects is 2 cm, the focal length of the condensing lens is $f_1 = 10$ cm, and the wavelength of the light source is $\lambda = 600$ nm, calculate the source size requirements along the vertical and the horizontal directions.

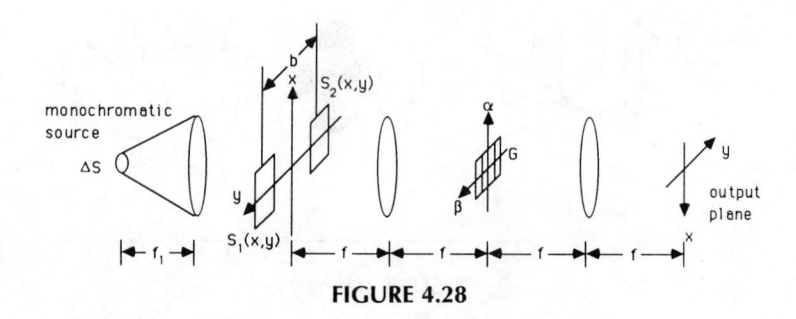

FIGURE 4.28

4.12 Suppose the mutual coherence function at the input plane of a partially coherent optical signal processing system is computed as given by

$$\Gamma(x) = \frac{1}{2}[\delta(x - h_0) + \delta(x + h_0)] + \delta(x),$$

where $x = x_2 - x_2'$. Evaluate a source encoding mask $s(x_1)$ so that the specified mutual coherence function can be obtained with the encoded extended source.

4.13 With reference to Young's experiment of Figure 4.5, if we wish to extend the source encoding concept over a three-dimensional space near a three-dimensional extended source:
  (a) Describe the appropriate encoding process such that a high degree of the mutual coherence at plane P_1 may be obtained.
  (b) Estimate the increased available light power at P_1.

4.14 Consider a spatially incoherent processor, as depicted in Figure 4.29. We assume that the spatial coherence function at the input plane is given by

$$\Gamma(|x - x'|) = \text{rect}\left[\frac{|x - x'|}{\Delta x}\right],$$

which is independent of y.
  (a) Evaluate the transmittance function of the source encoding mask.
  (b) Is the source encoding mask of part (a) physically realizable? Give the reason for your answer.
  (c) Design a physically realizable source encoding mask that has a coherence distance equal to $2\Delta x$.

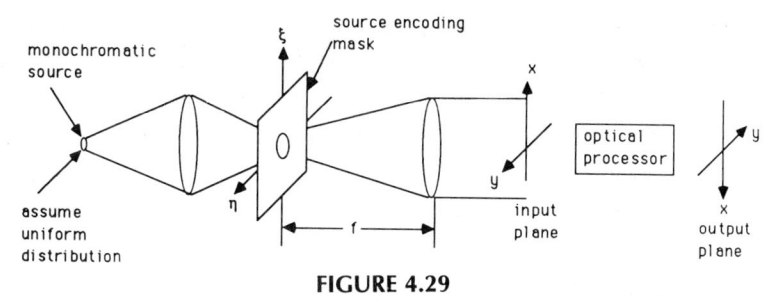

FIGURE 4.29

4.15 Suppose that the amplitude transmittance of an input object transparency is

$$T(x, y) = s(x, y)[1 + \text{sgn}(\cos p_0 x)],$$

where

$$\text{sgn}(\cos p_0 x) \triangleq \begin{cases} 1, & \cos(p_0 x) > 0, \\ 0, & \cos(p_0 x) = 0, \\ -1, & \cos(p_0 x) < 0, \end{cases}$$

p_0 is the spatial sampling frequency, $s(x, y)$ is the input signal, and (x, y) is the spatial coordinate system. Assuming that the sampling frequency is more than twice the spatial bandwidth of $s(x, y)$, show that the input signal $s(x, y)$ can be recovered with a white-light optical information processing technique. Why does this optical processing operation not require a coherent source?

4.16 Let us consider the white-light multi-image regeneration technique.
  (a) Design a set of diffraction grating filters so that an $m \times n$ array of images can be generated.
  (b) If we assume that a white-light point source is used and that the spatial bandwidth of the input object is about 20 lines/mm, what are the minimum spatial frequency and the maximum spectral bandwidth requirements of the grating filters by which the minimum color blurring of the regenerated images can be obtained.

4.17 Referring to the white-light photographic image deblurring of Section 4.6.1, if the linear smeared length is about 1 mm, then:
  (a) What are the spatial and temporal coherence requirements for the deblurring process with an incoherent source?
  (b) In order to achieve the spatial coherence requirement, what is the requirement of the light source?
  (c) In order to obtain the temporal coherence requirement, what is the minimum sample frequency of the diffraction grating $T(x)$?

4.18 With reference to Problem 4.17:
  (a) Design a fan-shaped deblurring filter such that the deblurring can take place with the whole spectral band of the white-light source.
  (b) Referring to the fan-shaped deblurring filter in part (a), evaluate the deblurred image intensity at the output image plane.

4.19 If the spatial-frequency limit of the blurred image of Problem 4.18 is about 25 lines/mm, estimate the degree of the deblurring error.

4.20 A distant object moves at a variable speed, at which it is recorded on photographic film. If the amplitude transmittance of this recorded smeared image is

$$T(x, y) = s(x, y) * \left[\exp\left(-\frac{x^2}{2}\right) \text{rect}\left(\frac{x}{2}\right) \right], \quad |x| \leq 1 \text{ mm},$$

where $s(x, y)$ is the object image, design a white-light optical processing system and the fan-shaped spatial filter to deblur the image. (*Note:* The source size, the frequency, and the size of the deblurred filter should be specified.)

4.21 Assume that the object image is linearly smeared in the x direction and then in the y direction so that the transmittance of the recorded photographic image is

$$T(x, y) = s(x, y) * \text{rect}\left(\frac{x}{\Delta x}\right)\text{rect}\left(\frac{y}{\Delta y}\right),$$

where $s(x, y)$ is the unsmeared object image, and Δx and Δy are the smeared length in the x and y axes, respectively. Design a white-light optical processor with the deblurring filters to unsmear the image.

4.22 Consider the image subtraction with the encoded extended source discussed in Section 4.6.2. Assume that the spatial frequencies of the input object transparencies are about 10 lines/mm.
  (a) Calculate the temporal coherence requirement.
  (b) If the main separation of the two input object transparencies is 20 mm and the focal length of the achromatic transform lenses is 300 mm, design a spatial filter and a source encoding mask to produce point-pair spatial coherence for the processing operation.
  (c) Calculate the visibility of the subtracted image.

4.23 Consider the image subtraction of Problem 4.22. If a phase grating $T(x) = \exp[ip_0 x]$, where $p_0 = 100\pi$ rad/mm, is inserted in the input plane with the input object transparencies, design a source encoding mask and a fan-shaped spatial filter so that the subtraction process operation can take place with the whole spectral band of the light source.

4.24 We noted that image encoding for archival storage of color films takes place with spatial sampling. Let the amplitude transmittance of this encoded film be

$$t_p(x, y) = [T_r(x, y)(1 + \cos p_0 x) + T_b(x', y')(1 + \cos p_0 x')$$
$$+ T_g(x'', y'')(1 + \cos p_0 x'')]^{\gamma/2},$$

where $\gamma = \gamma_{n1}\gamma_{n2}$, and (x, y), (x', y'), and (x'', y'') are 0°, 60°, and 120° coordinate systems.
  (a) Referring to Figure 4.19, evaluate the complex Fourier spectra at the spatial frequency plane for $\gamma = 4$.
  (b) In color image retrieval, show that color cross talk cannot be eliminated.

156   PARTIALLY COHERENT PROCESSING

4.25 Given an image transparency containing only two primary-color images (e.g., red and green), if the encoding takes place sequentially with a sinusoidal grating rotated by 90° so that the amplitude transmittance of the encoded film is

$$t_p(x, y) = [T_r(x, y)(1 + \cos p_0 x) + T_g(x, y)(1 + \cos p_0 y)]^{\gamma/2},$$

where $\gamma = \gamma_{n1}\gamma_{n2}$, then:
- (a) Evaluate the Fourier spectra at the spatial-frequency plane for the case $\gamma \neq 2$.
- (b) For color image decoding, show that color cross talk can be completely eliminated.

4.26 With reference to the color image encoding process of Section 4.6.4, the same objective may be achieved by the white-light processing technique shown in Figure 4.30, where W is the extended white-light source, $s(x, y)$ is the color transparency, $T(x, y)$ is a two-dimensional sinusoidal grating, and P_3 is the output image plane. For simplicity, we assume that the input color object transparency $s(x, y)$ contains only red and green colors.
- (a) Calculate the corresponding Fourier spectra as a function of the spectral wavelength of the light source at plane p_2.
- (b) Evaluate the irradiance of the encoded image at the output plane p_3.

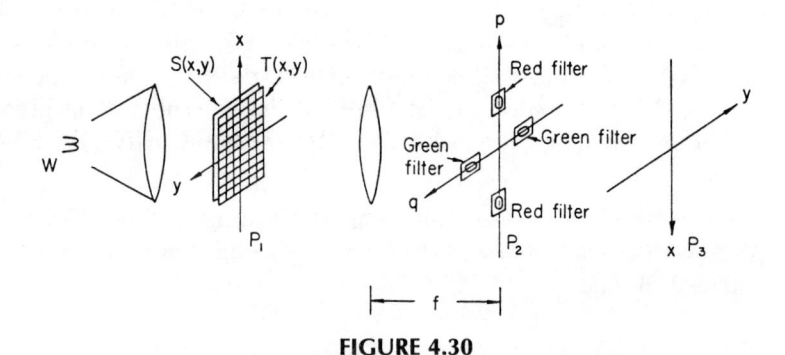

FIGURE 4.30

4.27 Let us consider spatial-frequency pseudocoloring of a black-and-white object transparency with a white-light processor. We assume that the low spatial-frequency content of the input object is known a priori.
- (a) Design a multicolor spatial filter so that the low and high spatial-frequency signals can be encoded in two different color transparencies.
- (b) Evaluate the intensity distribution of the pseudocolor image at the output plane.

PROBLEMS 157

(c) If precise spatial-frequency content of the input object is known, is it possible to color code the object with a multicolor spatial filter? If yes, provide an example.

4.28 (a) Design a real-time white-light density pseudocolor encodor with phase contrast reversal, utilizing a one-dimensional diffraction grating technique and color spatial filtering.

(b) Describe the technique of obtaining a phase contrast reversal filter, and design the density pseudocolor spatial filter.

(c) Through a step-by-step evaluation, show that real-time density pseudocolor encoding may be obtained by a white-light optical processing technique.

4.29 It is known that the integrated-circuit mask is generally a two-dimensional cross-grating-type pattern. The corresponding Fourier spectrum may be represented in a finite region of spatial frequency plane as depicted in Figure 4.31.

(a) Design a white-light optical processing technique for the integrated-circuit mask inspection.

(b) Carry out a detailed analysis to show that any defects can be easily detected through color coding.

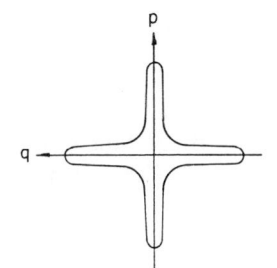

FIGURE 4.31

4.30 With reference to the linear smeared color image deblurring, we assume that the smeared length is 1 mm, the spatial frequency of the phase grating $T(x)$ is 100π rad/mm, and the focal length of the transformer lens is 300 mm.

(a) Design a color deblurring filter that takes the effects of the whole spectral band of the white-light source.

(b) Evaluate the spatial coherence and temporal requirement for the color image deblurring.

(c) Evaluate the requirement of source size to achieve an optimum utilization of the light source.

4.31 If the color image deblurring is performed by a fan-shaped deblurring filter, then:

(a) Evaluate the deblurred color image that takes place with the entire color spectral band of the white-light source.

158 PARTIALLY COHERENT PROCESSING

- (b) Show that the degree of deblurred errors depends upon the spatial frequency of the input sampling grating T and the size of the light source.

4.32 Let us consider color image subtraction with encoded incoherent sources.
- (a) Show that the color image subtraction technique can be extended to an encoded white-light source.
- (b) Let us assume that the input objects are spatial-frequency limited to ω rad/mm. Compute the minimum spatial-frequency requirement for the sampling grating, the source encoding mask, and the spatial filter.
- (c) Show that complex color image subtraction can be observed at the output plane of the white-light processor.

4.33 We wish to perform spatial-frequency pseudocolor encoding of an input object transparency with a white light.
- (a) Sketch a white-light processor that can perform this task.
- (b) We wish to encode low spatial frequency in red and high spatial frequency in blue. Sketch a spatial filter that can perform this operation.

4.34 The amplitude transmittance function of a multiplexed transparency, with a positive and a negative image is given by

$$t(x, y) = t_1(x, y)(1 + \cos p_0 x) + t_2(x, y)(1 + \cos q_0 y),$$

where t_1 and t_2 are the positive and negative image functions, and p_0 and q_0 are the spatial sampling frequencies along the x and y axes, respectively. If this encoded transparency is inserted at the input plane of the white-light processor shown in Figure 4.19:
- (a) Evaluate the smeared spectra at the Fourier plane.
- (b) If the focal length of the transform lens is $f = 300$ mm, and the sampling frequencies are $p_0 = 80\pi$ and $q_0 = 60\pi$ rad/mm, compute the smearing length of the Fourier spectra. Assume that the spectral lines of the white-light source vary in length from 350 to 750 nm.
- (c) Design a set of transparent color filters by which the density or gray levels of the image can be encoded in pseudocolors at the output plane.
- (d) Compute the irradiance of the pseudocolor image.

4.35 To illustrate the noise immunity of the partially coherent system of Figure 4.4, we assume that the narrow spectral band filters are contaminated with additive white Gaussian noise, that is, $H_n(\alpha, \beta) + n(\alpha, \beta)$. Show that the output signal-to-noise ratio improves when the white-light source is used.

4.36 With reference to the white-light signal processor of Figure 4.4, we assume that the input object transparency is contaminated with a random phase noise $\phi_n(x, y)$, that is, $f(x, y)e^{i\phi_n(x,y)}$.
 (a) Evaluate the output light field using coherent and incoherent illuminations, respectively.
 (b) Show that the phase noise immunity can be achieved by using incoherent light.

4.37 Refer to the preceding problem, if the input object is imbedded in an amplitude noise, that is, $f(x, y) + n(x, y)$:
 (a) Evaluate the output light distribution under the coherent and the incoherent regimes.
 (b) Show that it might not be possible to get rid of the amplitude noise by using either coherent or incoherent illuminations.

4.38 Referring to the white-light speech spectrograph of Figure 4.24, we assume that the focal length of the transform lens is $f = 500$ mm.
 (a) Compute the spatial-frequency requirement of the sampling grating if it were to generate a 4-kHz bandwidth spectrograph.
 (b) Determine the width of the optical window by which a 300-Hz analysis (called wide-band) spectrogram can be generated.
 (c) Repeat part (b) for a 100-Hz analysis (called narrow-band) spectrogram.

CHAPTER FIVE

Spatial Light Modulators and Detectors

Both parallelism and interconnection are inherent in optics. This is obvious from the image formed by a lens and has been known for centuries. In other words, a lens can be used to transmit two-dimensional information in space [5.1]. The formation of an image is one aspect of the interconnection property of photons. Photons are scattered or emitted from the object and then dispersed by the lens. They finally intersect such that a distribution similar to the original pattern of the object is formed at the image plane. Unlike electrons, photons are easily redirected in space by optical means. Photons do not interact with each other; therefore, they pass through each other without any change. However, this property causes this a problem with data manipulation: how to process information carried by photons with respect to other information carried by other photons.

Data manipulation is usually performed by a spatial light modulator (SLM). For example, the write-in beam generates an interaction between material in an SLM, and the change in the material affects the readout beam. Thus information carried by photons can be effectively altered by other information-carrying photons. The coherence of the readout beam is not affected; only amplitude, phase, or polarization is modulated, which allows coherent or holographic processing to take place.

SLMs are devices that can modulate some properties of an optical wavefront, such as amplitude or intensity by absorption, phase by refractive index, and polarization by rotation. These devices form a critical part of optical information processors since they serve as input transducers and signal converters, as well as performing several basic processing operations on the optical wavefront. The information-bearing signals for the SLM can be electrical or optical, leading to two major classes of SLMs: electrically and optically addressed SLMs.

An electrically addressed SLM is usually constructed with a pixel structure.

Thus, the local optical wavefront is modulated at each individual pixel by electric signals. The advantage of an electrically addressed SLM is its capability of interfacing with electronic and optical systems. However, isolated pixels are required. This causes multiple diffraction patterns in coherent processing, which diminishes the processed energy of the information carrier. In addition, space utilization is inefficient due to the dead zone between electrodes.

In principle, an optically addressed SLM consists of a continuous structure for performing the modulation function. In general, the addressing optical image produces electric charge distribution over modulation material that generates secondary effects for electrooptic modulation. In this context, an optically addressed SLM can be described as a combination of a detector and a modulator. The advantage of an optically addressed SLM is its capability of modulating light by another light beam. The common disadvantage of optically addressed SLMs is the expensive fabrication cost. However, some SLMs, such as photorefractive and electron-trapping devices may consist simply of a crystal or a thin film coated on a transparent substrate.

5.1 ACOUSTOOPTIC MODULATOR

The interaction of light waves with acoustic (sound) waves has been the basis of a large number of devices connected to various laser systems for display, information handling, optical signal processing, and numerous other applications requiring the spatial and temporal modulation of coherent light [5.2]. The underlying mechanism of acoustooptic interaction is simply the change induced in the refractive index of an optical medium by the presence of an acoustic wave. An acoustic wave is a traveling pressure disturbance that produces regions of compression and rarefaction in material. These density variations cause corresponding changes in the refractive index of the material.

Acoustooptic (AO) modulators are usually used in laser systems for the electronic control of the intensity and position of the laser beam. When an acoustic wave is launched into the optical medium, it generates a refractive index wave that behaves like a sinusoidal phase grating. An incident laser beam passing through this grating diffracts the laser beam into several levels. The angular position of the selected diffraction order (e.g., the first order) is linearly proportional to the acoustic frequency, so that the higher the frequency, the larger the diffraction angle. The intensity of the diffracted light depends on the power of the acoustic wave, so that the intensity can be modulated.

The interaction between light and the acoustic wave produces a Bragg diffraction effect, as illustrated in Figure 5.1. The beam of light is incident upon a plane acoustic wave in the AO cell. This acoustic wave is emitted by a transducer driven by an electric signal. At a certain critical angle of incidence θ_1, the incident beam produces a coherent diffraction at an angle θ_d. The

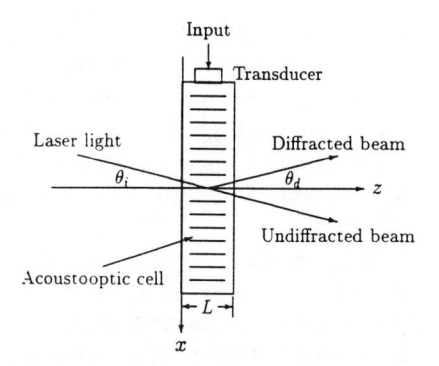

FIGURE 5.1 Operation of an acoustooptic cell.

second angle is known as the Bragg angle of diffraction and is given by

$$\sin \theta_d = \lambda/2\Lambda, \qquad (5.1)$$

where λ and Λ are the light and the acoustic wavelengths in the cell, respectively.

A variety of different AO materials are used depending on the laser parameters, such as laser wavelength, polarization, and power density. For the visible region and near-infrared region the modulators are usually made from dense flint glass, tellurium oxide (TeO_2), or fused quartz. At the infrared region, germanium is employed in an AO modulator. Lithium niobate ($LiNbO_3$) and gallium phosphide (GaP) are used for high-frequency signal processing devices.

There are certain physical constraints on the types of signal waveforms that can serve as input and the way in which AO modulators can be used. For example, acoustic waves emitted by the transducer into the medium usually cannot be seen if they are viewed by conventional optics. Moreover, the electric signals that drive the AO modulators must generally be band-pass in nature and have a frequency in the range of 1 MHz to 1 GHz. This restriction on input signals that are not originally band-pass in nature must be modulated with a carrier frequency that is suitable for input of the AO cell.

The limit of the rise and fall time of the AO modulator is the transit time of the acoustic wave propagation across the optical beam. A typical rise time for a 1-mm-diameter laser beam is around 150 ns. To achieve faster rise times, it is necessary to focus the laser beam and decrease the acoustic transit time. Also, in the AO interaction, the laser beam frequency is shifted by an amount equal to the acoustic frequency. This frequency shift can be used for heterodyne-detection applications, where precise phase information is measured.

5.2 MAGNETOOPTIC MODULATOR

A magnetooptic spatial light modulator (MOSLM) is a two-dimensional electronically addressed SLM [5.3]. The MOSLM is based on a magnetooptic effect generally known as the *Faraday effect*. The Faraday effect is a property of transparent substances that causes a rotation of polarization of light traversing the substance when the material is subjected to a magnetic field. The MOSLM consists of a square grid of magnetically bistable mesas (pixels) that can be used to modulate incident polarized light by the Faraday effect. The device can be electrically switched so that object patterns can be written with a computer. Thus this device could function as a programmable SLM.

The basic structure of the MOSLM is a bismuth-doped, magnetic iron-garnet film that is epitaxially deposited on a transparent, nonmagnetic garnet crystal substrate. The film is then etched into a square grid of magnetically bistable mesas, and current drive lines are deposited between them. The resulting device is an $n \times n$ matrix of mesas, as shown in Figure 5.2.

When linearly polarized light is incident on the device, the axis of the polarization of the transmitted light will be rotated by 45° clockwise for a magnetic state. The plane of polarization is rotated by 45° counterclockwise for opposite magnetic state, as shown in Figure 5.3. The magnetization state of the pixel can be changed by sending current to its two adjoining drive lines. An analyzer can convert the polarization rotation into a useful input for an optical processor. If the analyzer is set at the direction making a 45° angle with the original light polarization, intensity or brightness modulation will be obtained. Alternatively, the analyzer can be set at the direction parallel to the original light polarization to generate phase modulation, which is desired for the formation of a phase-only filter [5.4].

The MOSLM has a storage capability, since the magnetization state of the substance remains as a stable state. The state is switched by current. This current can generate heat, due to ohmic losses, that limits the performance of the MOSLM. The switching speed of the magnetic domain itself in these

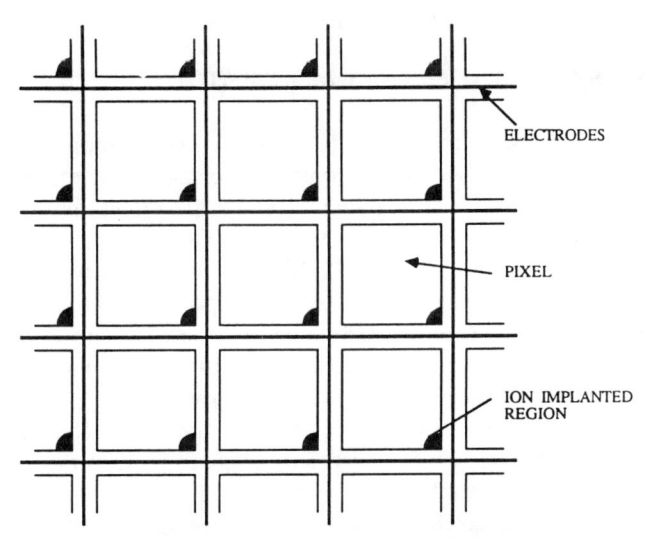

FIGURE 5.2 Structure of MOSLM pixels.

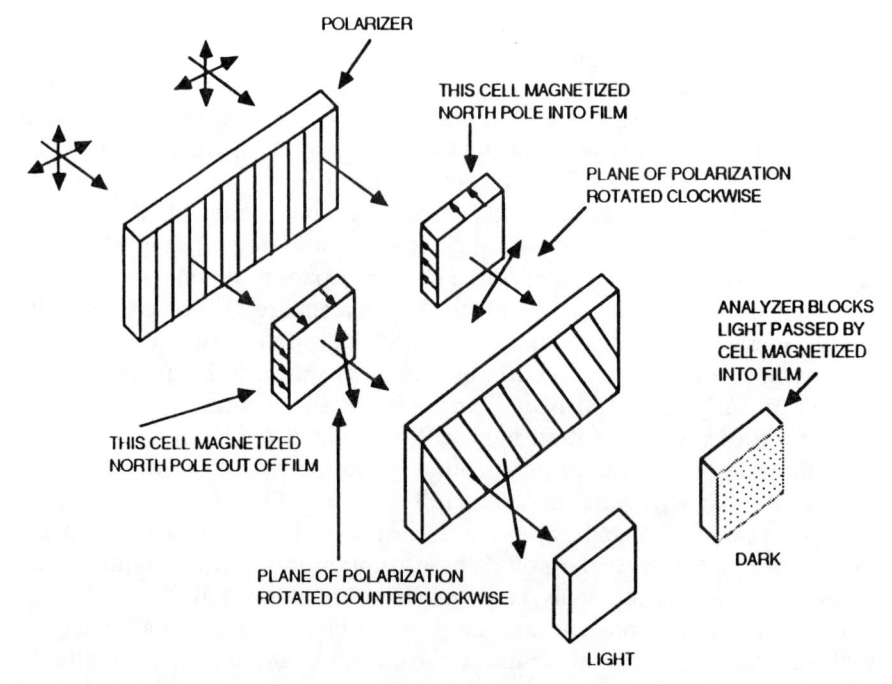

FIGURE 5.3 Operation of MOSLM as a light valve.

devices can be very fast—of the order of tens of nanoseconds. Also, 256 × 256 array devices are available. The typical pixel size is 60 μm, the frame rate is 100 Hz, and the contrast ratio is > 200:1; however, the transmittance of a bright pixel is only 5 percent.

5.3 POCKEL'S READOUT OPTICAL MODULATOR

A Pockel's readout optical modulator (PROM) is a two-dimensional optically addressed SLM that is based on an important electrooptic effect known as the *Pockel's effect* [5.2]. It is a linear electrooptic effect inasmuch as the induced birefringence is proportional to the applied electric field across an asymmetric crystal. Therefore, under Pockel's effect, the crystal can change the polarization of the light. The change of the polarization is controlled by the applied electric field. There are two common configurations referred to as *transverse* and *longitudinal*, depending on whether the applied electric field is perpendicular or parallel to the direction of propagation, respectively.

PROM is fabricated from various electrooptic crystals, such as ZnS, ZnSe, and $Bi_{12}SiO_{20}$ (BSO). The basic construction of the PROM device is shown in Figure 5.4. The electrooptic crystal wafer is sandwiched between two transparent electrodes and separated from them by an insulator. The crystal wafer

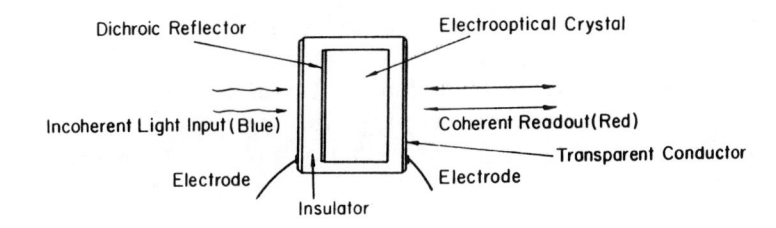

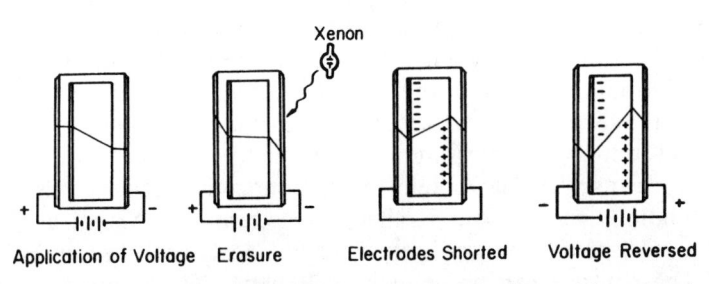

FIGURE 5.4 Composition of the PROM device and its operation.

is oriented in such a way that the field applied between the electrodes produces a longitudinal electrooptic effect. The operation of the PROM device is also illustrated in the figure. An applied dc voltage with an erase light pulse is used to create mobile carriers that cause the voltage V_0 in the active crystal to decay to zero. The polarity of the applied voltage is brought to zero and then reversed. When a total voltage of $2V_0$ appears across the crystal, the device is exposed to the illumination pattern of blue light. The voltage in the area exposed to the bright part of the input pattern decays because of the optically created mobile carriers, but the voltage in the dark area remains unchanged, thus converting the intensity pattern into a voltage pattern. The relation between input exposure and voltage across the crystal is given by

$$V_c = V_0 e^{-KE}, \tag{5.2}$$

where V_0 is the applied voltage and K is a positive constant. The readout is performed with a red linearly polarized light (e.g., He–Ne laser). For BSO, the crystal is 200 times more sensitive in the blue region (400 nm) than in the red region (633 nm). Therefore, reading with an He–Ne light source in real time does not produce significant voltage decay over a period of time.

The readout is performed by reflection. In this readout mode, the area of the crystal where the voltage across it has not been affected by the input light intensity acts like a half-wave retardation plate. The angle of polarization of the linearly polarized laser light input reflected by such an area is therefore rotated by 90°. Thus the light reflected by the area corresponding to the bright region has a polarization perpendicular to that of the dark region. The re-

166 SPATIAL LIGHT MODULATORS AND DETECTORS

flected light is then passed through a polarizer, and the amplitude of the transmitted light is attenuated according to the polarization of the input.

The theoretical curve for amplitude A of output coherent light versus exposure E of input incoherent light is plotted in Figure 5.5. We see that it has a transfer characteristic similar to that of a photographic film, a linear region with a range between $E = 2/K$ and $E = 0$, and a bias point at $E = 1/K$ (see Section 5.10).

The PROM device has some drawbacks, however. For example, the fabrication of the device still needs refinement to improve the uniformity and consistency of the crystal. In addition, the device needs a narrower band-pass in its spectral sensitivity. Any extended exposure to high-intensity readout light causes substantial decay of the crystal voltage, thus reducing the read amplitude of the device. Therefore, the device cannot be read over an extended period of time under strong illumination.

PROM can be used for incoherent-to-coherent conversion, amplitude and phase modulation, and optical parallel logic operation. A typical PROM requires 5 to 600 $\mu J/cm^2$ optical write energy. The typical resolution is 100 lines/mm. The contrast can be as high as 10000:1. The write–read–erase cycle can be repeated indefinitely, with operation at video frame rates (30 Hz). The write and erase times can be less than 0.1 ms.

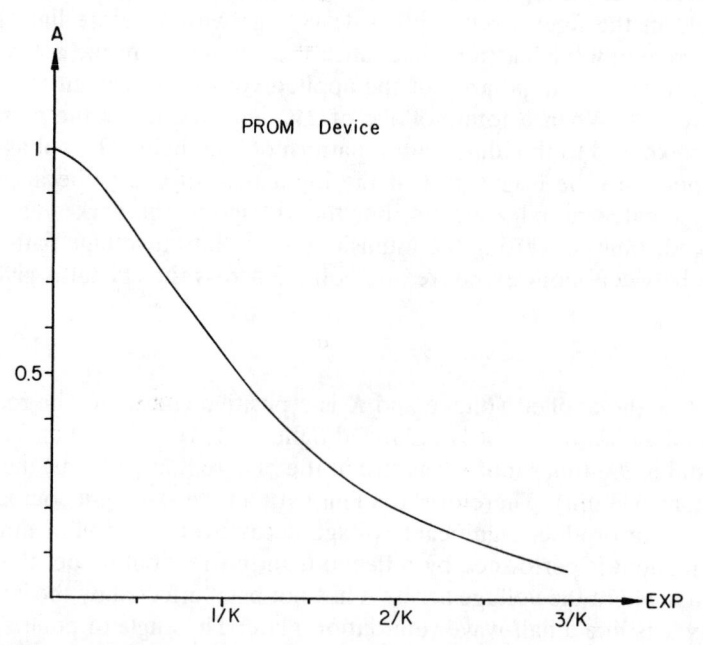

FIGURE 5.5 Amplitude reflectance of the PROM device as a function of exposure to input coherent light.

5.4 MICROCHANNEL PLATE MODULATOR

The microchannel plate spatial light modulator (MSLM) is another two-dimensional optically addressed SLM that has frequently been used in real-time optical signal processing and computing [5.5]. The MSLM is an optically addressed device that has a high level of optical sensitivity. The basic structure of an MSLM is illustrated in Figure 5.6. It consists of a photocathode, a microchannel plate (MCP), an accelerating mesh electrode, and an electrooptic crystal plate of $LiNbO_3$ that bears, on its inner side, a high-resistivity dielectric mirror to isolate the readout from the write-in side. Some MSLMs have more than one mesh electrode to improve the electrostatic imaging and focusing. All these components are seals in a vacuum tube.

The basic operation of an MSLM is shown in Figure 5.7. The write-in light (coherent or incoherent image) incident on the photocathode generates a photoelectron image, which is multiplied to about 10^5 times by the MCP, accelerated by the mesh electrode, and deposited on the dielectric mirror of the $LiNbO_3$ crystal plate. The process of electron multiplication is similar to that in an image intensifier tube. The resulting charge distribution, in combination with the biasing voltage, creates a spatially varying electric field within the crystal plate in the direction of the optical axis. This field in turn modulates the refractive indices of the crystal plate. Because of the birefringence property of the $LiNbO_3$ crystal, its refractive indices in the horizontal and vertical planes are modulated differently. Thus, after twice passing the crystal plane, the readout light, which was originally polarized in a plane bisecting the X and Y axes of the crystal plate, will have a relative phase retardation between its x and y components. The higher the charge density, the greater the phase retardation. If an analyzer is inserted in the readout light path as shown in the figure, a coherent image that is proportional to the input image can be obtained. Generally speaking, not only is the MSLM an incoherent-to-coherent converter, but it can be applied as a wavelength converter, as an input or output transducer, and to image plane or Fourier plane processing.

The versatility of the device comes from its architecture. As just described, photoelectron generation, intensification, transfer, deposit, readout light

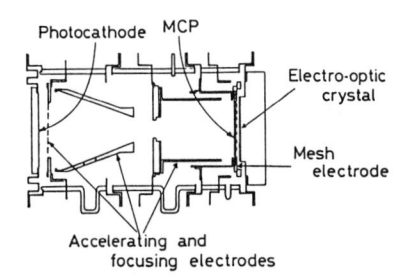

FIGURE 5.6 Structure of an MSLM.

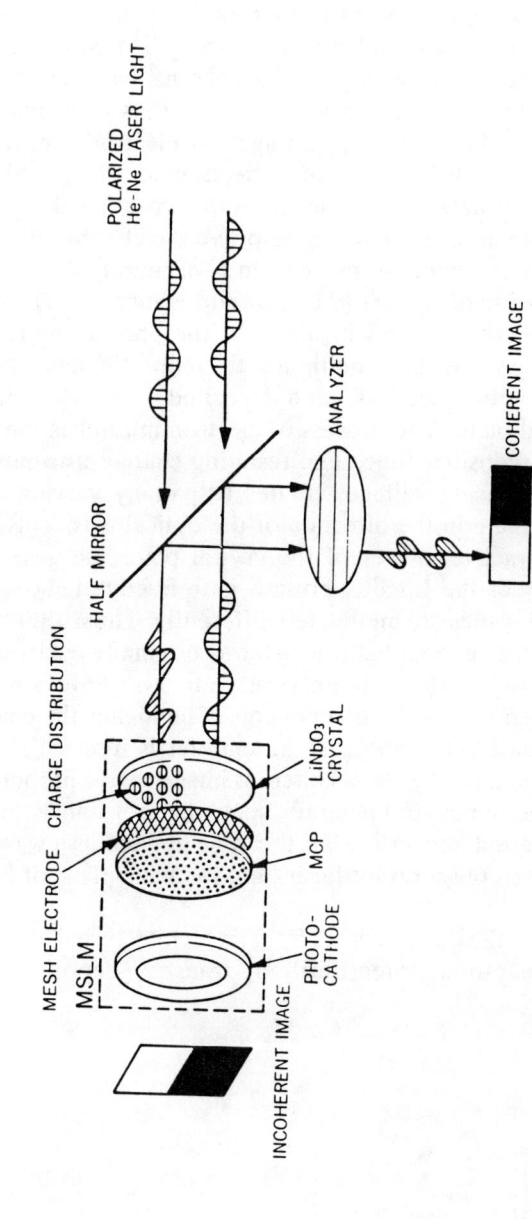

FIGURE 5.7 Operation of an MSLM as a light valve.

modulation, and detection are performed by each functional component. An important feature of an MSLM is that the device can hold an image memory (charge distribution) for a period of time. Since the output image is produced by the charge distribution, the MSLM can perform addition and subtraction by superimposing the charge distributions generated by two input images. Subtraction is performed by reversing the polarity of the biasing voltage. In addition, optical thresholding can be demonstrated by varying the biasing voltage [5.6].

The typical performance specifications of commercially available MSLMs are as follows. The spatial resolution is about 20 lines/mm, the contrast ratio is more than 1000:1, the input sensitivity is around 30 nJ/cm^2, the maximum readout light intensity is 0.1 W/cm^2, writing time response is about 10 ms, erasing time is about 20 ms, storage time is several days, and the input window diameter is 15 mm.

5.5 LIQUID CRYSTAL LIGHT VALVE

Another example of an optically addressed spatial light modulator is the liquid crystal light valve (LCLV) [5.7]. Most of us are familiar with liquid crystal materials from their use in the display panels of digital wristwatches and calculators. In fact, liquid crystal displays have found their way into portable laboratory equipments, kitchen appliances, automobile dashboards, and many other applications requiring good visibility, low power consumption, and special display geometries. Most of these applications use the liquid crystal in a twisted nematic cell; a segment of the cell is either opaque or transparent (binary), depending on the magnitude of the applied electric voltage. However, the LCLV combines the property of the twisted nematic cell in the off state with the property of electrically tunable birefringence to control transmittance over a wide continuous range in the on state.

A simplified sketch of a transmission-type twisted nematic cell is shown in Figure 5.8a. A thin layer (1 to 20 μm) of nematic liquid crystal is sandwiched

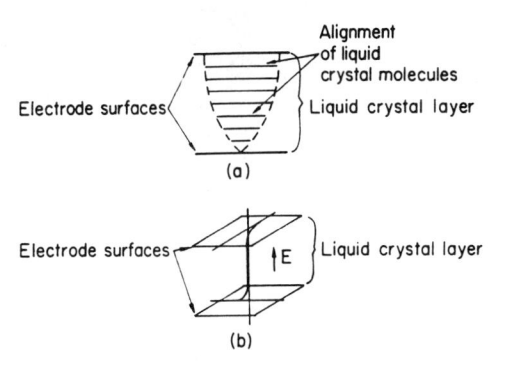

FIGURE 5.8 (a) Twisted nematic liquid crystal layer with no electric field applied. (b) Molecular alignment in the direction of the applied electric field E.

between two transparent electrode-coated glass plates. The electrode surfaces are treated to preferred direction of alignment for the liquid crystal molecules. The plates are so arranged that, with no electric voltage applied across the layer of liquid crystal molecules, the layer is twisted continuously by 90°. A polarizer and an analyzer are placed in front of and behind the sandwiched cell, respectively. The direction in which the light passing through the polarizer is polarized must be the same as the direction of molecular alignment at the front electrode surface. As the light passes through the twisted liquid crystal layer, its direction of polarization is also twisted by 90°. If we make the direction of polarization of the analyzer perpendicular to the direction of molecular alignment at the back electrode surface, the polarized light will not exit the cell, and the device will be in its dark state.

An interesting phenomenon occurs when a voltage is applied across the twisted nematic liquid crystal layer. The molecules tend to align themselves in the direction of the applied electric field—that is, perpendicular to the electrode surfaces. The resulting splay and bend of the molecules is shown in Figure 5.8b. Thus, if the polarizer and the analyzer have parallel directions of polarization, the polarized light will pass unaffected through the liquid crystal layer and the analyzer, which is the on state for a liquid crystal alphanumeric display. However, this on state behavior is not exhibited in the LCLV.

The LCLV takes advantage of the pure birefringence of the liquid crystal material in order to modulate the output laser beam while in the on state. Operation of the LCLV is clarified in the side view of Figure 5.9. An incoherent image is focused onto the photoconductor (CdS–CdTe) layer to gate

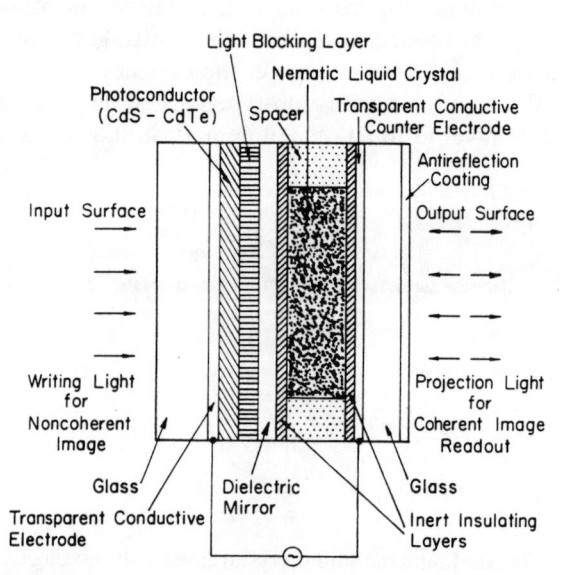

FIGURE 5.9 Side view of a liquid crystal light valve (LCLV) and its operation.

the applied alternating voltage to the liquid crystal layer in response to the input intensity at every point in the input space. Laser light illuminating the back of the LCLV is reflected back, but modulated by the birefringence of the liquid crystal layer at every point. In order to achieve this effect, the molecular alignment has a 45° twist between the two surfaces of the liquid crystal layer. The dielectric mirror plays an important role by providing optical isolation between the input incoherent light and the coherent readout beam. As with the MOSLM, a phase filter can be generated by properly orienting the analyzer.

In addition to incoherent-to-coherent conversion and other coherent processing applications, the LCLV is also used as a wavelength converter. An infrared image can be generated by passing an infrared beam through the LCLV, which is modulated by a visible image. This application is required for the test of military and remote-sensing equipment, which are generally operating in 3 to 5 μm and 8 to 12 μm bands [5.8]. It is worth noting that the resolution of the commercially available LCLV is about 60 lines/mm, and because of the slow response of the liquid crystals, the readout time is about 10 ms. The required write energy is typically 6 $\mu J/cm^2$.

5.6 LIQUID CRYSTAL TELEVISION

The liquid crystal television (LCTV) was originally produced as a pocket television set. With proper modification, a commercially available LCTV can be used as an electronically addressed SLM [5.9]. The basic structure of the LCTV is illustrated in Figure 5.10a. Two polarizing sheets are attached to the substrates with adhesive, one acting as the polarizer and the other as the analyzer. A plastic diffuser provides diffused illumination on one side, and a clear plastic window protects the device from dust on the opposite side. The pocket LCTV can be converted to a spatial light modulator as follows [5.2].

1. Open the case and break the hinge stops so that the LCTV screen can be open fully.
2. Disassemble the aluminum frame of the LCTV screen and remove the plastic diffuser and window from the frame.
3. Peel off the two polarizing sheets from the glass substrates.
4. Clean the substrates carefully with acetone.
5. Submerge the modified LCTV screen in an index-matching liquid gate, which will be used as a spatial light modulator, as illustrated in Figure 5.10b.

The last step is necessary to remove the phase noise distortion caused by the thin glass substrate. As consumer electronic technology rapidly progresses, new types of the LCTV screen, which can be modified to SLMs for coherent processing applications, will appear. To name two, they are LCTV display

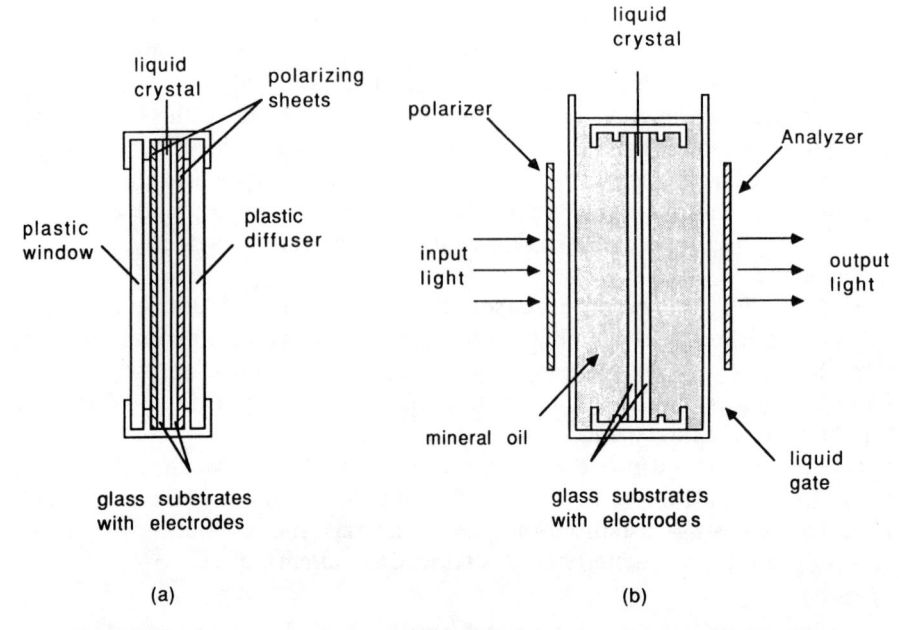

FIGURE 5.10 Structure of an LCTV. (*a*) Original structure. (*b*) Modified structure.

panels for projection TV and LCTV screens for video camera view finders. These newly introduced products generally show better contrast, resolution, and space–bandwidth product.

The LCTV is similar to the LCLV. The operation of an LCTV is illustrated in Figure 5.11. Each liquid crystal cell of the LCTV screen is a nematic liquid crystal twisted 90°. The cell is individually controlled by electronic signals. When no electric field is applied, the plane of polarization for linearly polarized light is rotated through 90° by the twisted liquid crystal molecules. Thus no light can be transmitted through the analyzer, as illustrated in the upper part of the figure. Under an applied electric field, however, the twist and the tilt of the molecules are altered, and the liquid crystal molecules attempt to align parallel with the applied field, which results in partial transmission of light through the analyzer. As the electric field increases further, all the liquid crystal molecules align in the direction of the applied field. The molecules do not affect the plane of polarization, so all the light passes through the analyzer, as shown in the lower part of the figure. In general, an analyzer parallel with (0°) and orthogonal to (90°) the polarizer will produce a positive and negative image, respectively. If the analyzer is set at 45°, a phase modulation can be obtained.

Varying the applied voltage at each liquid crystal cell allows light transmission to be varied. If the applied voltages of the LCTV screen are generated from a computer, a video camera, or a TV receiver, the LCTV screen can produce gray-scale images.

LIQUID CRYSTAL TELEVISION   173

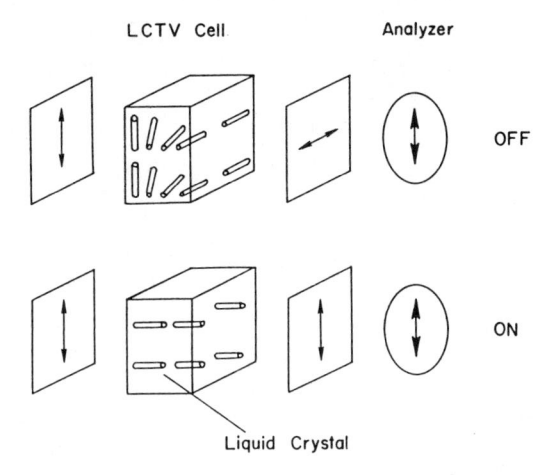

FIGURE 5.11   Basic operation of an LCTV as an SLM.

The major advantages of the LCTV are its low cost (because of mass production) and programmability, which make the device a very practical SLM for many optical signal processing, computing, and neural network applications. However, since LCTVs are made for consumer video display, the field rate is limited to 60 Hz, although the contrast, resolution, and the number of pixels are being significantly improved. At the present time, pixels of LCTV can be made smaller than 50 μm^2, with a contrast ratio better than 100:1.

An LCTV can also be used to generate an infrared scene for testing infrared imaging systems [5.10]. The infrared image generated by an LCTV is illustrated in Figure 5.12. A videotape containing dynamic scenes of tanks is used to drive the LCTV. A pair of infrared polarizers are used to replace the

FIGURE 5.12   Infrared image generated by an LCTV.

original visible light polarizers. The LCTV is illuminated with infrared light. The modulated infrared beam is detected by a CCD camera and displayed on a video monitor, as shown in Figure 5.12.

5.7 DEFORMABLE MIRROR DEVICE

Another example of an electronically addressed SLM is the deformable mirror device (DMD) [5.11]. The DMD involves the mechanical deformation of the modulator in response to electrostatic force. The modulating elements of the DMD are tiny metal mirrors. These mirrors are fabricated to form the cantilever beam structure over an underlying silicon address structure. A cross section of an individual mirror element is shown schematically in Figure 5.13. The mirror and the underlying address structure form an air-gap capacitor that is typically 2 to 3 μm wide. The addressing structure, which is a transistor array, allows a prescribed amount of charge to be deposited below each mirror. The amount of deflection of the mirror is determined by electrostatic attraction.

Each pixel consists of four cantilever-beam mirrors, each of which is approximately 12.7 μm^2. The 128 × 128-element array can be addressed by a single analog input with a data rate as high as 20 MHz. It is designed to operate at a rate of 150 frames/sec. In contrast to other SLMs, this particular SLM modulates the phase or the optical path length of the light beam. However, intensity modulation can be obtained by using a schlieren optical system. The contrast ratio of the resultant intensity modulation is approximately 2:1.

5.8 OPTICAL DISK

Optical disks have found numerous applications in the past decade. Especially, audio optical disks or compact disks (CDs) have been rapidly penetrating the consumer market. A CD can be utilized as an SLM to modulate the phase of the light beam as the DMD does (see Section 5.7). In the field of data storage, the optical disk system has been used for a computer peripheral

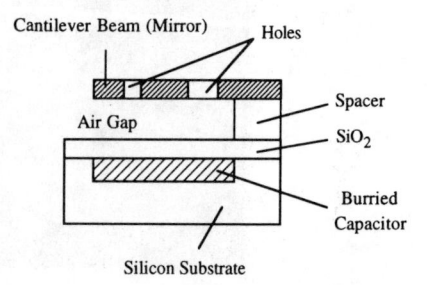

FIGURE 5.13 Side view of an element of a DMD.

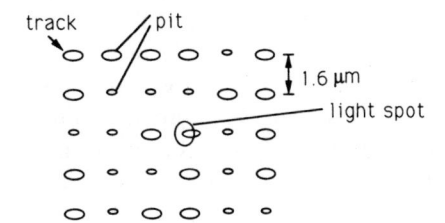

FIGURE 5.14 Structure of a compact disk.

device called CD-ROM (read-only memory). In principle, information is stored using a string of pits on the surface of the CD.

Figure 5.14 shows the basic structure of a CD. The recorded signal is encoded in the length of the pit and the spacing of the pits along the track. The distance between two adjacent tracks (track pitch) is 1.6 μm. The width of a pit is equal to a recording spot size of 0.5 to 0.7 μm. The light source used in the optical disk system is usually a GaAlAs semiconductor laser diode with a wavelength of 0.78 to 0.83 μm. The spot size of the readout beam is determined by the numerical aperture (NA) of the objective lens. Typically, $\lambda/NA = 1.55$ is chosen, so the effective diameter of the readout spot is approximately 1 μm. The spot size is larger than the width of a pit, but a single readout spot does not cover two tracks (see Figure 5.14).

The optical pickup is shown in Figure 5.15. When there is no pit (Figure 5.15a), the light will be fully reflected to the detector. When there is a pit, the focused beam will cover both pit and the surrounding land (Figure 5.15b). Keep in mind that both pit and land are coated with high-reflectivity material (e.g., Al), so light is reflected from both the pit and the land. The depth of pit is made such that the phase difference between the reflected light from a pit and a land is π. Consequently, should a destructive interference occur at the detector, less light will be detected. The pit depth is typically 0.13 μm.

We are interested, however, in the SLM aspect of an optical disk rather than its sequential data storage aspect. To function as an SLM, the optical

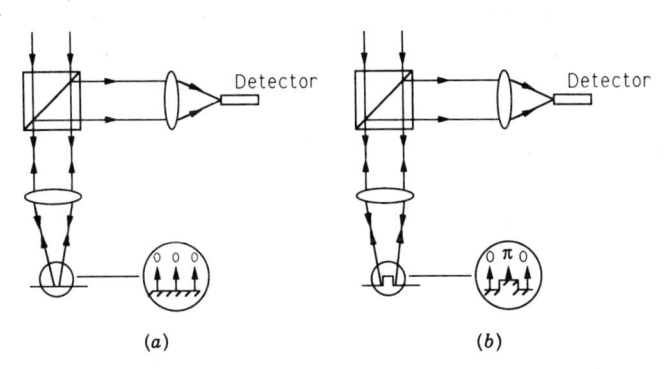

FIGURE 5.15 Optical pickup operation of a compact disk. (*a*) Bright reflection. (*b*) Dark reflection.

disk must be read out in parallel. As a consequence, the disk could be considered a pixelated SLM with 0.7-μm pixel diameter and 1.6-μm cross-track pixel spacing. While cross-track pixel spacing is set by a manufacturing standard (1.6 μm), along-track pixel spacing can be varied, so a similar 1.6-μm spacing can be selected. In contrast to other SLMs, the pixel format is not a Cartesian coordinate. The pixels (pits) are distributed on the tracks, which are concentric circles. However, if the readout collimated beam illuminates only a small sector of track, the polar format would be very close to the Cartesian coordinate. This small sector of an optical disk could consist of a large number of pixels when compared with that in an ordinary SLM. Since the pixel modulates the reflected light by a 0 or π phase shift, an optical disk can be used as a binary phase-modulating SLM. An optical disk can be employed to record and reconstruct a computer-generated hologram [5.12]. Further potential applications to neural network processing have been proposed [5.13]. This type of optical disk is inconvenient to optical engineers or researchers, since it requires the mastering process of CD.

While compact disks are primarily produced for the consumer market for which the copyright of the content (music, movie, or graphic and text) needs protection, an SLM optical disk must be easily writable by the user. An optical disk called WORM (write once, read many times) has also been commercially available. A WORM disk consists of either a polycarbonate or hardened-glass substrate and a recording layer made of a highly reflective substance (dye-polymer or tellurium alloy). As with the CD, the recording layer is covered by clear plastic to protect the recording medium. WORM disk systems use a laser beam to record data sequentially. A write beam burns a hole (pit) in the recoding medium to produce a change in the reflectivity. In contrast to the previously discussed compact disks, the WORM optical disk modulates the reflected intensity of the readout beam. A WORM optical disk system can be utilized for performing optical correlation [5.14]. The primary drawback of the system is that the disk is neither erasable nor rewritable.

An erasable and rewritable optical disk system is best represented by a magnetooptic (MO) disk akin to the MOSLM mentioned previously (see Section 5.2). The MO medium makes use of a recording material that at room temperature is resistant to changes in magnetization. The reversed magnetic field required to reduce the magnetization of the recording material to zero is called *coercivity*. In other words, the coercivity of the MO recording material at room temperature is quite high. The coercivity can be altered only at a high temperature that is defined as the *Curie point*. The typical Curie point of the MO material used is 150°C. The heat of the write laser beam brings the recording material to the Curie point. A bias magnet then reverses the magnetization of the heated area that represents a bit. As with the MOSLM, a low-power linearly polarized laser beam can be used to read the data on the MO disk. According to the Kerr magnetooptic effect, the polarization of the readout beam will be rotated to the left or right, depending on whether the magnetization of the recording material is upward or downward. At the present time, the typical rotation is less than 1°. In principle, the intensity modulation can be obtained by applying an analyzer.

5.9 PHOTOPLASTIC DEVICE

Photoplastic devices involve the surface deformation of a transparent layer, such that the phase of the light beam passing through the layer will be modulated [5.2]. The basic components of a photoplastic device are shown in Figure 5.16. The device is composed of a glass substrate that is coated with a transparent conductive layer (tin oxide or indium oxide), on the top of which is a layer of photoconductive material, followed by a layer of thermoplastic. For the photoconductor, poly-n-vinyl carbazole (PVK) sensitized with trinitrofluorenone (TNF) can be used with an ester resin thermoplastic (Hurculus Floral 105). The five steps in a typical operation cycle are shown in Figure 5.17. Before exposure, the device is charged either by a corona discharge or with a charging plate made of another transparent conductive material. The charging plate is separated from the device by a strip of 100-μ Mylar tape. After the charging process, the device can be exposed to the signal light that is usually an interference pattern of holographic fringes, which causes a variation in the charge pattern proportional to the intensity of the input light. The illuminated region displaces the charge from the transparent conductive layer to the photoplastic interface, which in turn reduces the surface potential of the outer surface of the thermoplastic, as shown in the figure. The device is then recharged to the original surface potential and developed by raising the temperature of the thermoplastic to the softening point and then rapidly reducing it to room temperature. The temperature

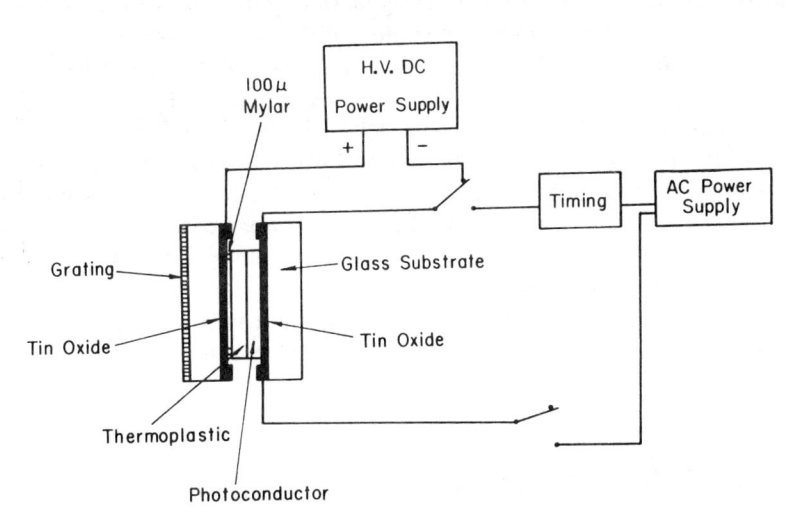

FIGURE 5.16 Composition of a photoplastic device.

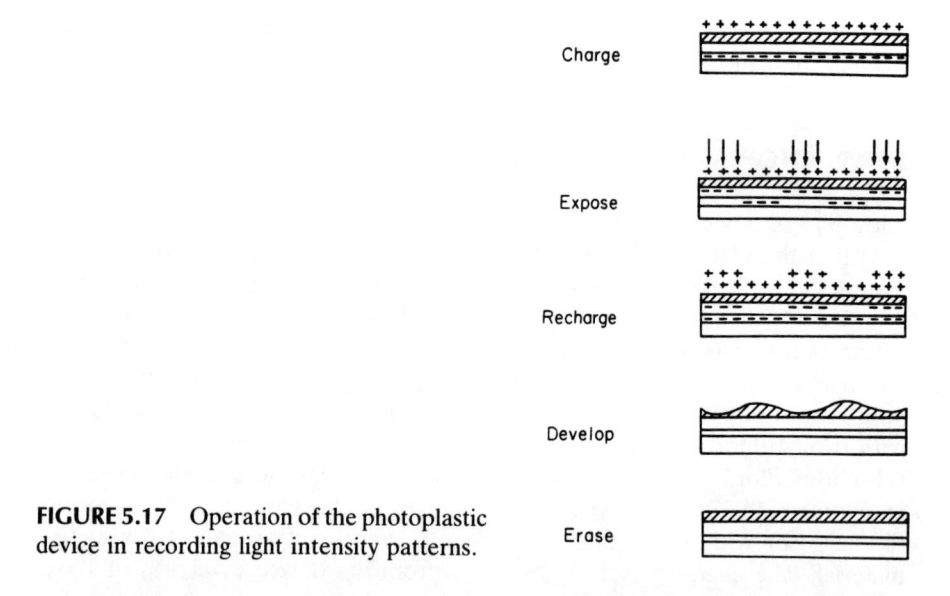

FIGURE 5.17 Operation of the photoplastic device in recording light intensity patterns.

reduction can be accomplished by passing an ac voltage pulse through the conductive layer. Surface deformation caused by the electrostatic force then produces a phase recording of the intensity of the input light. This recording can be erased by raising the temperature of the thermoplastic above the melting point, thus causing the surface tension of thermoplastic to flatten the surface deformation and erase the recording.

The frequency response of the photoplastic is poor at low frequencies. To use the device for recording signals with low spatial frequencies, we must modulate the signal with a sinusoidal signal of a spatial frequency corresponding to the peak of the frequency response of the device, which is typically 50 cycles/mm. This can be done by putting a sinusoidal grating in front of the thermoplastic device.

The advantage of the photoplastic device is its relatively low cost, which makes it a very practical recording device for use in holography, which does not require the wet processing that photographic film does. Its lifetime is limited to about 500 cycles, depending on laboratory conditions. The signal-to-noise ratio is relatively low because of the random thickness variation of the thermoplastic plate. Diffraction efficiencies of 10 percent with exposures of 60 μJ/cm^2 were reported, which is comparable to the sensitivity of a high-resolution photographic emulsion. The resolution can be higher than 2000 lines/mm.

5.10 PHOTOGRAPHIC FILM

Photographic film is the oldest spatial light modulator, although it is primarily considered a recording medium. The spatial light modulation effect of a photographic film is obvious, for instance, in a movie theater. The illuminating light is modulated by the movie films, and thus images are formed on the screen. In addition, photographic film or plates can be used for the synthesis of complex spatial filters, holograms, and two-dimensional signal transparencies for optical processing. There are other optical materials whose optical properties are similar to those of photographic film; however, the use of these materials is not as popular as the use of photographic film. It is indeed doubtful whether these new materials will ever replace photographic film.

Photographic film is generally composed of a base, made of a transparent glass plate or acetate film and a layer of photographic emulsion, as shown in Figure 5.18 [5.2]. The emulsion consists of a large number of tiny photosensitive silver halide particles, which are suspended more or less uniformly in a supporting gelatin. When the photographic emulsion is exposed to light, some of the silver halide grains absorb optical energy and undergo a complex physical change. Some of the grains that absorb sufficient light energy are immediately reduced, forming tiny metallic silver particles. These are the so-called development centers. The reduction to silver is completed by the chemical process of development. The grains that were not exposed or that have not absorbed sufficient optical energy will remain unchanged. If the developed film is then subjected to a chemical fixing process, the unexposed silver halide grains are removed, leaving only the metallic silver particles in the gelatin. These remaining grains are largely opaque at optical frequencies, so the transmittance of developed film depends on their density.

The relation of intensity transmittance to the density of the developed grains was first demonstrated in 1890 by F. Hurter and V. C. Driffield, who showed that the photographic density, the number of the metallic silver particles per unit area, is proportional to $-\log T_i$,

$$D = -\log T_i, \qquad (5.3)$$

where T_i is the intensity transmittance, which is defined as

$$T_i(x, y) = \left\langle \frac{I_o(x, y)}{I_i(x, y)} \right\rangle. \qquad (5.4)$$

The angle brackets, $\langle \rangle$, represent the localized ensemble average, and $I_i(x, y)$ and $I_o(x, y)$ are the input and output irradiances, respectively, at point (x, y).

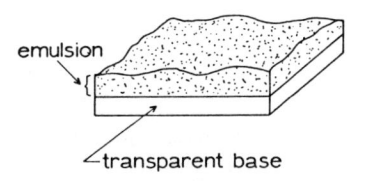

FIGURE 5.18 Section of a photographic film. The emulsion is composed of silver halide particles suspended in gelatin.

One of the most commonly used descriptions of the photosensitivity of a given photographic film is that given by the Hurter–Driffield curve, or the H-and-D curve, as shown in Figure 5.19. This curve is the plot of the density D of the developed grains versus the logarithm of the exposure E. The plot shows that if the exposure is below a certain level, the photographic density is quite independent of the exposure; this minimum density is usually referred as *gross fog*. As the exposure increases beyond the toe of the curve, the density begins to increase in direct proportion to log E. The slope of the straight-line portion of the H-and-D curve is usually referred as the *film gamma*, γ. If the exposure is increased beyond the straight-line portion of the H-and-D curve, after an intermediate region called the *shoulder*, the density saturates. In the saturated region there is no further increase in the density of the developed grains as the exposure increases.

Conventional photography is usually carried out within the linear region of the H-and-D curve. A film with a high-value gamma is called a high-contrast film, whereas one with a low-value gamma is referred as a low-contrast film, as illustrated in Figure 5.20. The value of γ is, however, affected not only by the type of photographic emulsion used but also by the chemical of the developer and the time taken by the developing process. In practice it is therefore possible to achieve a prescribed value of γ with a fair degree of accuracy by using suitable film, developer, and developing time.

If a given film is recorded in the straight-line region of the H-and-D curve, the photographic density may be written as

$$D = \gamma_n \log E - D_o, \qquad (5.5)$$

where the subscript n means that a negative film is being used, and $-D_o$ is

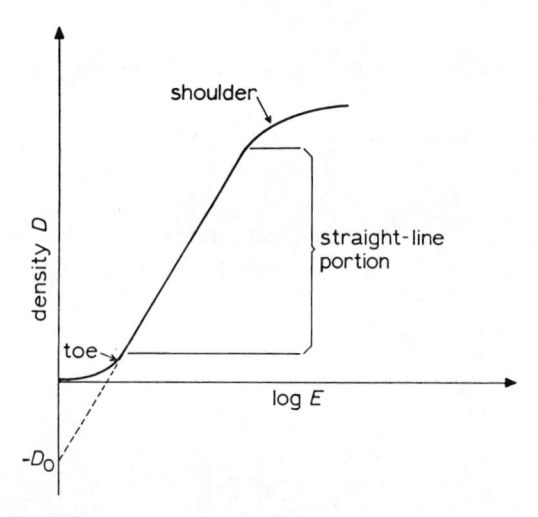

FIGURE 5.19 The Hurter–Driffield (H-and-D) curve.

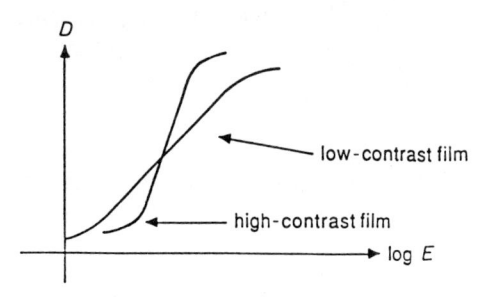

FIGURE 5.20 High- and low-gamma (γ) films.

the point where the projection of the straight-line portion of the H-and-D curve intercepts the density ordinate, as shown in Figure 5.19. By substituting Eq. 5.3 in Eq. 5.5, we get

$$\log T_{in} = -\gamma_n \log(It) + D_o, \tag{5.6}$$

where I is the incident irradiance and t is the exposure time. Note that the exposure of the film is given by $E = It$. Equation 5.6 can be written as

$$T_{in} = K_n I^{-\gamma_n}, \tag{5.7}$$

where $K_n = 10^{D_o} t^{-\gamma_n}$, is a positive constant.

It is apparent that intensity transmittance is highly nonlinear with respect exto the incident irradiance. It is, however, possible to obtain a positive linear relation between intensity transmittance and the incident irradiance. To do so requires a two-step process called *contact printing*.

In the first step a negative film is exposed, and in the second step another negative film is laid under the developed film. An incoherent light is then transmitted through the first film to expose the second film. By developing the second film to obtain the prescribed value of γ, we can obtain a positive transparency with a linear relation between intensity transmittance and the incident irradiance.

To illustrate this two-step process, let the resultant intensity transmittance of the second developed film (i.e., the positive transparency) be

$$T_{ip} = K_{n2} I_2^{-\gamma_{n2}}, \tag{5.8}$$

where K_{n2} is a positive constant, and the subscript $n2$ denotes the second-step negative. The irradiance I_2 that is incident on the second film can be written as

$$I_2 = I_1 T_{in}, \tag{5.9}$$

where

$$T_{in} = K_{n1} I^{-\gamma_{n1}}.$$

182 SPATIAL LIGHT MODULATORS AND DETECTORS

Here the subscript $n1$ denotes the first-step negative. The illuminating irradiance of the first film during contact printing is I_1, where I is the irradiance originally incident on the first film. By substituting Eq. 5.9 in Eq. 5.8, we get

$$T_{ip} = K I^{\gamma_{n1}\gamma_{n2}}, \tag{5.10}$$

where

$$K = K_{n2} K_{n1}^{-\gamma_{n2}} I_1^{-\gamma_{n2}}$$

is a positive constant. Thus, we see that a linear relation between the intensity transmittance of the positive transparency and the incident recording irradiance may be obtained if the overall gamma is made to be unity, that is $\gamma_{n1}\gamma_{n2} = 1$.

If the film is used as an SLM in a coherent system, it is more appropriate to use complex amplitude transmittance rather than intensity transmittance. Complex amplitude transmittance can be defined as

$$T(x, y) = [T_i(x, y)]^{1/2} e^{i\phi(x,y)}, \tag{5.11}$$

where T_i is the intensity transmittance, and $\phi(x, y)$ represents random phase retardations. Such phase retardations are primarily due to variations in the thickness of the emulsion. These variations are of two sorts: the coarse "outer-scale" variation, which is a departure from the optical flatness of the emulsion and base, and the fine "inner-scale" variation, which is caused by random fluctuation in the density of the developed silver grains. The silver grains do not swell uniformly in the surrounding gelatin. This fine-scale variation in emulsion thickness obviously depends on the exposure of the film.

In most practical applications, phase retardations caused by variations in the thickness of the emulsion can be removed by means of an index-matching liquid gate, as shown in Figure 5.21. Such a gate consists of two parallel, optically flat glass plates separated by a refractive-index-matching liquid, which is a liquid whose refractive index is very close to that of the film

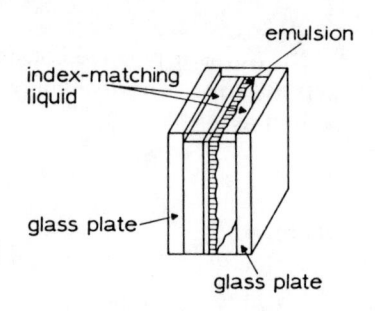

FIGURE 5.21 Refractive-index-matching liquid gate.

emulsion. If a developed film is submerged in the liquid gate, the overall complex amplitude transmittance can be written as

$$T(x, y) = [T_i(x, y)]^{1/2}, \tag{5.12}$$

which is a real function, with the random phase retardations removed.

By substituting the negative and positive transparencies of Eqs. 5.7 and 5.10 in Eq. 5.12, we have as the amplitude transmittances of these two transparencies

$$T_n = (T_{in})^{1/2} = K_n^{1/2} I^{-\gamma_n/2} = K_n^{1/2}(uu^*)^{-\gamma_n/2} \tag{5.13}$$

and

$$T_p = (T_{ip})^{1/2} = K^{1/2} I^{\gamma_{n1}\gamma_{n2}/2} = K^{1/2}(uu^*)^{\gamma_{n1}\gamma_{n2}/2}, \tag{5.14}$$

where u is the complex amplitude of the incident light field. Thus the amplitude transmittance of the two-step contact process can be written as

$$T = K_1 |u|^\gamma, \tag{5.15}$$

where K_1 is a positive constant and $\gamma = \gamma_{n1}\gamma_{n2}$. A linear relation between amplitude transmittance and the amplitude of the recording light field may be achieved by making the overall gamma equal to unity.

In practice, the first gamma is frequently chosen to be less than unity (e.g., $\gamma_{n1} = 1/2$), and the second gamma is chosen to be larger than two (e.g., $\gamma_{n2} = 4$). The overall gamma is therefore equal to two. This provides a square-law relation rather than linearity for intensity transmittance versus incident irradiance. As can be seen from Eq. 5.12, however, the relation for amplitude transmittance is linear.

In most coherent systems it is more convenient to use the transfer characteristic directly than to use the H-and-D curve. This direct transfer characteristic is frequently referred to as the T-E curve, for amplitude transmittance versus exposure, as shown in Figure 5.22. As we can see, if the film is properly exposed at an operating point that lies well within the linear region of the transfer characteristic of the T-E curve, then within a limited variation in exposure, the result will offer the best linear amplitude transmittance. If E_Q and T_Q ("quiescent") denote the corresponding bias exposure and amplitude transmittance, then within the linear region of the T-E curve, amplitude transmittance can be written as

$$T \simeq T_Q + \alpha(E - E_Q) = T_Q + \alpha'(\Delta|u|^2), \tag{5.16}$$

where α is the slope measured at the quiescent point of the T-E curve, and $\Delta|u|^2$ is the incremental intensity variation, $\alpha' = \alpha t$, where t is the exposure time.

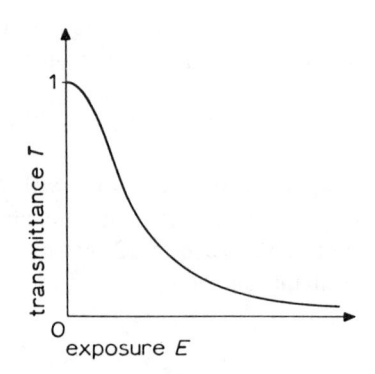

FIGURE 5.22 The amplitude transmittance versus exposure ($T-E$) curve of a photographic negative.

We conclude this section by reiterating that the constraint of the signal recorded within the linear region of the $T-E$ curve may not be necessary in some coherent optical systems. This is particularly so in holography, since the holographic construction is mostly a phase-modulated encoding. In general, photographic films have two major drawbacks: the wet development process is cumbersome, and, more importantly, the delay encountered in developing films is a major bottleneck in many optical processing systems. On the other hand, only a small amount of photon energy is required to generate a development center on the film. During the process of development, a development center is sufficient to change the whole grains composed of silver halides into metallic silver. In other words, the photographic recording (write-in) process involves a photon-induced latent image with development gain. Thus photographic films are usually 3 to 6 orders of magnitude more sensitive than other direct-recording materials. The development of photographic film will produce about 10^8 silver atoms for each absorbed photon. For example, the spatial resolution and the sensitivity of a Kodak SO253 holographic plate are 2500 lines/mm and 0.4 µJ/cm^2, respectively. Few SLMs can provide a better contrast ratio than that of photographic film.

5.11 ELECTRON-TRAPPING MATERIALS

The electron trapping (ET[1]) materials developed by Quantex Corporation can emit different output photons that correlate spatially in intensity with input photons. Although the ET device does not modulate the phase, amplitude, and polarization of the wavefront passing through it, it is similar to SLMs in that they both transfer and/or process information from a spatial format to an optical carrier [5.15, 5.16, 5.17, 5.18].

The ET materials are stimulable phosphors consisting of IIA–VIB compounds (alkaline-earth chalcogenides) with two specific rare-earth dopants added. An example of an ET material is SrS:Eu,Sm. Although the precise

[1]ET is the trademark of Quantex Corporation, 2 Research Court, Rockville, MD 20850.

details of the luminescence mechanism are not known, several empirical models have been proposed in the literature. The band gap and the mechanism for the light emission of an ET material are shown in Figure 5.23. Both the ground and excited states of each impurity exists within the band gap of the wide-band-gap (~4 eV) host material. Visible light excites an electron in the ground state of Eu^{2+} into its excited state. Some of the electrons at this higher energy level of the Eu^{2+} tunnel to the Sm^{3+} ions, where they remain trapped until stimulated by infrared light. The Sm^{2+} ions so formed are thermally stable deep traps of about 1.1 to 1.2 eV. Such a material has to be heated to about 450° C before the electrons are freed. Upon stimulation with infrared light (e.g., 1064 nm photons from a YAG:Nd laser), trapped electrons are released from the Sm^{2+} ions. These released electrons then tunnel back to the Eu ions, resulting in the characteristic Eu^{2+} emission when the electrons return to the ground state.

The operation of ET materials can be summarized as follows. Visible light (e.g., at 488 nm) excites electrons from their ground level into an electron trapping level so that optical information can be stored. The information is retrieved by returning the trapped electrons to the ground state, with an emission at 620–630 nm (orange to red light). The retrieval can be controlled, since the recombination of electrons from the trapping band to the ground level requires infrared light (e.g., 1064 nm). Obviously, the ET materials can be used to store optical information as trapped electrons [5.19].

In addition to storage, the ET materials are interesting as SLMs capable of performing multiplication, addition, and subtraction within a dynamic range covering four orders of magnitude. The orange/red emission intensity is pro-

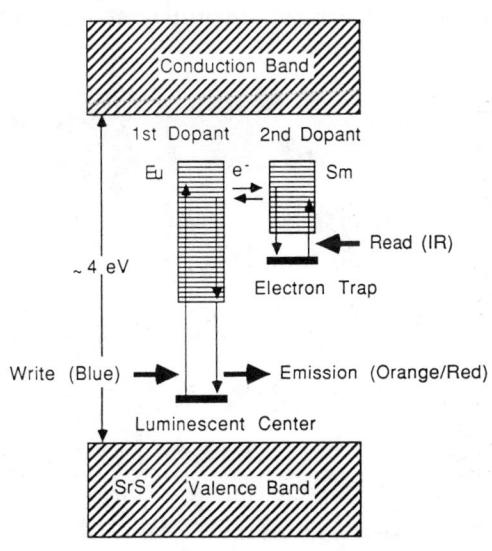

FIGURE 5.23 Band-gap structure of ET material and its operation.

186 SPATIAL LIGHT MODULATORS AND DETECTORS

portional to the product of the blue write-in intensity and the infrared readout intensity. The addition and subtraction are performed by increasing and decreasing the number of trapped electrons. These operations are physically carried out by exposing the ET material to blue and infrared light, respectively.

The ET device consists of an ET thin film coated on a transparent substrate. Thin films of ET materials can be fabricated by electron-beam deposition, sputtering, or other standard thin-film deposition technologies. The response time of ET materials to infrared light is less than 50 ns. The resolution of a fabricated 4-μm-thick ET thin film has been measured to be better than 80 lines/mm. The sensitivity of the fabricated ET thin film is 1 μJ/cm^2.

The application of ET thin film to instant photography is straightforward. A picture taken under sunlight with the ET photographic plate is shown in Figure 5.24. The ET plate was initially discharged. The recorded image was directly seen under an infrared light source in a dark room. Thus, absolutely no wet developing process is required. However, the infrared exposure results in the erasure of the recorded picture. The picture shown in Figure 5.24 was printed from a negative that was contact-printed with the emitting ET plate under infrared illumination.

The merit of the ET plate is its very large dynamic range (four orders of magnitude, as shown in Figure 5.25) as compared with that of conventional photographic film (typically two orders of magnitude). In addition, the ET plate is reusable. The drawback is that the ET plate cannot be kept as a hard copy, since the contrast rapidly degrades under infrared exposure. However, this can be an advantage for certain applications such as document security, in that only one reading may be possible. Obviously, exposure to blue light will also destroy information.

The ET plate can also be used for recording an infrared picture in a controlled environment, that is, an environment with sufficient infrared il-

FIGURE 5.24 Optical image detected and stored using ET material.

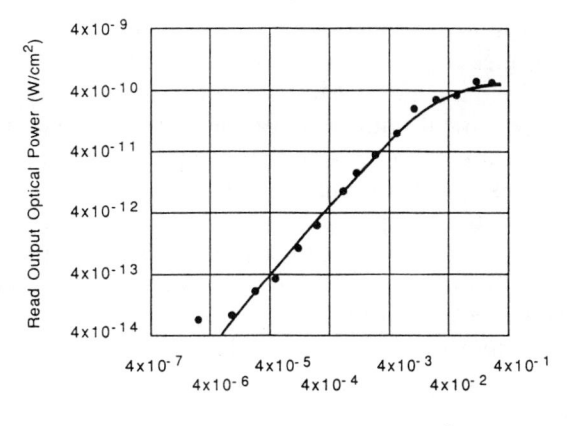

FIGURE 5.25 Dynamic range of ET material.

lumination and objects with high infrared reflectivity. In this application, the ET plate is first uniformly charged with visible light before it is exposed to an infrared image. The picture is then taken by employing a near-infrared filter. The recorded image can be seen (in a negative version) under infrared exposure in a dark room.

5.12 PHOTOREFRACTIVE MATERIALS

Like electron trapping materials, photorefractive materials contain electron traps [5.20]. Exposure of photorefractive materials to light excites electrons from traps to the conduction band where electrons can freely move. In contrast, electrons tunnel through only a very short distance in the electron trapping materials. In photorefractive materials, the concentration of free electrons diffuses thermally or drifts under applied or internal electric fields and become retrapped preferably in regions of low-intensity light. The space–charge buildup continues until the field completely cancels the effect of diffusion and drift and makes the current zero throughout. The resulting charge distribution modifies the refractive index of the material through the linear electrooptic Pockel's effect (see Section 5.3).

Popular photorefractive materials include: $LiNbO_3$, $Sr_{0.75}Ba_{0.25}Nb_2O_6$ (SBN), $Bi_{12}SiO_{20}$ (BSO), $Bi_{12}GeO_{20}$ (BGO), and $KTa_{0.65}Nb_{0.35}O_3$ (KTN). The electron traps are generated by intrinsic defects and residual impurities. Thus a pure crystal will not demonstrate the photorefractive effect. The sensitivity and the resultant diffraction efficiency can be dramatically increased by doping iron (Fe) into the crystal lattice. For example, Fe_2O_3 is added when a crystal of $LiNbO_3$ is grown by means of the Czochralski process. Iron enters the crystal lattice as Fe^{2+} and Fe^{3+} ions. These two species of iron ions are

188 SPATIAL LIGHT MODULATORS AND DETECTORS

initially evenly distributed throughout the crystal. When Fe^{2+} is exposed to the input light, an electron is excited to the conduction band of the crystal lattice, and Fe^{2+} becomes Fe^{3+}. Migration of electrons occurs in the conduction band of the crystal until they become trapped once more by Fe^{3+} ions in the low-intensity regions. Note that electrons may be trapped in the high-intensity regions, but they immediately escape from the traps. In the low-intensity regions the trapped electrons cannot easily escape from the traps. The operation of the photorefractive effect is schematically shown in Figure 5.26. Typically, an Fe-doped $LiNbO_3$ crystal has a resolution power of as high as 4000 lines/mm, which is very useful for real-time holography, and write-in sensitivity is of the order of 1 J/cm^2. A diffraction efficiency of the recorded volume hologram of higher than 90 percent has been reported in the literature.

5.13 CHARGE-COUPLED DEVICES

The charge-coupled device (CCD) is not a spatial light modulator but an image detector. The output of the CCD is an electronic signal. However, the electronic signal can be used to drive an electronically addressed SLM such as a LCTV. Thus the combination of a CCD camera and a LCTV is equivalent to an optically addressed SLM such as a LCLV. The combination can be operated at the standard video frame rates of 60 fields/sec interlaced to produce 30 frames/sec.

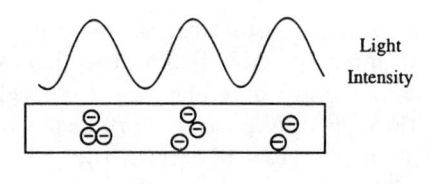

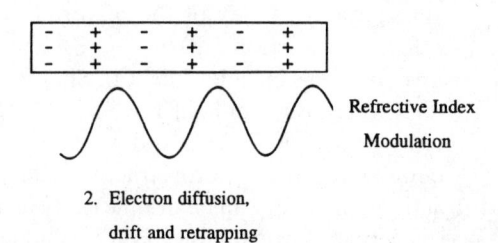

FIGURE 5.26 Operation of photorefractive material in recording light intensity patterns.

The CCD consists of an array of tiny capacitors that form isolated potential wells in the silicon substrate [5.2]. The potential well is shown schematically in Figure 5.27. A thin layer of silicon dioxide is grown on a section of silicon and a transparent electrode is applied as a gate over the oxide to form a tiny capacitor. When a positive electrical potential is applied to the electrode, a depletion region or electron potential well is created in the silicon substrate under the gate. When the silicon is exposed to light, a pair of electron-hole will be generated. The free electrons generated by incoming photons in the vicinity of the capacitor are stored and integrated in the well.

The quantity of electrons in the well is detected at the edge of the CCD by transfering the charge package. The principle of the propagation of potential wells is illustrated in Figure 5.28. In phase 1, gates G2 and G5 are turned on while others are off. Thus electrons are collected in wells W3 and W5. In phase 2, G2, G3, G5, and G6 are on; thus, wells W2 and W3 merge to make a wider well. Similarly, G5 and G6 form a single well. In phase 3, only G3 and G6 are turned on. Therefore, the electrons previously in W2

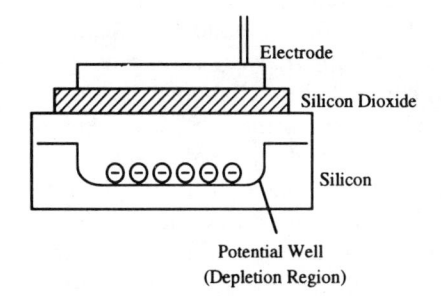

FIGURE 5.27 Structure of a pixel in a CCD.

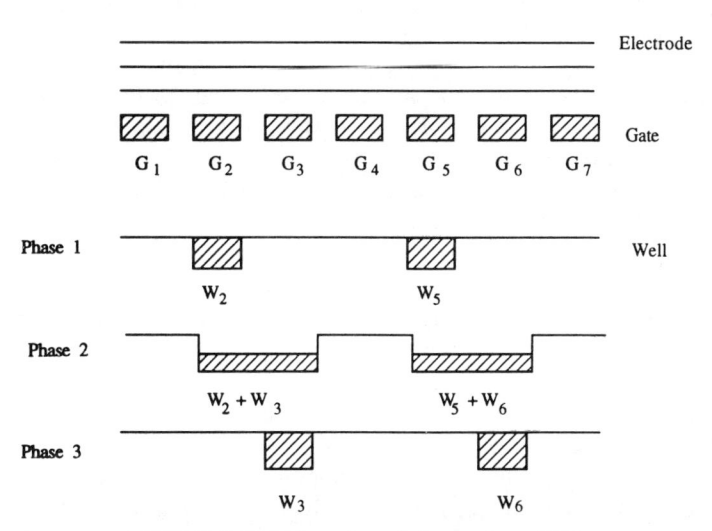

FIGURE 5.28 Transfer of charge in a CCD.

are now shifted and stored in W3, and the electrons of W5 are transferred to W6 in a similar way. By repeating this process, all charge packages will arrive at the edge to be detected.

CCD array detectors are available in 256 × 256 to 1024 × 1024 pixels. Each pixel is 20 μm square. The linear dynamic range depends on the noise level, which is typically 100. However, a dynamic range of 40,000 is possible. The sensitivity is of the order of 10^{-8} W/cm^2 (0.07 lux). Moreover, higher sensitivity can be achieved by integrating and storing data over relatively long periods of time. When the device is cooled, the integration time can be as long as several minutes. When adequate light is available, exposure times of less than 1 ns can be set, thus allowing the capture of high-speed events without blur.

5.14 QUANTUM WELL MODULATORS

Quantum well devices are attractive because they are based on quantum phoenomena rather than on classic physics. Conventional electronic devices such as transistors are not quantum devices. In these classic solid-state devices, the signal-bearing electrons can be considered balls that are rolling down a slope. As with the motion of balls that is controlled by changing the slope, the motion of electrons can be controlled by varying the electric potential between two terminals. If a ball is placed in a well, the ball requires an adequate amount of energy to throw it higher than the wall of the pit so it can escape from the well. Similarly, the potential given in a classic device must be higher than the intrinsic barrier in order to keep electrons moving. However, quantum mechanics tell us that electrons are also waves. As a consequence, electrons may escape from the well although their energy is much lower than the barrier.

The potential barrier can be generated at the interface of different semiconductor layers. A compositional superlattice consisting of GaAs and GaAlAs layers is the most popular structure at the present time. The layers are grown by molecular beam epitaxy (MBE). First, a layer of GaAs is grown, then a very thin layer of GaAlAs, then another layer of GaAs, and so forth. Each thin GaAlAs layer creates a potential barrier. The GaAs layer therefore becomes a quantum well between two potential barriers, as shown in Figure 5.29. The resonant tunneling effect can take place in this single quantum well or in multiple quantum wells. Figure 5.29 shows a quantum well with eigenvalues E_1 and E_2 and a potential barrier of E_B ($E_1 < E_2 < E_B$). When the quantum well device is not connected to any electric bias voltage, obviously no electrons pass through the quantum well, and the current is off (Figure 5.29a). Setting the bias voltage, E_1, will generate resonant tunneling (Figure 5.29b). In other words, in resonant tunneling, the energy of the incident electrons is aligned with one of the eigenvalues of the quantum well, and thus the tunneling current is much greater than that for off-resonance. However,

QUANTUM WELL MODULATORS   191

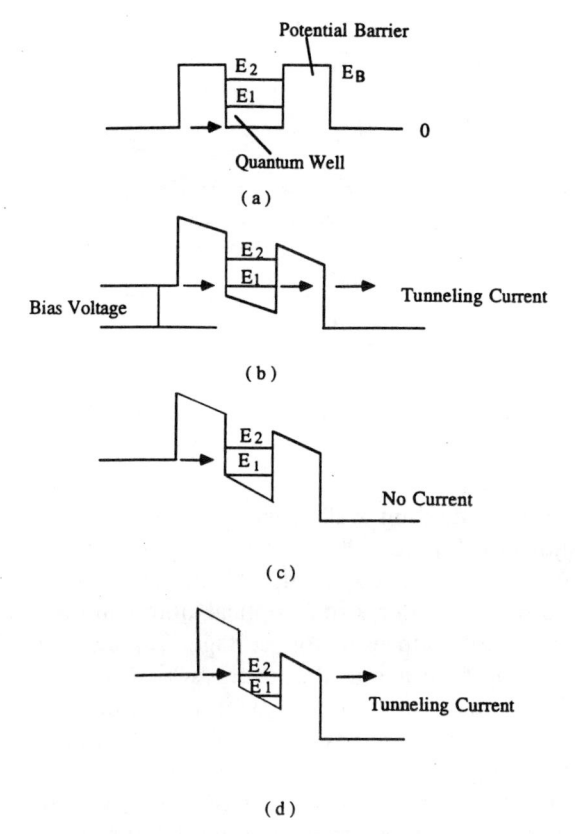

FIGURE 5.29 Resonant tunneling in a quantum well.

when the bias is increased to more than E_1, the resonant effect disappears until the bias achieves E_2 (Figure 5.29c and d). The advantage is now apparent. The switching energy can be as low as E_1, which is extremely low as compared with E_B. Note that classic solid-state devices require E_B to switch the device from the off state to the on state. Secondly, the switching time does not depend on the drift of the electrons (as balls roll down a slope), since electron behaves like a quantum wave. People believe it can oscillate as high as 1 THz, which is far beyond the cutoff frequency of any transistor.

An example of quantum well spatial light modulators is the self-electrooptic effect device (SEED) developed by Bell Laboratories [5.21]. The operation of the SEED makes use of the quantum confined Stark effect (QCSE), which describes the changes in optical absorption of quantum well materials when electric fields are applied perpendicular to the quantum well layers. The sharp optical absorption edge near the band-gap energy can be shifted to lower energies by this field. For incident wavelengths near the zero-field absorption peak, when an electric field is applied to quantum well layers, their absorption decreases. Without an electric field they absorb light readily. The SEED

192 SPATIAL LIGHT MODULATORS AND DETECTORS

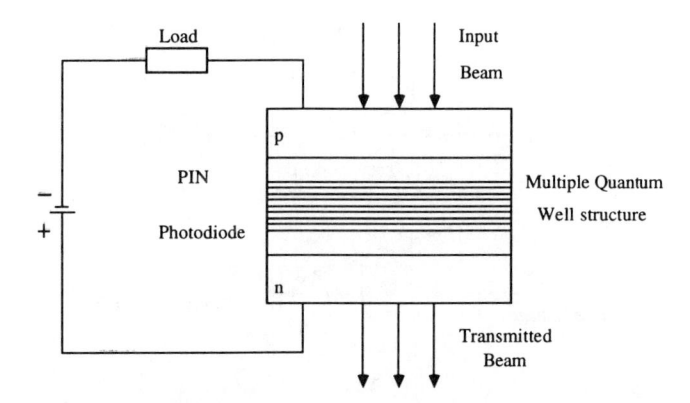

FIGURE 5.30 Structure of a pixel of SEED.

consists of multiple quantum well layers placed inside a PIN photodiode detector, as shown in Figure 5.30. In the dark state, the PIN diode detects no light, no photocurrent is generated, and the field across the layers introduces low absorption. Under strong optical illumination the photocurrent generated in the SEED induces a large voltage drop across the load, thereby reducing the electric field across the layers, which, in turn, increases light absorption. The increased absorption generates an increasingly larger photocurrent until the device becomes totally opaque. Thus low-intensity inputs are transmitted and high-intensity inputs are blocked. Note that at slightly longer wavelengths, absorption may decrease with decreasing field.

A 6 × 6-array SEED linear spatial light modulator [5.22] can be operated with two wavelengths. A red beam from a He–Ne laser (632.8 nm) is used for writing. The write beam is absorbed in the top photodiode, while a readout infrared beam (859.2 nm) is transmitted through the entire device. The modulation in the linear mode is performed as follows. The power subtracted from the infrared read beam is proportional to the incident red write beam. Each mesa of the array is 60 μm^2 with a 30-μm^2 optical window. Although theoretical switching energy and time are extremely low and fast, respectively, in practice they are limited by the electronic circuit employed. Practical switching times range between microseconds and seconds, in contrast to the theoretical values of a few picoseconds. The switching energy is 5 $\mu J/cm^2$, which some people believe can be decreased to lower than 1 $\mu J/cm^2$. The main drawback of quantum well spatial light modulators is their very low contrast ratio, which is about 2:1 at the present time.

REFERENCES

5.1 F. T. S. Yu, *Optical Information Processing*, Wiley–Interscience, New York, 1983.

5.2 F. T. S. Yu and I. C. Khoo, *Principle of Optical Engineering*, Wiley, New York, 1992.

5.3 W. E. Ross, D. Psaltis, and R. H. Anderson, "Two Dimensional Magneto-Optic Spatial Light Modulator for Signal Processing," *Opt. Eng.*, 22 (1983): 485.

5.4 D. Psaltis, E. Paek, and S. Venkatesh, "Optical Image Correlation with a Binary Spatial Light Modulator," *Opt. Eng.*, 23 (1984): 698.

5.5 C. Ward, A. D. Fisher, D. M. Cocco, and M. Y. Burmawi, "Microchannel Spatial Light Modulator," *Opt. Lett.* 3 (1978): 196.

5.6 C. Ward and J. Thackara, "Operating Modes of the Microchannel Spatial Light Modulator," *Opt. Eng.*, 22 (1983): 695.

5.7 Grinberg *et al.*, "A New Real Time Non-Coherent to Coherent Light Image Converter: The Hybrid Field Liquid Crystal Light Valve," *Opt. Eng.* 14 (1975): 217.

5.8 M. S. Welkowsky, R. A. Forber, C. S. Wu, and M. E. Pedinoff, "Visible-to-Infrared Image Converter Using the Hughes Liquid Crystal Light Valve," *Proc. SPIE* 825 (1987): 193.

5.9 H. K. Liu, J. A. Davis, and R. A. Lilly, "Optical Data Processing Properties of a Liquid Crystal Television Spatial Light Modulator," *Opt. Lett.* 10 (1985): 635.

5.10 S. Jutamulia, G. M. Storti, W. M. Seiderman, J. Lindmayer, and D. A. Gregory, "Infrared Signal Processing Using a Liquid Crystal Television," *Opt. Eng.* 30 (1991): 178.

5.11 D. A. Gregory *et al.*, "Optical Characteristics of a Deformable-Mirror Spatial Light Modulator," *Opt. Lett.* 13 (1988): 10.

5.12 T. Yatagai, J. G. Camacho-Basillio, and H. Onda, "Recording of Computer Generated Holograms on an Optical Disk Master," *Appl. Opt.* 28 (1989): 1042.

5.13 T. Lu, K. Choi, S. Wu, X. Xu, and F. T. S. Yu, "Optical Disk Based Neural Network," *Appl. Opt.* 28 (1989): 4722.

5.14 D. Psaltis, M. A. Neifeld, and A. Yamamura, "Image Correlators Using Optical Memory Disks," *Opt. Lett.* 14 (1989): 429.

5.15 S. Jutamulia, G. M. Storti, J. Lindmayer, and W. Seiderman, "Use of Electron Trapping Materials in Optical Signal Processing. 1: Parallel Boolean Logic," *Appl. Opt.* 29 (1990): 4806.

5.16 S. Jutamulia, G. M. Storti, J. Lindmayer, and W. Seiderman, "Use of Electron Trapping Materials in Optical Signal Processing. 2: 2D Associative Memory," *Appl. Opt.* 30 (1991): 2879.

5.17 S. Jutamulia, G. M. Storti, J. Lindmayer, and W. Seiderman, "Use of Electron Trapping Materials in Optical Signal Processing. 3: Modifiable Hopfield Type Neural Networks," *Appl. Opt.* 30 (1991): 1786.

5.18 S. Jutamulia, G. M. Storti, W. Seiderman, J. Lindmayer, and D. A. Gregory, "Use of Electron Trapping Materials in Optical Signal Processing. 4: Parallel Incoherent Image Subtraction," *Appl. Opt.* To be published.

5.19 S. Jutamulia, G. M. Storti, W. Seiderman, and J. Lindmayer, "Erasable Optical 3D Memory Using Novel Electron Trapping (ET) Materials," *Proc. SPIE* 1401 (1990): 113.

5.20 L. Solymar and D. J. Cooke, *Volume Holography and Volume Gratings*, Academic Press, London, 1981.

5.21 D. A. B. Miller et al., "Novel Hybrid Optically Bistable Switch: The Quantum Well Self-Electro-Optic Effect Device," *Appl. Phys. Lett.* 45 (1984): 13.

5.22 G. Livescu, D. A. B. Miller, J. E. Henry, A. C. Gossard, and J. H. English, "Spatial Light Modulator and Optical Dynamic Memory Using a 6 × 6 Array of Self-Electro-Optic-Effect Devices," *Opt. Lett.* 13 (1988): 297.

PROBLEMS

5.1 An AO cell is depicted in Figure 5.31. What is the rise time of the AO cell in terms of v_A (acoustic wave velocity) and W (window in the AO cell)? The rise time is the time delay between the time when the AO cell launches an acoustic wave and the time when the deflected light can be detected.

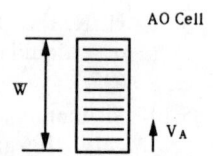

FIGURE 5.31

5.2 An AO cell with $W = 1$ mm, $v_A = 5 \times 10^3$ m/sec is employed to modulate digital optical signals, as shown in Figure 5.32.

   (a) What is the bandwidth of the signal?

   (b) Can you suggest how to reduce the rise time and thus to increase the signal bandwidth? What is the trade-off? Show how to achieve a 1-GHz bandwidth employing the system given in Figure 5.32.

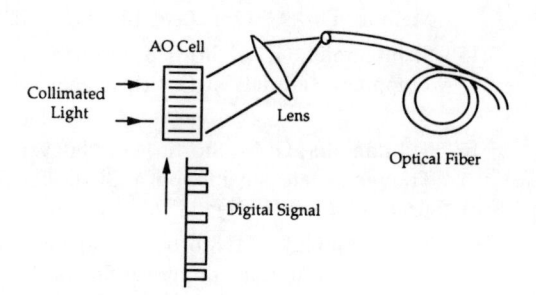

FIGURE 5.32

5.3 Describe how to utilize an AO cell as a scanner.

5.4 Assume the MOSLM rotates light polarization by $-45°$ and $45°$ for a binary input of 0 and 1, respectively.

   (a) Describe how to implement a binary phase filter using a MOSLM.

   (b) If the MOSLM rotates only by $-9°$ and $9°$, what are the intensity transmittances of the phase filter? (*Hint*: Use Malus's law.)

5.5 A MOSLM with the pixel structure $p(x, y)$ displays a spatial pattern $f(x, y)$.
  (a) What is the pattern at the Fourier-transform plane in terms of $p(x, y)$ and $f(x, y)$?
  (b) Draw schematically the patterns at the MOSLM and at the Fourier plane.

5.6 Do we have to align the polarization of the readout light to a specific axis of the MOSLM? Explain why.

5.7 Given the Kerr law for a PROM

$$n_1 - n_2 = k\lambda E^2,$$

where n_1 and n_2 are the refractive indices of light with planes of polarization parallel and perpendicular to the applied electric field E, respectively, k is Kerr's constant, and λ is the wavelength of light:
  (a) Show that for the applied voltage V_h to produce half-wave phase retardation, that is, to rotate the polarization plane by 90°, is

$$V_h = \sqrt{(m + 1/2)d/2k},$$

  where m is an integer and d is the thickness of the crystal. (*Hint*: To produce half-wave retardation, the phase difference of the ordinary wave (n_1) and the extraordinary wave (n_2) is $\Delta\phi = \pi$, 3π, 5π, ..., at the exit of the retardation plate).
  (b) If we change the wavelength of the readout light, do we have to tune the applied voltage?

5.8 (a) Referring to the Kerr law given in Problem 5.7, describe what happens if the readout light is polarized parallel to the polarization of either the ordinary or extraordinary ray.
  (b) What condition is needed for the polarization of the readout beam to properly operate a PROM device?

5.9 Referring to Figure 5.5, design a two-dimensional parallel NOR optical logic gate using a PROM device. The truth table for NOR functions is as follows:

Input A	Input B	NOR
0	0	1
0	1	0
1	0	0
1	1	0

(*Hint*: Utilize thresholded output.)

196 SPATIAL LIGHT MODULATORS AND DETECTORS

5.10 Given that the input sensitivity of the MSLM is 30 nJ/cm², the writing time response is 10 ms, and its maximum allowed readout light intensity is 0.1 W/cm², what is the maximum gain?

5.11 A monochrome slide is projected on the input side of an MSLM. If a white-light beam is used for the readout, we will get a color output. Explain why.

5.12 A photomultiplier can detect very-low-intensity light based on a multiplication process as shown in Figure 5.33. This device allows a photon to eject an electron from a photocathode. The photomultiplier then amplifies this feeble photocurrent by accelerating the electron onto successive dynodes, from which additional electrons are easily ejected. Similar to an MSLM, the image intensifier also employs a microchannel plate (MCP). The MCP contains a bundle of microscopic hollow tubes whose insides are coated with a dynode-type multiplication surface so that every tube functions as a tiny photomultiplier. Electrons ejected from the photocathode are multiplied by the MCP. In the image intensifier, secondary electrons hit the phosphor with enough energy to give off a bright flash of light. On the other hand, these secondary electrons are deposited and thus they generate a static electric field across the crystal in the MSLM. Assume that the thickness of the MCP is 1 mm and that it consists of a bundle of 10-μm hollow, internally coated glass tubes.

(a) What is the resolution of the MCP in terms of lines/mm?

(b) If one electron creates on the order of five secondary electrons, and the total gain is 10^7, how many times do electrons hit the coating of the hollow glass tubes?

(c) If the thickness of the MCP becomes twice as large (i.e., 2 mm), what is the gain?

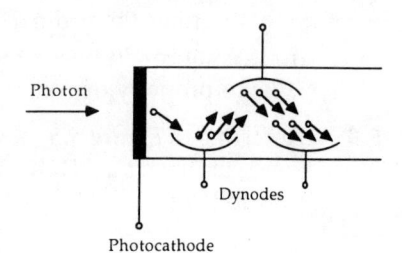

FIGURE 5.33

5.13 An LCLV can generate a large-screen monochrome display from a TV monitor. Draw a schematic diagram for this application.

5.14 (a) Describe that the system shown in Figure 5.34 can be used as a memory.

(b) Can we use the system shown in Figure 5.35 as a memory? Why?

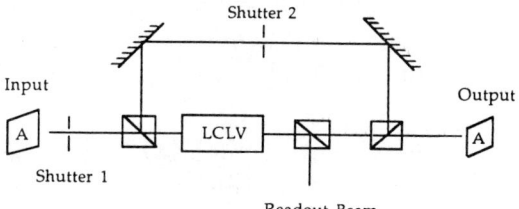

FIGURE 5.34

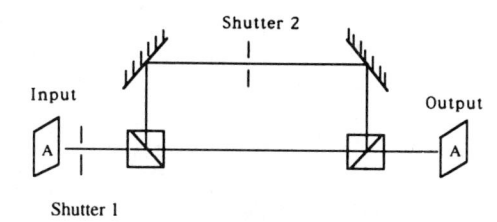

FIGURE 5.35

5.15 What is the power required of a laser to write a 25-mm² grating pattern onto an LCLV with 6-µJ/cm² sensitivity and 10-ms response time? Assume that the original laser pencil-beam cross-section area is 5 mm².

5.16 If the scanning procedure of the LCTV is exactly the same as that of a TV monitor, which is a point-by-point scanning process, can we obtain the Fourier transform of the pattern shown on the LCTV? Describe under what conditions the answer is yes or no.

5.17 Without an analyzer, can we observe:
   (a) The pattern written on the LCTV?
   (b) The Fourier spectra of the pattern written on the LCTV? Explain why.

5.18 Suppose the LCTV is weakly phase modulated by function $f(x, y)$, where $f(x, y) \ll 1$. The transmittance function becomes $t(x, y) = \exp[-if(x, y)]$. What are the Fourier power spectra at a specific diffraction order?

5.19 Show a schematic diagram of a system based on the ray tracing necessary to observe a binary pattern that is electronically written on the DMD, as shown in Figure 5.36.

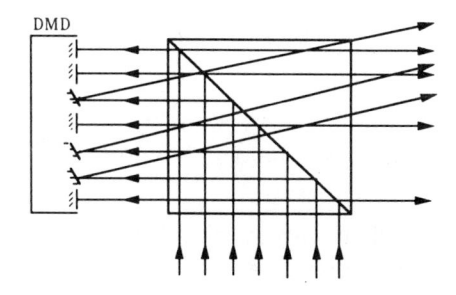

FIGURE 5.36

198 SPATIAL LIGHT MODULATORS AND DETECTORS

5.20 Why does the size of the readout beam have to be larger than the width of the pit on a nonerasable CD? On the other hand, why does the beam size have to be smaller than the size of the pit on a WORM and an MO disk?

5.21 Figure 5.37 shows the surface structure of the CD. Determine the pit depth, d, in terms of the wavelength of light, λ, and the refractive index of the clear coating, n. If $\lambda = 0.78$ μm, and $n = 1.5$, what is d?

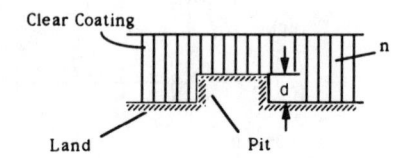

FIGURE 5.37

5.22 When a 120-mm CD is employed as an SLM, what is the number of pixels in the 1-mm^2 area close to the edge of the CD?

5.23 Figure 5.38 shows the basic pickup optics for a CD system. Show that the maximum collectable light at the detector is only 25 percent of the emitted light from the laser. Assuming that the laser emits linearly polarized light, show that by employing a polarized beam splitter and a quarter-wave plate, the maximum collectable light get to be 100 percent.

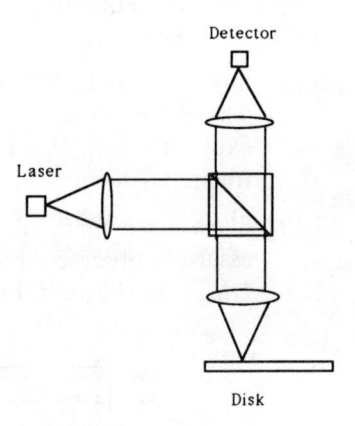

FIGURE 5.38

5.24 Why is a photoplastic device good for a hologram but not appropriate for photographic uses?

5.25 A thin phase grating can be made by using a photoplastic device. The thin phase grating can be expressed as

$$t(x, y) = \exp[i\alpha \cos(2\pi by)]$$
$$= \sum i^n J_n(\alpha)\exp(in2\pi by),$$

where J_n is the Bessel function of the first kind and the nth order, and α is a constant. Show that the maximum efficiency is 33.9 percent. (*Hint*: Use a Bessel function table.)

5.26 Given the Hurter–Driffield (H-and-D) curve of a certain photographic film, as shown in Figure 5.39:
  (a) Evaluate the gamma (γ) of the film.
  (b) Write a linear equation to represent the straight-line region of the H-and-D curve.

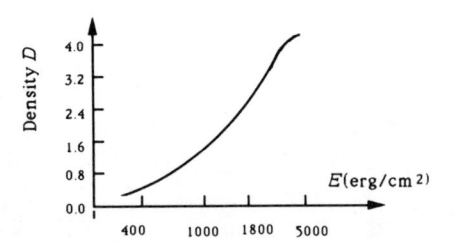

FIGURE 5.39

5.27 Using the H-and-D curve given in Figure 5.39:
  (a) Plot the amplitude transmittance versus the linear exposure (T–E) curve of the film.
  (b) Write a linear equation to represent the linear region of the T–E curve.

5.28 Consider two negative image transparencies, where the intensity transmittances are given by T_{n1} and T_{n2}, respectively. These two transparencies are simultaneously encoded on a photographic plate, as shown in Figure 5.40. Assumed that the photographic plate has a linear T–E curve.
  (a) Calculate the amplitude transmittance of the recorded photographic plate.
  (b) Show that the transmittance of the recorded transparency is a composite positive image of T_{n1} and T_{n2}.

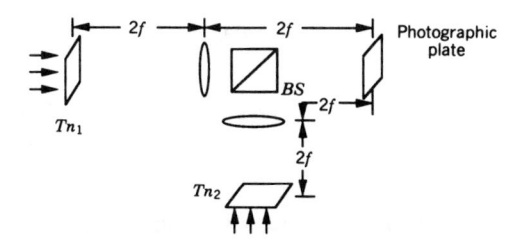

FIGURE 5.40

200 SPATIAL LIGHT MODULATORS AND DETECTORS

5.29 A photographic plate is used to record the joint Fourier-transform power spectra $I(p, q)$, as shown in Figure 5.41a. The developed photographic plate is then put in the input plane to produce correlation spots in the Fourier plane, as shown in Figure 5.41b. What are the Fourier power spectra in Figure 5.41b if gamma $(\gamma) = 2$ is produced in the photographic development process? Assume $I(p, q)$ are close to 1. (*Hint*: $x^{-1} = 1 - (x - 1) + (x - 1)^2 - (x - 1)^3 + \cdots$.)

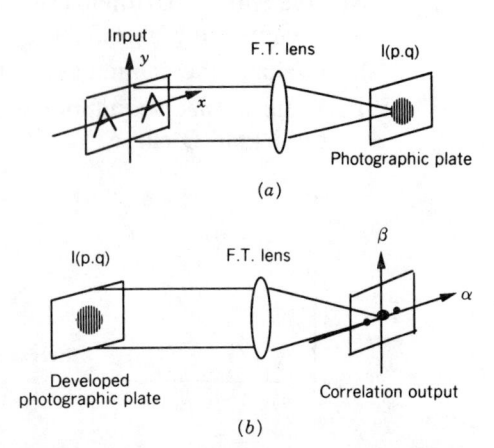

FIGURE 5.41

5.30 The amplitude transmittance of a grating recorded on a photographic plate can be expressed schematically as in Figure 5.42. What is the diffraction efficiency when the photographic plate is illuminated by a plane wave?

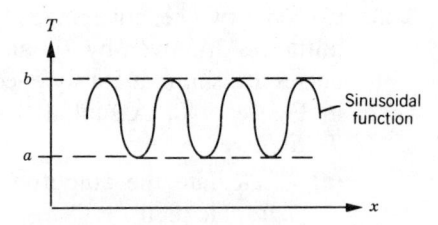

FIGURE 5.42

5.31 Regarding their high sensitivities, describe an analogy between a photographic plate and an image intensifier.

5.32 Show how to perform image addition and image subtraction using ET film.

5.33 What is the optical gain of ET film? Assume the quantum efficiencies of the ET film to blue and infrared exposures are 10 and 5 percent, respectively.

5.34 An optical switch is shown in Figure 5.43. When the blue input is low,

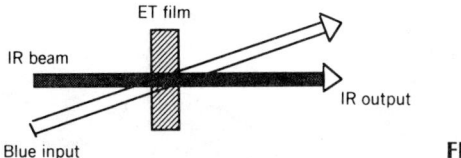

FIGURE 5.43

what is the status of the infrared output? When the blue input is high, what is the infrared output? Explain why.

5.35 Can we employ an ET thin film to record and reconstruct a hologram? Explain why.

5.36 We want to write a hologram into a photorefractive crystal that has a sensitivity of 200 nJ/μm^2 using an Ar laser with 10-mW output at 488 nm. Assume all the laser light can be utilized and focused onto an area of 0.5 × 0.5 mm^2. How long is the required exposure time?

5.37 A photorefractive crystal can be considered as a thick phase grating such as an AO cell. What is its maximum diffraction efficiency?

5.38 Optical phase conjugation is an interesting optical phenomenon that is schematically described in Figure 5.44. A conventional plane mirror reflects the incident light according to Snell's law. On the other hand, the beam reflected by a phase conjugator retraces its original path, so that the incident light returns exactly upon itself. Show schematically how to generate a phase-conjugated light from an incident light by employing a photorefractive crystal.

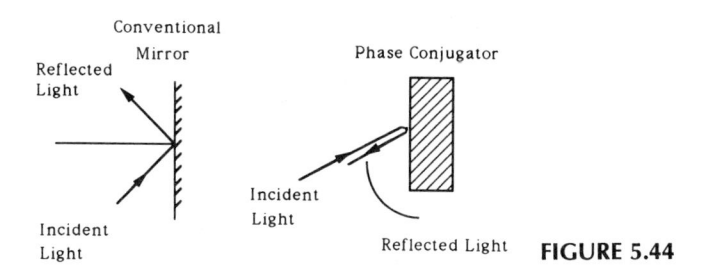

FIGURE 5.44

5.39 Assume that a photorefractive crystal is employed as holographic storage that stores a 256 × 256 bit pattern for a supercomputer. The stored pattern is read out by a laser beam. The reconstructed holographic image is detected by a CCD with the same 256 × 256 pixels, as shown in Figure 5.45. Each pixel is 20 × 20 μm^2, and the sensitivity is 10^{-6} W/cm^2. If the diffraction efficiency of the hologram is 10 percent, what is the minimum laser power required to read the memory?

FIGURE 5.45

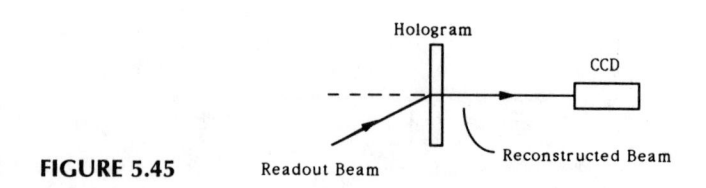

Hologram / CCD / Readout Beam / Reconstructed Beam

5.40 Assume that the absorption curve of a multiple quantum well structure is shifted to the right under an applied electric field, as shown in Figure 5.46. Describe how to utilize this characteristic to make both a positive-feedback and a negative-feedback SEED circuit with only one wavelength.

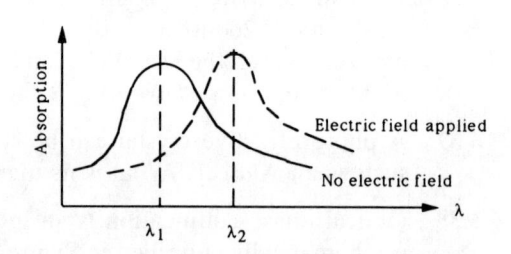

FIGURE 5.46

CHAPTER SIX

Hybrid-Optical Signal Processing

Two-dimensional optical processing has been used in a wide variety of applications in which the large-capacity and parallel-processing capabilities of optics are exploited. The areas of particular interest are image correlation for pattern recognition, image subtraction for machine vision, and numerical processing for optical computing. Although optical correlators that rely on general holographic filtering techniques have been introduced, the concept of programmability in optical signal processing is more recent. The trend is primarily due to recent advances in sophisticated spatial light modulators and photorefractive crystals that allow us to construct various types of real-time hybrid-optical signal-processing systems. The systems can be compactly packaged, and so, in theory, can be used for on-board processing in space stations.

Although there are innumerable techniques available for the implementation of real-time optical processing, we restrict our discussion to a few architectures and applications that would be of general interest to our readers. There are a great number of contributors to this field, and we apologize for not being able to include all their work.

6.1 MICROCOMPUTER-BASED OPTICAL PROCESSORS

It is apparent that at the current stage, a purely optical signal processor has some drawbacks, which make certain tasks difficult or impossible to implement. The first is that optical systems are difficult to *program*, in the sense of programming general-purpose digital electronic computers. A purely optical system can be designed to perform specific tasks (analogous to a *hard-wired* electronic computer), but cannot be used where more flexibility is required. A second problem is that a system based on Fourier optics is naturally analog, in which great accuracy is difficult to achieve. A third problem is that optical systems by themselves cannot be used to make decisions, as some electronic counterparts can. Even the simplest type of decision making is based on the comparison of the output with a stored value, such that the operation cannot be performed without the intervention of electronics.

Moreover, the deficiencies of the optical system happens to be the strong points of its electronic counterparts. For instance, accuracy, controlability, and programmability are the traits of digital computers. Thus, the concept of combining the optical system with its electronic counterparts is rather natural as a means of applying the rapid processing and parallelism of optics to a wider range of applications. In this section, we apply this concept to a general-purpose microcomputer-based optical signal processor.

The first approach to the microcomputer-based optical processor is using a 4-f (f-focal length) optical processing configuration, in which the input object and the spatial filter are generated by programmable spatial light modulators (SLMs), as shown in Figure 6.1. For instance, a programmable complex conjugate Fourier transform of reference patterns is generated with the SLM2 using a microcomputer, through which cross-correlation between the input object and the reference pattern can be detected by a CCD array detector. The detected signal can be fed back to the microcomputer for display and for decision making. Thus, we see that a programmable real-time optical signal processor can be realized using this 4-f architecture, if an SLM with sufficient space–bandwidth product (SBP) and resolution is available for the display of the computer-generated complex spatial filter.

The second approach to the hybrid-optical processor is to use a joint Fourier transform configuration, in which both the input object and the spatial impulse response of the filter function can be simultaneously displayed at the input SLM1, as shown in Figure 6.2. For instance, programmable spatial reference functions can be generated side by side with the input object, such that the joint transform power spectrum (JTPS) can be detected by CCD1 [6.1]. By displaying the JTPS on the SLM2, via the microcomputer, cross-correlation between the input object and the reference function can be obtained at the

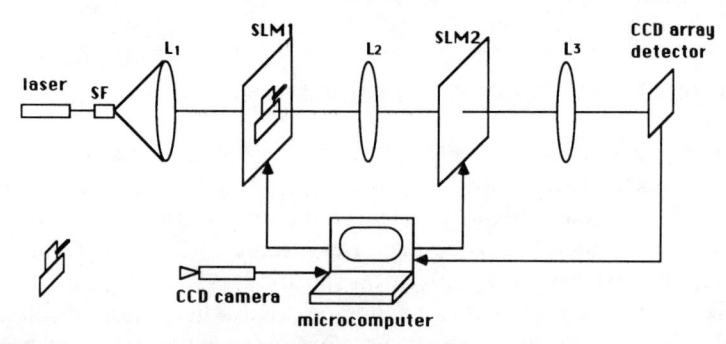

FIGURE 6.1 A microcomputer-based optical processor. *Note:* L_1 is the collimated lens and L_2 and L_3 represent the Fourier-transform lenses.

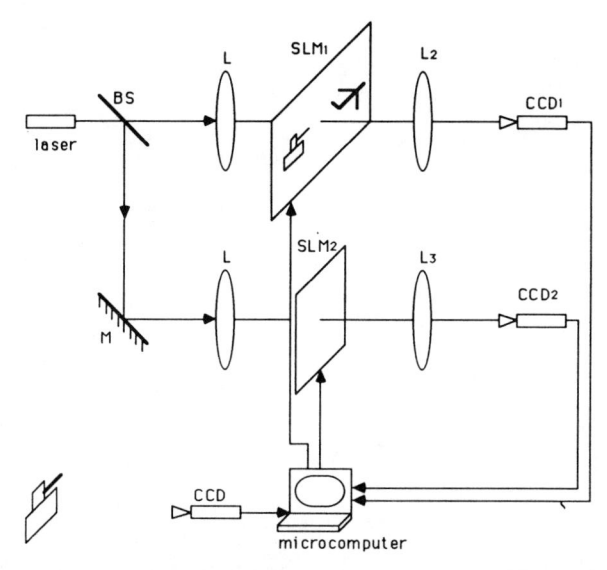

FIGURE 6.2 A microcomputer-based joint-transform processor. *Note:* BS is the beam splitter; L is the collimated lens; and L_2 and L_3 are the Fourier-transform lenses.

back focal plane of the Fourier-transform lens L_3. Thus, we see that a real-time hybrid-optical processor can be constructed using the joint transform architecture.

Although the functions of the hybrid-optical configurations of the 4-f and the joint transform architectures are basically the same, there is one major distinction between them. The spatial filter synthesis (e.g., Fourier hologram) is *independent* of the input signal, whereas the joint power spectrum displayed on the SLM2 (i.e., joint transform filter) are *dependent* on the input signal. Thus, nonlinear filtering can generally be used in the 4-f system, but cannot be generally applied to joint transform architectures, because, for one thing, it would produce poor performance (e.g., false alarms and lower output signal-to-noise ratio [6.2],[6.3]).

6.2 PROGRAMMABLE JOINT TRANSFORM CORRELATOR

Let us illustrate a technique for performing a real-time joint transform correlation, as shown in Figure 6.3 [6.4], [6.5]. A programmable spatial light modulator [e.g., magnetooptic (MOSLM) and liquid crystal television (LCTV)] is used to display both the real-time input object and a set of reference images. The rate of the proposed system would be dependent upon the cycle time of the LCLV. The resolution of the current MOSLM and LCLV is about 14 lines/mm and 30 lines/mm, respectively. Measured at the 50 percent modulation transfer function (MTF), the resolution of the overall system would

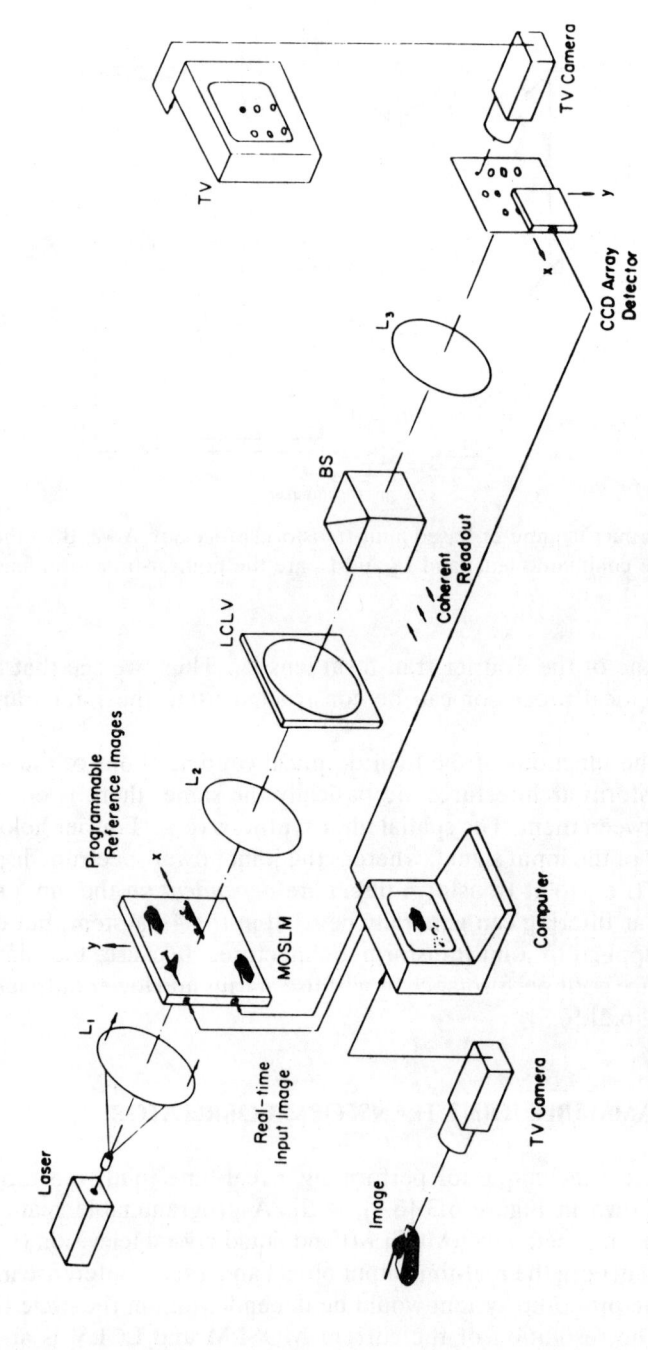

FIGURE 6.3 A real-time programmable joint-transform correlator. *Note*: L_2 and L_3 are Fourier transform lenses; BS is the beam splitter.

depend more on the MOSLM. Even if 50 percent resolution reduction is used for the overall system performance, this would correspond to a resolution of about 7 lines/mm, which is certainly a good-quality image for image correlation. Thus, within the current state of the art, a real-time programmable optical correlator as applied to automatic pattern recognition is feasible.

The contrast ratio of the MOSLM could be as high as 1000:1 under coherent illumination, which is suitable for input object generation; whereas, the contrast ratio of the LCLV is about 100:1, which is usable by a square-law detector. As an experimental demonstration, we provide the result obtained using this joint transform architecture, as shown in Fig. 6.4. A set of input objects (i.e., the Roman letter A) generated by the MOSLM is shown in Figure 6.4a, while the output irradiance with the photometer scan traces is shown Figure 6.4b. From this result we see that two distinctive correlation peaks can be easily identified.

The aforementioned architecture was further implemented using a single LCTV that replaced the MOSLM and the LCLV [6.1], as conceptually shown in Figure 6.2. There are, however, three major objections to using commercially available liquid crystal TVs for optical processing applications: (1) their low contrast ratio, (2) their phase nonuniformity, and (3) their low resolution and low SBP. These problems must be minimized if an LCTV is to be used as a spatial light modulator in a coherent optical system. The contrast uniformity can be improved by replacing the original poor plastic polarizers of the LCTV with high-quality ones, and immersion of the LCTV in a liquid gate aids in correcting the phase variations. Although the SBP of the LCTV is constant, in theory an image can be enlarged to compensate for the low resolution of the LCTV. In practice, however, the detail of the image cannot be enlarged too much because the correlation signal might become buried in the dc pattern characteristic of joint transform correlators.

To verify the implementation of this new architecture, especially the usefulness of LCTVs, a preliminary experiment was performed. Processing speed was ignored in favor of exploring the contrast and resolution limitations of the LCTV. A schematic diagram of the preliminary experimental setup is shown in Figure 6.5.

A microcomputer was employed to generate object and reference patterns simultaneously on the LCTV. A collimated coherent beam is incident on the LCTV, which was disassembled and immersed in a liquid gate. The joint transform of the object and reference patterns is performed by lens L_3. If the object and reference patterns are identical, the joint transform spectrum consists of a fringe structure. The fringe structure was recorded by a vidicon onto a video tape. The recorded tape of the fringe structure was then replayed using the same LCTV. The correlation signal, if it existed, was then displayed on the TV monitor. In this preliminary investigation, five fringes or more produced recognizable correlation spots.

An illustration of these results is shown in Figure 6.6. Figure 6.6a shows the images of two microcomputer-generated fighters as a simulation of the

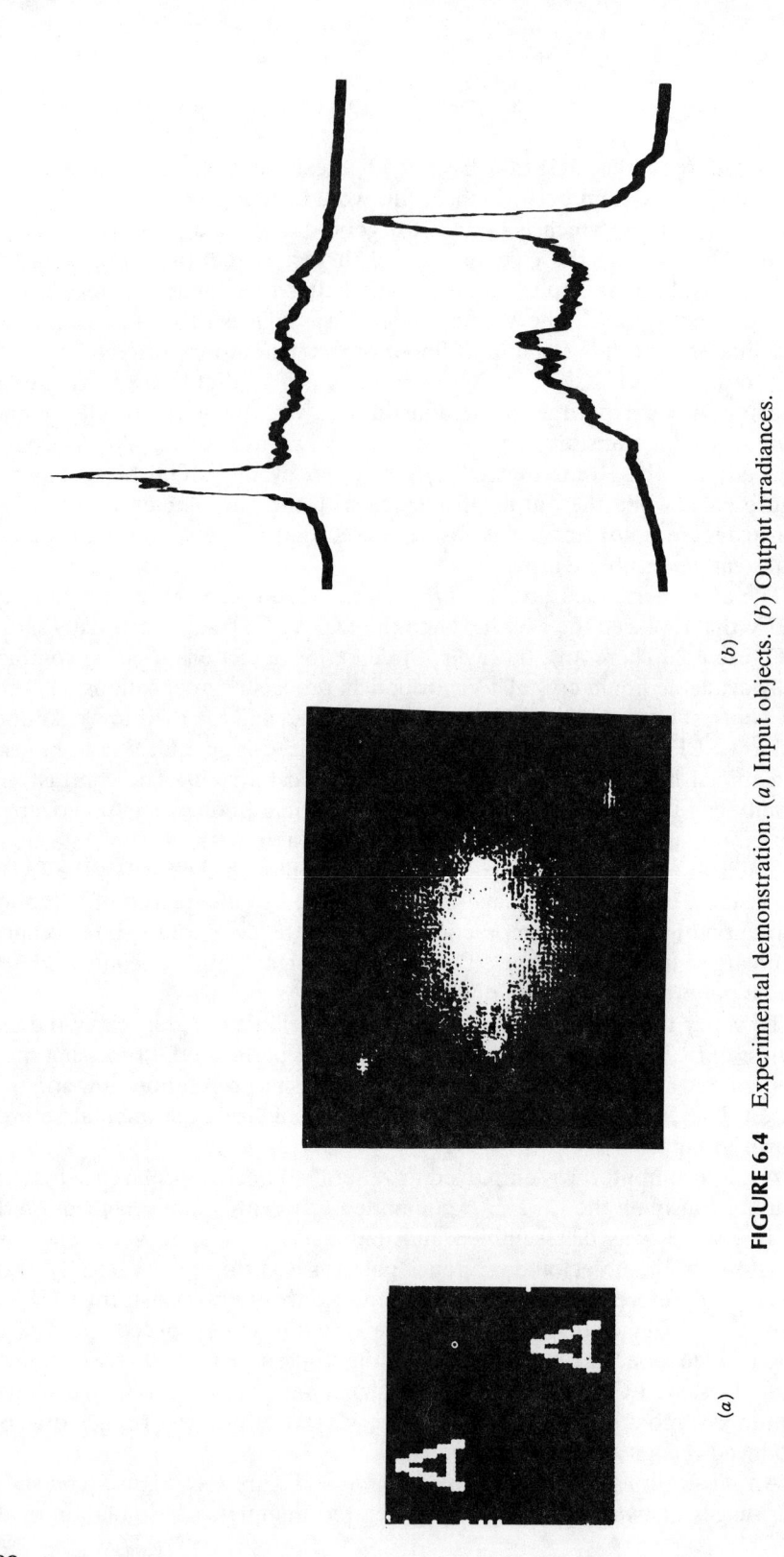

FIGURE 6.4 Experimental demonstration. (*a*) Input objects. (*b*) Output irradiances.

HIGH EFFICIENCY JOINT TRANSFORM CORRELATOR 209

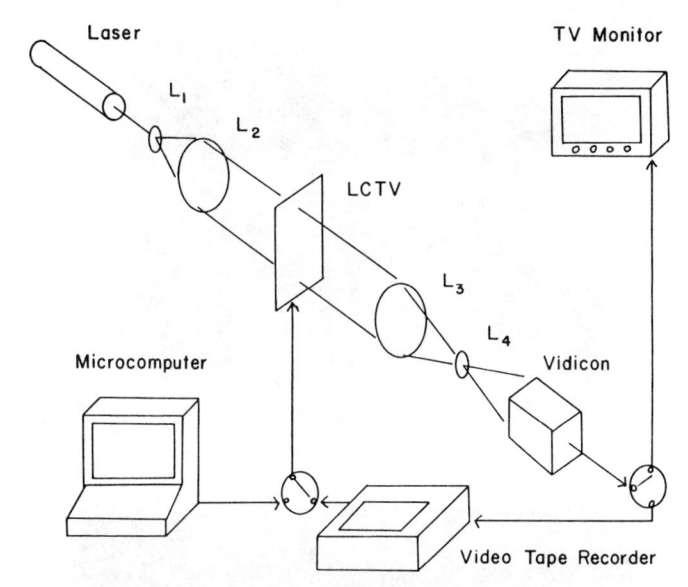

FIGURE 6.5 Schematic diagram of a programmable JTC employing a single LCTV.

input scene and reference object. Figure 6.6b and c are the left half of the correlation output and the extended dc patterns, respectively. A correlation spot is easily observed at the left part of the picture shown in Figure 6.6b. The scanning lines of the TV monitor are also shown in Figure 6.6b and c. In addition, when the simulated object was moved, the correlation spot moved accordingly, thus displaying translational invariance.

6.3 HIGH EFFICIENCY JOINT TRANSFORM CORRELATOR

A plane wave is used in a joint transform correlator to read out the joint transform power spectrum (JTPS), producing the following complex light field at the output plane:

$$u(x, y) = f(x, y) \circledast f(x, y) + g(x, y) \circledast g(x, y)$$
$$+ f(x, y) \circledast g(x + 2x_0, y) \qquad (6.1)$$
$$+ g(x, y) \circledast f(x - 2x_0, y),$$

where $2x_0$ is the separation between the two input functions $f(x, y)$ and $g(x, y)$, and $\circledast$ denotes the correlation operation. Note that the cross-correlation functions are diffracted around $(\pm 2x_0, 0)$. Since the JTPS is encoded within a small region of the square-law detector, the overall system

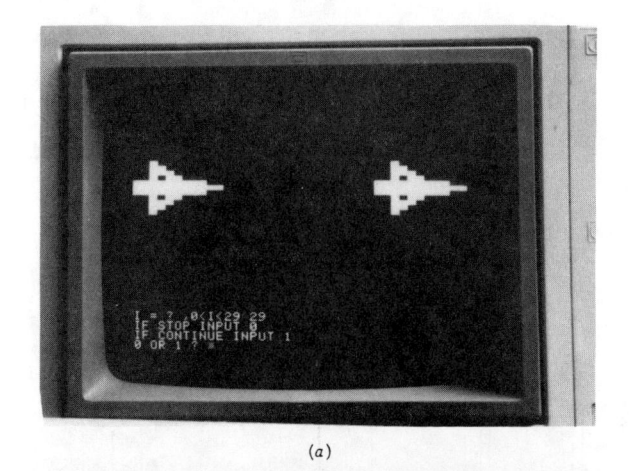

210 HYBRID-OPTICAL SIGNAL PROCESSING

(a)

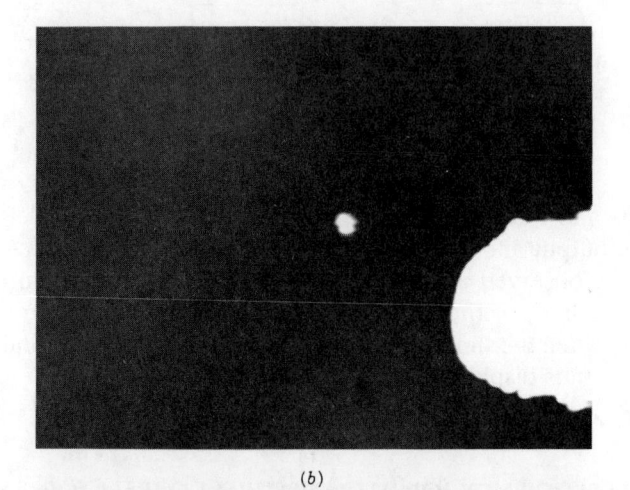

(b)

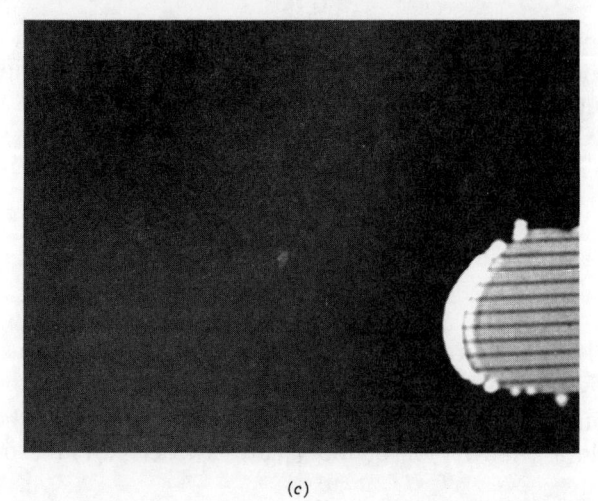

(c)

readout efficiency would be

$$\varepsilon = \varepsilon_m \frac{\iint |f(x, y) \circledast g(x, y)|^2 \, dx \, dy}{1/R \iint |u(x, y)|^2 \, dx \, dy}, \qquad (6.2)$$

where R is the ratio of the spectral size to the detector's dimension, and ε_m is the diffraction efficiency of the recording material. For example, if $f(x, y) = g(x, y)$, then $\varepsilon = \varepsilon_m R/6$. As an estimation, we assume that if $R = 1/35$ (for a 5 mm × 5 mm spectrum on a 35 mm × 25 mm film), then $\varepsilon = \varepsilon_m/210$. If a thin amplitude filter is used, then $\varepsilon_m = 6.25$ percent and $\varepsilon = 0.29$ percent; thus, we see that more than 97 percent of the power is wasted due to the R factor.

In this section, we discuss a hybrid-optical JTC in which the correlation diffraction efficiency can be dramatically increased, as suggested by Figure 6.7 [6.6]. Let us assume that the JTPS is picked up by the CCD1 array detector, by which it can be replicated into an $N \times N$ spectral array on SLM2. The corresponding amplitude transmittance is given by

$$T(p, q) = 2 \sum_{n=1}^{N} \sum_{m=1}^{N} |F(p - nd, q - md)|^2 \{1 + \cos[2x_0(p - nd)]\}, \qquad (6.3)$$

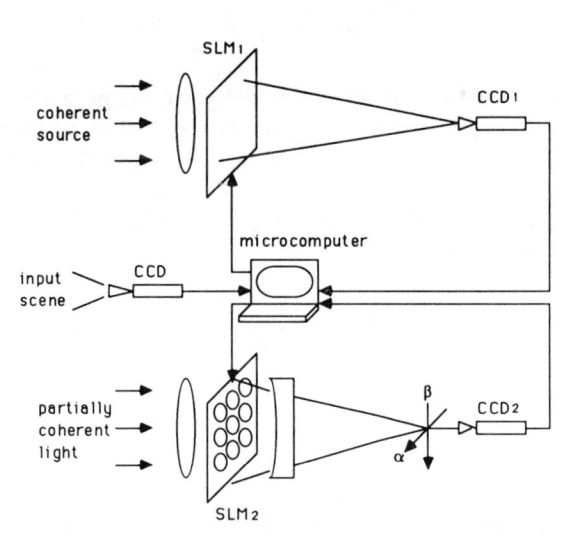

FIGURE 6.7 A High-efficiency joint transform correlator.

FIGURE 6.6 First experimental demonstration of the single LCTV–JTC. (*a*) identical input patterns displayed on the LCTV. (*b*) Correlation output of part (*a*). (*c*) dc output with no input pattern displayed on the LCTV.

where (p, q) is the angular spatial frequency coordinate system, and d is the bandwidth of the Fourier spectrum. Thus by coherent readout, the output intensity distribution would be

$$I_c(x, y) = \left| \sum_{n=1}^{N} \sum_{m=1}^{N} 2f(x, y) \circledast f(x, y)e^{i(ndx + mdy)} \right|^2$$

$$+ \left| \sum_{n=1}^{N} \sum_{m=1}^{N} f(x, y) \circledast f(x - 2x_0, y)e^{i(ndx + mdy - 4ndx_0)} \right|^2$$

$$+ \left| \sum_{n=1}^{N} \sum_{m=1}^{N} f(x, y) \circledast f(x + 2x_0, y)e^{i(ndx + mdy + 4ndx_0)} \right|^2 \quad (6.4)$$

It can be seen that if ndx is the integer multiple of 2π, the correlation peak intensity would be $(NN)^2$ times the conventional JTC. However, if it used a coherent readout, it would introduce coherent artifact noise.

On the other hand, by using a partial coherent readout, whose light source coherence width is assumed to be equal to the bandwidth of the Fourier spectrum, the output irradiance would be

$$I_{pc}(x, y) = NN[|2f(x, y) \circledast f(x, y)|^2$$

$$+ |f(x, y) \circledast f(x - 2x_0, y)|^2$$

$$+ |f(x, y) \circledast f(x + 2x_0, y)|^2]. \quad (6.5)$$

Thus, we see that correlation peak intensity would increase to $[1 + NN]$ times the JTC. We note that by using the partial coherent illumination, the coherent artifacts can be suppressed, thus increasing the output signal-to-noise ratio.

The overall correlation diffraction efficiency, when using partial coherent illumination, is given by

$$\varepsilon = N^2 \varepsilon_m \frac{\iint [f(x, y) \circledast f(x, y)]^2 \, dx \, dy}{1/R \iint |u(x, y)|^2 \, dx \, dy}, \quad (6.6)$$

which is increased by about N^2 times, as compared with Eq. 6.2.

To verify our discussion, we show the experimental results obtained by using coherent and partial coherent readouts in Figure 6.8. The results were obtained with a 3 × 3 replicated JTPS array. The correlation spots under coherent and partial coherent readouts are shown in Figure 6.8a and b, respectively. We see that the correlation intensity under the coherent readout

AUTONOMOUS TARGET TRACKING   213

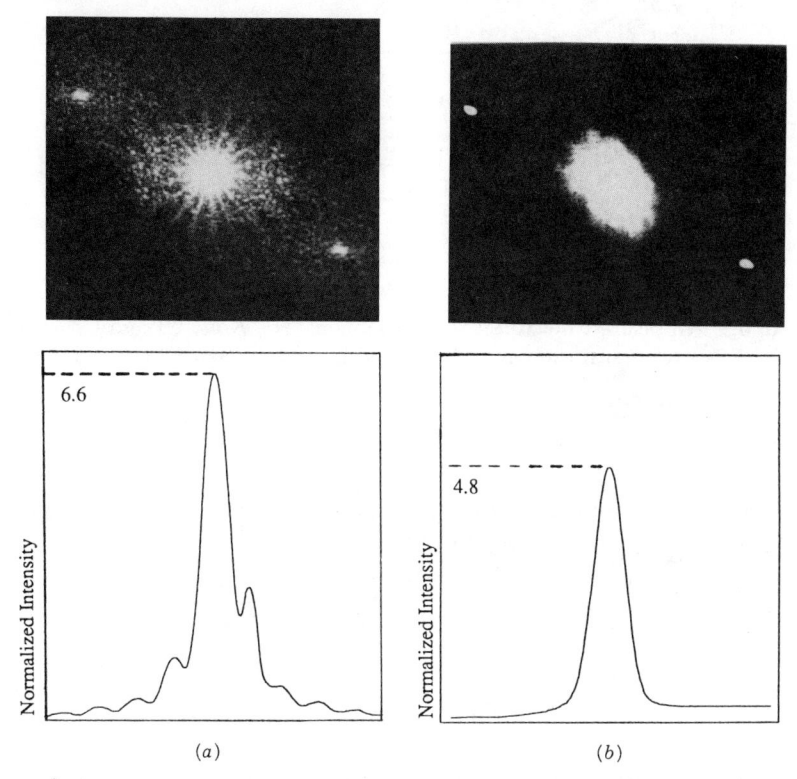

FIGURE 6.8 Output irradiance obtained with a 3 × 3 replicated JTPS array. (*a*) Using coherent readout. (*b*) Using partial coherent readout.

is higher and sharper than that under the partial coherent readout; however, the output signal-to-noise ratio seems to be lower in comparison with the partial coherent case. As discussed in Section 2.4, the JTCs can, in theory, perform all the processing operations that a 4-f processor can offer. Thus, the high-efficiency JTC can also be used as a generalized image processor.

6.4 AUTONOMOUS TARGET TRACKING

In this section, we discuss autonomous target tracking using a joint transform correlator (JTC) [6.7]. The idea is to correlate the object in the current frame with the object in the previous frame, such that the hybrid-optical system can be made adaptive by constantly updating the reference target with the dynamic object. The key element of the system is interfacing the LCTV with a microcomputer, as shown in Figure 6.9.

Let us assume that two sequential scenes of a moving object are displayed on the LCTV by a video frame grabber. The previous frame and the current

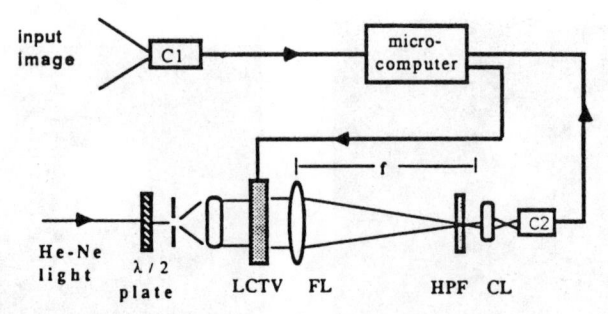

FIGURE 6.9 Optical architecture for the adaptive JTC. *Note:* C1 and C2 are CCD cameras; FL is the transform lens; CL is the camera lens; and HPF is the high-pass filter.

frame are positioned in the upper and lower half of the liquid crystal display (LCD), respectively, as depicted in Figure 6.10. Let

$$f_{t-1}\left(x - x_{t-1}, y - y_{t-1} - \frac{\alpha}{2}\right)$$

$$\text{and} \quad f_t\left(x - x_{t-1} - \delta x, y - y_{t-1} - \delta y + \frac{\alpha}{2}\right) \quad (6.7)$$

be the object functions, where 2α is the height of the display unit, t and $t - 1$ are the current and previous time frames, and $(\delta x, \delta y)$ is the relative translation of the object. Then the complex light field at the frequency plane is given by

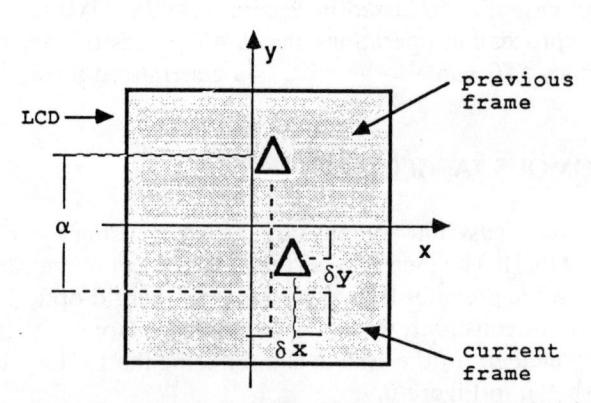

FIGURE 6.10 Two frames on the LCD. *Note:* 2α equals the height of the display unit.

$$T(u, v) = F_{t-1}(u, v)\exp\left\{-i2\pi\left[ux_{t-1} + v\left(y_{t-1} + \frac{\alpha}{2}\right)\right]\right\}$$
$$+ F_t(u, v)\exp\left\{-i2\pi\left[u(x_{t-1} + \delta x) + v\left(y_{t-1} + \delta y - \frac{\alpha}{2}\right)\right]\right\}. \quad (6.8)$$

The power spectrum recorded on the CCD camera C_2 is then sent back to the LCTV for an inverse Fourier transformation, in which the complex light field at the output plane becomes

$$\begin{aligned}C(x, y) &= \mathcal{F}^{-1}\{|T(u, v)|^2\} = R_{t,t}(x, y) \\ &+ R_{t-1,t-1}(x, y) + R_{t,t-1}(x + \delta x, y + \delta y - \alpha) \\ &+ R_{t-1,t}(x - \delta x, y - \delta y + \alpha),\end{aligned} \quad (6.9)$$

where

$$\begin{aligned}R_{m,n}(x, y) &= \mathcal{F}^{-1}\{F_m(u, v)F_n^*(u, v)\} \\ &= \int_{-\infty}^{+\infty}\int_{-\infty}^{+\infty} f_m(u, v)f_n^*(u - x, v - y)\, du\, dv\end{aligned}$$

is the correlation function between f_m and f_n. Note that the last two terms represent the cross-correlation terms, which are diffracted at $x_1 = \delta x$, $y_1 = (\delta y - \alpha)$ and $x_2 = \delta x$, $y_2 = (-\delta y + \alpha)$. Referring to our previous report [6.8], the angular and scale tolerances of the target in the JTC are roughly $\pm 5°$ and ± 10 percent, respectively. If we assume that the motion of the object is relatively slow as compared to the processing cycle of the correlator, we see that f_{t-1} correlates strongly with f_t, and that two high-intensity correlation peaks appear at the output plane, in which the new location of the object is given by

$$x_t = (x_{t-1} + x_1), \qquad y_t = (y_{t-1} + y_1 + \alpha). \quad (6.10)$$

A C language program can be used in the hybrid system to evaluate the object position. A block diagram of the system configuration is shown in Figure 6.11. Two video frame grabbers (IVG128 and AT428 from Datacube Inc.), which can digitize a full frame of input video signal into an image array, can be installed in the microcomputer. The video input of the AT428 board is connected to CCD camera C1, which is aimed at the object. The video output of the AT428 board is fed to the LCTV via a video/RF signal convertor. CCD camera C2 is connected to the IVG128 board and captures the joint transform power spectrum during the first half of the processing cycle. Since we do not use a video multiplexer, the recorded spectrum is sent from the IVG board to the AT board before it can be displayed on the LCTV. During the second

216 HYBRID-OPTICAL SIGNAL PROCESSING

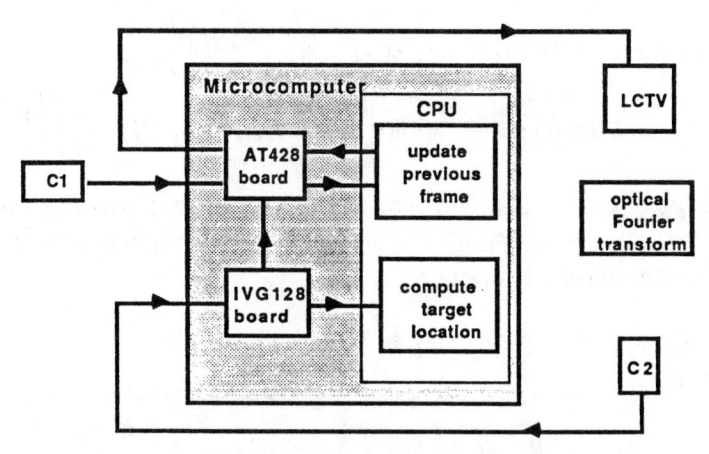

FIGURE 6.11 Optical–digital interface diagram.

half of the cycle, the correlation result is captured by camera C2, and the peak location is determined by sequentially scanning the image array for the pixel with maximum intensity. A position-sensitive detector or a parallel-array detector would definitely increase the time of detection. In spite of these hardware limitations, the system can run at approximately 1.2 sec/cycle. It is possible for the hybrid system to run at half the video frame frequency, which is $\frac{1}{2} \times 30 = 15$ cycles/sec, if specialized supporting hardware is used.

To describe the performance of the system: camera C1 was first focused on a stationary object, by which the correlation between two identical scenes is captured by camera C2. By slightly modifying the program, the original image is locked at the upper half of the LCD, and the updating input frame is always displayed on the lower half. The program is then set to run for 300 cycles, and the distribution of the correlation peak locations is plotted in Figure 6.12. The jittery video signal amplified by the low resolution of the LCTV might be one of the sources of error that cause fluctuation in the data. The deviation of the peak value is higher in the y direction because there are more pixels in this direction than in the x direction. Nevertheless, a standard deviation of less than a 0.5 pixel unit is a fairly acceptable result. Next, we translate the object along the x direction and then the y direction, respectively. Plots of the correlation peak as a function of the object's translation are shown in Figure 6.13. The result shows an excellent linear relationship between the object space and the correlation space, for which the scale factor can be evaluated in terms of the distance in the object space (or in the video system's space) per pixel unit. It is noted that the aspect ratio of the image array is given by

$$\text{Aspect ratio} = \frac{\text{monitor screen height} \times \text{number of horizontal pixels}}{\text{monitor screen width} \times \text{number of vertical pixels}},$$

(6.11)

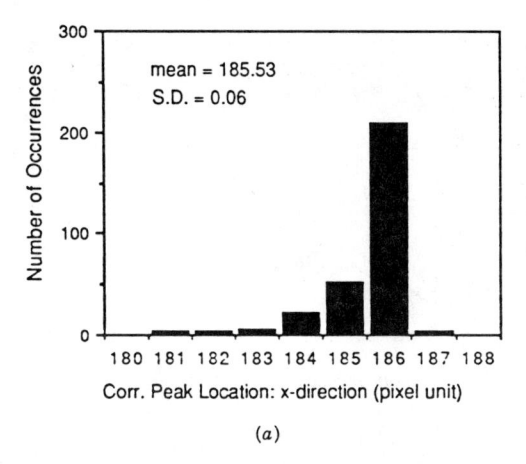

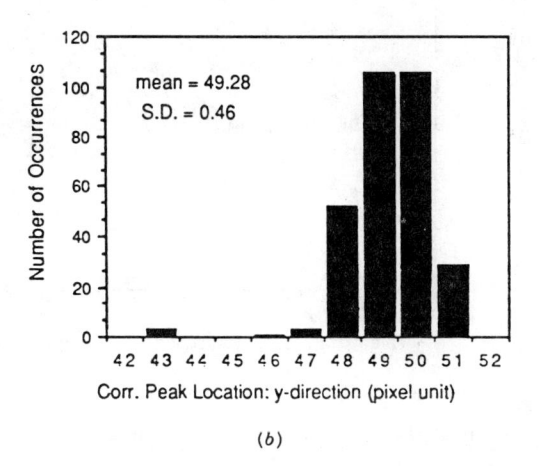

FIGURE 6.12 Distributions of the correlation peaks in 300 JTC cycles. (*a*) For the *x* direction. (*b*) For the *y* direction.

which is basically a measurement of the pixel element's height-to-width ratio. Comparing the number with the *x*, *y* scale factor ratio, we can check the overall accuracy performance of the system.

To test the actual performance, a tank-shaped graphical image was used as the next test object. The tank was set to revolve in an elliptical path, as shown in Figure 6.14*a*. The original program that updates both halves of the LCD was set to run autonomously. Figures 6.14*b* and *c* show the locations of the tank tracked, and proper *x*- and *y*-direction scale factors are used in the plots. Excellent tracking of the object's location is obtained at the end of the first revolution. However, after four revolutions, some deviations of the tracked points from the correct loci are observed. This deviation reveals that detection errors are accumulated during each correlation cycle, and are

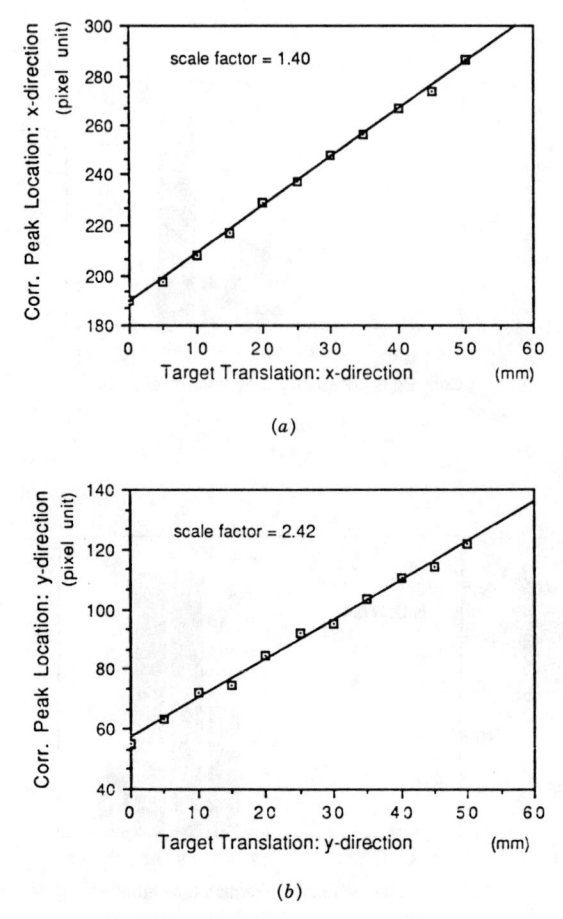

FIGURE 6.13 Location of the correlation peak as a function of object translation. (a) For the x direction. (b) For the y direction.

a general problem in object tracking based on the correlation between images in sequential frames.

One major merit of the proposed technique is its adaptive property. Let us assume that we have a situation in which a camera mounted on a moving space vehicle is focused on a fixed target on the ground for automatic navigation, as shown in Figure 6.15. As the space vehicle approaches the target, the detected scenes change continuously; the target size appears to be larger; and its orientation and shape also change due to the different angles caused by the motion of the vehicle. Using computer-aided design graphics, a three-dimensional tree-like object was created as a target on the ground. Nine image sequences simulating exactly the same scenes as captured by the moving space vehicle were recorded from a CAD terminal, as shown in Figure 6.16. The hybrid tracking system has little difficulty in correlating targets on dif-

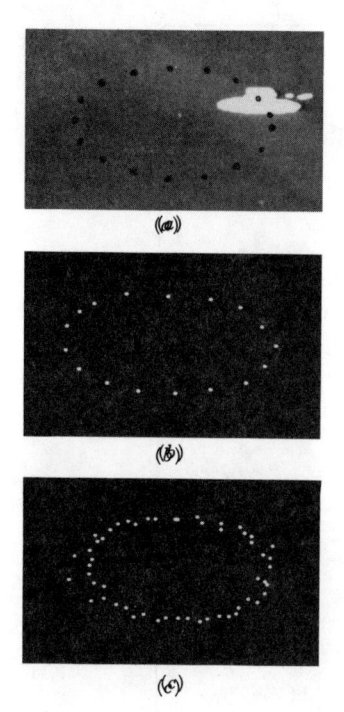

DATA ASSOCIATION MULTITARGET TRACKING 219

FIGURE 6.14 (*a*) An object revolves in an elliptical path at 21 sec/rev. The dark dots are the hand track of the tank's position at each of the JTC cycles. (*b*) The tracked positions of the tank after 1 revolution. (*c*) The same after 4 revolutions.

ferent frames; even the targets on the first and last frames look very different. Figure 6.17 shows the tracked location of the target as seen from the vehicle's coordinate frame.

In concluding this section, we stress that the adaptive property of the hybrid-optical system allows the tracking of a target even though the orientation, scale, and perspective change during the course of its motion. The simplicity and compactness of the system strongly suggest that it can be used in various civilian, military, and aerospace applications. We have made some elementary tests and obtained satisfactory results at an operating speed of 1.2 sec/cycle. Nevertheless, this result does not reflect the potential improvement, in terms of speed, accuracy, and reliability, one might expect from a more specialized implementation of the technique.

6.5 DATA ASSOCIATION MULTITARGET TRACKING

In this section, we describe a hybrid-optical technique for tackling a multitarget tracking problem. Let us assume that there are multiple targets whose dynamic states (e.g., locations and velocities) are to be evaluated in a motion sequence. A new scene is captured at every frame by an optical sensor. The space–bandwidth product in each frame is so high that it is extremely difficult for an all-electronic computer to process them on a real-time basis. Although

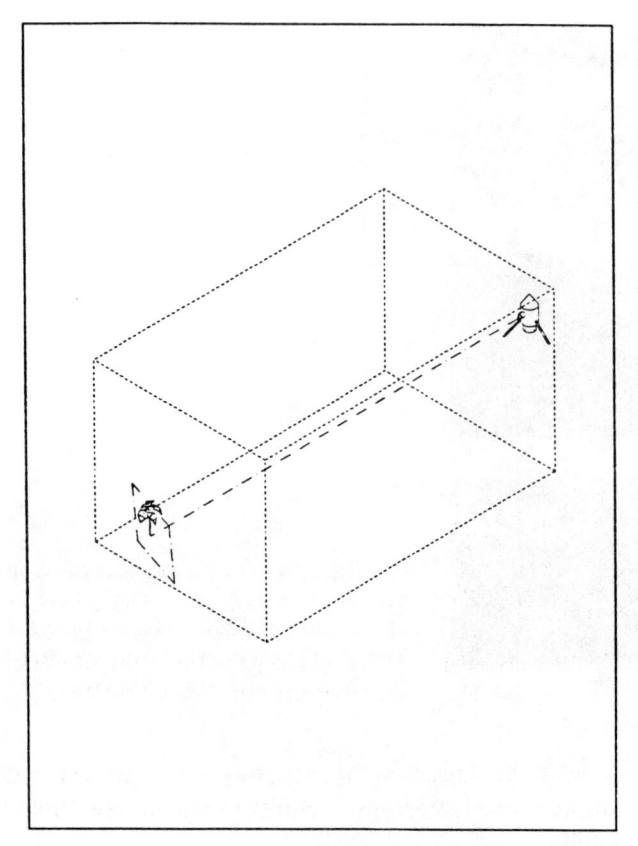

FIGURE 6.15 A camera on a space vehicle aimed at a fixed target on the ground for purposes of automatic navigation.

parallel processing can be performed by an optical system, it is not feasible to build an optical system that performs precise decision making. The hybrid optical system that we propose uses a joint transform correlator to carry out the correlation operation, and a data association algorithm for multiple target tracking. The advantages of a joint transform correlator (JTC) are simplicity, easier alignment, and the avoidance of matched filter synthesis. A JTC is also capable of adapting to new input scenes, thus allowing the previous frame to be used as a reference image for correlation with the target in the current frame (see Section 6.4). Assuming that the processing cycle of the system is sufficiently short, a target will look much the same after a few sequential frames, and hence strong correlation peaks are produced. The position measurements of the correlation peaks can be interpreted as the average velocities of the targets within the tracking system. Based on these measurements, the dynamic states of the targets can be updated. Since multiple correlation peaks are produced in a multitarget tracking problem, a data association algorithm

FIGURE 6.16 A sequence of nine images are recorded from a CAD terminal, simulating the exact scenes as captured by a camera mounted on a moving space vehicle. Only frames 1, 5, and 9 are shown here.

FIGURE 6.17 Tracked positions of the ground target as seen from the vehicle's coordinate frame.

should be employed to associate each of the peaks with the correct path of its target's motion [6.9].

Assume that $f^n(x, y)$, with $n = 1$ to N, represents the moving targets in an image sequence. Two sequential scenes displayed on the input plane of the hybrid JTC shown in Figure 6.18, such that the previous frame $(k - 1)$ and the current frame (k) are positioned in the upper and lower halves of the LCTV, as given by

$$T(x, y) = \sum_{n=1}^{N} f_{k-1}^n\left(x - x_{k-1}^n, y - y_{k-1}^n - \frac{\alpha}{2}\right)$$

$$+ \sum_{n=1}^{N} f_k^n\left(x - x_{k-1}^n - \delta x_k^n, y - y_{k-1}^n - \delta y_k^n + \frac{\alpha}{2}\right), \quad (6.12)$$

where 2α is the height of the LCTV aperture, (x_{k-1}^n, y_{k-1}^n) are the locations of the targets in the $k - 1$ frame, and $(\delta x_k^n, \delta y_k^n)$ are the relative translations. The corresponding joint transform power spectrum (JTPS) is given by

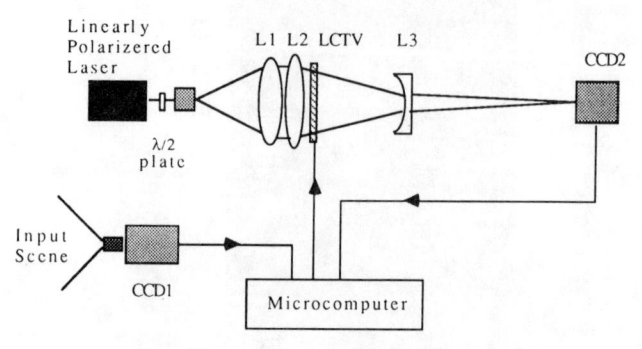

FIGURE 6.18 A hybrid-optical JTC.

$$C(x,y) = \sum_{n=1}^{N}\sum_{m=1}^{N} R_{k-1,k-1}^{m,n}(x + x_{k-1}^m - x_{k-1}^n, y + y_{k-1}^m - y_{k-1}^n)$$
$$+ \sum_{n=1}^{N}\sum_{m=1}^{N} R_{k,k}^{m,n}(x + x_{k-1}^m - \delta x_k^m - x_{k-1}^n + \delta x_k^n, y + y_{k-1}^m - \delta y_k^m - y_{k-1}^n + \delta y_k^n)$$
$$+ \sum_{n=1}^{N}\sum_{m=1}^{N} R_{k-1,k}^{m,n}(x + x_{k-1}^m - x_{k-1}^n + \delta x_k^n, y + y_{k-1}^m - y_{k-1}^n + \delta y_k^n + \alpha)$$
$$+ \sum_{n=1}^{N}\sum_{m=1}^{N} R_{k-1,k}^{m,n}(x + x_{k-1}^m - \delta x_k^m - x_{k-1}^n, y + y_{k-1}^m - \delta y_k^m - y_{k-1}^n - \alpha), \quad (6.13)$$

where

$$R_{k,k'}^{m,n}(x - \alpha, y - \beta) = f_k^m(x,y) \circledast f_{k'}^n(x,y) * \delta(x - \alpha, y - \beta) \quad (6.14)$$

is the correlation function f_k^m, and f_k^n, located at (α, β) and $\circledast$ and $*$ denote the correlation and convolution operations, respectively.

Note that the correlation between the same target in the k frame and the $k - 1$ frame, given as $R_{k,k-1}^{n,n}$, are diffracted around $(\delta x_k^n, \delta y_k^n + \alpha)$ and $(-\delta x_k^n, -\delta y_k^n - \alpha)$, and that the other terms $(R_{k,k-1}^{m,n},$ and $R_{k,k}^{m,n}$ for $m \neq n$) represent the cross-correlation functions between target m and target n. We further assume that the target functions do not look alike, which would cause the intercorrelations among them to be weaker. Furthermore, the size and the gray level of the targets are also assumed to be relatively congruous with each other so that the correlation peaks produced by $R_{k,k-1}^{n,n}$ are not significantly different.

By translating the coordinate origin from the optical axis to $(0, \alpha)$, the correlation peaks generated from the same target in the $k - 1$ and k frames are then located at $(\delta x_k^n, \delta y_k^n)$, a new coordinate system. If these correlation peaks are associated with the proper target motions, the locations of the targets in the k frame can be represented as

$$x_k^n = x_{k-1}^n + \delta x_k^n, \quad y_k^n = y_{k-1}^n + \delta y_k^n, \quad n = 1 \text{ to } N. \quad (6.15)$$

This equation shows that the new locations of the targets can be updated based on their locations in the previous frame and the position measurements of the correlation peaks. It is apparent that the k and $k + 1$ frames can be sent to the input plane in the next tracking cycle, and that multiple targets can thus be traced simultaneously in near-real-time mode. We also see that the position of the correlation peak represents the average velocity of a target of the sampling interval δt, that is,

$$\bar{x} = \frac{\delta x}{\delta t}, \quad \bar{y} = \frac{\delta y}{\delta t}. \quad (6.16)$$

For instance, targets moving at a constant velocity product stationary correlation peaks, while those moving with constant acceleration produce correlation peaks that are located at equally separated intervals on a straight line, and stationary targets produce correlation peaks located at the origin of the new coordinate plane.

We now describe a parameter-based data association algorithm using a Kalman filtering model. It is assumed that the sampling interval δt is sufficiently short, so that the dynamic parameters (velocity, acceleration, angular velocity, etc.) of the targets are fairly consistent within a few sequential frames. Thus, given the dynamic parameters of a target in the k frame, the parameters in the next frame are predictable. If we let $z(k)$ be the measurement at the k frame and $\hat{z}(k|k-1)$ be the predicted measurement in the k frame based upon the information evaluated up to the $k-1$ frame, then the innovation (or measurement residue) can be defined as

$$v(k) = z(k) - \hat{z}(k|k-1), \qquad (6.17)$$

which can be used to evaluate the likelihood association between $z(k)$ and the target under consideration. In stochastic models, one would evaluate the normalized squared distance D from the measured $z(k)$ to the current track:

$$D = v'S^{-1}v. \qquad (6.18)$$

where v' is the transpose of v, and S is the innovation covariance of the target, which is basically the variance of the estimated states. The values of $\hat{z}(k|k-1)$, S, and the like can be evaluated by applying a standard Kalman filter to the dynamic model. The use of Kalman filtering in stochastic modeling is a well known subject on its own and so will not be discussed here. Interested readers can refer to the text by Mayback [6.10].

As an example, the data association process can be carried out as follows:

STEP 1:

At the $k-1$ frame, the dynamic parameters of the N targets are determined at track 1 to N.

STEP 2:

At the k frame, N new measurements, given as $a, b, \ldots N$, are made. The normalized square distances are then computed:

$$D_{1a} = v'_{1a}S_1^{-1}v_{1a}, \qquad D_{1b} = v'_{1b}S_1^{-1}v_{1b}, \ldots,$$

and similarly for $D_{2a}, D_{2b}, \ldots, D_{3a}, \ldots$.

STEP 3:

The most likely association is given by choosing the possible combination of D's that yields the minimum sum.

To initiate the tracker, all the measurements in the first few tracking cycles are used to set up multiple potential tracks. Tracks that have inconsistent dynamic parameters are dropped until only a single track is assigned to each target. Recall that the measurement in each cycle is the average velocity of a target during the sampling period. Therefore, dynamic parameters can be assigned quickly in a few cycles: only two or three cycles are needed to determine targets with constant velocity or constant acceleration. The tracking scheme discussed so far, does not, however, determine the initial positions of the targets in the first frame, nor, due to its nature, does it assign measurements to the targets. Therefore, an initial acquisition scheme is needed to perform this task before the start of the adaptive tracker. The task can be done by using prestored reference images located at fixed positions at the image plane.

To demonstrate the ability of the tracking algorithm, a motion sequence of three targets was generated as shown in Figure 6.19. A target-tracking model was then set up as follows. First, the dynamic state of the target at the k frame was defined as

$$\mathbf{x}(k) \equiv \begin{pmatrix} x(k) \\ \dot{x}(k) \end{pmatrix}. \tag{6.19}$$

Since motion along each coordinate can be decoupled, we only need to consider one direction. Acceleration and maneuvering of the targets can be handled by including processing noise n in the dynamic equation

$$\mathbf{x}(k+1) = \begin{pmatrix} 1 & 1 \\ 0 & 1 \end{pmatrix} \mathbf{x}(k) + \begin{pmatrix} 1 \\ 1 \end{pmatrix} n, \tag{6.20}$$

so the measurement is

$$z(k) = (0 \ \ 1)\mathbf{x}(k) + w, \tag{6.21}$$

where w is the measurement noise. A Kalman filtering process can therefore be applied to the tracking problem. The innovation covariance S can be computed so the normalized squared distance D in Eq. 6.18 can be evaluated,

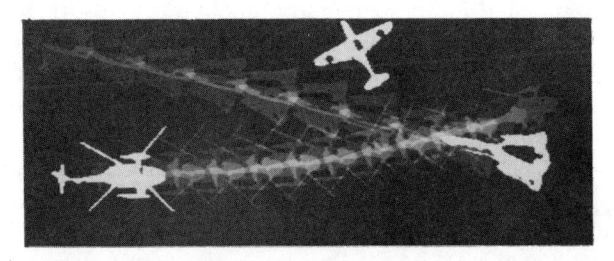

FIGURE 6.19 Motion sequence of three targets. The helicopter and jet are moving from bottom to top and the aeroplane is stationary.

and the data association process described in the preceding section can be carried out. However, our goal here is to demonstrate the capability of the optical tracker and to illustrate the data association algorithm. Therefore, in order to show the basic performance rather than the filtered results in this example, we simply assume a noise-free measurement situation ($w = 0$), which immediately sets the gain of the filter to one. The updated dynamic states of the target are then solely determined by the new measurements, and the predicted measurement is given by

$$\hat{z}(k|k-1) = z(k-1). \tag{6.22}$$

For simplicity, the value of S is also assigned as the variance of the target's velocity in a number of tracing cycles.

A computer program that controls the joint transform process as well as the data association process can be written. To initiate the coordinate, the system is first set to run with a stationary object as input, and the position of the correlation peak thus generated is assigned as the origin of the velocity plane coordinate. The tracking program is then set to run autonomously, with the motion sequence in Figure 6.20 as inputs. The computer program was written in Microsoft C, which ran on a microcomputer using an INTEL 386 processor operated at 25 MHz, and the processing time for a tracking cycle was approximately 0.7 sec. Figures 6.21a and b show the images as displayed on the LCTV and the corresponding correlation spots generated during each step of the tracking cycle. To avoid unnecessary data transfer, the current frame is alternatively loaded onto the upper and lower half of the LCTV during every tracking cycle. This modification generates a correlation plane whose coordinate axes are inverted at each cycle, and the location of the measurements has to be interpreted accordingly. The final results are shown in Figure 6.21, in which the actual locations of the targets are also provided for comparison at each step of the tracking system. As can be seen, a relatively simple hybrid-optical architecture is capable of tracking multiple targets rather accurately.

6.6 ACOUSTOOPTIC SPACE INTEGRATOR

Acoustooptic (AO) signal correlators have been of particular interest for such applications as matched filters, ambiguity function processors, and spectrum analyzers [6.11]–[6.17], in which real-time processing is indispensable. A variety of architectures for signal correlators have been developed. These architectures can be categorized into two basic types: multiplicative and additive. In the multiplicative type, the laser beam is sequentially modulated by two successive AO cells and detected by a photodetector array. In the additive type, the laser beam is split into two paths, each of which is singly modulated by an AO cell and combined on a photodetector array where square-law mixing takes place.

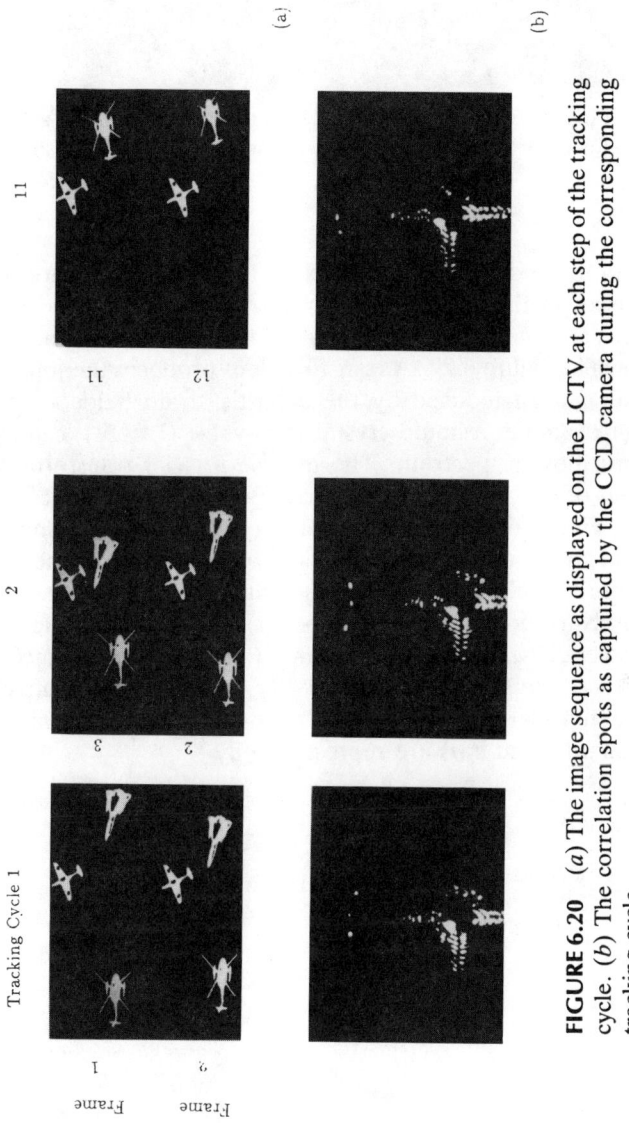

FIGURE 6.20 (*a*) The image sequence as displayed on the LCTV at each step of the tracking cycle. (*b*) The correlation spots as captured by the CCD camera during the corresponding tracking cycle.

228 HYBRID-OPTICAL SIGNAL PROCESSING

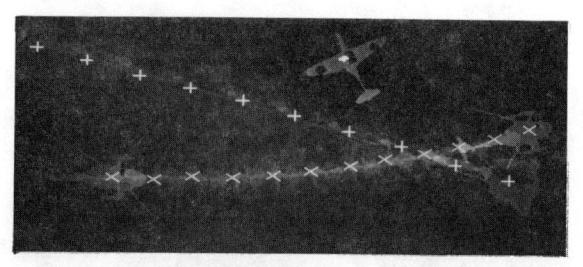

FIGURE 6.21 Final results obtained after eleven tracking cycles. The actual locations of the targets at each of the tracing cycles are also given for comparison.

In this section, we discuss an architecture for a real-time space-integrating correlator based on the joint transform correlator [6.18]. Two parallel on-plane AO cells are employed to convert electrical signals into acoustic strain fields, as shown in Figure 6.22. A transform lens produces the joint transform of the optical pattern induced by the acoustic strain fields. A square-law converter, for example, a liquid crystal light valve (LCLV), can extract the joint transform power spectrum. The inverse Fourier transform of the coherent readout of the square-law converter provides the cross-correlation of input signals. Figure 6.23 gives the geometry of the input plane. Two AO cells (AO_1 and AO_2) with dimensions a and b are inserted in the input plane with centers at $(a/2, h/2)$ and $(a/2, -h/2)$. Both AO cells are operating in the Bragg regime. Narrow-band input signals $s_1(t)$ and $s_2(t)$ induce acoustic strain fields in the AO cells, in which we assume that the transmittance functions of AO_1 and AO_2 are $g_1(x, y - h/2, t)$ and $g_2(x, y + h/2, t)$, respectively, where h is a separation between two cells, and t denotes the time variable. Now let us assume that $s_1(t)$ and $s_2(t)$ are represented by

$$s_1(t) = a_1(t)\cos[\omega t + \phi_1(t)] = \tilde{s}_1(t) + \tilde{s}_1^*(t), \tag{6.23}$$

$$s_2(t) = a_2(t)\cos[\omega t + \phi_2(t)] = \tilde{s}_2(t) + \tilde{s}_2^*(t), \tag{6.24}$$

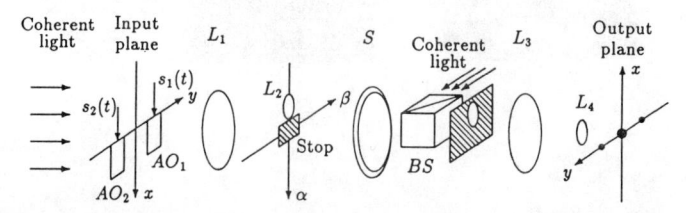

FIGURE 6.22 Optical setup for an acoustooptic signal correlator. *Note:* AO_1 and AO_2 are the acoustooptic cells; L_1 and L_3 are the transform lenses; L_2 and L_4 are the magnifying lenses; S is the square-law converter; BS is the beam splitter.

ACOUSTOOPTIC SPACE INTEGRATOR   229

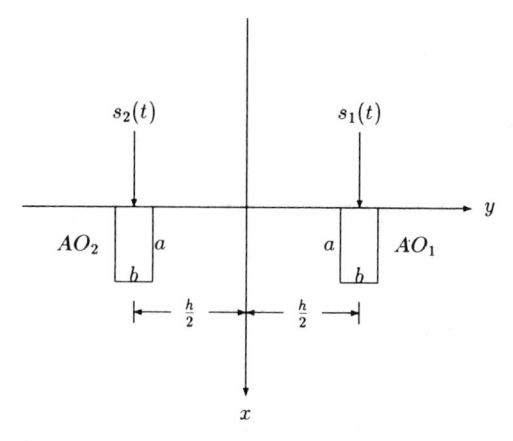

FIGURE 6.23 The geometry of a two-cell system.

where

$$\tilde{s}_1(t) = \frac{1}{2}\tilde{a}_1(t)\exp(i\omega t), \tag{6.25}$$

$$\tilde{s}_2(t) = \frac{1}{2}\tilde{a}_2(t)\exp(i\omega t), \tag{6.26}$$

$$\tilde{a}_1(t) = a_1(t)\exp[i\phi_1(t)], \tag{6.27}$$

$$\tilde{a}_2(t) = a_2(t)\exp[i\phi_2(t)], \tag{6.28}$$

Here $\tilde{a}_1(t)$ and $\tilde{a}_2(t)$ represent complex envelopes of $s_1(t)$ and $s_2(t)$ respectively; $\phi_1(t)$ and $\phi_2(t)$ represent phase factors; ω is a carrier frequency; the superscript asterisk represents the complex conjugate, and the terms $\tilde{s}_1(t)$ and $\tilde{s}_2(t)$, having no negative frequency component, are the analytic signals associated with $s_1(t)$ and $s_2(t)$. The two terms of Eqs. 6.23 and 6.24 correspond to the downshifted (-1) diffraction order and upshifted ($+1$) diffraction order. Either downshifted or upshifted diffraction order can be observed in the Bragg regime. In the following discussion, we assume the downshifted components $\tilde{s}_1(t)$ and $\tilde{s}_2(t)$.

By taking the input end of the AO cells as the origin of the x axis, $g_1(x, y, t)$ and $g_2(x, y, t)$ can be written as

$$g_1(x, y, t) = \exp\left[i\gamma \tilde{s}_1\left(t - \frac{x}{v}\right)\right]w(x, y), \tag{6.29}$$

$$g_2(x, y, t) = \exp\left[i\gamma \tilde{s}_2\left(t - \frac{x}{v}\right)\right]w(x, y), \tag{6.30}$$

where

$$w(x, y) = \begin{cases} 1, & 0 \le x \le a, \; -\dfrac{b}{2} \le y \le \dfrac{b}{2}, \\ 0, & \text{otherwise,} \end{cases}$$

γ is the modulation depth, and v is sound velocity in the AO cells. For small γ, Eqs. 6.29 and 6.30 can be approximated by the following equalities:

$$g_1(x, y, t) \simeq \left[1 + i\gamma \tilde{s}_1\left(t - \frac{x}{v}\right)\right] w(x, y), \tag{6.31}$$

$$g_2(x, y, t) \simeq \left[1 + i\gamma \tilde{s}_2\left(t - \frac{x}{v}\right)\right] w(x, y), \tag{6.32}$$

The first terms in the brackets correspond to zero-order diffractions that are eliminated by spatial filtering as giving by

$$g_1(x, y, t) \simeq i\gamma \tilde{s}_1\left(t - \frac{x}{v}\right) w(x, y), \tag{6.33}$$

$$g_2(x, y, t) \simeq i\gamma \tilde{s}_2\left(t - \frac{x}{v}\right) w(x, y). \tag{6.34}$$

It is apparent that the complex light field at the focal plane of lens L_1 can be written as

$$\begin{aligned} G(\alpha, \beta, t) &= \mathscr{F}\left\{ g_1\left(x, y - \frac{h}{2}, t\right) + g_2\left(x, y + \frac{h}{2}, t\right) \right\} \\ &= \exp\left(-\frac{ih\beta}{2}\right) G_1(\alpha, \beta, t) + \exp\left(\frac{ih\beta}{2}\right) G_2(\alpha, \beta, t), \end{aligned} \tag{6.35}$$

where $G_1(\alpha, \beta, t)$ and $G_2(\alpha, \beta, t)$ are the Fourier spectra of $g_1(x, y, t)$ and $g_2(x, y, t)$, respectively.

Interference fringes are generated by the modulation of $G_1(\alpha, \beta, t)$ and $G_2(\alpha, \beta, t)$ by which they are magnified by L_2 onto the square-law converter S. The intensity distribution at the output end of the square-law converter is given by

$$\begin{aligned} |G(\alpha, \beta, t)|^2 &= |G_1(\alpha, \beta, t)|^2 + |G_2(\alpha, \beta, t)|^2 \\ &\quad + \exp(-ih\beta) G_1(\alpha, \beta, t) G_2^*(\alpha, \beta, t) \\ &\quad \exp(ih\beta) G_1^*(\alpha, \beta, t) G_2(\alpha, \beta, t), \end{aligned} \tag{6.36}$$

where the magnification constant is omitted for simplicity.

By coherent readout the complex light distribution at the output plane can be shown as

$$g(x, y, t) = [R_{11}(x, y, t) + R_{22}(x, y, t) + R_{12}(x, y - h, t) + R_{21}(x, y + h, t)], \tag{6.37}$$

where

$$R_{ij}(x, y, t) = \mathcal{F}^{-1}\{G_i(\alpha, \beta, t)G_j^*(\alpha, \beta, t)\}$$

$$= \int_{-\infty}^{+\infty}\int_{-\infty}^{+\infty} g_i(\alpha + x, \beta + y, t)g_j^*(\alpha, \beta, t)d\alpha\, d\beta, \tag{6.38}$$

the asterisk and the superscript asterisk represent the convolution operation and the complex conjugate, respectively; R_{11} and R_{22} are the autocorrelation functions that appear at the origin of the output plane; R_{12} and R_{21} are the cross-correlation terms that are centered around $y = h$ and $y = -h$, respectively. We note that these cross-correlation patterns are magnified by lens L_4 for the convenience of observation.

By substituting Eqs. 6.25 and 6.26 into inequalities 6.33 and 6.34, and ignoring the window effect w, the intensity distribution at $y = h$ can be shown as

$$|R_{12}(x, 0, t)|^2 = \frac{\gamma^2 b^2 y^2}{16} \left|r_{12}\left(-\frac{x}{v}, t\right)\right|^2, \tag{6.39}$$

which is proportional to the square value of the cross-correlation of $\tilde{a}_1$ and $\tilde{a}_2$, that is,

$$r_{12}(x, t) = \int_{-\infty}^{+\infty} \tilde{a}_1(t + \alpha + x)\tilde{a}_2^*(t + \alpha)\, d\alpha. \tag{6.40}$$

We stress that if the signal duration is longer than the cell length or the effect of $w(x, y)$ cannot be ignored, only partial correlation can be obtained. We further note that the cross-correlation can be obtained only if the frame rate of the square-law converter is sufficiently high. For example, if the signal takes 10 μs to fulfill the aperture of the AO cell, the necessary frame rate is about 100 kHz. Unfortunately, with the current stage of technology, such a high frame rate is not achievable in existing square-law converters.

For the purposes of experimental demonstration, we assume that a sinusoidal signal at frequency 65 MHz is applied to both AO cells. The separation h between cells is about 15 mm. The aperture dimensions $a = 5$ mm $b = 3$ mm were selected to be sufficiently small so that a larger main lobe could be obtained. Figure 6.24a shows the interference fingers of the joint transform power spectrum, in which the fringe size is equal to $\lambda f/h$, where f is the focal

232 HYBRID-OPTICAL SIGNAL PROCESSING

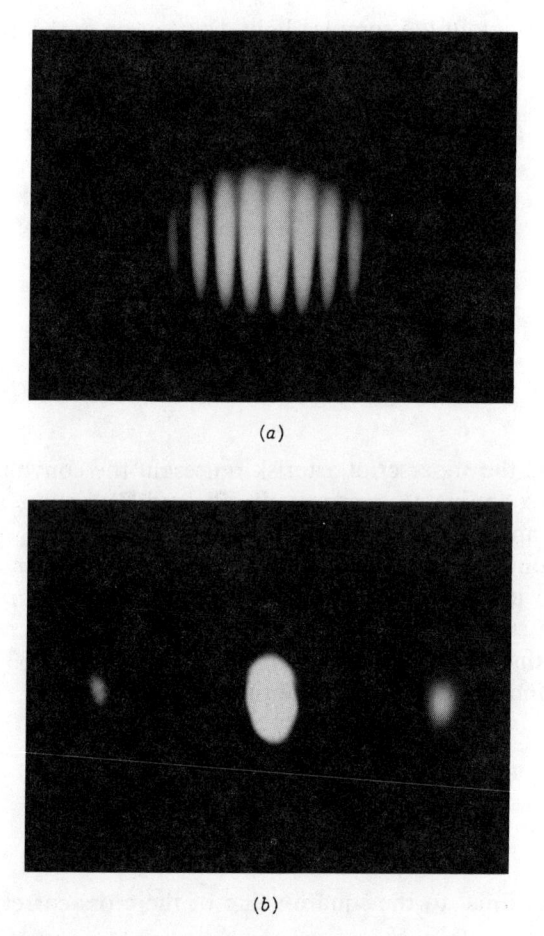

FIGURE 6.24 Experimental results. (*a*) Write-in JTPS. (*b*) Output correlation peaks. The center spot is the zero-order diffraction.

length of lens L_1, and λ is the wavelength of illumination. The corresponding readout correlation spots are shown in Figure 6.24*b*.

6.7 MULTIPLE-FREQUENCY-SHIFT KEYING SIGNAL DETECTION

In the preceding section, we discussed an acoustooptic space integrator, in which two AO cells were used to produce cross-correlation between two temporal signals. We note that the proposed system is capable of processing signals that are modulated by frequency-shift keying (FSK).

In this section we expand the concept for a multiple AO cell system that deals with multiple-frequency signals, so that higher communication throughout can be obtained. The proposed multicell system is suitable for the application of detecting multiple-frequency-shift keying (MFSK) communication signals [6.19].

Figure 6.25a shows a schematic diagram of an acoustooptic joint transform correlator, which consists of an array of AO cells at the input plane and a liquid crystal light valve (LCLV) acting as a square-law detector for the composite Fourier-to-power-spectrum conversion. The geometrical locations of the AO cells at the input plane are shown in Figure 6.25b. One of the AO cells, which is referred to as a reference cell, is driven by a local reference signal $s_0(t)$. We assume $N - 1$ number of signals $s_n(t)$, received from a communication path, are fed into the other $N - 1$ AO cells, which are called *signal cells*. If all the signal cells are equally spaced on the right-hand side of the input plane, then the reference cell would be placed on the left-hand side at a distance $(N - 1)h$ apart from the optical axis, where h is the spacing of the signal cells. Thus, the cross-correlations among received signals would be diffracted within a distance $(N - 2)h$ from the optical axis, while the cross-correlation between reference and received signals would be diffracted away from those undesired correlation spots.

Now assume that the input signals $s_n(t)$ are narrow-band signals, which can be decomposed into the sum of two analytic signals

$$s_n(t) = \tilde{s}_n(t) + \tilde{s}_n^*(t), \qquad n = 0, 1, 2, \ldots, N - 1. \qquad (6.41)$$

The corresponding transmittance functions of the AO cells can be approximated by (Section 6.6)

$$g_n(x, y, t) \simeq i\gamma \tilde{s}_n(t - x/v) w_n(x, y), \qquad n = 0, 1, 2, \ldots, N - 1, \qquad (6.42)$$

where γ and $w_n(x, y)$ are the modulation depth and the window function of the AO cells, respectively. Note that the window function represents not only the aperture size but also includes the uniformity of illumination, misalignment factor, and roughness of the crystal. Thus, the light distribution emerging from the AO cells can be written as

$$E(x, y, t) = g_0(x, y + (N - 1)h, t)$$
$$+ \sum_{n=1}^{N-1} g_n(x, y - h(n - 1), t). \qquad (6.43)$$

The Fourier transform can be projected through transform lens L_1 onto the input end of a square-law converter (i.e., LCLV). Lens L_2 is used to magnify the joint Fourier spectra, so that the interference fringes would be within the resolution limit of the LCLV. Since the readout light field of the square-law converter is proportional to the square modulus of this Fourier

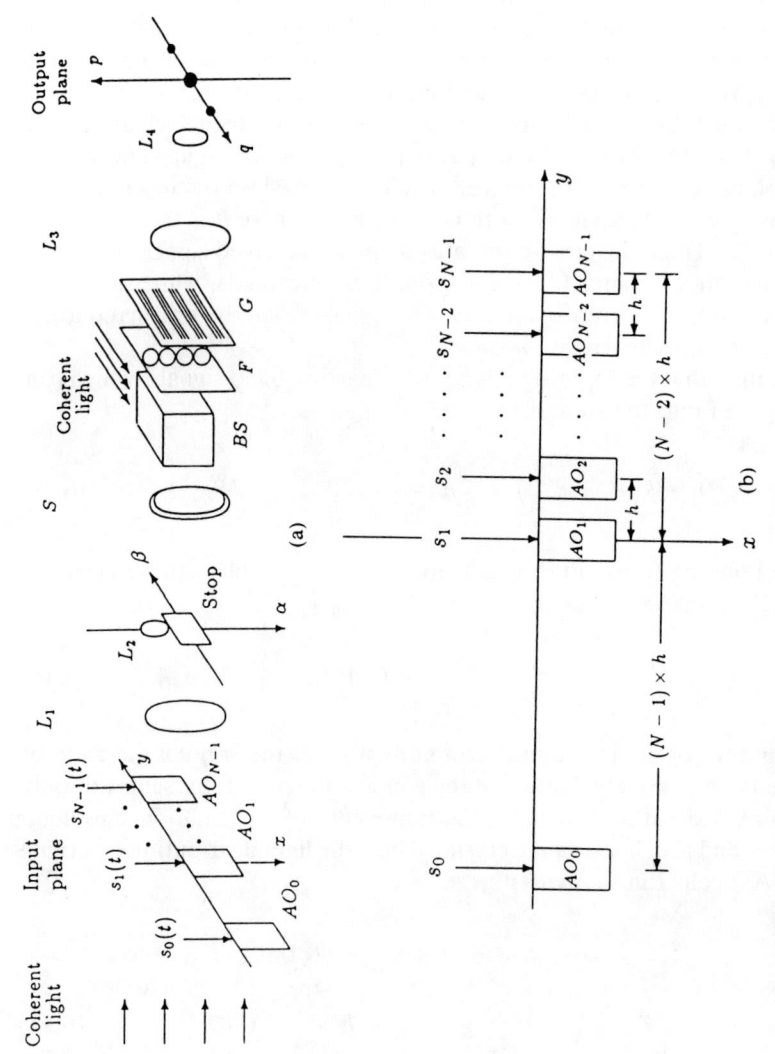

FIGURE 6.25 (a) Multicell-multifrequency acoustooptic JTC. *Note:* AO's are the acoustooptic cells; L_1 and L_3 are the transform lenses; L_2 and L_4 are the magnifying lenses; S is the square-law converter; BS is the beam splitter; F is the spatial filter; G is the grating. (b) The geometry of the multicell system.

MULTIPLE-FREQUENCY-SHIFT KEYING SIGNAL DETECTION 235

transform, we have

$$|E(\alpha, \beta, t)|^2 = \sum_{n=0}^{N-1} |G_n(\alpha, \beta, t)|^2$$

$$= \sum_{n=1}^{N-1} G_0(\alpha, \beta, t) G_n^*(\alpha, \beta, t) \exp[ih(N + n - 2)]$$

$$+ \sum_{n=1}^{N-1} G_0^*(\alpha, \beta, t) G_n(\alpha, \beta, t) \exp[ih(N + n - 2)]$$

$$+ \sum_{n=1}^{N-1} \sum_{m=1}^{N-1} G_n(\alpha, \beta, t) G_m^*(\alpha, \beta, t) \exp[ih(n - m)], \quad (6.44)$$

where $G_n(\alpha, \beta, t)$ are the Fourier transforms of $g_n(x, y, t)$.

The complex light distribution at the output plane would be

$$E(p, q, t) = \sum_{n=0}^{N-1} R_{nn}(p, q, t)$$

$$+ \sum_{n=1}^{N-1} R_{0n}(p, q + h(N + n - 2), t)$$

$$+ \sum_{n=1}^{N-1} R_{n0}(p, q - h(N + n - 2), t)$$

$$+ \sum_{n=1}^{N-1} \sum_{m=1}^{N-1} R_{nm}(p, q - h(n - m), t), \quad (6.45)$$

where

$$R_{nm}(p, q, t) = \int_{-\infty}^{+\infty} \int_{-\infty}^{+\infty} g_n(\alpha + p, \beta + q) g_m^*(\alpha, \beta, t) \, d\alpha \, d\beta.$$

The first summation represents the autocorrelation terms of the input signals, which are diffracted at the origin of the output plane. The second and third summations correspond to the cross-correlations between the reference and the input signal terms, which are diffracted in the vicinity of $[0, \pm h(N + n - 2)]$. These correlation spots can be separated if the spacing h is sufficiently large. The last summation represents the undesired cross-correlations of the input signals, which would be diffracted within the distance $(N - 2)h$ from the optical axis. Notice that these terms are separated from the desired reference to input signal correlation spots.

Also note that, if they match the reference frequencies, the correlation spots from the second and third summations represent the frequency content of the input signals. The position of each correlation spot indicates that the signal cell has the same frequency components as the reference cell. Because the frequency components are diffracted to the same correlation spots, the actual temporal frequencies cannot be determined.

To overcome this problem, gratings of different spatial frequencies are added behind the square-law converter, as shown in the figure. A linear array of band-pass spatial filters is also introduced to reduce the zero-order diffraction component. Since the AO cells diffract incident light at different angles, a series of Fourier spectra along the vertical axis can be obtained. If a signal contains one of the frequency components of the reference cell, linear interference fringes would be produced in the corresponding Fourier spot, thus determining the horizontal location of the output correlation spots. The gratings behind the square-law converter separate the superimposed correlation spots in the vertical direction. One of the possible arrangements of the output correlation spots is shown in Figure 6.26. The correlation spots within the dashed box represent the frequency content of the input signal cells.

Since efficient diffraction by the AO cell occurs at the Bragg angle, the signal should be implemented around the Bragg frequency. The incoming wide-band signal is divided into small subbands that fit into the bandwidth of the AO cells. The center frequency of each subband is then translated to the Bragg frequency before being input to the AO cells. We assume that there are $N - 1$ signal cells and that each subband has M frequency-division channels. The system can then deal with $M(N - 1)$ channels simultaneously.

A block diagram of the proposed receiving system is given in Figure 6.27. The first frequency converter selects the appropriate communication band, and demodulates the signal to the intermediate frequency that is the Bragg frequency of the system. The secondary frequency converters are used to translate the center frequency of the subbands to the appropriate Bragg fre-

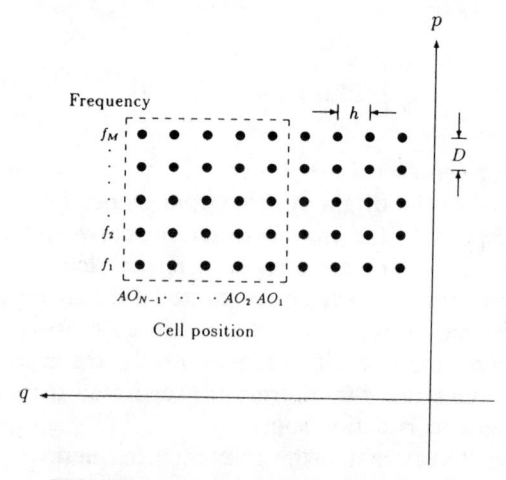

FIGURE 6.26 Output correlation spots.

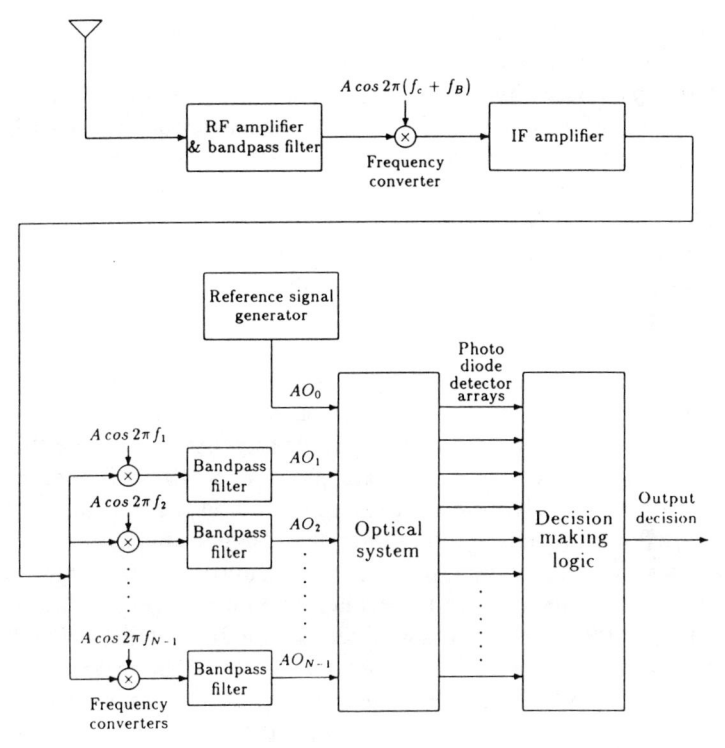

FIGURE 6.27 A block diagram representation of an acoustooptic frequency-hopping signal receiver.

quency of the AO cells. After band-pass filtering, these signals are fed into an array of AO cells. Output correlation spots can be read out by photodiode array detectors. By passing these detected correlation spots through a thresholding logic network, the highest probable received signal can be displayed at the system output. The basic bottleneck of the proposed system is the square-law converter (e.g., LCLV), which has a response time on the order of milliseconds. It also has a very limited dynamic range.

6.8 OPTICAL-DISK-BASED CORRELATOR

With the latest development and improvement of many real-time addressable spatial light modulators (SLMs), pattern recognition using optical correlation techniques has become more realistic. Yet a single input image might need to correlate with a huge library of reference images before a match can be found; therefore, the lack of large-capacity information storage devices that can provide a high-speed readout capability is still a major drawback to a practical optical correlation system. Optical disks (ODs), which have been developed in recent years as mass-storage media in many consumer products, are excellent candidates for this task. Psaltis *et al.* [6.20] and Lu *et al.* [6.21] have recently proposed the use of optical disks in correlation systems and in neural networks, respectively. In this section, we present an optical-disk-based joint transform correlation system as part of the continued effort to advance the realization of a practical optical correlator. The system employs an electrically addressable SLM to display the input image, and an optical disk to provide the reference image in a joint transform correlator (JTC) architecture. The major merits of the system are (1) high operation speed; (2) large information capacity; (3) shift invariance correlation; (4) relaxed in optical alignment.

The architecture of the proposed system is shown in Figure 6.28 [6.22]. A target captured by a video camera is first displayed on an electrically addressed SLM1. A beam expansion/reduction system is then used to reduce the image size of the input image m times. For example, if f1 = 10 × f2, then 10 times reduction is obtained. The reference image stored on the optical disk is read out in parallel and magnified by another set of expansion lenses to m times so that the image sizes of the reference image and input target are identical (i.e., $m \times n$ is the dimension ratio between the input target displayed on the SLM and that of the reference image stored on the optical disk). The Fourier transform of the two images, which are now comparable in size, is carried out by transform lens FL1, through which the joint transform power spectrum (JTPS) is recorded onto an optically addressed SLM2, which operates as a square-law converter. After the Fourier transform of the power spectrum has been taken, the correlation result is readily available and is recorded by a

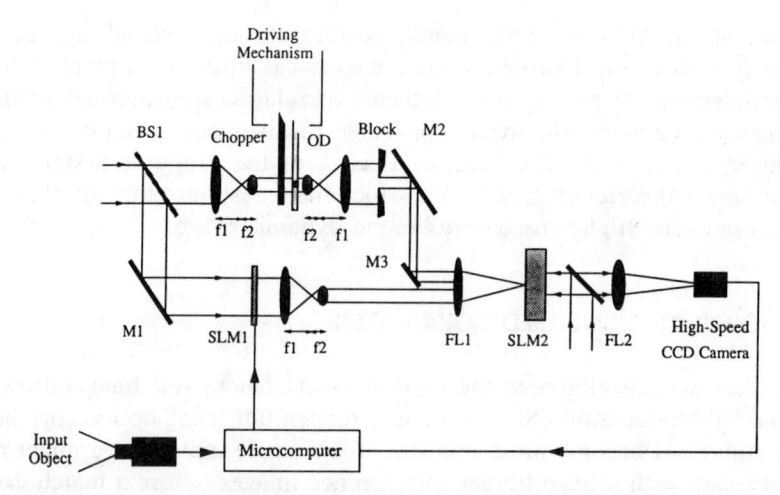

FIGURE 6.28 An optical-disk-based transform architecture. *Note:* FL1 and FL2 are Fourier-transform lenses; OD is an optical disk; SLM1 is the electronic addressable spatial modulator; SLM2 is the optical addressable SLM.

high-speed CCD camera located at the output plane. The optical disk advances to the next reference image, and a new correlation is made, and so on until a match is found.

We note that the unavoidable difference in transmission factor between the OD system and SLM1 introduces unequal illumination on the Fourier plane. As pointed out by Gregory *et al.* [6.23], the performance of the JTC, in terms of the correlation peak intensity, will then be affected. Optimum performance is obtained when the illumination of the input target and reference image are identical. This can be achieved by properly choosing the reflectance/transmittance ratio of the beam splitter BS1.

Because of the limited resolution of the optically addressed modulator SLM2, an upper threshold spatial frequency is imposed on the JTPS. This problem can be solved by either inserting an imaging lens in front of the SLM2 to magnify the power spectrum, or by adding a negative lens (concave lens) behind the transform lenses so that the effective focal lengths of these lenses are significantly increased, which in turn decreases the spatial frequency on the Fourier plane.

Generally, the dynamic range of the JTPS largely exceeds the limited dynamic range of modulator SLM2, and so cannot be recorded linearly. One approach to handling this difficulty is simply to adjust the laser light intensity so that the low-frequency component of the JTPS is saturated, and the higher frequency component is optimally recorded on the SLM2. This enhances the correlation of objects with high-frequency compositions (e.g., edge-enhanced images). However, objects with strong dc components will not be effectively correlated. Nonetheless, light intensity written on the SLM2 can be adjusted accordingly to give optimum correlation results.

Note that neither the Fourier transform on the input images nor the power spectrum strictly require that the object be located at the front focal plane of the transform lens. The distance between the SLMs and the transform lenses in the system can be made as short as possible, hence reducing the physical dimensions of the system.

It has been proposed that the transparent write-once, read-many-times OD be used in this architecture. To record the library of reference images onto the OD, a laser beam is focused on an approximately 0.5-μm spot on the photosensitive layer of the OD to record each pixel of the images sequentially. This method results in the reference images being recorded in binary form [6.20]. Images with gray scale can be recorded by area modulation of the spots on the OD, for which the gray-level images can be read out by using the differential interferometric technique proposed by Rilum and Tanguay [6.24].

If binary images of a 200 × 200 pixels format are to be recorded, each image would occupy a 0.2 × 0.2-mm^2 block on the OD. If we assume 0.01-mm spacing between adjacent blocks, then more than 27,000 reference images can be recorded on a single 120-mm-diameter OD. Since the block size is very small, the minute phase variation caused by the nonuniform thickness of the OD's plastic cover can be neglected. However, if the cover is too coarse for coherent processing, ODs with optical quality covers should be used.

The light source should be gated at a frequency synchronized with the image access time of the OD so as to freeze the image on the rotating OD. To estimate the sequential access time for a block of 0.2×0.2 mm^2 on a standard OD, we assume that the average revolution speed is 1122 rev/min, the average radius is 40 mm, and that all the images are scanned sequentially on each consecutive band of the OD. The minimum access time is then approximately 40 μs. To further estimate the operation speed of this system, assume that an optically addressed ferroelectric liquid crystal spatial light modulator is used as the square-law detector, the response time of which is between 10 μs and 155 μs [6.25]. To complete one correlation process, we assume that the response time of the slower device is used, that is, 40–155 μs. This is the same as performing more than 6400 correlations per second, a number that can hardly be matched by using current electronic technology.

It must be mentioned that in JTC architecture, the reference images in its spatial domain, rather than its complex Fourier spectrum in the frequency domain, are directly recorded onto the OD. The massive computation in generating the Fourier-transform holograms of the references, as required in a 4-f Vander Lugt correlator, can be avoided. Moreover, due to the shift invariance property of the JTC architecture, the strict mechanical alignment of the OD can be relaxed: That is, the parallel readout beam can be expanded to more than the block size of the reference image, on the optical disk, and proper image selection can be made through a window at plane P1.

REFERENCES

6.1 F. T. S. Yu, S. Jutamulia, T. W. Liu, and D. A. Gregory, "Adaptive Real-Time Pattern Recognition Using a Liquid Crystal TV Based Joint Transform Correlator," *Appl. Opt.* 26 (1987): 1370.

6.2 F. T. S. Yu, F. Cheng, T. Nagata, and D. A. Gregory, "Effects of Fringe Binarization of Multiobject Joint Transform Correlator," *Appl. Opt.* 28 (1989): 2988.

6.3 F. T. S. Yu, Q. W. Song, Y. S. Cheng, and D. A. Gregory, "Comparison of Detection Efficiencies for Vander Lugt and Joint Transform Correlators," *Appl. Opt.*, 29 (1990): 225.

6.4 F. T. S. Yu and X. J. Lu, "A Programmable Joint Transform Correlator," *Opt. Commun.* 52 (1984): 10.

6.5 F. T. S. Yu and J. E. Ludman, "A Microcomputer Based Programmable Optical Correlator for Automatic Pattern Recognition and Identification," *Opt. Lett.* 11 (1986): 395.

6.6 F. T. S. Yu, E. C. Tam, and D. A. Gregory, "High-Efficiency Joint-Transform Correlator," *Opt. Lett.* 15 (1990): 1029.

6.7 E. C. Tam, F. T. S. Yu, D. A. Gregory, and R. Juday, "Autonomous Real-Time Object Tracking with an Adaptive Joint Transform Correlator," *Opt. Eng.* 29 (1990): 314.

6.8 F. T. S. Yu, X. Li, E. C. Tam, S. Jutamulia, and D. A. Gregory, "Detection of Rotational and Scale Varying Objects with a Programmable Joint Transform Correlator," *Proc. SPIE* 1053 (1989): 253.

6.9 E. C. Tam, F. T. S. Yu, A. Tanone, D. A. Gregory, and R. D. Juday, "Data Association Multiple Target Tracking Using a Phase-Mostly Liquid Crystal Television," *Opt. Eng.* 29 (1990): 1114.

6.10 P. Mayback, *Stochastic Models, Estimation and Controls*, Academic Press, New York, 1979.

6.11 W. T. Maloney, "Acousto-Optical Approaches to Radar Signal Processing," *IEEE Spectrum* 6 (1969): 40.

6.12 J. N. Lee, "Optical and Acousto-Optical Techniques in Radar and Sonar," in *Optical Computing*, J. A. Neff, Ed. [*Proc. SPIE* 456 (1984): 96].

6.13 T. M. Turpin, "Spectrum Analysis Using Optical Processing," *Proc. IEEE* 69 (1981): 79.

6.14 R. A. Sprague, "A Review of Acousto-Optic Signal Correlators," *Opt. Eng.* 16(5) (1977): 467.

6.15 W. T. Rhodes, "Acousto-Optic Signal Processing; Convolution and Correlation," *Proc. IEEE* 69 (1981): 65.

6.16 N. J. Berg and J. N. Lee, *Acousto-Optic Signal Processing*, Dekker, New York, 1983.

6.17 A. Korpel, *Acousto-Optics*, Dekker, New York, 1988.

6.18 F. T. S. Yu and T. Nagata, "Optical Architecture for Acousto-Optic Space Integrating Correlator," *Opt. Eng.* 27 (1988): 507.

6.19 F. T. S. Yu and T. Nagata, "MFSK Signal Detection Using Acousto-Optic Joint Transform Correlator," *Micro. Opt. Tech. Lett.* 1 (1988): 190.

6.20 D. Psaltis, M. A. Neifeld, and A. Yamamura, "Image Correlators Using Optical Memory Disks," *Opt. Lett.* 14 (1989): 429.

6.21 T. Lu, K. Choi, S. Wu, X. Xu, and F. T. S. Yu, "Optical Disk Based Neural Network," *Appl. Opt.* 28 (1989): 4722.

6.22 F. T. S. Yu, E. C. Tam, T. W. Lu, E. Nishihara, and T. Nishikawa, "Optical Disk Based Joint Transform Correlator," *Appl. Opt.* 30 (1991): 915.

6.23 D. A. Gregory, J. Loudin and F. T. S. Yu, "Illumination Dependence of the Joint Transform Correlator," *Appl. Opt.* 28 (1989): 3288.

6.24 J. H. Rilum and A. R. Tanguay, Jr., "Utilization of Optical Memory Disks for Optical Information Processing," in *Technical Digest of OSA Annual Meeting* (Optical Society of America, Washington, D.C., 1988), paper MI5.

6.25 D. A. Jared, K. M. Johnson, and G. Moddel, "Joint Transform Correlation Using Optically Addressed Chiral Smectic Liquid Crystal Spatial Light Modulators," in *Technical Digest of OSA Annual Meeting* (Optical Society of America, Washington, D.C., 1989), paper THI5.

PROBLEMS

6.1 Consider the microcomputer-based optical processor of Figure 6.1. Assume that the operation speed is mostly limited by the addressing time of the SLMs and the response time of the CCD array detector.

242 HYBRID-OPTICAL SIGNAL PROCESSING

If the addressing time of the SLMs is 60 frames/sec and the response time of the CCD detector array is 50 frames/sec, calculate the operation speed of the processor.

6.2 Suppose that the resolutions of the SLMs is given by 100 lines/mm and the CCD array detector is given as 20 lines/mm, referring to the preceding problem, compute the space–bandwidth product of the hybrid-optical processor.

6.3 Assuming that the spatial frequency content of the SLM1 is given as 10 lines/mm, calculate the space–bandwidth requirement for the SLM2 for a Vander Lugt spatial filter. We assume that the focal length of the transform lens is 400 mm.

6.4 Referring to the 4-f optical processor of Figure 6.1 and the joint transform architecture of Figure 6.2:
  (a) State the basic advantages and disadvantages of these two processors.
  (b) Calculate the spatial carrier frequency requirements for the SLM2.
  (c) Evaluate the input spatial coherence requirements of these two processors.

6.5 Suppose that the addressing times of the SLMs and the response time of the CCDs are given by 1/60 sec and 1/50 sec, respectively:
  (a) Calculate the operating speed of the joint transform correlator.
  (b) Comment on the result of part (a) with respect to the result obtained in Problem 6.1.

6.6 Let us assume that K number of input images are displayed on the magnetooptic device (MOSLM) shown in Figure 6.3, in which these images are written by

$$f(x, y) = \sum_{k=1}^{K} f_k(x - a_k, y - b_k),$$

where (a_k, b_k) denotes the position of the kth input image. Since the MOSLM has the inherent grating structure by which the amplitude transmittance is given by

$$t(x, y) = f(x, y)g(x, y),$$

where $g(x, y)$ represents a two-dimensional grating function of MOSLM:
  (a) Compute the output complex light distribution.
  (b) Identify the output auto- and cross-correlation terms of part (a).
  (c) To ensure the nonoverlapping distributions, determine the required locations of the input functions.

6.7 To avoid the overlapping cross-correlation distributions, the symmetric locations of the object functions on the MOSLM should be broken, for example,

$$f(x, y) = f_1(x - a, y - b) + f_2(x, y - b)$$
$$+ f_3(x - a, y) + f_4(x, y + b).$$

Determine the output cross-correlation distributions.

6.8 Referring to the real-time joint transform correlator of Figure 6.3, in which we assume that the addressing time of the MOSLM and the LCTV are given by 1/1200 sec and 1/60 sec, respectively:
  (a) Calculate the operation speed of the correlator.
  (b) Compare part (a) with the result obtained in Problem 6.1
  (c) Although MOSLM can be parallelly addressed, what are the major drawbacks of this device?

6.9 Consider the single LCTV joint transform correlator shown in Figure 6.5. Assuming that the joint transform power spectrum, detected by the CCD array detector, can be immediately fed back for correlation operation:
  (a) Compute the duty cycle of the JTC.
  (b) What are the advantages and the disadvantages of the single-SLM JTC compared with the conventional two-SLM JTC.
  (c) If the JTPS can be replicated into the $N \times N$ array over the liquid crystal panel, compute the ratio of the correlation intensity as compared with the single JTPS case.
  (d) Calculate the duty cycle of part (c).

6.10 Referring Problem 6.9:
  (a) Show that the information content of the JTC is primarily determined by the carrier spatial frequency of the JTPS.
  (b) By properly replicating the JTPS, compute the optimum correlator diffraction efficiency.

6.11 Suppose the size of a square-law converter (i.e., LCTV) is given as 4×4 cm². If the angle's spatial frequency bandwidth of the signal is 10 lines/mm, the focal length of joint transform lens is 500 mm, and the wavelength of the light source is 600 nm, compute the optimum number of joint transform power spectra that can be replicated within the device's panel.

6.12 Referring to Problem 6.11, if the set of replicated power spectra is illuminated by spatial coherent light:
  (a) Calculate the spatial coherence requirement of the source.

244 HYBRID-OPTICAL SIGNAL PROCESSING

- **(b)** Show that the signal-to-noise ratio of the correlation peak improved as compared with coherent illumination.
- **(c)** Calculate the accuracy of the detection under strictly coherent and the spatially coherent illuminations, respectively.
- **(d)** Compute the correlation peaks of part (c).

6.13 Referring to the single spatial light modulation JTC of Figure 6.5. Assuming that the dimension of the CCD camera is 2 cm in diameter, and ignoring the HPF and CL elements of the system:
- **(a)** Calculate the allowable separation of the input functions by which the output correlation peaks can both be detected by the CCD camera.
- **(b)** Assuming that the input functions are separated to the maximum extent in part (a), and the resolution of the CCD camera is 20 lines/mm, calculate the required focal length of the transform lens.

6.14 It may be seen from Problem 6.13 that the required focal length of the transform lens is indeed very long.
- **(a)** Show that by introducing a concave lens the effective focal length of the system can be dramatically increased.
- **(b)** Given that the focal lengths of the transform lens and the concave lens are 38 cm and 10 cm, respectively, calculate the location of the concave lens such that the effective focal length would be 5 m.
- **(c)** On the other hand, if the physical distance from the transform lens to the CCD detector is fixed at 50 cm, calculate the required focal length and the location of the concave lens by which the effective focal length would be 5 m.

6.15 Referring to the autonomous target tracking of Section 6.4, Figure 6.13a shows the location of the correlation peak as a function of the target's translation in the x direction. By considering the limited resolution of the array detector, find the minimum speed of the target that can be properly tracked using the JTC of Figure 6.7. Assume that the correlation cycle is 0.05 sec.

6.16 Referring to the role of the position of the correlation peak as a function of target motion in Figure 6.13:
- **(a)** Determine the aspect ratio of the image array.
- **(b)** Assuming that the target is revolving in a circular path and the system is set to run autonomously, calculate the tracking errors after five revolutions.

6.17 Consider the dynamic state of the target at the kth frame given by Eq. 6.19. Since the velocity and the acceleration of the target can be handled

PROBLEMS 245

by the JTC system of Figure 6.18, describe a Kalman filtering procedure so that multitarget tracking can be performed by the proposed hybrid-optical system.

6.18 Consider the acoustooptic cell time-integrator shown in Figure 6.29:
  (a) Calculate and sketch the Fourier spectra distribution.
  (b) Design a spatial filter such that the time-integrating signal can be detected by a photodetector array.
  (c) Compute the output time-integrating signal.

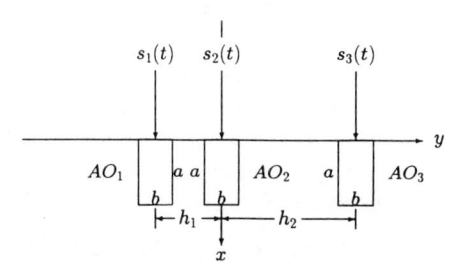

FIGURE 6.29

6.19 Instead of using the two cascaded acoustooptic cells of Problem 6.18, a one-cell architecture is depicted in Figure 6.30.
  (a) Describe the performance of this system.
  (b) Determine the spectra distribution at P_2.
  (c) Calculate the associated time-integrated intensity at the output plane.

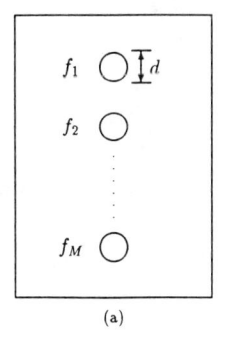

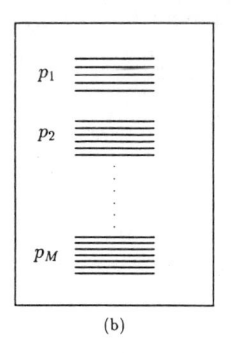

FIGURE 6.30

6.20 If the time signals take about 20 μs to to fill the apertures of the acoustooptic cells of Figure 6.22:
  (a) Calculate the necessary frame rate for the square-law converter to respond to the AO cells.
  (b) If the square-law converter can respond faster than the AO cells, what would the operation speed of the system be?

246 HYBRID-OPTICAL SIGNAL PROCESSING

6.21 Refer to the AO cell correlator of Figure 6.22. It is assumed that the readout from the square-law converter is proportional to the integral of the write-in intensity over the response time T_r. Suppose that two sinusoidal signals with slightly different frequencies Ω_1 and Ω_2 are, respectively, fed into AO_1 and AO_2. Find the frequency difference $\Delta\Omega = |\Omega_1 - \Omega_2|$ that would reduce the correlation peak to one-half of the maximum intensity.

6.22 We assumed that the AO correlator is expanded to a three-cell system, as shown in Figure 6.29. Assuming that the cells are driven by the same sinusoidal signal, derive an equation for the output light field, and identify the correlation peaks.

6.23 Referring to the preceding problem, we assume that two reference frequencies F_1 and F_2 are fed into AO_1 and AO_3, respectively, and that AO_2 is driven by a received signal whose frequency is to be determined. Determine the allowable frequency difference between F_1 and F_2 so that the system can resolve the received signal.

6.24 Refer to the multicell architecture of Figure 6.25. We let the diameter of the spatial filter be d, as shown in Figure 6.29, and the grating frequency be

$$p_i = p_0 + (i - 1)\Delta p, \quad (i = 1, 2, \ldots, M).$$

Determine the minimum Δp and p_0 such that M minus the signal frequencies can actually be resolved.

6.25 Suppose that the square-law converter has a response time equal to the AO cells and assume it has an infinite dynamic range.
   (a) Calculate the space–bandwidth product of the MFSK system of Figure 6.25.
   (b) Compare part (a) with the space–bandwidth product of a conventional joint transform system.

6.26 The optical disk-based joint transform correlator (ODJTC) of Figure 6.28 can be represented by the block diagram of Figure 6.31, where FL represents the Fourier transform system and PBS is the polarized

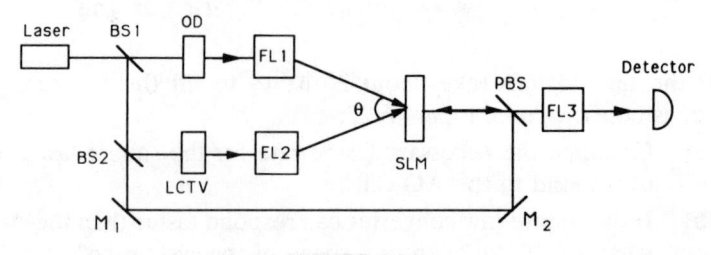

FIGURE 6.31

beam splitter. Let $f(x, y)$ and $g(mx, my)$ be the input and the magnified OD reference function, respectively. Assuming that the 2-f Fourier-transform system is used in ODJTC:

(a) Determine the relationship of the focal length between FL1 and FL2.

(b) Assuming that the space–bandwidth product of the input and the reference OD functions are identical, compute the requirement of the Fourier-transform lenses.

(c) Letting the space–bandwidth product of part (b) be W, determine the required incident angle ϑ formed by the input and the reference beams. (*Hint:* The focal depth of the Fourier-transform lens is given in Eq. 2.69.)

6.27 One of the basic constraints of the ODJTC is the continuous movement of the OD reference functions. For simplicity, we assume that the motion of the OD reference is restricted to the meridian plane perpendicular to the optical axis of FL1 of Figure 6.31.

(a) Calculate the transmittance of the OD-based joint transform hologram.

(b) Assuming that the allowable tolerance of the shifted fringes is limited to 1/10 cycle, calculate the allowable displacement of the OD during the operation cycle.

6.28 Consider the ODJTC as depicted in Figure 6.32. We assume that the input function is located behind the joint transform lens FL2 and also that the focal length of FL2 is f_2.

(a) Calculate the Fourier spectrum of $f(x, y)$ at the SLM.

(b) To match the quadratic phase factors of the input and reference OD functions, determine the location of the OD.

(c) Compute the position tolerance of the OD. Assume that $m = 10$, SBP $= 200$, $b = 20$ mm, and $\lambda = 0.5$ μm.

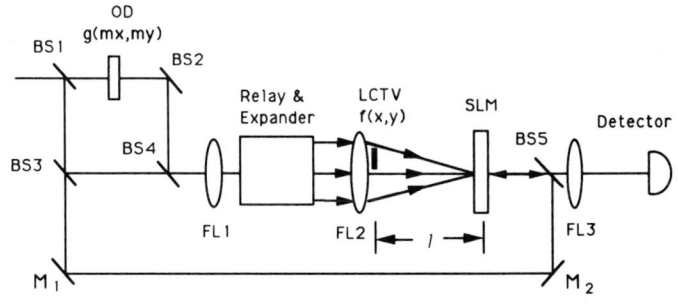

FIGURE 6.32

6.29 We note that the line and continuous tone patterns can be encoded onto the optical disk in the pit array, thus allowing the encoded OD patterns to be addressed in parallel. Assuming that the encoding is in binary-form:

(a) Describe two encoding techniques for the OD images.

(b) Are the techniques in part (a) suitable for both binary and gray-scale image patterns? Explain.

6.30 Referring to the ODJTC of Figure 6.31, the duty cycle of the LCTV is 33 ms and the response time of the SLM is about 10 to 155 μm. Suppose that the disk size is 120 mm in diameter and that it is rotating at 1000 rpm. We further assume that the OD pattern size is about 0.5×0.5 mm^2 with 0.01 mm spacings, and that the patterns are recorded between radii of 30 and 55-mm within the disk. Calculate the average operating speed of the system.

CHAPTER SEVEN

Photorefractive Crystal Signal Processing

In recent years, advances in photorefractive materials have stimulated interest in the application of phase conjugation techniques to a number of signal-processing problems [7.1]. Currently, the phase conjugation mirror, based on the self-pumped configuration [7.2] in photorefractive crystals, exhibits reflectivities as high as 70 percent, while requiring only a few tens of milliwatts of optical input power. Thus, this extends the range of practical applications of phase conjugation mirrors to real-time optical signal-processing capabilities. Although there are myriad photorefractive crystals in optical processing, in this chapter we restrict ourselves to illustrating only a few applications. In view of the great number of published papers in this area, we apologize for the possible omission of references in this context.

7.1 PHASE CONJUGATION OPTICAL CORRELATOR

In this section, we discuss application of photorefractive material to a joint transform correlator (JTC) [7.3]. In most coherent image-processing applications, the input objects must be free from any phase distortion. The input objects of a real-time optical processor are usually generated by a spatial light modulator (SLM); however, most SLMs introduce phase distortion, which can severely degrade its processing capability. Although liquid gates may be used to compensate for the phase distortion to some extent, they can only remove the external distortion from the devices. In addition, although they have the disadvantages of critical alignment and cumbersome fabrication, holographic optical elements (HOE) may provide another means of phase distortion removal.

Another problem common to the JTC, as well as to other coherent correlators, is that the width of the correlation spot is too broad and the cross-correlation intensity is too high. To improve the accuracy of detection, the object functions can be preencoded. The inherent nonlinearities in phase conjugation may be used for the encoding process.

Let us now consider a four-wave mixing JTC, as shown in Figure 7.1, in which the object beam is applied to the input of a JTC. This configuration has two major advantages.

1. The phase distortion due to the input SLM can be automatically compensated for by the conjugated wavefront.
2. The additional modulation produced by phase conjugation can be used to improve the accuracy of detection.

In this figure, the readout beam is adjusted beyond the coherent length with respect to the writing beams; thus, the setup represents a two-wave mixing configuration. Notice that the expanded collimated laser beam is divided into three paths: the one directed toward the photorefractive crystal (e.g., BSO) serves as the reference beam; the second illuminates input objects O_1 and O_2, which are imaged onto the crystal; and the third (directed by M1, M5, M4) serves as the readout beam. It can be seen that the reconstructed beam from the crystal is imaged back to the input objects for phase removal. After passing through the input objects, the beam is then joint transformed in the output plane P_0, via the beam splitter BS_3. We notice that a half-wave plate Q is used to rotate the polarization of the readout beam, and an analyzer A is used to reduce the light scattered from the optical elements in the system.

With reference to the optical configuration in Figure 7.1, the object beam can be written as

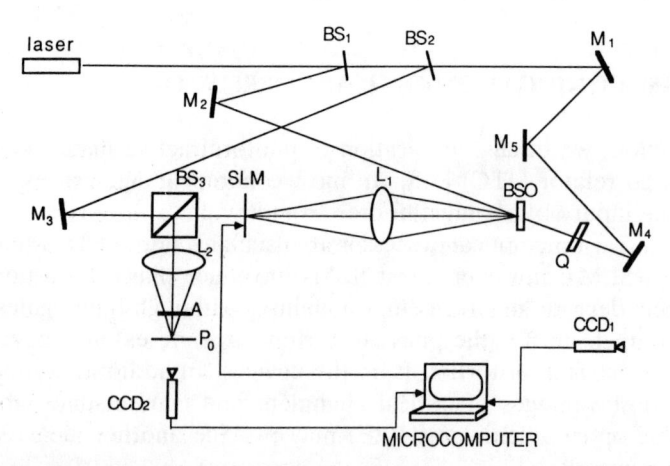

FIGURE 7.1 Experimental setup. *Note:* BS is the beam splitter; M is the mirror; O_1 and O_2 are input objects; Q is the quarter-wave plate; A is the analyzer; L_1 is the imaging lens; L_2 is the transform lens; P_0 is the output plane.

PHASE CONJUGATION OPTICAL CORRELATOR

$$O(x, y)\exp[i\phi(x, y)] = O_1(x - b, y)\exp[i\phi_1(x - b, y)]$$
$$+ O_2(x + b, y)\exp[i\phi_2(x + b, y)], \quad (7.1)$$

where O_1, O_2, ϕ_1, and ϕ_2 are the amplitude and phase distortion of the input objects, respectively; b is the mean separation of the two input objects; and O_1, O_2 are assumed positive real. At the image plane (i.e., the crystal), the object beam is given by

$$O\left(\frac{x}{M}, \frac{y}{M}\right)\exp\left[i\phi\left(\frac{x}{M}, \frac{y}{M}\right)\right]\exp\left[ik\frac{x^2 + y^2}{2L}\right], \quad (7.2)$$

where M represents the magnification factor of the imaging system; $L = s - f$; where s is the image distance and f is the focal length of lens L_1; and $k = 2\pi/\lambda$, where λ is the wavelength of the light source.

Thus, the reconstructed beam emerging from the crystal is given by

$$O'\left(\frac{x}{M}, \frac{y}{M}\right)\exp\left[-i\phi\left(\frac{x}{M}, \frac{y}{M}\right)\right]$$
$$\times \exp\left[-ik\frac{x^2 + y^2}{2L}\right]\exp\left[i\theta\left(\frac{x}{M}, \frac{y}{M}\right)\right]. \quad (7.3)$$

Notice that this expression does not represent the exact phase conjugation of expression 7.2. The amplitude distribution of $O'(x, y)$ deviates somewhat from $O(x, y)$, which is primarily due to the nonlinearity of the crystal. However, a phase shift $\theta(x, y)$ between the phase conjugation and the reconstructed beam is also introduced, which is dependent on the intensity ratio R of the object beam and the reference beam. If there is no voltage applied on the BSO crystal, $\theta(x, y)$ would represent a constant phase of 90°.

The reconstructed beam, imaged back on the object plane, can be written as

$$O'(x, y)\exp[-i\phi(x, y)]\exp[i\theta(x, y)]. \quad (7.4)$$

After passing through the input objects, the complex light distribution becomes

$$O(x, y)O'(x, y)\exp[i\theta(x, y)], \quad (7.5)$$

which removes the phase distortion $\phi(x, y)$ of the input objects.

To demonstrate phase compensation with the phase conjugate technique, we provide Figure 7.2, in which a pair of input objects is added with a random phase plate (Figure 7.2a). Their joint transform spectrum is shown in Figure 7.2b, in which the spectrum is severely corrupted by the phase disturbances.

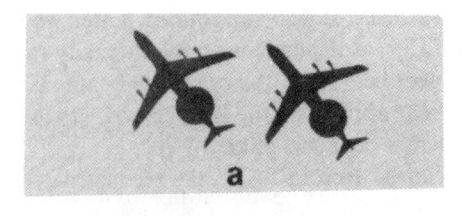

FIGURE 7.2 Joint Fourier transform spectra. (*a*) Input objects with random noise. (*b*) Their joint transform spectrum. (*c*) The joint transform spectrum with phase compensation.

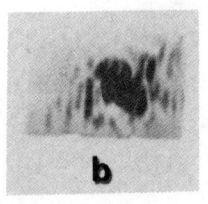

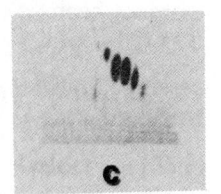

However, with the phase compensation technique, the spectrum is relatively free from disturbance, as shown in Figure 7.2c. In addition, the output correlation spots for these two cases are shown in Figure 7.3, in which we see that phase compensation takes place when the phase conjugation technique is used.

We stress that incremental modulation of the reconstructed beam can be used for preencoding to improve the correlation characteristics. Accordingly, the incremental modulation is dependent on the object and reference beam ratio R [7.4], as defined by

$$R(x, y) = \frac{O^2(x/M, y/M)}{I_r}, \tag{7.6}$$

where I_r is the intensity of the reference beam.

The phase modulation $\theta(x, y)$ represents the phase difference between the conjugation of the object beam and the actual reconstruction beam (see Eq. 7.3), which is due to the interaction between the writing beams. According to Vahey [7.5], the phase deviation between the writing beams, which varies along the propagation within the crystal, can be expressed as

$$\psi(z) = \psi(0) - \cot(\phi_g) \ln\left(\frac{\cosh[Q(z)]}{\cosh[Q(0)]}\right), \tag{7.7}$$

where

$$Q(z) = 2\Gamma z \sin(\phi_g) + \tan^{-1}[(1 - R)/(1 + R)], \tag{7.8}$$

where Γ is the coupling constant, ϕ_g is the phase shift between the writing interference pattern and the induced index grating, and $\psi(0)$ is the initial phase deviation between the writing beams. This phase variation produces

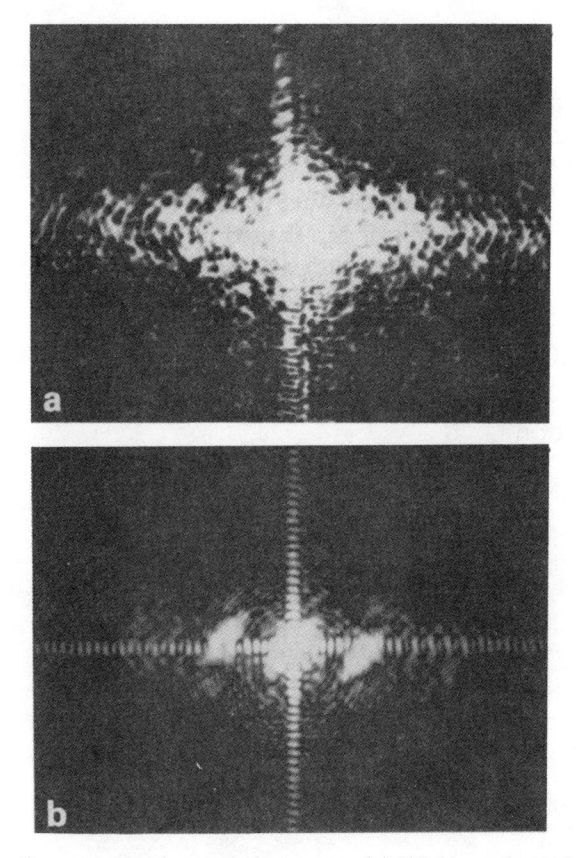

FIGURE 7.3 Reconstructed correlation spots. (*a*) Without phase compensation. (*b*) With phase compensation.

grating bending within the crystal. When a readout beam illuminates the crystal, the reconstructed wavefront from the bent volume grating has a phase shift $\theta(x, y)$ relative to the conjugate wavefront of the object beam. From Eqs. 7.7, 7.8, and 7.6, we notice that the phase shift $\theta(x, y)$ is dependent on R and is directly related to the object intensity distribution $O(x, y)$. Therefore, the phase modulation $\theta(x, y)$ can be utilized to encode the object functions. A computer-simulated result is shown in Figure 7.4, in which we see that additional phase encoding improves the accuracy of detection of the JTC.

Furthermore, object encoding can also be accomplished with amplitude modulation. It is obvious that $O'(x, y)$ is proportional to the diffraction efficiency ε of the phase grating within the crystal. The diffraction efficiency ε of the phase grating in a photorefractive material is related to the intensity ratio R of two writing beams as [7.1],

$$\varepsilon(x, y) \propto \begin{cases} R, & R < 1, \\ \dfrac{1}{R}, & R > 1. \end{cases} \tag{7.9}$$

254 PHOTOREFRACTIVE CRYSTAL SIGNAL PROCESSING

(a)

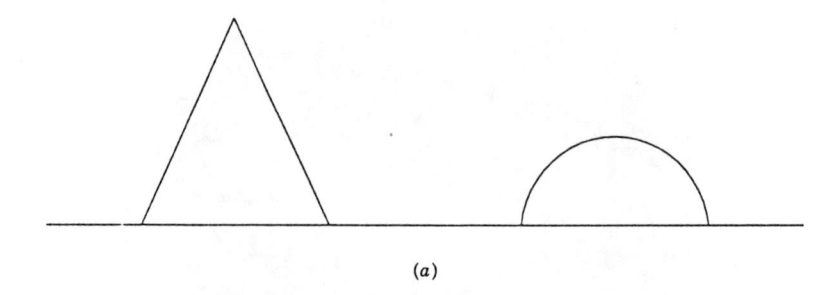

Correlation

(b)

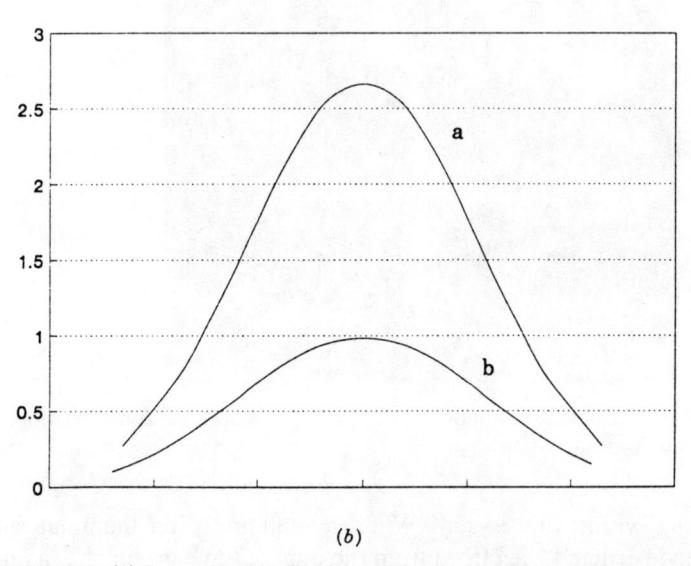

FIGURE 7.4 (a) Intensity distribution of the input objects to be correlated. (b) Correlation without phase encoding: a, autocorrelation; b, cross-correlation. (c) Correlation with phase encoding: a, autocorrelation; b, cross-correlation.

Thus, different amplitude encoding may be accomplished by controlling the intensity of the reference beam, for example, edge enhancement, which is a desirable preprocessing in a JTC.

7.2 RECONFIGURABLE INTERCONNECTIONS

It is well known that a photorefractive crystal hologram can have high diffraction efficiency, and high angular and wavelength selectivities. In this sec-

Correlation

(c)

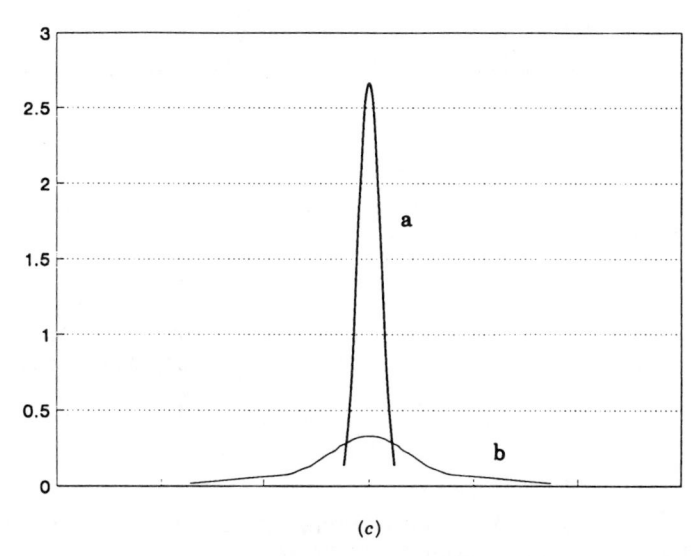

FIGURE 7.4 *(Continued)*

tion, we start by discussing the performance of transmission and reflection holograms based on coupled wave theory and law of refraction. Reconfigurable optical interconnections using wavelength tuning and spatial division techniques are discussed [7.6]–[7.7]. A small amount in wavelength tuning can be used to realize a large number of reconfigurable interconnections, which can be obtained by choosing the writing angle and the thickness of the crystal. For the spatial division method, the interconnection patterns can be recorded as a series of pinhole holograms in the crystal. This series of pinhole holograms can be reconstructed using an array of light sources and by simply translating a pinhole (generated by an SLM). Thus, the interconnection pattern can be reconfigured.

7.2.1 Properties of Volume Holograms

First we discuss some basic properties of volume holograms. We assume that two write-in beams forming an angle 2ϑ enter into a photorefractive material, as shown in Figure 7.5. The vector magnitude of the interference grating within the crystal can be written as

$$|k| = \frac{4\pi\eta \sin \vartheta}{\lambda}, \tag{7.10}$$

where λ is the writing wavelength and η is the refractive index of the crystal. If the readout wavelength deviates from λ by $\Delta\lambda$, then the Bragg diffraction

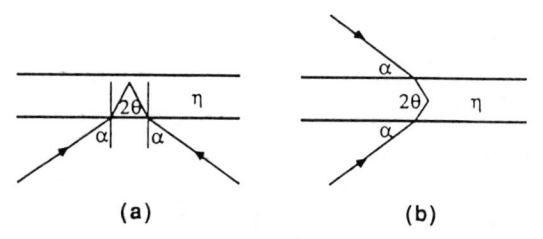

FIGURE 7.5 Writing angle inside and outside the recording media. (*a*) Transmission hologram. (*b*) Reflection hologram.

condition requires a change of $\Delta\vartheta$. By using the momentum conservation, the relationship between $\Delta\lambda$ and $\Delta\vartheta$ can be second-order approximated as given by

$$\frac{\Delta\lambda}{\lambda} = \frac{1}{2}\left[\cot(\vartheta)\Delta\vartheta - \frac{1}{2}\Delta\vartheta^2\right], \quad (7.11)$$

for which the change of λ should be compensated for by the change of ϑ. We call 2ϑ the internal writing angle within the crystal. Notice that the external writing angle 2α is different from the internal writing angle 2ϑ. By applying the law of refraction to Eq. 7.11 for the unslanted transmission holograms of Figure 7.5*a*, we have

$$\Delta\vartheta_t = \frac{\cos\alpha}{\sqrt{\eta^2 - \sin^2\alpha}}\Delta\alpha, \quad (7.12)$$

and

$$\left\{\frac{\Delta\lambda}{\lambda}\right\}_t = \frac{1}{2}\left[\cot(\alpha)\Delta\alpha - \frac{1}{2}\frac{\cos^2\alpha}{\eta^2 - \sin^2\alpha}(\Delta\alpha)^2\right], \quad (7.13)$$

where the subscript t signifies the transmission hologram. As with unslanted reflection hologram of Figure 7.5*b*, we have

$$\Delta\vartheta_r = \frac{\sin\alpha}{\sqrt{\eta^2 - \cos^2\alpha}}\Delta\alpha, \quad (7.14)$$

and

$$\left\{\frac{\Delta\lambda}{\lambda}\right\}_r = \frac{1}{2}\left[\frac{\sin\alpha\cos\alpha}{\eta^2 - \cos^2\alpha}\Delta\alpha - \frac{1}{2}\frac{\sin^2\alpha}{\eta^2 - \cos^2\alpha}(\Delta\alpha)^2\right], \quad (7.15)$$

where the subscript r signifies the reflection hologram and 2α represents the external write-in angle. We note that only the second-order terms in Eqs. 7.13 and 7.15 are significant as α approaches 90°. However, we shall consider cases for α in the region (10°–80°), and all second-order terms can be neglected. The reciprocal of the dispersions (i.e., $(1/\lambda)(d\lambda/d\alpha)$ for transmission and reflection holograms as functions of external write-in angle α (from Eqs. 7.13 and 7.15) are shown in Figure 7.6a and b, respectively. We see that under the same write-in angle 2α, the reflection hologram would provide higher dispersion, because of the refraction at the surface of the photorefractive crystal. Since the refractive index of the crystal is higher than the index of air, the internal angle ϑ is less than the external angle α for the transmission hologram, and $\vartheta > \alpha$ for the reflection hologram. This means that for the same external angle α, the reflection hologram would have a higher dispersion. On the other hand, when α approaches 0°, the angular magnification $(\Delta\alpha/\Delta\vartheta)$ becomes larger due to refraction, as can be deduced from Eq. 7.14. This would also cause higher dispersion in reflection holograms. In the region between $\alpha = 30°$ and 60°, a uniform dispersion is observed for the reflection hologram.

To analyze the angular and wavelength selectivities of volume holograms, we refer to the coupled wave theory obtained by Kogelnik [7.8]. Let us assume that the multiple diffraction process can be neglected for the multiexposure hologram. The problem can be treated with weak coupling approximation. Thus from coupled wave theory, the normalized diffraction efficiency for the unslanted transmission hologram can be expressed as

$$\varepsilon_t = \frac{\sin^2(\nu^2 + \zeta^2)^{1/2}}{(1 + \zeta^2/\nu^2)}, \qquad (7.16)$$

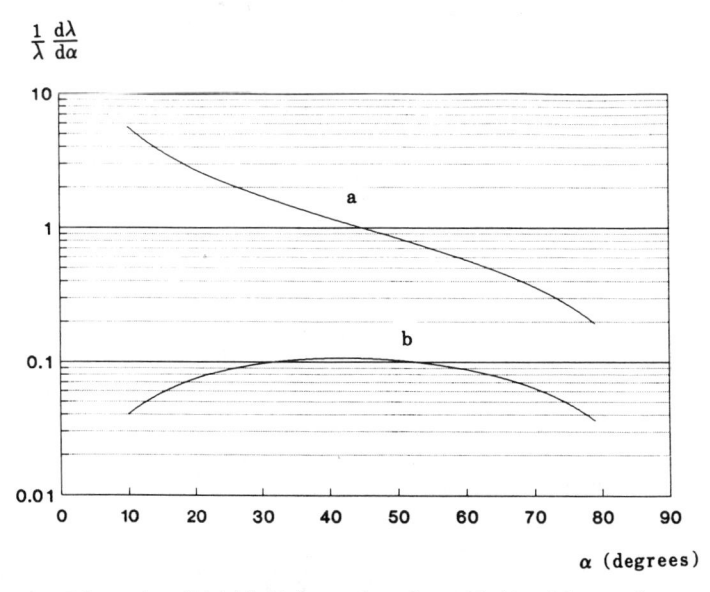

FIGURE 7.6 Dispersion $(1/\lambda)(d\lambda/d\alpha)$ as a function of half-writing angle α, $\eta = 2.28$. (a) Transmission hologram. (b) Reflection hologram.

where $v = \pi\eta_1 d/\lambda \cos\theta$, η_1 is the amplitude of the spatial modulation of the refractive index, d is the thickness of the hologram, and

$$\zeta = \frac{2\pi\eta d \sin\theta}{\lambda} \Delta\vartheta$$

$$= -\frac{\pi\eta d}{\lambda} \frac{\sin^2\vartheta}{\cos\vartheta} \frac{\Delta\lambda}{\lambda},$$

is known as the *dephasing parameter*, which is dependent upon the reading angular deviation $\Delta\vartheta$ and the reading wavelength deviation $(\Delta\lambda/\lambda)$.

For the weak coupling approximation (i.e., $|v| \ll |\zeta|$), Eq. 7.16 can be simplified to read

$$\varepsilon_t = v^2 \text{sinc}^2\zeta. \tag{7.17}$$

The angular and wavelength selectivities of the holograms can be defined by the full width of the main lobe of the sinc function and are given by

$$\{\Delta\vartheta\}_t = \frac{\lambda}{\eta d \sin\vartheta}, \tag{7.18}$$

and

$$\left\{\frac{\Delta\lambda}{\lambda}\right\}_t = \frac{\lambda \cos\vartheta}{\eta d \sin^2\vartheta}, \tag{7.19}$$

Referring to Eq. 7.12 and the law of refraction, we find that

$$\{\Delta\alpha\}_t = \frac{\sqrt{\eta^2 - \sin^2\alpha}}{\sin\alpha \cos\alpha} \frac{\lambda}{d}, \tag{7.20}$$

and

$$\left\{\frac{\Delta\lambda}{\lambda}\right\}_t = \frac{\sqrt{\eta^2 - \sin^2\alpha}}{\sin^2\alpha} \frac{\lambda}{d}. \tag{7.21}$$

As with unslanted reflection hologram, the *normalized diffraction efficiency* can be expressed as

$$\varepsilon_r = \frac{1}{[1 + \{1 - (\zeta^2/v^2)\}/\sinh(v^2 - \zeta^2)^{1/2}]}, \tag{7.22}$$

where

$$\nu = \frac{i\pi\eta d}{\lambda \sin \vartheta},$$

$$\zeta = \frac{2\pi\eta d \cos \vartheta}{\lambda} \Delta\vartheta,$$

$$= \frac{-\pi\eta d \sin \vartheta}{\lambda} \frac{\Delta\lambda}{\lambda}.$$

For the weak coupling case (i.e., $|\nu| << |\zeta|$), Eq. 7.22 can be reduced to the following expression:

$$\varepsilon_r = |\nu|^2 \text{sinc}^2 \zeta. \tag{7.23}$$

The equations for the angular and wavelength selectivities of unslanted reflection holograms can be derived, such as,

$$\{\Delta\alpha\}_r = \frac{\sqrt{\eta^2 - \cos^2\alpha}}{\sin \alpha \cos \alpha} \frac{\lambda}{d}, \tag{7.24}$$

and

$$\left\{\frac{\Delta\lambda}{\lambda}\right\}_r = \frac{1}{\sqrt{\eta^2 - \cos^2\alpha}} \frac{\lambda}{d}, \tag{7.25}$$

where the subscript r signifies the reflection hologram.

Figure 7.7 shows the angular selectivities, $(\Delta\alpha)_t$ and $(\Delta\alpha)_r$, as functions of external write-in angle α, where the values of $\Delta\alpha$ have been normalized by λ/d. From this figure, we see that the optimal values occur at

$$(\alpha_t)_{\text{opt}} = \sin^{-1}\sqrt{\eta(\eta - \sqrt{\eta^2 - 1})}, \tag{7.26}$$

and

$$(\alpha_r)_{\text{opt}} = \cos^{-1}\sqrt{\eta(\eta - \sqrt{\eta^2 - 1})}, \tag{7.27}$$

respectively. For example, if $\eta = 2.28$ for LiNbO$_3$ crystal, $(\alpha_t)_{\text{opt}} = 46.5°$ and $(\alpha_r)_{\text{opt}} = 43.5°$. We further note that in the region of $\alpha = 30° - 60°$, the hologram has the sharpest angular selectivity both for transmission and reflection holograms.

Figure 7.8 shows the wavelength selectivities, $\{\Delta\lambda/\lambda\}_t$ and $\{\Delta\lambda/\lambda\}_r$, as functions of α. From this figure, we see that the wavelength selectivity for trans-

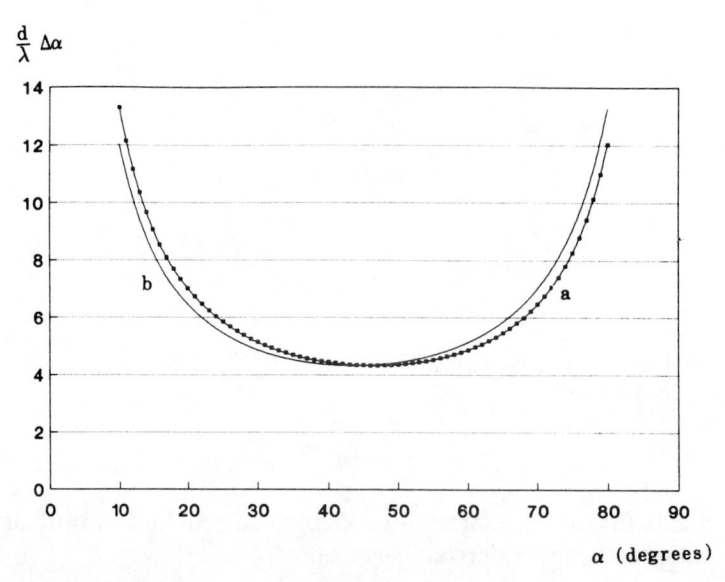

260 PHOTOREFRACTIVE CRYSTAL SIGNAL PROCESSING

FIGURE 7.7 Angular selectivity of volume holograms normalized by λ/d, $\eta = 2.28$. (*a*) Transmission hologram. (*b*) Reflection hologram.

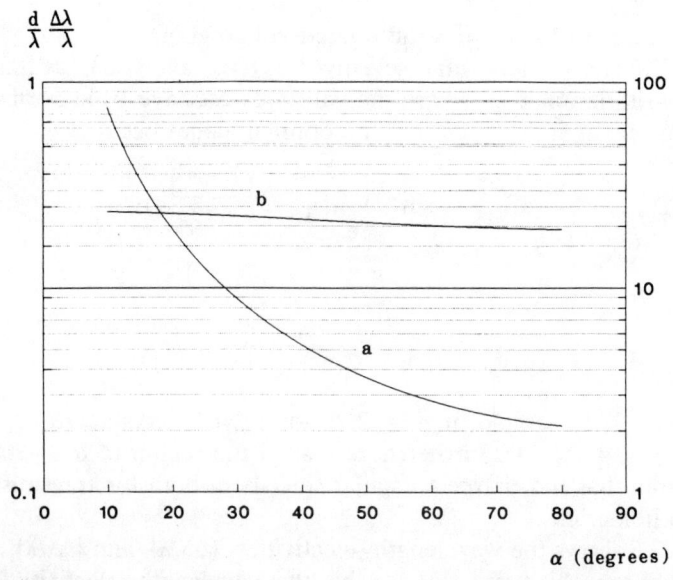

FIGURE 7.8 Wavelength selectivity of volume holograms normalized by λ/d, $\eta = 2.28$. (*a*) Transmission hologram. (*b*) Reflection hologram.

mission holograms increases as α increases. However, transmission holograms generally have a poorer wavelength selectivity than the reflection hologram. The wavelength selectivity of the reflection hologram is relatively uniform over α, which is about $0.45\,\lambda/d$.

The diffracted wavevectors can be determined from the principle of momentum conservation. Let us assume that the holographic recording medium is infinitely extended in the x and the y directions, and has a finite thickness d in the z direction. A *dephasing wave vector* can be defined as

$$\Delta \mathbf{k} = \mathbf{k}_1 - \mathbf{k}_2 - \mathbf{k}_3 + \mathbf{k}_4. \tag{7.28}$$

where $\mathbf{k}_1$ and $\mathbf{k}_2$ are the two writing wavevectors, $\mathbf{k}_3$ is the reading wavevector, and $\mathbf{k}_4$ is the diffracted wavevector. In terms of momentum conservation, it is required that,

$$(\Delta k)_x = (\Delta k)_y = 0. \tag{7.29}$$

Thus, the z component of Δk is directly related to the dephasing parameter ζ in Eq. 7.16 by

$$\zeta = (\Delta k)_z \cdot d. \tag{7.30}$$

Equation 7.16 can be used to determine the diffracted wave vector as shown in Figure 7.9. For simplicity, we assume that all the wave vectors are in the

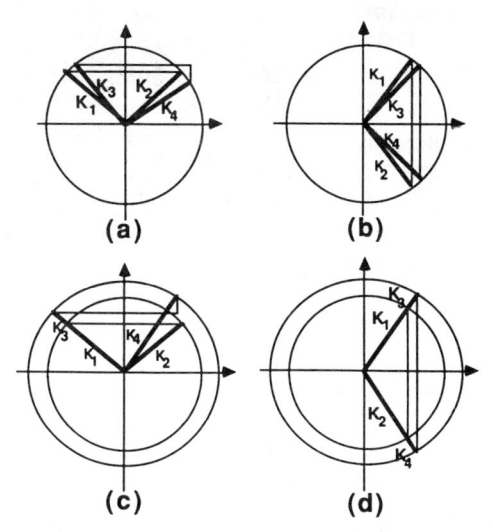

FIGURE 7.9 Diffracted wave vectors derived according to momentum conservation (the horizontal components of the dephasing vector should always be zero). (*a*) Transmission hologram with incident angular deviation. (*b*) Reflection hologram with incident angular deviation. (*c*) Transmission hologram with reading wavelength deviation. (*d*) Reflection hologram with reading wavelength deviation.

x-z plane. Figure 7.9*a* shows that the reading angle of the transmission hologram deviates by $\Delta\vartheta$ from the write-in angle ϑ. By referring to Eq. 7.29, we see that the diffracted wave vector should deviate $-\Delta\vartheta$ in the first-order approximation. The wave-vector diagram for the reflection hologram is shown in Figure 7.9*b*. In this figure we see that the angular deviations of the reading and writing wave vectors are identical. Figures 7.9*c* and *d* show the effects due to reading wavelength dephasing. For the transmission hologram (i.e., Figure 7.9*c*), the diffracted wave vector deviates by $\Delta\vartheta$, so for the first order approximation, we have

$$\Delta\vartheta = 2 \tan \vartheta \frac{\Delta\lambda}{\lambda}. \tag{7.31}$$

This indicates that for a finite wavelength bandwidth, the deviation will cause the diffracted focal spot to smear. However, reflection holograms do not suffer from such focal spot smearing, since the wave vectors for unslanted reflection holograms are always symmetrical about the *x* axis.

7:2.2 Reconfigurability with Wavelength Tuning

The principle of the reconfigurable interconnection using wavelength tuning can be seen in Figure 7.10. The grating vectors **OA** and **OB** are written in the photorefractive crystal with an angular separation of $\Delta\vartheta$. When the grating **OA** is read out with wave vector **OC**, the diffracted wave vector is denoted by **AC** (CE is the perpendicular bisector of **OA**). On the other hand, if grating **OB** is read out in the same direction, the magnitude of the reading vector should be changed to **OD**. The diffracted wave vector deviates from **AC** by $2\Delta\vartheta$. Thus, by changing the wavelength, we can read different gratings in the same reading direction. Since different gratings cause different diffraction angles, reconfigurable optical interconnections can be realized in this simple fashion. The interconnection pattern was recorded in the volume hologram earlier, for which the angular and wavelength selectivities should be high enough to prevent cross talk between channels. We assume that if the range of tunable wavelengths $[\Delta\lambda/\lambda]$ of a laser diode is about 0.01 [7.9] (i.e., $\Delta\lambda/\lambda \approx 0.01$), and the required angular deviation is $2\Delta\alpha = 0.2$ rad, then α should

FIGURE 7.10 The principle of reconfigurable optical interconnects with volume holograms. Two grating vectors **OA** and **OB** have the same magnitude and an angular separation of $\Delta\vartheta$. **CE** and **DF** are the perpendicular bisectors of **OA** and **OB**.

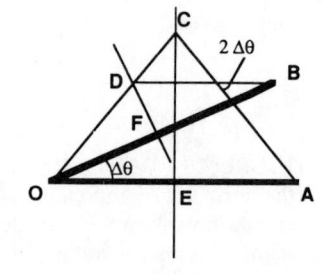

be > 84° for transmission holograms (from Figure 7.6a). We note that this angle would require a large recording crystal (i.e., about $a/\cos\alpha$, where a is the laser beam diameter). However, for reflection holograms, α is about 45° (from Figure 7.6b), which is in fact the optimum angle for angular selectivity, and this angle is also more convenient to work with in practice.

The choice of thickness d of the photorefractive crystal should allow the bandwidth of the hologram to be equal to or greater than the signal bandwidth. If the modulation frequency of the laser diode is Δf, then $\{\Delta\lambda/\lambda\}_s = \lambda\Delta f/c$, where c is the velocity of light and the subscript s signifies signal. Substituting this relationship in Eq. 7.25, we see that thickness d of the crystal should satisfy the following inequality:

$$d \leq \frac{\lambda}{\sqrt{\eta^2 - \cos^2\alpha}} \frac{1}{\{\Delta\lambda/\lambda\}_s} = d_{max}, \qquad (7.32)$$

where the subscript s denotes the relative signal bandwidth. Notice that the corresponding angular selectivity of $(\Delta\alpha)_r$ can be obtained from Eq. 7.24. If we took $(\Delta\alpha)_c = 3(\Delta\alpha)_r$ as the angular separation between channels, the cross talk due to the sidelobes of the sinc function would be less than -20 dB, where the subscript c signifies channel. The wavelength interval $\{\Delta\lambda/\lambda\}_c$ can be derived from Eq. 7.15, and it can be used as the longitudinal mode spacing of laser diodes for wavelength tuning. This would require the effective optical cavity length to be

$$\eta_l L = \frac{\lambda}{2\{\Delta\lambda/\lambda\}_c}, \qquad (7.33)$$

where η_l is the refractive index of the laser medium, and L is the physical length of the cavity.

For example, using an LiNbO$_3$ crystal ($\eta = 2.28$) as the recording medium, $\alpha = 45°$, $\Delta f = 10$ GHz, and $\lambda = 680$ nm; the relative signal bandwidth is $\{\Delta\lambda/\lambda\}_s = 2.4 \times 10^{-5}$; the thickness of the photorefractive crystal is $d_{max} = 13.8$mm; the angular selectivity is $(\Delta\alpha)_r = 2.1 \times 10^{-4}$; and the angular separation between channels is $(\Delta\alpha)_c = 6.3 \times 10^{-4}$. For 0.1-rad angular deviation, one would have about 160 channels with a wavelength tuning range $\Delta\lambda/\lambda$ of about 0.01. The wavelength interval between channels is $\{\Delta\lambda/\lambda\}_c = 6.7 \times 10^{-5}$ and the effective cavity optical length of laser diode is $\eta_l L = 5$ mm. If $0.1\{\Delta\lambda/\lambda\}_s$ is used as the required relative wavelength stability, we would have the required wavelength stability of laser diodes, such as $(\Delta\lambda)_{stability} = 0.16$ nm. This is possible for a single laser diode at the present time.

A possible configuration of a reconfigurable optical crossbar structure is shown in Figure 7.11. Multiple reflection gratings are written in a piece of z-cut LiNbO$_3$ crystal. The writing light can be derived from a dye laser of an He–Ne Laser ($\lambda = 632.8$ nm) and the reading light can be derived from an array of laser diodes ($\lambda = 680.0$ nm). The wavelength difference between

FIGURE 7.11 Reconfigurable optical crossbar. C-z-cut LiNbO$_3$ crystal. *Note:* L$_1$ and L$_2$ are the collimating and focusing lenses; P$_1$ and P$_2$ are the input and output planes; LA and DA are the laser-diode array and line-detector array on planes P$_1$ and P$_2$.

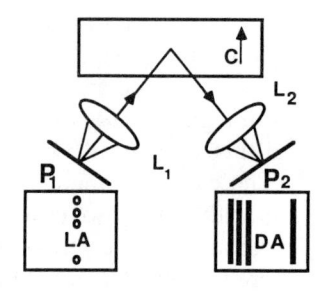

write-in and reading may be compensated for by modifying the write-in angle according to the dispersion relation. The writing process is performed at a fixed writing angle and multiple exposures are carried out by rotating the crystal with an angular separation equal to the required channel separation. The exposure procedure given by Strasser *et al.* [7.10] should be adopted to make the diffraction efficiencies of different channels uniform. After writing, a fixing procedure as described by Staeble *et al.* [7.11] should be used to fix the holograms in the crystal. A linear laser diode array is arranged along the nondispersion direction at the input plane. Since it is in the nondispersion direction, there would be no wavelength tunable range limitation for the separations between laser diodes, provided the total extent of the array is within the paraxial approximation. A one-dimensional line-detector array is placed at the output plane with the space between the line detectors equal to two times the channel separation, as previously given. Different laser diodes can use the same set of gratings in the crystal. In the nondispersion direction, the light beams are reflected according to the law of reflection. By independently controlling the wavelength of the laser diodes, a reconfigurable electrooptical crossbar architecture can be realized in practice.

7.2.3 Reconfigurability with Spatial Division

Another possible architecture for reconfigurable interconnections with photorefractive volume holograms is spatial division. A page-oriented holographic setup is shown in Figure 7.12. We apply the pinhole hologram technique as proposed by Xu *et al.* [7.12]. The angular selectivity of the recorded volume hologram would have a larger storage capacity as compared with thin holographic plates. The recording arrangement is shown in Figure 7.12*a*, in which an SLM is in the focal plane of the condenser lens L$_1$ and the interconnection pattern masks are placed at the page plane P. The object beam B is focused by L$_1$, and after passing the SLM the beam is directed toward the recording medium. We note that the SLM is used to generate a movable pinhole that allows only the object beam to pass in one direction. In other words, the interconnection mask is illuminated by the object beam in one direction, where the pinhole of SLM is set at a spatial location to allow the object beam to pass through. It can be seen that a set of interconnection masks can be

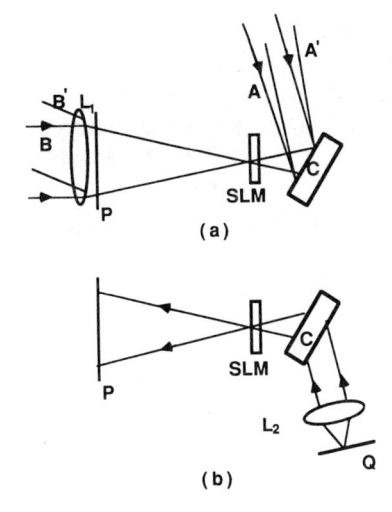

FIGURE 7.12 Geometry for reconfigurable interconnections with spatial division. (a) Recording setup. (b) Reading setup. *Note:* L_1 is the condensing lens; L_2 is the collimating lens; C is the recording media; P is the page plane; Q is the laser diode plane.

encoded in the crystal for a given reference beam A by moving the SLM pinhole position and changing the object beam B'. Similarly, another set of interconnection pattern masks can be encoded for another reference beam A', and so on. In the readout process, a one-dimensional laser diode array is placed at the front focal plane Q of the collimating lens L_2, as shown in Figure 7.12b. Each diode generates a reading beam that is conjugate to a specific reference beam A. When the SLM pinhole is set at one position, a set of interconnection patterns is diffracted and projected onto the page plane P. As the pinhole position is moved, the interconnection patterns change. Thus, we see that the interconnections between the laser diode array and the page plane can be made reconfigurable by a programming SLM.

Unlike the wavelength-tuning reconfigurable interconnection, the spatial division reconfiguration requires low wavelength selectivity (not sensitive to the wavelength). Based on the comparisons of the volume holograms discussed in Section 7.1, we should use transmission-type holograms for interconnections. To have a higher angular selectivity, the average write-in angle (2α) should be about 90°. If the thickness of the photorefractive crystal (i.e., $LiNbO_3$) is about 1 to 2 cm, then the bandwidth of the hologram would be much wider than the signal bandwidth, as can be seen in Figure 7.8a. Referring to Figure 7.7a, the angular selectivity is found to be $(\Delta\alpha)_t = 5\lambda/d = 3.4 \times 10^{-4}$. If $3(\Delta\alpha)_t$ is used as the channel separation and assuming 30° angular range, there would be about 10^3 useful interconnection channels in the photorefractive crystal. Due to the degeneration of Bragg diffraction, only a one-dimensional laser diode can be used. If the full range of $N \times N$ SLM pinholes is used, the total number of interconnection patterns would be $M = N^2 \times K$, where K is the number of channels (i.e., the number of laser diodes).

In theory, this architecture can be used for massive information storage. For example, if $N = 32$, $K = 10^3$, the total number, M, of patterns (or pictures) would be 10^6, which is about the capacity of 10 hours of TV programming. This architecture does not require high space-bandwidth product of the SLM (only 32 × 32). The requirement of the pinhole size is about $m\lambda f/a$, where $m \times m$ is the number of pixels, a is the size of the pictures, and f is the focal length of the condenser lens L_1. The size of the SLM is about $mN\lambda f/a$. For instance, if $m = 512$, $N = 32$, $\lambda = 680$ nm, $f/a = 2$, the required size of the SLM is about 23 mm × 23 mm. The main advantage of this architecture is its rapid and random access to the pictures, in contrast with the sequential access in optical disks.

In practice the total number M of interconnection patterns, which can be recorded in the photorefractive hologram, is basically limited by the maximum index modulation $\Delta\eta$ of the photorefractive material. With reference to Solyman and Cooke's calculation, the number of interconnection patterns is about [7.13]

$$M = \frac{\pi}{\varepsilon^{1/2}} \frac{\eta_1}{\eta} \frac{d}{\lambda}. \qquad (7.34)$$

For example, given $\Delta\eta \sim 10^{-3}$, if $\varepsilon \sim 10^{-3}$, $d = 2$ cm, and $\lambda = 680$ nm for an ion-doped $LiNbO_3$ photorefractive crystal, then the total number of interconnection patterns would be $M \sim 1.2 \times 10^3$. We stress that higher storage capacity would be expected if recording materials with higher $\Delta\eta$ are available.

The experimental setup for the reconfigurable interconnections with *wavelength tuning* is shown in Figure 7.13. The laser beam is divided into two parts by a polarizing beam splitter. A half-wave plate is used to rotate the polarization of one beam so that the reflection hologram is formed in ordinary polarization. A piece of y-cut $LiNbO_3$ crystal 1 mm thick is employed as the recording medium. The write-in angle 2α of beam A and beam B is about 150°. Since we do not have a z-cut crystal, in order to have a grating vector component on the c axis, the writing arrangement should be asymmetrical. Beam A is arranged to be perpendicular to the crystal surface. The wavelength used for writing is 632.8 nm. Eight exposures were made by rotating the

FIGURE 7.13 Experimental setup. C-y-cut LiNbO$_3$. *Note:* PBS is the polarizing beam splitter; $\lambda/2$ is a half-wave plate; M indicates the mirrors; L is the focusing lens; P is the output plane.

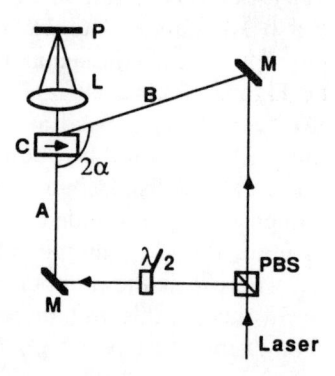

FIGURE 7.14 Readout light spots with eight different wavelengths.

crystal with 0.8° steps. A tunable dye laser is used to read the hologram in the same direction as beam B. The reconstructed light field is collected by a focusing lens L onto the output plane P. It is therefore apparent that holographic gratings can be read out one at a time by simply tuning the wavelength of the dye laser. The readout spots from eight gratings encoded in the crystal using different wavelengths is shown in Figure 7.14. Figure 7.15 shows the linear relationship of the reconstruction wavelength and the deflection angle. It is clear that the write-in angle (i.e., 2α) can be calculated from the slope of the straight line using the dispersion relation of Eq. 7.11, which is given by $2\alpha = 148.5°$.

The experimental setup for *spatial division* reconfigurable interconnections

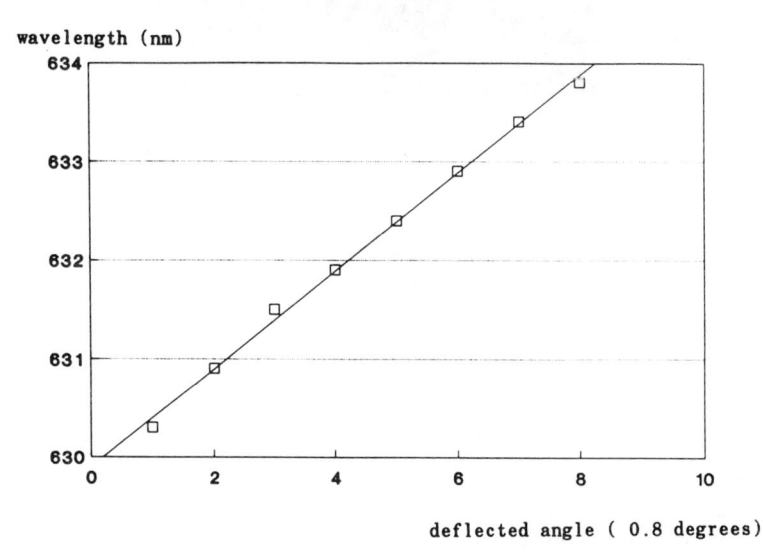

FIGURE 7.15 Reconstruction wavelength as a function of the deflected angle.

is basically the same as shown in Figure 7.12, except that here we use one laser beam illumination in different directions, instead of a laser diode array. In our experiment we employed a movable pinhole as the SLM pinhole. The moving step of the pinhole is about 1 mm, the focal length of the condenser lens is 250 mm. Figure 7.16a shows three reconstructed patterns for the same pinhole position from three different reading directions. The angular separation of the reading beams is ~1°. Figure 7.16b shows the six focal spots reconstructed at the SLM plane with a single reading direction. If these six focal spots are projected onto the page plane, six interconnection patterns would overlap. To separate the overlapping patterns, a pinhole can be used to select one focal spot at a time. Thus, nonoverlapping patterns can be sequentially displayed on the page plane.

To conclude this section, we point out that reflection photorefractive holograms have higher and more uniform dispersions, which is more suitable for reconfigurable optical interconnections with limited tunable wavelength range. If the thickness of the crystal is properly selected, it is possible to satisfy the communication channel bandwidth. In theory, a large number of reconfigurable optical interconnections with high channel bandwidth (e.g., 10^{10} Hz) can be achieved by using a reflection hologram.

We have also shown that transmission photorefractive holograms are more suitable for the spatial division scheme. Since the hologram is encoded in the form of pinhole holograms, the optical interconnection pattern from each laser diode illumination can easily be reconfigured by a programmable SLM.

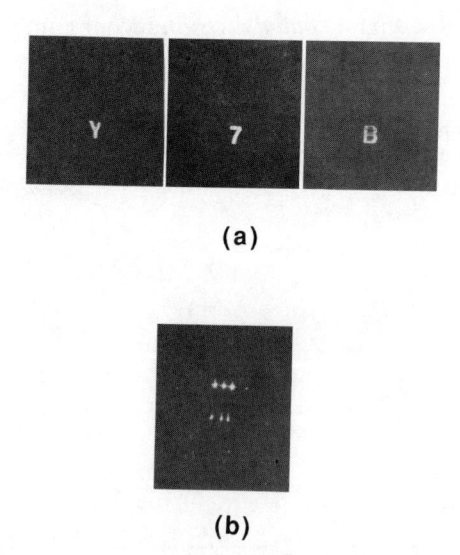

FIGURE 7.16 Interconnections reconfigurable with spatial division. (*a*) Reconstructed patterns on the page plane using three different reading directions with the same pinhole positions. (*b*) Six focal spots reconstructed on the SLM plane by one reading beam.

Nevertheless, for both the wavelength tuning and the spatial division schemes, the maximum number of interconnections stored in a volume hologram is limited by the maximum index modulations of the photorefractive material.

7.3 MULTIPLEXED PHOTOREFRACTIVE MATCHED FILTERS

Recently, multiplexing of filters in photorefractive materials has attracted much attention. By measuring the maximum phase shift achieved in a deep volume hologram and calculating an exposure schedule for recording multiple equally diffracting holograms, Hong et al. have estimated that over 1000 holograms could be recorded in a 4-mm-thick $BaTiO_3$ crystal [7.14]. The holograms can be recorded in the crystal using angular or wavelength multiplexing techniques. By using a fixed image position, and changing the angular position of the reference beam, Mok et al. have reported recording 500 high-resolution, uniformly diffracting volume holograms in a single $LiNbO_3$ crystal [7.15]. By writing holograms sequentially and changing the writing wavelength between exposures, multiple holograms can be recorded in the crystal. This wavelength multiplexing technique has the advantage that neither the object nor the reference beam needs to be changed in the writing or reading process, even though the two processes can be used together to further increase the multiplexing capabilities. This technique has been used in holographic film in which matched filters were multiplexed [7.16]. However, the thin-film emulsion leads to low wavelength selectivity, and the filters are difficult to produce. In addition, the system was not able to quickly update the reference patterns.

In this section we investigate wavelength multiplexed matched spatial filters using a photorefractive $LiNbO_3$ crystal [7.17]. Referring to the coupled-mode analysis of Kogelnik [7.8], we analyze the wavelength multiplexing capacity of reflection-type matched spatial filters. By integrating over the thickness of the crystal, as was suggested by Gheen and Cheng [7.18], we show that thick crystal filters exhibit high wavelength selectivity and retain a good degree of the shift invariance. Thus, by recording single-wavelength filters, and reading out the filters with a multiwavelength source, parallel pattern recognition can be performed.

It is well known that volume holograms offer high diffraction efficiency and high angular and wavelength selectivities. Reflection volume holograms have a much higher wavelength selectivity than transmission volume holograms, while the angular selectivity of the holograms remain similar. For this reason, we chose to use reflection volume holograms for matched filter synthesis. Using the weak coupling approximation, where multiple diffractions are ignored, the wavelength selectivity of the reflection hologram can be expressed as [7.6]

$$\left(\frac{\Delta\lambda}{\lambda}\right)_r = \frac{1}{\sqrt{\eta^2 - \cos^2\alpha}} \frac{\lambda}{d}, \qquad (7.35)$$

270 PHOTOREFRACTIVE CRYSTAL SIGNAL PROCESSING

where λ is the central wavelength of the writing beam, d is the thickness of the crystal, η is the refractive index of the crystal, and α is the external angle shown in Figure 7.5b.

The shift invariant property of the spatial filter can be determined by using layer integration over the thickness of the crystal, as proposed by Gheen and Cheng [7.18]. Figure 7.17 is a schematic diagram of the synthesis of a reflection-type matched spatial filter. Without loss of generality, we use a one-dimensional representation for the analysis, in which $q_1(x_1)$ represents the reference image that is located at the front focal plane of the transform lens L. For a given point x_1, a wave represented by wave vector $\mathbf{k}_1(x_1, \lambda_1)$ is incident at the photorefractive crystal. The reference beam, which is a plane wave represented by wave vector $\mathbf{k}_0(\lambda_1)$, is incident on the opposite side of the crystal. Thus, it is apparent that a reflection-type matched filter can be recorded in the crystal. Let $q_2(x_2)$ be the readout beam representing the input object that is to be detected. Thus, each point x_2 would produce a readout wave vector $\mathbf{k}_2(x_2, \lambda_2)$ for which the reconstructed wave vector is $\mathbf{k}_3(x_3, \lambda_2)$, where x_3 denotes the output coordinate plane. The wave vector representations in the crystal can be expressed as,

$$\mathbf{k}_0(\lambda_1) = -\frac{\eta}{\lambda_1}\hat{z}$$

$$\mathbf{k}_1(\lambda_1) = \frac{x_1}{\lambda_1}\hat{u} + \frac{\eta}{\lambda_1}\left(1 - \frac{x_1^2}{2\eta^2}\right)\hat{z},$$

$$\mathbf{k}_2(\lambda_2) = \frac{x_2}{\lambda_2}\hat{u} + \frac{\eta}{\lambda_2}\left(1 - \frac{x_2^2}{2\eta^2}\right)\hat{z},$$

$$\mathbf{k}_3(\lambda_2) = \frac{x_3}{\lambda_2}\hat{u} + \frac{\eta}{\lambda_2}\left(1 - \frac{x_3^2}{2\eta^2}\right)\hat{z}, \qquad (7.36)$$

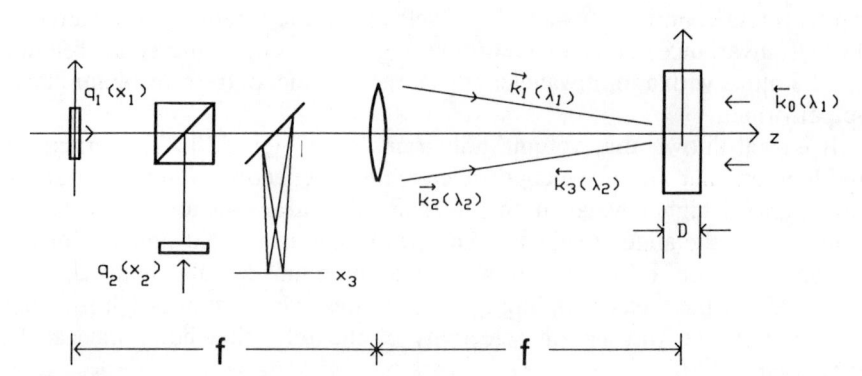

FIGURE 7.17 Geometry for reflection matched filter. *Note:* x_1, x_2, and x_3 are reference, input, and output plane, respectively; $\mathbf{k}_0$, $\mathbf{k}_1$, $\mathbf{k}_2$, $\mathbf{k}_3$, are reference, writing, reading, and readout wave vectors, respectively.

where x_s have been normalized by focal length f, and $\hat{z}$ and $\hat{u}$ are the unit vectors along and normal to the optical axis of the system, respectively. The output correlation signal can be expressed by the following integral equation:

$$R(x_3) = A \left| \iiiint q_1^*(x_1) q_2(x_2) \exp\left[i2\pi\Delta k(u\hat{u} + z\hat{z})\right] dx_1 dx_2 du dz \right|^2, \quad (7.37)$$

where $\Delta \mathbf{k}$ represents the Bragg *dephasing* vector,

$$\Delta \mathbf{k} = \mathbf{k}_0 - \mathbf{k}_1 + \mathbf{k}_2 - \mathbf{k}_3. \quad (7.38)$$

For simplicity, assume that the size of the crystal is infinite in the $\hat{u}$ direction; therefore, the $\hat{u}$ component of the Bragg dephasing wave vector must be zero. From Eq. 7.38, we have

$$\frac{x_1}{\lambda_1} - \frac{x_2 + x_3}{\lambda_2} = 0. \quad (7.39)$$

It follows that

$$x_2 = \left(1 - \frac{\Delta\lambda}{\lambda_1}\right) x_1 - x_3, \quad (7.40)$$

where $\Delta\lambda = \lambda_1 - \lambda_2$. Since the relative wavelength difference, $\Delta\lambda/\lambda_1$, is small, the third-order terms can be neglected. Thus, the $\hat{z}$ component of the Bragg dephasing vector can be written as

$$\Delta k_z = \frac{1}{\eta\lambda_1}\left[2\eta^2 \frac{\Delta\lambda}{\lambda_1} - x_3(x_1 - x_3)\right]. \quad (7.41)$$

By substituting Eqs. 7.40 and 7.41 into Eq. 7.37, and integrating with respect to u, z, and x_2, the correlation signal is

$$R(x_3) = A \left| \int q_1^*(x_1) q_2\left[\left(1 - \frac{\Delta\lambda}{\lambda_1}\right)x_1 - x_3\right] \right.$$

$$\left. \times \mathrm{sinc}\left(\frac{\pi D}{\eta\lambda_1}\left[2\eta^2 \frac{\Delta\lambda}{\lambda_1} - x_3(x_1 - x_3)\right]\right) dx_1 \right|^2. \quad (7.42)$$

Referring to the sinc factor, one can evaluate the wavelength selectivity and the shift-invariant properties of the thick crystal filter. If the input object is centered with respect to the reference function (i.e., $x_1 = x_2$), then the filter would respond to the wavelength variations that satisfy the following inequality:

$$\left|\frac{\Delta\lambda}{\lambda_1}\right| < \frac{\lambda_1}{\eta D}. \quad (7.43)$$

This result is essentially the same as that obtained with coupled wave theory in Eq. 7.35, when the beams are perpendicular to the surface of the crystal.

On the other hand, if the readout and the writing wavelength are identical, then the filter would respond to object shifting that satisfies the following inequality:

$$\left|\frac{x_3(x_1 - x_3)}{f^2}\right|_{max} < \frac{\lambda_1}{\eta D}, \quad (7.44)$$

where f represents the focal length of the transform lens, and D is the thickness of the crystal.

By substituting Eq. 7.40 into Eq. 7.44, and letting $x_3 = x_1 - \Delta x$, we have

$$|\Delta x(x_1 - \Delta x)|_{max} < \frac{\lambda_1 f^2}{\eta D}. \quad (7.45)$$

This inequality shows that the allowable shift, Δx, is dependent on the half-width of the input object $(x_1 - \Delta x)_{max}$, the thickness of the crystal, and the focal length of the lens. It follows that the wavelength selectivity and shift-invariance property are dependent on the thickness of the crystal. In addition, by changing the effective focal length f of the system, a desired shift invariance for a given thickness of the crystal can be obtained [Section 7.1].

Figure 7.18 shows the optical setup that was used for the experiments. The beam splitter separates the beam into a reference beam that enters the crystal from the right, and an object beam that illuminates the input plane, which is transformed by lens L_1 onto a 1-mm-thick $LiNbO_3$ crystal. These two beams interfer in the crystal to form a reflection-type matched filter. After the filter has been recorded, the reference beam is blocked, and an input object to be correlated with the filter is placed in the input plane. The light scattered by the filter forms an output signal that is transformed by lens L_2 onto the output CCD detector, which is connected to a video monitor for real-time observation.

In the first experimental demonstration, we tested the wavelength multiplexing capabilities of a $LiNbO_3$ crystal. By using $\lambda = 488$ nm, $d = 1$ mm, and $\eta = 2.25$ in Eq. 7.43, we found that the filter should not respond for wavelength shifts of $\Delta\lambda > 0.106$ nm. We recorded individual matched filters using wavelengths 457.9, 465.8, 488, and 496.5 nm. Reading out these filters

MULTIPLEXED PHOTOREFRACTIVE MATCHED FILTERS 273

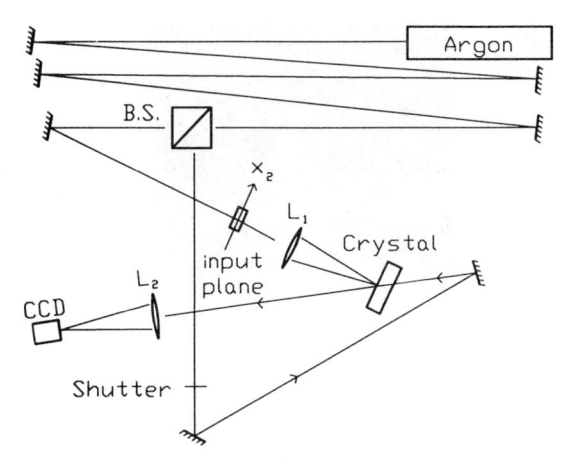

FIGURE 7.18 Experimental setup.

with wavelengths that were different from the recorded wavelength produced no visible output signal. Next, a multiplexed filter using the previously cited wavelengths was recorded of the capital letters D, F, K, and J. Figure 7.19a shows the output autocorrelation spot of a letter D using wavelength 457.9 nm. The corresponding intensity profile of the autocorrelation signal detected by the CCD camera is shown in Figure 7.19b. In this figure, we see that a high-intensity correlation peak was obtained. Figure 7.19c shows the output cross-correlation of this filter with an input object C using a wavelength 457.9 nm. It is apparent that no detectable peak was observed. Thus, we have seen that the wavelength multiplexing capabilities of the crystal filter are in good agreement with our analysis.

In the second experiment the shift-invariant property of the crystal filter was verified. By using $\lambda = 488$ nm, $\eta = 2.25$, $d = 1$ mm, and the effective focal length $f = 1$ m, in Eq. 6.94, it is clear that $[\Delta x(x_1 - \Delta x)]$ must be less than 216 mm^2. The objects that were used for this experiment have a half-width of 1.3 mm, for which the shift invariance expression reduces to $\Delta x_{max} <$ 16 cm, which is much larger than the beam diameter. A reflection-type filter of capital letter O, centered at the input plane, was recorded, The corresponding output autocorrelation signal is shown in Figure 7.20a. Next, a transparency consisting of two Os and an X, as shown in Figure 7.20b, was inserted at the input plane of the optical system. The letters were moved about 9 mm with respect to the position of the reference object of the filter. The corresponding output correlation spots are shown in Figure 7.20c, where two strong correlation spots are observable, as well as a weak cross-correlation distribution. The input beam in this experiment had a usable radius of about ~1.2 cm, and beyond this radius the beam exhibited rapid amplitude variations. Next, the input object was shifted within the beam, and we found that very little amplitude variation in the correlation peak intensity was observed. As before, the experimental results show good agreement with the analysis.

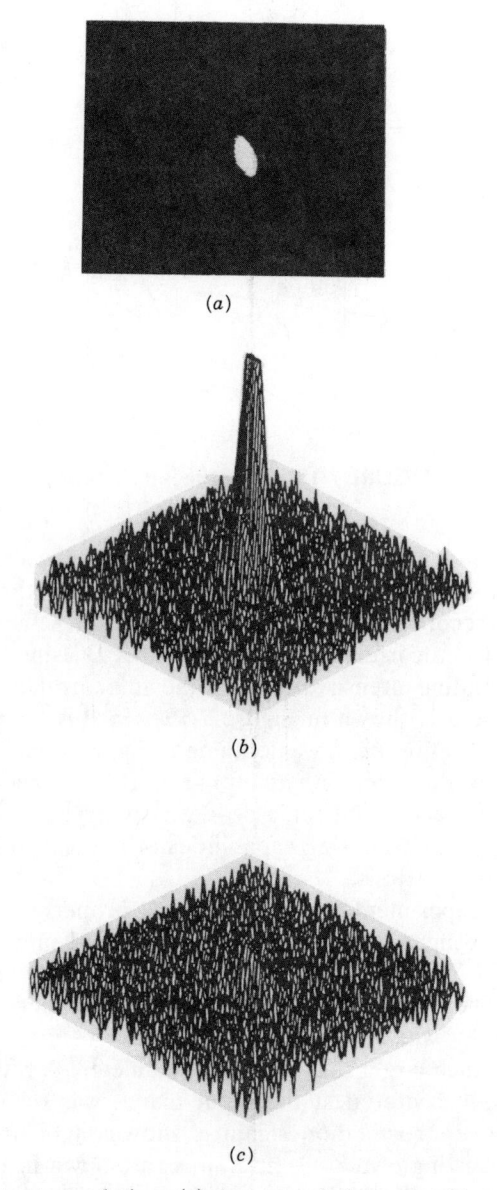

274 PHOTOREFRACTIVE CRYSTAL SIGNAL PROCESSING

FIGURE 7.19 Output correlation. (*a*) Autocorrelation spot of letter *D*. (*b*) Intensity plot of (*a*). (*c*) Cross-correlation with letter *C*, using the same wavelength.

FIGURE 7.20 Shift-invariance property of reflection volume filter. (*a*) Autocorrelation of letter O. (*b*) Input object consisting of two Os and an X. (*c*) Output correlation spots.

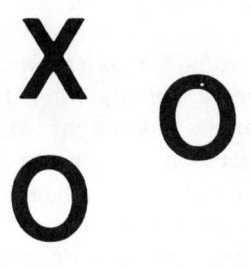

MULTIPLEXED PHOTOREFRACTIVE MATCHED FILTERS 275

(a)

(b)

(c)

7.4 OPTICAL NOVELTY FILTER

Techniques for using photorefractive effects for novelty filtering, such as the four-wave mixing interferometric method [7.19], the two-wave mixing beam depleting [7.20], and the beam fanning technique [7.21], have recently been suggested by several investigators. In theory, the phase distortion in the interferometer, due to any stationary object, would be compensated for by the phase conjugation, and hence only moving objects would be displayed on the output of the interferometer. In practice, however, the nonuniformity of the photorefractive material cannot be completely compensated for. In addition, the nonuniform intensity distribution of the incident light may cause problems. Furthermore, it is rather complicated to set up a two-arm interferometer configuration, and it is extremely difficult to obtain a perfect null output field.

In this section, we discuss a phase carrier frequency technique to produce novelty filtering [7.22]. The features of this technique are that it does not require a high-intensity laser and the configuration is simpler. Since the filter is located in the Fourier plane, it is a shift-invariant system. Thus we see that if the phase object is compensated for with the phase conjugated beam, only the dc component would emerge from the filter. It is clear that if the dc term is blocked at the Fourier plane, a null output would result for the stationary object. However, if the object is in motion, the high-frequency components of the object will be observed at the output plane, in which the low-frequency contents as well as the dc component of the moving object are lost. In order to solve this problem, a phase grating carrier can be used to shift the spectrum of the moving object out of the origin. Thus by using one of the diffraction orders, the moving object can be perceived at the output plane.

Two cases are discussed in the following: in the first case, we assume a moving phase object with a stationary phase carrier frequency (grating). Let $\phi(x, y; t)$ be the moving phase object for which the encoded object beam is given by

$$A = \exp[i\phi(x, y; 0)\sin 2\pi f_0 x], \qquad (7.46)$$

where f_0 is the carrier frequency of the phase grating. Thus the corresponding phase conjugate beam derived from the phase conjugate mirror is given by

$$A^* = \exp[-i\phi(x, y; 0)\sin 2\pi f_0 x]. \qquad (7.47)$$

Thus for a given time t, which is assumed to be shorter than the response time of the phase conjugate mirror, A^* would remain unchanged, although the phase object is $\phi(x, y; t + \Delta t)$. If the phase conjugate beam passes through the object again, the output beam can be written as

$$B = \exp\{i[\phi(x, y; t) - \phi(x, y; t + \Delta t)]\sin 2\pi f_0 x\}. \qquad (7.48)$$

If we assume that the carrier frequency f_0 is much higher than the bandwidth of the object, then Eq. 7.48 can be written in the following form:

$$B \simeq \sum_{m=-\infty}^{m=\infty} J_m(\Delta\phi(x, y; t, \Delta t))e^{i2\pi m f_0 x}, \qquad (7.49)$$

where the difference between the object at $t = 0$ and $t = t$ is given by $\Delta\phi(x, y; t) = \phi(x, y; 0) - \Delta(x, y; t)$. From this result we see that each diffraction order contains the $\Delta\phi(x, y; t)$ distribution. Notice that when $\Delta\phi(x, y, t) = 0$, the dc component is the only nonzero term in Eq. 7.49. Therefore, by blocking all but one of the diffraction orders, a null output distribution is expected.

Suppose, we assume an object moving along with a phase carrier frequency at a constant velocity v for the second case, then the output light field can be written as

$$B = \exp\{i[\phi(x - vt, y)\sin 2\pi f_0(x - vt) - \phi(x, y)\sin 2\pi f_0 x]\}. \qquad (7.50)$$

By further assuming that $f_0 \gg B$, Eq. 7.50 can be written as

$$B \simeq \sum_m \{J_m[\phi(x - vt, y)\cos 2\pi f_0 vt - \phi(x, y)]$$
$$- iJ_m[\phi(x - vt, y)\sin 2\pi f_0 vt]\}e^{i2\pi m f_0 x}. \qquad (7.51)$$

Thus the average intensity for the mth-order term would be

$$I_m = \langle J_m^2[\phi(x - vt, y)\cos 2\pi f_0 vt - \phi(x, y)]\rangle$$
$$+ \langle J_m^2[\phi(x - vt, y)\sin 2\pi f_0 vt]\rangle, \qquad (7.52)$$

where $\langle\ \rangle$ denotes the time ensemble average. Thus we see that each of the diffraction orders has the information content of the object at the starting and at the ending positions. Furthermore, for $v = 0$, that is, a stationary object, $I_m = 0$ (except the zero order). Therefore, by selecting one of the diffraction orders, a moving object can be tracked.

For purposes of experimental demonstration, we used the setup shown in Figure 7.21. An argon laser beam is divided into beams A, B, and C using two beam splitters. A BSO crystal biased with a 3-kV/cm transverse electric field is used as a phase conjugate mirror. Beams B and C are used as the pump beams, and beam A is directed to the input object transparency O. Thus a phase conjugate beam, generated by the crystal, will pass through the object transparency. Notice that the input object O is imaged onto the crystal by lens L_1, and the output light field is imaged by lens L_2 onto the CCD camera, in which a small aperture to select the specific diffraction order is incorporated. The input object encoded with a grating structure is shown in

278 PHOTOREFRACTIVE CRYSTAL SIGNAL PROCESSING

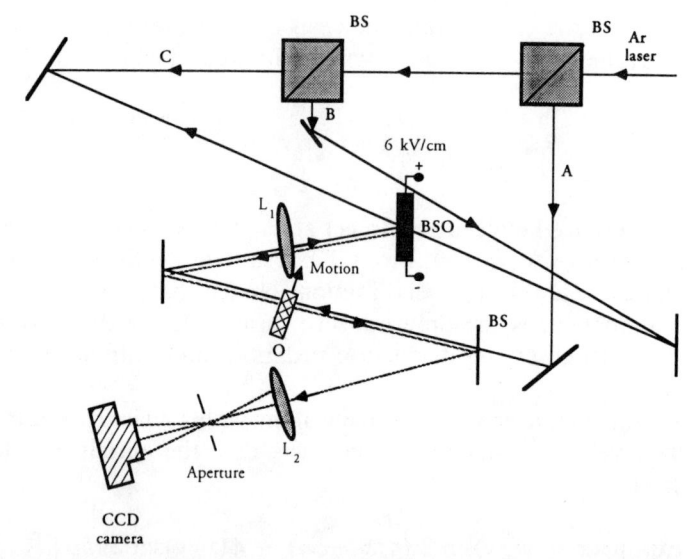

FIGURE 7.21 Experimental setup for novelty filtering with phase carrier frequency.

Figure 7.22 in which the grating frequency f_0 is approximately 4 lines/mm. Needless to say, a phase carrier encoded object may be obtained by using a conventional bleaching process.

The spectrum of a stationary object at the Fourier plane is shown in Figure 7.23a, in which the high diffraction orders appear very weak. This figure demonstrates that the input phase object (with phase grating) was compensated for by the phase conjugation. However, since the object is moving, the high diffraction orders appeared as shown in Figure 7.23b. If one of the first diffraction orders is selected, the output image can be captured by the CCD camera. Figures 7.24(a) and (b) show output results obtained for moving and

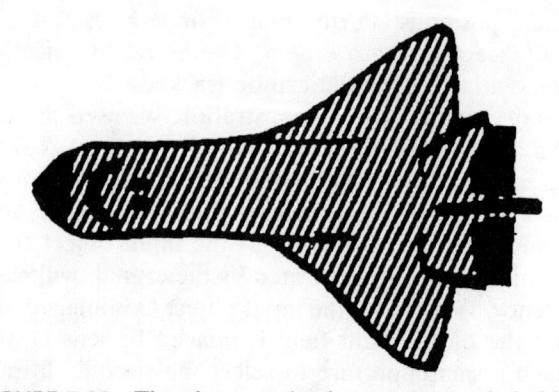

FIGURE 7.22 The phase carrier frequency encoded object.

OPTICAL NOVELTY FILTER 279

(a)

(b)

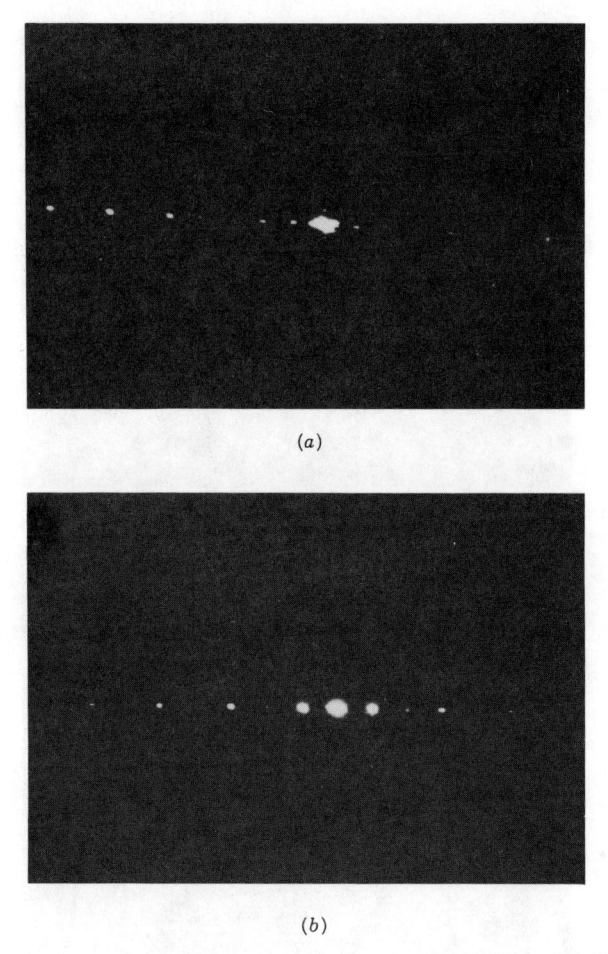

FIGURE 7.23 The spectral distribution of the novelty filter. (a) For a stationary object. (b) For a moving object.

stationary objects, respectively. From these results, we have shown that a moving object can be reconstructed at the output plane.

The frequency of the phase carrier is mainly limited by the nonuniformity of the photorefractive crystal. The use of the imaging lens L_1 minimizes the effect of the nonuniformity of the crystal. Since only a small conical region within the crystal is used, it only affects the image quality for each object point. In our experiments the crystal thickness is 10 mm, and we used a carrier frequency of up to 10 lines/mm. However, for gratings of higher frequency, the phase compensation cannot be fully completed, as shown in Figure 7.23a. In concluding this section, we have shown that the phase carrier frequency technique has the advantages of high response speed, a low laser intensity

280 PHOTOREFRACTIVE CRYSTAL SIGNAL PROCESSING

(a)

(b)

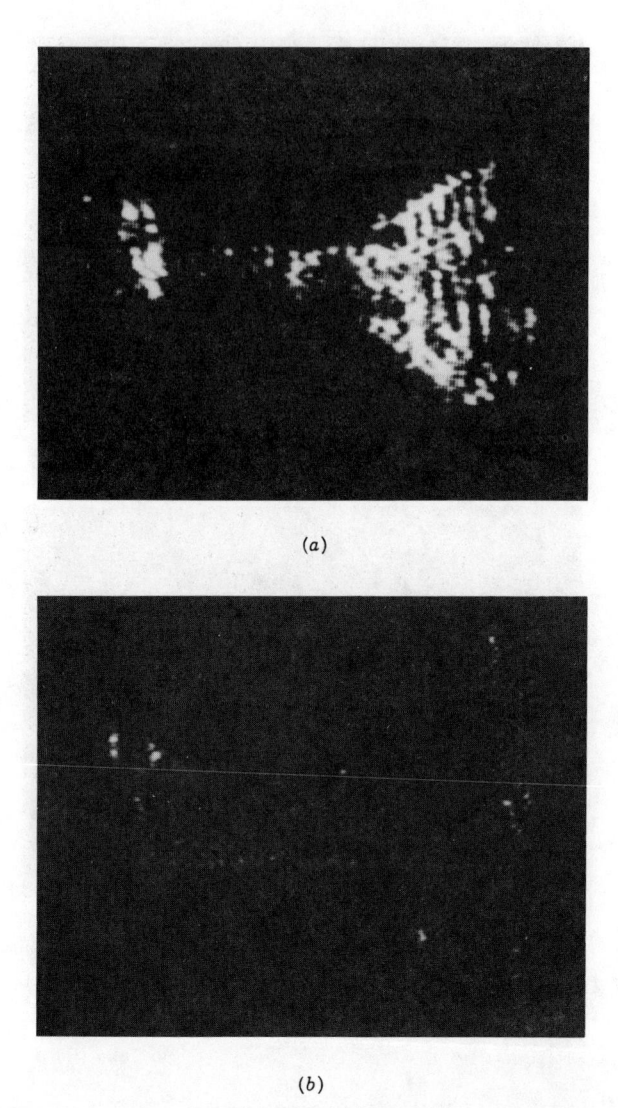

FIGURE 7.24 The output image distributions using the filter. (a) For a moving object. (b) For a stationary object.

requirement, and a simpler configuration. Also, this technique may offer a real-time target tracking application.

7.5 COMPACT JOINT TRANSFORM CORRELATOR USING A THICK CRYSTAL

One of the important aspects for a correlator must be a rapid-update capability, for which an updatable matched filter is required. Spatial light modulators (SLM) may be the possible solution to this problem; however, the state-of-the-art SLM cannot fulfill these demands, because of its low resolution, low contrast, low efficiency, and poor optical quality. Although photorefractive materials have been shown promising effects for real-time spatial filter synthesis, one of the major impediments is the Bragg diffraction limitation. In other words, when a thick crystal is used, the object width and the allowed shift are severely limited [7.23],[7.24].

In this section [7.25], we discuss a simple technique for alleviating this problem. The autocorrelation peak intensity of a JTC, as a function of the shift distance S, can be expressed as [7.18]

$$R(s) = \left| \int |O_1(x_1 - h)|^2 \, \text{sinc}\left[\frac{\pi d(x_1 - h)(2h - S)}{\eta \lambda f^2} \right] dx_1 \right|^2, \quad (7.53)$$

where $O_1(x_1)$ is the object function, d and η are the thickness and refractive index of the crystal, respectively, f is the focal length of the transform lens, and $2h$ is the separation between two input objects. The integration contains two windows, the object and the sinc function, which are both centered at $x_1 = h$. The Bragg limitation is imposed by the correlator with the window of the sinc function, which limits both the object width and the object separation. To increase the width of the window of the sinc function, a long focal length has to be used. This would make the correlator unacceptably large for practical purposes.

To deal with this shortcoming, we used a negative lens along with the transform lens to form a Gallilean telescope, by which a very long effective focal length can be obtained, as shown in Figure 7.25. A similar technique used to alleviate the low-resolution problem of the SLMs was reported by Davis et al. [7.26]. It can be shown that the effective focal length of the correlator is equal to

$$f = \frac{f_2(f_1 - L)}{f_1 - f_2 - L} + L, \quad (7.54)$$

where f_1, f_2 are the focal length of lenses L_1 and L_2 (usually $f_1 > f_2$), and L is the distance between the two lenses. The magnification of the focal length is equal to

$$M = \frac{f_1(f_2 + L) - 2f_2 L - L^2}{f_1(f_1 - f_2 - L)}. \quad (7.55)$$

We note that when the distance between the two lenses varies from f_1 to $f_1 - f_2$, the effective focal length varies from f_1 to infinity.

As an experimental demonstration, a compact JTC using the BSO photorefractive crystal shown in Figure 7.25 is utilized. The focal length of the transform lens is about 300 mm, and the crystal is about 10 mm thick and

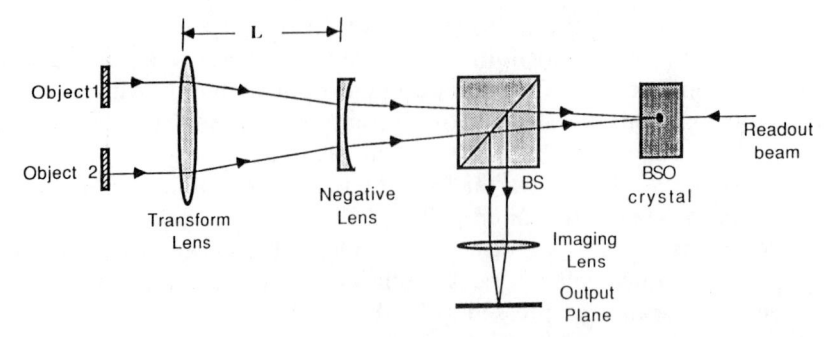

282 PHOTOREFRACTIVE CRYSTAL SIGNAL PROCESSING

FIGURE 7.25 One-dimensional compression technique using a Gallilean telescope.

operates under a 6 kV/cm transverse electric field. In our experiments, two input objects, letters "O" and "X" (about 2.5 mm), are used for auto- and cross-correlation operations. The separation between the input object varies from 6 mm to 17 mm. The photorefractive holograms are recorded using a 480-nm Ar laser, for which the output correlation peak is detected by a CCD camera. First, without the Gallilean telescope (removing the negative lens), no output correlation peak is observed due to the Bragg diffraction limitation. After the telescope was introduced ($M = 5$), the output correlation peak was as shown in Figure 7.26, in which the autocorrelation peaks (using the letter

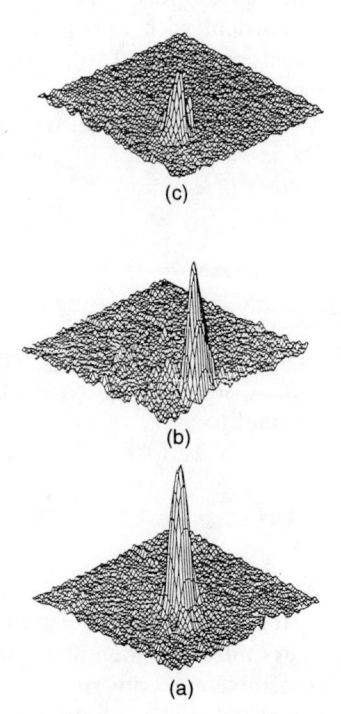

FIGURE 7.26 Output autocorrelation distribution of the letter "O" for various object separations. (*a*) 11 mm. (*b*) 13 mm. (*c*) 17 mm.

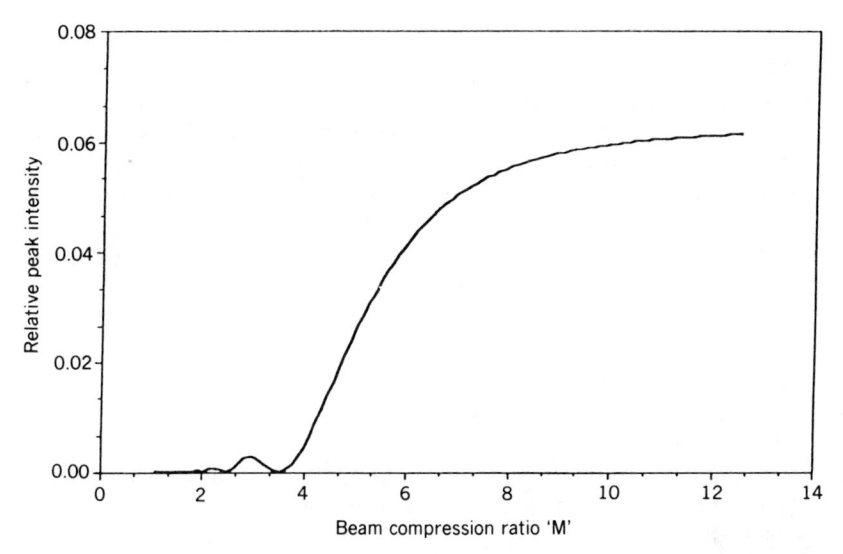

FIGURE 7.27 Relative peak intensity as a function of the beam compression ratio M.

"O") are obtained with increasing object separation. These results show that the use of the Gallilean telescope can effectively alleviate the Bragg limitation in a JTC.

To compute the correlation peak intensity of the function of M given in Eq. 7.53, we assume that the focal length of the transform lens $f = 10$ cm, the wavelength $\lambda = 488$ nm, and input objects are limited by 2.5-mm rectangular widths separated by a distance of 15 mm. The refractive index of the crystal is 2.54 with a thickness of 1 cm. The computed results of the relative correlation peak intensity as a function of object beam compression ratio, M, are shown in Figure 7.27. From this plot, we see that the peak intensity rapidly increases as M increases from 4 to 8, and then tapers off beyond $M = 8$. Notice that if a transform lens of $8f$ is employed to achieve the same results, the size of the correlator would be unacceptable.

We should also note that while the effective focal length increases M-fold, the scale of the transform spectrum is also increased M-fold. To preserve the space–bandwidth product of the JTC, the transverse size of the crystal should be increased by the same factor of M.

REFERENCES

7.1 R. A. Fisher, Ed., *Optical Phase Conjugation*, Academic Press, New York, 1983.

7.2 J. Feinberg, "Self-Pumped, Continuous-Wave Phase Conjugator Using Internal Reflection," *Opt. Lett.* 7 (1982): 486.

7.3 F. T. S. Yu, S. Wu and A. W. Mayers, "Applications of Phase Conjugation to a Joint Transform Correlator," *Opt. Commun.* 71 (1989): 156.

7.4 E. Ochoa, L. Hesselink, and J. W. Goodman, "Real-Time Intensity Inversion Using Two-Wave and Four-Wave Mixing in Photorefractive $Bi_{12}G_eO_{20}$," *Appl. Opt.* 24 (1985): 1826.

7.5 D. W. Vahey, "A Nonlinear Coupled-Wave Theory of Holographic Storage in Ferroelectric Materials," *J. Appl. Phys.* 46 (1975): 3510.

7.6 S. Wu, Q. Song, A. Mayers, D. A. Gregory, and F. T. S. Yu, "Reconfigurable Interconnections Using Photorefractive Holograms," *Appl. Opt.* 29 (1990): 1118.

7.7 P. Yeh, A. E. T. Chiou, and J. Hong, "Optical Interconnection Using Photorefractive Dynamic Holograms," *Appl. Opt.* 27 (1988): 2093.

7.8 H. Kogelnik, "Coupled Wave Theory for Thick Hologram Grating," *Bell Syst. Tech. J.* 48 (1969): 2902.

7.9 E. Bradley, P. K. L. Yu, and A. R. Jonston, "System Issues Relating to Diode Requirements for VLSI Holographic Optical Interconnections," *Opt. Eng.* 28 (1989): 201.

7.10 A. C. Strasser, E. S. Maniloff, K. M. Johnson, and S. D. D. Goggin, "Procedure for Recording Multiple-Exposure Holograms with Equal Diffractions Efficiency in Photorefractive Media," *Opt. Lett.* 14 (1989): 6.

7.11 L. Staeble, W. J. Burke, W. Phillips, and J. J. Amodei, "Multiple Storage and Erasure of Fixed Holograms of Fe-Doped $LiNbO_3$," *Appl. Phys. Lett.* 26 (1975): 182.

7.12 S. Xu, G. Mendes, S. Hart, and J. C. Dainty, "Pinhole Hologram and Its Applications," *Opt. Lett.* 14 (1989): 107.

7.13 L. Solyman and D. J. Cooke, *Volume Holography and Volume Grating*, Academic Press, New York, 1981.

7.14 J. H. Hong, P. Yeh, D. Psaltis, and D. Brady, "Diffraction Efficiency of Strong Volume Holograms," *Opt. Lett.* 15 (1990): 344.

7.15 F. Mok, M. Tackett, and H. M. Stoll, "Uniform Diffraction Angle-Multiplexed Hologram in $LiNbO_3$," in *Digest of Annual Meeting of the Optical Society of America*, TUG2 (1989).

7.16 S. K. Case, "Pattern Recognition with Wavelength-Multiplexed Filters," *Appl. Opt.* 18 (1979): 1890.

7.17 F. T. S. Yu, S. Wu, A. W. Mayers and S. Rajan, "Wavelength Multiplexed Reflection Matched Spatial Filters Using $LiNbO_3$," *Opt. Commun.* 81 (1991): 343.

7.18 G. Gheen and L. J. Cheng, "Optical Correlators with Fast Updating Speed Using Photorefractive Semiconductor Materials," *Appl. Opt.* 27 (1988): 2756.

7.19 D. Z. Anderson, D. M. Liniger, and J. Feinberg, "Optical Tracking Novelty Filter," *Opt. Lett.* 12 (1987): 123.

7.20 M. Cronin-Golomb, A. M. Brenacki, C. Lin, and H. Kong, "Photorefractive Time Diffraction of Coherent Images," *Opt. Lett.* 12 (1987): 1029.

7.21 J. E. Ford, Y. Fainman, and S. H. Lee, "Time Integrating Interferometry Using Photorefractive Fanout," *Opt. Lett.* 13 (1988): 1856.

7.22 F. T. S. Yu, S. Wu, S. Rajan, A. Mayers, and D. A. Gregory, "Optical Novelty Filtering Using Phase Carrier Frequency," *Opt. Commun.* (1992).

7.23 B. Loiseaux, G. Illiaquer, and J. P. Huignard, "Dynamic Optical Cross-Correlator Using a Liquid Crystal Light Valve and a Bismuth Silicon Oxide Crystal in the Fourier Plane," *Opt. Eng.* 24 (1985): 144.

7.24 M. G. Nicholson, I. R. Cooper, M. W. McCall, and C. R. Petts, "Simple Computation Model of Image Correlation by Four-Wave Mixing in Photorefractive Media," *Appl. Opt.* 6 (1987): 278.

7.25 F. T. S. Yu, S. Wu, S. Rajan, and D. A. Gregory, "Compact Joint Transform Correlator Using a Thick Photorefractive Crystal," *Appl. Opt.* (1992): 2416.

7.26 J. A. Davis, M. A. Waring, G. W. Bach, R. A. Lilly, and D. M. Cotrell, "Compact Optical Correlator Design," *Appl. Opt.* 28 (1989): 10.

PROBLEMS

7.1 We showed in Section 7.1 that phase distortion introduced by an SLM in a joint transform correlator can be compensated for by using a nonlinear photorefractive crystal. If a nonuniform photorefractive crystal is used, illustrate whether phase compensation can be achieved.

7.2 State the major advantages and disadvantages of using a phase-encoding technique in a joint transform correlator.

7.3 By using the four-wave mixing technique, draw an optical architecture and show that an image contrast reversal can be performed.

7.4 Repeat Problem 7.3 for edge enhancement.

7.5 Sketch a two-wave mixing architecture, and show that wavefront-distortion compensation can indeed be accomplished with the optical setup.

7.6 Referring to Section 7.2 on reconfigurable interconnections, calculate the optimum writing angle such that the photorefractive crystal hologram would be sensitive to wavelength variation.

7.7 Given a photorefractive crystal volume holographic process, derive a general Bragg diffraction condition by using volume scattering theory.

7.8 Two grating vectors has been written into a thick photorefractive crystal with a 45° writing beam. Assuming that the angular separation of this set of gratings is about 2° and that the constructing wavelength is $\lambda = 514$ nm, calculate the readout wavelength difference from the second grating vector for the same reading angle.

7.9 Assuming that a 10-mm-thick $LiNbO_3$ photorefractive crystal is used for a transmission-type hologram, and assuming that the wavelength of the light source is $\lambda = 514$ nm and the writing angle is about 45°, compute the allowable reading angular deviation.

7.10 Repeat Problem 7.9 for a reflection-type hologram.

7.11 Draw a vector diagram to represent the reading direction for the two-grating structure in a photorefractive crystal using the same reading wavelength. Assume that the same amplitude is used and the angular separation is $\Delta\theta$.

7.12 Referring to the spatial division scheme shown in Figure 7.12, assume that the SLM has 256 × 256 pixel arrays and that the pixel size at P (the interconnection pattern) is about 50 μm. Calculate the minimum angular separation between the object illuminator beams B and B'. Notice that the illuminating wavelength is $\lambda = 480$ nm.

7.13 Referring to the reflection-type matched filtering in Figure 7.13, state the major advantages of using this type of photorefactive crystal filter. Are there any major disadvantages? Explain.

7.14 A 1-mm-thick $LiNbO_3$ photorefractive crystal is used for a reflection-type matched filter. Assuming that the writing wavelength is $\lambda = 500$ nm and that the refractive index of the crystal is $\eta = 2.28$, calculate the minimum writing-wavelength separation for a wavelength-multiplexed filter.

7.15 Referring to Problem 7.14, if the object size has a width of 2 mm, and the focal length of the transform lens is 100 mm, what would be the allowable shift of the object?

7.16 Referring to the compact joint transform correlator of Section 7.5, assume that a 10-mm-thick $LiNbO_3$ crystal is used for the joint transform filter and that the illuminating wavelength is $\lambda = 500$ nm. If the object separation is about $2h = 10$ mm and the focal length of the transform lens is 300 mm, calculate the maximum allowable width of the object.

7.17 Referring to Problem 7.16, if a 20-mm object width is used, what would the composite optical system used? Assume that the separation between the transform and the negative lenses (Figure 7.25) is about 200 mm.

7.18 State the major advantages and disadvantages of using the phase carrier technique for novelty filtering.

CHAPTER EIGHT

Digital-Optical Computing

Traditionally, optics deals with two-dimensional image formation, plus the generation, propagation, and detection of light waves [8.1], [8.2]. But the reaffirmation of the parallelism of optical processing and the development of picosecond and femtosecond optical switching devices have thrust optics into the nontraditional area of digital computing. The motivation for digital optical computing comes from the need for higher performance general-purpose digital computers. High-performance computers are especially necessary for weather prediction, computational aerodynamics, flight simulation, remote sensing, artificial intelligence, simulation of nuclear reactors, and military uses.

There has always been a demand for faster computers, and computer scientists and engineers have used two methods to achieved higher performance [8.3]. First, they have increased the speed of the circuitry (herd of elephants approach). Second, they have increased the number of operations that can take place concurrently, through either pipelining or parallelism (army of ants approach). In other words, two directions can be taken; device and architecture. While device is a purely physical and an engineering issue, architecture is not merely a conceptual issue.

The multiprocessor structure in a parallel architecture requires a complex interconnection among processors that is difficult to achieve using wires or planar microcircuits. However, both parallelism and interconnection are inherent in optics. Unlike electrons, photons are easily redirected in space by optical means and do not interact with each other. To process the information carried by photons, which can be considered optical buses, special optical devices, such as spatial light modulators (SLMs), are employed as multiprocessors. Each spatial element (pixel) of the SLM can be seen as a single bit processor. The interconnection that provides the communication pattern among processors can be implemented using a lens, grating, optical fibers, or a hologram. Thus, parallel architectures of a single-instruction stream, multiple-data stream (SIMD), multiple-instruction stream, single-data stream (MISD), and multiple-instruction stream, multiple-data stream (MIMD) defined by Flynn [8.3] are very likely implementable by optical means.

Since the basic operation performed by a processor in a computer is a Boolean logic function, the multiprocessor-like SLM should be able to perform all 16 Boolean functions. The logic function is a nonlinear operation that can be realized by a combination of linear addition and multiplication, and nonlinear thresholding. The optical logic gates based on SLM described in this chapter utilize either the intrinsic thresholding capability of the SLM or the external thresholding that can be done electronically by a light-detecting device or a simple mathematical operation in a host electronic computer. For a simplified comparison, the Cray-1 supercomputer with 100 megaflops may be equivalent to an SLM with 1000 × 1000 pixels and 3200 frames per second.

Another trend in optical computing is the investigation of the high-speed switch based on nonlinear optical bistability. The goal of this effort is to fabricate a new optical switch with higher speed and lower energy as compared with its electronic counterpart. It should also be noted that optical processors are immune to electromagnetic interference.

The field of optical computing is quite broad, and includes many different ideas and possibilities. It is not well-defined and nearly any operation in which an optical device or phenomenon can be used for numeric and symbolic computation can be categorized as optical computing [8.4]. However, we restrict ourselves to a few topics that would have general interest to our readers. In view of the large amount of literature on the subject, this chapter is by no means complete, and we apologize for not being able to include all of these references (see [8.5]–[8.8]).

8.1 SHADOW-CASTING LOGIC

A digital computer can be described as a finite-state machine whose physical realization requires numerous Boolean logic gates. A Boolean logic operation basically consists of two inputs and a single output, where the variables of an expression represent only logical 0 and 1. Table 8.1 shows, in regular order, all 16 possible positive logic functions that might result from combining two binary variables. For simplicity, positive logic is discussed throughout the book; however, the analysis can be modified straightforwardly to include negative logic.

Since an optical detector is sensitive to light intensity (optical energy), it is very logical choice to represent binary numbers 0 and 1 with dark and bright states, respectively. Zero means no energy input to or output from a gate; 1 means a package of energy input to or output from a gate. It is apparent that some difficulty would occur when a logical 1 has to be the output from 0s (e.g., NOR, XNOR, NAND), because no energy can be physically generated for 1 (bright) from 0s (dark). The method of shadow casting invented by Tanida and Ichioka [8.9] ingeniously solves the problem by initially en-

TABLE 8.1. Sixteen Possible Functions of Two Binary Variables for Positive Logic

Input		Output															
A	B	F0	F1	F2	F3	F4	F5	F6	F7	F8	F9	F10	F11	F12	F13	F14	F15
0	0	0	0	0	0	0	0	0	0	1	1	1	1	1	1	1	1
0	1	0	0	0	0	1	1	1	1	0	0	0	0	1	1	1	1
1	0	0	0	1	1	0	0	1	1	0	0	1	1	0	0	1	1
1	1	0	1	0	1	0	1	0	1	0	1	0	1	0	1	0	1
FUNCTION NAME		0	AND	$A\bar{B}$	A	$\bar{A}B$	B	XOR	OR	NOR	XNOR	$\bar{B}$	$A+\bar{B}$	$\bar{A}$	$\bar{A}+B$	NAND	1

290 DIGITAL-OPTICAL COMPUTING

coding 1 and 0 in a dual rail form; that is, 1 is represented by bright and dark elements, and 0 is represented by dark and bright elements. Thus 1 and 0 carry the same amount of total energy, although they have inverse spatial patterns. The final output is, however, in the form of a single element, that is, bright state or dark state.

The shadow-casting logic essentially performs all sixteen Boolean logic functions based on the combination of the NOT, AND, and OR functions. In the input plane, 1 and 0 are encoded with four cells, as shown in Figure 8.1a. The 1 of output A is encoded as a horizontal opaque and transparent stripe pattern, and 0 is the inverse (and horizontal) pattern of 1. The 1 of input B is encoded as a vertical opaque and transparent stripe pattern, and 0 is the inverse (and vertical) pattern of 1. The two spatially encoded binary images of A and B are placed in contact, which is equivalent to an AND operation, as shown in Figure 8.1b. If the uncoded 1 and 0 are represented by transparent and opaque cells, respectively, this coding procedure provides four AND operations, that is, AB, $A\bar{B}$, $\bar{A}B$, and $\bar{A}\bar{B}$, simultaneously, as shown in Figure 8.1b. This superposed image is the input coded image of the optical logic array processor, and is set in the input plane. Four spatially distributed light-emitting diodes (LEDs) are employed to illuminate the encoded input. The shadows from each LED will be cast onto an output screen, as shown in Figure 8.2. A decoding mask is needed to extract only the true output. The shadow casting is essentially a selective OR operation among AB, $A\bar{B}$, $\bar{A}B$, and $\bar{A}\bar{B}$. If the on–off states of the LEDs are denoted by α, β, γ and δ (where on is 1, and off is 0), the shadow-casting output can be expressed as follows:

$$G = \alpha(AB) + \beta(A\bar{B}) + \gamma(\bar{A}B) + \delta(\bar{A}\bar{B}), \tag{8.1}$$

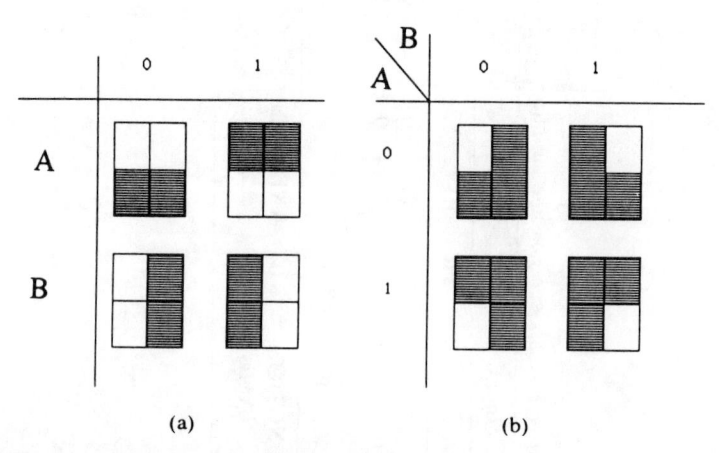

FIGURE 8.1 (*a*) Encoded input patterns. (*b*) Product of the input patterns in the shadow-casting logic array processor.

SHADOW-CASTING LOGIC   291

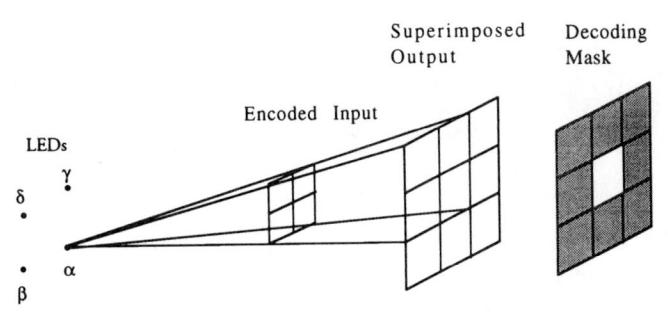

FIGURE 8.2 The original shadow-casting logic array processor. The shadows of the encoded input generated by four LEDs are superimposed.

which is the intensity at the overlapping cell. The complete combination of α, β, γ, and δ for generating the 16 Boolean functions is given in Table 8.2.

Since an encoding step is required, a computer may have to be employed to perform this encoding task. A schematic diagram of a hybrid-optical logic array processor is depicted in Figure 8.3 [8.10]. Computer-encoded inputs A and B are displayed on LCTV1 and LCTV2, respectively. In this hybrid scheme, a uniform illumination instead of four LEDs is used. However, an additional optical mask, LCTV3, is employed to determine the values of α, β, γ, and δ. The OR operation expressed by Eq. 8.1 is performed electronically rather than optically by shadow casting. This has the advantage that no space is needed for shadow casting nor is an output decoding mask needed. The problems with this system are (1) the encoding operation may slow down

TABLE 8.2. Generation of Sixteen Boolean Functions

	α	β	γ	δ
F0	0	0	0	0
F1	1	0	0	0
F2	0	1	0	0
F3	1	1	0	0
F4	0	0	1	0
F5	1	0	1	0
F6	0	1	1	0
F7	1	1	1	0
F8	0	0	0	1
F9	1	0	0	1
F10	0	1	0	1
F11	1	1	0	1
F12	0	0	1	1
F13	1	0	1	1
F14	0	1	1	1
F15	1	1	1	1

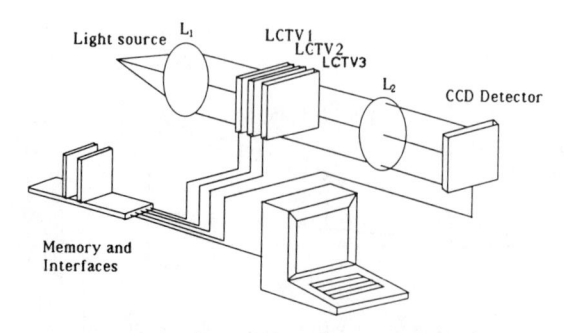

FIGURE 8.3 Shadow-casting logic processor using cascaded LCTVs.

the whole process (which always plagues a coded shadow-casting method), and (2) if the OR operation expressed by Eq. 8.1 is performed in parallel, a large number of electronic OR gates and wire intercommunications are required, and if it is performed sequentially, a longer processing time is required.

Many advanced architectures and algorithms based on shadow-casting logic have been reported [8.11], [8.12]. All these logic processors use encoded inputs. If the coding is done by electronic means, the overall processing speed will be substantially reduced. On the other hand, the optical output is also an encoded pattern that requires a decoding mask to obtain only the true output. Although the decoding process is parallel, and thus takes no significant processing time, the decoding mask does change the format of the output. A noncoded shadow-casting logic array that is free from the difficulties mentioned previously was proposed, as shown in Figure 8.4 [8.13].

An electronically addressed SLM, such as an LCTV, can be driven by a computer or TV camera to write an image on it. The negation can be done easily by rotating the LCTV's analyzer by 90° without altering the electronic signal or software processing. The electronic signal of input A is split into four individual SLMs. Two of them display input A, and the other two display $\bar{A}$. Input B follows a similar procedure to generate two Bs and two $\bar{B}$s. The products of AB, A$\bar{B}$, $\bar{A}$B, and $\bar{A}\bar{B}$ are straightforwardly obtained by putting two corresponding SLMs up to each other. Finally, beam splitters combine

FIGURE 8.4 Noncoded shadow-casting logic array processor. *Note:* S is the light source; BS is the beam splitter; and M indicates a mirror.

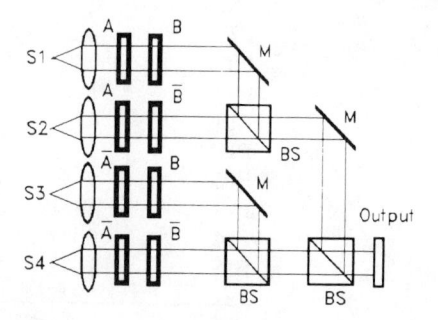

AB, A$\overline{\text{B}}$, $\overline{\text{A}}$B and $\overline{\text{AB}}$. The logic functions are controlled by the on-off state (α, β, γ, and δ) of the illuminating light (S1, S2, S3, and S4), as given in Table 8.2.

The implementation of these logic functions using LCTVs is straightforward, since no electronic signal modification or software data manipulation is required to encode inputs A and B. Although it seems that more SLMs are needed (four times as many), there is no increase in the space–bandwidth product of the system. In the original shadow-casting logic array, four pixels are used to represent a binary number 1 or 0, while a binary number can be represented by only one pixel in the noncoded system. The use of four sets of individual SLMs is to utilize fully the capability of LCTV to form a negative image by simply rotating the analyzer by 90°. This method can eliminate the bottleneck of the shadow-casting optical parallel logic array, which is introduced by the coding process.

8.2 POLARIZATION LOGIC

The two characteristic states of optical bistability (logical 1 and logical 0) can be associated not only with intensity but also with polarization [8.14], although the final states should be converted to intensity, which is the only parameter that can be detected by a square-law (energy) detector. Many optical logical gates employing polarization modulation SLMs have been reported [8.15]–[8.17].

For instance, optical parallel logic can be implemented using MOSLMs [8.18]. Taking advantage of the ability of a polarization modulation-type SLM to reverse the output by simply rotating its analyzer by 90°, the Boolean functions F1, F2, F4, F6, F8, and F9 shown in Table 8.1 can be straightforwardly implemented using the multiplicative configuration shown in Figure 8.5. To perform XOR (F6), polarizer P2 is removed, while the direction of P3 is set parallel to that of P1. When there is 90° polarization rotation for passing through an SLM (logical 1) and no rotation for an off SLM (logical 0), only different state combinations (0, 1) and (1, 0) result in a nonzero output. Ideally, XNOR (F9) could be performed as XOR with a 90° rotated polarizer P3. It is also obvious that functions F7, F11, F13, and F14 can be implemented using the additive configuration, as shown in Figure 8.6.

The Boolean functions can also be performed using only the configuration

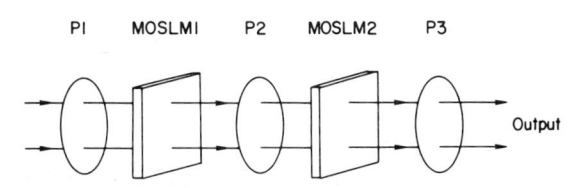

FIGURE 8.5 Multiplicative configuration for logic operations. *Note:* P is the polarizer.

294 DIGITAL-OPTICAL COMPUTING

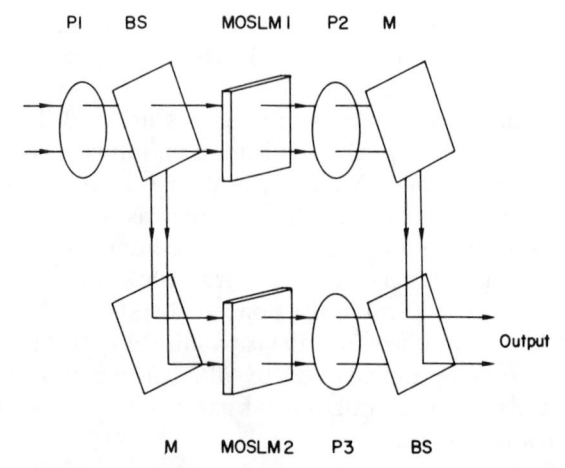

FIGURE 8.6 Additive configuration for logic operations. *Note:* P is the polarizer; BS is the beam splitter; and M indicates mirror.

shown in Figure 8.7 [8.19]. Based on NOT and AND operations, 14 optical parallel logic gates (excluding XOR and XNOR) can be implemented by this structure. To perform XOR and XNOR, the polarizer between two the SLMs (LCTV1 and LCTV2) is removed. This configuration is explained schematically in Figure 8.8 [8.20]. Note that in the off-off state, no light is transmitted through the LCTV2. To get an XNOR output, LCTV3 reverses an XOR output from LCTV2.

It is seen that two SLMs are required to construct a two-input XOR logic gate. Since the liquid crystal materials in the SLM absorb light, the cascading of SLMs results in an exponential energy loss. If the transmittance of an SLM is t, the transmittance of two cascading SLMs will be t^2 ($0 \leq t \leq 1$). The use

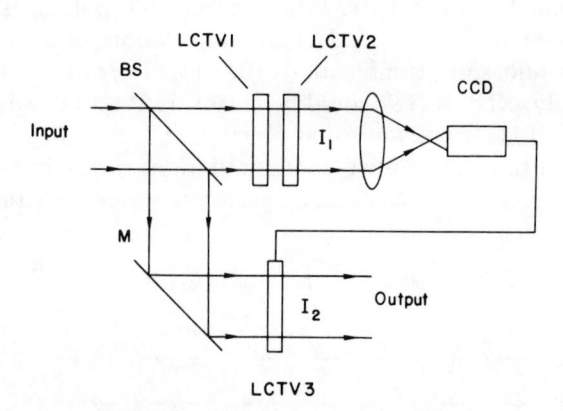

FIGURE 8.7 Logic array processor using LCTVs and CCD based on NOT and AND functions.

POLARIZATION LOGIC 295

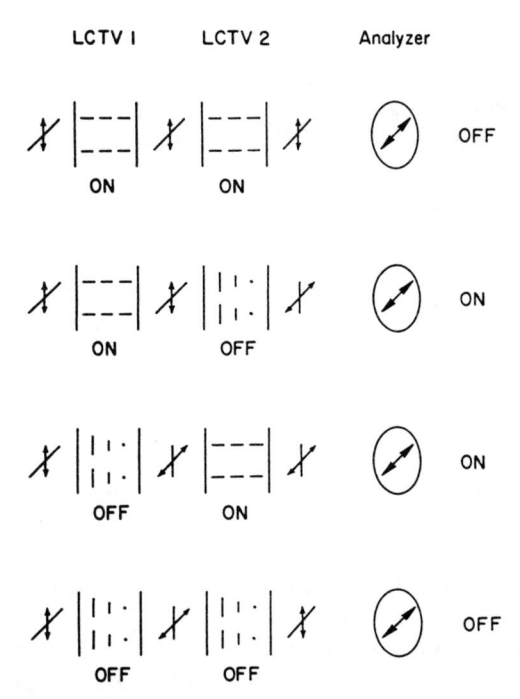

FIGURE 8.8 XOR operation of two cascaded LCTVs. No polarizer is between the two LCTVs.

of a single SLM for a two-input logic gate will significantly reduce the energy loss and the complexity of the optical system. The synthesis of an XOR and XNOR gate using a single electronically addressed SLM [8.21] is discussed in the following paragraphs.

The polarization rotation is controlled by the electric field applied at each pixel. For the nematic twisted liquid crystal structure that is generally used for an LCTV, the presence of a static electric field cancels the rotation of polarization, while the absence of the field results in the rotation of polarization. The electric field is generated by two transparent electrodes that sandwich the liquid crystals materials. It is possible to construct an XOR or XNOR gate using a single LCTV as follows. Input A is connected to one electrode and input B is connected to another electrode. The logical 1 and 0 are represented by a positive and zero voltage, respectively. It is clear that combinations (0, 0) and (1, 1) generate no electric field, since there is no potential difference between the two electrodes. Thus the light polarization will be rotated by 90° due to the twisted liquid crystal molecular structure. Combinations (0, 1) and (1, 0) generate electric fields in opposite directions. However, in both cases the twisted molecular structure will be aligned perpendicular to the light polarization (parallel with the light propagation), such that no polarization rotation is performed. This method is not only applicable to LCTVs, but can also be applied to any type of electrooptic display device

296 DIGITAL-OPTICAL COMPUTING

that is operated with electric fields; for instance, an electroluminescent (EL) lamp [8.21].

It is worth mentioning that an MSLM can be employed for performing XOR and XNOR operations [8.22]. The output intensity from an MSLM is [8.23]

$$I(x, y) = I_o \sin^2[c_1 V_b + c_2 I_w(x, y)], \qquad (8.2)$$

where I_o is the uniform readout illumination intensity, c_1 is a constant determined by the crystal plate, c_2 is a parametric constant depending on the bias voltages on the electrodes, V_b is the bias voltage across the crystal plate, and $I_w(x, y)$ is the intensity of the write-in light. By setting $c_1 V_b = c_2 I_i = \pi$, the output intensity would be zero if the write-in intensity were either zero or I_i. If the write-in intensity were $I_i/2$, the output intensity would be I_o, which is the maximum. This relationship between input and output intensities is illustrated in Figure 8.9, and corresponds to the XOR of the input operands. Figure 8.10 illustrates sixteen Boolean functions obtained using three LCTVs for multiplicative and additive configurations and an MSLM for XOR and XNOR operations [8.22].

The XOR operation is a basic operation for binary addition and subtraction. In a half-adder, which is the adder of two 1-bit numbers, carry and sum are determined by AND and XOR operations, respectively. Since polarization modulation-type SLMs are capable of performing AND and XOR functions, an optical half-adder can be constructed. A full-adder is the adder of two numbers with more than one bit in which the carry from the previous lower order bit's addition must taken into account. An optical full-adder can be implemented in the same way. In particular, an optical binary adder using LCTV has already been demonstrated [8.24].

Another example of optical logic circuit is the flip-flop array. A flip-flop has two inputs corresponding to two stable states. It is called flip-flop because application of a suitable input pulse causes the device to "flip" into the corresponding state and remain in that state until a pulse on the other input causes it to "flop" into the other state. A flip-flop can be implemented by a pair of NOR gates. Since an LCLV can perform NOR operation, two LCLVs can be arranged in an optical circuit to implement an optical flip-flop [8.25].

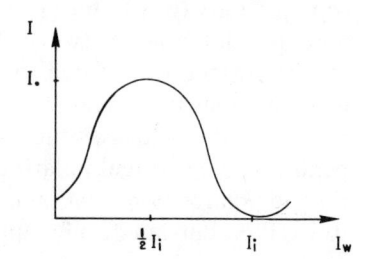

FIGURE 8.9 Relationship of the input and output intensities of the MSLM to the XOR function.

ELECTRON TRAPPING LOGIC 297

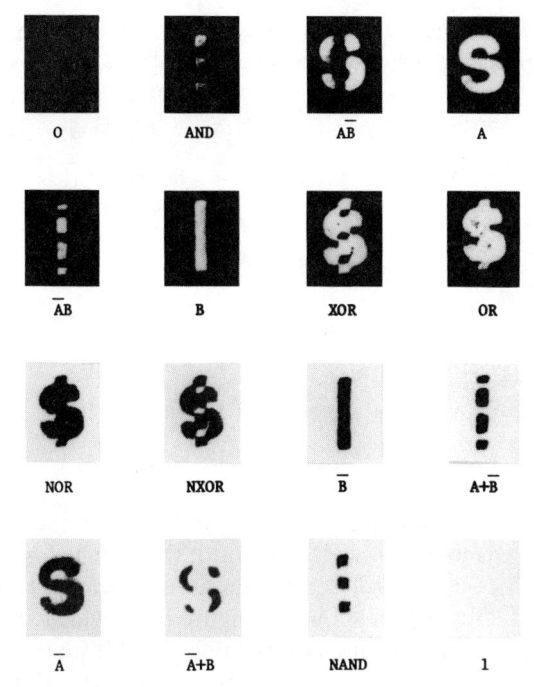

FIGURE 8.10 Sixteen Boolean functions obtained by the array processor employing LCTVs and MSLM.

It is apparent that a flip-flop can hold digital data. Therefore, an optical flip-flop can be employed as primary memory in an optical computer.

8.3 ELECTRON TRAPPING LOGIC

With reference to de Morgan's theorem, a Boolean function of inputs A and B can be constructed by a proper combination of other functions. The electron trapping (ET) materials have the inherent capability of performing AND and NOT functions [8.26]. To perform A.B, inputs A and B are illuminated with blue and infrared light, respectively. Superposition of the blue A and infrared B on the ET materials generates an orange emission equivalent to A.B. The NOT operation is performed as follows. First, a uniform blue light floods the ET materials. Next, the input A is illuminated with infrared to erase A from the ET materials, and, finally, an infrared uniform illumination produces $\bar{A}$. Operation $\bar{A}$.B is performed by (1) uniform blue illumination, (2) input A with IR illumination, (3) input B with IR illumination. Operation $\bar{A}.\bar{B}$ is performed by (1) uniform blue illumination, (2) input A with IR illumination, (3) input B with IR illumination, and (4) uniform IR illumination.

All 16 Boolean operations shown in Table 8.1 can be generated by some combination of functions that can be directly performed by the ET materials, also known as spatial light rebroadcasters (SLR) [8.27, 8.8], as follows [8.26]:

F0	= 0	F1	= A · B
F2	= A · $\overline{B}$	F3	= A
F4	= $\overline{A}$ · B	F5	= B
F6	= A · $\overline{B}$ + $\overline{A}$ · B	F7	= A + B
F8	= $\overline{A}$ · $\overline{B}$	F9	= $\overline{A}$ · $\overline{B}$ + A · B
F10	= $\overline{B}$	F11	= A + $\overline{B}$
F12	= $\overline{A}$	F13	= $\overline{A}$ + B
F14	= $\overline{A}$ + $\overline{B}$	F15	= 1

where 0 stands for no illumination and 1 stands for uniform blue and IR illumination. The symbol + is an OR operator that can be implemented using a beam splitter. The basic optical setup is shown in Figure 8.11. An experiment has been conducted [8.26], as shown in Figure 8.12, which shows the experimental data of Boolean logic operations employing ET materials. Two masks were used for representing input A and B with a vertical and a horizontal bar, respectively.

A binary addition based on electron trapping logic was also demonstrated [8.26]. A binary half-adder simply consists of an XOR gate for sum and an AND gate for carry. To realize a full addition, the carry from the half addition of the less significant bit must be taken into account. Therefore, logic gates with three inputs are required. This precludes the use of ET materials, since they have only two inputs for a logic operation, as shown previously. To overcome this problem, a parallel flow, iterative algorithm is used for an ET

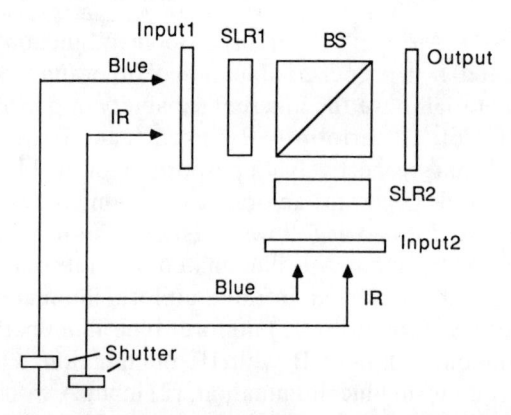

FIGURE 8.11 Logic array processor using electron trapping materials. SLR stands for spatial light rebroadcaster, which is a thin film of electron trapping material.

ELECTRON TRAPPING LOGIC   299

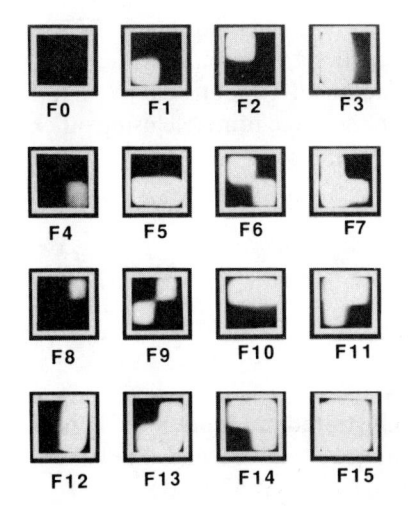

FIGURE 8.12 Sixteen Boolean functions obtained by the electron trapping processor.

material based architecture. An example of four-bit addition that needs four iterations is given in Figure 8.13. The advantage of this algorithm is that a full addition can be performed by a series of shift-and-logic operations repeatedly using the same two-input ET logic device. In theory, shifting can be performed optically by a mirror. Parallel logic operations, that is, XOR and AND, are performed by an ET logic device. The shifted intermediate output

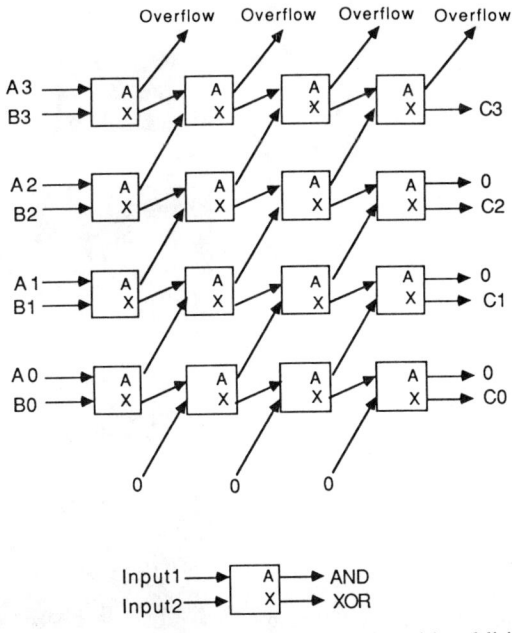

FIGURE 8.13 Parallel algorithm for four-bit addition.

300 DIGITAL-OPTICAL COMPUTING

can be fed back to the logic device through a CCD-microcomputer-LCTV system. The combination of CCD–LCTV functions essentially as a wavelength converter from orange emission to blue and IR input beams. A full optical system can also be constructed based on the same principle using other optically addressed SLMs as wavelength converters.

The addition was as follows:

$$\begin{array}{r} 1\ 0\ 0\ 1 \\ +\ \ 0\ 1\ 0\ 1 \\ \hline 1\ 1\ 1\ 0 \end{array}$$

The experimental procedure and results are illustrated in Figure 8.14. Figure 8.14a and b show two masks representing input A = 1001 and input B = 0101, respectively. The experimental results of E = (A AND B) and D = (A XOR B) performed by an ET logic device are shown in Figure 8.14c and d. Two masks simulating shifted-E and D, as shown in Figure 8.14e and f, were used as inputs for the second cycle. The results of G = (D AND shifted-E) and F = (D XOR shifted-E) are shown in Figure 8.14g and h. Since G consists of only zero bits, F is the final output of the addition, which is 1110.

The advantages of using ET materials are reportedly (1) large amounts of data can be processed in parallel, since the SBP of ET materials is potentially much larger than that of currently available SLMs; (2) an extremely high

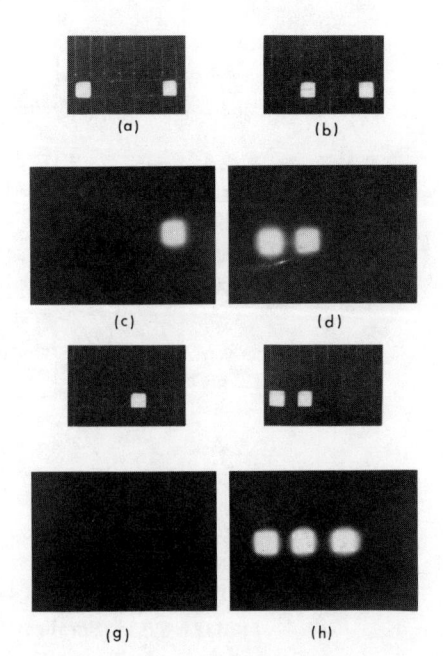

FIGURE 8.14 Experimental result of four-bit addition. See text for detailed explanation.

signal-to-noise ratio (SNR) is obtained, since the input and output are carried by different wavelengths; (3) a basic operation such as AND can be performed at about several tens of nanoseconds; and (4) the fabrication of an ET logic device is potentially very cost effective. The main disadvantages are that wavelength conversion is required for cascadability, and some operations require four cycles, with a consequent reduction in speed.

8.4 SYMBOLIC SUBSTITUTION LOGIC

Symbolic substitution was first proposed by Huang [8.28] as a means of utilizing the parallelism of optics to perform digital computing. In this method, specific logic patterns are substituted into new logic patterns in parallel according to a given transformation rule. It has been pointed out that symbolic substitution can be applied to Boolean logic, binary arithmetic, artificial intelligence, Turing machine, and so forth [8.29].

An optical implementation is shown in Figure 8.15 [8.30]. In this example, a pattern of four points arranged as a cross is turned into four points at the corners of a square. Step A shows the input pattern. The input pattern generates four identical patterns at step B. Each of the generated patterns is shifted right, down, left, and up, respectively, at step C. The four patterns of step C are superimposed at step D. Step E is a threshold that allows only a point with maximum intensity passing through it. Step F shows the point after threshold. The pattern of step F generates four identical patterns at step G. Each of the generated patterns is shifted left-up, right-up, left-down, and right-down, respectively, at step H. Superposition of four shifted patterns results in a substitution output at step I.

Symbolic substitution is essentially a combination of the recognition and substitution phases. Symbolic substitution recognizes not only a combination

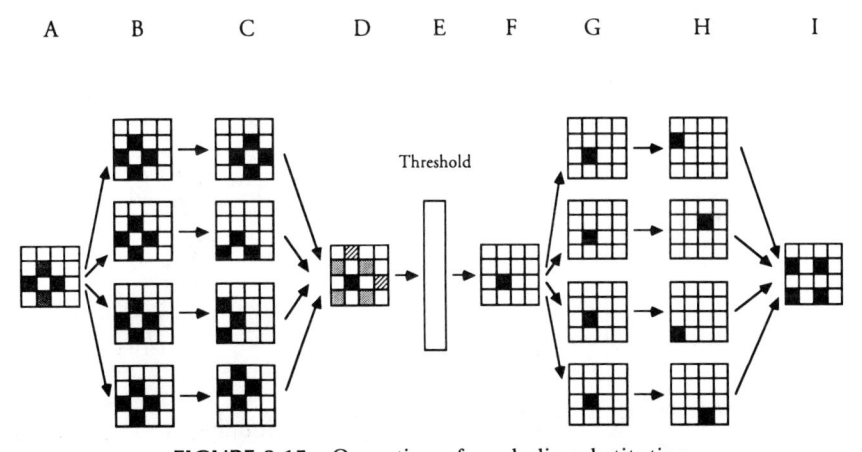

FIGURE 8.15 Operation of symbolic substitution.

of bits but also the relative location of these bits. The output is not just a single bit, but rather a combination of bits positioned in a particular manner, as shown in Figure 8.16a. A method of optical associative memory can be applied to implement a symbolic substitution logic system [8.31]. Logical 1 and logical 0 can be encoded in certain spatial patterns instead of bright and dark or polarization direction. For example, the logic pattern shown in Figure 8.16a can be encoded into the patterns shown in Figure 8.16b, where logical 1 and 0 are encoded into a cross and a ring, respectively.

The first method uses a matched spatial filter (MSF) to recognize input patterns. The autocorrelation spots (assumed to be delta functions) are convolved with the desired output pattern so that each correlated input pattern produces an output pattern. The optical setup is schematically depicted in Figure 8.17. MSF1 and MSF2 are Fourier-transform holograms of input and output patterns, respectively. To depress the output pattern that comes from cross-correlation, the thresholding process is applied at the correlation and output plane.

The second method makes use of a specially designed computer-generated hologram (CGH). By using a CGH, an input image is converted into another associative image. The optical setup of this second method is shown schematically in Figure 8.18. An experiment verified this optical computing method [8.32]. Instead of a CGH, a joint Fourier-transform hologram of an input and an output is recorded beforehand. The output is then generated optically by illuminating the hologram with the input pattern. To perform a Boolean operation, the AND function, for instance, four associative memories are required, corresponding to four possible combinations of two inputs.

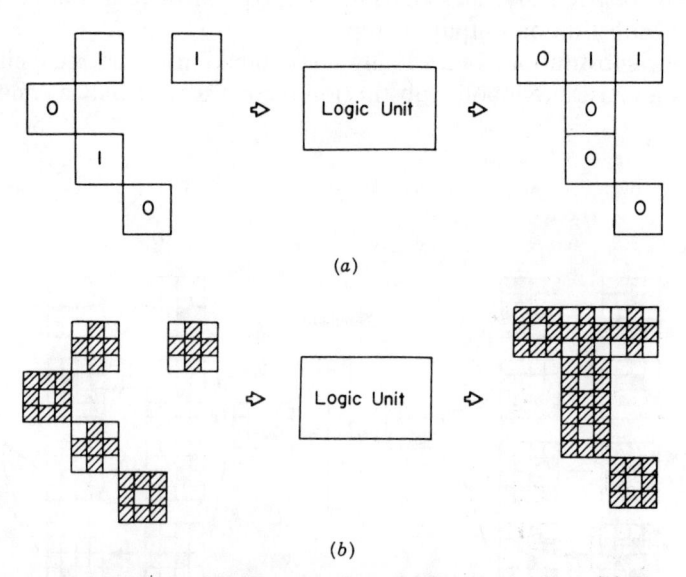

FIGURE 8.16 (a) Conceptual diagram of symbolic substitution. (b) Encoded logic patterns for the symbolic substitution processor.

SYMBOLIC SUBSTITUTION LOGIC 303

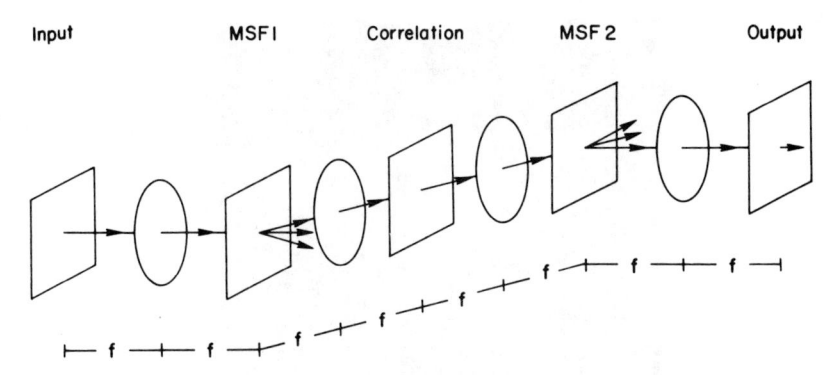

FIGURE 8.17 Symbolic substitution using matched spatial filters (MSFs).

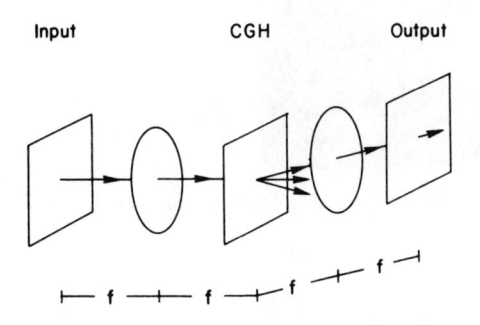

FIGURE 8.18 Symbolic substitution using an associative memory-type hologram.

An optical half-adder based on symbolic substitution was demonstrated [8.32], in which the sum obtained from XOR and the carry obtained from AND can be produced simultaneously from the same data. This is an example of the realization of multiple-instruction stream, multiple-data stream (MIMD) architecture using the parallelism of optics. Four combinations of sum and carry are illustrated in Figure 8.19. The experimental result of parallel half

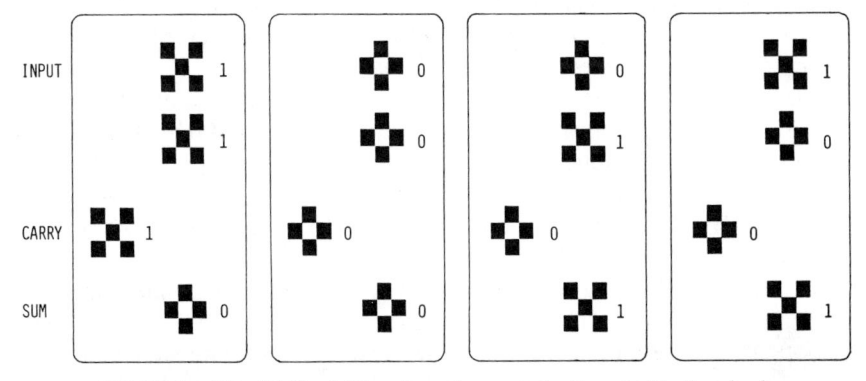

FIGURE 8.19 Half addition based on symbolic substitution logic.

304 DIGITAL-OPTICAL COMPUTING

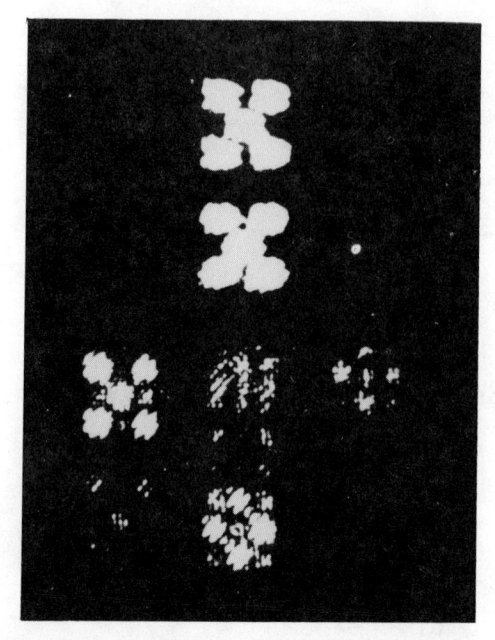

FIGURE 8.20 Experimental result of half addition using holographic symbolic substitution.

addition, that is, sum and carry obtained in parallel, is depicted in Figure 8.20. This picture was taken from the video monitor after thresholding. Although cross-correlation still exists, the dominant output is apparently the correct logic pattern. The main merit of the holographic symbolic substitution is that any substitution can be performed in one simple step.

8.5 HOLOGRAPHIC LOGIC

The implementation of symbolic substitution mentioned earlier [8.32] can also be classified in the holographic logic, since a method of holographic associative memory is used. It is mentioned [8.31] that the matching of the input and the reference can be performed by correlation. The matching of the input and the reference can also be done by performing an XOR or NAND operation [8.33]. If the input pattern matches the reference pattern, the XOR output will be uniformly zero or totally dark. However, this matching output (which is dark) has to be converted into electronic signals before the next optical processing can be performed.

The parallel XOR output is essentially the intensity of a binary amplitude image subtraction [8.20]. Image subtraction can be performed by many optical means [8.1]. Optical image synthesis by complex amplitude subtraction was originally proposed by Gabor *et al.* [8.34]. The technique involves successive

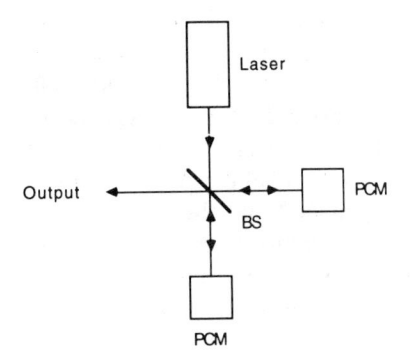

FIGURE 8.21 Phase conjugate Michelson interferometer.

recordings of two complex diffraction patterns on a holographic plate and the subsequent reproduction of the relatively out-of-phase composite hologram images. Bromley et al. [8.35] described a holographic subtraction technique, by which a real-time image and a previously recorded hologram image can be subtracted. This technique is the basis for performing holographic logic for truth-table lookup data processing [8.33], which implements Boolean logic and arithmetic by relating input binary digit pattern to output binary digit pattern.

Alternatively, this holographic technique should be able to perform Boolean logic on the bit basis rather than the pattern basis. The method of image subtraction based on phase conjugation, which is usually applied to real-time holography, is described as follows [8.36]. A phase conjugate mirror (PCM) is a device that behaves like a retroreflective mirror. More important, an incident beam to the PCM will be phase conjugated and propagate backward, retracing its path. A phase conjugate Michelson interferometer consists of two self-pumped $BaTiO_3$ (photorefractive material) crystals as PCMs replacing ordinary mirrors, as shown in Figure 8.21. An incident laser beam is split by beam splitter BS into two components, which are retroreflected back by the PCMs. According to Stokes' principle of time reversibility, when the two phase conjugate beams recombine at the beam splitter, a time-reversed replica of the incident beam is generated. This beam propagates backward, retracing the original incident beam path. Thus there is no light at the output; the total darkness is a result of time reversal. This fundamental phenomenon has been observed experimentally [8.37]. The image subtraction can be performed by placing two input transparencies between BS and the two PCMs, respectively. When the images are in binary form, the resultant intensity of the subtraction represents XOR output [8.38].

8.6 LOGIC BASED ON OPTICAL BISTABILITY

Unlike the optical logics mentioned earlier, which are logical extensions of parallel optical processing, optical bistability [8.39], [8.40] can be seen as an

306 DIGITAL-OPTICAL COMPUTING

attempt to mimic electronic devices using better optical devices. Better functional performance, such as power, speed, heat generation, stability, and uniformity, as compared to transistors is expected. Bistability is normally represented by the hysteresis loop depicted in Figure 8.22. Initially, the output (intensity) remains low until the input (intensity) is increased beyond some critical value or threshold T_2. The output then remains high while the input is decreased until another critical value T_1 is reached and the device jumps to the off state. This phenomenon is called *bistability* because two stable output states exist for the same value of the input between T_1 and T_2. An important property of bistability is that it has memory. This can be seen by noting that the response of the device at any moment is not determined solely by the value of the input at the moment, but rather by the value of the input as well as the state the device is in. This is a very useful property for implementing full optical circuits emulating electronic digital circuits that eventually build up a full-scale computer.

A Fabry–Perot etalon is employed in an optical bistable device. The Fabry–Perot etalon is an interferometer consisting of two half-mirrors that are optically flat and fixed accurately parallel to one another with a separation. Light entering the etalon through one of the half-mirrors bounces back and forth in it. At each reflection, some of the light is transmitted through the half-mirrors. The transmitted light is composed of rays that reflect differently in the etalon. If all these rays are in phase, the transmitted light will be high. On the other hand, if all rays are relatively out of phase, they will cancel each other and the transmitted light will be low. The phase of the ray is determined by the frequency of the light, the separation of the two half-mirrors, and the refractive index of the medium in the etalon.

Optical bistability is usually achieved by inserting a nonlinear medium, such as GaAs, ZnS, ZnSe, CuCl, InSb, InAs, and CdS, inside the Fabry–Perot etalon [8.39]. The nonlinear medium, normally a thin semiconductor slab, has an intensity-dependent index of refraction. The semiconductor slab has flat, parallel faces that have high-reflectivity and are dielectrically coated, forming a Fabry–Perot etalon that provides optical feedback. The etalon is initially detuned at low light intensity; but for sufficiently high incident intensity, the induced refractive index change sweeps the Fabry–Perot peak

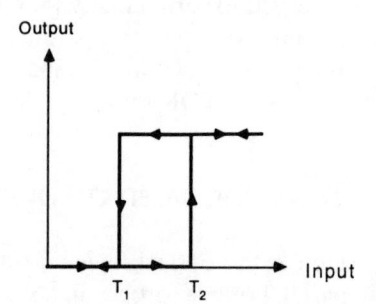

FIGURE 8.22 Relationship between input and output showing bistability. *Note:* T indicates threshold.

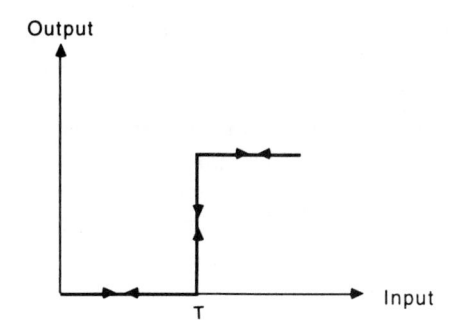

FIGURE 8.23 Relationship between input and output, showing nonlinear threshold T.

into resonance with the laser, switching the device on very rapidly. Switch-off is accomplished in a similar way, with accompanying hysteresis.

The switching operation of optical bistability is based on classic optical phenomena, that is, constructive or destructive interference. This operation can also be achieved by a multilayer interference filter. Another type of bistable device is made by a multilayer sandwich of alternately high (ZnSe or ZnS) and low (ThF$_4$) refractive index material [8.40]. The high index material is usually nonlinear.

The logic operation is performed by changing the bistability characteristic shown in Figure 8.22 to the single-threshold characteristic shown in Figure 8.23 [8.41]. The degree of initial detuning from resonance is a critical parameter and determines the width of the hysteresis loop, that is, the range of input power over which the device is bistable, as well as the power required to induce switching. Thus adjustment of this parameter by altering the etalon optical thickness or the illumination wavelength permits tuning of the input–output characteristic. If the input frequency is near enough to the resonant frequency, the bistable region becomes very narrow and eventually disappears, as shown in Figure 8.23. The schematic diagram for logic operations is depicted in Figure 8.24, where A and B are input signal beams with low power, and H is the hold beam with higher power. When both inputs are zero, the intensity of the hold beam is below the threshold, and the etalon is in the off resonant state. The AND operation is accomplished by setting

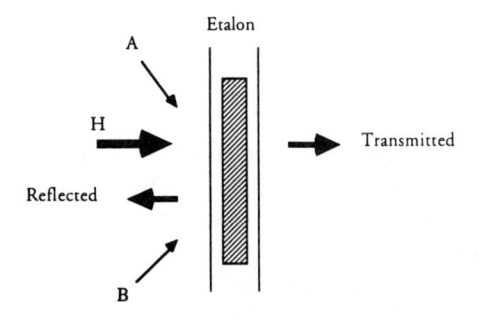

FIGURE 8.24 Schematic diagram of an optical logic gate based on nonlinear optics. *Note:* A and B are input; H is the hold beam; transmitted and reflected beams of H are the complementary outputs.

308   DIGITAL-OPTICAL COMPUTING

the input intensity low enough so that both inputs are required to switch on the etalon. On the other hand, the OR operation is executed by setting the input intensity sufficiently high so that only one input is required to switch on the etalon. Since the reflected beam is the complement of the transmitted beam of the etalon, a single etalon provides two complementary outputs, that is, when the transmitted beam is an AND function, the reflected beam is a NAND function. Therefore the optical bistable device can inherently perform AND, NAND, OR, and NOR operations. All 16 Boolean functions can be implemented by combining these four basic operations.

8.7   OPTICAL INTERCONNECT AND PERFECT SHUFFLE

The logic functions mentioned in the previous section are nonlinear processes in which input signals interact to produce output signals. In addition to logic gates, a digital computer also requires interconnections between such nonlinear processors. It is obvious that when the computer structure becomes more complex, wire interconnections between processors are increasingly difficult to implement. The application of free-space optical interconnection as demonstrated by the formation of images by a lens is very likely able to replace the complex wire interconnection. Thus, the signal can be carried by photons that travel in free space. Unlike electrons, photons do not interact with each other.

Speed is one of the most important features of computer performance. The computational speed of a computer is limited not only by the speed of the nonlinear processors or switches, but also by the speed of interconnection, which is inversely proportional to the time required for the signal traveling from one switch to another. The speed of wire interconnection apparently cannot be increased by simply scaling down the system, as pointed out by Huang [8.28]. As the length of a wire is shrunk by a factor of α and the cross-sectional area of the wire is reduced by a factor of α^2, the capacitance of the wire will decrease by a factor of α while the resistance will increase by a factor of α. The net result is that the RC time constant remains the same, the signal propagation time remains the same, and thus the time it takes for a signal to get from one switch to another will remain constant, independent of scaling. It seems that optical interconnect might be free from the difficulty mentioned previously.

Optical interconnect is not only useful for optical computing purpose, but it is also the most modest, realistic, and near-term application of optics to electronic computers, after the introduction of the optical disk. An optical interconnect [8.42] that can be implemented using fibers, integrated optical waveguides, free-space propagation by lenses, or holograms, can be used for clock distribution and data communication in an electronic computer with different levels: on chips, between chips, between boards, and between cabinets. As an illustration, the implementation of perfect shuffle as a particular example of optical interconnect is described in the following paragraphs.

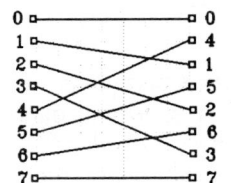

OPTICAL INTERCONNECT AND PERFECT SHUFFLE   309

```
0 o────────────o 0
1 o╲         ╱─o 4
2 o ╲       ╱  o 1
3 o  ╲     ╱   o 5
4 o   ╲   ╱    o 2
5 o    ╲ ╱     o 6
6 o     ╳      o 3
7 o────────────o 7
```
FIGURE 8.25 An 8-bit perfect shuffle.

Interconnection networks are developed to construct a concurrent processing system by interconnecting a large number of processors and memory modules. The perfect shuffle is an interconnection primitive between local processors for parallel computation. The significance of a perfect shuffle in performing interconnection was first realized by Stone [8.43] and then by Wu and Feng [8.44]. The perfect shuffle is one of the most useful and universal regular interconnects. It is commonly used for sorting, interconnecting array processors, permutation networks, and for special algorithms such as the fast Fourier transform (FFT) [8.42]–[8.44]. An 8-bit perfect shuffle is shown schematically in Figure 8.25. The optical implementations of a perfect shuffle have been demonstrated using diffractive optics and refractive optics [8.45]–[8.49], which require imaging components such as lenses, prisms, gratings, mirrors, and beam splitters.

A simple method for demonstrating an optical implementation of a perfect shuffle is given in Figure 8.26 [8.50]. Note that the output is arranged in an inverse version for the sake of geometric simplicity. For this particular geometry, only two and four windows are required on the first and second mask, respectively. The source (left side) and sink (right side) arrays have the same structure with spacing a. The distance from source to sink is $7a$. It is convenient to use a geometrical analysis to determine the position and size of the windows as well as the location of the two masks. One can easily determine that the distance between the first mask and the source array (input plane) is $7a/3$ and that the second mask is located $7a/5$ from the sink array (output plane). To minimize diffraction effects and to maximize the power transferred, large windows are preferred. However, to keep the system free from cross talk, the width of the window on the second mask must be $d < 4a/5$, and that of the first mask must be $d' < a/3$, as shown in Figure 8.26. The method is easily extended to three-dimensional interconnects for two-dimensional source and

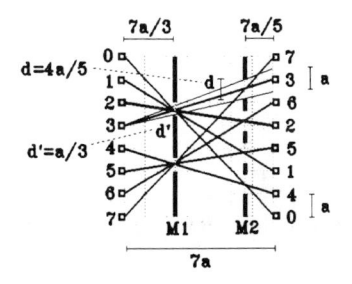

FIGURE 8.26 Optical perfect shuffle based on shadow casting.

sink arrays. However, the drawback is the power loss due to the fan-out and absorption by the masks.

The implementation of a perfect shuffle using an imaging system is given below [8.49]. The optical setup is depicted in Figure 8.27. Two sets of data are designated by $s_1(x, y)$ and $s_2(x, y)$, which are separated by a distance 2β at the input plane. With coherent illumination, the complex light distribution at the spatial frequency plane can be described as

$$E(p, q) = S_1(p, q)e^{-i\beta q} + S_2(p, q)e^{i\beta q}, \quad (8.4)$$

where $S_1(p, q)$ and $S_2(p, q)$ are the Fourier spectra of the input data $s_1(x, y)$ and $s_2(x, y)$, respectively. To implement a perfect shuffle, we place a sinusoidal grating in the spatial frequency plane. The sinusoidal grating formula is

$$H(q) = \tfrac{1}{2}\{1 + \cos[(\beta + \Delta\beta)q]\}, \quad (8.5)$$

where $\Delta\beta$ is a small displacement constant. Thus, the output light field distribution can be shown as

$$\begin{aligned}I(x, y) = &\tfrac{1}{2}s_1(x, y - \beta) + \tfrac{1}{2}s_2(x, y + \beta)\\ &+ \tfrac{1}{4}[s_1(x, y + \Delta\beta) + s_2(x, y - \Delta\beta)]\\ &+ \tfrac{1}{4}s_1(x, y - 2\beta - \Delta\beta) + \tfrac{1}{4}s_2(x, y + 2\beta + \Delta\beta).\end{aligned} \quad (8.6)$$

From the third term of Eq. 8.6, we see that $s_1(x, y)$ and $s_2(x, y)$ are slightly shifted in opposite directions along the Y axis. If the incremental shift $\Delta\beta$ is equal to the separation between the processing data, s_1 and s_2 would be perfectly interlaced. Thus the two sets of input data would be perfectly shuffled. The experimental result is shown in Figure 8.28. Note that the input and output formats are not compatible. This incompatibility will present no problem, however, if we tailor the design of either the input or output data system.

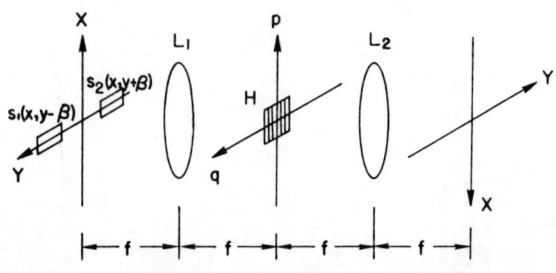

FIGURE 8.27 Optical perfect shuffle based on Fourier imaging.

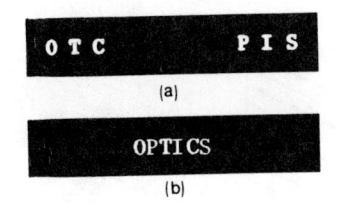

FIGURE 8.28 Experimental result of perfect shuffle using the system shown in Figure 8.27.

8.8 MATRIX–VECTOR MULTIPLIER AND CROSSBAR SWITCH

The optical matrix-vector multiplier was originally proposed by Goodman *et al.* [8.51] as shown in Figure 8.29. The elements of the vector are entered in parallel by controlling the intensities of N light-emitting diodes (LEDs). Spherical lens L_1 and cylindrical lens L_2 combine to image the LED array horizontally onto the matrix mask M while spreading the light from any single LED vertically to fill an entire column of the matrix mask M, which consists of $N \times N$ elements. Another combination of a cylindrical lens L_3 (perpendicular to cylindrical lens L_2) and a spherical lens L_4 collects all the light from a given row and brings it into focus on one element of a vertical array of N photodetectors. Each photodetector measures the value of one element of the output vector that is the product of the matrix–vector multiplication. This configuration can be further simplified by fabricating line-shape LEDs and a line-shape detector array as depicted in Figure 8.30. Note that line-shape LEDs can be replaced by an SLM with a uniform illumination.

Many important problems can be solved by the iterative multiplication of a vector by a matrix. Applications include finding eigenvalues and eigenvectors, solving systems of simultaneous linear equations, computing the discrete Fourier transform, and implementation of neural networks. As an example, the implementation of the Hopfield neural net is briefly described.

The neural network typically consists of several layers of neurons. Two successive neuron layers are connected by an interconnection net. If the neuron structure in a layer is represented by a vector, then the interconnect can be represented by a matrix. An analog matrix–vector multiplication, therefore, is a key operation in a neural network, as is nonlinear thresholding. To explain the interaction between an input and the memory, the Hopfield

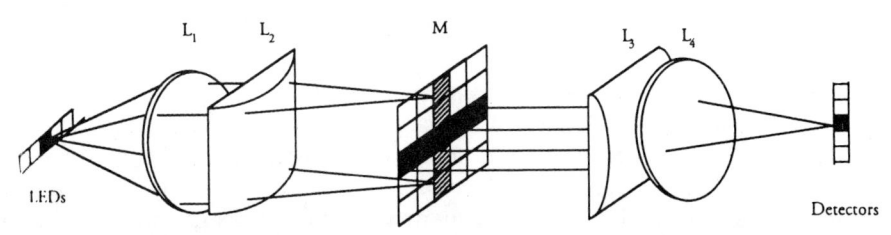

FIGURE 8.29 Schematic diagram of an optical matrix-vector multiplier.

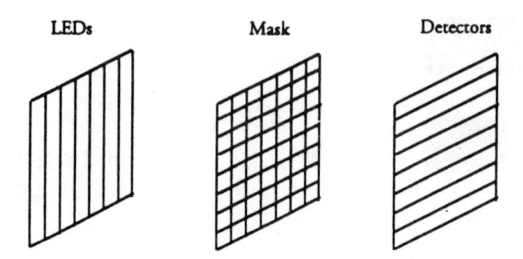

FIGURE 8.30 Optical matrix-vector multiplier using lineshape LEDs and detectors.

neural network model [8.52] defines an associative memory retrieval process that is equivalent to a matrix–vector multiplication expressed as

$$V_i \to 1 \quad \text{if} \quad \sum T_{ij}V_j > 0,$$
$$V_i \to 0 \quad \text{if} \quad \sum T_{ij}V_j \leq 0, \tag{8.7}$$

where V_i and V_j are the output and the input binary vectors, respectively, and T_{ij} is the nonbinary interconnect matrix. The matrix–vector multiplication $\sum T_{ij}V_j$ can be performed optically in parallel [8.53], [8.21]. An optical neural network is described in detail in the next chapter.

If the matrix is binary, the matrix–vector multiplier becomes a crossbar switch. The *crossbar switch* is a general switching device that can connect any of N inputs to any of N outputs; this is also called *global interconnect*. Crossbar switches are usually not implemented in electronic computers because they would require N^2 individual switches; however, they are used in telephone exchanges. On the other hand, an optical crossbar interconnected signal processor would be very useful for performing fast Fourier transforms (FFT) and correlations by taking advantage of the reconfigurability and parallel processing of crossbar interconnect [8.54]. Also, the optical crossbar switch can be employed to implement a programmable logic array (PLA) [8.55]. The electronic PLA contains a two-level, AND–OR circuit on a single chip. The number of AND and OR gates and their inputs is fixed for a given PLA. A PLA can be used as a read-only memory (ROM) for the implementation of combinational logic.

8.9 SYSTOLIC PROCESSOR AND DIGITAL TRANSFORM

The systolic matrix–vector multiplier was originally invented by Kung to implement parallel processing for VLSI circuits [8.56]. The engagement matrix–vector multiplier, which is a variation of systolic processor, is shown in Figure 8.31 [8.57]. The components of vector B are shifted into multiplier-adder modules starting at time t_0. Subsequent vector components are clocked in contiguously at t_1 for b_2, t_2 for b_3, and so on. At time t_0, b_1 is multiplied with

SYSTOLIC PROCESSOR AND DIGITAL TRANSFORM 313

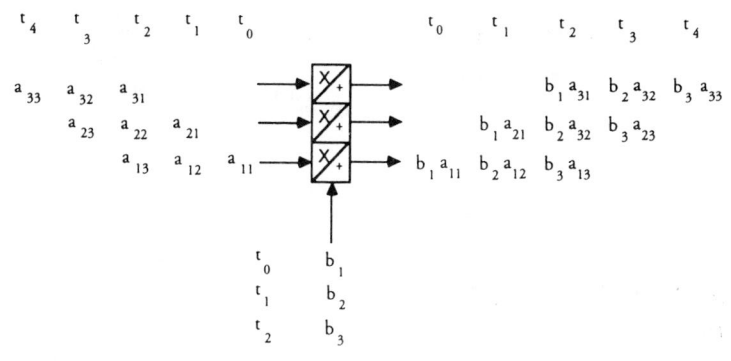

FIGURE 8.31 Conceptual diagram of engagement systolic array processor.

a_{11} in module 1. The resultant $b_1 a_{11}$ is retained within the module to be added to the next product. At time t_1, b_1 is shifted to module 2 to multiply with a_{21}. At the same time, b_2 enters module 1 to multiply with a_{12}, which forms the second product of the output vector component. Consequently, module 1 now contains the sum $b_1 a_{11} + b_2 a_{12}$. This process continues until all the output vector components have been formed. In all, $(2N - 1)$ clock cycles that employs N multiplier-adder modules are required. The main advantage of a systolic processor is that optical matrix–vector multiplication can be performed in the high-accuracy digital mode. This was demonstrated by Guilfoyle [8.58] based on the principle of digital multiplication by analog convolution [8.59].

A discrete linear transformation (DLT) system can be characterized by an impulse response h_{mn}. The input–output relationship of such a system can be summarized by the following equation

$$g_m = \sum f_n h_{mn}. \tag{8.8}$$

Since the output g_m and the input f_n can be considered vectors, the preceding equation can be represented by a matrix–vector multiplication, where h_{mn} is known as a transform matrix. Thus, the different DLTs would have different matrices. We now illustrate a few frequently used DLTs.

The discrete Fourier transform (DFT) is defined by

$$F_m = (1/N) \sum f_n \exp[-i2\pi mn/N], \tag{8.9}$$

where $n = 0, 1, \ldots, N - 1$, and

$$h_{mn} = \exp[-i2\pi mn/N], \tag{8.10}$$

is also known as the *transform kernel*. To implement the DFT transformation in an optical processor, we present the complex transform matrix with real elements. The corresponding real transform matrices can be written as

$$\text{Re}[h_{mn}] = \cos \frac{2\pi mn}{N}, \tag{8.11}$$

$$\text{Im}[h_{mn}] = \sin \frac{2\pi mn}{N}, \tag{8.12}$$

which are the well-known discrete consine transform (DCT) and discrete sine transform (DST).

The relationship between the real and imaginary parts of an analytic signal can be described by the Hilbert transform. The discrete Hilbert transform (DHT) matrix can be written as

$$\begin{aligned} h_{mn} &= 2\,\frac{\sin^2\left[\pi(m-n)/2\right]}{\pi(m-n)}, & m - n \neq 0, \\ &= 0, & m - n = 0. \end{aligned} \tag{8.13}$$

Another frequently used linear transform is the Chirp-Z transform, which can be used to compute the DFT coefficients. The discrete Chirp-Z transform

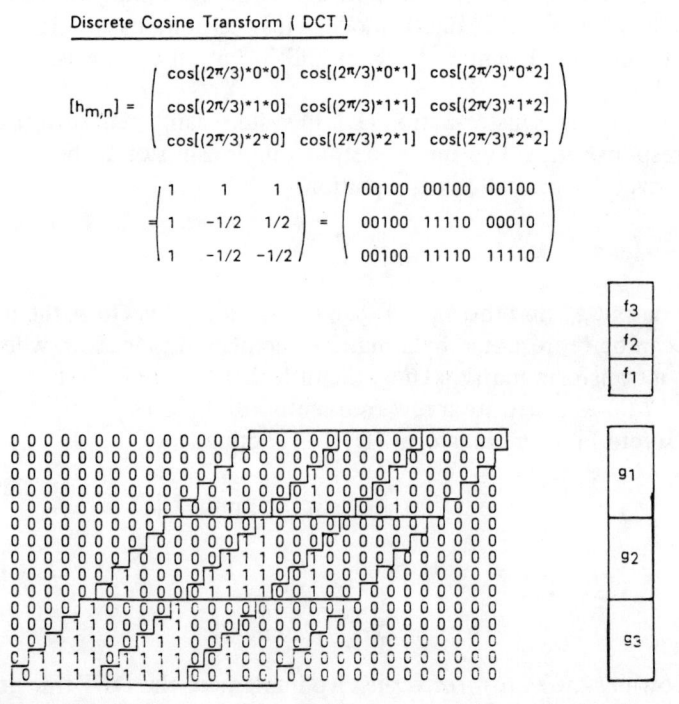

FIGURE 8.32 Transformation matrix for discrete cosine transform using two's complement representation.

(DCZT) matrix can be written as

$$h_{mn} = \exp \frac{i\pi(m-n)^2}{N}. \qquad (8.14)$$

Since the DLT can be viewed as the result of a digital matrix–vector multiplication, systolic processing can be used to implement it. By combining the systolic array processing technique and the two's complement representation, a DLT can be performed with a digital optical processor. As compared with the analog optical processor, the technique has high accuracy and a low error rate. Also, it is compatible with other digital processors.

Two's complement representation has been applied to improving the accuracy of matrix multiplication [8.60]. Two's complement numbers provide a binary representation of both positive and negative values, and facilitate subtraction by the same logic hardware that is used for addition. In a b-bit two's complement number, the most significant bit is the sign. The remaining $b-1$ bits represent its magnitude. Examples for DCT and DST are given in Figures 8.32 and 8.33 [8.61]. The digital transform matrices are encoded in two's complement representation and arranged in systolic engagement form.

Discrete Sine Transform (DST)

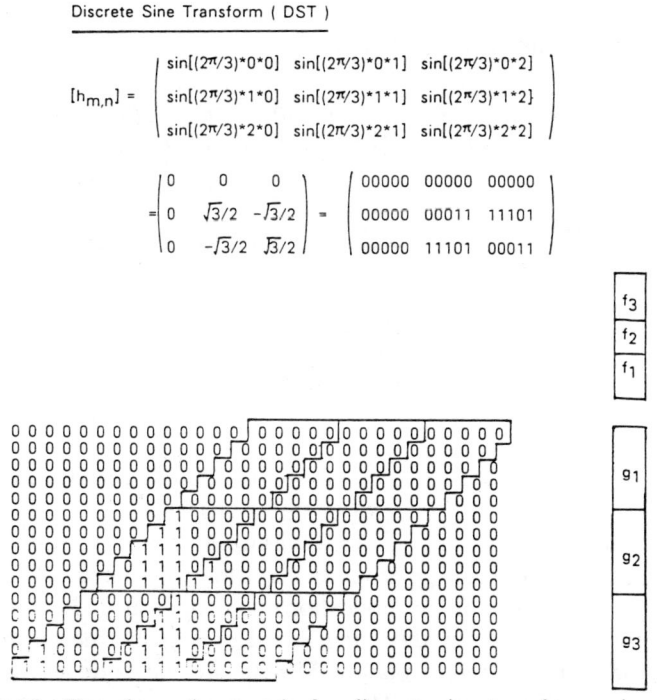

$$[h_{m,n}] = \begin{pmatrix} \sin[(2\pi/3)*0*0] & \sin[(2\pi/3)*0*1] & \sin[(2\pi/3)*0*2] \\ \sin[(2\pi/3)*1*0] & \sin[(2\pi/3)*1*1] & \sin[(2\pi/3)*1*2] \\ \sin[(2\pi/3)*2*0] & \sin[(2\pi/3)*2*1] & \sin[(2\pi/3)*2*2] \end{pmatrix}$$

$$= \begin{pmatrix} 0 & 0 & 0 \\ 0 & \sqrt{3}/2 & -\sqrt{3}/2 \\ 0 & -\sqrt{3}/2 & \sqrt{3}/2 \end{pmatrix} = \begin{pmatrix} 00000 & 00000 & 00000 \\ 00000 & 00011 & 11101 \\ 00000 & 11101 & 00011 \end{pmatrix}$$

FIGURE 8.33 Transformation matrix for discrete sine transform using two's complement representation.

8.10 MATRIX–MATRIX MULTIPLIER

The matrix–matrix multiplier is a mathematical extension from the matrix–vector multiplier. Matrix–vector multiplication naturally matches with the optical system as demonstrated in Figure 8.29. In contrast, the implementation of the matrix–matrix multiplier requires a more complex optical arrangement. Matrix–matrix multipliers may be needed to change or process matrices that will eventually be used in a matrix–vector multiplier. The general survey of optical matrix algebraic processors was given by Athale [8.62], in which various matrix–vector and matrix–matrix multipliers were discussed. Further extension to a multiple (more than two) matrix multiplier was also reported [8.63]. The following is an example of the optical implementation of a matrix–matrix multiplier.

Matrix–matrix multiplication can be computed by successive outer-product operations as follows:

$$\begin{bmatrix} a_{11} & a_{12} & a_{13} \\ a_{21} & a_{22} & a_{23} \\ a_{31} & a_{32} & a_{33} \end{bmatrix} \begin{bmatrix} b_{11} & b_{12} & b_{13} \\ b_{21} & b_{22} & b_{23} \\ b_{31} & b_{32} & b_{33} \end{bmatrix} = \begin{bmatrix} a_{11} \\ a_{21} \\ a_{31} \end{bmatrix} \begin{bmatrix} b_{11} & b_{12} & b_{13} \end{bmatrix}$$

$$+ \begin{bmatrix} a_{12} \\ a_{22} \\ a_{32} \end{bmatrix} \begin{bmatrix} b_{21} & b_{22} & b_{23} \end{bmatrix} + \begin{bmatrix} a_{13} \\ a_{23} \\ a_{33} \end{bmatrix} \begin{bmatrix} b_{31} & b_{32} & b_{33} \end{bmatrix} \qquad (8.15)$$

Since the outer-product can be expressed as

$$\begin{bmatrix} a_{11} \\ a_{21} \\ a_{31} \end{bmatrix} \begin{bmatrix} b_{11} & b_{12} & b_{13} \end{bmatrix} = \begin{bmatrix} a_{11}b_{11} & a_{11}b_{12} & a_{11}b_{13} \\ a_{21}b_{11} & a_{21}b_{12} & a_{21}b_{13} \\ a_{31}b_{11} & a_{31}b_{12} & a_{31}b_{13} \end{bmatrix}, \qquad (8.16)$$

the outer product can be obtained by simply butting two SLMS against each other. The two SLMs display matrices

$$\begin{bmatrix} a_{11} & a_{11} & a_{11} \\ a_{21} & a_{21} & a_{21} \\ a_{31} & a_{31} & a_{31} \end{bmatrix} \quad \text{and} \quad \begin{bmatrix} b_{11} & b_{12} & b_{13} \\ b_{11} & b_{12} & b_{13} \\ b_{11} & b_{12} & b_{13} \end{bmatrix},$$

respectively. Therefore, Eq. 8.16 can be realized optically as shown in Figure 8.34 [8.64]. Each pair of SLMs performs the multiplication of the outer products, while beam splitters perform the addition of the outer products.

We can see that the basic operations for a matrix–matrix multiplication (as well as a matrix–vector multiplication) are addition and multiplication (sum and product). In the method mentioned previously, the multiplication is optically performed using a pair of SLMs, and the addition is optically performed using a beam splitter. The whole combinational operation is com-

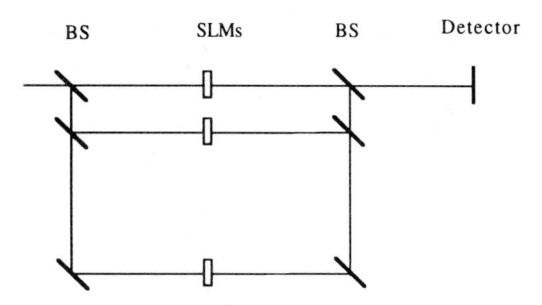

FIGURE 8.34 Matrix–matrix multiplier based on outer product.

pleted in one cycle. The addition, however, can be performed electronically in a sequential operation. That means that only a pair of SLMs is required in the system. The multiplication is performed sequentially in more than one cycle. The advantage is that fewer SLMs are needed. The trade-off is the increase in processing time. This approach is generally called *systolic processing* [8.56],[8.62].

Figure 8.35 illustrates an example of systolic array matrix operation [8.64]. Two transmission-type SLMs are placed close together and in registration in the input plane. By successively shifting the A and B systolic array matrix formats into two SLMs, we can obtain the product of matrices A and B with a time-integrating CCD detector at the output plane. Although only tow SLMs are required, the computation time needed for performing an $n \times n$ matrix–matrix multiplication with b-bit number would be $(2nb - 1) + (n - 1)$ times that needed by the outer-product processor. Figure 8.36 shows two matrices, each with 3×3 elements, that are encoded in binary form before multiplication takes place. Note that the principle of optical matrix–matrix multiplier described herewith is not limited to binary operation; an analog matrix–matrix multiplication can be performed as well or easier. By utilizing the two's complement representation and defining the 5-bit word length, this conversion results in 3×5 binary matrices.

Figure 8.37 shows the systolic outer-product matrix multiplier [8.64]. The optical processor consists of $n \times n = 3 \times 3 = 9$ pieces of SLM with $b \times b$

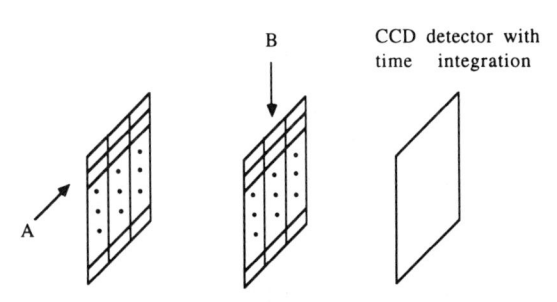

FIGURE 8.35 Matrix–matrix multiplier based on systolic array.

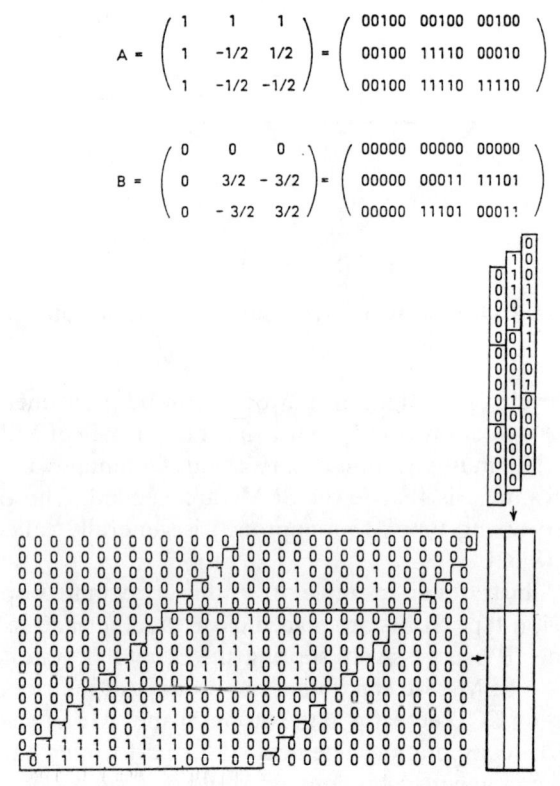

$$A = \begin{pmatrix} 1 & 1 & 1 \\ 1 & -1/2 & 1/2 \\ 1 & -1/2 & -1/2 \end{pmatrix} = \begin{pmatrix} 00100 & 00100 & 00100 \\ 00100 & 11110 & 00010 \\ 00100 & 11110 & 11110 \end{pmatrix}$$

$$B = \begin{pmatrix} 0 & 0 & 0 \\ 0 & 3/2 & -3/2 \\ 0 & -3/2 & 3/2 \end{pmatrix} = \begin{pmatrix} 00000 & 00000 & 00000 \\ 00000 & 00011 & 11101 \\ 00000 & 11101 & 00011 \end{pmatrix}$$

FIGURE 8.36 Example of matrix–matrix multiplication using the system shown in Figure 8.35.

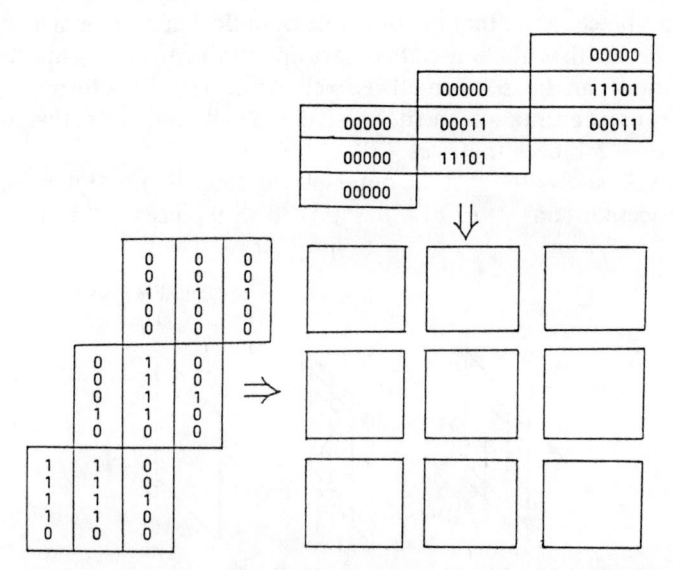

FIGURE 8.37 Matrix–matrix multiplication based on the systolic outer-product method.

= 5 × 5 pixels each. Note that the systolic array format representation of matrices A and B differs from the systolic formats described previously. By sequentially shifting the row and column elements of A and B into the SLMs, we can implement the $a_{ij}b_{kl}$ multiplication at each step, with an outer-product operation that has been performed in the 5 × 5 SLM. The result can be integrated in relation to time with a CCD detector at the output plane. Since more SLMs are employed in parallel, the matrix–matrix multiplication can be completed in fewer steps.

8.11 EXPERT SYSTEM AND ARTIFICIAL INTELLIGENCE

An expert system is one of the most common commercial applications of artificial intelligence (AI). Expert systems have been developed to assist a manager with complex planning and scheduling tasks, in diagnosing diseases, in locating mineral deposits, and so forth [8.65]. A popular approach to an expert system is to use IF–THEN rules. These rules say that if a certain kind of situation arises, then a certain kind of action can be taken. There are two basic control strategies for applying the established IF–THEN rules. The first strategy is to select a goal to be achieved to and then to scan the rules backward to find those whose consequent actions can achieve the goal. This is known as *goal-driven backward chaining*. Most existing expert systems use such a backward-chaining strategy. A different strategy is to scan forward through the rules until one is found whose antecedents match assertions in the data base. The rule is applied, updating the data base, and the scanning resumes. This process continues until either a goal state is reached or no applicable rules are found. This strategy is known as *data-driven forward chaining*. The data-driven forward-chaining strategy may approach the ideal parallel system, and would thus be suitable for an optical inference engine. It should be noticed that sequential reasoning in an electronic-inference engine is replaced by parallel reasoning in an optical-inference engine. A relatively simple architecture for an optical-inference engine based on parallel propositional logic, which gives an exact assertion, is described as follows [8.66].

The problem to be solved by an expert system is usually represented by an AND/OR graph, which is a network combining a number of IF–THEN rules. Basically, only AND and OR gates are required to perform the inferences. A simple example of an AND/OR graph is shown in Figure 8.38. LCTVs can be used to implement the parallel data-driven forward-chaining strategy for the AND/OR graph shown in the figure. A hybrid expert system, utilizing LCTVs to do inference processing and an electronic computer to control LCTVs, for storing a knowledge base and to input and output data (i.e., human–machine interfacing), is employed.

A pair of LCTVs can perform all 16 Boolean logic functions with two inputs. Two different optical configurations are required for AND and OR gates [8.18]. It is thus less convenient to implement an AND/OR graph using

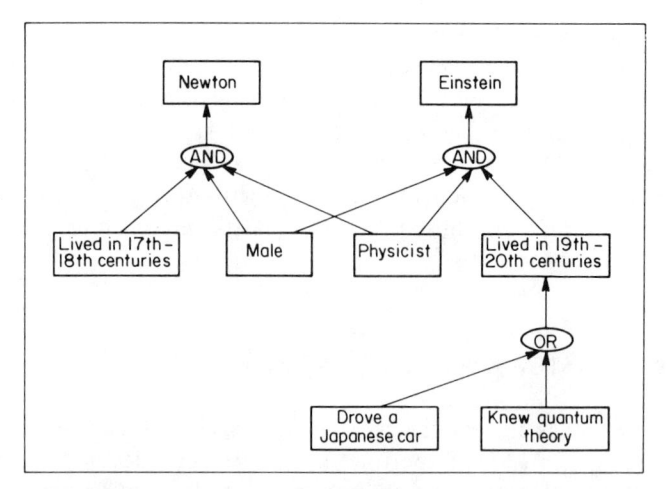

FIGURE 8.38 Example of AND/OR graph for an expert system.

different optical configurations for AND and OR gates, because it is not reconfigurable by software and, consequently, it is not flexible. The same configuration can be employed for AND and OR functions using the principle of sum-and-threshold [8.41]. However, if we use a nonzero background level for the transmittance of an LCTV screen, AND and OR functions are directly available with the same configuration based on the principle of product-and-threshold, where zero-magnitude input never exists (though logical 1 and logical 0, of course, exist). This suggests a new class of optical logic gates having more than two inputs.

For instance, let us consider that off-pixel and on-pixel have 1 and 2 transmittances in an arbitrary unit, respectively. The threshold level for the resultant transmittance can be set to determine the logic function as either AND or OR. If the threshold is 2, an OR function is obtained. On the other hand, the AND function is obtained by setting the threshold equal to 3. To implement the AND/OR graph shown in Figure 8.38, three LCTVs are arranged in tandem to form three-input AND or OR gates. The resultant transmittances are listed in Table 8.3. It is clear that the threshold selections at 2 and 6 result in OR and AND functions, respectively.

A computer is used to store and update the knowledge base, to write symbols (logic patterns) on the LCTVs, and to control the whole operation. The search based on the AND/OR graph shown in Figure 8.38 may be completed in two cycles. Each cycle performs one to two inference rules in parallel. The knowledge base is updated after each cycle. An LCTV display consists of about 140 × 120 pixels. To perform less than 140 inference rules in parallel, a vertical line can be used instead of a pixel to represent a fact. A cylindrical lens then focuses the vertical line onto an element of the array detector. This optical setup further introduces fault tolerance due to defects associated with the LCTV and any other noise. The detected signal is fed back into a computer to be thresholded and to complete one cycle.

EXPERT SYSTEM AND ARTIFICIAL INTELLIGENCE 321

TABLE 8.3. Resultant Transmittance of Three LCTVs

LCTV1	LCTV2	LCTV3	Resultant	OR	AND
1 (off)	1 (off)	1 (off)	1	off	off
1 (off)	1 (off)	2 (on)	2	on	off
1 (off)	2 (on)	1 (off)	2	on	off
1 (off)	2 (on)	2 (on)	4	on	off
2 (on)	1 (off)	1 (off)	2	on	off
2 (on)	1 (off)	2 (on)	4	on	off
2 (on)	2 (on)	1 (off)	4	on	off
2 (on)	2 (on)	2 (on)	8	on	on

The following discussion explains the operation of the system in detail for this particular example. The facts: DROVE A JAPANESE CAR; KNEW QUANTUM THEORY; PHYSICIST; MALE; LIVED IN 17TH-18TH CENTURIES; must be input into the computer to generate a symbolic representation. The intermediate results from a cycle may be used to update the knowledge base that is needed for the subsequent inference cycles. For instance, results from the first cycle are used to generate symbols for the second cycle. For a given example—which is: DROVE A JAPANESE CAR = NO; KNEW QUANTUM THEORY = YES; PHYSICIST = YES; MALE = YES; LIVED IN 17TH-18TH CENTURIES = NO—the generated symbols are illustrated in Figure 8.39. If a logic gate is operated by only two inputs, then the other input is set off, and the thresholds for the OR and AND functions are 2 and 3, respectively. The first cycle will update the knowledge base with the fact LIVED IN 19TH-20TH CENTURIES = YES, which shows that the fact EINSTEIN is finally YES, while the other alternative is NO.

In the aforementioned example, when the fact MALE is YES, the chances for NEWTON and EINSTEIN are the same. In contrast, medical diagnostic expert systems are usually based on the probabilistic principle. If a symptom is positive, there are uneven probabilities for different diseases. The optical expert system for diagnosis use was described by McAulay [8.67]. The data base may be used to establish a list of apriori probabilities, $p(e_i|h_j)$, the conditional probability that an event or symptom e_i will be present given a specified hypothesis or illness h_j. The expert system is then used to compute the aposteriori probabilities, $p(h_j|e_i)$, the probability of a specified illness h_j, given a specified symptom e_i. After the patient has answered a number of questions, the illness or illnesses with the highest probabilities are the most likely hypotheses. The Bayes theorem provides an equation for obtaining the aposteriori probabilities from the apriori one

$$p(h_j|e_i) = \frac{p(e_i|h_j)p(h_j)}{p(e_i|h_j)p(h_j) + p(e_i|\bar{h}_j)p(\bar{h}_j)}, \qquad (8.17)$$

where, $\bar{h}_j$ is not-h_j, and $p(\bar{h}_j) = 1 - p(h_j)$. The theorem can be extended to

322 DIGITAL-OPTICAL COMPUTING

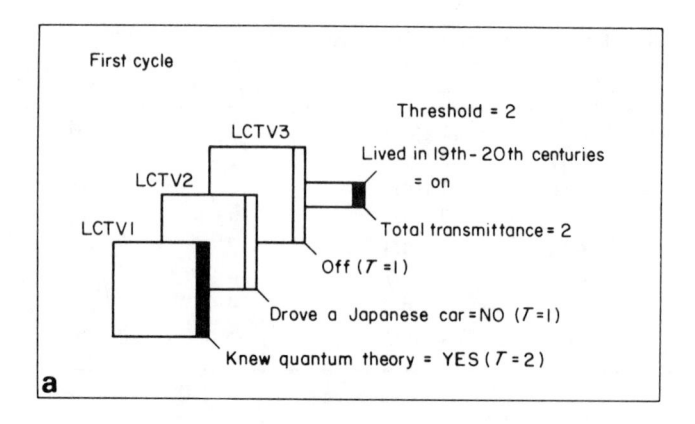

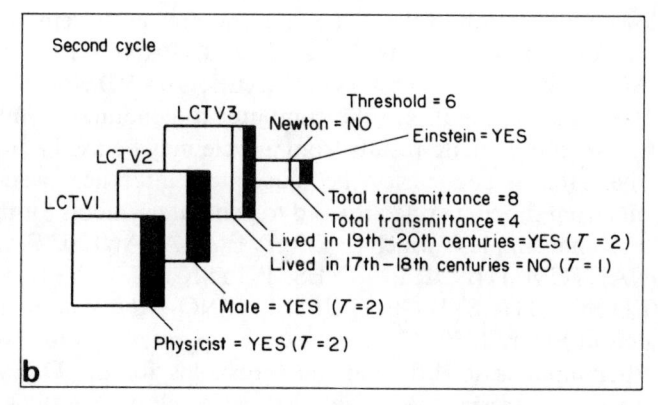

FIGURE 8.39 Operation of inference. Symbols are generated on LCTVs at (*a*) the first cycle, and (*b*) the second cycle. *Note:* Black stripes represent on-pixels (transmittance = 2); white stripes represent off-pixels (transmittance = 1).

multiple events and circumstances. Two terms in the denominator (one is identical to the numerator) can be obtained using optical matrix–vector multipliers. If a response to the ith event has been received, a unit signal is entered at this input, while all other inputs remain zero. These inputs form the input vector. The apriori probabilities $p(e_i|h_j)$ form the interconnection matrix. The elements of the output vector are multiplied by the corresponding $p(h_j)$, which are known from statistics for the region and patient profile.

Both the deterministic and probabilistic examples given previously are based on relatively simple proposition calculus, in which a true or false fact is simply a statement without any arguments. Optical expert systems based on predicate calculus have been proposed by Warde and Kottas [8.68] and Jau *et al.* [8.69]. These systems are based on the production system paradigm, where facts and rules constitute a knowledge base. Facts define the relationship between objects, and rules define the procedures for deriving new relations from existing ones. PROLOG (which has been selected as the basis for the Japanese fifth-generation computers) is a popular AI language that implements the production system paradigm.

An AI system generally consists of a knowledge base and an inference engine. The inference engine accepts as input a set of facts and a set of rules from the knowledge base and one or more queries. The output of the inference engine is a set of specific conclusions that are logically inferred from the facts and rules in response to the queries. For example, a set of data could be a set of names of people.

$$D = \{\text{Ann, Beth, Carol, David, Edward, Frank}\}. \qquad (8.18)$$

A set of relationships for D might be possible relationships between the people, such as marriage, mother, father, male, and female. Let this set of relationships be denoted by

$$R = \{\text{married-to, mother-of, father-of, son-of,} \atop \text{daughter-of, child-of, is-male, is-female}\}. \qquad (8.19)$$

The data objects and relationships are linked as a collection of facts and rules that relate the elements of D and R. In this example, the fact could be defined as

David married-to Ann,
Edward married-to Beth,
David father-of Carol,
Edward father-of Frank.

The query addressed to this knowledge base is "Who is the mother of Carol?" or ?mother-of Carol. The PROLOG code for these expressions is as follows:

married-to(david, ann),
married-to(edward, beth),
father-of(david, carol),
father-of(edward, frank),

and the query ?-mother-of(X,carol).

In the mapping-template optical-inference engine [8.68], mapping templates are used to store the relationships between the data objects, and are thus defined by the facts. Conclusions are assigned to queries by applying these mapping templates to the data objects in the order prescribed by the rules. The married-to and father-of facts are represented by two-dimensional mapping templates as shown in Figures 8.40a and b, respectively. Operation of the ?mother-of Carol query is performed as follows. An SLM—for example, an LCTV—is used to display the mapping template for the father-of

324 DIGITAL-OPTICAL COMPUTING

Father-of

	A	B	C	D	E	F
A						
B						
C				■		
D						
E						
F					■	

(a)

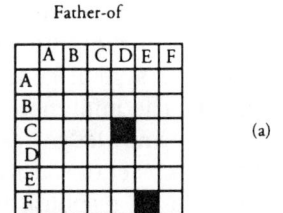

Married-to

	A	B	C	D	E	F
A				■		
B					■	
C						
D						
E						
F						

(b)

FIGURE 8.40 Templates showing the relationship of (*a*) father-of, and (*b*) married-to.

facts (Figure 8.40*a*). The query data Carol will turn on a horizontal line of C to illuminate the LCTV. This is a two-dimensional optical AND operation between the horizontal line and the LCTV display. The transmittance from the LCTV will be low, except that the element (D, C) being high indicates that David is the father of Carol. The bright spot at (D, C) is then expanded optically (using a cylindrical lens) to form a vertical line, and is projected onto another LCTV showing the mapping template of the married-to facts (Figure 8.40*b*). Consequently, the transmittance from the second LCTV shows only one bright spot at (D, A). The bright spot is now expanded horizontally so that it can be detected by the detector A. This indicates the conclusion Ann.

It is very interesting to notice that the mapping template method can also be performed using an algebraic matrix operation [8.69]. The married-to facts is represented by the binary matrix

$$[MT] = \begin{matrix} & \begin{matrix} A & B & C & D & E & F \end{matrix} \\ \begin{matrix} A \\ B \\ C \\ D \\ E \\ F \end{matrix} & \begin{bmatrix} 0 & 0 & 0 & 0 & 0 & 0 \\ 0 & 0 & 0 & 0 & 0 & 0 \\ 0 & 0 & 0 & 0 & 0 & 0 \\ 1 & 0 & 0 & 0 & 0 & 0 \\ 0 & 1 & 0 & 0 & 0 & 0 \\ 0 & 0 & 0 & 0 & 0 & 0 \end{bmatrix} \end{matrix},$$

and the father-of facts is represented by another binary matrix

$$[FO] = \begin{array}{c} A \\ B \\ C \\ D \\ E \\ F \end{array} \begin{matrix} A & B & C & D & E & F \end{matrix} \\ \begin{bmatrix} 0 & 0 & 0 & 0 & 0 & 0 \\ 0 & 0 & 0 & 0 & 0 & 0 \\ 0 & 0 & 0 & 0 & 0 & 0 \\ 0 & 0 & 1 & 0 & 0 & 0 \\ 0 & 0 & 0 & 0 & 0 & 1 \\ 0 & 0 & 0 & 0 & 0 & 0 \end{bmatrix}.$$

The query ?mother-of Carol can be answered by a rule

$$X \text{ mother-of Carol, IF } Y \text{ married-to } X \text{ AND } Y \text{ father-of Carol,} \quad (8.20)$$

which involves two facts connected by a rule. We may consider that, in general, a rule is a function of facts. A new fact can be concluded, from the function, through a sequence of logic operations applied to the known facts. In the matrix encoding method, logic operations between relations are carried out by thresholding the matrix–matrix product for the AND operation and by thresholding the matrix–matrix sum for the OR operation. Equation 8.20 can be used to generate new facts of mother-of as follows:

$$[MO] = [MT][FO], \quad (8.21)$$

Equation 8.21 yields

$$[MO] = \begin{array}{c} A \\ B \\ C \\ D \\ E \\ F \end{array} \begin{matrix} A & B & C & D & E & F \end{matrix} \\ \begin{bmatrix} 0 & 0 & 1 & 0 & 0 & 0 \\ 0 & 0 & 0 & 0 & 0 & 1 \\ 0 & 0 & 0 & 0 & 0 & 0 \\ 0 & 0 & 0 & 0 & 0 & 0 \\ 0 & 0 & 0 & 0 & 0 & 0 \\ 0 & 0 & 0 & 0 & 0 & 0 \end{bmatrix}.$$

to get the conclusion for the query ?mother-to Carol, a matrix–vector multiplication is performed, in which the input vector is [A = 0, B = 0, C = 1, D = 0, E = 0, F = 0]. The output vector is obtained as follows:

$$\begin{bmatrix} 0 & 0 & 1 & 0 & 0 & 0 \\ 0 & 0 & 0 & 0 & 0 & 1 \\ 0 & 0 & 0 & 0 & 0 & 0 \\ 0 & 0 & 0 & 0 & 0 & 0 \\ 0 & 0 & 0 & 0 & 0 & 0 \\ 0 & 0 & 0 & 0 & 0 & 0 \end{bmatrix} \begin{bmatrix} 0 \\ 0 \\ 1 \\ 0 \\ 0 \\ 0 \end{bmatrix} = \begin{array}{c} A \\ B \\ C \\ D \\ E \\ F \end{array} \begin{bmatrix} 1 \\ 0 \\ 0 \\ 0 \\ 0 \\ 0 \end{bmatrix}. \quad (8.22)$$

Since the output vector is [A = 1, B = 0, C = 0, D = 0, E = 0, F = 0], the conclusion is Ann. We conclude that optical matrix–vector and matrix–matrix multipliers can be applied to artificial intelligence.

REFERENCES

8.1 F. T. S. Yu, *Optical Information Processing*, Wiley–Interscience, New York, 1983.

8.2 F. T. S. Yu and I. C. Khoo, *Principle of Optical Engineering*, Wiley, New York, 1992.

8.3 M. J. Quinn, *Designing Efficient Algorithms for Parallel Computers*, McGraw-Hill, New York, 1987.

8.4 D. G. Feitelson, *Optical Computing*, MIT Press, Cambridge, Mass., 1988.

8.5 H. H. Arsenault, T. Szoplik, and B. Macukow, Eds., *Optical Processing and Computing*, Academic Press, San Diego, 1989.

8.6 R. Arrathoon, Ed., *Optical Computing, Digital and Symbolic*, Dekker, New York, 1989.

8.7 M. Murdocca, *A Digital Design Methodology for Optical Computing*, MIT Press, Cambridge, Mass., 1990.

8.8 A. D. McAulay, *Optical Computer Architectures*, Wiley, New York, 1991.

8.9 J. Tanida and Y. Ichioka, "Optical Logic Array Processor Using Shadow-grams," *J. Opt. Soc. Am.* 73 (1983): 800.

8.10 F. T. S. Yu, Y. Jin, and C. Zhang, "Symbolic Logic Processor Using Cascaded Liquid Crystal Televisions (LCTVs)," *Microwave Opt. Tech. Lett.* 2 (1989): 309.

8.11 Y. Li, G. Eichmann, and R. R. Alfano, "Optical Computing Using Hybrid Encoded Shadow Casting," *Appl. Opt.* 25 (1986): 2636.

8.12 M. A. Karim, A. A. Awwal, and A. K. Cherri, "Polarization-Encoded Optical Shadow-Casting Logic Units: Design," *Appl. Opt.* 26 (1987): 2720.

8.13 S. Jutamulia and G. Storti, "Noncoded Shadow-Casting Logic Array," *Appl. Opt.* 28 (1989): 4517.

8.14 A. W. Lohmann, "Polarization and Optical Logic," *Appl. Opt.* 25 (1986): 1528.

8.15 R. A. Athale and S. H. Lee, "Development of an Optical Parallel Logic Device and a Half-Adder Circuit for Digital Optical Processing," *Opt. Eng.* 18 (1979): 513.

8.16 T. Minemoto, K. Okamoto, and K. Miyamoto, "Optical Parallel Logic Gate Using Spatial Light Modulators with the Pockels Effect," *Appl Opt.* 24 (1985): 2055.

8.17 M. T. Fatehi, K. C. Wasmundt, and S. A. Collins, Jr., "Optical Logic Gates Using Liquid Crystal Light Valve: Implementation and Application Example," *Appl. Opt.* 20 (1981): 2250.

8.18 F. T. S. Yu, S. Jutamulia, and T. Lu, "Optical Parallel Logic Based on Magneto-Optic Spatial Light Modulator," *Opt. Commun.* 63 (1987): 225.

8.19 F. T. S. Yu, S. Jutamulia, and D. A. Gregory, "Optical Parallel Logic Gates Using Inexpensive Liquid-Crystal Televisions," *Opt. Lett.* 12 (1987): 1050.

8.20 F. T. S. Yu, S. Jutamulia, and D. A. Gregory, "Real-Time Liquid Crystal TV XOR- and XNOR-Gate Binary Image Subtraction Technique," *Appl. Opt.* 26 (1987): 2738.

8.21 S. Jutamulia, G. M. Storti, J. Lindmayer, and W. Seiderman, "Use of Electron Trapping Materials in Optical Signal Processing. 3: Modifiable Hopfield Type Neutral Networks," *Appl. Opt.* 30 (1991): 1786.

8.22 F. T. S. Yu, Q. W. Song, and X. J. Lu, "Implementation of Boolean Logic Gates Using a Microchannel Spatial Light Modulator with Liquid-Crystal Televisions," *Opt. Lett.* 12 (1987): 962.

8.23 F. T. S. Yu, Q. W. Song, and X. J. Lu, "Operating Characteristics and Applications of a Microchannel Spatial Light Modulator Under White-Light Illumination," *Appl. Opt.* 26 (1987): 2743.

8.24 Y. Jin and F. T. S. Yu, "Optical Binary Adder Using Liquid Crystal Television," *Opt. Commun.* 65 (1988): 11.

8.25 M. T. Fatehi, K. C. Wasmundt, and S. A. Collins, Jr., "Optical Flip-Flops and Logic Circuits Using Liquid Crystal Light Valve," *Appl. Opt.* 23 (1984): 2163.

8.26 A. D. McAulay, "Optical Analog to Digital Converter Using Optical Logic and Table Look-Up," *Opt. Eng.* 29 (1990): 114.

8.27 S. Jutamulia, G. M. Storti, J. Lindmayer, and W. Seiderman, "Use of Electron Trapping Materials in Optical Signal Processing. 1: Parallel Boolean Logic," *Appl. Opt.* 29 (1990): 4806.

8.28 A. Huang, "Parallel Algorithms for Optical Digital Computers," in *Tenth International Optical Computing Conference, Proc. SPIE* 422 (1983): 13.

8.29 K.-H. Brenner, A. Huang, and N. Streibl, "Digital Optical Computing with Symbolic Substitution," *Appl. Opt.* 25 (1986): 3054.

8.30 M. J. Murdocca, "Digital Optical Computing with One-Rule Cellular Automata," *Appl. Opt.* 26 (1987): 682.

8.31 F. T. S. Yu and S. Jutamulia, "Implementation of Symbolic Substitution Logic Using Optical Associative Memories," *Appl. Opt.* 26 (1987): 2293.

8.32 F. T. S. Yu, C. Zhang, and S. Jutamulia, "Application of One-Step Holographic Associative Memories to Symbolic Substitution," *Opt. Eng.* 27 (1988): 399.

8.33 C. C. Guest and T. K. Gaylord, "Truth-Table Look-Up Optical Processing Utilizing Binary and Residue Arithmetic," *Appl. Opt.* 19 (1980): 1201.

8.34 D. Gabor, G. W. Stroke, R. Restrick, A. Funkhouser, and D. Brumm, "Optical Image Synthesis (Complex Amplitude Addition and Subtraction) by Holographic Fourier Transformation," *Phys. Lett.* 18 (1965): 116

8.35 K. Bromley, M. A. Monahan, J. F. Bryan, and B. J. Thompson, "Holographic Subtraction," *Appl. Opt.* 10 (1971): 174.

8.36 P. Yeh, A. E. Chiou, J. Hong, P. Beckwith, T. Chang, and M. Khoshnevisan, "Photorefractive Nonlinear Optics and Optical Computing," *Opt. Eng.* 28 (1989): 328.

8.37 M. D. Ewbank, P. Yeh, M. Khoshnevisan, and J. Feinberg, "Time Reversal by an Interferometer with Coupled Phase Conjugators," *Opt. Lett.* 10 (1985): 282.

8.38 A. E. Chiou and P. Yeh, "Parallel Image Subtraction Using a Phase-Conjugate Michelson Interferometer," *Opt. Lett.* 11 (1986): 306.

8.39 N. Peyghambarian and H. M. Gibbs, "Optical Bistability for Optical Signal Processing and Computing," *Opt. Eng.* 24 (1985): 68.
8.40 S. D. Smith, A. C. Walker, B. S. Wherrett, F. A. P. Tooley, N. Craft, J. G. H. Mathew, M. R. Taghizadeh, I. Redmond, and R. J. Campbell, "Restoring Optical Logic: Demonstration of Extensible All-Optical Digital Systems," *Opt. Eng.* 26 (1987): 45.
8.41 A. C. Walker, "Application of Bistable Optical Logic Gate Arrays to All-Optical Digital Parallel Processing," *Appl. Opt.* 25 (1986): 1578.
8.42 J. W. Goodman, F. J. Leonberger, S.-Y. Kung, R. A. Athale, "Optical Interconnections for VLSI Systems," *Proc. IEEE* 72 (1984): 850.
8.43 H. S. Stone, "Parallel Processing with the Perfect Shuffle," *IEEE Trans. Comput.* C-20 (1971): 153.
8.44 C. L. Wu and T. Y. Feng, "The Universality of the Shuffle-Exchange Network," *IEEE Trans. Comput.* C-30 (1981): 324.
8.45 A. W. Lohmann, W. Stork, and G. Stucke, "Optical Perfect Shuffle," *Appl. Opt.* 25 (1986): 1530.
8.46 G. Eichmann and Y. Li, "Compact Optical Generalized Perfect Shuffle," *Appl. Opt.* 26 (1987): 1167.
8.47 K.-H. Brenner and A. Huang, "Optical Implementation of the Perfect Shuffle Interconnection," *Appl. Opt.* 27 (1988): 135.
8.48 C. W. Stirk, R. A. Athale, and M. W. Haney, "Folded Perfect Shuffle Optical Processor," *Appl. Opt.* 27 (1988): 202.
8.49 Q. W. Song and F. T. S. Yu, "Generalized Perfect Shuffle Using Optical Spatial Filtering," *Appl. Opt.* 27 (1988): 1222.
8.50 S. Jutamulia and G. Storti, "Incoherent Optical Interconnects (Perfect Shuffle) Based On Shadow Casting," *Appl. Opt.* 28 (1989): 4262.
8.51 J. W. Goodman, A. R. Dias, and L. M. Woody, "Fully Parallel, High-Speed Incoherent Optical Method for Performing Discrete Fourier Transforms," *Opt. Lett.* 2 (1978): 1.
8.52 J. J. Hopfield, "Neural Networks and Physical Systems with Emergent Collective Computational Abilities," *Proc. Natl. Acad. Sci. U.S.A.* 79 (1982): 2554.
8.53 D. Psaltis and N. Farhat, "Optical Information Processing Based on an Associative-Memory Model of Neural Nets with Thresholding and Feedback," *Opt. Lett.* 10 (1985): 98.
8.54 A. D. McAulay, "Optical Crossbar Interconnected Digital Signal Processor with Basic Algorithms," *Opt. Eng.* 25 (1986): 82.
8.55 R. Arrathoon, "Historical Perspectives: Optical Crossbars and Optical Computing," *Proc. SPIE*, 752 (1987): 2.
8.56 H. T. Kung, "Why Systolic Architecture?" *Computer* 15 (1982): 37.
8.57 H. J. Caulfield, W. T. Rhodes, M. J. Foster, and S. Horvitz, "Optical Implementation of Systolic Array Processing," *Opt. Commun.* 40 (1981): 86.
8.58 P. S. Guilfoyle, "Systolic Acousto-Optic Binary Convolver," *Opt. Eng.* 23 (1984): 20.
8.59 D. Psaltis, D. Casasent, D. Neft, and M. Carlotto, "Accurate Numerical Computation by Optical Convolution," in *1980 International Optical Computing Conference, Proc. SPIE* 232 (1980): 151.

8.60 R. P. Bocker, "Optical Digital RUBIC (Rapid Unbiased Bipolar Incoherent Calculator) Cube Processor," *Opt. Eng.* 23 (1984): 26.

8.61 F. T. S. Yu, M. F. Cao, and T. W. Lu, "A Hybrid Optical System for Linear Transformation Processing," *Proc. SPIE* 698 (1986): 276.

8.62 R. A. Athale, "Optical Matrix Algebraic Processor: A Survay," in *Tenth International Optical Computing Conference, Proc. SPIE* 422 (1983): 24.

8.63 F. T. S. Yu and T. Lu, "Digital Optical Architectures for Multiple Matrix Multiplication," *Opt. Commun.* 71 (1989): 39.

8.64 F. T. S. Yu and M. F. Cao, "Digital Optical Matrix Multiplication Based On a Systolic Outer-Product Method," *Opt. Eng.* 26 (1987): 1229.

8.65 F. Hayes-Roth, D. A. Waterman, and D. B. Lenat, Eds. *Building Expert Systems*, Addison-Wesley, Reading, Mass., 1983.

8.66 S. Jutamulia, G. Storti, X. Li, "Expert Systems Based On LCTV AND/OR Logic," *Opt. Laser Technol.* 21 (1989): 392.

8.67 A. D. McAulay, "Real-Time Optical Expert Systems," *Appl. Opt.* 26 (1987): 1927.

8.68 C. Warde and J. Kottas, "Hybrid Optical Inference Machines: Architectural Considerations," *Appl. Opt.* 25 (1986): 940.

8.69 J. Y. Jau, F. Kiamilev, Y. Fainman, S. Esener, and S. H. Lee, "Optical Expert System Based On Matrix-Algebraic Formulation," *Appl. Opt.* 27 (1988): 5170.

PROBLEMS

8.1 Figure 8.41 shows the geometry of the shadow-casting array processor. Show that

$$b = \frac{da}{d-a} \quad \text{and} \quad z_2 = \frac{a}{(d-a)} z_1.$$

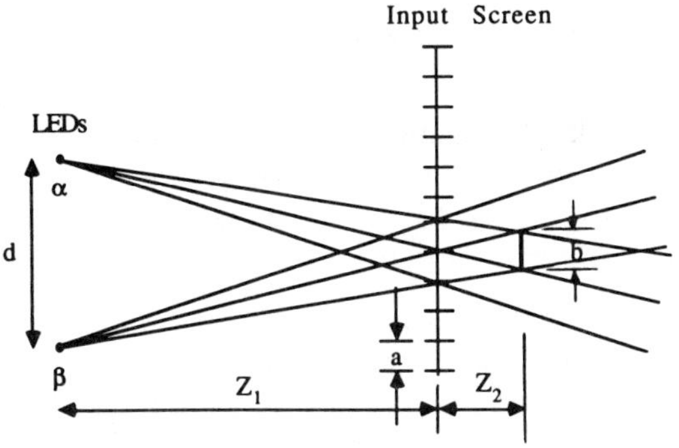

FIGURE 8.41

8.2 In order to suppress diffraction effect at the output of the shadow-casting array processor (see Figure 8.41):

(a) Should a be small or large?

(b) Should z_2 be small or large?
(c) Should z_1 be small or large?

Explain your answers in detail.

(d) When the diffraction effect is minimized, what is the trade-off?

8.3 Shadow casting is basically the superposition of four shadows produced by four LEDs. How do four images produced by half-mirrors perform the same task? Show the optical setup and give a detailed explanation.

8.4 Figure 8.42 shows a two-mask shadow-casting image processor. Two transparencies $f(x, y)$ and $g(x, y)$ (both are real functions) are arranged in tandem in the processor. Show that the output is the correlation

$$o(\alpha, \beta) = \iint f\left(\frac{x - \alpha d}{f}, \frac{y - \beta d}{f}\right) g(x, y)\, dx\, dy.$$

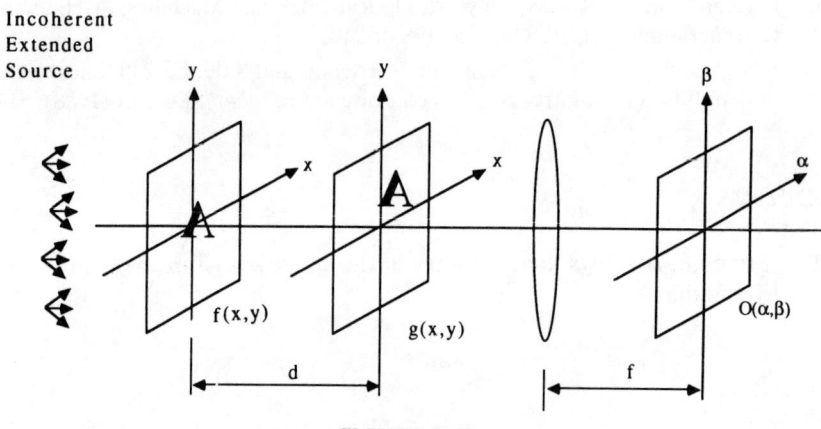

FIGURE 8.42

8.5 Ideally, an MOSLM rotates light polarization by $+45°$ for logical 1 and $-45°$ for logical 0. Show that the XNOR function can be implemented using two MOSLMs based on the arrangement shown in Figure 8.8 (i.e., no polarization between two SLMs).

8.6 In reality, the MOSLM rotates light polarization by $+9°$ and $-9°$. What are the intensities of the outputs of (00), (01), (10), and (11), using the configuration of Problem 8.5?

8.7 Assuming that an LCLV has a threshold characteristic for its input-output relation, show the implementation of the OR and NOR gates using a LCLV.

8.8 A flip-flop consisting of two NOR gates is shown in Figure 8.43. Design an optical circuit using LCLV NOR gates.

FIGURE 8.43

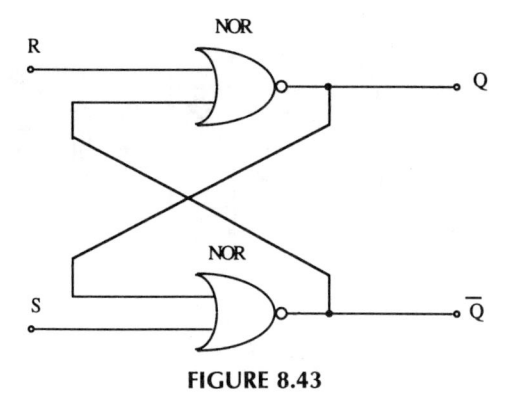

8.9 **(a)** Explain in detail that the optical setup depicted in Figure 8.44 functions as a half-adder. A = 0011 and B = 0101. Note that $\lambda/2$ plate rotates the polarization of light by 90°.
  (b) What are the binary patterns of outputs C and D?
  (c) Which is sum? Which is carry?

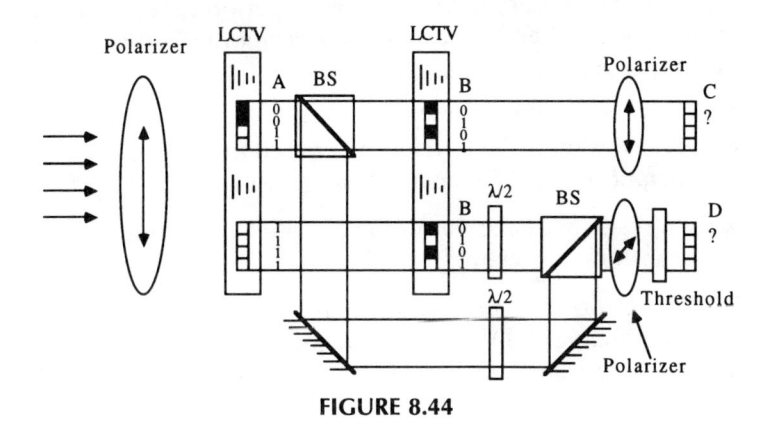

FIGURE 8.44

8.10 An LCTV has 140 × 120 pixels and 30 frames per second. What is the throughput of an LCTV logic processor in terms of bits/second?

8.11 Assume that the ET thin film has a resolution of 80 lines/mm, and the response time of the ET thin film to infrared stimulation is 50 ns.
  (a) What is the possible maximum throughput of an array logic processor using 1 × 1 cm² ET thin film?
  (b) Mention any factors that may decrease the throughput in practice.

8.12 Provided that LCTV1 and LCTV2 can display an array input or its negation, show that a noncoding shadow-casting logic can be performed using the optical setup shown in Figure 8.45.

FIGURE 8.45

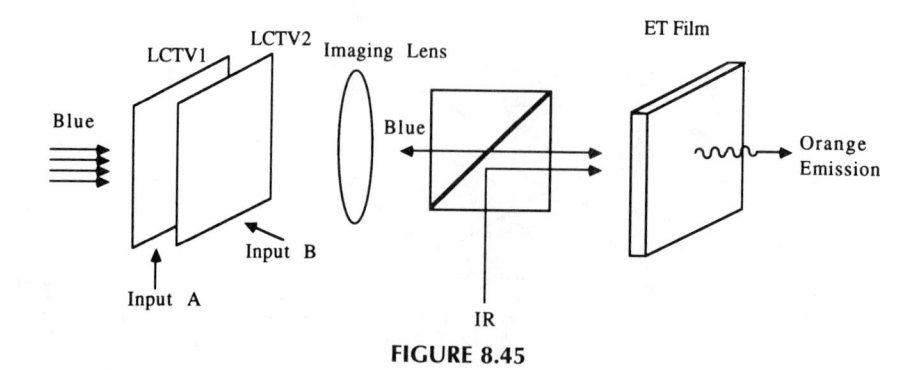

8.13 Show step by step the addition of (3 + 6) using the parallel addition algorithm given in Figure 8.13.

8.14 Draw a diagram and give a mathematical explanation in terms of Fourier operators that show the implementation of symbolic substitution using a joint Fourier-transform hologram.

8.15 A joint transform hologram is made to perform the substitution rule (10) → 0, where 1 and 0 are encoded as a cross and a ring, respectively.
   (a) What is the output of (11)?
   (b) Does the output contain 0 (a ring)?
   (c) If yes, what is the difference between the output of (11) and the output of (10)? Compare their intensities.

8.16 Draw a diagram of the performing symbolic substitution based on a joint transform correlator.

8.17 We can perform the recognition step for symbolic substitution using electron trapping (ET) material, as shown in Figure 8.46, in which the infrared pattern should be smaller than the blue pattern. The blue light

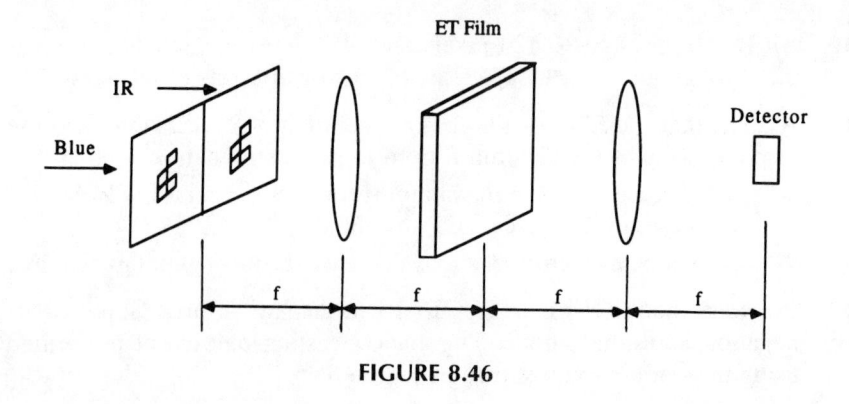

FIGURE 8.46

is from an Ar laser ($\lambda = 488$ nm), and the infrared light is from a YAG:Nd laser ($\lambda = 1064$ nm).

(a) What is the scale ratio between the blue and infrared patterns?

(b) What is the disadvantage of this system as compared with a joint transform correlator?

8.18 Show that the binary amplitude image subtraction is equivalent to an XOR logic function.

8.19 What is the difference between pattern matching based on XOR (or XNOR) and AND functions? Use vectors (110101) and (110000).

8.20 What is the difference between pattern matching based on logic operation such as XOR and AND and the optical correlation?

8.21 If logical 1 of input A is encoded with a vertical grating, and logical 1 of input B is encoded with a horizontal grating, what logic function is implemented by the optical system shown in Figure 8.47?

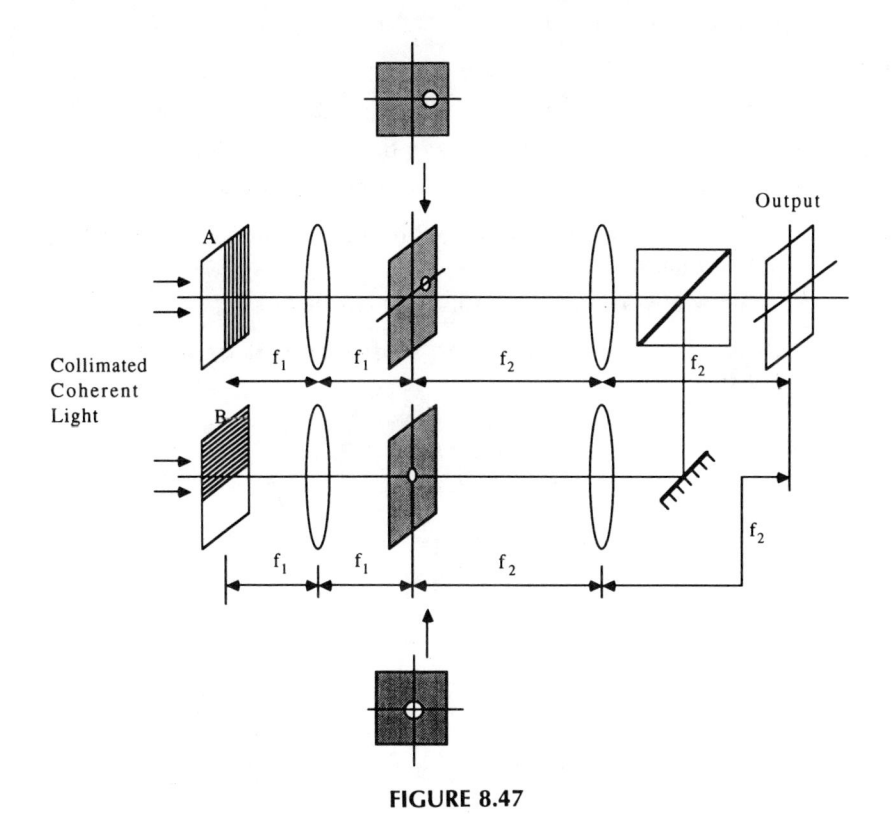

FIGURE 8.47

8.22 What logic function is implemented by the optical system shown in Figure 8.48?

334 DIGITAL-OPTICAL COMPUTING

FIGURE 8.48

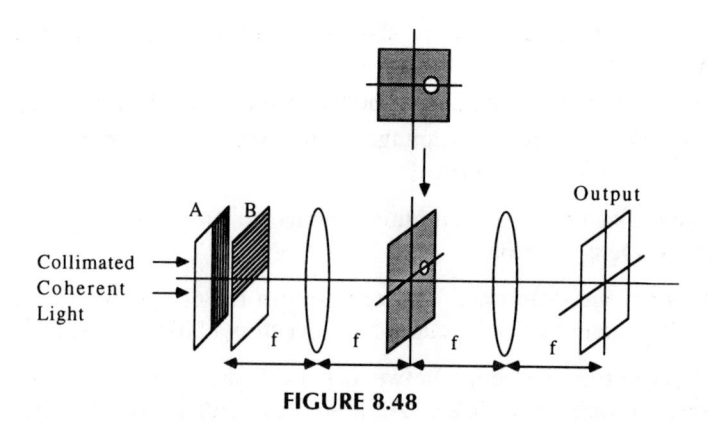

8.23 A Fabry–Perot etalon with distance $d = 20\lambda$ is filled with nonlinear material having $n = 2.5$. Determine whether the transmitted light of a normal incident light is in the on or off state. To switch the state of the transmitted light, how much is $\Delta n/n$ required?

8.24 Show that all 16 Boolean logic gates can be implemented as combinations of AND, NAND, OR, and NOR gates.

8.25 **(a)** Describe a half-adder using optical bistability logic gates.
  (b) Describe a flip-flop using optical bistability logic gates.

8.26 **(a)** Show how to implement an 8-bit perfect shuffle simply by using two pinholes.
  (b) Show how to implement it using two lenses.

8.27 What is the output of the perfect shuffle network depicted in Figure 8.49?

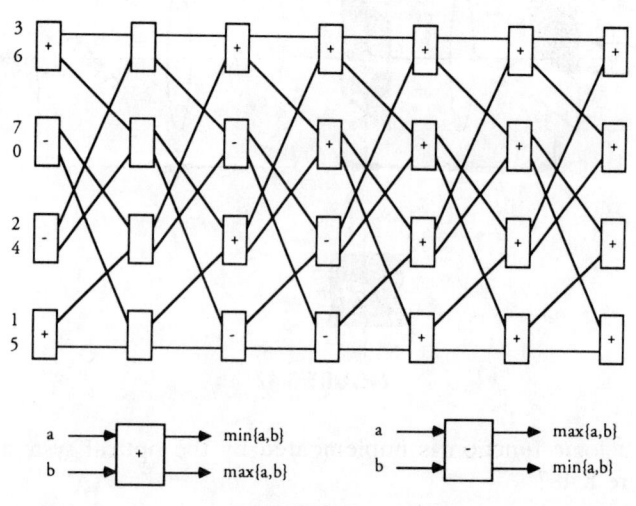

FIGURE 8.49

8.28 Repeat Problem 8.27 for the input:

$$2, 3, 1, 7, 4, 6, 5, 0.$$

8.29 Design an 8-bit perfect shuffle using a crossbar switch.

8.30 In a matrix–vector multiplier, the vector is given by a transmission-type one-dimensional SLM, and the matrix is given by transmission-type two-dimensional SLM. Design an optical setup with three cylindrical lenses and one spherical lens, if a coherent point source (e.g., a laser beam that is focused on and passes through a pinhole) is available.

8.31 **(a)** How many steps are required to complete a matrix–vector multiplication using the system of Problem 8.30?

(b) How many steps are required to complete a matrix–vector multiplication using the systolic engagement system shown in Figure 8.31?

8.32 An ET thin film can be used for matrix–vector multiplication. The matrix pattern can be written into the thin film with blue light, and the extended vector pattern can be written with infrared light. The direct product of the two patterns is obtained as an orange colored luminescent emission from the thin film, as shown in Figure 8.50. The emission is incoherent. Can we use any lens to focus the emission light from the ET thin film into a line so that the linear detector can be used? Note that the element of the output vector is focused onto a pixel of the linear detector. Explain your answer.

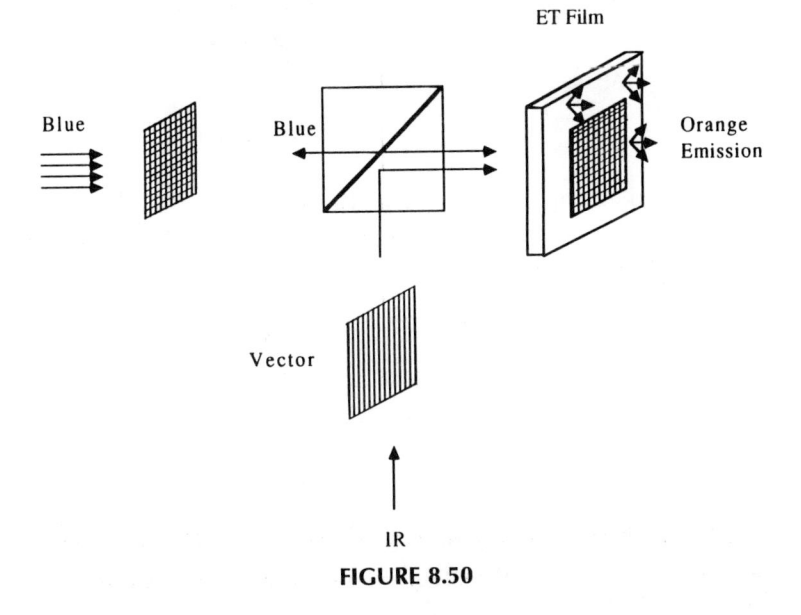

FIGURE 8.50

8.33 The product of 5 × 3 can be obtained by performing the (optical) convolution of two binary arrays as follows:

$$5 = (101)$$
$$3 = (011)$$
$$(101) \text{ convolves } (011) = (01111) = 15.$$

Show step by step the convolution process to perform the multiplication of 5 × 4.

8.34 Repeat Problem 8.33 for multiplication of 29 × 14.

8.35 Two's complement numbers provide a binary representation of both positive and negative values, and facilitate subtraction by the same logic circuits in the microprocessor that are used for addition. In a two's complement number, the most significant bit is the sign. The sign bit of a positive number is 0, while the sign bit of a negative number is 1. An example is given as follows:

Decimal +127:   Sign   Magnitude
                         +   1111111

Two's complement representation: 01111111.

Decimal −127:

+127:	01111111
Complement:	10000000
Add 1:	1
	10000001

Two's complement representation: 10000001.
The two's complement representation of decimal +127 can also be obtained from that of decimal −127.

−127:	10000001
Complement:	01111110
Add 1:	1
	01111111

Two's complement representation of decimal +127: 01111111.

    (a) Determine the two's complement representation of decimal −26 (8-bit).

- **(b)** Determine the two's complement representation of decimal + 26 from the −26 obtained in Part (a).

8.36 **(a)** Give the 3 × 3 transform matrix of a discrete Hilbert transform for $n = 0, 1, 2$ and $m = 0, 1, 2$.
- **(b)** Give the transform matrix in two's complement representation for a 5-bit word.

8.37 Show that a systolic array matrix–matrix multiplication (Figure 8.36) requires $(2nb - 1) + (n - 1)$ steps.

8.38 **(a)** A linear four-terminal (electrical) network is depicted in Figure 8.51. Suppose these equations hold:

$$E_1 = AE_2 + BI_2,$$
$$I_1 = CE_2 + DI_2,$$

where A, B, C, and D are constants. Write these equations in matrix–vector multiplication form. The matrix is called the transmission matrix T.

- **(b)** Considering the two identical networks in cascade as shown in Figure 8.52, find I_2 and E_1 in terms of I_3 and E_3. Show that the overall transmission matrix is T^2.

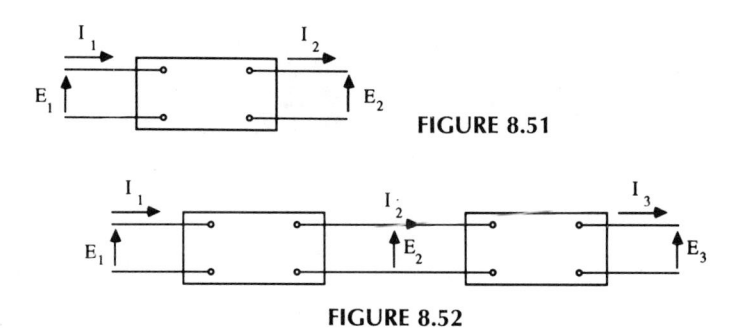

FIGURE 8.51

FIGURE 8.52

8.39 Show the AND/OR graph of the production rules given as follows:

IF: The exhaust is smoky, and
 The car is backfiring, and
 There is a lack of power,
THEN: The carburetor fuel mix is too rich.
IF: There is a lack of power, and
 There is a gray deposit on the spark plugs, and
 The engine is overheats,
THEN: The carburetor fuel mix is too weak.
IF: The carburetor fuel is too rich, or
 The carburetor fuel mix is too weak,

THEN: The carburetor fuel mix needs to be adjusted.

8.40 Given the facts in a family tree:

father-of (Bob, Paul)
father-of (Dave, John)
father-of (Mike, Tom)
father-of (Dave, Mike)
father-of (John, Bob).

Based on the matrix algebraic method, determine:

Who is the grandfather of Tom?
Who is the grandfather of Bob?
Who is the grandfather of Paul?
Who is the great-grandfather of Paul?

8.41 Show the procedure using the mapping template method for Problem 8.40.

CHAPTER NINE

Optical Neural Networks

It is well accepted that digital computers can solve computational problems, such as addition, subtraction, multiplication, division, thousands of times faster and more accurately than human brains. However, cognitive tasks, such as pattern recognition, understanding and speaking a natural language, retrieving contextual information, and guiding a mechanical hand, can be performed more naturally and efficiently by the human brain, for these tasks are beyond the reach of the modern digital computer. It is in fact for this reason, engineers would like to simulate an artificial neural network for computing.

9.1 ASPECTS OF NEURAL NETWORKS

The human brain consists of millions of neurons and each neuron is interconnected to thousands of other neurons. The technology underlying the development of artificial neural networks (ANNs) draws heavily on cognitive psychology and biological models of human memory, learning, and perception. They attempt to implement the useful computational properties exhibited by the biological nervous systems. In other words, neural network research tries to simulate the structure of a massively interconnected biological neural network, by which information processing can be performed in a parallel and associative manner. There are, however, some fundamental differences between digital computers and the ANNs. For instance, in an ANN, every neuron performs simple logical operations, whereas in digital computers, data processing relies on the central processing unit (CPU). In addition, ANNs exhibit such characteristics of learning as improving the performances, adapting the environments, and coping with disruptions. On the other hand, digital computers are programmed with rigid rules, which must be manually reprogrammed for better solution. Moreover, neural networks can process inexact, ambiguous, fuzzy data that do not exactly match the stored information, while electronic computers cannot adjust the specific definitions and rules with which they are programmed, to accommodate new, inexact, degraded, or contradictory input.

A neural network consists of a collection of processing elements, that is, neurons. Each neuron has many input signals, but only one output signal, which is fanned out along many pathways to other neurons. These pathways connect the neurons into a network, as shown in Figure 9.1. The processing that each neuron does is determined by a transfer function—a mathematical formula that defines the neuron's output as a function of the input signals. Every connection entering a neuron has an adaptive coefficient called *weight* assigned to it. The weight determines the connection strength between neurons. The weights can be changed by a learning law—a rule that modifies the weights in response to the input signals and the value supplied by the transfer function. The learning law allows the neuron's response to change with time, depending upon the nature of the input signals. This is the means by which the network adapts itself to the environment and so organizes information within itself—in short, learns.

There are generally two kinds of learning, namely, *supervised* and *unsupervised*. In supervised learning, a teacher is required to supply the network with both input data and the desired output data, such as training exemplars (e.g., references). The network has to be taught when to learn and when to process information, but it cannot do both at the same time. In unsupervised learning, the network is given input data but no desired output data; instead, after each trail or series of trails, it is given an evaluation rule that evaluates its performance. It can learn an unknown input during the process, and it presents more or less the nature of human self-learning ability.

Many neural network models have been developed in the past several decades (e.g., Fukushima, 1969; Hopfield, 1982; Kohonen, 1984; Rumelhart and Zipser, 1986; Lippmann, 1987; and Carpenter and Grossberg, 1988; i.e., [9.1]–[9.6]). Hopfield, Perceptron, error-driven back-propagation, and Boltzman machine are some of the supervised learning models; adaptive resonance theory (ART), neocognitron, Madline, and Kohonen self-organizing feature map models are among the best known unsupervised learning models.

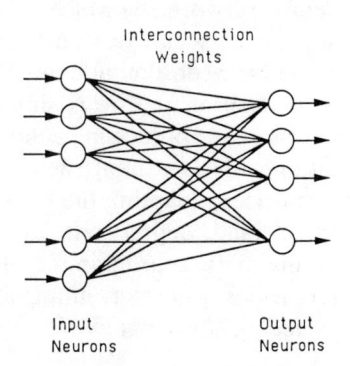

FIGURE 9.1 A single layer fully interconnected neural network.

Generally speaking, a neural network of N neurons has N^2 interconnections. The transfer function of the network can be a threshold function, that is, a step function, making the state of a neuron binary (0 or 1), or a sigmoid function, which gives a neuron analog values. As illustrated in Figure 9.2, the state of the ith neuron in the network can be expressed mathematically by the following iterative equation

$$u_i = f\left\{\sum_{j=1}^{N} T_{ij} u_j - \theta_i\right\}, \qquad (9.1)$$

where u_i is the activation potential of the ith neuron, T_{ij} is the interconnection weight (called *associative memory*) between the jth neuron and the ith neuron, and f is a nonlinear transfer function, which we assume is a thresholding function that can be written as

$$f(x) = \begin{cases} 1, & x > 0, \\ 0, & x \leq 0. \end{cases} \qquad (9.2)$$

Thus we see that the operation of a neuron is simply a nonlinear transfer operation of the sum of weighted input signals. In other words, the mathematical expression can be represented by a *matrix–vector* product and a nonlinear operator:

$$\mathbf{U} = f\{\mathbf{TV}\}, \qquad (9.3)$$

where $\mathbf{U}$ is the state vector or output vector of the neural network, $\mathbf{V}$ stands for the input vector, and $\mathbf{T}$ is defined as the *interconnection weight matrix* (IWM) or associative memory.

Neural networks are models and algorithms that can be simulated on conventional computers, but are best implemented on special-purpose computational hardware. Very large-scale integration (VLSI) technology has been used to design and synthesize neural network operations. However, for a

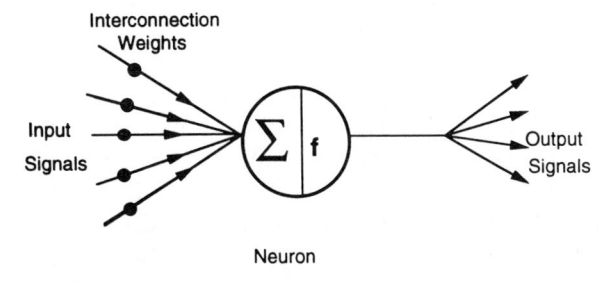

FIGURE 9.2 A mathematical model of a neuron.

single-layer neural network, in general, the number of interconnections is the square of the number of neurons composing a given network. For example, a fully interconnected network of 10^4 neurons requires 10^8 interconnections, which is beyond the reach of state-of-the-art VLSI technology. On the other hand, optics offers the advantages of the parallel processing and massive interconnection capabilities for the design of large-scale optoelectronic neurocomputers (Farhat *et al.*, 1985; Lalann *et al.*, 1987; Athale *et al.*, 1986; Wu *et al.*, 1989; and Yu *et al.*, 1989; i.e., [9.7]–[9.11]). Since light beams can pass through three-dimensional space without interfering with each other, optical systems can provide higher space–bandwidth-product operation than can their electronic counterparts. These unique properties of optics have stimulated great interest among neural network researchers for designing hybrid-optical architectures that can perform neural network operations at high speed.

To our knowledge, the first optoelectronic neural network was proposed by Farhat *et al.* [9.7]. Since then several other optical neural network architectures have been proposed, for example, associative memory using liquid crystal light values (LCLV) (Psaltis et al. [9.12] and [9.13]), hybrid optical neural networks using programmable spatial light modulators (SLMs) (Johnson *et al.* [9.14]), and the optical ring resonator (Anderson and Erie [9.15]). Numerous papers have recently been published in the neural network area, and we apologize for not being able to cite all of them in this chapter. In short, this present chapter provides the reader with a bird's-eye view of optical neural networks. It is not, however, our intention to cover the vast domain of neural networks; for this the reader should consult the works by Rosenblatt, Fukushima, Hopfield, Farhat, and Psaltis [9.16]–[9.18] [9.12].

9.2 OPTICAL ASSOCIATIVE MEMORY

There has been a great deal of interest in the possibility of implementing associative memory using optical techniques, much of it centered around the implementation of neural network models. The associative memory is a process in which the presence of a complete or partial input directly results in a predetermined output. The neural network shown in Figure 9.1 is one of the possible implementations for associative memory. A neural network attempts to mimic the real structure and function of neurons, as was shown in Figure 9.2.

It is interesting to note, however, that we do not necessarily have to exactly mimic a human brain in order to design a special-purpose cognitive machine, just as it is not necessary to exactly imitate a bird in order to make a flying machine [9.19]. In this section, we review the model of a hybrid electrooptical associative memory based on an inner-product model (a neural network is based on an outer-product model, i.e., matrix–vector multiplication results in an outer product). The inner-product model is implemented by employing a new class of photonic materials, called *electron trapping* (ET) *materials* [9.20].

Optical correlators have been widely used to perform space invariant pattern recognition (see Chapter 2). An optical pattern recognizer usually has a bank of memories. The match of an input and a memory is indicated by the presence of a strong correlation output. A correlation is essentially a space invariant inner product. The correlation spot resembling a point source can be further used to reconstruct a hologram or to simply project a picture as a recalled output. If the recalled output is identical to the memory, the system is categorized as *autoassociative*. If the recalled output is not the memory, the system is *heteroassociative*.

In order to be able to recall different stored memories, the inner product must not be space invariant. The position of a noninvariant correlation peak will indicate the match of the input with a certain memory. Therefore, an optical associative memory retrieval process can be decomposed by first taking multiple noninvariant inner products in parallel and then multiplying the inner products by the corresponding memories. A holographic process is not essential. Several associative memory models based on inner product have been proposed and demonstrated.

Liu *et al.* [9.21] demonstrated a procedure consisting of the following steps: (1) computation of the inner product of the input and each memory, (2) multiplication of each inner product by the corresponding memory, and (3) summation of these products over all of the memories to produce the final result. The associative memory output is obtained by thresholding the final result. If the output is not the associative memory, the output can be fed back as a new input until the process converges.

Since a correlation peak is proportional to the inner product, the method shown by Liu *et al.* is equivalent to the holographic method shown by Paek and Psaltis [9.22]. Paek and Psaltis's procedure is (1) take the correlation at the origin of the input and each memory, (2) multiply each correlation coefficient by the corresponding memory, which is equivalent to multiplying the Fourier-transform hologram of each memory by the corresponding correlation coefficient and reconstructing that weighted Fourier-transform hologram, and (3) sum the reconstructed holographic image over all the memories to produce the final result.

Although the methods just mentioned may approximate a biological neural process, many iteration steps might be required to make the output agree with the associative memory from a noisy input. Furthermore, a rarely available two-dimensional optical threshold is required. In practice, this problem can be eliminated by changing the order of thresholding and thus forming a noniterative association akin to the winner-take-all algorithm. Note that it may not be a pure imitation of a biological process, but it could be useful in some practical applications. The algorithm can be expressed as follows:

$$o(x, y) = m^k(x, y),$$

if

$$\iint m^k(x, y)i(x, y)\, dx\, dy \geq U, \qquad (9.4)$$

where $o(x, y)$ and $i(x, y)$ are the output and the input, respectively, $m^k(x, y)$ is the kth stored memory, and U is an arbitrary constant. This algorithm is similar to that of the symbolic substitution by correlation [9.23], and is similar to the method of controlled nonlinearity in the correlation domain proposed by Athale *et al.* [9.9], as well as to holographic associative memory [9.24].

Based on this algorithm, two operations are needed to obtain an associative memory $o(x, y)$: (1) compute the inner product of the input and each memory, and (2) if the inner product equals or exceeds the threshold, then the output is the corresponding memory.

Applying Parseval's theorem, it is apparent that the inner product of the input and memory in the space domain equals the inner product in the Fourier domain as follows:

$$\iint m^k(x, y)i(x, y)\, dx\, dy = \iint M^k(p, q)I(-p, -q)\, dp\, dq, \qquad (9.5)$$

where $M^k(p, q)$ and $I(p, q)$ are the Fourier spectra of $m^k(x, y)$ and $i(x, y)$, respectively. Substitution of Eq. 9.5 into Eq. 9.4 yields

$$o(x, y) = m^k(x, y)$$

if

$$\iint M^k(p, q)I(-p, -q)\, dp\, dq \geq U. \qquad (9.6)$$

In Eq. 9.4, $m^k(x, y)$ and $i(x, y)$ are always real and positive; however, their Fourier spectra may be complex and bipolar. Therefore, the realization of Eq. 9.6 is not trivial. In fact, the association can be alternatively performed based on the following condition:

$$\iint |M^k(p, q)|^2 |I(p, q)|^2\, dp\, dq \geq U', \qquad (9.7)$$

where U' is a proper threshold value.

Jutamulia *et al.* [9.25] have demonstrated that the left-hand side of Eq. 9.7 can be used for object identification and counting as follows:

$$\iint |M^k(p, q)|^2 |I(p, q)|^2\, dp\, dq = \{\mathcal{F}[|M^k|^2|I|^2]\}_{x=0, y=0}, \qquad (9.8)$$

where $\mathcal{F}$ stands for taking a Fourier transform. Equation 9.8 can be further manipulated to be

$$\{\mathcal{F}[(M^k I^*)(M^k I^*)^*]\}_{x=0,y=0} = \{[\mathcal{F}(M^k I^*)] \circledast [\mathcal{F}(M^k I^*)]\}_{x=0,y=0}$$
$$= \{[m^k \circledast i] \circledast [m^k \circledast i]\}_{x=0,y=0}, \quad (9.9)$$

where * and $\circledast$ indicate a complex conjugate and correlation, respectively. Equation 9.9 is the autocorrelation peak value (the autocorrelation peak is always at the origin) of $[m^k \circledast i]$, which is the correlation of $m^k(x, y)$ and $i(x, y)$. Equation 9.9 is proportional to the number of peaks from the first correlation ($m^k \circledast i$) that can be used for object identification and counting application [9.25], although information regarding the position of the first correlation peak is lost. Since Eq. 9.9 can be utilized to count specific objects, Eq. 9.7 can be used for pattern matching (i.e., counting a specific object to be either zero or one) for associative memory.

The alternate approach shown in Eq. 9.7 is as follows: (1) compute the inner product of the Fourier power spectra of the input and each memory, and (2) do the same as in the previous approach, only with a different threshold value.

The ET materials (see Section 5.11) can be employed as an incoherent spatial light modulator (also called *spatial light rebroadcaster* (SLR) by McAulay [9.26]) in an associative memory retrieval system. The absorption of blue photons by the ET materials results in the excitation and capture of electrons by electron traps in the ET materials. The trapped electrons are then removed by infrared illumination. The absorption of infrared photons by the ET materials stimulates the trapped electrons to return to their original ground state. The recombination produces orange light. The orange emission intensity is proportional to the product of the blue write-in intensity and infrared readout intensity. The ET materials, which have a large dynamic range, can be utilized as an analog multiplier to perform the intensity inner product.

The architecture for the space domain approach is given in Figure 9.3. A lenslet array generates multiple images from an input onto an ET device (SLR). To write a memory, the memory is placed at the input plane and illuminated using blue light. A mask is employed to select only one location on the ET device for a distinctive memory. The writing process is then repeated for the whole memory. The association is performed when an input is illuminated with infrared light. The multiple infrared images are incident onto the ET device. Consequently, orange light will be emitted from the ET device as the product of the input and individually stored memories. The orange emission integrated by another lenslet array represents the inner products of the input and the individual memories. A detector array is employed to convert the optical inner products to electronic signals that can be easily thresholded. The thresholded electronic signal will drive the corresponding LED and project an associative memory at the output plane. Note that the electronic thresholding scheme does not degrade the speed of the association,

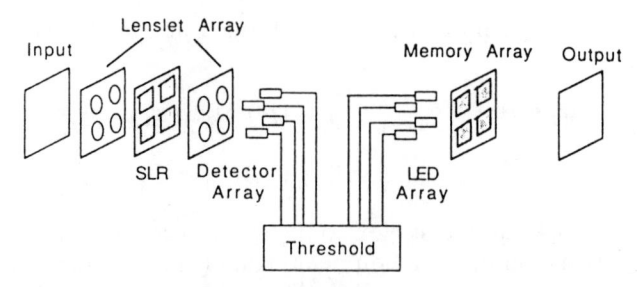

FIGURE 9.3 Hybrid electrooptical architecture for two-dimensional associative memories based on the inner product in the spatial domain.

because it is a fully parallel structure. An important point is that the number of electronic thresholds is the number of associative memories and not the huge number of neurons. Thus, the complexity introduced by electronic thresholding is still tolerable.

In the architecture of the Fourier domain approach, the input is displayed on a pixel-structured SLM, such as an LCTV or magnetooptic SLM (MOSLM). Under collimated coherent illumination, multiple Fourier spectra of the input are inherently generated at the focal plane of the Fourier-transform lens. To record a memory, the memory is displayed on the input screen and illuminated by collimated blue light. A mask is placed at the spectrum plane so that only one selected spectrum passes. The spectrum is then written into the ET device at that selected position. Other memories can be written following a similar procedure with a different selection of spectrum order.

To retrieve a memory, the input is illuminated with collimated coherent infrared light to generate multiple Fourier spectra. Each spectrum reads out a different memory in parallel at the ET device. The resultant emission is then integrated onto the detector by a lens of the lenslet array. Electronic thresholding is then performed in a similar manner to the architecture for the former approach. If the input is sufficiently matched with a memory—that is, the detected signal is higher than the threshold—the corresponding LED will be on, and the memory will be projected onto the output plane. Note that in order to keep the correct scale of the Fourier spectra, one must use lenses with different focal lengths or place the input at different distances behind the lens for the recording and retrieving process [9.27].

Preliminary experiments have been made [9.20]. The memory is stored in a 4-μm-thick ET thin film by exposure to blue light (488 nm) from an Ar laser. The input is projected with infrared light (1064 nm) from a YAG laser onto the ET thin film that generated orange light. The intensity of the orange emission is proportional to the product of the input and the memory. The integrated intensity is proportional to the inner product. The detected electronic signal is then thresholded. The thresholded signal will finally recall the associated memory by turning on the LED for that memory. These experimental data are shown in Figure 9.4.

OPTICAL ASSOCIATIVE MEMORY 347

Stored Memory	Input	Inner Product	Thresholded Signal	Output

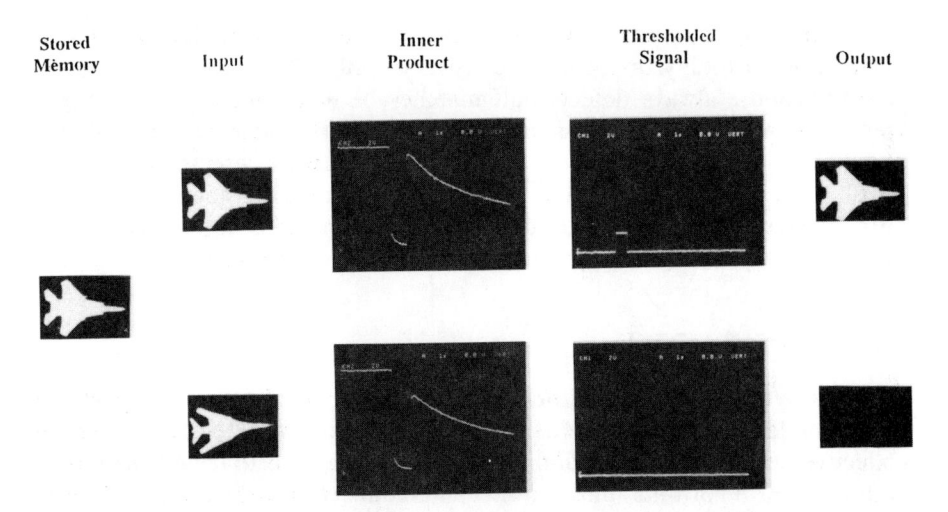

FIGURE 9.4 Experimental data of optical associative memory using ET thin film.

The signal from the detector consists of a peak whose height is proportional to the inner product. The lower curve at the left of the peak existed before the infrared input was incident onto the ET thin film. The exponential decay curve from the peak is due to the decay of the luminescent intensity of the ET thin film. It is obvious that the resolution and contrast of the output are independent of the input and the ET storage medium. Coherent noise is not present at the recalled output, since it is simply an incoherent projection of a high-quality picture, not a holographic reconstruction.

There are two basic matching schemes, namely, XNOR and AND. In Boolean algebra, it is known that

$$A \text{ XNOR } B = (A \text{ AND } B) \text{ OR } (\overline{A} \text{ AND } \overline{B}), \qquad (9.10)$$

where $\overline{A}$ and $\overline{B}$ are the negation of A and B, respectively. This will result in different inner-product calculations, so that the AND scheme performs only half of the matching performed in the XNOR scheme. However, the essence of the information is not reduced since $(\overline{A} \text{ AND } \overline{B})$ and $(A \text{ AND } B)$ are not independent.

In fact, these two matching schemes based on XNOR and AND functions should be applied in different circumstances. For symbolic computation in which "0" is a piece of information as well as "1," the XNOR matching scheme is applied. However, for two-dimensional associative memory in imaging and object recognition, the AND (multiplicative) matching scheme is preferred. In the XNOR scheme, the match between "0" of the background in a memory scene with "0" of the background in an input scene contributes positively to the inner product. This contribution is generally not required for associative imaging memories to obtain a high ratio between auto-inner-product and cross-inner-product.

In a real-world situation, when the input pattern is just a uniform distribution (i.e., a totally bright input consists of only "1"s), the space domain XNOR scheme always detects half matches between input and all stored memories, provided that the memory consists of the same number of "1"s and "0"s. On the other hand, the AND scheme always detects full matches for all memories. Consequently, the whole memory is considered an associative memory. However, the Fourier domain approach is not subject to this drawback, because it simply blocks the intense dc component.

9.3 HOPFIELD MODEL

A neural network is a large information-processing architecture composed of many simple processing elements interconnected in parallel to achieve certain collective computational capabilities. The essence of neural networks is to embed serial algorithms into parallel interconnected architectures. Consequently, a neural net will provide faster (due to a shorter algorithm) and more accurate (due to a distributed structure) computations when compared to serial computers. Neural networks are especially useful for optimization, association, and recognition.

A neural network consists of interconnections and nonlinear thresholdings. A high-density interconnection could be implemented with optics, and supplementary electronics may perform the thresholding. A neural network model is basically represented by a matrix–vector multiplication that provides the required outer product. The matrix–vector multiplication can be easily performed optically employing two orthogonal cylindrical lenses (see Section 8.8), where the vector and matrix represent a one-dimensional input and an interconnection weight function, respectively.

An associative memory is considered a fundamental neural network. A complete or partial image of a known input recalls a predetermined associative output. An associative memory is recalled by linking the outer product of the input and the distributed memory. If the input is a one-dimensional vector, the distributed memory is then a two-dimensional matrix. If only one set of orthogonal vectors can exist, an arbitrary input (a member of the orthogonal set) will associate with only one predetermined output, and the cross talk is zero. When the input vector is a slightly distorted memory (i.e., not a member of the orthogonal set), the desired output cannot be retrieved, the output will be a linear combination of several associative memories that is unrecognized.

Regarding this problem, Hopfield [9.2] proposed a mathematical model wherein the desired output can be retrieved from a distorted input after several nonlinear iterations. The Hopfield model states that an associative memory retrieval process is equivalent to an iterative thresholded matrix–vector outer product expressed as follows:

$$\begin{aligned} \mathbf{V}_i &\to 1 \quad \text{if} \quad \sum_{j=1}^{N} \mathbf{T}_{ij} \mathbf{V}_j \geq 0, \\ \mathbf{V}_i &\to 0 \quad \phantom{\text{if} \quad \sum_{j=1}^{N} \mathbf{T}_{ij} \mathbf{V}_j} < 0, \end{aligned} \quad (9.11)$$

where V_i is the binary output and V_j is the binary input. This process is repeated by using the previous output as the new input, until the output is the same as the input. In other words, the iterative process converges on the associative memory. The interconnection matrix T_{ij} is defined by the following supervised learning:

$$\begin{aligned} T_{ij} &= \sum_{m=1}^{M} (2V_i^m - 1)(2V_j^m - 1), & \text{for } i \neq j, \\ &= 0, & \text{for } i = j, \end{aligned} \qquad (9.12)$$

where V_i^m and V_j^m (whose values are either 1 or 0) are the ith and jth elements of the mth binary memory vector V^m. Note that the interconnection matrix T_{ij} is differerently formulated if the elements of the binary vector are defined either 1 or -1 (instead of 1 or 0).

Because the memory is distributed in the interconnection matrix, many other memories can be overlaid in the same interconnection matrix. It is only necessary to calculate the interconnection separately for each memory and add each to the interconnection to the memories already in storage. However, problems arise if memories are too numerous. The number of memory vectors that can be stored effectively is only about 15 percent of the number of neurons in a layer.

The features of the Hopfield model are (1) it is based on an outer-product operation, (2) the interconnection matrix is determined by the supervised learning rule expressed in Eq. 9.12, (3) it involves a nonlinear threshold function, (4) the desired output from a distorted or incomplete input can be obtained after some iterations, and (5) the interconnection matrix does not necessarily change after a noniterative learning. The most important merit of the model is that it correctly recognizes and associates distorted or partial input signals. However, the required iterations may slow down the signal-processing time.

In addition to various electronic implementations, the first optoelectronic neural network was proposed by Farhat et al. [9.7], in which a crossbar architecture (see Figure 8.29) is used to carry out the matrix–vector multiplication operations for implementing the Hopfield model. In their proposed architecture, an LED array representing the input vector illuminates the SLM that represents the interconnection weight matrix (IWM) that results in the matrix–vector multiplication. The output vector is then detected by a photodiode array for amplification and thresholding before returning for the next iteration. For a two-dimensional input, which is no longer a vector but a matrix, Farhat and Psaltis [9.12] used a two-dimensional array as an input feature composer, interconnecting it with a synaptic mask by a lenslet array, as shown in Figure 9.5. The array of interconnective signals can be picked up by a photoconductor array. By electronically summing this array of signals and then thresholding, the signal can be fed back for the next iteration. After Farhat and Psaltis, many optical architectures for the Hopfield model have

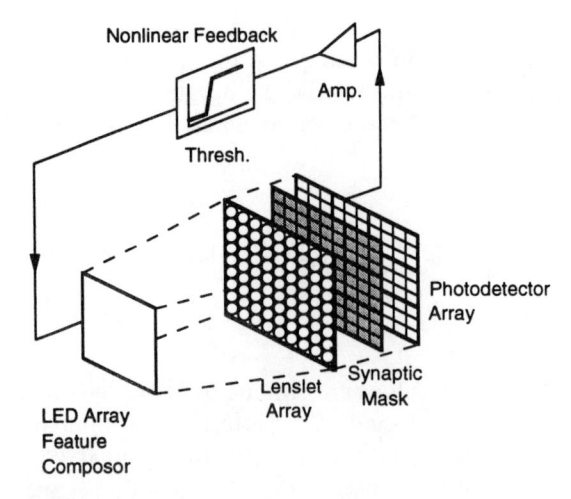

FIGURE 9.5 Two-dimensional optical neural network.

been reported, among them an implementation using an ET thin film to represent the IWM [9.28].

9.4 BACK-PROPAGATION MODEL

The Hopfield model mentioned earlier is useful for associative memory, however it cannot be used for complex computations. A classic example is that of an XOR gate that cannot be implemented by a simple input–output layer network [9.29]. This can also be understood from the view point of fundamental logic processing [9.30]. A neuron is exactly the same with a threshold logic gate that performs sum-of-weighted-product and thresholding. The AND and OR are vertex gates; thus, they can be easily realized using threshold logic gates. However, the XOR gate cannot be realized using a single threshold logic gate. This suggests that a neuron cannot perform the XOR operation. However, multilayer neural networks are able to perform XOR or other complex computational tasks.

It should not be difficult to determine the interconnection for an input-output network when the values or states of the input and the output are known. However, it would be very difficult to determine the interconnections between layers in a multilayer network, provided that only the states of the input and output layers were known. Regarding this problem, Rumelhart *et al.* [9.29] have proposed the back-propagation method.

This method is applied to the formation of correct interconnections for hidden layers in a multilayer network. To generate interconnections for known input–output pairs, random interconnections are assigned as the starting point. During the first phase the input is presented and propagated forward through the multilayer network to compute the output. This actual output is then compared with the desired output, resulting in an error signal. The second phase involves a backward pass through the network during which the error signal is passed to each layer in the network and the appropriate weight changes are made.

The outer product for multilayer neural networks is given as follows:

$$n_j = \sum_i w_{ji} o_i, \tag{9.13}$$

where n_j is the output before a nonlinear transformation, w_{ji} is the weight of the interconnection, and o_i is the output of the previous layer (*i*th layer). The output for that layer (*j*th layer) is

$$o_j = f_j(n_j), \tag{9.14}$$

where f_j is a differentiable and nondecreasing response function for a nonlinear transformation. Notice that the hard threshold function is not differentiable. The output expressed in Eq. 9.14 then becomes the input for the next layer, as expressed in Eq. 9.13. This computation is continued until the final output is obtained. Since the final output from this actual computation may not be the same as the desired output, the interconnections between layers will have to be corrected.

The rule for changing weights is

$$\Delta w_{ji} = \eta \delta_j o_i, \tag{9.15}$$

where Δw_{ji} is the change to be made to the weight from the *i*th to the *j*th unit, η is a constant called the *learning rate*, and o_i is the *i*th element of the input vector. The error signal for the last layer is

$$\delta_j = (t_j - o_j) f_j'(n_j), \tag{9.16}$$

where t_j and o_j are the desired (target or teacher) and actual outputs, respectively, and $f_j'(n_j)$ is a derivative of the nonlinear response function. Whenever the layer is not the output layer, the error signal is computed as follows:

$$\delta_j = f_j'(n_j) \sum_k \delta_k w_{kj}, \tag{9.17}$$

where the *j*th layer is prior to the *k*th layer in the forward direction. This propagates the error back one layer, and the same process can be repeated for every layer. An example of f_j is given by

$$f_j(n_j) = o_j = \frac{1}{1 + \exp[-(n_j + \theta_j)]}, \tag{9.18}$$

where θ_j is a bias. Thus the derivative becomes

$$f'_j(n_j) = \frac{\partial o_j}{\partial n_j} = o_j(1 - o_j). \tag{9.19}$$

Assume that we have a neural network (input, output, and a hidden layer) and a pair of input–outputs supervised learning is provided. The training algorithm used is given by

Step 1: Set w_{ji} (IWM of input and hidden layers) and w_{kj} (IWM of hidden and output layers), θ_j and θ_k to small random values.
Step 2: Determine learning rate η and error limit E.
Step 3: Input the known input o_i.
Step 4: Compute $n_j = \Sigma_i w_{ji} o_i$.
Step 5: Compute $o_j = 1/\{1 + \exp[-(n_j + \theta_j)]\}$.
Step 6: Compute $n_k = \Sigma_j w_{kj} o_j$.
Step 7: Compute $o_k = 1/\{1 + \exp[-(n_k + \theta_k)]\}$.
Step 8: Compute error $e_k = t_k - o_k$, where t_k is the desired output.
Step 9: Compute $\delta_k = e_k o_k (1 - o_k)$.
Step 10: Compute $\Delta w_{kj} = \eta \delta_k o_j$.
Step 11: Compute $\delta_j = o_j(1 - o_j) \Sigma_k \delta_k w_{kj}$.
Step 12: Compute $\Delta w_{ji} = \eta \delta_j o_i$.
Step 13: Correct IWMs:

$$w_{ji}^{\text{new}} = w_{ji}^{\text{old}} + \Delta w_{ji},$$
$$w_{kj}^{\text{new}} = w_{kj}^{\text{old}} + \Delta w_{kj}.$$

Step 14: Repeat the process from step 3 until e_k is smaller than E.

The features of the back-propagation model are (1) the interconnection is formed after an iterative error correction process (the consequence is that no specific explicit algorithms is needed to write a program as long as the input–output pair is known); and (2) after the correct interconnection is formed, the computation can be performed in one step.

Optical implementation for back-propagation neural network was discussed by Psaltis *et al.* [9.31]. They proposed an architecture using a photorefractive crystal for the implementation of the IWMs; thus, the IWMs could be corrected or changed optically. The feedforward and back-propagation networks were physically the same network. However, no single SLM has the characteristics of both transfer functions required by steps 7 and 11 for the feedforward and back-propagation signals, respectively. A hybrid electrooptic system should be relatively easy to implement for the back-propagation neural network.

Among the various applications, Gorman and Sejnowski [9.32] have used the back-propagation learning algorithm to train the neural network to classify sonar returns from an undersea metal cylinder and a cylindrical-shaped rock of comparable size.

9.5 AN ADAPTIVE OPTICAL NEURAL NETWORK

In recent years attention has been drawn to the problems of optical implementation of neural networks. Recently, a two-dimensional optical neural network was proposed by Farhat and Psaltis, for which they used the basic concept of a matrix–vector optical processor [9.12]. They used a linear array of LEDs as an input feature composer, which is interconnected to a synaptic mask by a lenslet array. To provide the network with self-organization and learning capabilities, a fine-resolution programmable SLM with a large number of distinguishable gray levels was needed for the generation of the IWM. However, currently available SLMs have relatively small space–bandwidth product and very limited gray levels, which makes it difficult to implement such an optical neural network. In addition, the interconnective part of the iterative equation has to be either electronically added or used as an array of light integrating elements, which would either slow down the operation or pose severe optical alignment problem. In this section, we describe a hybrid-optical architecture that alleviates these disadvantages. First we illustrate the architecture using a high-resolution video monitor to display the IWM [9.10], [9.33], as shown in Figure 9.6. The architecture has the advantage of providing the incoherent light source, and of alleviating the constraints of the low resolution and dynamic range of the SLM. Use of the video monitor has, however, other disadvantages; for example, its physical size makes the system rather large, and the curvature of the monitor screen causes some alignment problems. To eliminate these problems, we have developed a compact optical neural network using *inexpensive* pocket-sized liquid-crystal televisions (LCTVs) [9.11], as shown in Figure 9.7.

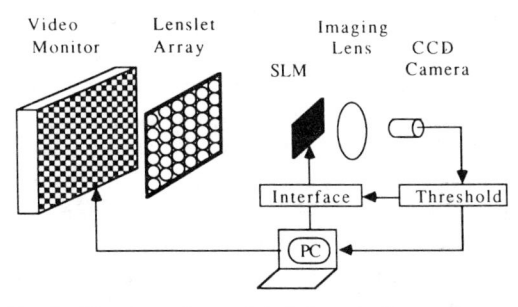

FIGURE 9.6 Schematic diagram of an adaptive optical neural network using a video monitor.

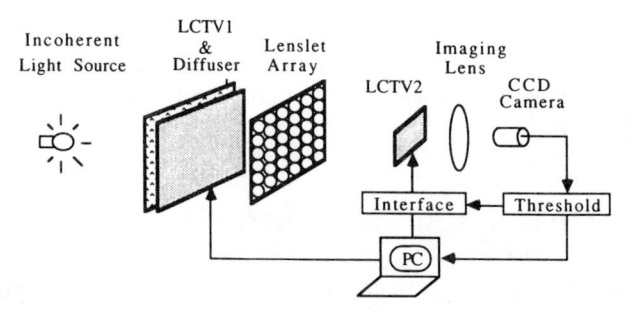

FIGURE 9.7 Schematic diagram of an LCTV optical neural network.

Mention must be made of the major differences of this architecture compared to the matrix–vector processor of Farhat and Psaltis. These are that the positions of the input feature composer and the synaptic mask been exchanged, so that the IWM is generated by the LCTV. In addition, this optical arrangement allows the summation of the interconnectivity between the input vector and the IWM to be performed purely by optics.

Generally speaking, an N-neuron network requires up to N^2 interconnections. It is apparent that, for a two-dimensional $N \times N$ neuron network, the iterative equation suggested by Hopfield (see Section 9.3) can be extended:

$$v_{lk}(n+1) = f\left[\sum_{i=1}^{N}\sum_{j=1}^{N} \mathbf{T}_{lkij} v_{ij}(n)\right], \qquad (9.20)$$

where v_{lk} represents the state of the lkth neuron in an $N \times N$ space and $\mathbf{T}_{lkij}$ is a four-dimensional interconnection weight matrix. Note that the matrix $\mathbf{T}$ can be partitioned into an array of two-dimensional submatrices $\mathbf{T}_{11ij}$, $\mathbf{T}_{12ij}$, ..., $\mathbf{T}_{NNij}$, in which each submatrix is of $N \times N$ size. Thus we see that a four-dimensional associative memory matrix can be displayed as an $N^2 \times N^2$ two-dimensional array representation, as shown in Figure 9.8.

In recent developments of the LCTV, the imaging quality has been reported to be close to that of the commercially available high-resolution video monitors. For instance, the contrast ratio of a recent LCTV, with built-in thin-film transistors, was higher than 30:1, and the dynamic range was approximately 16 gray levels, which can be continuously adjusted. We have developed the an optical architecture using an Hitachi Model C5-LC1 5-in. (12.7-cm) color LCTV to display the IWM and a Seiko Model LVD-202 2.7-in. (6.9-cm) color LCTV to display the input patterns. The resolutions of these LCTVs are 256×420 pixels and 220×330 pixels, respectively.

A diagram of a compact LCTV optical neural network is shown in Figure 9.7. A neural network with $8 \times 8 = 64$ fully interconnected neurons was recently built, with an 80-W xenon-arc lamp as the incoherent light source. In the present architecture, the Hitachi LCTV (LCTV1) is used for the gen-

AN ADEQUATE OPTICAL NEURAL NETWORK   355

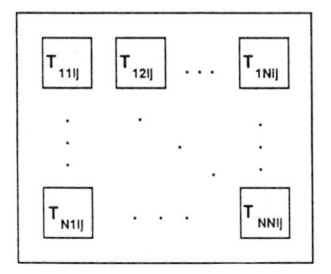

FIGURE 9.8 Partition of a four-dimensional weight matrix T_{lkij} into an array of T_{11ij}, T_{12ij}, ... T_{NNij} submatrices.

eration of the IWM, which consists of an 8×8 array of submatrices, with each submatrix having 8×8 elements. This IWM is then displayed on a fine diffuser immediately behind LCTV1. The Seiko LCTV (LCTV2) is used as an input device for the generation of the input patterns. The lenslet array, which consists of 8×8 lenses, provides the interconnections between the IWM and the input pattern. Each lens of the lenslet array images each of the IWM submatrices onto the input LCTV2 to establish the proper interconnections. Thus we see that the input matrix (i.e., LCTV2) is superimposed onto and multiplied (or interconnected) by all the IWM submatrices. This represents the connective part of Eq. 9.20, that is,

$$\sum_{i=1}^{N} \sum_{j=1}^{N} T_{lkij} v_{ij}(n). \tag{9.21}$$

The transmitted light field behind the LCTV2 is collected by the imaging lens, focused at the lenslet array, and imaged onto a charge-coupled-device (CCD) array detector, as illustrated in Figure 9.9. The signals collected by the CCD camera are then sent to a thresholding circuit, and the final results are fed back to the LCTV2 for a second iteration. Note that the data flow in the optical system is controlled primarily by a microcomputer (PC). For instance, the IWMs and the input patterns can be written onto the LCTV1 and the LCTV2 through the PC, and the PC can also make decisions based

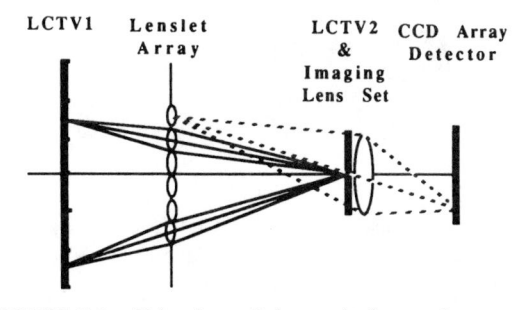

FIGURE 9.9 Side view of the optical neural network.

on the output results of the neural network. Thus the proposed LCTV optical neural network is indeed a programmable and *adaptive* neural network.

We now illustrate an image reconstruction process based on the system just described. With reference to the Hopfield model, four Roman letters, A, B, W, and X, are stored in the memory matrix **T**. Each letter occupies an 8×8 array pixel, as shown in Figure 9.10a. The positive and negative parts of the memory matrix **T** are shown in Figures 9.10b and c, respectively. As depicted in Figure 9.10d a partial image of A is fed to the input SLM. By sequentially displaying the positive and negative parts of the memory matrix on the LCTV1, the output signal arrays can be picked up by the CCD detector and then sent to the microcomputer for subtraction and thresholding operations. A partially recovered pattern is obtained at the output end, as shown in the middle of Figure 9.10d. Since the output pattern is not complete, it is fed back to the input SLM for the next iteration. A more completely recovered pattern is obtained as shown on the right-hand side of Figure 9.10d. Needless to say, the positive and negative parts of IWM can be added with a bias level to avoid the negative quantity, for which a single-step operation can be achieved.

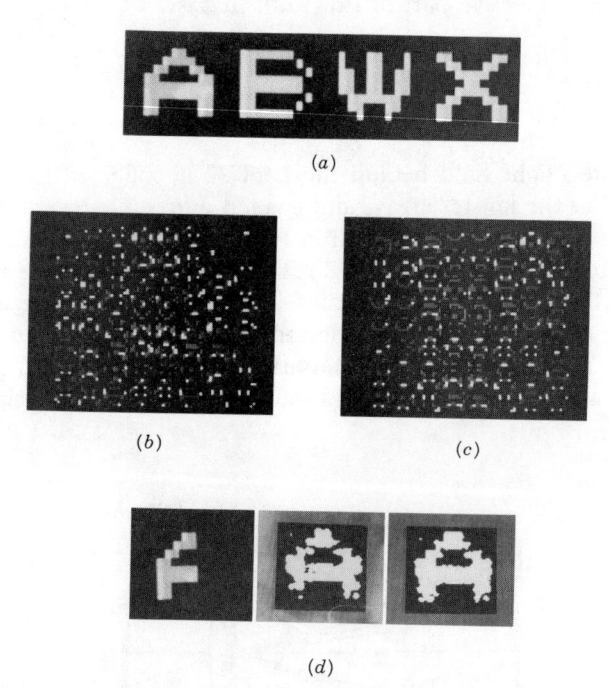

FIGURE 9.10 Experimental results of the Hopfield model. (*a*) Training set. (*b*) and (*c*) Positive and negative weight matrices, respectively. (*d*) Reconstruction using the optical neural network.

9.6 ORTHOGONAL PROJECTION ALGORITHM

The error-correction ability of the Hopfield model is effective when we assume that the stored vectors are significantly different, and its correction ability decreases rapidly as the number of stored patterns increases. To obtain the desired results, the number of vectors **M** stored in the Hopfield model should be significantly smaller than the number of neurons in the network, as pointed out by McEliece *et al.* [9.34], that is, **M** < $N/4 \ln N$. In practice, however, the stored vectors are generally not independent, which produces ambiguous output results.

We note that orthogonization techniques have been used in associative memory and digital image processing [9.3]. In this section, we use the orthogonal projection (OP) algorithm to improve the error-correction ability of the optical neural network, as described below.

Let us consider an N-dimensional vector space consisting of a set of **M** vectors $\mathbf{V}^{(m)}$, which are used to construct an interconnection weight matrix **T**. The basic concept of the OP algorithm is to project each vector $\mathbf{V}^{(m_0)}$ within the vector set $\{\mathbf{V}^{(m)}\}$ onto the orthogonal subspace spanned by the independent vectors $\mathbf{V}^{*(m)}$, $m = 1, 2, \ldots, m_0 - 1$. The orthogonal projection vector can be described by the Gram-Schmidt orthogonalization procedure [9.35] as

$$\mathbf{V}^{*(m_0)} = \mathbf{V}^{(m_0)} - \sum_{m=1}^{m_0-1} \frac{[\mathbf{V}^{(m)}, \mathbf{V}^{*(m)}]}{\|\mathbf{V}^{*(m)}\|} \mathbf{V}^{*(m)}, \qquad (9.22)$$

where $[\mathbf{V}^{(m)}, \mathbf{V}^{*(m)}]$ denotes the inner product, and $\|\mathbf{V}^{*(m)}\|$ is the norm of $\mathbf{V}^{*(m)}$.

Hence, for a given matrix $\mathbf{T}^{(m-1)}$, the recursive algorithm for the associative memory matrix $\mathbf{T}^{(m)}$ can be expressed as

$$\mathbf{T}^{(m)} = \begin{cases} \mathbf{T}^{(m-1)} + [\mathbf{U}^{(m)} - \mathbf{T}^{(m-1)}\mathbf{V}^{(m)}] \dfrac{\mathbf{V}^{*(m)T}}{\|\mathbf{V}^{*(m)}\|}, & \text{for } \|\mathbf{V}^{*(m)}\| \neq 0, \\ \mathbf{T}^{(m-1)}, & \text{otherwise,} \end{cases}$$

(9.23)

where $\mathbf{U}^{(m)}$ stands for the desired output vector, and the initial memory matrix $\mathbf{T}^{(0)}$ can be either zero or an identity matrix.

Using the OP algorithm described earlier, we can conduct computer simulations of the proposed optical neural network; the result is shown in Figure 9.11. Note that four Roman letters, shown in Figure 9.10*a*, are used for the reference patterns. Applying Eqs. 9.22 and 9.23, we construct the associative memory matrix T; the positive and negative parts of T are shown in Figures 9.11*a* and *b*. The reconstructions of a partial pattern of A using the OP and Hopfield models are shown in Figures 9.11*c* and *d*, respectively. The successive patterns in these figures represent the successive iterations. Thus we see

358 OPTICAL NEURAL NETWORKS

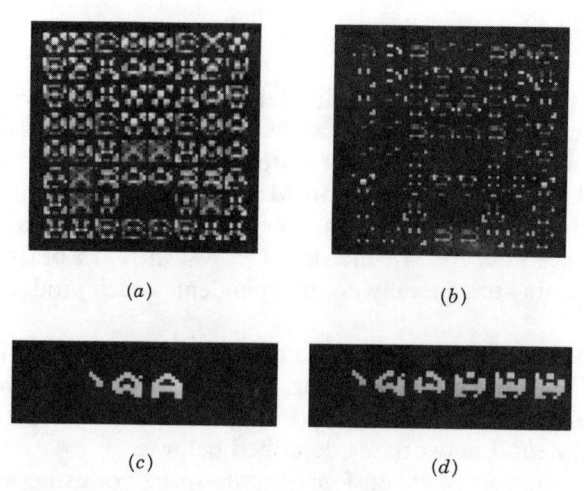

FIGURE 9.11 (a) and (b) Positive and negative weight matrices using the OP algorithm. (c) Reconstruction using the OP algorithm. (d) Reconstruction using the Hopfield model.

that the OP algorithm is more robust and has a higher convergent speed when compared to the Hopfield model. Furthermore, in this example, the OP algorithm requires only two iterative operations to obtain the correct result (Figure 9.11c). In contrast, the Hopfield model converges into a local minimum, which gives an incorrect result (Figure 9.11d).

The numerical analysis of the robustness of an 8 × 8-neuron single-layer neural network is evaluated. Twenty-six Roman letters are used as the reference patterns, each occupying an 8 × 8-pixel array. The average Hamming distance of the reference patterns is about 26 pixels, and the minimum distance is 4 pixels. We assume that the input patterns are embedded in random noise, where the input SNRs are chosen to be about 5 dB (i.e., 50 percent noise), 7 dB (i.e., 33 percent noise), and 10 dB (i.e., 10 percent noise), respectively. Figure 9.12 graphs the output error pixels against the number of stored patterns for various values of input SNRs. From this figure we see that using the Hopfield model the neural network becomes unstable after storing five reference patterns. However, using the OP algorithm, the neural network can retrieve all the letters with 50 percent input noise. We also note that the error-correction ability decreases substantially as input noise and the number of stored patterns increase. Even so, the OP algorithm still provides better error-correction capability.

9.7 MULTILEVEL RECOGNITION ALGORITHM

For the case of an ill-conditioned weight matrix, the Hamming distances between the stored vectors are very short, which may result in incorrect

MULTILEVEL RECOGNITION ALGORITHM 359

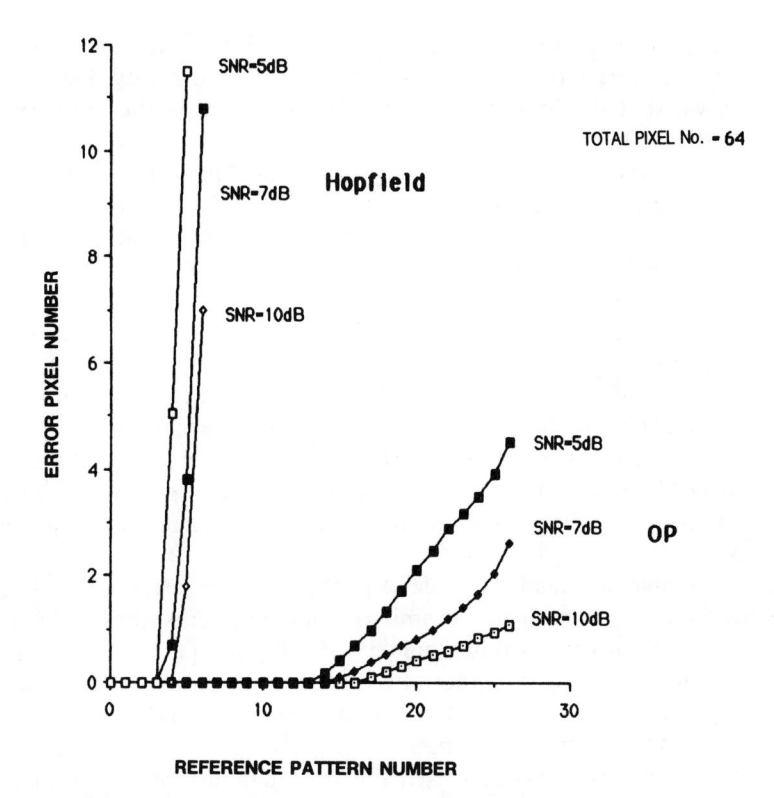

FIGURE 9.12 Performance of the Hopfield and the OP models.

results. For example, four Roman letters, T, I, O, and G, are stored in the associative memory matrix, as shown in Figure 9.13a. Although the input partial image of G contains the main features, the Hopfield neural network fails to reproduce the pattern, which results in the output falling into a local minima, as shown in Figure 9.13b. We note that, in some cases, the output would not converge to the correct result, even when the input is exactly the same as one of the reference patterns. In other words, the Hopfield model is effective only in dealing with independent patterns.

FIGURE 9.13 (a) Four Roman letters stored in the memory mask. (b) Obtained by the Hopfield model.

From the preceding example we see that the smaller the Hamming distances among the stored patterns, the less the error-correction ability. However, it is also known that the less information there is stored in the memory, the more effectively the neural network can correct the error. Using the advantages of the programmability of the proposed optical neural network, a multilevel recognition (MR) algorithm is developed. This algorithm adopts the *tree search strategy*, which increases the error-correction ability by reducing the number of vectors stored in each memory matrix [9.36]. The MR algorithm first classifies the reference patterns into subgroups and then develops a tree structure according to the similarity (i.e., Hamming distance) of the reference patterns. A smaller number of reference patterns can be stored in the memory matrix built for each subgroup. The MR algorithm then changes the memory matrices with reference to the Hamming distances between the intermediate result and the patterns in different subgroups. In this manner, the storage capacity is not limited by the size of the neural network. However, the tradeoff is that the processing speed is slowed due to changes in the memory matrices.

As an example, we again consider the four Roman letters shown in the preceding figure. According to the similarity of the patterns, these four letters can be classified into two groups, namely, [O, G] and [T, I]. Letters T and O are arbitrarily selected from these two subgroups to form a root group [T, O], as shown in Figure 9.14a. Instead of constructing an associative memory matrix T_{TIOG}, three submemory matrices, T_{TO}, T_{OG}, and T_{TI}, are composed and stored in the microcomputer. In the first demonstration, the memory matrix T_{OT} is displayed on the LCTV1 and an input vector V', which represents the partial image of G, is presented on the input LCTV2 of the system. After converging to a stable state, the output vector V^* is compared using

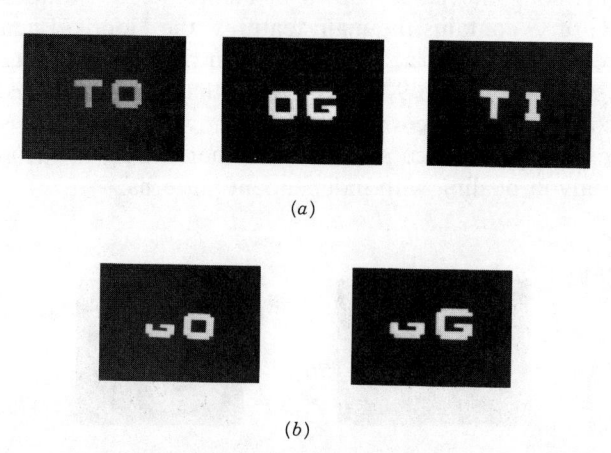

FIGURE 9.14 (*a*) The three subgroups of letters used in the MR algorithm. (*b*) Reconstruction of the letter G by T_{TO} and T_{OG}, respectively.

V'=G

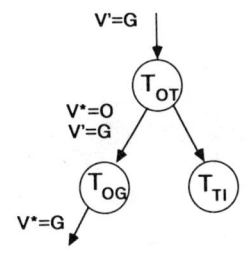

V*=O
V'=G

T_{OT}

T_{OG} T_{TI}

V*=G

FIGURE 9.15 Flowchart diagram of the MR algorithm.

the Hamming distance as the criterion of comparison with the stored vectors O and T. If the Hamming distance between the vectors $\mathbf{V}^*$ and O is shorter than that of T, the memory matrix T_{OG} will be used to replace the matrix T_{OT}. Afterward, the input vector $\mathbf{V}^*$ is fed into the network for a new round of iteration, in which the letter G is retrieved as shown in Figure 9.14b. A flowchart diagram to illustrate this tree search operation is given in Figure 9.15.

9.8 INTERPATTERN ASSOCIATION MODEL

Neural networks have been shown to be effective in pattern recognition. For recognition of a given set of reference patterns, there are two schemes to construct the associative memory matrix (i.e., IWM). The first is the so-called *intrapattern association*, which emphasizes the association of elements within each reference pattern. For example, in the Hopfield model, the outer products of the reference patterns are added to form the interconnection weight matrix. This type of approach may create an unstable or ill-conditioned network if the reference patterns are not independent of each other. The second scheme is an *interpattern association* (IPA), wherein the interconnection weight matrix is constructed by emphasizing the association between reference patterns. Where the reference patterns are similar to each other (e.g., human faces, fingerprints, handwriting characteristics), the special features of each pattern become very important in pattern recognition. Therefore, in constructing the interconnection weight matrix [9.37], it is necessary to consider the relationships between the special and common features among the reference patterns.

For example, a set of three overlapping patterns A, B, and C are situated in a pattern space, as illustrated in Figure 9.16. These patterns can be divided into seven subspaces: I, II, and III are the special subspaces of patterns A, B, and C, respectively; IV, V, and VI are the common subspaces of A and B, B and C, C and A, respectively; VII is the common subspace of A, B, and C. The rest can be defined as an empty set Ø. These subspaces can be expressed by the following logic functions: $\wedge$, $\vee$, and $\overline{}$, which stand for

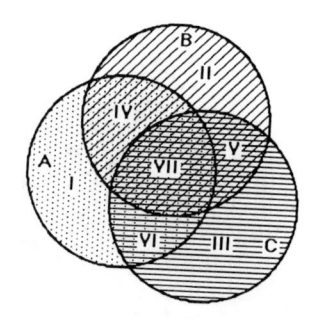

FIGURE 9.16 Common and special subspaces of three reference patterns.

the logic AND, OR, and NOT operations,

$$\text{I} = A \wedge \overline{(B \vee C)},$$
$$\text{II} = B \wedge \overline{(A \vee C)},$$
$$\text{III} = C \wedge \overline{(A \vee B)},$$
$$\text{IV} = (A \wedge B) \wedge \overline{C},$$
$$\text{V} = (B \wedge C) \wedge \overline{A},$$
$$\text{VI} = (C \wedge A) \wedge \overline{B},$$
$$\text{VII} = (A \wedge B \wedge C) \wedge \overline{\emptyset}, \qquad (9.24)$$

respectively.

We can now start building the interconnections between the input and the output neurons, using this set of logic functions to determine the excitory, the inhibitory, and the null interconnections. For instance, if an input neutron in area VII is "on," it can only excite the output neurons within subspace VII and have no connection with the output neurons in the other subspaces. On the other hand, if an input neuron in V is "on," it will excite the output neurons in V and VII, but inhibit the output neurons in I; similarly for input neurons in IV or VI. Furthermore, if an input neuron is "on" in I, it will excite all the output neurons in pattern A (i.e., I, IV, VI, and VII), but inhibit the output neurons in $(B \vee C) \wedge \overline{A}$ (i.e., areas II, III, and V); similarly for the other subspaces.

By using the *principles of induction*, the logic function rule can be extended to M reference patterns, such as

$$X = P \wedge \overline{Q}, \qquad (9.25)$$

where

$$P = p_1 \wedge p_2 \wedge \cdots \wedge p_n,$$
$$Q = q_1 \vee q_2 \vee \cdots \vee q_m.$$

Here $p_1, p_2, \ldots, p_m$ and $q_1, q_2, \ldots, q_m$ are reference patterns, and $n + m = M$ is the total number of reference patterns. The input neurons in area X must excite (i.e., having positive connections with) all the output neurons in area P, inhibit (i.e., having negative connections with) all output neurons in area $Q \wedge \overline{P'}$, where P' is defined by

$$P' = p_1 \vee p_2 \vee \cdots \vee p_n, \tag{9.26}$$

and have no connection with the output neurons in the remaining areas. For simplicity, the connection strengths (i.e., weights) are defined as 1 for positive connections, -1 for negative connections, and 0 for no connection. Thus the IPA neural network can be constructed in a simple *three-state* structure.

To further illustrate the construction of the IPA model, A, B, and C are assumed to be the three 2×2 array patterns shown in Figure 9.17a. The pixel–pattern relationship is given in Table 9.1. It is apparent that pixel 1 represents the common feature of A, B, and C, pixel 2 is the common feature of A and B, pixel 3 is the common feature of A and C, and pixel 4 represents the special feature of C.

By applying the preceding logic operations [9.24], a tristate interconnection neural network can be constructed, as illustrated in Figure 9.17b. This is a one-layer neural network with four input neurons and four output neurons. Each neuron is matched to one pixel of the reference patterns. For example, the first input neurons corresponds to pixel 1 of the input pattern, and excites only the first output neuron. The second input neuron (the corresponding pixel belongs to patterns A and B) excites both the first and second output

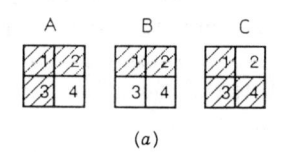

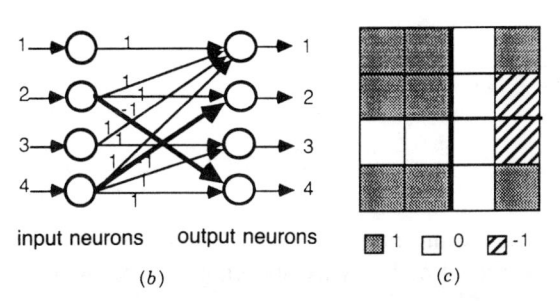

FIGURE 9.17 Example of the construction of an IPA neural network. (*a*) Three reference patterns. (*b*) One-layer neural net. (*c*) Interconnection weight matrix.

364   OPTICAL NEURAL NETWORKS

TABLE 9.1. Pixel–Pattern Relationship of Three Reference Patterns

Pattern \ Pixel	1	2	3	4
A	1	1	1	0
B	1	1	0	0
C	1	0	1	1

neurons, while inhibiting the fourth output neuron, which belongs to the special subspace of pattern C.

We can now partition the four-dimensional IWM into a two-dimensional submatrix array, as illustrated in Figure 9.17c. The IWM can be divided into four blocks, in which each block corresponds to one output neuron. The four elements in one block represent the four neurons at the input end. For example, since all four elements in the upper-left block have a value of 1, either one of the four input neurons can excite the first output neuron. As another example, the first and third elements in the upper-right block are 0, the second element has a value of 1, and the fourth element is -1. From this example we can determine that the first and third input neurons have no connection to the second output neuron, the second input neuron excites the second output neuron, and the fourth input neuron inhibits the second output neuron.

To simplify the logic operations, an *equivalent rule* is developed as follows. This rule can be used to construct the IWM by examining the pixel–pattern relationships. We stress that these rules for IWMs are simple and straightforward, which is suitable for computer calculations. Let us define $D_{l,i}$ as a two-dimensional matrix that corresponds to the two-dimensional array in Table 9.1, where l and i denote the row and column numbers. If we let d_i be the number of patterns that are in state 1 at the ith pixel, then we can determine by summing the elements in the ith column of Table 9.1, that is,

$$d_i = \sum_{l=1}^{M} D_{l,i}. \qquad (9.27)$$

Let us also define k_{ij}:

$$k_{ij} = \sum_{l=1}^{M} D_{l,i} D_{l,j}, \qquad (9.28)$$

which is the sum of the product of columns i and j in Table 9.1. Then we can construct an IPA neural network by applying the following logical rules:

1. If $k_{ij} = \min(d_i, d_j)$,

when $d_i < d_j$, pixel i must excite pixel j, but pixel j must not excite pixel i;

when $d_i = d_j$, pixels i and j must excite each other;

when $d_i > d_j$, pixel j must excite pixel i, but pixel i must not excite pixel j;

2. If $0 < k_{ij} < \min(d_i, d_j)$, pixels i and j have no connection to each other.
3. If $k_{ij} = 0$,

when $d_i \neq 0$ and $d_j \neq 0$, pixels i and j must have no connection to each other.

It is the differences rather than the similarities among patterns that are used for pattern recognition. Just as in some other neural network algorithms, the Hopfield model constructs the IWM by correlating the elements within each pattern, though it ignores the relationships among the reference patterns. For example, the IWM **T** of the Hopfield model for three reference patterns A, B, and C can generally be expressed as

$$\mathbf{T} = \mathbf{AA}^T + \mathbf{BB}^T + \mathbf{CC}^T, \tag{9.29}$$

where superscript T represents the transpose of the vectors.

If input pattern A is applied to the neural system, the output would be

$$\begin{aligned} V &= \mathbf{TA} \\ &= \mathbf{A}(\mathbf{A}^T\mathbf{A}) + \mathbf{B}(\mathbf{B}^T\mathbf{A}) + \mathbf{C}(\mathbf{C}^T\mathbf{A}), \end{aligned} \tag{9.30}$$

where $\mathbf{A}^T\mathbf{A}$ represents the autocorrelation of pattern A, while $\mathbf{B}^T\mathbf{A}$ and $\mathbf{C}^T\mathbf{A}$ are the respective cross-correlation between A and B, and A and C. If the differences between A, B and C are sufficiently large, the autocorrelation of A, B or C would be much larger than the cross-correlation between them, that is,

$$\mathbf{A}^T\mathbf{A} \gg \mathbf{B}^T\mathbf{A}, \qquad \mathbf{A}^T\mathbf{A} \gg \mathbf{C}^T\mathbf{A}. \tag{9.31}$$

Notice that in Eq. 9.31 pattern A has a larger weighting factor than patterns B and C, which means that patterns B and C can be considered noise. By choosing the proper threshold value, pattern A will be constructed at the output end of the neural network.

On the other hand, if A, B, and C are very similar, Eq. 9.31 no longer holds, the threshold value for the Hopfield model cannot be defined, and the network becomes unstable.

Computer simulations with an 8×8 neuron neural network are conducted for both the Hopfield and IPA models. The reference patterns considered are the 26 Roman letters lined up in sequence based on their similarities. Figure 9.18 shows that the error rate as a function of the number of reference

[Graph: Error Pixel Number vs Reference Pattern Number, comparing Hopfield and IPA models]

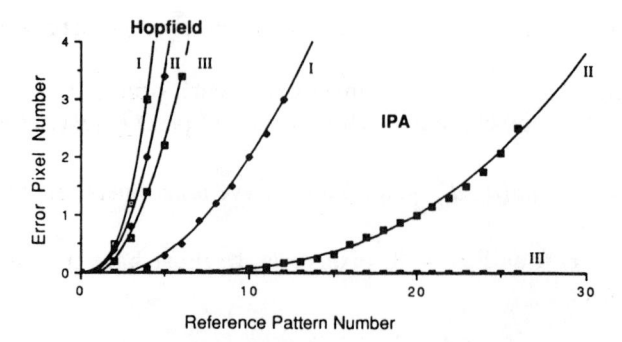

FIGURE 9.18 Comparison of the IPA and the Hopfield models. *Note*: I: 10 percent noise level; II: 5 percent noise level; III: No noise.

patterns. For the input SNR is about 7 dB, we notice that the Hopfield model becomes unstable to about 4 patterns, whereas the IPA model is quite stable to about 12 stored letters. Comparison is also made for noiseless input. In this condition, the IPA model can produce correct results for all 26 stored Roman letters, whereas the Hopfield model starts making significant errors when the number reference letters increases beyond 4 letters.

As an experiment, we used the Roman letters B, P, and R as the training set for constructing the IWMs, as shown in Figure 9.19a. The positive and negative parts of the IWMs for the IPA model are shown in Figures 9.19b and c, while those for the Hopfield model are displayed in Figures 9.19d and e. When we compare these two IWMs, we can see that the IPA model has two major advantages, namely, (1) fewer interconnections, and (2) fewer gray levels. The latter is significant because the IPA model requires only three gray levels to represent the IWM, whereas the Hopfield model needs $2M + 1$ gray levels, where M is the number of stored patterns.

The results of these two models are obtained from the input pattern B embedded in 30 percent random noise (SNR = 7 dB), as shown in Figure 9.19f. The output results are shown in Figures 9.19g and h, in which we see that the IPA model performs better.

9.9 HETEROASSOCIATION MODEL

We now discuss a heteroassociative neural network model using interpattern association to construct the IWM for pattern recognition. The special features of a reference pattern are generally more significant than the common features. The purpose of an IPA model is to determine whether the pixels in the pattern space belong to special or common features, and then set the

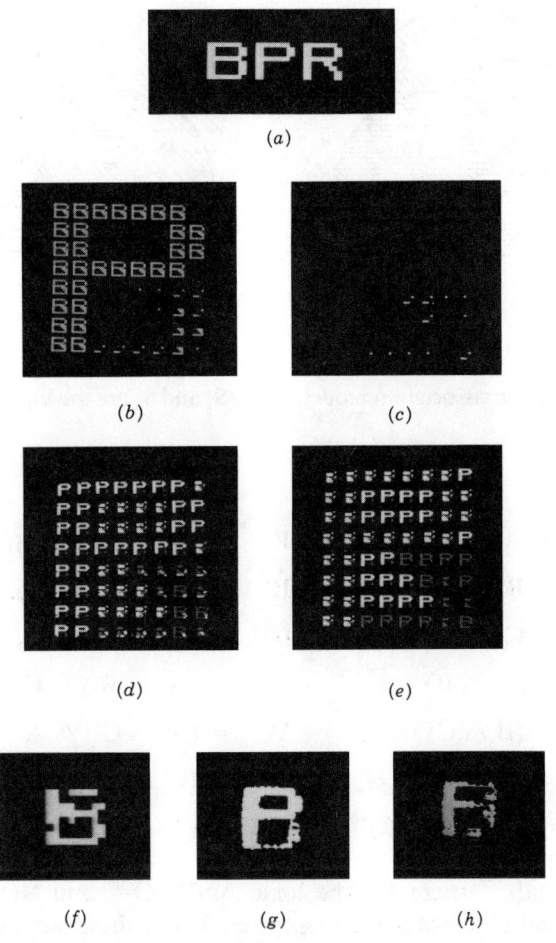

FIGURE 9.19 Experiments of an optical neurocomputer. (*a*) Three similar reference patterns. (*b*) and (*c*) Positive and negative IWMs of the IPA model. (*d*) and (*e*) Positive and negative IWMs of the Hopfield model, respectively. (*f*) Input pattern, SNR = 7 dB. (*g*) Pattern reconstruction using the IPA model. (*h*) Result using the Hopfield model.

excitatory or inhibitory interconnections based on logical relationships. We apply the IPA algorithm to the heteroassociation model [9.38]. For example, the overlapping input–output training sets shown in Figure 9.20 can be divided into subspaces, in which I, II and III are the special subspaces of input patterns A, B and C, respectively, IV, V and VI are the common subspaces for A and B, B and C, C and A, respectively, and VII is the common subspace for A, B and C. We do the same for output pattern space S_2. These subspaces in the input–output spaces can be determined by the following logical functions:

368 OPTICAL NEURAL NETWORKS

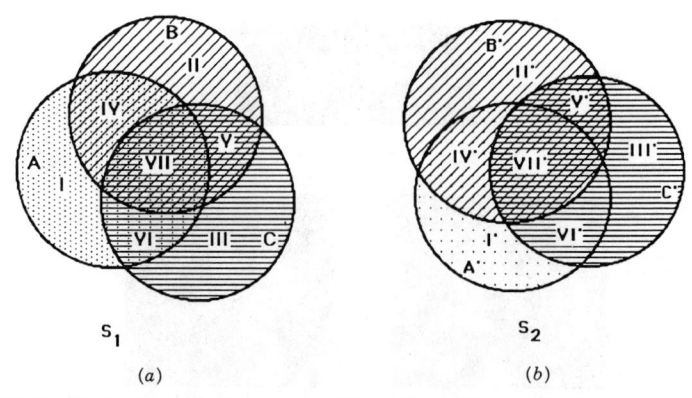

FIGURE 9.20 Heteroassociation model. *Note:* S_1 and S_2 are the input and the output pattern spaces.

$$\begin{aligned}
\text{I} &= A \wedge (\overline{B \vee C}), & \text{I}' &= A' \wedge (\overline{B' \vee C'}), \\
\text{II} &= B \wedge (\overline{A \vee C}), & \text{II}' &= B' \wedge (\overline{A' \vee C'}), \\
\text{III} &= C \wedge (\overline{A \vee B}), & \text{III}' &= C' \wedge (\overline{A' \vee B'}), \\
\text{IV} &= (A \wedge B) \wedge \overline{C}, & \text{IV}' &= (A' \wedge B') \wedge \overline{C'}, \\
\text{V} &= (B \wedge C) \wedge \overline{A}, & \text{V}' &= (B' \wedge C') \wedge \overline{A'}, \\
\text{VI} &= (C \wedge A) \wedge \overline{B}, & \text{VI}' &= (C' \wedge A') \wedge \overline{B'}, \\
\text{VII} &= (A \wedge B \wedge C) \wedge \overline{\emptyset}, & \text{VII}' &= (A' \wedge B' \wedge C') \wedge \overline{\emptyset}, & (9.32)
\end{aligned}$$

where $\wedge$, $\vee$ and $^-$ stand for the logic AND, OR, and NOT operations, respectively, and $\emptyset$ denotes the empty set. Using these simple logical operations, we can construct the IWM for the input and output neurons.

Let us consider the relationship of the input to output neurons as a mapping process for every pixel in the input space to the output space. For example, when a neuron (e.g., representing a pixel) in the input subspace VII is on, it implies that this neuron will excite all the neurons within output space VII', and it has null interconnection with the neurons in other output subspaces in S_2. However, when a neuron in the input subspace V is on, it will excite the neurons in output subspaces V' and VII', but inhibit the neurons in I'. Similarly, logical operations can also be applied to neurons in subspaces IV' or VI'.

In the case where a neuron is on in the input subspace I, it is implied that pattern A will appear at the input end, and that this neuron can excite all the neurons in output pattern A' (i.e. areas I', IV', VI' and VII'), and inhibit the neurons in subspaces $(B' \vee C') \wedge \overline{A'}$ (i.e. areas II', III' and V'). This is also true for the neurons in area II or III, which would excite output patterns

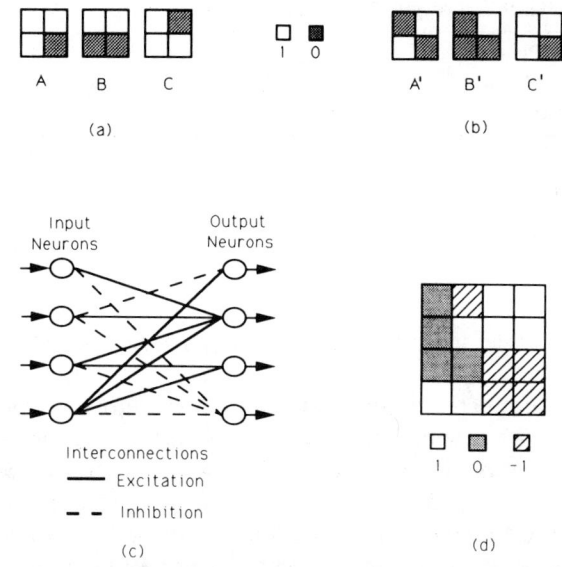

FIGURE 9.21 Construction of a heteroassociation IWM using the IPA model. (*a*) Input–output training sets. (*b*) A triastate neural network. (*c*) Heteroassociation IWM.

B' or C', and inhibit I', III', and VI', or I', II', and IV', respectively. Thus we see that a *heteroassociation* IWM can be constructed by logical rules.

Needless to say, by applying the *induction principle*, heteroassociation logical operations can be extended for M reference patterns, just like the one described in the preceding section.

To illustrate the construction of the heteroassociative IWM, we assume that A, B, C, A', B', and C' are the input–output training sets, as shown in Figures 9.21*a* and *b*. The corresponding input and output pattern–pixel relationships are given in Tables 9.2 and 9.3 respectively. As can be seen from the input pattern space S_1, pixel 1 (upper-left) is the common feature of A, B and C, pixel 2 is the common feature of A and B, pixel 3 is the common feature of A and C, while pixel 4 represents the special feature of C. Likewise,

TABLE 9.2. Input Pixel–Pattern Relationship

Pattern \ Pixel	1	2	3	4
A	1	1	1	0
B	1	1	0	0
C	1	0	1	1

TABLE 9.3. Output Pixel–Pattern Relationship

Pattern \ Pixel	1	2	3	4
A'	0	1	1	0
B'	0	1	0	0
C'	1	1	1	0

from the output pattern space S_2, pixel 3 represents the special feature of B', and so on.

A tristate-interconnection neural network can therefore be constructed as shown in Figure 9.21c. Notice that the second output neuron representing the common features of A', B', and C', has positive interconnections from all the input neurons. The fourth output neuron, a special feature of A', B' and C', is subjected to inhibition from all input neurons, while representing the common features of A, B, and C in the input pattern space. The corresponding IWM for the heteroassociation is constructed as shown in Figure 9.21d, in which 1, 0, −1 mean for excitation, no connection, and inhibition, respectively.

We now conduct the implementation of the heteroassociation model in the LCTV neural network of Figure 9.7 for character translation. A set of input–output training patterns is shown in Figure 9.22a, where the upper and lower rows are the corresponding Roman alphabets and Chinese characters. The heteroassociation IWMs using the IPA model are shown in Figures 9.22b and c, for Chinese to Roman and for Roman to Chinese, respectively. Although area encoding and the biasing method can be used to accommodate the negative values of the IWMs, for simplicity, the positive and negative parts of the IWMs are sequentially displayed in the LCTV1. Then a subtraction operation is performed by the microcomputer and the final results are obtained after the thresholding operation. Figures 9.22d and e show a set of experimental results, for partial inputs and their respective translated output patterns. Thus we have shown that the heteroassociation neural network can indeed perform character translations.

9.10 SPACE–TIME-SHARING ALGORITHM

For a fully interconnected neural network, every neuron has to be interconnected to the other neurons; for instance, 1000 neurons would require a million interconnections. Thus a very-high-resolution SLM is required for these massive interconnections. However, the resolution of the currently available SLMs is rather limited. This poses an obstacle in developing an

SPACE–TIME-SHARING ALGORITHM 371

(a)

(b)

(c)

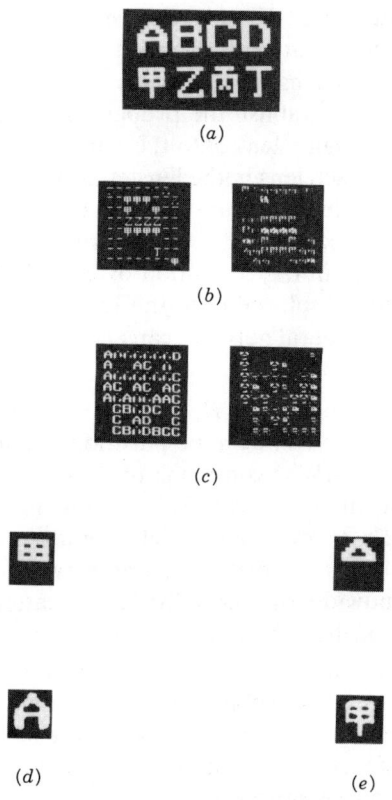

(d)   (e)

FIGURE 9.22 Character translations. (a) Roman–Chinese character training sets. (b) Positive (left) and negative (right) heteroassociation IWMs for Chinese-to-Roman translation. (c) Positive (left) and negative (right) heteroassociation IWMs for English-to-Chinese translation. (d) and (e) Partial input characters to the translated output characters.

optical neural network (ONN) for large-scale operation. In this section, we discuss a space–time-sharing technique to alleviate this constraint [9.39].

The iterative equation for an $N \times N$ neuron network, can be described by Eq. 9.20, that is,

$$\mathbf{V}_{lk}(n + 1) = f\left[\sum_{i=1}^{N} \sum_{j=1}^{N} \mathbf{T}_{lkij}\mathbf{U}_{ij}(n)\right], \qquad (9.33)$$

where n stands for the nth iteration, $f(')$ represents a nonlinear operator, $\mathbf{V}_{lk}$ and $\mathbf{U}_{ij}$ represent the state of the lkth and ijth neurons, respectively, and $\mathbf{T}_{lkij}$ is the connection strength from the lkth to ijth neurons. The term $[\mathbf{T}_{lkij}]$ is the interconnection weight matrix (IWM), which can be partitioned into an array of $N \times N$ submatrices, as shown in Figure 9.8 in Section 9.5.

372 OPTICAL NEURAL NETWORKS

The LCTV neural network (shown in Figure 9.7) is used for our discussion. In it, the IWM and the input pattern are displayed onto the LCTV1 and LCTV2, respectively. Each lens in the lenslet array images a specific submatrix onto the input LCTV2 to establish the proper interconnections. The lenslet array is imaged by the imaging lens onto the output plane, so that the overall intensity transmitted by each lens in the lenslet array is picked up by the CCD detector. We let the resolution of the LCTV1 be limited by $R \times R$ pixels, and the lenslet array be equal to $L \times L$ neurons. If the size of the IWM (i.e., $N \times N$) is larger than the resolution of the LCTV1, that is, $N^2 > R$, the IWM cannot be fully displayed onto the LCTV1. In the following cases, we discuss how a smaller neural network can accommodate a large size IWM.

Case I: For $N^2 > R$ and $LN < R$, we let $D = \text{int}(N/L)$, where int(') is an integer. The IWM can be partitioned into $D \times D$ sub-IWMs, with each sub-IWM consisting of $L \times L$ submatrices of $N \times N$ size, as shown in Figure 9.23. To complete the iterative operation of Eq. 9.21, $D \times D$ sequential operations of the sub-IWMs are required. Thus, a smaller neural network can handle a larger space–bandwidth product (SBP) input pattern through sequential operation of the sub-IWM.

Case II: For $N^2 > R$ and $LN > R$, we let $D = \text{int}(N/L)$ and $d = \text{int}(LN/R)$. In this case, the submatrices within the sub-IWMs are divided further into $d \times d$ submatrices, with each submatrix being $(N/d) \times (N/d)$ in size, as shown in Figure 9.24. Thus the iterative equation can be written as

$$\mathbf{V}_{lk}(n+1) = f\left[\sum_{p=0}^{d-1}\sum_{q=0}^{d-1}\left(\sum_{i=pd+1}^{(p+1)(N/d)}\sum_{j=qd+1}^{(q+1)(N/d)} \mathbf{T}_{lkij}\mathbf{U}_{ij}(n)\right)\right]. \tag{9.34}$$

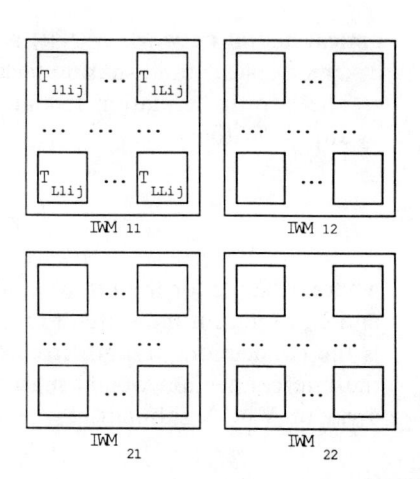

FIGURE 9.23 Partition of the IWM into $D \times D$ sub-IWMs, for $D = 2$.

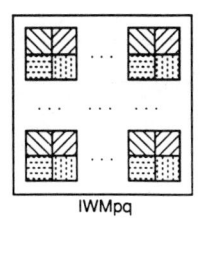

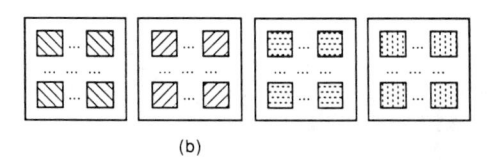

FIGURE 9.24 Partition of a sub-IWM into $d \times d$ submatrices, for $d = 2$. (*a*) The pqth sub-IWM. (*b*) $d \times d$ smaller submatrices.

If the input pattern is also partitioned into $d \times d$ submatrices, and each submatrix is $(N/d) \times (N/d)$ in size, then by sequentially displaying each of the IWM submatrices with respect to the input submatrices onto the LCTV1 and LCTV2, respectively, a very large SBP pattern can be processed with a smaller neural network. It is trivial that the processing speed is prolonged by $D^2 \times d^2$ times.

Generally speaking, the processing time increases as the square function of the space–bandwidth product of the input pattern, as given by:

$$T_2 = \left[\frac{(N_2 \times N_2)}{(N_1 \times N_1)}\right]^2 T_1 = \left(\frac{N_2}{N_1}\right)^4 T_1, \quad (N_2 > N_1 \geq L), \quad (9.35)$$

where T_2 and T_1 are the processing times for the input patterns for $N_2 \times N_2$ and $N_1 \times N_1$ resolution elements, respectively. This relationship is shown in Figure 9.25. For instance, if the resolution elements of the input pattern increase four times in each dimension, that is, $N_2 = 4N_1$, the processing time would be $4^4 = 256$ times longer.

As an experimental demonstration, we show that patterns with 12×12 resolution elements can be processed using a 6×6 neuron network. A 240×480-element Hitachi color LCTV (LCTV1) is used for displaying the IWM. Since each color pixel is composed of red, green, and blue elements, the resolution is actually reduced to 240×160 pixels. In the experiment, however, we have used 2×2 pixels for each interconnection weight, so the resolution of the LCTV1 is essentially reduced to 120×80 elements.

By referring to $N = 12$, $L = 6$, $R = 80$, and knowing that $N^2 =$

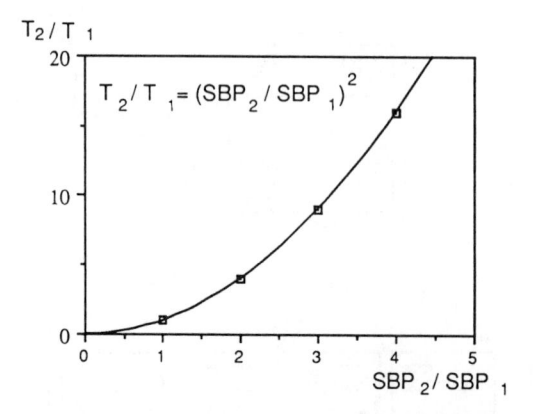

FIGURE 9.25 Processing time increases as a square of the SBP of the input pattern, for $SBP_2 = N_2 \times N_2$ and $SBP_1 = N_1 \times N_1$.

$144 > R$ and $LN = 72 < R$, we have $D = \text{int}(N/L) = 2$. The IWM can be divided into a 2×2 sub-IWM array and displayed one-by-one onto the LCTV1. If an input pattern is displayed on LCTV2, the signals collected by the CCD camera can be thresholded and then composed to produce an output pattern, which has an SBP four times larger than that of the optical neural network.

One of the experimental results is shown in Figure 9.26. The training set, which includes four cartoon patterns, is shown in Figure 9.26a. Each of these patterns is limited by a 12×12-pixel matrix. Figure 9.26b shows a partial image of the second cartoon figure with 12×5 pixels blocked out, as the input pattern. The sub-IWMs are then sequentially displayed, one by one, onto the LCTV1. Different parts of the output pattern are obtained, and one of the output parts is shown in Figure 9.26c. The final output pattern composed by the optical neural network is given in Figure 9.26d.

To further demonstrate the larger scale operation, a 24×24-neuron IWM is used. Since $N = 24$, $L = 6$, $R = 80$, $N^2 = 576 > R$, and $LN =$

FIGURE 9.26 Processing of a 12×12-element pattern by a 6×6 neuron network. (a) Four reference patterns stored in the IWM. (b) Partial input patterns. (c) One of the four 6×6 suboutput arrays. (d) Output-composed pattern.

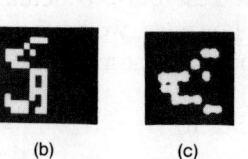

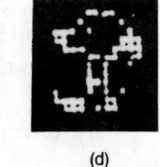

$94 > R$, we get $D = \text{int}(N/L) = 4$ and $d = \text{int}(LN/R) = 2$. Thus the IWM is partitioned into 4×4 sub-IWMs, with each sub-IWM divided into 2×2 smaller submatrices, as illustrated earlier in Figure 9.24. In this case, the input pattern is also divided into 2×2 submatrices, with each submatrix 12×12 in size. It is apparent that, by sequentially displaying the submatrices of the IWM and the input submatrices onto LCTV1 and LCTV2, respectively, a 24×24 output pattern can be obtained.

Figure 9.27a shows the training set of four 24×24-pixel cartoon patterns. A partial image of the third cartoon figure, shown in Figure 9.27b, is used as the input pattern, which is divided during the processing into 2×2 matrices, 12×12 in size. Four of sixteen 6×6 output parts are shown in Figure 9.27c. After going through all the partitions of the IWM, an output pattern is composed in Figure 9.27d. The whole process takes $D^2 \times d^2 = 64$ operations of the optical neural network.

In summary, we have used a space–time-sharing technique for large-scale neuron operation. We have shown that to achieve a large SBP of the system, additional expenditure of processing time is needed. The amount of processing time increases as the square function of the SBP of the input pattern.

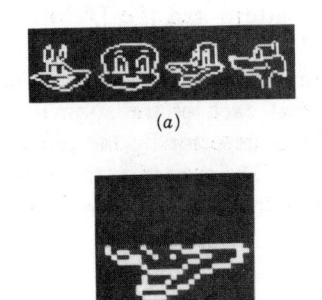

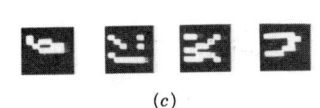

FIGURE 9.27 Simulated results of processing the 24×24-element pattern by a 6×6 neuron network. (a) Reference patterns stored in the IWM. (b) Partial input pattern. (c) Four of the sixteen 6×6 suboutput arrays. (d) Output-composed pattern.

9.11 THE COMPACT OPTICAL NEURAL NETWORK

In Section 9.5, we showed an optical architecture using liquid crystal television (LCTV), which uses a larger imaging lens. The numerical aperture of the imaging lens is large (about the order of 1/0.7), however, to image the lenslet array onto the output CCD detector. Thus, the architecture suffers the disadvantages of low light efficiency, high aberration, and increased size.

To alleviate these problems, we propose a new compact architecture using tightly cascaded LCTVs [9.40], as shown in Figure 9.28. Let us recall the iterative operation of a two-dimensional $N \times N$ neuron network, as given by,

$$\mathbf{V}_{lk}(n+1) = f\left[\sum_{i=1}^{N}\sum_{i=j}^{N} \mathbf{T}_{lkij}\mathbf{U}_{ij}(n)\right], \qquad (9.36)$$

Where $\mathbf{V}_{lk}$ and $\mathbf{U}_{ij}$ represent the state of the lkth and ijth neuron in the $N \times N$ neuron space, $\mathbf{T}_{lkij}$ is a four-dimensional IWM, and n represents the nth iteration. Notice that the matrix $\mathbf{T}$ can be partitioned into an array of two-dimensional submatrices $\mathbf{T}_{lk11}, \mathbf{T}_{lk12}, \ldots, \mathbf{T}_{lkNN}$, in which each submatrix is $N \times N$ in size. Thus, the IWM can be displayed as an $N^2 \times N^2$ array representation.

In the architecture of Figure 9.28, the input pattern and the IWM are displayed on the cascaded LCTVs, as illustrated in Figure 9.29. The light emerging through the cascaded LCTVs is apparently proportional to the product of $\mathbf{T}_{lkij}\mathbf{U}_{ij}(n)$ in Eq. 9.36. We can see that each of the submatrix $\mathbf{T}_{lkij}\mathbf{U}_{ij}(n)$ is superimposed as images onto the CCD detector by the lenslet array. Thus, the output intensity array from the CCD detector is the summation of the submatrices $\mathbf{T}_{lkij}\mathbf{U}_{ij}(n)$ over i and j. We stress that the summation

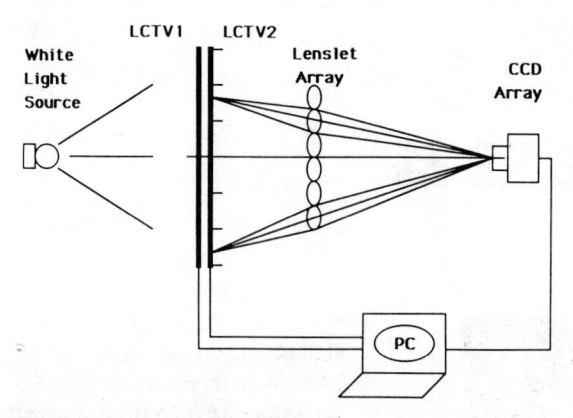

FIGURE 9.28 Compact ONN using cascaded LCTVs.

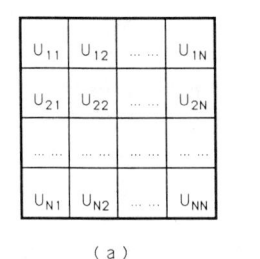

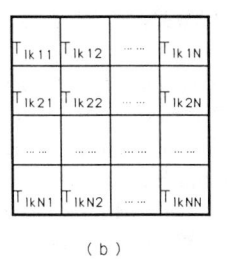

THE COMPACT OPTICAL NEURAL NETWORK

U_{11}	U_{12}	......	U_{1N}
U_{21}	U_{22}	......	U_{2N}
....	....	....	....
U_{N1}	U_{N2}	......	U_{NN}

(a)

T_{lk11}	T_{lk12}	......	T_{lk1N}
T_{lk21}	T_{lk22}	......	T_{lk2N}
....	....	....	....
T_{lkN1}	T_{lkN2}	......	T_{lkNN}

(b)

FIGURE 9.29 Formats of the input and the IWM. (*a*) Input pattern format. (*b*) IWM.

is carried out optically by the lenslet array. Needless to say, after the output signals are thresholded, the results can be fed back to the input LCTV via a microcomputer for the next iteration. Therefore, a closed-loop operation can be obtained with this system. Furthermore, with the elimination of the imaging lens, the system can be built more compactly. Moreover, by cascading the input pattern with the IWM, the output pattern pixels from the ONN remain the same shape as the input pattern, instead of as a circular shape as in the previous architectures shown in Figure 9.7 in Section 9.5.

As an experimental demonstration, we have used the Inter-pattern Association (IPA) model for the construction of the IWM. An IWM is shown in Figures 9.30*b* and *c* for the Roman letters A, B, C and D. A partial letter of A is shown in Figure 9.30*d* to the compact neural network; a recovery of the letter, using only one iteration, is shown in Figure 9.30*e*.

In short, we have built a compact ONN using tightly cascaded LCTVs. This optical architecture offers the advantages of compact size, easy alignment, higher light efficiency, better image quality, and very low cost.

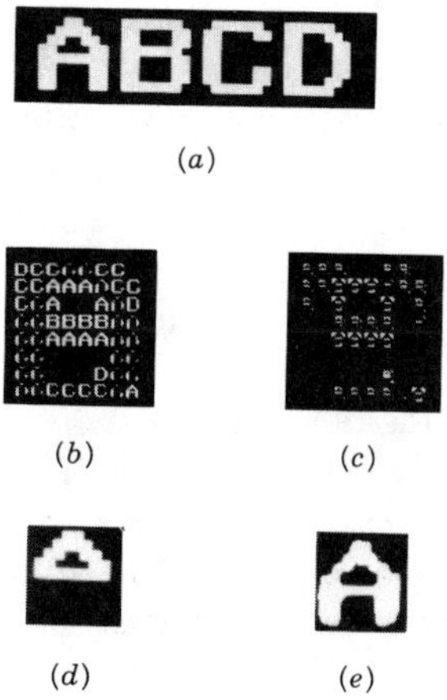

FIGURE 9.30 Result obtained with the cascaded LCTV neural network. (*a*) Input training set. (*b*) and (*c*) Positive and negative IWM. (*d*) Partial input. (*e*) Reconstructed pattern.

9.12 INFORMATION STORAGE CAPACITY

By contrast to the standard memory, where information is stored as an explicit quantity, the storage capacity of an associative memory is a complicated issue. However, associative memory must be a reasonable model for biological memory, on which a large number of simple, connected building blocks (i.e., the neurons) act individually in a random way, but in a specific task to accomplish the collective constitution of an organ. An important step in understanding collective systems is to quantify their ability in storing information and in carrying out computations.

The Hopfield neural network is a model of associative memory that is capable of storing information, as well as carrying out certain computational tasks, such as error correction, speech, and pattern recognitions.

In this section we introduce a definition of information capacity in which the upper and the lower bound storages can be found in a neural network. However, we restrict ourselves to a format of information storage that includes stable-state conditions in which an upper bound of vectors can be made stable in the model [9.41, chap. 5].

A neural network consists of $N \times N$ neurons, with the ith neuron in one of the two states: $u_i = -1$ (off) or $u_i = +1$ (on). The synaptic connections are undirected and have strengths that are fixed real numbers. We define the state vector u to be binary vector (± 1) whose ith component corresponds to the state of the ith neuron. Each neuron examines its input and then decides whether to turn itself on or off in the following manner: let the IWM **T** be an $N \times N$ positive real zero-diagonal symmetric matrix (i.e., $\mathbf{T}_{ij} = \mathbf{T}_{ji}$ and $\mathbf{T}_{ii} = 0$), for which the entries $\mathbf{T}_{ij}$ represent the strength (which may be negative) of the synaptic connection from the jth to ith neuron. We further let t_i be the threshold voltage of the ith neuron. If the weighted sum over all of its input is greater than or equal to t_i, the ith neuron turns on and its state becomes $+1$. However, if the sum is less than t_i, the neuron turns off and its state becomes -1. Thus the choice between **T** and t defines a special neural network with specific synaptic connection strengths and the threshold voltages of the neurons. We assume that the network starts has an initial state and that it runs with each neuron randomly and reevaluates itself independently. Often, the network enters a stable point in the state space in which all neurons remain in their current state after evaluating their inputs. This stable vector constitutes a stored word in the memory, and the basic operation of the network is to converge to a stable state if we initialize it with a nearby state vector.

Hopfield proposed a specific scheme for constructing the matrix **T**, which makes a given set of vectors $u^1, \ldots, u^K$ stable states in neural network. The scheme is based on the sum of the *outer products* of these vectors. Here no assumption is made about how the matrix **T** is constructed in terms of vectors $u^1, \ldots, u^K$, and all the results are valid even if the construction does not follow Hopfield's scheme.

Since the neural network represents a memory that stores information, it is appropriate to ask how much information can be stored in a network of N neurons. We use a familiar example to define the information capacity C. If we have a random-access memory (i.e., the RAM) with M addressable lines and one data line (an $M \times 1$ RAM, consisting of 2^M memory locations, where each location is accessed by an M-bit address and contains one bit of stored data), it is apparent that we can store 2^M bits. In other words, we can load the $M \times 1$ RAM with the string that is able to retrieve the whole string from the RAM.

There is another way to look at it. If we consider the string as a single object, we can store and retrieve any string (of length 2^M) in the $M \times 1$ RAM, and there are 2^{2^M} such distinguishable strings. Since the storage capacity can be defined as the logarithm of the number of distinguishable objects, it is trivial that the storage capacity of the $M \times 1$ RAM is

$$C = \log 2^{2^M} = 2^M \text{ bits}. \tag{9.37}$$

We now apply the preceding definition to a Hopfield model that has $N \times N$ neurons, for which we can find the upper and the lower bounds of information capacity C.

9.12.1 The Upper Bound

The question now becomes how many different sets of values for T_{ij} and t_i can we distinguish between merely by observing the state transition scheme of the neurons? The state transition scheme is determined by the number of distinguishable networks of $N \times N$ neurons. If this number is M, then the capacity of the network would be $C = \log M$ bits.

The key factor in estimating the number of distinguishable networks is the known estimate of the number of switching functions (linearly separable switching function are also called *threshold functions*). Switching function $f(x_1, x_2, \ldots, x_n)$ of n binary variables $x_1, x_2, \ldots, x_n$ is defined by assigning either -1 or $+1$ to each of the 2^n in $\{-1, +1\}^N$. A switching function $f(x_1, x_2, \ldots, x_n)$ of n variables is linearly *separable* if there exists a hyperplane Π in the n-dimensional space, which strictly separates the "on" set $f^{-1}(+1)$ and the "off" set $f^{-1}(-1)$. In other words, $f^{-1}(+1)$ lies on one side of Π and $f^{-1}(-1)$ on the other, and $\Pi \cap \{-1, +1\}^N$ is empty. Linearly separable switching functions are also called *threshold functions*. Winder [9.42] gave the following upper bound to the number of threshold functions of n variables defined on m points:

$$B_n^m \leq 2 \sum_{i=0}^{n} \frac{(m-1)!}{i!(m-i-1)!}. \tag{9.38}$$

The functions arrive at their upper bound in the following manner: Define an $(n + 1)$-dimensional space in which the coordinate axes correspond to the weights and to the threshold voltage. Consider a particular state u. Plot u as a hyperplane in the $n + 1$ space, so the set of all values of w_j and t satisfies the following equation:

$$\sum_{j=1}^{n} w_j u_j - t = 0. \quad (9.39)$$

Note that the hyperplane passes through the origin of the coordinate system, and this plane divides the space into two regions. Weights and threshold voltage from one of the regions make

$$\sum_{j=1}^{n} w_j u_j - t > 0, \quad (9.40)$$

and correspond to the threshold function of u being equal to 1. Weights and threshold voltage from the other region make

$$\sum_{j=1}^{n} w_j u_j - t < 0, \quad (9.41)$$

and correspond to the threshold function of u being equal to -1. Each of the m points gives a similar hyperplane. Thus we have m hyperplanes passing through the origin in the $n + 1$ space and partitioning the space into a number of regions, each of which corresponds to a threshold function. All points in any one of these regions correspond to values of w_j and t that produce the same threshold function. Two points in different regions correspond to two different functions, and at least one u out of the mu's is mapped to $+1$ by one function and mapped to -1 by the other. Therefore B_n^m is less than or equal to the maximum number of regions (called C_{n+1}^m) made by m hyperplanes passing through the origin in the $n + 1$ space. Assume $m - 1$ hyperplanes have made C_{n+1}^{m-1} regions in $n + 1$ space. We add the mth hyperplane to make as many more regions as possible. The mth hyperplane can intersect the other $m - 1$ hyperplanes in at most $m - 1$ hyperlines. The $m - 1$ hyperlines can at most partition the mth plane into C_n^{m-1} hyperplane regions, which is the same problem as experienced in n space. Since each region in the mth plane has been divided into a boundary between two regions in $n + 1$ space, we have added C_n^{m+1} regions to the other C_{n+1}^{m-1} regions determined by $m - 1$ planes. This means that we have

$$C_{n+1}^m = C_n^{m-1} + C_{n+1}^{m-1}. \quad (9.42)$$

The solution to this relation is given by

$$C_{n+1}^m = 2 \sum_{i=0}^{n} \frac{i!}{(m-1)!(i-m+1)!}, \quad (9.43)$$

which is the upper bound for B_n^m. If $m = 2^n$, that is, the threshold function is defined for every binary n-vector, then the upper bound for the number of fully defined threshold functions of n variables is given by

$$B_n^{2^n} \le 2 \sum_{i=0}^{n} \frac{(2^n - 1)!}{i!(2^n - i - 1)!} \le 2(n + 1) \times \frac{(2^n - 1)!}{n!(2^n - n - 1)!}$$

$$\le 2(n + 1) \frac{2^{n^2}}{n!} \le 2^{n^2}. \tag{9.44}$$

Since the action of each neuron simulates a general threshold function of $N - 1$ variables (i.e., the states of all the other neurons), we have at most $2^{(N-1)^2}$ such functions [9.43]. Since there are N neurons, there will be at most $(2^{(N-1)^2})^N$ distinguishable networks. The logarithm of this number is an upper bound for the information capacity, C, namely,

$$C \le \log(2^{(N-1)^2})^N = N(N - 1)^2 = O(N^3) \text{ bits.} \tag{9.45}$$

9.12.2 The Lower Bound

It is known from Abu-Mostafa and Jacques [9.43] that there are at least $2^{0.33n^2}$ threshold functions of n variables. The symmetry of matrix $\mathbf{T}$ makes the N threshold functions dependent, but we may take the submatrix of $\mathbf{T}$, consisting of the first $[N/2]$ rows and the last $[N/2]$ columns, and consider the partial threshold functions defined by this submatrix. Since the entries of this submatrix are independent, we have at least $[N/2]$ functions, each of which has $n = [N/2]$ variables. Therefore, the number of distinguishable networks is at least $(2^{0.33[N/2]^2})^{[N/2]}$. The logarithm of this number is a lower bound for the storage capacity C, namely

$$\log(2^{0.33[N/2]^2})^{N/2} = \frac{0.33}{8} N^3 \text{ bits} \le C. \tag{9.46}$$

From Eq. 9.45 we see that an N-neuron Hopfield network would have an information storage capacity on the order of N^3 bits.

The preceding results may be extended to the Inter-pattern Association (IPA) model. Since the associative memory $\mathbf{T}$ of the IPA model is a tristate-interconnection weight matrix, the storage capacity of the IPA model would be higher than the Hopfield network. As a rough estimation we consider that a switching function of n trial variables is defined by assigning $+1, 0$ or -1 to each of the 3^n points in the $\{-1, 0, +1\}^N$ network. After performing a derivation similar to that shown in the preceding section, the upper bound information storage capacity for the IPA model can be shown to be

$$C \le \log(3^{N^3}) \approx 1.6N^3 \text{ bits.} \tag{9.47}$$

9.13 MOMENT-INVARIANT NEUROCOMPUTING

In this section, we investigate the feasibility of using the image irradiance moments to replace the Hamming distance, which is generally used as a criterion for the convergence in neural computing. The moment $m_{p,q}$ of the image irradiance can be defined as

$$m_{p,q} = \int\!\!\int_{-\infty}^{\infty} x^p y^q f(x, y) \, dx \, dy, \qquad (9.48)$$

where $f(x, y)$ is assumed to be a continuous, bounded, and nonzero function. It should be noted that $m_{p,q}$ is not invariant to any distortions. In order to obtain moments that are invariant to translational change, we define the central moments $\mu_{p,q}$ as given by Hu [9.44].

$$\mu_{p,q} = \int\!\!\int_{-\infty}^{\infty} x^p y^q f(x + x_0, y + y_0) \, dx \, dy, \qquad (9.49)$$

where (x_0, y_0) are the coordinates of the centroid of the image irradiance;

$$x_0 = \frac{m_{1,0}}{m_{0,0}} \quad \text{and} \quad y_0 = \frac{m_{0,1}}{m_{0,0}}, \qquad (9.50)$$

and the zero-order moments $m_{0,0} = \mu_{0,0}$ represent the total image power.

Functions $\mu_{p,q}$ are not, however, invariant under a scale transformation. To overcome this inadequacy, the scale normalized moment was introduced, namely

$$v_{p,q} = \frac{\mu_{p,q}}{\mu_{0,0}^{1+(p+q)/2}}. \qquad (9.51)$$

It is now well known that for the second- and third-order central moments, we have the following functions that are invariant under position, scale, and rotation [9.44]:

$$\begin{aligned}
\phi_1 &= v_{2,0} + v_{0,2}, \\
\phi_2 &= (v_{2,0} - v_{0,2})^2 + 4v_{1,1}^2, \\
\phi_3 &= (v_{3,0} - 3v_{1,2})^2 + (3v_{2,1} - v_{0,3})^2, \\
\phi_4 &= (v_{3,0} + v_{1,2})^2 + (v_{2,1} + v_{0,3})^2,
\end{aligned} \qquad (9.52)$$

We note that, the first seven moments provide sufficient discrimination between alphabetical characters and also permit recognition of multisensor imagery [9.45], [9.46].

The Hopfield model can be summarized as follows: The first step is to assign connection weights between neurons, namely

$$T_{ij} = \sum_{\substack{m=1 \\ i \neq j}}^{M} f_{\mathbf{m}}(i) f_{\mathbf{m}}(j), \qquad i, j = 1, 2, \ldots, N, \qquad T_{ii} = 0. \qquad (9.53)$$

Here T_{ij} is the connection weight from neuron i to neuron j and $f_m(i)$ is the ith component of the vector **m** in a set containing **M** bipolar binary vectors. Every vector in this set represents an exemplar pattern and every component of a vector corresponds to a pixel in the exemplar pattern.

The second step is the initialization of the Hopfield net with the unknown input pattern that is described by vector $[\mathbf{f}_{m_0}(1), \mathbf{f}_{m_0}(2), \ldots, \mathbf{f}_{m_0}(N)]$. This step can be expressed by

$$g_0(i) = f_{m_0}(i), \qquad (9.54)$$

where $g_0(i)$ is the output of neuron i at the 0-th iteration of the network.

The third step describes the update rule,

$$g_{n+1}(j) = \text{sgn}\left[\sum_{i=0}^{N} T_{ij} g_n(i)\right], \qquad (9.55)$$

where $\text{sgn}[x] = -1$ if $x < 0$ and $+1$, othewise. The process of iteration is repeated until outputs remain unchanged with further iterations. Under some conditions, the outputs then represent the exemplar pattern that best matches the unknown input.

A Hopfield net with 64 neurons and thus 4096 weights was trained to recall four alphabetical characters A, C, E, and T as demonstrated in Figure 9.31 [9.47]. Every character is placed in a square unit area, as shown in Figure 9.32. The Hamming distances from character to character are listed in Table 9.4, and seven moment invariants calculated from Eq. 9.52 are listed in Table 9.5 and shown in Figure 9.33.

Figure 9.33 is divided into three parts: The first part (top) demonstrates

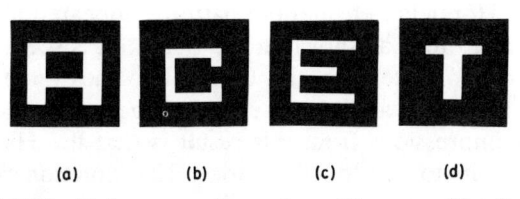

FIGURE 9.31 Reference patterns for a 64-neuron Hopfield net.

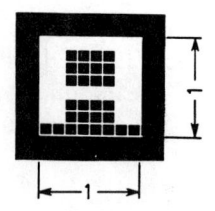

FIGURE 9.32 Dimension of the reference patterns.

TABLE 9.4. Hamming Distance–Pattern Relationship

Character	A	C	E	T
A	0	40	35	44
C	40	0	29	26
E	35	29	0	33
T	44	26	33	0

TABLE 9.5. Moment Invariances for the Four Exemplars

	A	C	E	T
ϕ_1	0.328	0.490	0.443	0.299
ϕ_2	8.40×10^{-3}	1.71×10^{-3}	6.17×10^{-3}	1.74×10^{-2}
ϕ_3	3.86×10^{-4}	7.75×10^{-4}	2.87×10^{-3}	1.67×10^{-2}
ϕ_4	3.55×10^{-5}	1.36×10^{-3}	3.32×10^{-3}	1.42×10^{-4}
ϕ_5	0	-1.39×10^{-6}	-1.03×10^{-5}	2.61×10^{-6}
ϕ_6	-3.25×10^{-6}	-5.60×10^{-5}	-2.61×10^{-4}	1.87×10^{-5}
ϕ_7	0	0	0	0

the whole process concerning the retrieval of the input pattern in four iterations in the Hopfield net; the second part shows the convergence of the Hamming distance; and the third part shows the variations of the ϕ-functions in the process of the four iterations.

The binary input pattern is a letter T that was corrupted by random noise that reversed each bit independently from 1 to 0 and vice versa with a probability near 0.1. The Hamming distance between the corrupted and the uncorrupted characters T is 5 bits. The corrupted pattern was presented to the input end of the Hopfield net, and the patterns appeared at the output end on iterations zero to four as shown in the figure. It is seen from this figure that when the network iterates, the output becomes increasingly like the correct exemplar pattern, and ultimately converges to it. A quantitative description of our impressions from this result is that the Hamming distance decreases from 5 bits to 0 in four iterations. This situation can be expressed by the following sequence:

MOMENT-INVARIANT NEUROCOMPUTING 385

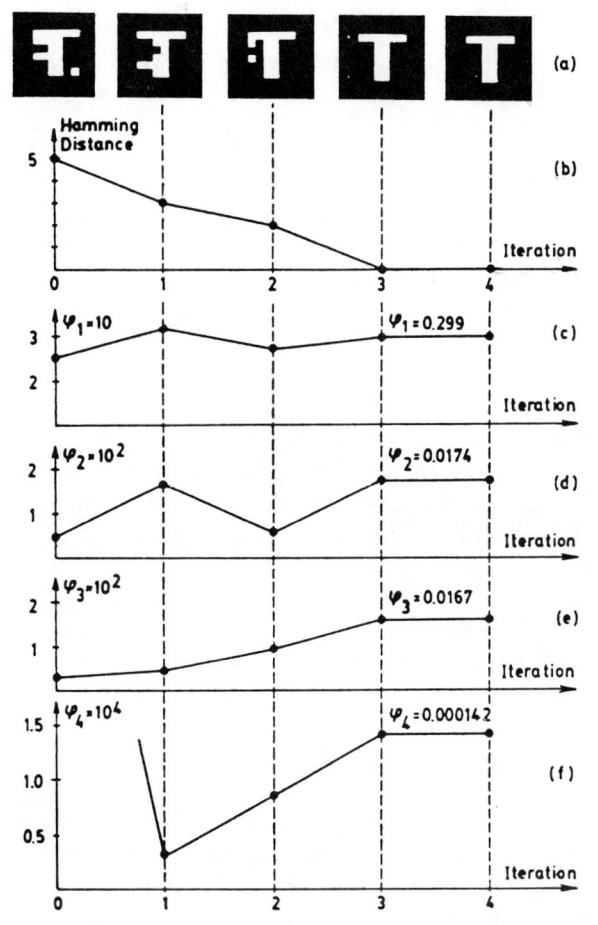

FIGURE 9.33 (*a*) Output patterns as number of iterations. (*b*) Convergence of the Hamming distance. (*c*) to (*f*) Convergence of the φ-functions.

$$\text{Hamming distance} = 5, 3, 2, 0 \ldots \text{(bits)}. \tag{9.56}$$

Unfortunately, the Hamming distance is not an image descriptor, so it cannot be used to discriminate between image patterns. For the purpose of pattern recognition, we suggest the use of moment invariants to show the convergence of collective computation in neutral nets. For example, function ϕ_1 of the character T converges to its stable value 0.299 (see Table 9.4) in the four iterations, as shown in the sequence.

$$\phi_1 = 0.255, 0.319, 0.277, 0.299, \ldots . \tag{9.57}$$

Instead of using the Hamming distance sequence expressed in Eq. 9.56, one can use the difference $\Delta\phi_i$ to show the convergence in neurocomputing:

$$|\Delta\phi_1| = 0.064, 0.042, 0.022, 0, \ldots$$
$$|\Delta\phi_2| = 0.012, 0.011, 0.012, 0, \ldots$$
$$\ldots \ldots \tag{9.58}$$

A comparison of the sequence of Eq. 9.56 with that of Eq. 9.58 shows that both of them are uniformly convergent to zero when the corrupted pattern is completely retrieved. However, sequences 9.58 provide information to discriminate between patterns under the basis of an examination of the quantitative difference between the values of moment invariants and the data listed in Table 9.5. This is the great advantage of replacing code description by an image description in neurocomputing.

In conclusion, it is known that ϕ_i is noise sensitive, so for neural nets it is not easy to make shift or distortion invariants without the use of an excessive number of training patterns. Nevertheless, we have proposed a method to combine the invariant moments with neurocomputing to make up their inadequacies: the distortion invariant, by the moments, and the noise immunity, by the neural nets.

9.14 SELF-ORGANIZING NEURAL NETWORK

Strictly speaking, two types of learning processes are used in the human brain: supervised and unsupervised [9.5]. If a teacher organizes the information and then teaches the students, it is obviously a supervised learning. For example, in an artificial neural network (ANN), both the input and desired output data must be provided as training examples. In other words, the ANN has to be taught when to learn and when to process the information. Therefore, if an unknown object is presented to the ANN during processing, the network may provide an erroneous output result.

On the other hand, in unsupervised learning (also called self-learning), the students learn by themselves, relying on some simple rules and their past experiences. In an ANN, only the input data are provided, while the desired output result is not. After a single trial or series of trials, an evaluation rule (previously provided to the neural network) is used to evaluate the performance of the network. Thus, we see that the network is capable of adapting and categorizing unknown objects. This kind of self-organizing process is a representation of the self-learning ability of the human brain.

In past decades, models of ANNs have been developed. A few examples of supervised learning models are the perceptron, error-driven back-propagation [9.29], the Hopfield models, and the Boltzmann machine; adaptive resonnance theory (ART) [9.4], neocognitron [9.16], madline, and the Kohonen self-organizing feature map [9.3] are some of the best known unsupervised learning models. Among the latter models, the Kohonen model is the simplest self-organizing algorithm, capable of performing statistical pattern recognition and classification, and it can be modified for optical neural network implementation [9.48].

9.14.1 Kohonen's Feature Map

Knowledge representation in human brains generally exists at different levels of abstraction and assumes the form of a feature map. The Kohonen model suggests a simple learning rule by which the interconnection weights between the input and output neurons are adjusted based on the matching score between the input and the memory. A single interconnection layer neural network, which consists of $N \times N$ input and $M \times M$ output neurons forming an input and output vector space, is illustrated in Figure 9.34, in which the nodes are also laterally interconnected. Let us assume that two-dimensional vectors (i.e., input patterns) are sequentially presented to the neural network:

$$x(t) = x_{ij}(t), \quad i, j = 1, 2, \ldots, N, \tag{9.59}$$

where t represents the time index, such as the iteration number in the discrete-time sequence, and (i, j) specifies the position of the input neuron. Thus, the output vectors of the neural network can be expressed as the weighted sum of the input vectors:

$$y_{lk}(t) = \sum_{i=1}^{N} \sum_{j=1}^{N} m_{lkij}(t) x_{ij}(t), \quad l, k = 1, 2, \ldots, M, \tag{9.60}$$

where $y_{lk}(t)$ represents the state of the (l, k)th neuron in the output space and $m_{lkij}(t)$ is the interconnection weight between the (i, j)th input and the (l, k)th output neurons. Equation 9.60 can also be written as a matrix innerproduct:)

$$\mathbf{y}_{lk}(t) = \mathbf{m}_{lk}(t)\mathbf{x}(t), \tag{9.61}$$

where $\mathbf{m}_{lk}(t)$ can be considered a two-dimensional vector in a four-dimensional memory matrix space, which can be expanded in an array of two-dimensional

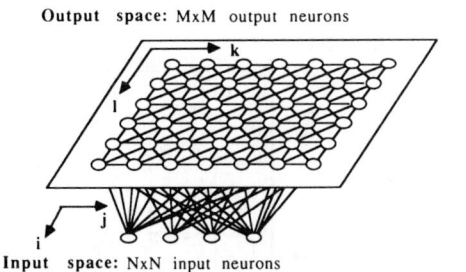

FIGURE 9.34 Single layer interconnected neural net.

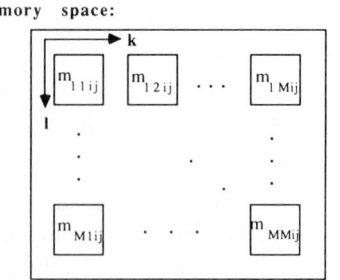

FIGURE 9.35 Memory vectors in the memory matrix space.

submatrices, as shown in Figure 9.35. Each submatrix can be written in the form

$$\mathbf{m}_{lk}(t) = \begin{bmatrix} m_{lk11}(t) & m_{lk12}(t) & \cdots & m_{lk1N}(t) \\ m_{lk21}(t) & m_{lk22}(t) & \cdots & m_{lk2N}(t) \\ \vdots & \vdots & & \vdots \\ m_{lkN1}(t) & m_{lkN2}(t) & \cdots & m_{lkNN}(t) \end{bmatrix}, \quad (9.62)$$

where the elements in each submatrix represent the associative weight factors from each of the input neurons to one output neuron.

Notice that the Kohonen model does not in general specify the desired output results. Instead, a similar matching criterion is defined in order to find the best match between the input vector and the memory vectors, and then to determine the best matching output node. The optimum matching score d_c, as defined by Kohonen, can be written as

$$d_c(t) = \|\mathbf{x}(t) - \mathbf{m}_c(t)\| = \min_{l,k} \{d_{lk}(t)\} = \min_{l,k} \{\|\mathbf{x}(t) - \mathbf{m}_{lk}(t)\|\}, \quad (9.63)$$

where $c = (l, k)^*$ represents the node in the output vector space at which a best match occurred, and $\|\cdot\|$ denotes the Euclidean distance operator.

After obtaining an optimum matching position c, the neighborhood $N_c(t)$ around the node c is further defined for modification, as shown in Figure 9.36. Notice that the memory matrix space is equivalent to the output space, in which each submatrix corresponds to an output node. As time progresses,

FIGURE 9.36 Neighborhood selection using Kohonen's self-learning algorithm: $N_c(t_1)$—the initial neighborhood—time proceeds, the neighborhood shrinks to $N_c(t_2)$ ..., until it reduces to one memory submatrix.

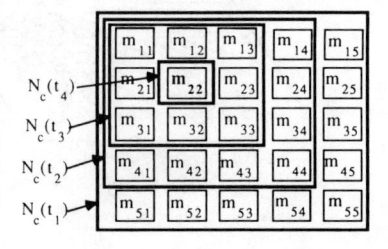

the neighborhood $N_c(t)$ slowly reduces to a neighborhood that consists of only the selected memory vector $\mathbf{m}_c$, as illustrated in the figure.

In addition, a simple algorithm is used to update the weight factors in the neighborhood topology, by which the similarity between the stored memory matrix $\mathbf{m}_{lk}(t)$ and the input vector $\mathbf{x}(t)$ increases. Notice that the input vectors can be either binary or analog patterns, while the memory vectors are updated in an analog incremental process. The adaptation formula of the algorithm can be written as

$$\mathbf{m}_{ik}(t+1) = \begin{cases} \mathbf{m}_{lk}(t) + a(t)[\mathbf{x}(t) - \mathbf{m}_{lk}(t)], & \text{for } lk \in N_c(t), \\ \mathbf{m}_{lk}(t), & \text{otherwise,} \end{cases} \quad (9.64)$$

where $0 < a(t) < 1$ represents a gain sequence, called the *learning speed*, that is usually a monotonically slowly decreasing function of t. In practice, the learning speed is assumed to be linear, which can be written as

$$a(t) = a(0) - \alpha t, \quad (9.65)$$

where α is a learning rate.

It must be said that the point density of the memory vectors tends to approximate the probability density function of the input vectors, which has been proved by Kohonen [9.3].

It should be noted that Eq. 9.63 can be expanded in the following form:

$$d_{lk} = \sum_{i=1}^{N} \sum_{j=1}^{N} [x_{ij}(t) - m_{lkij}(t)]^2$$

$$= \sum_{i=1}^{N} \sum_{j=1}^{N} x_{ij}^2(t) + \sum_{i=1}^{N} \sum_{j=1}^{N} m_{lkij}^2(t) - 2 \sum_{i=1}^{N} \sum_{j=1}^{N} m_{lkij}(t) x_{ij}(t), \quad (9.66)$$

where the first term is a constant with regard to the output position (l, k). If the weight vectors are normalized so that their autocorrelations (i.e., the sum of the squared weights from all inputs to each output node) are identical, then the second term also becomes a constant. Under this condition, the minimum Euclidean distance occurs whenever the third term becomes maximum, that is,

$$d_c(t) = \min_{l,k}\{d_{lk}(t)\} = \max_{l,k}\left\{ \sum_{i=1}^{N} \sum_{j=1}^{N} m_{lkij}(t) x_{ij}(t) \right\}, \quad (9.67)$$

which represents the output result of the neural network. In other words, selecting the minimum Euclidean distance between the memory vectors and the input pattern vector is equivalent to finding the maximum output node in the output space.

The maximum output node can be determined by using extensive lateral inhibition among the output nodes in the output space, which is known as the *MAXNET algorithm* [9.5]. The expression of the inhibited interconnections can be written as

$$y_{lk}(t+1) = f\left[y_{lk}(t) - \varepsilon \sum_{\substack{m=1 \\ (m,n) \neq (l,k)}}^{M} \sum_{n=1}^{M} y_{mn}(t)\right], l, k = 1, 2, \ldots, M, \qquad (9.68)$$

where f is a nonlinear operator over the output nodes and ε is an inhibition constant between the output nodes. For simplicity, we assume that the nonlinear operation $f(x)$ is a thresholding function, given by

$$f(x) = \begin{cases} 1, & x \geq a, \\ x, & b \leq x < a, \\ -1, & x < b, \end{cases} \qquad (9.69)$$

where a and b are arbitrary constants. Referring to the MAXNET algorithm, we see that each node excites itself and inhibits the other nodes during each iteration. Finally, only the maximum output node will retain data, while all of the other nodes will eventually go to zero. Since the MAXNET algorithm will always converge, for $\varepsilon < 1/M$, the maximum node can always be found [9.5].

9.14.2 Unsupervised Learning

Before applying the self-organizing model to the optical neural network (Figure 9.7), two major factors must be considered: one is the system components and alignment errors, the other is the effect of the parameters of the self-organizing system.

Since IWM submatrices are precisely interconnected with the input pattern vector by a lenslet array, the alignment of the interconnections is critical. Although the adjustment of lenses is formidable, it is rather simple to shift the IWM submatrices in the LCTV1. A set of test patterns can be displayed on LCTV1 and LCTV2. The test patterns are shifted in small steps according to the sharpness of the output pattern detected by the CCD camera. Thus, the interconnection alignment can be self-adjusted via the feedback loop.

The uniformity and stability of the light illumination also pose some problems to the accuracy of the output results. To alleviate the uniformity problem, a test is performed when a new input pattern vector is presented. During the test, all elements in the memory matrix are set to the same value, that is,

$$m_{lkij}(t_0) = 1, \quad l, k = 1, 2, \ldots, M, \quad i, j = 1, 2, \ldots, N. \qquad (9.70)$$

SELF-ORGANIZING NEURAL NETWORK 391

The output array can then be obtained:

$$\hat{y}_{lk}(t_0) = \sum_{i=1}^{N} \sum_{j=1}^{N} |x_{ij}(t_0)|, \quad l, k = 1, 2, \ldots, M. \quad (9.71)$$

The uniformity test array $\hat{Y}(t_0)$ is then divided by the output array during the self-learning and recognition processes:

$$y_{lk}^*(t) = \frac{y_{lk}(t)}{\hat{y}_{lk}(t_0)}, \quad l, k = 1, 2, \ldots, M, \quad (9.72)$$

where $Y^*(t)$ is the normalized output array in which the nonuniformity of the light illumination can be eliminated.

As an experimental demonstration, let four 8×8-pixel binary input patterns (i.e., a tree, a dog, a house, and an airplane) be sequentially presented at the input LCTV2, as shown in Figure 9.37a. Figure 9.37b shows the initial memory matrix as a random pattern. The first neighboring region is chosen as $N_c(0) = 5$, the initial learning speed is $a(0) = 0.01$, and the learning rate is selected as $\alpha = 0.00025$ per iteration. The output pattern picked up by the CCD camera must be normalized by Eq. 9.72. Then the location of the maximum output intensity can be identified by using the MAXNET algorithm. The memory submatrices in the neighborhood of the maximum output spot are adjusted according to the *adaptation rule* of the Kohonen model. The

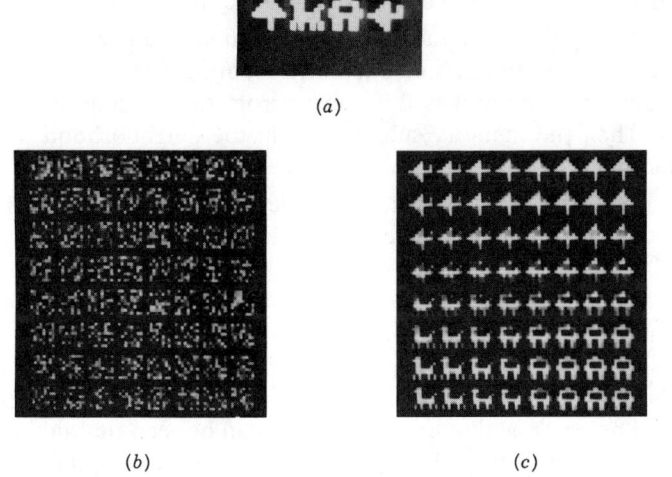

FIGURE 9.37 A self-organizing ONN using unsupervised learning. (*a*) Input training set. (*b*) Initial memory matrix space with random noise. (*c*) Final memory matrix space. The patterns are taken into the memory matrix; the tree is centered at (1, 8), the dog at (7, 1), the house at (7, 7), and the airplane at (1, 1).

updated memory matrix is then displayed on the LCTV1 for the next iteration, and so on. Due to the gray-level limitation in LCTV displays, a few iterations in the learning process may result in one noticeable gray-level change by the CCD detector array. Since the inputs are binary patterns, the center memory vector in the neighborhood region eventually converges to the binary input vector. Thus, the limited dynamic range of the LCTVs should not pose a major problem in our experiment. As shown in Figure 9.37c, after 400 iterations the memory has learned the four input patterns, mapping them around four overlapping regions in the IWM. The centers of these patterns are located at (1, 8), (7, 1), (7, 7), and (1, 1), respectively.

One of the major advantages of adaptive pattern recognition is learning the unknowns in addition to recognizing known objects. This task can be achieved by adding three criteria to the Kohonen learning rule, for which the matching rate R for pattern recognition can be defined as

$$R = \frac{\|Y_c(t)\|}{\|X(t)\|} = \frac{\sum_{i=1}^{N}\sum_{j=1}^{N} m_{cij}(t)x_{ij}(t)}{\sum_{i=1}^{N}\sum_{j=1}^{N} x_{ij}^2(t)}, \qquad (9.73)$$

where $\|\cdot\|$ is the norm operator. Let us assume that two constants F_1 and F_2 represent the matching and unmatching scores, by which $F_1 < 1$, $F_2 < 1$, and $F_1 > F_2$; then the criteria of the learning rules are as follows:

1. If $R \geq F_1$, the input object matches the memory submatrix at position c. Then the neural network recognizes the input object.
2. If $F_2 \leq R < F_1$, the input object is identified as a pattern that belongs to the class of patterns (i.e., submatrices) around location c. This shows that the input object has differences from the existing patterns in the class. Then the memory submatrices in the neighborhood of c should be modified to adapt to the new input pattern.
3. If $R < F_2$, the input object is considered to be an unknown pattern. Then a new category is developed to learn the unknown pattern using Eq. 9.73.

For example, F_1 and F_2 are selected as $F_1 = 95\%$ and $F_2 = 75\%$. A computer-simulated self-learning process is illustrated in Figure 9.38, in which four standardized Roman letters A, B, C, and D are sequentially presented to the neural network as the input objects. It can be seen that in the memory matrix, the locations of the submatrices reflect the similarity among the input patterns. The grouping of the submatrix locations is known as *Kohonen's feature map*, in which the patterns of similar features tend to stay close to each other. For example, B, C, and D are similar patterns; their submatrices are located on the same side of the memory matrix, centered at (8, 4), (6,

SELF-ORGANIZING NEURAL NETWORK 393

FIGURE 9.38 Feature map in the memory matrix space. Three similar patterns are located on the same side in this memory matrix: B is centered at (8, 4), C is at (6, 1), and D is at (8, 8), while A is at (1, 8).

1), and (8, 8), respectively, while pattern A sits in the opposite direction, location at (1, 8).

It should be noted that the inner products of the memory matrix are performed in parallel with the input pattern by optics, while the MAXNET algorithm, the thresholding, and the adaptive operations are carried-out by the microcomputer.

Our experience has shown that the best results in self-organization are obtained when the neighborhood of the memory matrix space is first selected as a wide region, and then allowed it to shrink as time proceeds. The linearly decreasing learning speed $a(t)$ is illustrated in Figure 9.39. Since $\alpha_1 > \alpha_2$, it is clear that $a_1(t)$ is a faster learning speed than $a_2(t)$. It is apparent that to reach the stable state of the memory matrix, $a_1(t)$ would require fewer iterations than $a_2(t)$. However, in real life, intensive training may not always be effective. With a slower learning speed, the memory matrix is more organized and also appears smoother. The price paid is obviously the training time required for using the slower learning speed. As an example, the memory matrix space adapted from the faster learning speed is shown in Figure 9.40a. Using $a(0) = 0.02$ and $\alpha = 0.00005$ after 400 iterations, similar patterns I, J, and T are adapted in the lower left part of the memory matrix, centered at (5, 1), (7, 2), and (8, 4), respectively, whereas pattern X submatrices occupy the upper right part, centered at (3, 8). Since pattern X is very different from the I, J, and T patterns in the memory space, using the slower learning rate, $\alpha = 0.000025$, pushes the pattern X submatrices further away to the upper right corner, centered at (1, 8) after 800 iterations, as shown in Figure 9.40b. In this figure, we see that the memory space is more topologically organized.

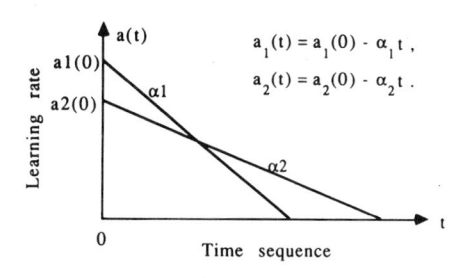

FIGURE 9.39 Fast and slow linear learning speeds.

$$a_1(t) = a_1(0) - \alpha_1 t$$
$$a_2(t) = a_2(0) - \alpha_2 t$$

394 OPTICAL NEURAL NETWORKS

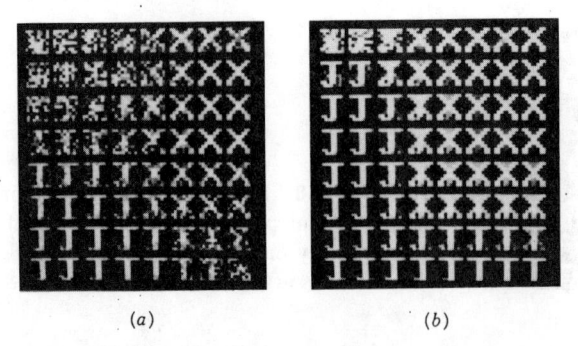

FIGURE 9.40 Memory matrix topology using linear learning speeds. (*a*) Fast learning rate with the centers of the similar patterns I at (5, 1), J at (7, 2), and T at (8, 4), and the center of the different pattern X at (3, 8). (*b*) Slow learning rate with the pattern X pushed further away to the upper right corner and centered at (1, 8). Notice that the memory space becomes topologically more organized and also appears smoother.

When similar patterns are presented at the input of a neural network, a new pattern may occasionally override the old pattern by selecting the same optimum position in the memory matrix space, with the old pattern gradually fading away. This phenomenon is similar to the learning process of humans: if one moves from New England to Southern Florida for a long period of time, one may forget the bitterness of the cold winters in the northern United States.

An example of this phenomenon has been simulated by computer, and is shown in Figure 9.41. An input pattern B is first presented to the optical neural network. The memory matrix adapts the pattern around the lower right corner, centered around (8, 8), as shown in Figure 9.41*a*. A second pattern E is presented to the neural network at a later time. Since pattern E is similar to pattern B, it picks the same spot (8, 8) in the memory matrix space as its maximum output point. As seen in Figure 9.41*b*, the memory submatrices of B are taken over by E after 100 iterations. If one wishes to preserve the old memory while new knowledge is learned, one of two ways can be used. In one the memory has to be refreshed by repeatedly reviewing the previous input patterns, which takes a lot of computational time and may cause confusion. Another way is to set a rule in the learning process: a new pattern should not take the output nodes within certain regions of the old patterns in the memory matrix, that is their center spots. This rule can be expressed as follows:

$$d_c(t_n) = \max_{(l,k)\notin R_e(t_n)} \left\{ \sum_{i=1}^{N} \sum_{j=1}^{N} m_{lkij}(t_n)x_{ij}(t_n) \right\} \quad (9.74)$$

where $R_e(t_n)$ consists of the output nodes of $d_c(t_1)$, $d_c(t_2)$ ..., $d_c(t_{n-1})$ and

SELF-ORGANIZING NEURAL NETWORK   395

(a)

(b)

Memory Space:

(c)

(d)

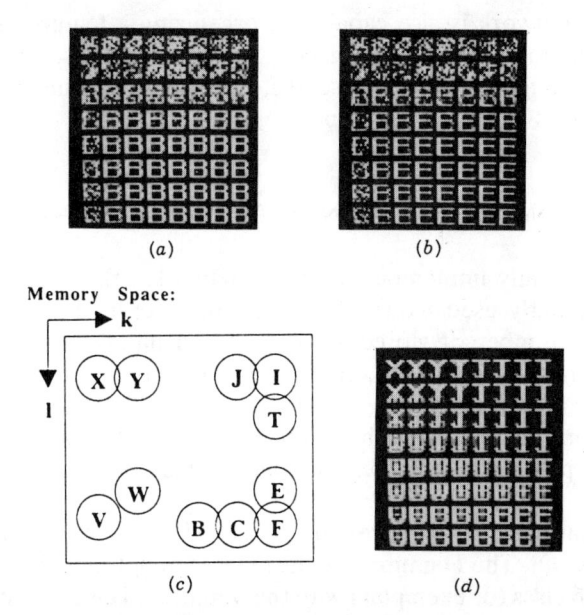

FIGURE 9.41 Topological memory matrix space showing learning without erasing the old memory. (*a*) Pattern B in the memory matrix space. (*b*) Pattern B submatrices are erased, after pattern E is learned. (*c*) Forbidden regions in memory matrix space. (*d*) Learning new patterns without erasing old ones. The centers of the 11 patterns are B at (8, 4), C at (8, 6), E at (6, 8), F at (8, 8), I at (1, 8), J at (1, 6), T at (3, 8), V at (7, 1), W at (6, 3), X at (1, 1), and Y at (1, 3).

their neighboring regions, as illustrated in Figure 9.41c. The radii r_e of the forbidden region can be determined by experience (in our experiments, $r_e = 2$ was selected). After this rule is added to the Kohonen model, the 8 × 8 array neural net can easily remember 11 patterns without erasing similar patterns, as shown in Figure 9.41d. The centers of these 11 patterns in the memory matrix are B at (8, 4), C at (8, 6), E at (6, 8), F at (8, 8), I at (1, 8), J at (1, 6), T at (3, 8), V at (7, 1), W at (6, 3), X at (1, 1), and Y at (1, 3).

Although results can be obtained in the self-organizing optical neural network by adjusting the learning parameters, the best results were achieved through experience. In addition, since the original Kohonen model was not designed for pattern recognition, its self-organization and adaptive pattern recognition capabilities can be enhanced by incorporating more effective models, such as the Inter-pattern Association (IPA) model, when constructing the interconnection weight matrix during the learning process.

In conclusion, we have implemented the Kohonen self-organizing feature map in an optical neural network. This model has modified by matching criteria, which shows that the self-organizing optical neural network has the ability to develop new categories and that it can learn the unknowns. The optical neural network is also capable or organizing a feature map and preserving old memory while learning new knowledge. These abilities can be achieved by setting new matching scores, and by introducing the concept of forbidden regions in the memory space.

9.15 OPTICAL IMPLEMENTATION OF THE HAMMING NET

Among the optically implemented neural networks, the Hopfield model is the most frequently used model. However, the Hopfield model is severely limited in the number of stored patterns it can handle, particularly those patterns that are similar. Second, the Hopfield model requires a larger number of interconnections; for instance, for 10 stored 20 × 20-pixel patterns, 160,000 interconnections are needed. Third, the Hopfield network can converge to an erroneous pattern, called *spurious output*, that produces a "no match" result.

These limitations can, however, be alleviated by using the Hamming net model [9.5], [9.49]. The Hamming net is, in fact, an optimum image classifier, as it selects the class (or exemplar) with the minimum Hamming distance with respect to the input pattern. The Hamming distance is the number of bits of the input pattern that do not match the exemplar. The interconnections in a Hamming net are much less than those in the Hopfield network. Because it consults the preceding 10 (20 × 20-pixel) exemplars, the Hamming net needs only 4100 interconnections, as opposed to the 160,000 required by the Hopfield model. Moreover, by using a Hamming net, the network would not suffer from spurious outputs and would not produce "no match" results. In this section, a modified Hamming net algorithm is introduced to the LCTV neural network [9.50].

9.15 Hamming Net Model

The Hamming net is essentially a two-interconnection-layer neural network, as shown in Figure 9.42, that performs as a maximum likelihood image classifier. The first layer, known as the *Hamming layer*, calculates the Hamming distances between the input pattern and each exemplar (i.e., each class), and the second layer, known as *MAXNET*, selects the maximum output node.

Let us assume that M is the number of the bipolar exemplars stored in the neural network, for which each exemplar has N pixels. The first layer (i.e., the Hamming layer) has N input and M output neurons corresponding to N pixels and M classes, respectively. The interconnection weights in the first layer are determined by

$$W_{ij} = \frac{X_i^{(j)}}{2}, \quad (1 \leq i \leq N, \quad 1 \leq j \leq M), \tag{9.75}$$

where W_{ij} is the interconnection weight from the ith input neuron to the jth

OPTICAL IMPLEMENTATION OF THE HAMMING NET 397

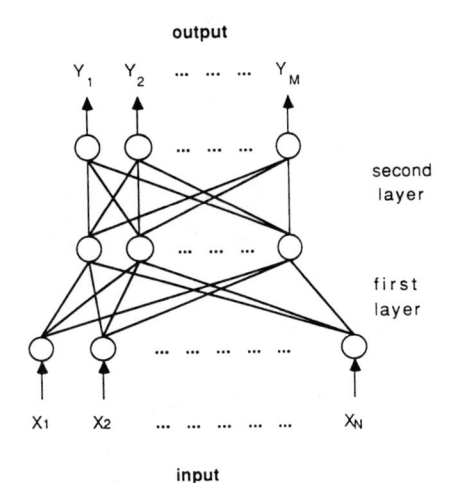

FIGURE 9.42 A Hamming net.

output neuron, and $X_i^{(j)}$ (which can be either $+1$ or -1) is the value of the ith pixel in the jth exemplar. The threshold values can be set at

$$\theta_j = \frac{N}{2}, \quad (1 \leq j \leq M). \tag{9.76}$$

Thus, when an unknown input pattern is presented at the input port, the output of the first layer is given by

$$U_j(0) = \sum_{i=1}^{N} (W_{ij} X_i) + \theta_j, \quad (1 \leq j \leq M). \tag{9.77}$$

It is apparent that the value for $U_j(0)$ (between 0 and N) is equal to the number of bits of the input pattern that match the bits of the jth exemplar, that is

$$U_j(0) = N - HD, \quad (1 \leq j \leq M), \tag{9.78}$$

where HD is the Hamming distance.

Although the Hamming net is theoretically sound, the second layer requires a high dynamic range SLM and successive iterations to produce a maximum output node. Notice that if the Hamming distance between an exemplar and the input pattern is larger than $N/2$, (i.e., more than half of the different bits), it is not required to send a nonzero signal to the second layer. We now discuss a modified model that enlarges the effect of the Hamming distance.

First we introduce the parameter α, $(0 < \alpha < 1)$, by which αN is the maximum Hamming distance that gives rise to a nonzero output signal from the first layer. The modified interconnection weights in the Hamming layer can be written as

398 OPTICAL NEURAL NETWORKS

$$W_{ij} = \frac{X_i^{(j)}}{2\alpha}, \quad (1 \le i \le N, \quad 1 \le j \le M), \quad (9.79)$$

and the threshold values are set at

$$\theta_j = N\left(1 - \frac{1}{2\alpha}\right), \quad (1 \le j \le M). \quad (9.80)$$

The output of the Hamming layer can therefore be written as

$$U_j(0) = f\left[\sum_{i=1}^{N} W_{ij}X_i + \theta_j\right] = \begin{cases} N - HD/\alpha & HD < \alpha N, \\ 0, & \text{otherwise,} \end{cases} \quad (9.81)$$

for $(1 < j < M)$, where

$$f(x) = \begin{cases} x, & x > 0 \\ 0, & x \le 0 \end{cases} \quad (9.82)$$

is a thresholding function.

Thus, by using this scheme, the Hamming distance between the input and the exemplar can be enlarged by a factor of $1/\alpha$, thus decreasing the dynamic range requirement of the SLM and the iterative cycles in the MAXNET.

In practice, however, the parameter α cannot be extremely small. It must be larger than the input noise tolerance of the network, or the Hamming layer would produce a zero output at the matching neuron. In our experiment, we set $\alpha = 0.5$ (to adapt within the dynamic range of a practical SLM), and assume that the input noise is about 20 percent. In this case, the interconnection weights of the Hamming layer are given by

$$W_{ij} = X_i^{(j)}, \quad (9.83)$$

the threshold level is

$$\theta_j = 0, \quad (9.84)$$

and the Hamming layer output is

$$U_j(0) = f\left[\sum_{i=1}^{N} W_{ij}X_i\right] = \begin{cases} N - 2HD, & HD < N/2, \\ 0, & \text{otherwise.} \end{cases} \quad (9.85)$$

Notice that the MAXNET has M input and M output neurons. The interconnection weight between the jth input and kth output neuron is given by

OPTICAL IMPLEMENTATION OF THE HAMMING NET 399

$$t_{jk} = \begin{cases} 1, & j = k, \\ -\varepsilon, & j \neq k, \end{cases} \quad (\varepsilon < \frac{1}{M}, \quad 1 \leq j, \quad k \leq M), \quad (9.86)$$

where ε is known as the *inhibition constant*. If the output signal of the Hamming layer is fed to the MAXNET, iterations are carried out as given by

$$U_k(n+1) = g\left[\sum_{j=1}^{M} t_{jk} U_j(n)\right]$$

$$= g\left[U_k(n) - \varepsilon \sum_{j \neq k} U_j(n)\right], \quad (1 \leq j, \quad k \leq M), \quad (9.87)$$

where $g(\cdot)$ is a nonlinear operator, which assumes a sigmoid function that represents the input–output transfer characteristic of the charge-coupled device (CCD) detector.

By successive iterations of the MAXNET, one of the output nodes will have a high-intensity value, while all of the other nodes will eventually go to zero. It has been proven that the MAXNET will always converge when $\varepsilon < (1/M)$ [9.49], [9.50], for which a maximum output node can always be found.

It is apparent that the Hamming net can also be used as an associative memory, if the examplar responding to the output of the MAXNET, rather than the intensity value, is displayed as the recalled pattern.

9.15.2 Optical Implementation

Figure 9.43 is a schematic diagram of an adaptive optical neural network for Hamming net implementation. The design of the system is described in Section 9.5. In brief, the IWM and the input pattern are displayed onto two liquid crystal televisions (LCTVs), respectively. The lenslet array is used to establish the optical interconnections, by which the light beam emerging from each of the IWM submatrices is superimposed onto the input LCTV2. The imaging

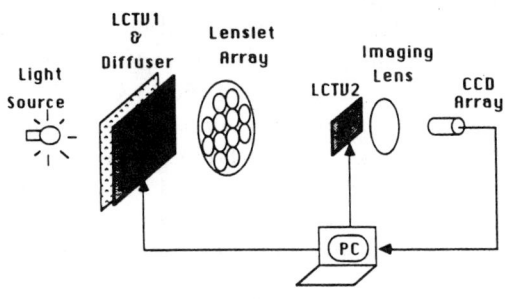

FIGURE 9.43 A hybrid-optical Hamming Net. The output signal is fed back for multilayer operation.

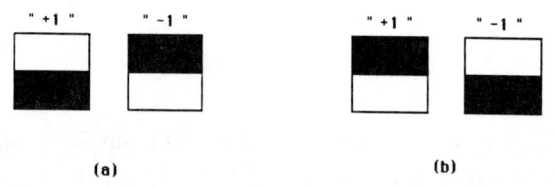

FIGURE 9.44 Area-modulation encoding for the IWM and the input patterns. (a) Pixel encodings for positive IWM and for positive input pattern. (b) Encodings for negative IWM and negative input.

lens is focused onto the CCD camera at the lenslet array so that the signals from the output array are detected. These signals can be thresholded and then fed back to the input LCTV2 for the next iteration.

As an experiment, we use 12 exemplars (i.e., classes) with each exemplar represented by an 8 × 8-pixel array. To achieve higher efficiency and minimize the primary aberration of the imaging lens, the lenslet array comprises 12 small lenses arranged within a circular formation that matches the aperture of the optical system. We note that in the first layer of the Hamming net, the IWM and the input pattern can both be bipolar signals. To achieve bipolar multiplication, the IWM and the input pattern are area modulated, as illustrated in Figure 9.44. For example, in the positive IWM, the value "+1" is encoded in such a way that the upper part of the pixel is transparent and the lower part is opaque, whereas the value "−1" is encoded such that the upper part is opaque and the lower part is transparent. Notice that the input pattern is encoded in the same manner, whereas the negative IWM is encoded in the inverse way. Thus when an encoded input pattern is fed onto the LCTV2, the encoded positive and negative parts of the IWM are sequentially displayed onto the LCTV1, and the output positive-part and negative-part intensities, collected by the CCD, are subtracted and thresholded via the microcomputer. Then the thresholded signal is fed back to the LCTV2 for the second layer (MAXNET) operation.

Figure 9.45a shows the 12 capital Roman letters used as the exemplars in the Hamming net. The positive and negative encoded IWM are shown in the Figures 9.45b and c, respectively, in which the IWMs are partitioned into 12 submatrices and each submatrix is represented by an 8 × 8-pixel array.

Since the number of input and output neurons in the MAXNET is equal to the number of exemplars, the IWM of the MAXNET is partitioned into 12 submatrices, with each submatrix containing 12 pixels. The area modulation can again be used to encode the bipolar IWM. As illustrated in Figure 9.46a, the transparent pixel represents the value "+1" in the positive IWM, while the pixel of value "$-\varepsilon = -1/16$" has only 1/16 of the transmitted area in the negative IWM. Figures 9.46b and 9.46c show the encoded positive and negative IWMs, respectively.

In the MAXNET, the input signal displayed on the LCTV2 is a nonnegative gray-level signal, and the performance of the Hamming net is primarily limited

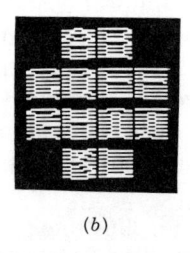

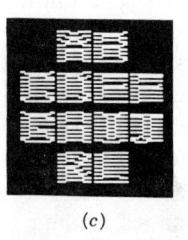

FIGURE 9.45 Exemplar set and the IWMs for the Hamming layer. (*a*) Twelve exemplars. (*b*) Encoded positive IWM. (*c*) Encoded negative IWM.

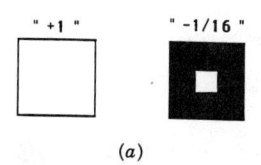

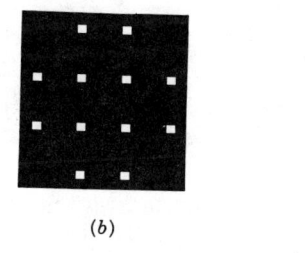

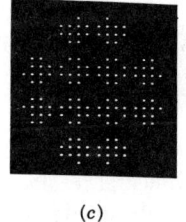

FIGURE 9.46 IWM for the MAXNET. (*a*) Pixel encoding for "t1" and "$-1/16$". (*b*) Encoded positive IWM. (*c*) Encoded negative IWM.

402 OPTICAL NEURAL NETWORKS

by the dynamic range of the LCTV2. To alleviate this constraint, an algorithm was developed, for which the dynamic range requirement imposed on the LCTV2 is relaxed by 50 percent (when $\alpha = 0.5$). Since each exemplar is represented by an 8×8-pixel array, the input signal $U_j(0)$ should have 32 (64/2) gray levels (based on Eq. 9.85). Under the white light illumination, however, the LCTV has a contrast ratio of about 16:1, which is only half the required dynamic range. Therefore, this neural network performs well only when the Hamming distances between each pair of exemplars are larger than 4 pixels.

The modified Hamming net increases the Hamming distance of the input signal of the MAXNET, which reduces the dynamic range requirement of the SLM and the cycles of iteration in the MAXNET. We stress that the sigmoid function representing the input–output transfer characteristic of the CCD detector can further reduce the iterative cycles. Since the dynamic range of the signal is rather large in MAXNET, the low-intensity signals that fall in the toe region of the CCD will be suppressed. According to Lippmann et al. [9.49], MAXNET usually converges in less than 10 iterations. However, using the hybrid-optical neural network, we have shown that it takes only two or three iterations.

The performance of the optical Hamming net is illustrated in Figure 9.47, where Figures 9.47a and e are two English letters "A" and "H" embedded in 20 percent random noise. The encoded input patterns are shown in Figures 9.47b and f, and the corresponding first layer outputs are shown in Figures 9.47c and g, respectively. Figure 9.47d is the output result of "A" from the MAXNET after two iterations, and Figure 9.47h is the output of "H" after three iterations. When these results are compared with the exemplars of

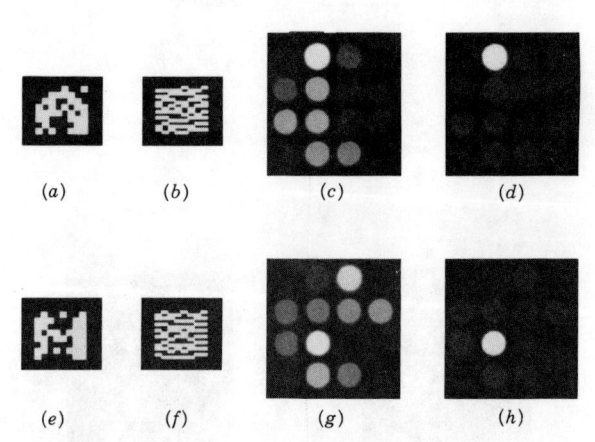

FIGURE 9.47 Experimental results. (a), (e) Input patterns embedded in 20 percent random noise. (b), (f) Encoded patterns of "A" and "H". (c), (g) Outputs from the first layer. (d), (h) Output from MAXNET after two iterations for "A" and three iterations for "H".

Figure 9.45a, we see that the Hamming net can be used for pattern classification. Compared with the Hopfield model, the Hamming net has a larger processing capacity, which can be seen from the demonstrations.

In addition, the converged output result from the MAXNET can be used to recall the examplar. If this recalled exemplar is displayed on an SLM as the final result, then the Hamming net has been used as an associative memory. We further note that the MAXNET used in an unsupervised learning network (Section 9.14) is carried out by the computer, whereas the MAXNET in the optical Hamming net is partially carried out by optics.

REFERENCES

9.1 K. Fukushima, "Visual Feature Extraction by a Multilayered Network of Analog Threshold Elements," *IEEE Trans. Syst. Sci. Cybern.* SSC-5 1969: 322.

9.2 J. J. Hopfield, "Neural Network and Physical System with Emergent Collective Computational Abilities," *Proc. Natl. Acad. Sci. U.S.A.* 79, 1982: 2554.

9.3 T. Kohonen, *Self-Organization and Associative Memory*, Springer-Verlag, Berlin/New York, 1984.

9.4 D. E. Rumelhart and D. Zipser, "Feature Discovery by Competitive Learning," in *Parallel Distributed Processing*, Vol. 1, Chap. 5, D. E. Rumelhart and J. L. McClelland, Eds., MIT Press, Cambridge, Mass., 1988.

9.5 R. P. Lippmann, "An Introduction to Computing with Neural Nets," *IEEE ASSP Magazine*, April (1987): 4–22.

9.6 G. A. Carpenter and S. Grossberg, "A Massively Parallel Architecture for a Self-Organizing Neural Pattern Recognition Machine," *Comput. Vision, Graphics, Image Process.* 37, (1987): 54.

9.7 N. H. Farhat, D. Psaltis, A. Prata, and E. Paek, "Optical Implementation of the Hopfield Model," *Appl. Opt.* 24, (1985): 1469.

9.8 P. Lalanne, J. Taboury, J. C. Saget, and P. Chavel, "An Extension of the Hopfield Model Suitable for Optical Implementation," *Proc. SPIE* 813 (1987): 27.

9.9 R. A. Athale, H. H. Szu, and C. B. Friedlander, "Optical Implementation of Associative Memory with Controlled Nonlinearity in the Correlation Domain," *Opt. Lett.* 11 (1986): 482.

9.10 S. Wu, T. Lu, X. Xu and F. T. S. Yu, "An Adaptive Optical Neural Network Using a High Resolution Video Monitor," *Micro. Opt. Tech. Lett.*, 2, (1989): 252.

9.11 F. T. S. Yu, T. Lu, X. Yang and D. A. Gregory, "Optical Neural Network with Pocket-Sized Liquid-Crystal Televisions," *Opt. Lett.*, 15, (1990): 863.

9.12 N. H. Farhat and D. Psaltis, "Optical Implementation of Associative Memory Based on Models of Neural Networks," *Optical Signal Processing*, ed. by J. L. Horner, *Academic Press*, New York, 1987.

9.13 D. Psaltis, J. Yu, X. G. Gu and H. Lee, "Optical Neural Nets Implemented with Volume Holograms," *Optical Computing, Tech. Digest Series*, 11, (1987): 129.

9.14 K. M. Johnson, M. A. Handschy and L. A. Pagano-Stauffer, "Optical Computing and Image Processing with Ferroelectric Liquid Crystals," *Opt. Eng.*, 26, (1987): 385.

9.15 D. Z. Anderson and M. C. Erie, "Resonator Memories and Optical Novelty Filter," *Appl. Opt.* 26, (1987): 434.

9.16 F. Rosenblatt, *Principles of Neurodynamics*, Spartan Books, Washington, DC, 1962.

9.17 K. Fukushima, "A Neural Network for Visual Pattern Recognition," Computer, 21, (1988): 65.

9.18 J. J. Hopfield, "Artificial Neural Networks," *IEEE Circuits and Devices Magazine*, 4, (1988): 3.

9.19 T. Lu, S. Wu, X. Xu and F. T. S. Yu, "A 2-D Programmable Optical Neural Network," *App. Opt.*, 28, (1989): 4908.

9.20 S. Jutamulia, G. M. Storti, J. Lindmayer, and W. Seiderman, "Use of Electron Trapping Materials in Optical Signal Processing. 2: Two-Dimensional Associative Memory," *Appl. Opt.* 30, (1991): 2879.

9.21 H. K. Liu, S. Y. Kung, and J. A. Davis, "Real-Time Optical Associative Retrieval Technique," *Opt. Eng.* 25, (1986): 853.

9.22 E. G. Paek and D. Psaltis, "Optical Associative Memory Using Fourier Transform Holograms," *Opt. Eng.* 26, (1987): 428.

9.23 F. T. S. Yu and S. Jutamulia, "Implementation of Symbolic Substitution Logic Using Optical Associative Memories," *Appl. Opt.* 26, (1987): 2293.

9.24 Y. Owechko, G. J. Dunning, E. Marom, and B. H. Soffer, "Holographic Associative Memory with Nonlinearities in the Correlation Domain," *Appl. Opt.* 26, (1987): 1900.

9.25 S. Jutamulia, H. Fujii, and T. Asakura, "Double Correlation Technique for Pattern Recognition and Counting," *Opt. Commun.* 43, (1982): 7.

9.26 A. D. McAulay, J. Wang, and C. Ma, "Optical Heteroassociative Memory Using Spatial Light Rebroadcasters," *Appl. Opt.* 29, (1990): 2067.

9.27 J. W. Goodman, *Introduction to Fourier Optics*, McGraw-Hill, New York, 1968, p. 88.

9.28 S. Jutamulia, G. M. Storti, J. Lindmayer, and W. Seiderman, "Use of Electron Trapping Materials in Optical Signal Processing. 3: Modifiable Hopfield Type Neural Networks," *Appl. Opt.* 30, (1991): 1786.

9.29 D. E. Rumelhart, G. E. Hinton, R. J. Williams, "Learning Internal Representations by Error Propagation," in *Parallel Distributed Processing*: Vol. 1, Chap. 8, D. E. Rumelhart and J. L. McClelland, Eds., MIT Press, Cambridge, Mass. 1988.

9.30 S. L. Hurst, *The Logical Processing of Digital Signals*, Crane Russak, New York, 1978.

9.31 D. Psaltis, D. Brady, and K. Wagner, "Adaptive Optical Networks Using Photorefractive Crystals," *Appl. Opt.* 27, (1988): 1752.

9.32 R. P. Gorman and T. J. Sejnowski, "Analysis of Hidden Units in a Layered Network Trained to Classify Sonar Target," *Neur. Network*, 1, (1988): 75.

9.33 T. Lu, S. Wu, X. Xu and F. T. S. Yu "A 2-D Programmable Optical Neural Network," *Appl. Opt.* 28, (1989): 4908.

9.34 R. J. McEliece, E. C. Posner, E. R. Rodemich and S. S. Venkatesh, "The Capacity of the Hopfield Associative Memory," *IEEE Trans. Inform. Theory*, IT-33, (1987): 461.

9.35 G. H. Golub and C. F. Van Loan, *Matrix Computation*, Johns Hopkins Press, Baltimore, 1983.

9.36 R. Hecht-Nielsen, "Performance Limits of Optical Electro-Optical, and Electronic Neurocomputers," *Proc. SPIE* 634, (1986): 277.

9.37 T. Lu, X. Xu, S. Wu and F. T. S. Yu, "A Neural Network Model Using Inter-Pattern Association (IPA)," *Appl. Opt.* 29, (1990): 284.

9.38 F. T. S. Yu, T. Lu, and X. Yang, "Optical Implementation of Hetero-Association Neural Network with Inter-pattern Association Model," *Int. J. Opt. Comput.*, 1, (1991): 129.

9.39 F. T. S. Yu, X. Yang, and T. Lu, "Space-Time Sharing Optical Neural Network," *Opt. Lett.*, 16, (1991): 247.

9.40 X. Yang, T. Lu, and F. T. S. Yu, "Compact Optical Neural Network Using Cascaded Liquid Crystal Televisions," *Appl. Opt.*, 29, (1990): 5223.

9.41 Y. Li "Applications of Moment Invariants to Neurocomputing for Pattern Recognition," Ph.D. Dissertation, The Pennsylvania State Univ., University Park, Pa., 1990.

9.42 R. O. Winder, "Threshold Logic," Ph.D. Dissertation, Princeton Univ., Princeton, N.J., 1962.

9.43 Y. S. Abu-Mostafa and J. M. St. Jacques, "Information Capacity of the Hopfield Model," *IEEE Trans. Inform. Theory*, IT-31, (1985): 461.

9.44 M. K. Hu, "Visual Pattern Recognition by Moment Invariants," *IRE Trans. Inform. Theory*, IT-8, (1959): 179.

9.45 M. R. Teague, "Image Analysis via the General Theory of Moments," *J. Opt. Soc. Am.* 70, (1980): 920.

9.46 D. Casasent and D. Psaltis, "Hybrid Processor to Compute Invariant Moments for Pattern Recognition," *Opt. Lett.* 5, (1980): 395.

9.47 Y. Li and F. T. S. Yu, "Variations of Irradiance Moments in Neurocomputing for Pattern Recognition," *Optik*, 86, (1991): 141.

9.48 T. Lu, F. T. S. Yu, and D. A. Gregory, "Self-Organizing Optical Neural Network for Unsupervised Learning," *Opt. Eng.* 29, (1990): 1107.

9.49 R. P. Lippmann, B. Gold, and M. L. Malpass, "A Comparison of Hamming and Hopfield Neural Nets for Pattern Classification," MIT Lincoln Lab. Tech. Rep. TR.769, 1987.

9.50 X. Yang and F. T. S. Yu, "Optical Implementation of Hamming Net," *Appl. Opt.*, 31 (1992): 3999.

PROBLEMS

9.1 Given an associative memory based on the outer product obtained by a matrix–vector multiplication:

406 OPTICAL NEURAL NETWORKS

$$a_i = \sum_j b_{ij} c_j,$$
$$b_{ij} = \sum_m v_i^m v_j^m,$$

where v^n is the mth memory vector. Show that a_i can be obtained from a linear combination of the memory vectors in which the coefficients are the inner products:

$$a_i = \sum_m v_i^m \sum_j v_j^m c_j.$$

9.2 Show that a correlation is an inner product.

9.3 Prove Eq. 9.5:

$$\iint m^k(x, y) i(x, y) \, dx \, dy = \iint M^k(p, q) I(-p, -q) \, dp \, dq,$$

where $M^k(p, q)$ and $I(p, q)$ are the Fourier transforms of $m^k(x, y)$ and $i(x, y)$, respectively.

9.4 Given two memory vectors

$$V^1 = (1, 1, 0, 0, 0, 1, 1)$$
$$V^2 = (0, 1, 1, 0, 0, 1, 0):$$

(a) What is the Hopfield interconnection matrix?
(b) What is the output when the input is V^1?
(c) What is the output when the input is $(1, 1, 0, 1, 0, 1, 1)$?

9.5 Using the IWM of Problem 9.4, what is the output when the input is $(1, 1, 0, 1, 0, 0, 1)$? Speculate why it occurs this way.

9.6 Figure 9.48 shows a two-layer network. Determine simple interconnection weights and the threshold value to perform:
(a) AND logic function.
(b) OR logic function.

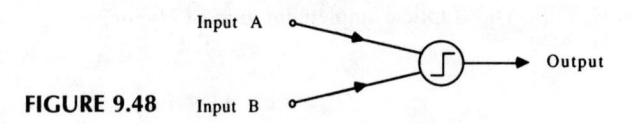

FIGURE 9.48

9.7 Figure 9.49 shows a network within a hidden layer. Determine the interconnection in the network using only $+1$ and -1 weights and 0.5 threshold for an XOR logic function.

```
Input A  ──────→(0.5)
          ╲  ╱          Output
           ╲╱      (0.5)──────→
           ╱╲
          ╱  ╲
Input B  ──────→(0.5)
```

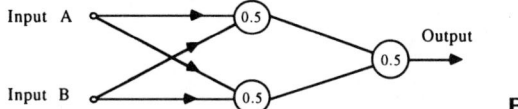

FIGURE 9.49

9.8 Referring to the LCTV optical neural network (ONN) of Figure 9.7:
  (a) Calculate the space–bandwidth product (SBP) and the resolution requirement for a 16 × 16-neuron network.
  (b) Repeat part (a) for an $N \times N$-neuron net.

9.9 Suppose that a 125-mm LCTV is used to display the IWM in the ONN shown in Figure 9.7. We assume that the ONN has 8 × 8 neurons, that each associative memory submatrix is 8 × 8 mm², and that the diameter and focal lengths of the lenses in the array are 6 mm and 60 mm, respectively. If the imaging lens is about 30 mm in diameter with a focal length of about 40 mm, estimate the physical size of the ONN.

9.10 Referring to the preceding problem, if the frame rate of the LCTVs is 30 frames per second:
  (a) Calculate the operation speed of the ONN.
  (b) To improve the operation speed of the ONN, show that, in theory, one can either increase the number of neurons or increase the frame rate of the SLM.

9.11 If we use a 3-in. color LCTV with 450 × 220 pixel elements and assume that the independent addressable pixels are 2 × 2 color pixel elements:
  (a) Evaluate the number of fully interconnected neurons that can be built using this LCTV.
  (b) If the number of output neurons is assumed to be 10, what would the input resolution requirement be?

9.12 Assume the size of a 450 × 220-pixel LCTV panel is 6 × 4 cm². If the LCTV is used to display the memory matrix (IWM) in an optical neuron network:
  (a) Compute the number of lenses required in the lenslet array for the fully interconnected network.
  (b) If the focal length of these lenses is 50 mm, compute the required diameter of the lenses to match an input pattern of 2 × 2 cm².

9.13 Assuming that the diffraction angle of the diffuser is 18°, and the transmittance of the LCTVs is 10 percent, estimate the power budget of the LCTV-based optical neural network of Problem 9.12.

9.14 Four binary patterns represented by a Venn diagram are shown in Figure 9.50. Simple logic operation can be performed to determine the

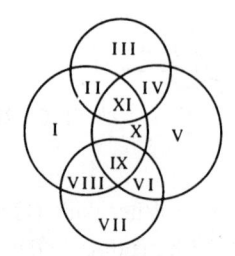

FIGURE 9.50

excitory and inhibitory interconnections between the input and the output neurons. With reference to this figure, describe the relationships between neurons in the following subsets:
 (a) I and II.
 (b) I and V.
 (c) VI and X.
 (d) IX and XI.
 (e) III and IX.

9.15 A set of the binary patterns shown in Figure 9.51 are to be stored in the IWM in a neural network:
 (a) Use a Hopfield model to construct a one-level neuron network.
 (b) With reference to part (a), construct the memory matrix.

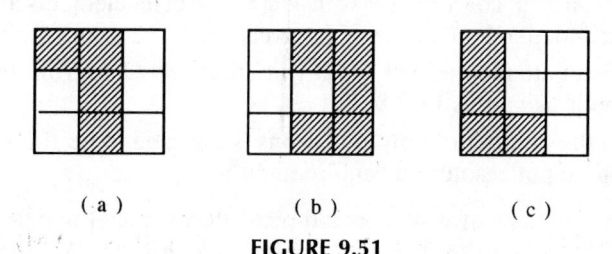

(a)   (b)   (c)

FIGURE 9.51

9.16 Repeating Problem 9.15 for the IPA model:
 (a) Determine the excitory and the inhibitory interconnections by logical operation.
 (b) Construct a one-level neural net.
 (c) Construct the IWM.
 (d) Compare the results of parts (b) and (c) with the results obtained in Problem 9.15.

9.17 Referring to the binary patterns of Figure 9.51, one would use the equivalent rule to construct an IPA–IWM.
 (a) Tabulate the pattern–pixel relationship.

(b) Use the equivalent rule to determine the excitory and the inhibitory interconnections.

   (c) Construct the IWM and compare it with part (c) of the preceding problem.

9.18 Write a software program for the construction of the IWM using the following models:

   (a) Hopfield models:

   (b) Orthogonal projection algorithm.

   (c) IPA model.

9.19 Referring to Problem 9.17:

   (a) Write a computer program for the construction of the IWM using the equivalent rule.

   (b) Verify the result of part (a) by comparing it with the result obtained in Problem 9.17.

9.20 Assuming that a set of Roman letters {X B T O} is to be stored in an 8 × 8 neuron network, construct the following IWMs:

   (a) For the Hopfield model.

   (b) For the orthogonal projection algorithm.

   (c) For the IPA model.

   (d) Compare the results of parts (a), (b), and (c)

9.21 A set of Roman letters {B P R F E H L} is to be stored in an 8 × 8 neuron network.

   (a) Construct a Hopfield memory matrix.

   (b) Construct an IPA memory matrix.

   (c) Show that the Hopfield model becomes unstable, but that the IPA model can recall the letters with unique certainty.

   (d) What is the minimum number of letters in this set that can be stored using the Hopfield model.

9.22 Using the same training set as in Problem 9.21:

   (a) Develop an orthogonal projection algorithm to construct the memory matrix.

   (b) Compare the IWM obtained in part (a) with the ones in parts (a) and (b) of Problem 9.21.

9.23 Estimate the minimum number of patterns that can be stored in an $N \times N$ neuron Hopfield network.

   (a) For 8 × 8 neurons.

   (b) For 64 × 64 neurons.

9.24 **(a)** Repeat Problem 9.23 with the IPA model.

   (b) Compare the results with those for the preceding problem.

410 OPTICAL NEURAL NETWORKS

9.25 Considering the input–output training set of Figure 9.52, and using the IPA model:
  (a) Develop a one-level heteroassociation neuron network.
  (b) Construct a heteroassociation IWM.
  (c) Estimate the number of storage patterns for a 4 × 4-neuron heteroassociation network.

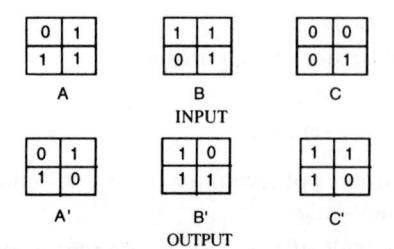

0	1		1	1		0	0
1	1		0	1		0	1

A B C
INPUT

0	1		1	0		1	1
1	0		1	1		1	0

A' B' C'

FIGURE 9.52   OUTPUT

9.26 **(a)** Develop a computer program using the IPA model for a heteroassociation neural network.
  (b) If the input–output patterns of Arabic numerals {1, 2, 3} are to be translated as Roman numeric {I, II, III}, construct a heteroassociation IWM for 8 × 8 neurons.
  (c) Construct a heteroassociation IWM to translate {I, II, III} as {1, 2, 3}.
  (d) Show that the partial input of an Arabic numeral will produce the correct Roman numeric translation.

9.27 **(a)** Calculate the space–bandwidth product and the resolution requirement for a 32 × 32 neuron network.
  (b) If the requirements of part (a) are to be used with a small space–bandwidth neuron network—for example, an 8 × 8 neuron net—and the LCTV has 200 × 240 pixels, calculate the additional processing time required to achieve the same result as part (a).

9.28 State some of the practical limitations using the space–time-sharing technique of Section 9.10.

9.29 State some major advantages and disadvantages of the cascaded LCTV neural network in Section 9.15 as compared with the architecture of Figure 9.17.

9.30 Suppose 75-mm LCTVs are used for a cascaded LCTV-based neural network. Assuming that for an 8 × 8 neuron net, the size of the memory submatrix is 6 × 6 mm^{-2}, and the lenses in the lenslet array are 3 mm in diameter and 60 mm in focal length:
  (a) Estimate the physical size of the cascaded LCTV neural network.
  (b) How much space is saved if one uses the architecture of Figure 9.7?

9.31 Given the high-efficiency optical neural network architecture shown in Figure 9.53, and assuming that the transmittance of the diffuser used in the cascaded LCTV network is 80 percent:
  (a) Calculate the light efficiency ratio between these two optical architectures.
  (b) Plot the light efficiency ratio of part (a) as a function of the number of neurons.

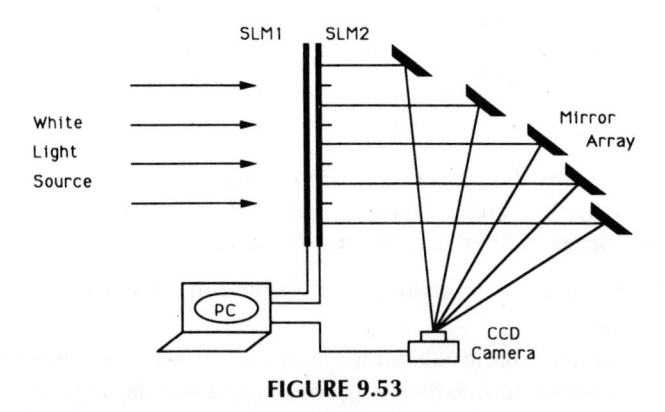

FIGURE 9.53

9.32 Referring to the information capacity in Section 9.12,
  (a) Calculate the information storage capacity of a Hopfield model with a 64 neuron network.
  (b) Repeat part (a) using the IPA model.

9.33 Prove the following inequality, which is used to estimate the upper bound storage capacity of the Hopfield model:

$$2(n+1)\frac{2^{n^2}}{n!} \leq 2^{n^2}.$$

9.34 Calculate the central moment $\mu_{p,q}$ ($p, q = 0, 1, 2, \ldots, 6$) for the binary patterns shown in Figure 9.54;
  (a)
  $$f(x, y) = \begin{cases} 1, & |x| \leq a, \quad |y| \leq a, \\ 0, & \text{otherwise.} \end{cases}$$

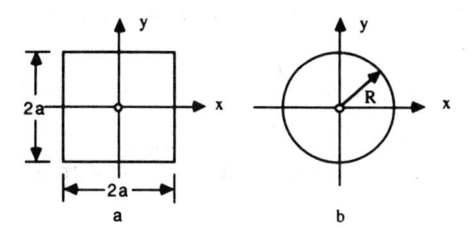

FIGURE 9.54

(b)
$$f(x, y) = \begin{cases} 1, & \sqrt{x^2 + y^2} \leq R, \\ 0, & \text{otherwise}. \end{cases}$$

9.35 Consider the binary patterns of A and C shown in Figure 9.55. Calculate the central moments for these two patterns.

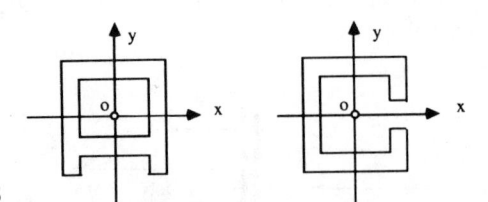

FIGURE 9.55

9.36 Assuming that the second-order moment μ_{20} for the patterns of A and C in Figure 9.55 are given by $\mu'_{2,0}$, and $\mu''_{2,0}$, respectively, calculate the second-order moment μ_{20} for the AC pattern.

9.37 Referring to moment-invariant neurocomputing as described in Section 9.13:
 (a) State the basic advantage and disadvantage of using moment-invariant neurocomputing for pattern recognition.
 (b) Draw a block diagram that describes the implementation to an LCTV-based neural network.

9.38 Given a set of Roman letters, represented by the 8 × 8-pixel elements shown in Figure 9.31:
 (a) Compute the binary-code moment invariants for this set of letters.
 (b) Assuming that the letters in part (a) are to be stored in an IPA neural network, construct the IWM.
 (c) An input letter T is translated one pixel to the right and then rotated 90°, calculate the binary-code moment-invariant representation.
 (d) If part (c) is presented to the input port of the IPA neural network, simulate the output result and show that the recognition is shift and rotation invariant.

9.39 What are the major differences in operation between the Kohonen and the Hopfield neural nets, shown in Figures 9.34 and 9.1, respectively.

9.40 Describe the effects and the strategies for selecting the neighborhood $N_c(t)$ in a Kohonen neural net.

9.41 What are the criteria for selecting the optimum node for an input pattern $X^*(t)$ presented to the Kohonen neural net.

9.42 Write a computer program to construct a Kohonen self-organizing neural network.

(a) Set different learning rates and describe the effects due to fast and to slow learnings.

(b) Set different matching and unmatching scores and observe the changes in the memory matrix.

9.43 Assume that the initial memory matrix in a Kohonen neural net is distributed by the 50 percent random noise shown in Figure 9.37b. A training set of Roman letters {A B C X} is to be stored in the self-organizing neural net, in which a linear learning speed is used, where $a(0) = 0.02$ and $\alpha = 0.00005$.

(a) Simulate the memory matrix space after 200 iterations.

(b) Repeat part (a) for 400 iterations.

(c) Compare the results of parts (a) and (b).

9.44 Refer to the preceding problem, but use $a(0) = 0.015$ and $\alpha = 0.000025$ for a slow learner.

(a) Simulate the memory matrix after 800 iterations.

(b) Compare part (a) with part (b) of the preceding problem.

9.45 To show that old memory may be taken over by the new memory, we assume that the memory matrix is distributed by the 50 percent error rate noise shown in Figure 9.38b, and that the artificial neural network is learning the letter P. Letting $a(0) = 0.02$ and $\alpha = 0.00005$ for a linear learning speed:

(a) Compute the memory matrix after 400 iterations.

(b) If the letter R is later repeatedly presented to the ANN, compute the memory matrix after 400 iterations and compare with part (a).

9.46 Referring to Figure 9.42, state the advantages of the Hamming net as compared with the Hopfield model and with experience.

9.47 Assuming that ten 16 × 16 pixel patterns are stored in the Hamming net:

(a) Calculate the total number of required interconnections.

(b) What would be the number of interconnections using the Hopfield model? Compare your answer with part (a).

9.48 (a) State the reasons that bipolar multiplication is used in the Hamming layer instead of binary multiplication.

(b) What is the definition of MAXNET?

9.49 Referring to the LCTV-based optical Hamming net shown in Figure 9.43, and assuming that the liquid crystal panel has 16 gray levels, estimate the capacity of the optical Hamming net.

Index

Acoustooptic signal processing, 226–237
  of FSK, 232
  of space integration, 226
Achromatic lens, 122
Achromatic processing, 121
Acoustooptic cell, 161
Adaptive optical neural networks, 353–354, 376, 399
Additivity property, 11
Amplitude filter, 81
Amplitude transmittance, 183
Angular selectivity, 258
Area modulation, 45, 111
  Signal processing of, 45
  Wide-band processing, 111
Artificial intelligence, 319
Artificial neural network (ANN), 339
Aspect ratio, 216
Associative memory, 341, 342
Autonomous target tracking, 213

Back-propagation NN, 350
Band-limited partially coherent processing, 121
Bayes Theorem, 321
Bistability, definition of, 306
Boolean logic function, 259, 291, 297
Bragg dephasing vector, 271
Bragg diffraction condition, 255
Broad-band matched filter, 140

Charge coupled device (CCD), 188
Chirp-Z transform, 314
Circular harmonic processing, 97
Coherence, 1–10
  complex degree of, 2
  distance, 4
  and signal processing, 38, 69
  length, 4
  longitudinal, 3, 9
  and mutual coherence function, 2
  measurement, 2
  partial coherence, 2
  spatial, 7
  temporal, 4, 9
  and visibility, 3
Color image processing, 134–149
Compact optical NN, 376
Complex spatial filtering, 39
  by partially coherent light, 117
  by matched filter, 39
  in signal detection, 39
  synthesis of, 40, 47
Complex transfer function, 118
Contact printing, 91
Converging lens, 17
Convolution, 41
  integral, 41
Correlation, 41
  function, 41
Correlators, 41
  joint transform, 42
  with photorefractive crystal, 249
  of Vander Lugt, 41
Crossbar switch, 311

Deformable mirror device (DMD), 174
Degree of coherence, 2
  definition of, 2
Density, photographic, 179
Dephasing parameter, 258
Dephasing wavevector, 261

415

416 INDEX

Detectors, 160
　CCD, 188
　film, 178
Diffraction efficiency, 258
　photorefractive crystal, 258–328
Digital-optical computing, 287–338
Discrete linear transformations, 313
　of chirp-z, 314
　of Hilbert, 314
Diverging lens, 17

Electro-optic devices, 160–192
Electron-trapping materials (ET), 184
Electron-trapping logic, 297
Ensemble average, 2, 179
　space, 179
　time, 2
Expert system, 319
Exposure, 180

Fabry-perot interferometer, 32, 47
Feature map, 391, 393
Filter synthesis, 40
　performed by lens, 20
　processor, 38
　of Van Cittert Zernike theorem, 126
Fraunhofer diffraction, 31
　definition of, 31
　Fourier transform property of, 52
Free space impulse response, 18
Fresnel-Kirchhoff theory, 17
Fresnel-Kirchhoff integral, 19

Gamma of photographic film, 180

H and D curve, 180
Hamming net, 396
　of optical implementation, 399
Heteroassociation, 366
High efficiency JTC, 209
Hilbert transform, 61, 314
Hopfield model, 348, 356, 365
Holographic logic, 304
Holography (photorefractive), 255
　properties of, 255
　JT hologram, 54
　reflection hologram, 259, 261
　transmission hologram, 259, 261
Homogeneity, definition of, 12
Homomorphic filtering, 90
Hough transform, 100
Hurter-Driffield (H-D) curve, 180
Hybrid-optical processing, 203–240
　microcomputer based, 203

Image restoration, 79, 134
　by coherent processing, 79
　by incoherent light, 134
Image subtraction, 83
　by coherent processing, 83
　by incoherent light, 136
Image sampling, 126
Impulse response, 12
　definition of, 12, 38
　intensity, 37
　spatial, 18
Incoherent imaging system, 37
Index of refraction, 182
　of liquid gate, 182
Information capacity, 357, 378
　of Hopfield, 357
　of lower bound, 381
　of IPA, 381
　of upper bound, 379
Interconnections, 340
Interconnection weight, 341
Interconnection weight matrix (IWM), 341
Interferometry, 10
　Fabry-Perot, 32
　Michelson, 10
　Young's experiment, 3
Intensity, 37
　impulse response, 37
　transfer function, 118
Invariance of linear system, 12
Inverse filter, 79
Inverse Fourier transform, 23
Inverse synthetic-aperture radar, 75
Interpattern association (IPA), 361
Iterative equation, 341, 354, 376

Joint transform correlators, 24, 50, 205
　for autonomous tracking, 213
　compact JTC, 280
　of high efficiency, 209
　of microcomputer based, 205
　for multitarget tracking, 219
　nonconventional, 50
　with photorefractive crystal, 249, 280
　using single SLM, 209
Joint transform hologram, 54
Joint transform processor, 42

Kalman filter, 224
Kirchhoff's integral, 19
　See also Fresnel-Kirchhoff theory, 17
Kohonen feature map, 387
Kohonen model, 387

INDEX 417

LCLV neural networks, 354, 376, 399
Lenses, 13
  achromatic, 122
  converging, 16
  diverging, 17
  Fourier transform property, 20
  negative, 17
  phase transformation by, 13
  positive, 16
  simple lenses, 18
  thin lenses, 13
Linear spatially invariant system, 12, 18, 21
Liquid crystal light valve (LCLV), 169
Liquid crystal television (LCTV), 171
Liquid gate, 182
Logarithm transformation, 91
Logic operations, 288–308
  Boolean, 289, 291
  electron trapping, 297
  gate, 307
  holographic, 304
  logic processors, 291–308
  polarization, 293
  shadow-casting, 288
  symbolic substitution, 301
  using optical bistability, 305

Magnetooptic modulator (MOSLM), 162
Matched filter, 41, 47, 140, 269
Matching rate, 392
Matrix-matrix multiplier, 316
Matrix-vector multiplier, 311
MAXNET, 390, 396
Mellin-transform, 95
Michelson interferometer, 10, 305
Michelson's visibility, 3
Microchannel plate modulator (MSLM), 167
Microcomputer based processors, 203
Models of ANNs, 348–375
  back-propagation, 350
  heteroassociation, 366
  Hamming net, 396
  Hopfield, 348
  interpattern association, 361
  Kohonen, 387
  moment-invariant, 382
  multilevel recognition, 358
  orthogonal projection, 357
  space-time-sharing, 370
Modulators, 161
Moment-Invariant, 382
MOSLM, 162
MSLM, 119
Multilevel recognition, 358

Multiplexed matched filters, 269
Multitarget tracking, 219
Mutual coherence function, 2
  of self coherence, 2
Mutual intensity function, 35

Neural networks, 339–403
  aspect of, 339
  of Hamming, 396
  of Hopfield, 348
  of Kohonen, 387
  of IPA, 361
  of multilevel recognition, 358
  of OP, 357
  optical implementation, 350, 353, 354, 376
  of space-time-sharing, 370
Neuron model, 341
Noise performance, 127
  of white-light processor, 127
Nonconventional joint-transform correlator, 50
Nonlinear filtering, 47, 90
Novelty filter, 276

Optical associative memory, 342
Optical bistability logic, 305
Optical computing, 287–337
Optical disk, 174
Optical-disk-based correlator, 237
Optical interconnects, 308
Optical logic processors, 292–307
Optical perfect shuffle, 308
Optical signal processing, 34, 203
  acousto optic processing, 226
  achromatic processing, 121
  band-limited incoherent processing, 121
  by Hough transform, 100
  circular harmonic, 97
  coherent, 34
  complex spatial filtering in, 39
  image correlation, 41
  image filtering, 39
  incoherent, 37, 120
  of computing, 287
  of hybrid processing, 203
  of optical-disk-based, 237
  partially coherent processing, 117
  polychromatic processing, 134–148
  photorefractive crystal, 249
  signal detections, 41
  spatial partial coherence, 120
  and white-light processing, 123
  wide-band processing, 84
Optical neural networks, 339–413

INDEX

Optimum matching score, 388
Optimum spatial filtering, 47
Orthogonal projection model (OP), 357
OTF, 119

Paraxial approximation, 16, 18
Partial coherence, 1
   basic aspects, 1-10
Partially coherent processing, 1, 117
Perfect shuffle, 308
Phase compensation, 253
Phase conjugate JTC, 249
Phase-only filter, 50
Phase-preserving filter, 50
Phase transformation, 14
   of thin lenses, 13
   positive lens, 16
   negative lens, 17
Photodetectors, 178, 184, 188
   CCD, 188
   ET, 184
   film, 178
   photomultiplier, 196
Photographic film, 178
   amplitude transmittance of, 182
   basic properties of, 179
   complex transmittance of, 182
   contact printing, 181
   density of, 176
   exposure of, 180
   gamma, 180
   Hurter-Driffield curve, 180
   intensity transmittance of, 179
   T-E curve, 184
   used in a liquid gate, 182
Photoplastic device, 177
Photorefractive crystal holograms, 255-262
Photorefractive materials, 187
Photorefractive signal processing, 249-283
   compact JTC, 280
   matched filtering, 269
   novelty filter, 276
   phase conjugation JTC, 249
   reconfigurable interconnects, 254
Pockel effect modulator, 164
Polarization logic, 293
Principle of superposition, 11
Processors, 34
   coherent, 38
   incoherent, 37
PROM, 164
Pseudocolor encoding, 144
Pseudoscopic imaging, 144, 147

Quantum well modulators, 190
Quasi Fourier transformation, 52

Radar imaging, 69
Reconfigurable interconnections, 254
   of angular selectivity, 258
   with spatial division, 204
   of wavelength tuning, 262
Reconfigurable optical crossbar, 264
Response of linear system, 12
Restoring blurred image, 79, 134

Self-coherence, 2
Sensitivity, 100
Scale invariant, 95
Shadow-casting, 288
Side-looking radar, 70
Signal detection, 39, 43
Source encoding, 124
Space-time-sharing, 370
Spatial coherence, 7, 35
Spatial incoherence, 36
Spatial impulse response, 12, 18
Spatial filtering, 38
   Optimum filtering, 47
Spatial light modulators (SLM), 160-185
Spatial light rebroadcaster, 345
Spatially partially coherent processing, 120
Spatially invariant, 12
Superposition, principle of, 11
Supervised learning, 340
Symbolic substitution, 301
Synthetic-aperture radar, 69
System transform, 10
Systolic array processor, 312

T-E curve, 184
Target tracking, 213, 219
Temporal coherence, 6, 9
Thin lens:
   definition of, 13
   Fourier transform property of, 20
   phase transform, 13
Transfer function, 118
   of coherent system, 118
   of incoherent system, 118, 119
   of linear system, 12
   of photographic plate, 184
   of thin lens, 14
Tree-search strategy, 360

Unsupervised learning, 340, 390

Van Citter-Zernike theorem, 3, 36, 126
Vander Lugt correlator, 40
Visibility, 3

Wavelength selectivity, 258
White-light optical processing, 123
  color retrieval, 142
  complex filtering, 123, 140
  generation of speech spectrograms, 147
  image deblurring, 134
  image subtraction, 136
  polychromatic processing, 134, 136, 142, 144
  pseudocolor encoding, 144
Wide-band signal processing, 84
  by area modulation, 110
  by intensity modulation, 84

Young's experiment, 3